THE 4000-FOOTERS OF THE

WHITE MOUNTAINS

The 4000-Footers
of the
White Mountains

SECOND EDITION

Steven D. Smith
Mike Dickerman

Bondcliff Books · Littleton, New Hampshire

DISCLAIMER: Every effort was made to ensure that the information in this book was accurate at press time. However, trail conditions are subject to change. We would appreciate hearing of any changes. Also, readers should note that hiking in the mountains is a potentially hazardous activity. Weather and trail conditions can change rapidly. Proper gear, clothing, conditioning, and knowledge are prerequisites for a safe journey. Readers are responsible for their own actions and safety, and are urged to exercise caution and sound judgment. Use of this guide is at the reader's own risk. The authors and publisher assume no responsibility.

Design and text composition by Passumpsic Publishing,
    St. Johnsbury, Vermont
Printed in the United States by Sherwin Dodge Printers,
    Littleton, New Hampshire

PHOTOGRAPH CREDITS
    Ken Stampfer: pages 117, 207, 240, 252, 329, 379
    Harold Emerson: page 453
    All other photographs by the authors

Additional copies of this book may be obtained directly from:
    Bondcliff Books
    P.O. Box 385
    Littleton, NH 03561

Contents

Acknowledgments

The authors would like to thank the many fine companions, too numerous to list here, who have accompanied them on their treks to the 4000-footers over the last three decades. Steve would like to make special note of Bill Vecchio, with whom he did most of the 4000-footers, finishing on Owl's Head in 1981. Thanks also go to Gene Daniell, longtime record-keeper of the Four Thousand Footer Club and the final authority on all matters concerning White Mountain peakbagging; Ken Stampfer, for contributing a number of fine photos; P. Thompson Davis, for reviewing and improving the geology notes; and Laura Waterman and the late Guy Waterman, for inspiration. For helpful information and comments for the second edition, we also thank Allen Koop, Mohamed Ellozy, Tom Ryan, Cathy Goodwin, Dave Govatski, Keith D'Alessandro, and staff and volunteers from the WMNF, AMC, RMC, and WODC.

Scott Cahoon of Passumpsic Publishing performed his usual layout magic with an unwieldy manuscript, and the folks at Sherwin Dodge Printers have been great, as always.

Thanks also to National Geographic Maps for use of their excellent Topo! software to create the locator map for the peaks. For more information on their map CD products, visit www.topo.com.

We owe a great debt to our respective spouses, Jeanne Dickerman and Carol Smith, for their unending patience and unwavering support as we plodded through this time-consuming project.

And with deep appreciation, we thank all those who have been stewards of the trails we are so privileged to enjoy, from the early trailblazers of the nineteenth century to the legions of volunteers who wield hoe, saw and clippers to keep our paths in good health today.

Any errors of commission or omission are the sole responsibility of the authors.

THE 4000-FOOTERS OF THE
WHITE MOUNTAINS

Introduction

Do you enjoy hiking in the White Mountains?

Have you ever been a stamp collector?

If you answer "yes" to both of the above, you are a likely candidate to become a member of the Four Thousand Footer Club (FTFC) of the White Mountains, sponsored by the Appalachian Mountain Club (AMC). Perhaps you already are a member, officially or unofficially. In either case, this book is written for you.

Hikers who aspire to join this hardy group practice the art of "peakbagging," a form of goal-oriented hiking in which one climbs, on foot, a given set of mountains defined by location and elevation. In New Hampshire's White Mountains, peakbaggers set their course for the 48 summits that rise 4000 feet or more above sea level, from mighty Mt. Washington (6288 ft.) down to lowly Mt. Tecumseh and Mt. Isolation (4003 ft.). As defined by the AMC, to qualify as a 4000-footer a peak must rise at least 200 ft. above the low point of a ridge that connects it with a higher neighbor. The list appears on pages 600–601 of the current (2007) edition of the authoritative *AMC White Mountain Guide*, and on pages 540-41 of this guide.

A quick scan shows such time-honored White Mountain favorites as Washington, Lafayette and Moosilauke. But other names—Hancock, Cabot, Bond, Owl's Head, Isolation—may be unfamiliar even to seasoned White Mountain trampers. And that's exactly why some AMC members created the FTFC back in 1957. Their intent was to entice hikers away from the well-trampled trade routes on the Presidential and Franconia Ranges and out to these lesser-known peaks. (See below for more on the history of the FTFC.)

Five decades later, the FTFC can rightfully be declared a hiking phenomenon. At the end of 2007 the club boasted over 8,800 members, each of whom has received a nifty red, white and blue patch and illustrated scroll attesting to their extensive travels across the White Mountains. Probably thousands more have completed the list but not bothered to apply for official recognition.

As Gene Daniell, longtime Secretary of the FTFC and editor of the *AMC Guide* notes, climbing the 4000-footers is an extremely democratic activity. The White Mountains are small indeed (though feisty at times) when compared to the world's great ranges, and they are very accessible. You need bring only reasonably sturdy legs and lungs, some basic hiking gear, and a strong dash of persistence.

1

White Mountain peakbaggers come in all shapes and sizes. They can be as young as five or as old as seventy-five. There are even a number of trail-hardened canines who have climbed them all. It's a great family venture, and kids, especially, seem to take pride in the accomplishment.

There are many reasons to climb the 4000-footers aside from merely checking them off the list. Hikers who never venture away from the familiar destinations miss out on some exceptionally beautiful corners of the mountains, whether it be the wilderness panorama from the sharp peak of West Bond, the back-door view of Mt. Washington from lonely Mt. Isolation, the striking lake country views from Mt. Whiteface, or the North Country feel of Mt. Cabot. Along the way you'll sample every flavor of White Mountain trail, from the smooth railroad grades in the Pemigewasset Wilderness to the breath-stealing scrambles up the steep flanks of East Osceola, the Hancocks and the Wildcats.

Of course, every club has its rites of passage, and many FTFC members will say that the ascent of Owl's Head is the true test of a peakbagger's devotion. This wooded hump rises deep in the Pemigewasset Wilderness and affords, after a nine-mile slog in, a wonderful fifty-foot view composed entirely of balsam firs. (Some hikers maintain that Owl's Head suffers from overly bad press, for there is a unique view from a rock slide below the summit, and the trek does take you through some lovely remote country.)

How does one get started on climbing the 4000-footers? If you're an experienced hiker who has scaled some of the major peaks such as Washington, Lafayette or Moosilauke, you already have a good idea of the equipment, preparation and effort you'll need. If you haven't done much hiking, start small and start slow. Try some shorter and easier hikes such as Welch and Dickey Mtns. near Waterville Valley, Hedgehog Mtn. on the Kancamagus Highway, Mt. Pemigewasset in Franconia Notch, or Mt. Willard in Crawford Notch. Each of these hikes is in the 3- to 5-mile round trip range, with about 1000 to 1800 ft. of climbing—a good workout, but less demanding than a 4000-footer. For specifics on hiking gear and safety, look below to the section on "Hiking Advice."

If you find the above-mentioned moderate hikes to your liking, you're ready to graduate to some of the easier 4000-footers. Some of the best "starter" peaks, relatively short with good views, include Mt. Jackson, Mt. Tecumseh, Mt. Tom, Mt. Pierce, Cannon Mtn., and Mt. Osceola from Tripoli Rd. Once you've cut a few notches on your hiking stick, you may find that you're hooked on this 4000-footer game. You can spend many pleasurable hours planning routes with this guide and the *AMC Guide* and its accompanying trail maps. For more information and an application for the FTFC, send a self-addressed stamped envelope to: Four Thousand Footer Committee, Appalachian Mountain Club, 5 Joy St., Boston, MA 02108.

If you're an energetic hiker with lots of free time, you could finish the 4000-footers in one or two busy summers. But most folks spread their peakbagging out over several years or even decades, leaving plenty of time for other hiking pursuits. Gene Daniell will tell you that in climbing the 4000-footers, the race does not go to the swift. "Most hikers find that it was the pursuit of the goal and not the accomplishment that was the real pleasure," he says.

And what happens when you finally bag all 48 peaks? It seems that very few hikers hang up their boots once they get their patch and scroll. Rather, they return to favorite peaks time and again, sometimes trying out new routes to the summits, or fan out and explore other corners of the mountains.

For those incurably afflicted with the peakbagging bug, there are more lists: the New England 4000-footers, the Northeast one hundred and eleven 4000-footers (including the Adirondacks and Catskills), the bush-whack challenges of the New England Hundred Highest, and so forth. Or one can indulge in any number of variations on the White Mountain list, such as climbing them in winter, in order of height, or in one con-tinuous trip.

The end result is, hopefully, that a hiker who climbs the 4000-footers comes away with a deeper appreciation of the mountain world, a knowl-edge he or she can share with other hikers just starting out. That, in turn, may lead to a commitment to preserve and protect the fragile beauty of the mountains, be it through involvement in trail maintenance or some other avenue. The peakbagger then becomes not merely a collector of mountains, but a steward of the mountains as well. And that's a worthy goal in any hiker's book.

History of the Four Thousand Footer Club

Peakbagging in the Northeastern mountains got its start in New York's rugged Adirondacks in 1918, when two teen-age brothers, Bob and George Marshall, and the family's guide, Herb Clark, began climbing all the mountains in that region exceeding 4000 ft. The requirement was that a mountain must rise at least 300 ft. above its col with a higher neighbor, or be at least ¾ mile distant. In 1925 they stood on their forty-sixth and final summit, Mount Emmons. Of the 46 peaks, only 14 then had trails, and eight had apparently never been climbed before. (Bob Marshall went on to become a ground-breaking conservationist and founder of The Wilderness Society.)

In 1937 the first "Forty-Sixers" club was formed in Troy, New York, to be succeeded by today's "Adirondack Forty-Sixers" in 1948. Through 2007, over 6,200 hikers had followed in the footsteps of Clark and the Marshalls to bag all the Adirondack high peaks. Although more recent surveys showed that four of the original peaks actually failed to top the 4000-ft. mark, a reverence for tradition has kept these summits on the Adirondack 46er list. The founder of peakbagging in the White Mountains was Nathaniel L. Goodrich, librarian at Dartmouth College, avid mountain explorer, and renowned AMC trailman in the "golden era" of trail building from about 1915–1930. (Goodrich and cohorts Charles W. Blood, Paul R. Jenks and Karl P. Harrington laid out such classic routes as Webster Cliff Trail, Garfield Ridge Trail, Kinsman Ridge Trail and Wildcat Ridge Trail. Their work on these "through trails" unified what had previously been several disconnected clusters of trails; see Laura and Guy Waterman's *Forest and Crag*.) In a December 1931 article in *Appalachia*, the journal of the AMC, Goodrich proposed a list of 36 White Mountain 4000-footers that he had climbed, stipulating that each peak must rise at least 300 ft. above any ridge connecting it with a higher 4000-ft. neighbor. He noted that his 300-ft. benchmark was arbitrary and could easily be changed to 200 ft. or 400 ft.

ORIGINAL LIST OF WHITE MOUNTAIN 4000-FOOTERS
Includes elevations as of 1931

Washington	6284	South Carter	4645	Tripyramid, N.	4140
Adams	5805	Garfield	4485	Passaconaway	4116
Jefferson	5725	Liberty	4460	Cannon	4077
Monroe	5390	Hancock	4430	Hale	4077
Madison	5380	Wildcat "A"	4415	Wildcat "E"	4070
Lafayette	5249	Kinsman, S.	4363	Moriah	4065
South Twin	4926	Flume	4327	Tom	4040
Carter Dome	4860	Osceola	4326	Hancock, E.	4035
Moosilauke	4810	Zealand	4301	Owl's Head	4023
Pleasant	4775	Field	4300	Waumbek	4020
Bond	4714	Osceola, E.	4185	Jackson	4012
Carrigain	4647	Cabot	4170	Tecumseh	4004

By 1934, AMC member Francis B. "Mully" Parsons had climbed Goodrich's original list of 36 peaks, getting inaccessible Hancock on his second try and climbing Owl's Head from Greenleaf Hut. Goodrich had since expanded his list to include 51 peaks with names and a total of 88 with stated elevations. Parsons went on to complete the list of 51, and also a list of New England 4000-footers, by 1949. He published his list and an account of his climbs in the December 1949 *Appalachia*.

In the summer of 1948 Mr. and Mrs. J. Daniel McKenzie climbed all the 4000-footers of Vermont, New Hampshire *and* New York, a remarkable feat described in the June 1958 *Appalachia*. Dana C. Backus, who started climbing the peaks as a member of the AMC trail crew in 1923, finished

Goodrich's 36 peaks in 1953, including the required bushwhack ascents of Hancock and Owl's Head. Of the latter peak, he wrote in the December 1953 *Appalachia*, "My clothing was ripped to ribbons. Scarcely enough was left of my shirt to flag a wheelbarrow, but I had at last reached the top of Owl's Head." In the summer of 1956 AMC member Roderick Gould climbed Goodrich's 36 peaks, plus two more—Willey and West Bond—that he had determined were additional qualifiers under the 300-ft. rise rule.

Meanwhile, Walter C. "Gus" Merrill distributed Goodrich's expanded list of 51 named peaks, and several AMC climbers completed this group of mountains in the mid-1950s. At a meeting of the club's General Outings Committee, Edwin Scotcher suggested that a Four Thousand Footer Club (FTFC) be created, similar to the Adirondack Forty-Sixers. The committee saw it as a way to introduce climbers to new areas, away from the familiar Presidential and Franconia Ranges, thereby boosting participation in the club's organized outings. In March 1957 a sub-committee composed of Parsons, Merrill, Barbara Richardson and Albert S. Robertson sent a letter to the governing AMC Council requesting approval for the idea. The letter included a design for a shoulder patch created by artist Mark Fowler. The Council approved the idea but asked that the list of 51 peaks be modified using a specific benchmark, rather than selecting mountains merely on the basis of having a name.

After exchanging letters with officials of the Adirondack Forty-Sixers, the AMC Four Thousand Footer Club committee held a map party at Parsons' home, using the 1955 *AMC White Mountain Guide*, the latest U.S. Geological Survey topographic maps, and magnifying glasses. They decided to use a 200-ft. rule, and the list was accepted by the AMC Council. After adding South Hancock and dropping Old Speck in Maine, the committee ended up with a list of 46 peaks—the same number of 4000-footers as the Adirondacks.

In May 1957 an AMC trip placed about 40 climbers on the summit of then-trailless North Hancock. Roderick Gould became the first to complete the new "official" list on May 26. Thomas S. Lamb followed on September 2. The next to finish, on September 14, were the eminent mountaineers, Miriam Underhill and Robert L. M. Underhill. On September 21 forty-one trampers summitted on South Hancock, including seven more finishers, and by year's end, the total of "four-thousanders" was nineteen, counting Goodrich and Parsons from the 1930s.

The first FTFC awards ceremony was held by the committee on April 26, 1958, including presentation of the aforementioned shoulder patch and a scroll designed by renowned cartographer Erwin Raisz, still in use today. Starting in 1959 the awards were given as part of the AMC Annual Meeting, but soon the numbers became too great and in January 1967 the awards gathering became its own separate event, held in the

Cabot Auditorium at the AMC offices in Boston. Now held in April and moved a few years ago to the middle school in Stratham, New Hampshire, the FTFC awards evening continues as an annual event attended by hundreds.

The official list of 4000-footers was published in the June 1958 issue of *Appalachia*, along with climbing directions for the summits without maintained trails—Cabot, Waumbek, Tom, Zealand, Owl's Head, West Bond and the Hancocks. In August of that year "Red Mac" MacGregor, who had climbed his first peak in 1911 and in the 1920s was the first manager of the AMC hut system, became the senior member of the FTFC at age 74.

"AMC 4000-Footer Club Spurs Climbers" read a *Boston Globe* headline in September 1958. A wave of peakbagging enthusiasm swept through the ranks of the AMC. There were sixteen finishers in 1958 and another dozen in 1959. New members were listed annually in *Appalachia*, and by 1962 the membership was at 129. A year-and-a-half later the roster had swelled to 199, including seven-year old Sarah Merrow and a mongrel named Friskie. "Herd paths" developed on the trailless peaks, and one-by-one these summits acquired official, maintained trails, though to this day the path up Owl's Head is technically not considered a trail.

Right after the FTFC became official, Miriam and Robert Underhill launched a new peakbagging venture—climbing the mountains in winter. This, wrote Miriam, "would present an even more sporting challenge than ambling up the well-trodden trails in summer." As originators of the game, the Underhills could set the rules—climbs must be made during calendar winter, typically between December 22 and March 20. "'Snow on the ground' and other namby-pamby criteria definitely did not count." As described by Miriam in the December 1967 *Appalachia*, the treks to the more remote peaks in those days of unbroken trails were true winter epics, in some cases requiring several return trips.

On December 23, 1960, the Underhills became the first to complete the winter peaks by cramponing to the top of cloud-wreathed Mt. Jefferson in the company of several friends. The temperature was −8°F with a 72 mph wind. Remarkably, Miriam was 62 and Robert 71 at the time. In February 1962, atop Mt. Monroe, Merle Whitcomb became the third hiker (and second woman) to complete the "winter 4000." The feat was not repeated again until 1967, and through the winter of 2007–2008, just 409 trampers had done the 48 peaks in winter, less than 5 percent of those who had finished the list in summer.

Winter seems to inspire some peakbaggers. Among the more remarkable snow-season feats have been climbing the peaks by moonlight (Fred Hunt), standing atop each summit at midnight (Mike Bromberg) and making ascents of each peak from all four points of the compass (Guy Waterman). Equally astonishing is the scaling of each peak in every month of the year (Gene Daniell, and, as of this writing, seven others). See the Appendix for more on these and other unusual spins on peakbagging.

A dozen years after the creation of the FTFC, one of its founders, Al Robertson, looked back with satisfaction. "The response far exceeded our expectations," he wrote in the June 1969 *Appalachia*. "At times, Guyot Shelter looked like Times Square! Climbers of the 1910 to 1940 era dusted off their gear and reappeared upon the scene. . . . More importantly, the list was attractive to new climbers."

From 1966 through 2007, at least one hundred hikers have finished the White Mountain 4000-footers each year, with notable surges in activity in the early 1970s and throughout the 1990s and into the twenty-first century, with over two hundred finishers per year. Famous peakbaggers have included the late Meldrim Thomson, governor of New Hampshire in the 1970s, U.S. Supreme Court Justice David Souter, and N.H. Congressman Jeb Bradley.

As peakbagging caught on, new lists were developed—the New England 4000-footers in 1964 (adding 12 peaks in Maine and 5 in Vermont), the Northeast 111 in 1967 (adding the Adirondacks and Catskills), and the New England Hundred Highest, also in 1967 (including a dozen or so peaks accessible only by map-and-compass bushwhacks.) These lists are all officially recognized by the present AMC Four Thousand Footer Committee.

The publication of a new South Twin Mountain quadrangle by the U.S. Geological Survey led to the addition of two new peaks to the White Mountain 4000-footer list. Galehead Mtn. was put on the roster in 1975, and in 1980 the magnificent Bondcliff became 4000-footer No. 48.

Over the years peakbaggers and the FTFC have not been without their critics. As a wave of new backpackers swept over the mountains in the early 1970s, some observers concluded that the club had done its job too well. In a June 1973 *Appalachia* article, then editor Phil Levin proposed the abolition of the FTFC. Heated correspondence, pro and con, followed in succeeding issues. Meanwhile, a new magazine called *Backpacker* ran an article gloomily entitled "Is Peak-bagging Dead?"

Critics have charged that peakbagging introduces, in Levin's words, "an undesirable artificiality into the natural scenery of the mountains." The peakbagger, it's said, is obsessed with a numbers game that demeans the mountain experience. Peakbaggers also have been taken to task for affecting use patterns and attracting more hikers to fragile trails and once-undisturbed summits. The results, critics say, are increased trail erosion and a loss of solitude in the mountains.

Supporters of peakbagging have countered that the way one enjoys the mountains is a matter of individual choice, as long as it does not detract from others' experiences, or degrade the mountains themselves. They add that most hikers who take up "the list" are already active hikers, and that many FTFC members are involved in trail maintenance and other stewardship activities. (For an excellent summary of the peak-bagging debate, see Laura and Guy Waterman's *Forest and Crag* and *Backwoods Ethics*.)

Over the last three decades the FTFC has flourished under the guidance of Committee Chairs such as Dick Stevens, Bruce Brown, Gene Daniell, Deane Morrison, Tom Sawyer and Eric Savage, ardent peakbaggers all. It seems likely that peakbagging is here to stay, and that for many it can be a magnificent obsession, opening new horizons and deepening one's commitment to cherish and protect the mountain world. Nathaniel Goodrich, the man who started it all in the White Mountains, spoke for generations of peakbaggers to follow when he wrote, "Yes, I have done the lot, and wish heartily there were more."

The AMC Four Thousand Footer Club Today

The FTFC is administered by a nine-person volunteer committee comprised of active hikers and peakbaggers. Committee members process applications, answer correspondence, maintain the Club's website (www.amc4000footer.org), and organize the annual awards dinner. The Club's website includes information on the New Hampshire and New England 4000-Footers and New England Hundred Highest, application forms, pointers about the "rules" of this peakbagging game, and the awards dinner.

Each year the FTFC donates thousands of dollars raised from membership dues, donations and sale of T-shirts and patches to organizations that undertake trail maintenance and other mountain stewardship activities. Often a major portion of the proceeds is given to the AMC Trails Department, earmarked for a specific project(s). Committee members also volunteer time to trail maintenance, whether individually or through work on the Club's adopted trail, currently the Passaconaway Cutoff.

A Note on Rules

Peakbagging is a game, and games have rules. One of the rules for the FTFC is that the hiker must ascend and descend the mountain(s) on foot, starting and ending at a trailhead. Mountain bikes may not be used on the trails (e.g. the Lincoln Woods Trail for an approach to Owl's Head or the Bonds). Nor can an automobile, tramway, ski lift or other mechanical conveyance be used in either direction. In winter, skis and snowshoes and sleds are allowed, but snowmobiles are not, even on roads that are open to cars in summer. The basic idea is that the use of machines is not in the spirit of the game.

One question beginning peakbaggers often ask is whether multiple summits can be climbed and counted on one hike. The answer is "Yes!" If, for example, you hike the loop over North and South Hancock, both summits "count" for your list. For more information on rules of the game, see the FAQ on the Club website.

Hiking Advice

With some basic precautions, knowledge and common sense, hiking the 4000-footers can be a safe and enjoyable experience. Among the many good "how-to" hiking books, an excellent, Northeastern-oriented resource is Dan H. Allen's *Don't Die on the Mountain*.

Season
The regular hiking season runs from about Memorial Day to Columbus Day. Earlier in the spring there is likely to be mud on the lower slopes and

HikeSafe Hiker Responsibility Code

You are responsible for yourself, so be prepared:

1. **With knowledge and gear.** Become self-reliant by learning about the terrain, conditions, local weather and your equipment before you start.
2. **To leave your plans.** Tell someone where you are going, the trails you are hiking, when you will return and your emergency plans.
3. **To stay together.** When you start as a group, hike as a group, end as a group. Pace your hike to the slowest person.
4. **To turn back.** Weather changes quickly in the mountains. Fatigue and unexpected conditions can also affect your hike. Know your limitations and when to postpone your hike. The mountains will be there another day.
5. **For emergencies.** Even if you are headed out for just an hour, an injury, severe weather or a wrong turn could become life threatening. Don't assume you will be rescued; know how to rescue yourself.
6. **To share the hiker code with others.**

HikeSafe: It's Your Responsibility.

The Hiker Responsibility Code was developed and is endorsed by the White Mountain National Forest and New Hampshire Fish and Game.

www.hikesafe.com

snow at higher elevations, in big snow years lasting even into June on the high, wooded ridges. Snow and ice may cloak the trails up high in late fall, and the days are considerably shorter. The conditions in the early spring and late fall "shoulder seasons" often catch hikers by surprise; at these times of year you should be prepared to deal with winter-like conditions. Special gear, clothing and knowledge are needed for winter hiking; see below.

Weather

Though fine, sunny summer days are common enough, at other times these mountains serve up some of the wildest weather on the continent. Be prepared for quick weather changes! Several storm tracks converge in this region, frequently lashing the upper slopes with wind, rain, snow and ice. On April 12, 1934, workers at the Mt. Washington Observatory clocked a wind blast of 231 mph—a world record that still stands today. The *average* wind speed at the summit is 35 mph. Snow has fallen in every month of the year and the top of Mt. Washington is in the clouds 55 to 60 percent of the time. These mountains deserve respect!

Hikers venturing to the high peaks should always check the forecast. It is likely to be 20 or more degrees colder at the summit than in the valley, and significantly windier and cloudier. Be especially cautious early or late in the season. Make alternate plans if the weatherman calls for a stormy day. Avoid stream crossings if heavy rain has occurred or is predicted. Even if good conditions are forecast, be prepared to head down if the weather takes an unfavorable turn. Many have died of exposure on these slopes, even in summer and fall. Thunderstorms are extremely dangerous to hikers on exposed ridges—keep a wary eye out for them.

Recorded White Mountain local forecasts can be obtained by calling 603–356–5030 (Conway), 603–444–2656 (Littleton), or 603–356–2137 (Mt. Washington Observatory). Perhaps the most useful website is www. mountwashington.org (Mt. Washington Observatory). The Observatory's "Higher Summits Forecast" is prepared early each morning and provides expected weather conditions, temperatures and wind speeds and directions for the higher Presidentials. Other weather sites include www .weather.com, www.accuweather.com and www.weather.gov.

Choosing a Hike

When deciding where to go hiking, several factors should be considered —weather, the fitness, ability and ambition of your group, stream crossings, available daylight, and the length, steepness, elevation gain, exposure and roughness of the trail. If you're new to hiking the high peaks, start with easier trips before working your way up to the longer, more difficult hikes. Stay within your limits! Strenuous ascents of the high Presidentials and long trips like Owl's Head, the Bonds and Mt. Isolation are challenging treks that are not suited for beginners. Leave word of your itinerary and expected return time with family or friends.

Clothing and Footwear

Dress for the season, elevation and weather. In cooler temperatures, layering is the key. Wool and synthetics are far better than cotton for warmth and insulating value, especially when wet. Hence the maxim, "cotton kills." In particular, blue jeans should be avoided for serious hiking. We always bring plenty of extra layers, even on hot days. When hiking to higher elevations, especially above treeline, bring rain and wind outerwear, an insulating jacket or sweater, extra shirts and socks, long pants, hat and gloves. 4000-footer trails are often rough, rocky and rooty, and are slippery when wet; wear sturdy, broken-in boots and wool/synthetic socks.

In Your Pack

In addition to the extra clothing mentioned above, we recommend bringing these items in a good-sized pack for a 4000-footer day hike: at least two quarts of water, lunch and high-energy snacks, map/guidebook, compass, watch, sunscreen, first aid kit, at least two flashlights or headlamps with extra bulbs and batteries, insect repellent (black flies and mosquitoes are worst in June), pocket knife, rope or cord, toilet paper, sunglasses, waterproof matches, camera, binoculars and bandanas (very useful). Lining your pack with a large plastic garbage bag will keep clothing dry. Trekking poles or a walking stick can be very helpful for balance on rugged trails and at stream crossings. We would like to re-emphasize bringing flashlights or headlamps, which can make the difference between a comfortable sleep at home and a nerve-wracking, unexpected night in the woods.

Maps

A good topographic trail map is essential. Highly recommended are the series of maps that come with the indispensable *AMC White Mountain Guide*; they may be purchased separately on waterproof Tyvek, including a four-map package for the entire WMNF. Routes can also be planned using the online version of the *White Mountain Guide* at www.outdoors .org (inexpensive subscription required). One of the neat features of this is that you can view trails on Google Earth satellite imagery. Another excellent choice is the waterproof Map Adventures map that comes with the *White Mountain Map Book*; it, too, can be purchased separately. The entire WMNF is covered by two good maps produced by National Geographic's Trails Illustrated. The Randolph Mountain Club, Wonalancet Out Door Club and Waterville Valley Athletic and Improvement Association have fine maps for the Northern Presidentials, Sandwich Range, and Waterville area, respectively. Bradford Washburn's map of the Presidential Range (published by AMC) is highly detailed and accurate. The

Wilderness Map Company publishes several fine "close-up" maps of specific areas. U.S. Geological Survey maps are unmatched for showing topographic detail, though trail locations may be inaccurate on older maps. The National Geographic/Topo! CDs for New England contain all the relevant USGS maps.

On the Trail

Set a steady, moderate pace that is comfortable for all in your group. Establish a turn-around time and stick to it, leaving plenty of time to get out before dark. (Darkness comes earlier in late summer and fall.) Watch your footing carefully on rocky, rooty and steep sections, especially when wet, and at stream crossings. Follow trail markings (blazes and cairns) and signs carefully, particularly above treeline and at junctions and stream crossings. Keep your group together and always wait up at trail junctions so no one goes astray. Filter or treat all surface water before drinking.

Prevent Hypothermia

Stay as warm and dry as possible in cool, damp weather. Hypothermia, the lethal chilling of the body core, can occur in summer, especially in wet, windy weather above treeline. Early signs include shivering, clumsiness, slurred speech and apathy. Get the victim into warm, dry clothing ASAP, before the condition worsens.

Rescue

Hikers should be as self-reliant as possible, but accidents do occur. There are highly capable and dedicated groups of search-and-rescue professionals and volunteers in the White Mountains. In an emergency situation, one hiker should stay with the victim and others should hike out for help. (Hence the maxim that four persons make a safer hiking party.) A cell phone *can* be a lifesaver, but there are many places in the mountains where you cannot get reception. Call 911 or the N.H. State Police emergency line, 1–800–525–5555. Note that under recent New Hampshire legislation, rescue calls that are unnecessary or due to negligent actions may result in a hefty fine for the calling party.

Winter

The snowy months can be an exhilarating and exciting season for hiking the high peaks. However, the combination of cold, snow of many varieties (sometimes very deep), ice, rain (ugh!), bitter winds, difficult route-finding and short days require great caution and appropriate clothing and gear. Snowshoes with aggressive crampons and insulated boots are needed on the winter trails, and full crampons and ice axe are necessities above treeline. On hard-packed trails below treeline, traction devices such as Stabilicers or Microspikes may be useful, but they are no substitute for crampons on solid ice.

In recent years there have been many more people out on the winter trails, and popular routes to 4000-footers are usually packed out soon after a snowstorm. However, if your party is the first to go in after a storm, or is using a less-traveled route, you will face the challenges of trail-breaking and route-finding. After several relatively light snowfall seasons, in 2007–2008 Mother Nature provided peakbaggers near-record snowfalls to contend with in some areas of the mountains. Winter beginners should *not* start with a 4000-footer. Try shorter, easier trips first, preferably in the company of experienced winter trampers. The AMC offers many organized trips and workshops throughout the winter. An extensive treatise on winter hiking is beyond the scope of this book; for that we refer you to the following resources: *Winterwise*, by John M. Dunn; *AMC Guide to Winter Camping*, by Stephen Gorman; *Don't Die on the Mountain*, by Dan H. Allen; and *Snowshoe Hikes in the White Mountains*, by Steven D. Smith.

The winter notes included under each individual mountain chapter are access and route tips specific to those peaks and are intended for experienced winter trekkers. Among the information provided is the winter status of access roads (many of which are closed) and parking. A useful resource for winter hikers is the website, www.viewsfromthetop.com, which has a section where trampers post "Trail Conditions" from recent hikes and another for more detailed "Trip Reports." These can provide current information on snow conditions, stream crossings and other variables. In addition to its Higher Summits Forecast, the weather page on www.mountwashington.org has a link to a useful "Backcountry Weather and Trail Conditions" report. For hiking on the Presidentials, the daily avalanche forecast for Tuckerman and Huntington ravines and other good information is found at www.tuckerman.org.

WMNF Parking Passes

In 1997 Congress directed the White Mountain National Forest (WMNF) and other National Forests to develop a parking permit program to provide recreation funding. Moneys raised are used for repair and maintenance of campgrounds, trails and shelters, for wildlife habitat enhancement, and for interpretive programs. You *must* have a parking pass to park at many trailheads on WMNF land, which is shaded in green on the Appalachian Mountain Club's trail maps. There are four options for parking passes:

Daily Pass	$ 3.00	Purchased at trailhead; self-service tube
7-Day Pass	$ 5.00	Purchased at stores or ranger stations
Annual Pass	$20.00	Purchased at stores or ranger stations
Household Pass *(two cars)*	$25.00	Purchased at stores or ranger stations

If you plan on frequent hikes from WMNF trailheads, you're better off getting an annual pass.

Protecting the Mountain Environment

All hikers have a responsibility to minimize our impact on the mountain environment. The objective is to Leave No Trace (LNT)—the name of a national organization dedicated to promoting outdoor ethics (www .lnt.org).

- Carry out what you carry in, and pick up any litter you find.
- Stay on the marked trails; please don't widen muddy spots, trample trailside vegetation or shortcut switchbacks, especially above treeline.
- Avoid hiking during spring and late fall "mud season," when trails are vulnerable to erosion.
- The call of nature should be answered at least 200 feet from any stream, water source or trail, and waste should be buried in a cat hole 6 to 8 inches deep. LNT advocates packing out used toilet paper in double Ziploc bags.
- Do not pick wildflowers or disturb wildlife.
- Limit your hiking group to 10 persons or less. Keep loud voices and noise to a minimum—other hikers will appreciate it.
- Keep dogs under control, or leave them at home. Don't let dogs wander off trail in the fragile alpine zone.
- If camping, use an established, legal site at least 200 feet off the trail. Some areas in the Whites are off-limits to camping, including the alpine zone and anyplace within one quarter-mile of huts, shelters and roads; the WMNF publishes an updated Backcountry Camping Rules brochure each year.
- Use a stove in preference to building fires; if you do build a fire, be extremely careful and erase all traces when you leave. Keep a clean campsite and hang your food so as not to tempt bears residing in the area.

Trail Stewardship

We strongly encourage all hikers climbing the 4000-footers to devote at least one day a year to trail maintenance. Over the last 30 years usage of trails in the White Mountains has greatly increased, while funds available for trail maintenance have declined, a victim of lean Forest Service budgets. The professional crews and dedicated core volunteers of the various maintaining organizations perform yeoman's work each year, but they can only do so much. Only with the help of additional volunteers can the 1200 miles of trails in the Whites be kept open for the enjoyment of hikers. Helping out with the trails gives you a sense of stewardship that goes beyond the bagging of peaks. Most volunteer trail work is not overly strenuous, and with a good group of people it can be a lot of fun.

There are numerous opportunities to participate in trail maintenance, from "adopting" your own trail to spending a day or even a week working on a specific project with an organized "crew."

Adopt-A-Trail Program

When you "adopt" a trail you agree to take over the basic maintenance of a section of trail, typically one to two miles in length. The most important work is the regular cleaning of drainages that divert water off the trail, essential to preventing trail erosion. Adopters also cut back brush, paint blazes, clear blowdown and pick up litter. Sponsoring organizations generally request that adopters make three trips per year to their chosen trail. The two largest Adopt-A-Trail programs are available through the AMC and WMNF. Similar programs are run by other groups. In most of these programs tools and training are provided for trail adopters. If you're interested in adopting a particular trail, look in the *AMC White Mountain Guide* to see what organization maintains it, and contact them to see if it or others are available; contact information is listed below.

Trail Work Days

If you don't want to take on the responsibility of adopting a trail, there are many work days sponsored by the various maintaining organizations such as AMC, RMC, WODC and Trailwrights throughout the hiking season. Two of the biggest single efforts are National Trails Day in early June and New Hampshire Trails Day in mid-July.

Donations

For hikers who truly do not have extra time to work on the trails, donations are always welcome. Funds are needed to purchase tools and supplies, and to hire highly skilled professional crews for major trail projects. The AMC Four Thousand Footer Committee maintains a trail fund supported by FTFC members who choose to contribute above the nominal basic dues cost. Such contributions can be mailed to: AMC Four Thousand Footer Committee, 5 Joy Street, Boston, MA 02108. Donations may also be made to the organizations listed below; be sure to specify that the funds are to be used for trail maintenance.

Trail Maintaining Organizations

Appalachian Mountain Club: Maintains over 300 miles of trails in the Whites. In addition to the club's official trails program, based at Pinkham Notch, many chapters have their own volunteer crews. 603–466–2721; www.outdoors.org; AMC Trails, PO Box 298, Gorham, NH 03581.

Chatham Trails Association: Oversees numerous trails in Evans Notch area. www.chathamtrails.org

Chocorua Mountain Club: Maintains several trails on Mt. Chocorua and Mt. Paugus.

Cohos Trail Association: Oversees the 160-mile Cohos Trail from Crawford Notch to the Canadian border. www.cohostrail.org.

Dartmouth Outing Club: Responsible for many trails in Mt. Moosilauke area. dartmouth.outing.club@dartmouth.edu; 603–646–2834.

New Hampshire Department of Parks: Responsible for trails in Franconia Notch and Crawford Notch State Parks. 603–271–3556; www.nhparks.state.nh.us; PO Box 1856, Concord, NH 03302.

Randolph Mountain Club: Maintains over 100 miles on Northern Presidentials and in Randolph valley. www.randolphmountainclub.org; Randolph Mountain Club, Randolph, NH 03570.

Squam Lakes Association: Maintains 40 miles of trails in the Squam Range and on Sandwich Dome. 603–968–7336; www.squamlakes.org; PO Box 204, Holderness, NH 03245.

Trailwrights: This dedicated group offers work trips and workshops on trails throughout the state. They also have their own list of seventy-two 4000-footers, using different criteria than the AMC list. The Trailwrights list includes several bushwhack peaks. To qualify for membership, you must climb each peak individually, and must complete 72 hours of trail work. Contact them for more info. www.Trailwrights.org; PO Box 1945, Hillsboro, NH 03244.

Waterville Valley Athletic & Improvement Association: Oversees many trails in the Waterville Valley area. www.wvaia.org; PO Box 412, Waterville Valley, NH 03215.

White Mountain National Forest: Maintains over 600 miles of trails in the Whites. 603–466–2713; www.fs.fed.us/r9/forests/white_mountain /; 300 Glen Rd., Gorham, NH 03581.

Wonalancet Out Door Club: Works on 52 miles of trails in the Sandwich Range. www.wodc.org; HCR 64, Box 5, Wonalancet, NH 03897.

White Mountains History in a Nutshell

The White Mountains are a range rich in history, adding great interest to climbs of the high peaks. In the individual chapters for the 4000-footers we list "Historical Highlights"—significant events that occurred on or around the mountains. The very brief historical summary presented here will provide a basic context for these events.

Native Americans inhabited parts of the White Mountain region, primarily in valleys around the fringes of the mountains. The Abenaki tribes who lived here seldom ventured high into the mountains, where powerful deities were thought to dwell. Abenaki place names are sprinkled around the White Mountains, and several mountains, including one 4000-footer, Mt. Passaconaway, were named after Abenaki chiefs.

Exploration of the mountains by colonists began with Darby Field's bold ascent of Mt. Washington in 1642, accompanied by two Indian guides. In the late 1700s and early 1800s numerous scientific explorations were conducted, especially in the Presidential Range. Among the more notable was the Belknap–Cutler expedition in 1784. Botanists poked into every nook and cranny in the 1820s and 1830s, and several Presidential Range features are named after them.

Meanwhile, white settlers began occupying valleys around the mountains in the late 1700s and early 1800s. The most famous pioneer clan was the Crawfords, who established inns at Crawford Notch and essentially founded the tourist industry in the White Mountains. Many of the first recreational hikers in the region were lured by the guide service offered by the Crawfords and the trails they established on the Presidential Range. Small hostelries were also established in other areas of the Whites.

The coming of the railroads and the construction of numerous hotels, many of the "grand" variety, launched the "golden era" of White Mountain tourism in the mid and late 1800s. Writers such as Thomas Starr King inspired visitors to get out and drink in the mountain scenery. Trails and bridle paths were built on several mountains, and in places like Waterville Valley entire networks of hiking paths were laid out.

The last three decades of the 1800s brought an era of intensive exploration and trail-building. Many mountain areas were visited for the first time during Charles H. Hitchcock's state geological survey from 1869 to 1871. The founding of the Appalachian Mountain Club in 1876 fostered additional probing into remote corners of the Whites, along with a flurry of trail-building. By century's end, hundreds of miles of paths had been cut, most notably on the Northern Presidentials, by such trail-blazers as J. Rayner Edmands (known for his comfortably graded paths), Eugene B. Cook, William H. Peek, and William G. Nowell. For many years hikers were guided by Moses Sweetser's comprehensive *The White Mountains: A Handbook for Travelers*, first published in 1876. In 1907 the AMC published its first guide to the trails of the Whites, and that has been the standard-bearer ever since.

The decades from the 1870s into the 1920s and 1930s saw intensive logging in the White Mountains. Timber barons such as Lincoln's infamous James E. Henry laid logging railroads into remote corners of the mountains to haul out the timber; a number of these old grades serve as trails today. Clearcutting was the order of the day, and fires kindled in logging slash consumed vast acreages, the worst occurring in 1903.

In response to abusive logging and the destructive fires that followed, conservation groups led by the Society for the Protection of NH Forests successfully lobbied Congress to pass the Weeks Act in 1911, authorizing the creation of National Forests in the East. Several hundred thousand acres were soon acquired by the U.S. Forest Service for the White

Mountain National Forest (WMNF). Today the WMNF spreads across some 780,000 acres. These lands are managed under the multiple use concept for recreation, water, timber, wildlife and other uses. Six Wilderness areas totaling 148,000 acres are left in an undisturbed state. About 45 percent of the WMNF is open to timber harvesting on a sustainable basis.

The years from about 1915 to the mid-1930s brought the expansion and unification of the White Mountains trail system and the development of the chain of AMC huts. Four AMC trail architects—Nathaniel L. Goodrich, Paul R. Jenks, Charles W. Blood, and Karl P. Harrington—were key figures in this era, along with the legendary hut system manager, Joe Dodge. The 1938 hurricane wrought havoc on many trails, and some were abandoned in its wake. Others were abandoned during and after World War II due to lack of use and manpower. The new mobility afforded to tourists and hikers with the coming of the automobile age made it easier than ever to get to—and around—the mountains. This spelled the end for most of the grand hotels.

A tremendous surge in hiking and backpacking in the late 1960s and early 1970s brought intensive pressure to bear on trails and backcountry facilities, forcing land managers to evolve new methods of coping with heavy use. The continued popularity of hiking into the twenty-first century has brought an increasing focus on trail maintenance. It has also fostered the development of a new "leave-no-trace" wilderness ethic, encouraging hikers to tread lightly on the land.

For a comprehensive and fascinating history of hiking in the White Mountains and the Northeast in general, we highly recommend Laura and Guy Waterman's *Forest and Crag*. For an interesting history of the Whites with an environmental angle, see Christopher Johnson's *This Grand and Magnificent Place*.

White Mountains Geology

The geologic history of the Whites dates back some 500 million years, when the area was covered by a prehistoric ocean and the edge of the North American continent was 100 miles or more to the west of New Hampshire. Over time sand, silt and mud were deposited on the floor of the sea and compressed into sedimentary rocks such as sandstones and shales. About 460 million years ago, a chain of volcanic islands resulted from the collision of the North American and Eurasian continental plates. Lofty peaks were thrust up to the west of New Hampshire. Intense heat and pressure transformed the sedimentary rocks into harder metamorphic ("changed") rocks.

Starting about 375 million years ago, after millions of years of erosion wore down the first mountain range, the continental plates of Europe and Africa collided with North America. Again, mountains were folded and thrust skyward, and the sedimentary rocks were molded into tough, erosion-resistant metamorphic rocks. These rocks—primarily schist, quartzite and gneiss—make up most of the Presidential and Carter Ranges and Mt. Moosilauke. Thus in the Granite State the very highest mountains are not composed of granite at all. Exposures of this metamorphic rock often show prominent foliation and folding, the latter indicating the tremendous pressures involved in their formation.

Most of the other mountains in the Whites, especially in the central and western regions, are made up of igneous ("firemade") rocks, which formed when magma (molten rock) welled up in the earth's crust. These are the granites and similar rocks for which New Hampshire is famous. The first such intrusion took place about 350 million years ago during the collision of the continents; a prominent rock of this time is Kinsman quartz monzonite, found in the Kinsman Range and in places on the lower slopes of the Franconia Range.

The largest intrusion of igneous rock, known as the "White Mountain Magma Series," occurred about 200 million years ago, as the continental plates were tearing apart. Some of this magma erupted above ground as lava, forming the Moat volcanics; these volcanic rocks were largely eroded away over the ages and are found in only a few places today. Some magma migrated into fractures in the crust and cooled into "dikes" or semi-circular "ring-dikes" (as seen with Mt. Waumbek and the Pliny Range). Other igneous rocks formed in large "plutons" far underground. Common rocks of this type include Conway granite and Mt. Osceola granite.

Millions of years of erosion have worn the White Mountains down from what may once have been far loftier heights, exposing the underlying metamorphic and igneous bedrock we see today. The most dramatic sculpting of the landscape in the last 2 million years has been accomplished by glaciers. Two types of glaciers carved the mountains of New Hampshire—the smaller valley glaciers that plucked out the steep headwalls and broad floors of glacial cirques such as Tuckerman, Huntington and King Ravines, the Great Gulf, and the Sandwich Range's Bowl, and the continental glaciers that once covered even the top of Mt. Washington. Ice streams within the continental ice sheets carved U-shaped troughs from V-shaped valleys such as Pinkham, Crawford and Franconia Notches. Glaciers advanced and retreated several times; the last pullback took place about 12,000 years ago.

Evidence of continental glaciation can be viewed in many places on and around the 4000-footers. Besides the great scoops of the cirques and notches, individual ledges ("sheepbacks" or "roches moutonnees") and entire mountains (such as Mts. Monroe, Garfield and Galehead) were shaped by the ice flow, showing gentle slopes on the north side, where the glacier moved uphill, and a steep face on the south side, where the ice plucked rock away as it ground downslope. Other signs of glaciation include scratches and striations on exposed ledges, glacial "erratic" boulders that were deposited by the glacier far from their point of origin, and pond basins, such as the Lakes of the Clouds, that were scooped out of the bedrock. Most of the soil in the White Mountains is glacial till—a jumbled mix of rocks, sand and clay left when the last ice sheet receded.

After the demise of the glaciers, frost action continued to work on the bedrock. When water freezes to ice, it expands with a power sufficient to shatter rock. Countless freeze-thaw cycles have left desolate jumbles of boulders around the cones of the higher Presidential peaks. The same process created the Old Man of the Mountain on the side of Cannon Mtn., and finally brought it down, in 2003. Frost action working on smaller rocks above treeline has created visible patterns—circles and stripes—on the alpine lawns.

Minor modifications of the mountain landscape still take place today, largely in the form of landslides. These occur on steep slopes (25 to 35 degrees) when heavy rains saturate thin soil cover, sending a cascade of soil, vegetation and rock roaring down the mountainside. The deadly Willey Slide of 1826 is the most famous of these, though the scar has long since revegetated. Several new slides fell in the mid-1990s on Mt. Osceola, North Twin, Mt. Pierce and the west side of the Bond–Guyot–South Twin ridge.

For those interested in such things, we have included in the Appendix a list of basic bedrock types for the 4000-footers culled from a series of geological bulletins produced by the state of New Hampshire.

Life on the Mountainsides

In terms of vegetation and climate, ascending a 4000-footer is like traveling to the northern reaches of Canada. Every 1000-foot rise in elevation has about the same effect as heading about 230 miles north—you lose 3 degrees in average temperature and gain 8 inches in annual precipitation. The climate is colder, wetter and windier at higher elevations, making life harsher for plants, animals and hikers. Distinctive zones of vegetation have evolved in response to these altitudinal gradients. In one day you climb from the temperate world of the valley floor to the arctic-alpine world above treeline. Although there are many local variations, the zones listed below are typical of what you will encounter on your way up one of the higher peaks. For further reference consult the many excellent field guides available. Three guides published by AMC Books are especially pertinent to the Whites: *Field Guide to the New England Alpine Summits*, by Nancy G. Slack and Alison W. Bell; *At Timberline*, by Frederic L. Steele (out of print); and *North Woods*, by Peter J. Marchand.

Northern Hardwood Forest

ELEVATION: Up to 2000–2500 ft., higher on some slopes

TREES: The dominant species of this light, airy, leafy forest—famous for its fall foliage displays—are sugar maple, yellow birch, and American beech. May also include paper birch, white ash, red maple, white pine, quaking aspen, Eastern hemlock, red spruce, balsam fir, black and pin cherry, and red oak. Hemlocks often dominate in cool, moist ravines. Paper birch forms lovely groves in burned areas, and also in the transition zone between the hardwoods below and the conifers above. Common shrubs in the hardwood zone are hobblebush, striped maple, and mountain maple.

WILDFLOWERS: Spring: red and painted trilliums, trout lily, bellwort, violets. Early summer: pink lady's slipper, bluebead lily, wood sorrel, purple twisted stalk, wild sarsaparilla, bunchberry, goldthread, starflower, Canada mayflower

BIRDS: Red-eyed and solitary vireos, scarlet tanager, white-breasted nuthatch, rose-breasted grosbeak, veery, wood thrush, hermit thrush, black-throated blue, black-throated green, Canada and black-and-white warblers, ovenbird, redstart, wood pewee, least flycatcher, black-capped chickadee, blue jay, yellow-bellied sapsucker, pileated, downy and hairy woodpeckers, broad-winged and red-tailed hawks, barred owl, ruffed grouse

MAMMALS: eastern chipmunk, white-tailed deer, moose (look for large, cloven tracks, tooth scrapings on young trees, "cow pies" in summer and heaps of large pellets in colder seasons), black bear (look for claw marks on beech trunks), coyote, white-footed mouse, porcupine, short-tailed weasel, fisher, raccoon, bobcat, snowshoe hare

Spruce–Fir Forest

ELEVATION: ca. 2500–3500 ft.

TREES: Red spruce and balsam fir dominate in the dark, shady conifer forests at these elevations. They are well-adapted to the cold, wet climate and thin, acidic, nutrient-poor soil found here. To tell them apart: spruce needles can be easily rolled between thumb and forefinger, while the flat needles of the fir cannot. These woods may be wonderfully open or frightfully thick and tangled, and are often carpeted with mosses or ferns. Other trees common at this elevation include mountain ash and the pinkish-barked, heart-leaved variety of paper birch, with striped and mountain maple also hanging in.

WILDFLOWERS: Bunchberry, wood sorrel, bluebead lily, Canada mayflower, starflower, goldthread, twinflower, wood aster, large-leaved goldenrod. Flowers that occur at all elevations will bloom later in the higher terrain.

BIRDS: Winter wren (loud, tinkling, trilling song), Swainson's thrush, boreal chickadee (with a brown cap, quite tame), spruce grouse (absurdly tame), white-throated sparrow (song is a sad, sweet whistle), yellow-bellied flycatcher, golden-crowned and ruby-crowned kinglets, yellow-rumped, magnolia, bay-breasted, blackpoll, Blackburnian (up to ca. 3000 ft.), and Nashville warblers, black-backed woodpecker, common junco, Canada or gray jay (the bold "whisky jack" or "camp robber" who will gladly take food from your hand), red-breasted nuthatch, purple finch, pine siskin, white-winged crossbill (irregular). Around ponds: rusty blackbird. Near cliffs: common raven.

MAMMALS: Red squirrel, moose (who even range above treeline on occasion), snowshoe hare, and others who venture up from the hardwoods.

Balsam Fir Forest

ELEVATION: ca. 3500–4500 ft.

TREES: Above 3500 ft. the adaptable and prolific balsam fir dominates until the low scrub at treeline is reached. These woods may be open and mature or wracked with blowdown and crammed with scrubby young growth. A remarkable phenomenon is the "fir wave," a band of dead and dying trees that slowly migrates up or down the slope in the direction of the prevailing wind, appearing as a gray band from a distance. These are thought to be caused by a combination of wind and icing. In places gnarled, scrubby heart-leaved paper birches and mountain ash hold their own with the firs. As elevation increases, the woods become more stunted.

WILDFLOWERS: Similar to spruce–fir forest.

BIRDS: A number of the spruce–fir species range into this zone. An additional specialty at this elevation is the much sought-after Bicknell's thrush.

MAMMALS: Similar to spruce–fir forest.

Krummholz Zone

ELEVATION: ca. 4500–4800 ft.

TREES: At this elevation, a zone of tension between the forest and the alpine zone, the trees are stunted and twisted; krummholz means "crooked wood" in German. Balsam fir and black spruce are the dominant trees.

BIRDS: White-throated sparrow, common junco, blackpoll and yellow-rumped warblers, Bicknell's thrush. Other species may venture up from the lower conifer forests.

Alpine Zone

ELEVATION: Above ca. 4800 ft.; treeline is sometimes lower, sometimes higher depending on wind exposure and other factors.

WILDFLOWERS: The hardy, low-lying plants that thrive in this harsh realm of cold, snow, fog, rain, ice, rock and relentless wind, where trees cannot survive, are famous for their colorful early summer blooms, especially on the "lawns" around Mt. Washington. There are dozens of plants to see up here, and several distinct communities have evolved in response to local micro-climates. The AMC's *Field Guide to the Alpine Summits* is an excellent resource. Most conspicuous in June are the white blooms of diapensia, the magenta of Lapland rosebay and the pink of alpine azalea. Later in the summer the small white flowers of mountain sandwort bloom profusely. Another conspicuous plant is the grass-like Bigelow's sedge, which carpets the alpine meadows. Above treeline, hikers should be constantly aware of the fragility of this plant life—one careless step can crunch away years of hard-won growth. Please stay on marked trails, or bare rock, at all times.

BIRDS: Only a handful of birds nest in the alpine zone, mainly the species mentioned under the krummholz zone.

MAMMALS: Various mice, shrews and voles, even an occasional woodchuck.

Using This Guide

What started out as a simple almanac-type guide to the White Mountain 4000-footers soon evolved into the much lengthier tome you're reading now. As we "researched" the peaks, we came to appreciate the unique qualities of each mountain—its physical attributes, its history, its trail approaches, and the views afforded (or not) from its summit. This has greatly enhanced our enjoyment of the mountains. We hope it does the same for you.

The chapters for each peak, or pair or trio of summits (e.g., Kinsmans, Bonds), are broken down into the seven sections listed below.

Mountain Facts
- Elevation in feet and meters.
- Ranking of height among the 48 peaks.
- What mountain range and towns and / or townships the mountains are located in.
- Which United States Geological Survey (USGS) topographic quadrangles cover the mountains. These are 7½′ (1:24,000 or 1:25,000 scale) maps.

Geography
This presents a physical description of the mountain(s), including major ridges, spurs, streams, ravines and other outstanding features. We recommend having a trail or topographic map on hand as you read this section.

Nomenclature

The origins of the mountains' names are described here. In many cases the names of ravines or other features on the mountain are also included in the discussion. Readily available references on White Mountain nomenclature are *Place Names of the White Mountains*, by Robert and Mary Julyan, and *The White Mountains: Names, Places & Legends*, by John T. B. Mudge.

Historical Highlights

Presented in time-line fashion, this section lists major events occurring on or around the mountains, including first ascents (if known), interesting explorations, dates of trail and shelter construction and other noteworthy events. Invaluable references for compiling this information included many older editions of the *AMC White Mountain Guide* and the AMC's journal, *Appalachia*, and Laura and Guy Waterman's comprehensive history of Northeastern hiking, *Forest and Crag*.

Trail Approaches

In this section we present summaries and descriptions of the major trail approaches to each mountain. Many 4000-footers are blessed with a wonderful variety of trails, and rather than covering only the "standard" routes, we have included many more for those who wish to seek out less-traveled ways to the high peaks. By one count there are 144 different major trail approaches to the peaks. For each approach there is a summary of round trip distance and elevation gain, brief trailhead directions, and a guidebook-style narrative of the trail route. A few of the steeper trails are not recommended for descent and are listed as one-way routes to the summit, with descent via an alternate trail. Loop and point-to-point traverse options, sometimes involving multiple summits, are mentioned where appropriate.

No trail maps are included here; these trail descriptions are intended for use with a good White Mountain trail map. We suggest that every hiker aiming to climb the 4000-footers obtain a copy of the latest *AMC White Mountain Guide* (28th edition, 2007). This authoritative guide describes every maintained hiking trail in the mountains and comes with a complete set of trail maps that covers all the 4000-footers. Most mileages and elevation gains in our descriptions were obtained from the *AMC Guide*. Another excellent resource is the *White Mountains Map Book* by Map Adventures, which includes an easy-to-read, waterproof map that covers all the 4000-footers.

Winter

These are notes on access and routes intended for use by experienced winter hikers who are considering snow-season ascents. Winter beginners should gain experience at lower elevations before attempting any of the higher peaks, especially those above treeline, where dangers are multiplied in winter.

View Guide

In days of old, meaning the mid-to-late 1800s, summit views were a bigger deal than they seem today. The guidebooks of that era, most notably Moses Sweetser's *The White Mountains: A Handbook for Travelers*, placed special emphasis on description and appreciation of summit views, extending into many pages of small print. Panoramic sketches were also provided for a few of the notable vistas. This latter art was resurrected in 1995 with the publication of *Scudder's White Mountain Viewing Guide*, a labor of love compiled over two decades by Brent E. Scudder. Among the 54 panoramas included in the 2005 second edition of Scudder's book are 15 from White Mountain 4000-footers (listed below) and two more from close neighbors Mt. Hight and The Horn.

In this book we have included detailed descriptions of the views from all the summits that grant you an outlook, plus a few other vantage points along popular trail approaches. If you're lucky enough to get a clear day, you can while away your summit stay with the appropriate View Guide, used in conjunction with a trail map and compass, and a Scudder's panorama if available.

At the end of the View Guide we list the number of other White Mountain 4000-footer summits that can be seen from the peak in question. On the wooded summits this is, of course, a somewhat theoretical notion. For a fuller discourse on this matter, refer to the Appendix item, "How Many 4000-Footers Can You See?"

Scudder's panoramas are available for these 4000-footers:

Mt. Adams	Mt. Flume	Mt. Moosilauke
Mt. Bond	Mt. Isolation	Mt. Osceola
Cannon Mtn.	Mt. Jackson	South Twin Mtn.
Mt. Carrigain	South Kinsman Mtn.	Mt. Washington
Mt. Eisenhower	Mt. Lafayette	Wildcat D

Abbreviations

AMC	Appalachian Mountain Club
ca.	circa (about, approximately)
DOC	Dartmouth Outing Club
E	east
FR	Forest Road (in WMNF)
ft.	feet, foot
jct.	junction
L	left
m	meters

mi.	miles
N	north
R	right
Rd.	Road
RMC	Randolph Mountain Club
RR	Railroad
S	south
USFS	United States Forest Service
USGS	United States Geological Survey
W	west
WMNF	White Mountain National Forest
WODC	Wonalancet Out Door Club
yds.	yards

The Mountains

The forty-eight 4000-ft. peaks covered in this book are arranged in eight groups according to their location in a prominent range or region.

Presidential Range/Dry River

This is the area most identified with the Whites and includes the region's five highest summits. The showpieces are the high, barren, rock-strewn peak of Mt. Washington, a legend among mountains for its ferocious weather and rich human history, and the great bouldery pyramids of the Northern Presidentials—Mts. Adams, Jefferson and Madison. Here also are the spectacular glacial cirques such as Tuckerman Ravine and the Great Gulf. But there is also much to like about the gentler Southern Presidentials—craggy Mt. Monroe, the bald dome of Mt. Eisenhower, the rounded swell of Mt. Pierce and the rocky nubble of Mt. Jackson, all rising between the Bretton Woods intervale and the remote Dry River valley. And many hikers are surprised by the beauty of lonely Mt. Isolation out on Montalban Ridge in the heart of the Presidential Range–Dry River Wilderness.

Wildcats–Carter Range

This is the long, high rampart east of the Presidentials, rising between Pinkham Notch and the spacious Wild River Wilderness: the pair of rugged, rocky Wildcats, the lofty, mostly wooded trio of Carter Dome and Middle and South Carter, and ledgy Mt. Moriah. Carter Notch is the most spectacular feature of this beautiful range.

Zealand–Crawford Region

These are the lower wooded peaks west of Crawford Notch, surrounding the pretty Zealand River valley and the NE section of the Pemigewasset

Wilderness. Included are the three peaks of the Willey Range—Mt. Tom, Mt. Field and the imposing Mt. Willey—and Zealand Mtn. and Mt. Hale in the lesser range of the Little River Mountains.

Pemigewasset Wilderness

This section includes the peaks around and within the heart of the largest Wilderness area in the Whites. To the south rise the Hancocks and mighty Mt. Carrigain; to the north, Galehead Mtn. and the sentinel-like Mt. Garfield. Running through the middle of the area is the high Twin Range with its string of open summits, including the two Twins and the trio of remote and lovely Bond peaks, highlighted by the incomparable Bondcliff and the airy perch of West Bond. And deep in the western Pemi is the solitary, lurking mass of Owl's Head Mtn.

Franconia Range

This is the second highest range in the Whites, offering four open summits on a lofty ridge between the Pemigewasset Wilderness and Franconia Notch. Mts. Lafayette and Lincoln are home to the second largest alpine zone in the Whites; the skywalk between them is second to none. Also distinctive are Mt. Liberty's rocky peak and the slide-raked face of Mt. Flume.

Kinsman–Moosilauke region

These are the western high peaks of the Whites, on the far side of Franconia Notch. These include rugged Cannon Mtn. with its ski area and thousand-foot cliff, the two Kinsmans, with their ledgy peaks and high mountain ponds, and Mt. Moosilauke, the gentle, bald-topped giant that is the favorite of many a tramper.

Sandwich Range and Waterville Valley

These peaks hold down the southern front of the Whites, dividing the higher ranges to the north from the lake country to the south. In the fine Sandwich Range Wilderness, a quieter corner of the mountains, are found four low but rugged peaks: Mt. Passaconaway and Mt. Whiteface, with the great valley of The Bowl between them, and the "official" two of the three Tripyramids, noted for their huge slides. On the NW side of the Waterville Valley are the two Osceolas, scored with cliffs and slides, and ski-trailed Mt. Tecumseh.

North Country

Though mostly wooded, Mt. Waumbek and Mt. Cabot offer a nice remote aura thanks to their northern setting beyond the major ranges and highways. Their gentle ridges, carpeted in firs and ferns, offer some of the most pleasant hiking in the Whites.

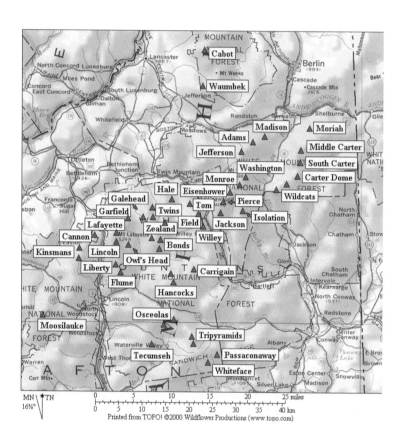

MN \ ⭑TN
16½°

0   5   10   15   20   25 miles

0   10   20   25   30   35   40 km

Printed from TOPO! ©2000 Wildflower Productions (www.topo.com)

PRESIDENTIAL RANGE
AND DRY RIVER

Mount Adams

ELEVATION: 5799 ft. / 1768 m   ORDER OF HEIGHT: 2
LOCATION: Northern Presidential Range, Town of Randolph,
  Townships of Low and Burbanks Grant and Thompson
  and Meserve Purchase
USGS MAP: 7½′ Mount Washington

Geography

With a summit elevation of 5799 ft., Mount Adams is the second highest peak in New England, but there is nothing else second-rate about this
ruggedly spectacular mountain. Some maintain that it's the most interesting of all the 4000-footers. Mt. Adams lies just a few miles N of Mt. Washington along the curving, barren ridgecrest of the Northern Presidential
Range. It is flanked by two impressive neighbors—Mt. Madison on the
NE and Mt. Jefferson to the SW. The upper part of the mountain is a pyramid of frost-riven rock thrusting 1000 ft. above timberline, and the 360-
degree view from its open peak is among the best in the Whites.

As seen from elsewhere in the mountains, the summit of Mt. Adams,
"presents the apperance of a symmetrical pyramid," wrote nineteenth-
century guidebook author Moses F. Sweetser. "It is exceeded by no other
in picturesque grandeur and alpine character, on account of its sharp and
slender peak and of the profound ravines which traverse its flanks."

The sharp peak of Adams is surrounded by several subsidiary peaks.
Mt. John Quincy Adams (5410 ft.) is a rugged, rocky hump that towers
above the Adams–Madison col, accessible via a boulder scramble from
the Air Line and providing impressive views into Madison Gulf. Mt. Sam
Adams (5585 ft.) is a prominent peaklet W of the main summit, with a
lesser knob, Adams 4 (5355 ft.) just to the N. Adams 5 (5274 ft.) is a small
rocky nubble along the ridge that extends from Sam Adams to Edmands
Col. All four of these "Adams Family" sub-peaks are on the "Trailwrights
72" list. In the col between Adams and Sam Adams is Thunderstorm Junction, a major trail intersection marked by a huge cairn. Gray Knob (4481
ft.) is a minor eminence on Nowell Ridge near the cabin of the same

The south slopes of Mount Adams rise steeply out of the Great Gulf.

name maintained by the Randolph Mountain Club (RMC), caretaker of most of the many miles of trails on Adams.

Magnificent ravines, carved out thousands of years ago by alpine glaciers, ring the mountain on practically all sides. The most impressive of the ravines are the Great Gulf—the huge glacial cirque drained by the West Branch of the Peabody River and separating the mountain from nearby Mt. Washington—and rugged King Ravine, with its 1100-ft. headwall topped by the craggy "Gateway" and its boulder-strewn floor, gouged into the N side of the mountain. The "rock glacier" on the floor of King Ravine is a labyrinth of huge boulders that can be visited via two short but challenging RMC paths. Mt. Adams shares three other cirques with its neighboring mountains: Castle Ravine to the W, Jefferson Ravine to the S, and Madison Gulf to the E; the latter two are tributary ravines to the Great Gulf.

Several prominent ridges run N and NW from the summit down towards the Moose River and US 2 in the Randolph valley. From summit to valley floor there is an elevation drop of nearly 4500 ft. Durand Ridge, the more northerly of the lot, is a steep, sharp ridge flanked by King Ravine to the W and the V-shaped Snyder Brook valley to the E. The narrow, upper portion of the ridge running above treeline is known as the Knife Edge. Nowell Ridge is a broad ridge with several spurs NW of Mt. Adams, bordered by King Ravine on the E and Cascade Ravine on the SW. On its lower slopes at ca. 2500 ft. are the minor viewpoints of White Cliff and Bog Ledge. The lesser Israel Ridge is the next ridge to the W, between Cascade and Castle Ravines; its lower end is known as Emerald Tongue. Emerald Bluff (4025 ft.) is a fine viewpoint on the edge of Israel Ridge overlooking Castle Ravine. Several lesser defined, unnamed ridges, strewn with scrubby scree slopes, drop off steeply to the mountain's S and into the depths of the Great Gulf; the steep-sided SE shoulder was once called The Buttress.

In the col between Mts. Adams and Madison, just a short distance from the Appalchian Mountain Club's Madison Spring Hut, lies Star Lake (4896 ft.), a tiny, shallow tarn in a bigger-than-life setting. Storm Lake, an even smaller pool of water near the junction of the Israel Ridge and Gulfside Trails, is located on Adams's long, gently sloping SW ridge some 5200 ft. above sea level. This bare SW ridge leads about a mile from the peak of Sam Adams down to Edmands Col (4938 ft.), named for J. Rayner Edmands, perhaps the best known of the early Randolph area trail builders. This wild, windswept saddle between Castle and Jefferson Ravines marks the low point on the ridge between the summits of Mt. Adams and Jefferson.

Numerous streams flow out of Mt. Adams's nothern ravines, and along these brooks are many scenic waterfalls accessed by the RMC's extensive trail network. Among the largest of these streams is Snyder Brook, which drains the long, twisting, non-glacial valley between Mt. Madison's Gordon Ridge and Mt. Adams's Durand Ridge. Cascades found along Snyder Brook include Duck, Salmacis, Tama, Salroc and Gordon Falls.

Out of King Ravine flow the icy waters of Cold Brook, which originates beneath the boulder field at the floor of the ravine and flows out over Mossy Fall. Probably its best known waterfall is Cold Brook Fall, which is easily accessed just 0.75 mi. from the Appalachia parking lot. Spur Brook, a western tributary of Cold Brook, features Chandler Fall, Canyon Fall and Spur Brook Falls.

Cascade Brook, rich in waterfalls, including the beautiful First and Second Cascades, drains Cascade Ravine and joins Castle Brook from Castle Ravine at the Forks of the Israel to form the W-flowing Israel River. Mystic Stream, a tributary of the Israel, drains the NW slopes of Nowell Ridge. On the lower N slopes of Nowell Ridge are the headwaters of the Moose River, which flows E through Randolph valley.

An unusual note about Mt. Adams is that it is a sacred mountain to members of the Aetherius Society, whose symbols are painted on rocks near the summit.

Nomenclature

The mountain was named on July 31, 1820, by members of the Weeks–Brackett party of Lancaster, which that day was guided to the summit of Mt. Washington by legendary innkeeper and local pioneer Ethan Allen

Crawford. The summit was named in honor of the nation's second President, John Adams (1735–1826). The Lancaster party, which included Adino N. Brackett, John W. Weeks, General John Wilson, Charles J. Stuart, N. S. Dennison, and Samuel A. Pearson (all of Lancaster) and mapmaker and New Hampshire Secretary of State, Philip Carrigain, also gave names to most of the other peaks in the Presidential Range. For many years, however, there was some confusion over the naming of the peaks, especially those of today's Mts. Adams and Jefferson. Several early maps of the White Mountain region mislabeled the summits, transposing the names of the two peaks.

Several of the mountain's sub-peaks have received their own Adams-related names. These include Mt. John Quincy Adams, Mt. Sam Adams, Adams 4 and Adams 5. Collectively they are known as the "Adams Family" of peaks. John Q. Adams (1767–1848) was the son of John Adams and the nation's sixth president. Sam Adams (1722–1803) was a Revolutionary War hero and a signer of the Declaration of Independence. He was also a former governor of Massachusetts, and his name now graces a popular New England brew.

King Ravine, the great glacial cirque cut into Mt. Adams's northern flanks is named for Rev. Thomas Starr King, author of the classic book, *The White Hills: Their Legends, Landscape and Poetry* (1859), and an early explorer of the ravine. Durand Ridge, the steep, rugged ridge running N from the summit, was named by frequent visitor and local trailbuilder William Peek in honor of the Town of Randolph's original grantees, the Durand family of London. Nowell Ridge, on the W side of King Ravine, is named for Dr. William Grey Nowell, a longtime summer resident of Randolph and an enthusiastic AMC explorer and trailbuilder in the late nineteenth century.

Historical Highlights

First Ascent: One month after the Weeks–Brackett climbed Mt. Washington in 1820 and assigned names to the various Presidential Range summits, three of its members (Adino Brackett, John W. Weeks and Charles J. Stuart), along with Richard Eastman, returned to the range for six more days of exploration. During this trip they climbed to the summits of all the Northern Peaks, including Mt. Adams, and are credited with the first recorded ascents of Mts. Adams, Madison and Jefferson.

Ca. 1829: Botanist J. W. Robbins (for whom the rare alpine flower Robbins cinquefoil is named) explores Northern Presidentials and Great Gulf.

1854: Benjamin Osgood climbs mountain, places register, bottle at summit. By 1866, register contains 12 names, by 1876, 20 names.

1857: Thomas Starr King and Gorham guide James Gordon lead party on first ascent of King Ravine. Epic climb takes nine hours from road to

Gateway at top of ravine. In his 1859 *The White Hills*, Starr King writes of, "Wide detours around piles of ragged rocks; cautious fordings of deep-cut torrents; breathless clambers over intrusive ridges; and long crackling conflicts with obstinate thickets consumed our time and strength, and gave many a tear to garments and shoes and hands. . . . The last few rods of the passage out of the ravine led us up a narrow and smooth gateway, quite steep, and carpeted with grass. We sat some time in it, looking at the rocky desolation and horror just about us, balanced by the lovely lines into which the verdure of the western ramparts was broken . . ."

1865: Members of Alpine Club of Williamstown, Mass.—first organized hking club in America—traverse Northern Peaks of Presidentials after spending previous night atop Mt. Washington.

1874: In survey report, state geologist Charles H. Hitchcock writes, "Any lover of mountain scenery must yearn to stand upon the top of Mt. Adams."

1875–76: Charles Lowe and William Nowell build Lowe's Path up Mt. Adams. Early users of path are required to pay nominal "toll."

1876: Lowe cuts new branch trail up through King Ravine.

1877: Ravine House at northern base of mountain opens. Building, dating back to 1850s, was earlier known as Mt. Madison House.

1881: Lowe and Charles E. Fay ascend King Ravine headwall by course of Cold Brook. Account of climb appears in *Appalachia*. Benjamin F. Osgood cuts first trail into Great Gulf, but it is abandoned by turn of century. Cabin–Cascades Trail is cut across slope of Nowell Ridge, leading to camp on Lowe's Path.

1882–1884: Air Line Trail up Durand Ridge—shortest route up Mt. Adams from Randolph—is built. Upper portion above treeline is constructed by Laban Watson, E. B. Cook. Lower portion built by Cook, William Peek.

1883: Original Scar Trail is constructed by Cook and Peek, also called "Wabash Avenue." Path has been opened into Cascade Ravine.

1884: Samuel Scudder, William Pickering, Laban Watson, Hubbard Hunt and two others makes unsuccessful winter attempt on summit. They ascend to area near today's Thunderstorm Junction, but are forced to turn back by wind, fog and bitter cold.

1884: AMC builds first section of Gulfside Trail from Madison–Adams col to Air Line. E. B. Cook completes Amphibrach up valley of Cold Brook; original trail splits into E and W branches. W branch connects with "Chicago Avenue" path built by W.H. Peek.

1885: Trail is cut from Air Line into King Ravine; two decades later it is obliterated by logging.

1886: Fire breaks out in King Ravine and sweeps up E wall over Knife Edge into Snyder Brook ravine.

1887: Charles Lowe makes first recorded winter ascent of summit.

1888: AMC constructs Madison Spring Hut in Madison–Adams col. New path has been cut up Cascade Ravine.

1889: William Nowell, others, build Log Cabin beside Lowe's Path.

1892: J. Rayner Edmands begins work on Israel Ridge Path, linking valley with summit of Mt. Adams. Also constructs birchbark shelter (The Perch) at head of Castle Ravine and Cascade Camp on Cascade Brook. He builds network of pleasure paths in Cascade Ravine, accessing upper cascades, and another along Israel Ridge past viewpoints at "Tip o' the Tongue" and Emerald Bluff. In this year he also starts extending Gulfside Trail (originally called Highland Path) SW from Air Line by Gateway of King Ravine; within several years this trail connects Northern Peaks with Mt. Washington.

1893: Edmands builds The Link as connecting trail along lower slopes of Adams.

1893–1899: Randolph Path from lower Howker Ridge Trail to Jefferson–Adams col built by Edmands.

1895–1897: Edmands builds graded Valley Way from Appalachia to Madison Hut, using some sections of earlier trails up Snyder Brook valley.

1899–1900: Torrey and Moore families build Spur Cabin W of Spur Brook at ca. 3200 ft.

1899–1901: Edmands builds graded Short Line path, providing easier access to King Ravine.

1900–1902: Spur Trail from Randolph Path to Lowe's Path (just below Thunderstorm Jct.) is cut by Charles C. Torrey.

1903–1905: Gray Knob Trail is built from Spur Trail to Randolph Path by Charles C. Torrey and others.

Ca. 1903–1907: Heavy logging disrupts many trails on Northern Peaks, extending 2 mi. up trails such as Israel Ridge, King Ravine and Air Line. Lower section of Israel Ridge Path is obliterated beyond restoration.

1905: E. Y. Hincks builds Gray Knob cabin just E of Gray Knob, a small hump on crest of Nowell Ridge.

1908: New trail from Star Lake (near Madison Hut) to summit is constructed.

1908–1910: Under direction of Warren Hart, series of audacious trails is built in Great Gulf: Great Gulf Trail up valley in 1908; Adams Slide Trail, one of steepest in mountains, and Buttress Trail, both on S face of Adams, in 1909; and Madison Gulf Trail in 1910.

1909: Crag Camp, situated on ridge at edge of King Ravine, is built as private camp by Nelson H. Smith. Hincks Trail is cut from Spur Trail to Gray Knob Cabin by Carroll Hincks.

1910: Randolph Mountain Club (RMC) is formed, soon begins restoring damaged trails on Northern Peaks.

1915–1919: RMC members cut new trail up Castle Ravine to Edmands Col.

1916: New Brookside path is built from Salmacis Fall to Valley Way just below Madison Hut.

1927: Cascade Camp is destroyed by flood, nearby trails disrupted.

1929: Derelict Spur Cabin is razed by WMNF.

Early 1930s: Louis F. Cutter lays out Cliffway, Monaway and Ladderback, pleasure paths on lower Nowell Ridge.

1932: RMC directors vote to adopt and maintain previously unofficial Great Gully Trail up King Ravine. Upper section of trail is relocated in 1933 to complete direct link to Gulfside Trail, Lowe's Path.

1935: Scar Trail is rebuilt by RMC.

1937: Chemin des Dames, connecting King Ravine with Air Line, is adopted by RMC; route was first made in 1920s.

1938: The Perch is blown away by September hurricane.

1939: RMC takes over maintenance of Crag Camp and Gray Knob Cabin.

1940: October fire guts Madison Hut. By August of following year, AMC, under leadership of legendary hutmaster Joe Dodge, reopens hut to hikers.

1948: RMC builds new Perch as memorial to Louis Cutter, well-known mapmaker and tireless RMC trail builder and maintainer in early 1900s. Perch Path is extended to Gray Knob Trail.

1962: Ravine House closes.

1964: Great Gulf Wilderness created by Congress, includes S and E slopes of Adams.

1969: Landslide damages forest near Mossy Fall in King Ravine.

1970: Klaus Goetze of RMC oversees cutting of Emerald Trail up side of Castle Ravine to Emerald Bluff.

Early 1970s: Adams Slide Trail abandoned.

1985: Original Log Cabin razed, replaced by RMC with new open-door shelter.

1989: New insulated and closed Gray Knob cabin built by RMC.

1994: Original Crag Camp razed and is replaced by new camp accommodating 20 hikers.

1998: January ice storm shatters hardwood forest on lower N slopes of Adams; herculean effort by RMC clears thousands of fallen trees from trails.

Trail Approaches

Mt. Adams has a multitude of possible trail approaches, especially from US 2 to the N, for the northern slopes of the mountain have the densest network of footpaths in the White Mountains. This is one of the toughest ascents in the Whites, involving nearly 4500 ft. of elevation gain in 4½ to 5 mi. of relentless uphill. The upper cone of the mountain is a jumble of broken rock, devoid of trees and any protection from the elements.

The climb should only be undertaken in favorable weather conditions, and all above-treeline precautions that apply to Mt. Washington are of equal importance when climbing Adams. Allow plenty of time for this very strenuous trip, which includes much tedious boulder-hopping in its upper reaches.

North Approaches from US 2

Many trail combinations can be used to climb Adams from the N. Six major routes, some with optional variations, are described here, from E to W. Connecting trails make numerous loops possible. The bottoms of trails starting from US 2 can be linked via the old cinder-surfaced RR grade now known as the Presidential Range Rail Trail. For full descriptions of all trails on the northern slopes, see the AMC *White Mountain Guide* or the RMC's *Randolph Paths*.

North Approaches from Appalachia

TRAILHEAD (1306 ft.): The large parking area at Appalachia is one of the major trailheads in the Whites. It's located on the S side of US 2, 5.5 mi. W of NH 16 in Gorham and 2 mi. E of Lowe's Store in Randolph. Various loops can be fashioned from the routes described here.

Valley Way, Gulfside Trail, Air Line
9.4 mi. round trip, 4500-ft. elevation gain

This relatively moderate route follows the steady and sheltered Valley Way—a wide, rocky trade route in places—to AMC'S Madison Hut, from which the exposed boulder-climb up the summit cone is undertaken. If doing a loop, this is a preferred way to descend. From parking area, follow blue-blazed Valley Way across old railroad grade and powerline (where Air Line forks R) and into woods. Climb moderately through hardwoods and then small area of old-growth hemlocks, passing several trail junctions: Maple Walk on L just into woods, Sylvan Way at 0.2 mi., and Fallsway on L at 0.5 mi. (Upper section of Fallsway parallels Valley Way and offers views of pretty Tama Fall on Snyder Brook.) Fallsway soon rejoins from L. Just beyond jct. R with Beechwood Way at 0.8 mi., Valley Way bears R (as Brookside diverges L) and climbs pitch to jct. with Randolph Path at 0.9 mi. / 1953 ft.

Valley Way now climbs steadily along slope high above Snyder Brook, bearing L (E), then R (S) into fine birch glade. Pass jct. with Scar Trail on R at 2.1 mi. / 2811 ft. and cross Watson Path at 2.4 mi. / 3175 ft. Long, steady climb continues up lower E slope of Durand Ridge, passing jct. L with Lower Bruin at 2.8 mi. / 3584 ft., side trail R to Valley Way Campsite (2 tent platforms) at 3.1 mi., and jct. R with Upper Bruin at 3.3 mi. / 4150 ft. Valley Way now climbs more steeply with rocky footing up headwall of ravine, with brook mostly close by on L except for one short loop out to R (W) at 4450 ft. Emerge from scrub and at 3.8 mi. / 4800 ft., just past jct. R with Air Line Cutoff, reach jct. with Gulfside and Star Lake Trails, 100 ft. below Madison Hut.

Turn R here on Gulfside Trail and climb easily through scrub, then steadily in open with many rock steps, to jct. R with Air Line on plateau at 4.1 mi. / 5125 ft.; look back for imposing view of Mt. Madison's massive pyramid. (Short detour to R on Air Line provides spectacular view down into Gateway of King Ravine.) Continue ahead on Gulfside as the trails coincide, then in 250 ft. turn L off Gulfside onto upper part of Air Line, which climbs SSW up open, boulder-strewn cone, passing to W of John Quincy Adams. Much of climb requires strenuous boulder-hopping. After easier section near col with John Quincy Adams, relentlessly rocky climb steepens and continues steady to sharp, small summit at 4.7 mi. / 5799 ft.

Note: A slightly longer but easier route, with better footing, is to continue following Gulfside Trail for 0.6 mi. SW from its jct. with Air Line, then turn L on Lowe's Path for moderate 0.3 mi. climb to summit. This adds 0.3 mi. each way to distance.

BROOKSIDE OPTION

This pleasant, lightly used trail offers a nice alternative to the middle section of the heavily traveled Valley Way. At a point 0.8 mi. up Valley Way from Appalachia, just past jct. with Beechwood Way, turn L onto path known as Brookside. In short distance Randolph Path joins from R and combined trails cross Snyder Brook on large rocks (former bridge at this site was washed out in 2005). On far side, bear R on Brookside as Randolph Path veers L and Inlook Trail continues ahead. Brookside climbs along stream, then recrosses to W side at 1.1 mi. from Appalachia and ascends moderately. Next section traverses high up on slope through beautiful white birch forest with good footing and ocassional peeks at cliffs on lower Gordon Ridge. Trail then comes back near brook, passes jct. L with Kelton Trail at 2.0 mi. / 2750 ft., and becomes steeper and rougher. Pass pretty Salmacis Fall on L (limited view N from top) and climb to jct. R with Watson Path at 2.5 mi. / 3250 ft. Bear L and follow Watson Path for short distance past large boulder on L, then bear R on Lower Bruin. (Short detour L here provides view of Duck Fall on Snyder Brook.) Lower Bruin makes steep, rough climb, then eases off to join Valley Way at 2.8 mi. / 3584 ft. Distance is same as direct route via Valley Way.

STAR LAKE TRAIL OPTION

This trail offers a steep, rugged alternative route from Madison Hut to summit of Adams, with unusual views. From hut, Star Lake Trail climbs easily S in open to Madison–Adams col. At 0.2 mi. from hut Parapet Trail forks L. Bear R on Star Lake Trail, passing by W side of Star Lake, sprinkled with lichen-dotted rocks. Beyond jct. L with Buttress Trail at 0.3 mi., slab below John Quincy Adams through scrub, then begin brutal climb up E side of main summit—very steep and rocky, with large boulders and some ledge scrambling in upper section. Look back for interesting views of Mt. Madison rising above Star Lake. Near top swing R across rocky shoulder and reach summit at 1.0 mi. from hut with 1000-ft. elevation gain. Total distance from trailhead is 4.8 mi.

Air Line
8.6 mi. round trip, 4500-ft. elevation gain

This is the shortest route to Adams, and provides maximum views with its traverse of the exposed Knife Edge on upper Durand Ridge; the looks into King Ravine are especially dramatic. From Appalachia parking, follow Air Line / Valley Way across old railroad grade and into powerline swath, where Air Line diverges R. Climb at easy to moderate grades through hardwoods, passing several trail junctions. Cross Sylvan Way at 0.2 mi. and Beechwood Way at 0.6 mi. (and brook just beyond). Short Line diverges R at 0.8 mi., and at 0.9 mi./2000 ft. Air Line meets Randolph Path, follows it to R for 75 ft., then diverges L. Grade soon steepens, and trail becomes very steep and rocky at 2700 ft. as it struggles up NW end of Durand Ridge; near bottom of steep climb, at 1.6 mi., short path L leads to spring. Grade eases at 2.4 mi. / 3700 ft. where Scar Trail comes in from L. Climb is steady to treeline at 3.0 mi. / 4350 ft., where Air Line emerges from scrub onto exposed ledges. For next 0.5 mi. there are outstanding views W down into and across King Ravine and N to Crescent, Pliny and Pilot Ranges and distant horizons, and also down into Snyder Brook valley to E, where stream-carved V-shape contrasts with glacier-carved U-shape of King Ravine. While ambling up open ledges among wild, jutting rock formations, pass jct. L with Upper Bruin at 3.1 mi. and jct. R with Chemin Des Dames from King Ravine at 3.2 mi. / 4475 ft. in tiny col. Scenic, view-rich climb continues up Knife Edge to jct. L with Air Line Cutoff at 3.5 mi. / 4800 ft. Air Line now climbs fairly steeply to shelf above headwall of King Ravine; follow markings carefully as footway is not well-defined in this area. At 3.7 mi. / 5100 ft. King Ravine Trail departs R to descend through dramatic slabs of Gateway of cirque. In 200 ft. Air Line meets Gulfside Trail, turns R to follow it for 250 ft., then bears L to ascend steadily and at times steeply up boulder-heaped cone of Adams, with much strenuous rock-hopping, as described above, reaching summit at 4.3 mi. / 5799 ft.

SCAR TRAIL OPTION
An alternate, longer approach, with more moderate grades, better footing, and an interesting view, can be made to Air Line at the point where it meets the Scar Trail at 3700 ft. on Durand Ridge. Follow Valley Way to jct. R with Scar Trail at 2.1 mi. / 2811 ft. Turn R on Scar Trail and ascend

The headwall of King Ravine presents an imposing obstacle to hikers attacking Mount Adams from the north.

moderately for 0.2 mi. to fork where Scar Trail goes L and Scar Loop goes R. Bear R on Scar Loop and quickly scramble up steep ledge to view-point known as Durand Scar (ca. 3150 ft.); here there are good views up valley of Snyder Brook to Adams and Madison and out to N. Scar Loop continues steady, winding climb with some limited vistas, then drops off ledge and rejoins main Scar Trail at 2.5 mi. / 3275 ft. From here Scar Trail winds up at moderate grades through deep conifer forest to Air Line at 3.1 mi. / 3700 ft. This is 0.7 mi. longer than direct route via Air Line, with same elevation gain. One-way distance to summit of Adams via this route and upper half of Air Line is 5.0 mi.

Lower Air Line, Short Line, King Ravine Trail, Upper Air Line
4.6 mi. one way, 4500-ft. elevation gain

Many hikers deem the ascent through King Ravine the most spectacular route to Adams, especially when combined with a return down Durand Ridge on Air Line (8.9 mi. loop). Traverse of King Ravine involves rough and difficult scrambling over boulders and ledges and is not advisable in wet weather or for descent.

From Appalachia parking follow Air Line for 0.8 mi. and bear R onto Short Line, which ascends moderately through hardwoods with good footing. Randolph Path joins from L at 1.3 mi. / 2275 ft. and splits R at 1.7 mi. / 2500 ft. as Short Line veers L. Becoming rockier and wilder, with ocasional slippery footing, Short Line leads S up valley of Cold Brook into lower area of King Ravine, climbing at moderate grade. Reach jct. with King Ravine Trail coming up from R at 2.7 mi. / 3150 ft. and follow it ahead into ravine, quickly reaching Mossy Fall on R, spilling between two boulders; for best view of cascade one must hop rocks out onto stream.

Ascent now becomes steep and rugged up through floor of ravine amidst scrub growth and huge boulders, with several fairly challenging scrambles; some boulders have deep holes between them that may make some hikers uncomfortable. Scramble up large rock on R offers good view back down ravine. At 3.1 mi. / 3700 ft., on upper floor of cirque, trail swings R, and emerges in open at jct. L with Chemin Des Dames (see below). Here King Ravine Trail jogs R, emerges in open, and splits; easier but still somewhat difficult route of main trail, "Elevated," is to L and offers fine views, while "Subway," to R, features difficult scrambling over and under massive boulders, with one leap of faith near the start and several narrow passages through caves. By this jct. there are several sitting rocks with impressive views up to ravine walls. The two routes rejoin in ca. 150 yds. (Elevated) or 200 yds. (Subway), and very steep Great Gully Trail leaves on R at 3.2 mi. / 3775 ft. (see below). Then short, rough, scrambly loop path (similar to Subway) diverges R for Ice Caves, where ice is indeed found well into summer. After it rejoins, King Ravine Trail commences very steep, rough ascent of headwall (1100 ft. in 0.5 mi.), with frequent ledge and boulder scrambling. Follow markings carefully. Steep grade calls for frequent pauses to admire stunning views back down ravine. Near top of headwall trail climbs up through cut known as "The Gateway," with smooth rock slabs up on R and rough crags on L, and emerges at jct. with Air Line at 4.0 mi. / 5100 ft., with fine view L to a remarkably pyramidal Mt. Madison. From here follow Air Line 0.6 mi. to summit of Adams, as described above.

Chemin des Dames, the shortest and least difficult (but still challenging) route out of King Ravine, provides the option to visit the floor of the cirque, then gaze down into its depths from the Knife Edge on Durand Ridge. It climbs ca. 800 ft. in just 0.4 mi., with scrambling over talus (some of it loose) and some ledges. Follow Air Line, Short Line and King Ravine Trail for 3.1 mi. to jct. with Chemin des Dames on floor of King Ravine (3700 ft.), as described above. Before ascending Chemin, proceed a few yds. farther up King Ravine Trail to open rocks with dramatic views up to ravine walls. Part of Chemin route can be seen on steep talus on E side. From jct., Chemin des Dames meanders short distance E across floor of ravine, then climbs steadily through scrub and boulders. Soon it emerges on large, steep talus slope, angles L, and climbs steeply up the rocks, some of which are loose. Follow cairns and yellow blazes carefully.

Near top of talus slope, at ca. 4000 ft., is spacious ledge perch on R with great view of ravine. Trail continues up talus past large quartz boulder, then enters birch and conifer scrub, negotiating ledge scramble and then a squeeze through cave-like formation known as Tunnel Rock or Orange Squeezer at ca. 4100 ft. Trail now jogs L and R, climbing steeply through scrub, swings L around ledges and over crevice, and continues up rocky footway. Soon wild projecting crags are seen above and trail bends R to climb in open along base of these ledges, with loose gravelly footing. Pass under uppermost crags and reach Air Line at 4475 ft., 0.4 mi. from floor of ravine. From here, follow Air Line 1.1 mi. to summit; total distance for ascent by this route is 4.6 mi. one-way with 4500-ft. elevation gain.

GREAT GULLY TRAIL OPTION
Experienced hikers looking for a challenging and often solitary climb can ascend from floor of King Ravine to Thunderstorm Junction via the spectacular and lightly-used Great Gully Trail, which rises 1700 ft. in just 1.0 mi. This blue-blazed RMC trail diverges R from King Ravine Trail 3.2 mi. from Appalachia and 0.1 mi. above Chemin des Dames jct.; this is just above upper jct. with Subway. Elevation here is 3775 ft. It runs at easy grades SW across floor of ravine for ca. 0.1 mi., soon ascends steadily, then steepens through scrubby birch and fern growth with several boulder scrambles and partial views. A 3.5 mi. / 4250 ft. trail emerges in open on rocky brookbed and climbs short distance to shelf at foot of high, thin cascade, with rocky precipices looming on either side. In midsummer yellow blooms of arnica can be seen on steep ledges beside cascade. Flat ledges make this a delightful resting spot. Here trail turns sharp R and scrambles up ledges with dropoff on R, swings L up through scrub, then L again for difficult scramble up under overhanging ledge where most hikers will have to remove pack; this spot is protected from dropoff by rock on L. Trail emerges on airy viewpoint overlooking cascade, swings R again for scramble with dropoff on R, then L and up to spectacular open viewpoint even with top of cascade, where one can look straight down the gully. Trail continues very steeply up through scrub, then swings L to brook at 4625 ft., and climbs up it a few yds. It exits L from brook, swings R, and continues steeply up on L side of gully, with one fairly challenging scramble. Continue very steep and scrambly ascent up jumbled rocks, making one tricky traverse to R beside dropoff. Farther up trail climbs up talus through low scrub; look back for views down to floor of ravine and across to headwall, with Durand Ridge and Mt. Madison beyond. Look for L turn off talus at ca. 5200 ft. Trail follows line of cairns up open sedgy slope, soon bending R at easier grade, and continues on faint footway up to Thunderstorm Junction at 4.2 mi. / 5490 ft. Here Lowe's Path comes in sharp R and Gulfside Trail sharp L. Continue up Lowe's Path, a moderately graded rock hop for 0.3 mi. to summit. Distance from Appalachia

to summit via this route is 4.5 mi. one-way with 4500-ft. elevation gain. Great Gully Trail is emphatically not recommended for descent.

Amphibrach, Spur Trail, Lowe's Path
10.2 mi. round trip, 4500-ft. elevation gain

This is a less-used, slightly longer approach with good views along the W edge of King Ravine from the Spur Trail. From Appalachia parking, follow Air Line / Valley Way across old railroad grade and into powerline clearing. Bear R here on Air Line, and in 100 yds. R again on The Link. This path runs W at easy grade with good footing, bearing L twice where logging roads join from R. After passing jcts. L with Beechwood Way and Sylvan Way, it crosses Cold Brook on Memorial Bridge at 0.7 mi. / 1425 ft.; Cold Brook Fall can be seen upstream. Just past bridge swing L on Amphibrach (Link goes straight) and climb S at moderate grade with mostly good footing on W side of Cold Brook, soon passing side path L to pool at base of Cold Brook Fall, well worth short detour. At 1.8 mi. / 2200 ft. pass jct. R with Monaway (where side path on L leads 200 ft. down to pretty spot called Coldspur Ledges) and cross Spur Brook just beyond. Cross Cliffway at 2.2 mi. / 2550 ft. and climb steadily to five-way jct., "The Pentadoi," at 2.6 mi. / 2925 ft.

Turn R on Randolph Path, cross Spur Brook, and quickly bear L onto Spur Trail for steep, rocky climb, at first along cascades on brook, then farther away from stream. At 2.7 mi. side path L leads 100 yds. down to ledges at base of lofty Chandler Fall, with limited view N, and at 2.9 mi. / 3450 ft. Hincks Trail leaves on R. (Hincks Trail climbs steadily, at times steeply, for 0.7 mi. to Gray Knob Cabin with 950-ft. elevation gain.) Spur Trail recrosses brook and continues steep, rough climb up E spur of Nowell Ridge. At 3.4 mi. short side path L leads to Lower Crag and good view into King Ravine, and RMC Crag Camp, spectacularly perched on W rim of cirque, is reached at 3.5 mi. / 4247 ft.; Gray Knob Trail splits R just beyond. Spur Trail remains steep, passing 100-yd. side path L to Knight's Castle, airy ledge perch above ravine with superb view, at 3.7 mi. / 4600 ft. Emerge from scrub at 3.9 mi. and climb steadily up E side of Nowell Ridge, with continuous views, to meet Lowe's Path at 4.7 mi. / 5425 ft. Turn L on Lowe's Path and reach Thunderstorm Jct. (5490 ft.) in less than 0.1 mi. Continue up Lowe's Path at moderate grade over broken rock to summit of Adams at 5.1 mi. / 5799 ft.

North Approach from Lowe's Store

Lowe's Path
9.4 mi. round trip, 4450-ft. elevation gain

TRAILHEAD (1375 ft.): Park at Lowe's Store on US 2 in Randolph (check in at store to pay nominal parking fee, not covered by WMNF Parking

Pass) and walk 100 yds. W on US 2 to sign for Lowe's Path on S side of road.

This straightforward climb is generally considered the "easiest" route to Adams, with a steep middle section but otherwise mostly moderate grades on the long climb up Nowell Ridge. The upper 1.5 mi. is above treeline. From road, trail enters woods and passes sign giving history of route. Cross old railroad grade and powerline and ascend moderately through hardwoods. Cross Link at 1.7 mi. / 2475 ft. King Ravine Trail forks L at 1.8 mi. Grade becomes steeper after switchback at ca. 3000 ft., leading to RMC's Log Cabin on L at 2.4 mi. / 3263 ft. Here Cabin–Cascades Trail splits R. Ascent remains steep with rough footing, crossing Randolph Path at 2.7 mi. / 3600 ft. (Follow route carefully at this jct. as Randolph Path, diverging R, looks more obvious than Lowe's Path, which continues ahead.) Trail rises steeply to crest of Nowell Ridge at ca. 4300 ft., then grade eases to jct. L with short trail called "The Quay," and with Gray Knob Trail just beyond, at 3.2 mi. / 4400 ft; both lead in short distance to Gray Knob Cabin. At Quay jct. open ledgy area provides good view W.

Lowe's Path soon breaks above treeline and climbs steadily up broad, open rocky ridge, with wide views and full exposure to NW winds. Cross minor peak of Adams 4 at 4.1 mi. / 5355 ft. (high point is to R of trail) and continue up to giant cairn at Thunderstorm Jct. at 4.4 mi. / 5490 ft. Cross Gulfside Trail and make moderate climb up rock-strewn summit cone on Lowe's Path, reaching top of Adams at 4.7 mi. / 5799 ft.

North Approach from Bowman

Castle Trail, Israel Ridge Path, Lowe's Path

10.8 mi. round trip, 4200-ft. elevation gain
(add 0.2 mi. round trip for visit to Emerald Bluff)

TRAILHEAD (1500 ft.): This route starts at parking area at Bowman, on S side of US 2, 1.0 mi. W of Lowe's Store. Park on N side of old railroad grade (Presidential Range Rail Trail) as land is private beyond.

This is a fine hike for Adams-baggers looking for wild scenery off the beaten track. Highlights include waterfalls and a possible short side trip to Emerald Bluff, a superb viewpoint. From parking area, follow railroad grade to R for 100 yds., then turn L into woods just past gate. Cross pipeline clearing and traverse on level through logged area to WMNF boundary at 0.3 mi. Cross powerline clearing and turn L along bank for 150 ft. to crossing of Israel River, at 0.4 mi.; not an easy crossing and very tough at high water. On far bank turn L and walk alongside stream for 100 yds., then bear R up bank and follow old logging road on easy climb through open hardwoods. At 1.3 mi. / 1900 ft. bear L on Israel Ridge Path and re-cross river at 1.4 mi. Castle Ravine Trail leaves R at 1.7 mi. as Israel Ridge Path climbs rather steeply L up side of slope into Cascade Ravine, passing jcts. with Link (on L and then quickly on R) and Cabin–Cascades Trail (on L) at 2.5 mi. / 2800 ft. (Short side trip R on Link leads to ledge at top of First Cascade, scenic spot with limited view of Mt. Bowman.)

Path continues steeply up E side of Cascade Brook, scaling two short ladders and passing expansive open sloping ledges on R beside Second Cascade; this is fine rest spot with view of Mt. Bowman to W and northern Vermont to NW. A short distance farther, at 2.7 mi. / 2975 ft., trail crosses brook at head of cascade, briefly turns R downstream, then L. It now makes steep, rough climb up Israel Ridge through mossy virgin conifer forest, then slabs upward along E side of ridge, with two more ladders up steep ledges. At 3.5 mi. / 4050 ft. Emerald Trail comes in on R; Emerald Bluff, spectacular viewpoint overlooking Castle Ravine and Mt. Jefferson's Castellated Ridge, can be visited with easy side trip of 0.1 mi. each way; viewpoint is on side path R where Emerald Trail turns L for descent into ravine. Israel Ridge Path turns L at this jct., climbs to Perch Path at 3.7 mi., then turns R and climbs steadily through fir woods, then high scrub with views starting to appear. Swing R and break above treeline shortly before reaching jct. L with Randolph Path at 4.1 mi. / 4825 ft.

For next 0.5 mi. Israel Ridge Path offers continuous and ever-changing views, especially W and SW to Castellated Ridge, Castle Ravine and Mt. Jefferson. At 4.2 mi. Israel Ridge Path splits L off Randolph Path and ascends moderately up rocky W flank of Mt. Adams; in places footway is paved with flat rocks placed by J. R. Edmands' crews. Grade eases on grassy plateau shortly before reaching Gulfside Trail on SW ridge of Adams at 4.6 mi. / 5225 ft. (To R, Gulfside descends easily over open ridge 0.7 mi. to Edmands Col.) Turn L here as Israel Ridge Path and Gulfside Trail coincide, quickly passing tiny pool known as Storm Lake (sometimes dry in summer) on L, and descend slightly to lushly vegetated depression, where unreliable Peabody Spring is on L. Trail now rises moderately with rocky footing along S flank of Sam Adams. At 5.1 mi. / 5475 ft. diverge R off Gulfside on Israel Ridge Path, which climbs over tumbled rocks (follow cairns carefully) and joins Lowe's Path at 5.2 mi. Bear R here and rock hop up cone at moderate grade to summit at 5.4 mi. / 5799 ft.

Southwest Approach from Edmands Col

For those traversing the Northern Presidential ridge from Mt. Jefferson towards Mt. Adams, the gentle climb up Adams' SW ridge from Edmands Col provides a scenic and relatively easy stretch of above-treeline walking. From the col (4938 ft.), Gulfside Trail ascends gradually up the ledgy ridgecrest, passing wild and impressive crags. There are excellent views R into Jefferson Ravine, with the Carters and Mt. Washington beyond, back to Mt. Jefferson, and L to the Castellated Ridge and North Country. Easy to moderate climbing continues to a 5200-ft. shoulder with more fine views.

Trail skirts to L of small rocky peak of Adams 5 (5274 ft.) and soon reaches jct. L with Israel Ridge Path (5225 ft.) at 0.7 mi. from Edmands Col. From here, follow combined Israel Ridge Path / Gulfside Trail for 0.5 mi., Israel Ridge Path for 0.1 mi., and Lowe's Path for 0.2 mi., as described above under Israel Ridge Path route. Distance from Edmands Col to summit of Adams is 1.5 mi. with 900-ft. elevation gain.

South Approaches from Great Gulf

Backpackers or very strong day hikers can approach Mt. Adams from the Great Gulf Trail in the Great Gulf Wilderness. Great Gulf Trail starts at parking area (1350 ft.) on NH 16, 4.1 mi. N of AMC Pinkham Notch Camp and 6.5 mi. S of US 2 in Gorham. As described in Mt. Washington chapter, Great Gulf Trail leads at easy to moderate grades up valley of West Branch of Peabody River. For details on approach to Adams–Madison col via steep Madison Gulf Trail, leaving 2.8 mi. from Great Gulf trailhead, see chapter on Mt. Madison. One-way distance from Great Gulf trailhead to Adams summit via Great Gulf Trail, Madison Gulf Trail, Parapet Trail and Star Lake Trail is 6.5 mi. with 4500-ft. elevation gain.

Another possible approach is the Buttress Trail. This long route offers a great variety of scenery. From Great Gulf Trail, 4.5 mi. from trailhead, take Six Husbands Trail across West Branch (difficult at high water) and up at easy to moderate grade along Jefferson Brook to jct. R with Buttress Trail at 5.0 mi. / 3350 ft. Turn R on Buttress Trail, which immediately crosses Jefferson Brook, swings L where side path leads R to campsite area, then climbs to R turn leading up to extensive talus slope at 5.2 mi. Trail angles ENE up this steep, open slope of large rocks, with difficult footing but excellent views of Great Gulf, Jefferson's Knee and Jefferson Ravine. Trail reenters woods at top of talus and climbs steadily for 0.3 mi., then swings L (N) and eases at 5.5 mi / 3925 ft. It now traverses gently sloping wooded shoulder for some distance, passes reliable spring on L at 6.0 mi. / 4300 ft., and continues moderately up with rough footing. Pass under roof-like rock at 6.2 mi., then climb steeply with some scrambles to ledge with excellent views E and S at 6.4 mi. Trail now ascends in open, passing several perches on R with spectacular views of Mt. Madison rising from Madison Gulf. Trail then eases and traverses bouldery slope with rough footing, makes short descent, then climbs through high scrub to Star Lake Trail in Adams–Madison col at 6.9 mi. / 4900 ft. Turn L on Star Lake Trail for steep, rough climb up open rocks to summit of Adams at 7.6 mi. / 5799 ft.

Winter

Being the second highest peak in the Whites, but at the top of the list in terms of total elevation gain from start to finish, a winter hike to

Mt. Adams is a serious undertaking. As the upper mile or more of the climb is above treeline, hikers usually will be exposed to cold winds and treacherous footing featuring a mix of ice, snow and broken rock. Only strong and experienced hikers, fully equipped for extended above-treeline travel, should attempt this climb, and then, only in good weather. Full crampons are required. Lowe's Path and Valley Way, both with ample winter parking, are the most commonly used approach routes and are usually well packed-out through the winter. The Valley Way approach provides the opportunity for strong hikers to climb both Adams and Madison and is sheltered almost all the way to Madison Hut. The steep, wooded middle section of Lowe's Path tends to be icy through much of the season. Particular care should be taken to follow the correct route where several trails diverge at Thunderstorm Junction. The Air Line and Spur Trail routes receive some use in winter. Any of the routes through King Ravine will probably require technical climbing and in any case should be avoided due to avalanche danger. The Israel Ridge Path route and especially the Buttress Trail approach are rarely used in winter.

The RMC's Gray Knob Cabin, situated at the crest of Nowell Ridge just off Lowe's Path, operates on a year-round basis and is ideal as a base camp for hikers looking to ascend any of the northern peaks, but especially Mt. Adams. The insulated cabin accommodates up to 15 guests on a first come, first serve basis. An overnight fee is charged per person.

View Guide

Many hikers have long considered Mount Adams to possess the grandest view of all the White Mountain 4000-footers. "It rivals the magnificent sweep of being on Washington, without the foreground clutter, and with even more of a sense of the world dropping away on all sides," once wrote the late Guy Waterman, whose peakbagging credentials rival those of any White Mountain hiker.

The summits of more than 30 of New Hampshire's highest peaks can be seen from Adams's sharp crown, while many of Maine's highest peaks, including the jumble of 4000-footers in the Rangeley Lakes region, are also seen from the summit far to the NE.

The most dramatic summit view is that looking S and SW across the gaping chasm of the Great Gulf and Jefferson Ravine toward Mts. Washington and Jefferson. Washington's summit, with its myriad of mountaintop buildings and towers, lies just to the W of S, and towers 2000 ft. above the remote inner recesses of the Great Gulf. Sloping down from Washington's summit to the E (L) one sees the auto road twisting its way up the mountain from Pinkham Notch, while above and to the R is Chandler Ridge, with its two notable knobs, Nelson Crag and Ball Crag, seen side-by-side due S.

To the R of Washington along its long connecting ridge with Jefferson is the sharp double peak of Mt. Clay. Sandwich Dome and its spur, Jennings Peak, are seen in the distance through the Washington–Clay col. Just above the R (true) summit of Clay and in the middle distance is the round dome of Mt. Carrigain. On clear days distant Mt. Kearsarge is visible between Sandwich Dome and Carrigain, over the L summit of Clay, and on very clear days Mt. Monadnock can be spotted beyond Kearsarge on the L. Directly below Clay's summit spire, rising up out of the Great Gulf, is the wildly steep and narrow E ridge of Jefferson known as Jefferson's Knee. To the R of Clay are the East Peak and main summit of Mt. Osceola, with Mt. Tecumseh popping up between them and Osceola's Middle and West Peaks farther R.

Next to the R and closer is the extended ridge of Mt. Hancock, with South Hancock under Middle Osceola and North Hancock to the R of West Osceola, and NW Hancock out to the R, above the much nearer peak of Mt. Willey. Closer in under South Hancock and Middle Osceola, off the lower R slope of Clay, is the small bare summit of Pierce with its W ridge descending to the R. The sprawling Mt. Cardigan is seen in the distance above Willey and NW Hancock. The two peaks of East Scar Ridge peer over between North and NW Hancock, with a spur of Cardigan in the distance. The sharp Middle Scar Ridge is to the R of NW Hancock and Willey, with Cataloochee Mtn. above, then one sees Mt. Hitchcock under the L end of the broad main mass of Scar Ridge with Stinson Mtn. beyond. Mt. Field is to the R of Willey, joined by a long ridge. Loon Mtn. peers over the R side of Field, with the E ridge of Mt. Kineo above and Croydon Peak on the horizon to the L. To the R of and beyond Field are Carr Mtn. (L) and Mt. Kineo (R). Vermont's Mt. Ascutney is on the horizon to the R of Kineo, with the L half of Mt. Cushman below. Next to the R and close at hand to the SW is the barren summit of Mt. Jefferson, rising dramatically above the depths of Jefferson Ravine, with Mt. Bond's top just visible to the L of the 5716-ft. peak. Following Jefferson's W ridge down to Jefferson Notch, visible above in the distance are (L to R) Mt. Liberty's sharp peak peering over the Guyot–South Twin ridge, Mt. Moosilauke, South Twin, and Mts. Lincoln and Lafayette. North Twin is under Lafayette with Mt. Hale below, and North Kinsman (L) and the tip of Cannon Mtn. (R) are seen over the R shoulder of Lafayette. The ski slopes of Bretton Woods are seen on Mt. Rosebrook (L) and Mt. Oscar (R) low down in this direction, just over the slope of Jefferson, and close at hand and lower still is the rocky landscape of Edmands Col.

Farther R, looking WSW, Mt. Deception rises above Mt. Dartmouth in the nearby Dartmouth Range, on the opposite side of Jefferson Notch. In this direction a long chain of Green Mountains runs along the horizon, with bulky Breadloaf Mtn. identifiable to the R of Deception's sharp W Peak. The lowly twin knobs of Mts. Cleveland and Agassiz in Bethlehem are seen just above and to the R of the Dartmouth Range, with Vermont's lumpy Signal Mtn. range and then the long Mt. Abraham–Mt. Ellen ridge beyond. Distant Mt. Grant is to the L of the Signal Range's L end. To the R of the Dartmouth Range, looking due W over the nearby rocky piles of Mt. Sam Adams, is Cherry Mtn. in nearby Jefferson with its spur, Owl's Head, on its R. To the L of Cherry, some 80 mi. away, is Vermont's Camel's Hump, with Mt. Ethan Allen on its L. Vermont's Worcester Range is seen over Cherry and Owl's Head, and father R is sprawling Mt. Mansfield with the Sterling Range on its R. Cherry Pond, just 11 mi. distant, sparkles in the broad Jefferson Meadows seen above and to the R of Mt. Sam Adams. Farther R on the Vermont skyline are (L to R) Belvidere Mtn., Tillotson Peak and Haystack Mtn., with the paired Burke (L, under Haystack) and Umpire (R) Mtns. in front.

Next to the R the Jay Peaks in far northern Vermont loom on the horizon above US 2 and Jefferson village, with Adams 4 seen below the highway. To the R of the Jays and closer is East Haven Mtn. with Mt. Pisgah at Willoughby Gap peering over. In the back a range extends R from Jay Peak across into Canada, with the nearer Bald Mtn. in the Northeast Kingdom to the R, seen over the L slope of the nearby Pliny Range. Looking NW, the Pliny Range rises out of the village of Jefferson to Mts. Starr King (L) and Waumbek (R), with Mt. Pliny seen under Waumbek's long, level E ridge. East Mtn. in Vermont is seen beyond Starr King on the L, and the Sutton Mountains range in southern Quebec is on the horizon above Starr King. To the R of Waumbek's E ridge is rounded South Weeks, with Vermont's Gore Mtn. on the horizon. Lowe's Store can be seen down on the valley floor under the low point between Waumbek and South Weeks.

Next to the R the Pilot Range's Mt. Cabot, with its telltale talus field high on its S slope, rises above North Weeks, with Hutchins Mtn. peering over Cabot's L ridge and Brousseau (L, with visible cliffs) and Sable (R) Mtns. on the skyline. To Cabot's R are The Bulge and The Horn, two New England 100 Highest peaks, with the Pond of Safety below (in front of the E ridge of North Weeks) and Goback Mtn. in the distance over The Bulge. Vermont's broad Monadnock Mtn. is seen behind Goback on the R. To the R of The Horn is the lower Unknown Pond Peak, with the Nash Stream Mtns. beyond (L to R): West Peak, Castle Mtn., Sugarloaf with the bare Percy Peaks below, Bunnell Mtn., and Gore Mtn. Farther R, in the foreground, beyond the mouth of King Ravine, is Mt. Randolph in the Crescent Range with Lookout Ledge below. Above Mt. Randolph in the Kilkenny area (to the R of Unknown Pond Peak) are Rogers Ledge on the L and the long Deer Ridge on the R with cliff-faced Square Mtn. and Greens Ledge peering over. In the distance above these is well-named Long Mtn. with North Whitcomb (Muise) Mtn. rising in back on the R. To the R of Mt. Randolph is Mt. Crescent with the broad mass of Dixville

Peak beyond. Cave Mtn., Rice Mtn. and other North Country ridges are to the R of Dixville. Farther R, looking just E of N beyond the Knife Edge on Durand Ridge and the Randolph valley, is the double summit of Black Crescent Mtn. Magalloway Mtn. is seen on the horizon over the flatter R summit, with Quebec's Mt. Megantic behind it on the L. Down in the valley below the L summit of Black Crescent is Durand Lake. A bit farther R on the skyline is the distinctive truncated shape of Rump Mtn. on the New Hampshire–Maine border. Continuing to the R, the sharp peak of Mt. Dustan is seen under the skyline, then little, ledgy Jericho Mtn. is seen much closer with Aziscohos Mtn. and an array of more distant high ridges in the boundary country of NW Maine beyond. Next to the R, looking NNE, the waters of Lake Umbagog on the New Hampshire–Maine border are visible to the R of Aziscohos Mtn.; the wavy crest of West Kennebago Mtn. is to the R of the lake. Farther R the long flat crest of Cambridge Black Mtn. is seen beyond the city of Berlin, with still more NW Maine ridges in the distance, including the mass of East Kennebago Mtn. just R of the city.

Next to the R you look down on nearby rocky hump of Mt. John Quincy Adams, with Rt. 16 between Berlin and Gorham beyond and flat Red Ridge above in the middle distance. To the R of Red Ridge, above a low double knob, is the distant pointed peak of Coburn Mtn. in Maine. Farther R and closer, over a low, ledgy spur of Cascade Mtn. in the southern Mahoosucs, are the paired Bemis Mtn. (L) and Elephant Mtn. (R), with flat Old Blue Mtn. extending to the R of Elephant. The Horns and West Peak of Bigelow Mtn. near Flagstaff Lake are behind Elephant on the R, and Crocker Mtn. (L) and Saddleback Mtn. (R) are above Old Blue. Next to the R and much closer is Old Speck Mtn., highest of the Mahoosuc Range, with Mahoosuc Arm in front on the L and Baldpate Mtn. peering over in back on its R. Ledgy Mt. Hayes is low down in front of Old Speck, with the rocky Cascade Mtn. behind it on the L across a deep saddle and the elongated Bald Cap Mtn. farther R. Sugarloaf and Spaulding Mtns. are in the distance above Old Speck and Baldpate, with the sprawling Mt. Abraham to their R.

Close by to the NE you have a dramatic look down on Mt. Madison's sharp, bare summit, with tiny Star Lake nestled in the flat col at its base and the long, serrated Osgood Ridge stretching out to the R. In the Mahoosuc Range a bit L of Madison's peak (under the R end of Mt. Abraham) is Goose Eye Mtn., with Fulling Mill Mtn. immediately to its L and Mt. Success blending in underneath. Behind Goose Eye on the R is Sunday River Whitecap, with the Jackson Mtns. near Weld, Maine, on the horizon. Reflection Pool in the Androscoggin River is to the R of Madison's summit, with Lary Brook Mtn. in the Mahoosucs and Puzzle Mtn. near Grafton Notch above it and the distant pyramid of Mt. Blue in back on the R. Next to the R, above upper Osgood Ridge, are the higher summits of

the eastern Mahoosucs (L to R): Bear Mtn., Black Mtn. and Wheeler Mtn.
The distinctive duo of Bald and Saddleback Wind Mtns. are on the horizon
above Black and Wheeler. Continuing to the R, the N end of the Carter–
Moriah Range rises out of the Androscoggin valley to the three Moriah
summits, seen above the middle of Osgood Ridge. The ledgy hump of
Shelburne Moriah Mtn. is on the L above Middle Moriah, and Mt. Moriah
is to the R. The many lower summits S of Rumford, Maine, including Mt.
Zircon, Speckled and Black Mtns., and Spruce Mtn. are beyond the Mo-
riahs. Peabody Mtn. is seen through the gap between the Moriahs, and
Gammon (L) and Caribou (R) Mtns. on the E side of Evans Notch are vis-
ible above the rocky S ridge of Mt. Moriah. Haystack Mtn. extends R from
Caribou to Haystack Notch, with the wild crags of Imp Mtn. in front.

The high, wooded ridgecrest of the Carters dominates the E view
across the Peabody River valley, running across nearly to the SE, starting
with North Carter on the L (and the Imp Face cliff down in front on the
L) and extending across Mt. Lethe, Middle Carter and South Carter to
Mt. Hight and the giant, slide-scarred Carter Dome standing guard over
the Glen House clearing and NH 16 as it climbs toward Pinkham Notch.
On very clear days the bumpy chain of the Camden Hills on the Maine
coast can be espied above and to the L of North Carter. The much closer
East Royce is seen behind North Carter on the L, with the low ridge of
Butters Mtn. and the top of Redrock Mtn. cliff behind on the L. West
Royce (L) and Speckled Mtn. (R) peer over the col on the R side of North
Carter, with Maine's Streaked Mtn. on the horizon. The top of North
Baldface's Bicknell Ridge pokes over Zeta Pass between South Carter and
Hight. Wildcat A is to the R of Carter Dome, forming the W side of
Carter Notch. Chandler Mtn. is seen through the notch, with Kezar Pond
and the long crest of Maine's Pleasant Mtn. beyond. Part of Sebago Lake
can be seen beyond Pleasant. Mt. Shaw and the twin Gemini are behind
Wildcat C, the Doubleheads with Rickers Knoll behind are seen through
Wildcat Col, and farther R Kearsarge North rises above Wildcats D and
E and the Wildcat ski slopes. Maine's Saddleback Hills are beyond the
Doubleheads, and above Kearsarge North and successively farther are the
Burnt Meadow Mtns., the Bill Merrill Mtn. group, and the Clark Mtn.
range. Black Cap Mtn. is seen over the saddle between Kearsarge North
and its spur on the R, Bartlett Mtn. Farther R are the lower peaks of the
Green Hills, with Thorn Mtn. seen in front and part of Conway Lake
seen at their R base. Farther back and to the R, seen through Pinkham
Notch and beyond the slope descending L from Mt. Washington's Nelson
Crag, are various hills along the Maine–New Hampshire border, includ-
ing the double hump of Green Mtn. in Effingham, seen above a prominent section of the Mt. Washington Auto Road. The top of White Horse
Ledge peers over a low ridge of Little Attitash Mtn., in line with Green
Mtn. Farther R are South, Middle and North Moat with the Moose Mtns.

(L) and Copple Crown Mtn. (R) on the horizon, then the view swings up
to nearby Nelson Crag.

NO. OF 4000-FOOTERS VISIBLE: 31

Mount Eisenhower

ELEVATION: 4760 ft. / 1451 m   ORDER OF HEIGHT: 12
LOCATION: Southern Presidential Range, Townships of Chandlers
    Purchase, Sargents Purchase and Cutts Grant
USGS MAPS: 7½′ Stairs Mtn., 7½′ Mt. Washington

Geography

The round, symmetrical dome of Mt. Eisenhower is, as one nineteenth-
century guidebook author wrote, "the most conspicuous" peak in the
southern reaches of the Presidential Range. Situated approximately halfway between the peaks at the N end of Crawford Notch and massive
Mt. Washington, capstone of the Presidentials, Eisenhower is arguably
the finest of the peaks along this portion of New Hampshire's greatest
mountain range.

Mt. Eisenhower lies along the ridgeline between Mts. Pierce and
Franklin, and its most striking features are its massive, bare, dome-shaped
crown (seen especially well from the Bretton Woods–Crawford Notch
region) and its expansive, nearly flat summit area, some six acres in size.
A ledgy, knobby ridge extends to Mt. Pierce on the SW, while the barren
bulge of Mt. Franklin rises abruptly along the ridge to the NE.

As seen from the Bretton Woods side, several old, mostly revegetated
landslides scar the mountain's W slopes. Some of these landslides crashed
down the mountain in 1826, the year of the tragic Willey family slide in
nearby Crawford Notch. Abenaki Ravine, out of which flows Abenaki
Brook, cuts deep into the mountain slopes WSW of the summit dome;
a prominent slide fell at its head in the mid-1990s. Spur ridges run NW
and WNW from the summit, with Mt. Pleasant Brook flowing between
them. The Edmands Path ascends the WNW ridge.

To the E of the mountain is the great Dry River Valley, with Oakes
Gulf, a large glacial cirque, at its head between Mt. Monroe and Boott
Spur. The Dry River (or Mt. Washington River, as it is sometimes called)
drains to the S out of Oakes Gulf, converging with the Saco River at
the S end of Crawford Notch. Nearly all of the Dry River Valley lies in
the remote Presidential Range–Dry River Wilderness. Closer to the NE
of Eisenhower are two tributary SE-facing cirques, one between Mts.

Franklin and Monroe and the other between Mts. Franklin and Eisenhower. The steep SE face of Eisenhower's dome overlooks yet another cirque-like basin that drains S, then E into the main valley of Dry River. A long ridge extends S from the Eisenhower–Franklin col, enclosing this basin and providing a route for the Mt. Eisenhower Trail. At the base of this ridge, on the main river, is beautiful and secluded Dry River Falls, just off the Dry River Trail.

Near the NE base of Eisenhower's summit cone is Red Pond, a tiny mountain tarn once described by guidebook author Moses Sweetser as "a dull puddle of bad water." Red Pond is unique in that in times of heavy rain, it purportedly drains into both the Ammonoosuc and Saco River valleys. Its name is culled from the red moss that is so prolific in the general vicinity of Mount Eisenhower.

For years, a large pile of stones has marked the official summit of the peak, though this cairn is somewhat lower in elevation than in the past. On crystal clear days, with the aid of quality binoculars, it is possible to spot the summit cairn from as far as 15 miles away.

Nomenclature

The peak, originally known as Mount Pleasant or Pleasant Dome, was renamed in 1972 in honor of the nation's thirty-fourth president, Dwight D. Eisenhower. Until 1820, the mountain was a nameless, but prominent bump along the mountain ridge. It was first dubbed Mt. Pleasant by the Weeks–Brackett party, a group of mountain explorers from nearby Lancaster, led by Ethan Allen Crawford, who hiked up onto Mt. Washington to choose names for the peaks in the Presidentials. As there were not enough former presidents to go around for all the summits on the range, the group decided on the name "Pleasant" for the round, bald mountain. They may have been influenced by the toasts of a concoction called "O-be-joyful" that had been raised as each previous peak was christened. Other early names for the mountain were "Mt. Prospect," used by James Pierce in an 1824 article, "Dome Mountain," and "Pleasant Dome."

After President Eisenhower died in 1969, New Hampshire notable Sherman Adams, formerly Assistant to the President under Ike, led the effort to rename the mountain. The change was approved by the U.S. Board on Geographic Names, and the official dedication took place in 1972 at the Eisenhower Wayside Park by US 302. Many an observer has since noted the resemblance between the bare summit dome and Ike's bald pate.

Historical Highlights

First Ascent: Possibly by Darby Field and his Indian companions back in June 1642, during Field's monumental first ascent of Mt. Washington. Recently uncovered material seems to indicate that Field's route up the mountain may have taken him over several of the southern Presidential Range peaks (including Eisenhower), and not up and over Boott Spur, as previously thought.

1811: Capt. Alden Partridge, founder of Norwich University, traverses Southern Presidentials with guide Ethan Allen Crawford. Walk more or less follows route of soon-to-be-built Crawford Path.

1819: Crawfords construct footpath from top of Crawford Notch to Mt. Washington, following for most part ridgeline of Southern Presidentials. Trail runs over summit of mountain that one year later (1820) would be named Mount Pleasant by group of Lancastrians guided onto Presidentials by Ethan Allen Crawford.

1840: Crawfords upgrade Crawford Path over Southern Presidentials to bridle path.

Late 1840s: Second trail up Mt. Pleasant is established from Fabyan area at Bretton Woods. Trail serves as bridle path, similar to many others developed throughout the White Mountains during this time period.

1867: *Eastman's White Mountain Guide* notes that even though Crawford Path now bypasses main summit of Mt. Pleasant, an unmarked path can still be followed to its top. Horses, however, "can very seldom be induced to take" this loop trail over the summit.

Ca. 1870: Party from Charles H. Hitchcock's N.H. Geological Survey bushwhacks from Crawford Path at col between Eisenhower and Franklin down into Dry River Valley. Vol. II of published report notes "interesting series of falls on this river, 5 or 6 mi. above its junction with the Saco." J. H. Huntington writes description of what is now known as Dry River Falls, noting that main drop is 23 ft. high.

1890: Author Rev. Julius Ward says of view from mountaintop: "The ridge from the peak of Jefferson to that of Washington looks like the wall of a fortress laid close to the sky, and the whole range might bid defiance to the armaments of the world."

1892–1898: Saco Valley Lumber Company builds logging railroad up Dry River valley to SE of Mt. Eisenhower and logs much of valley. Line features a dozen trestles over river and extends to ca. 2700 ft., about where brook flowing from ravine SE of Eisenhower drains into Dry River. At peak of operation some 200–300 men are working in the woods, but line is short-lived, partly due to high maintenance costs. RR grade later used for part of Dry River Trail.

1896: After lengthy period of disuse, Fabyan bridle path from Bretton Woods is restored. The trail, known as the Mt. Pleasant Path, passes "Lucky Strike Spring" on ascent and connects with loop trail over summit about halfway up cone on S side of peak.

1906: AMC Snow-Shoe Section makes successful winter ascent of mountain.

1909: J. Rayner Edmands, architect of many of the trails criss-crossing the Northern Peaks of the Presidentials, relocates and grades portions of trail from Fabyan's to area just N of summit. The durability and quality of his work is still quite evident on the upper part of the trail, which is appropriately named the Edmands Path.

1916: *AMC Guide* notes that upper section of old Mt. Pleasant Path, connecting with loop trail over summit, diverges R off Edmands Path near stone gateway half-mile from upper terminus of new path in Pleasant–Franklin col.

1918: Willard Helburn and Henry Chamberlain complete first single-day winter traverse of Presidential Range peaks, including Mt. Pleasant. Despite stormy weather, group covers 22 miles in 14 hours and climbs over nine summits (including Monroe twice).

1919: AMC officially designates connecting trail from Crawford Path to summit as Mt. Pleasant Loop.

1928: Cut-off trail between Edmands Path, Mt. Pleasant Loop no longer warrants mention in *AMC Guide*.

1932: Dry River valley is added to WMNF; trail is soon opened up through valley, using portions of old logging railroad grade.

1934: First mention in AMC guide of new Mt. Pleasant Trail, opened a year earlier by CCC, linking Dry River valley to Crawford Path in Pleasant–Franklin col. Also, Edmands Path now listed as officially beginning on E side of Mt. Clinton Road, not at Bretton Woods, as previously described.

1972: Three years after N.H. legislature passes bill authorizing name change, ceremony is held near Bretton Woods to formally christen peak Mt. Eisenhower, in honor of WW II hero and former U. S. President Dwight D. Eisenhower. Representing Eisenhower clan at event is Julie Nixon Eisenhower, daughter of President Richard Nixon and wife of David Eisenhower, grandson of Ike.

Early 1970s: Upper part of Mt. Eisenhower Trail is relocated, along with lower part of Dry River Trail, the latter to eliminate dangerous river crossings at which two hikers had drowned.

1975: Ridges and valleys on E side of Eisenhower are included in new Presidential Range–Dry River Wilderness.

Mid-1990s: Prominent slide comes down at head of Abenaki Ravine.

Trail Approaches

West Approach from Mt. Clinton Road

Edmands Path, Mt. Eisenhower Loop
6.6 mi. round trip, 2750-ft. elevation gain

TRAILHEAD (2000 ft.): Parking area for Edmands Path is on E side of Mt. Clinton Road, 2.3 mi. N of US 302 at Crawford Notch and 1.3 mi. S of jct. of Base Road and Jefferson Notch Road.

If it's just Mt. Eisenhower that you're looking to climb, then the Edmands Path is the choice ascent route. This historic trail, sections of which date back more than 150 years, was masterfully reconstructed in 1909 by J. Rayner Edmands, one of the true pioneer White Mountain trail builders in the late nineteenth and early twentieth centuries. Grades are moderate, with no really steep sections. Though parts of the trail have eroded over the years, overall the footing is good for a trail to a high peak. The upper 0.5 mi. of this route is fully exposed to weather.

Blue-blazed trail starts off on level, easy grades, crosses two small brooks, and at 0.4 mi. crosses Abenaki Brook on plank bridge. On far side trail turns R onto old woods road, turns L off it at 0.7 mi., and soon begins moderate ascent through forest of maple, beech and birch. Steady, uneventful climb continues up into deep fir forest at ca. 3000 ft. At 2.2 mi. / 4000 ft., trail jogs R and L, passes through stone gateway, and climbs past small stream flowing over ledges (treacherous if icy) at 2.5 mi. / 4225 ft. After short, steep ledgy pitch above crossing, climb eases as trail begins graded traverse across NW ridge. Occasional views down to Bretton Woods and vicinity are gained on L.

Trail swings around nose of ridge and runs nearly level through scrub firs and stunted birches, with views N to Mt. Jefferson; Mt. Franklin looms close by to NE. Cross open talus slope on carefully laid rocks and emerge above treeline, reaching jct. with Mt. Eisenhower Loop at 2.9 mi. / 4450 ft., a short distance below loop's N jct. with Crawford Path. This is just SW of Eisenhower–Franklin col. Loop trail to summit leaves R, dips slightly with tiny Red Pond to L (short side path leads to shore of this often-mucky water body), then zigzags steeply in open up NE end of summit ridge. Ledges offer views up ridge to Mt. Franklin, down to Red Pond and out to Dry Diver valley. Grade then eases along tundra-like crest for pleasant stretch of walking with wide views. Summit, marked by large cairn and delineated resting / viewing area around it, is attained at 3.3 mi. / 4760 ft. When walking above timberline, especially on Eisenhower's summit cone, be sure to stay on marked trail to protect fragile alpine plants found along Presidential Range.

Southwest Approach from Mt. Clinton Rd.

Crawford Path, Mount Eisenhower Loop
9.4 mi. round trip, 3200-ft. elevation gain

TRAILHEAD (1900 ft.): This approach starts at parking area for Crawford Path on L (W) side of Mt. Clinton Rd., 0.1 mi. N of its jct. with US 302 near AMC Highland Center at top of Crawford Notch.

Another popular, but significantly longer, way to ascend Mt. Eisenhower is via the historic Crawford Path, constructed in 1819 by the pioneering Crawford family, from the top of Crawford Notch. Follow Crawford Connector to Crawford Path at 0.4 mi., then climb on steady grades (for details see Mt. Pierce chapter) and reach timberline at 3.1 mi. / 4250 ft.,

The summit view from Mount Eisenhower features an impressive view north towards Mounts Franklin, Monroe, and Washington.

where Webster Cliff Trail from summits of Mt. Pierce and Jackson comes in on R. (Summit of Pierce is 0.1 mi. up this trail.) Crawford Path descends gradually NE through patchy scrub, frequently passing over ledges with fine views in various directions. After passing over several minor humps along ridge, small stream is crossed in col at 3.8 mi. / ca. 4060 ft., then grade steepens as ascent of Eisenhower begins. S end of Mt. Eisenhower Loop to summit is reached at 4.3 mi. / 4425 ft. Diverge L onto loop trail for 0.4 mi., 335 ft. climb to summit, ascending steadily in open via switchbacks with continuous views, including Mt. Pierce close by to SW. Section that cuts across S side of summit after sharp R turn has especially good view of Dry River valley. Broad open summit and large cairn are attained at 4.7 mi. / 4760 ft.

Note: From either Edmands Path or Crawford Path approach, loop can be made over Eisenhower's summit using full 0.8 mi. length of Mt. Eisenhower Loop and looping back via 0.5 mi. section of Crawford Path that contours mostly through scrub, with some rough rocky footing, along steep SE slope of mountain.

South Approach from US 302 via Dry River Valley

**Dry River Trail, Mt. Eisenhower Trail, Crawford Path,
   Mt. Eisenhower Loop**
8.5 mi. one way, 3850-ft. elevation gain

TRAILHEAD (1205 ft.): This approach starts on Dry River Trail on E side of US 302 in Crawford Notch State Park, 0.3 mi. N of Dry River Campground. There is roadside parking for several cars.

Though seldom used by day hikers, this route provides an attractive hike up the remote Dry River valley and a spur ridge leading to the crest of the Southern Presidentials between Mts. Eisenhower and Franklin. With a car spot at Edmands Path trailhead, an interesting 11.8 mi. traverse is possible. Because of a potentially difficult crossing of Dry River, this route should not be attempted in high water. Also, note that trails in this Wilderness area are maintained to a lower standard and may be rough and obscure.

From trailhead, Dry River Trail follows old road at easy grade through fine hardwood forest for 0.5 mi., where Saco River Trail diverges L and path from Dry River Campground comes in on R. Here Dry River Trail joins old logging railroad grade and mostly follows it to edge of boulder-filled Dry River at 0.9 mi., where there is attractive pool downstream to R. Trail bears L here and climbs to bank, then descends back to riverside. Short steep sidehill climb leads to framed view of Mt. Washington at head of valley at 1.5 mi. / 1700 ft. Trail drops steeply to cross suspension footbridge at 1.7 mi. and continues up valley, with rough ups-and-downs, then nice section with easy walking on RR grade. (*Note*: The suspension bridge was seriously damaged by a flood in 2005 and was closed at that time for safety reasons. It is scheduled to be repaired in summer of 2008. Without the bridge this crossing is difficult and possibly dangerous in high water. For update call Saco Ranger Station at 604–447–5448.) Reach jct. L with Mt. Clinton Trail at 2.9 mi. / 1900 ft. Keep on Dry River Trail up valley, on rough section and then RR grade, crossing brook at 3.6 mi. At 4.2 mi. trail makes R turn up to higher bank and weaves through beautiful birches, passing old logging camp site. At 4.9 mi. / 2600 ft. cross Isolation Brook and reach jct. R with Isolation Trail. Stay on Dry River Trail along bank high above river, passing cleared outlook L up to high boreal ridge of Mt. Pierce.

At 5.2 mi. / 2650 ft. turn sharp L on Mt. Eisenhower Trail and descend to crossing of Dry River on large rocks—difficult in high water. (For scenic detour, continue 0.2 mi. ahead on Dry River Trail to short, obscure path that drops steeply L to pool at base of Dry River Falls, a wild, remote spot.) Mt. Eisenhower Trail heads downstream for 0.2 mi., then swings R (NW) and climbs easily to jct. L with Dry River Cutoff at 5.5 mi. Mt. Eisenhower Trail now climbs N up W side of ridge at varying grades. At ca. 6.5 mi. / 3300 ft. pass through blowdown areas with dense young growth and occasional views of Mts. Pierce and Jackson and Eisenhower's bald dome, and down into remote valley to W. Sharp R turn at 7.0 mi. / 3600 ft. leads to steeper, rocky ascent through thick woods. Partial views back to S and up to Eisenhower and Franklin begin at ca. 4000 ft., and trail attains crest of W ridge at 7.6 mi. / 4200 ft. Pass outlook on R with view SW and wind upward through high scrub to treeline and views back into Dry River valley. Continue in open across flat, broad ridge between Franklin and Eisenhower and meet Crawford Path at 7.9 mi. / 4475 ft.

Turn L on Crawford Path, descend slightly to sag on ridge, and climb by switchbacks to jct. R with Mt. Eisenhower Loop at 8.1 mi., with Red Pond to L. Turn R on Eisenhower Loop, quickly pass jct. R with Edmands Path, and climb 0.4 mi. / 300 ft. to summit at 8.5 mi. / 4760 ft.

Winter

For a variety of reasons, the hike up Mt. Eisenhower is considerably tougher in winter than in any other season. For starters, the standard ascent route, the Edmands Path, is difficult to reach as the Mt. Clinton Road receives sparse winter maintenance and the trailhead parking lot is not plowed. This means anyone wishing to ascend via this trail will most likely have to walk the road for 2.2 mi. just to get to the trailhead. More often than not, winter hikers will approach the peak from Mt. Pierce via the Crawford Path, and either double back via their ascent route or take the Edmands Path down to Mt. Clinton Road, and then walk out via the road to the Crawford Path parking lot. (Note that the upper, exposed part of Edmands Path may present a difficult and possibly dangerous sidehill in crusty or icy conditions.) From Mt. Pierce to Eisenhower's summit (and especially on the latter's bald, summit cone), the Crawford Path is at or above treeline and hikers are thus exposed to the elements. On the Presidentials, this can mean low or near zero visibility, heavy snow, extreme cold temperatures and dangerous winds. Full winter regalia, including crampons, is required. If, upon reaching treeline just below Mt. Pierce's summit, conditions are less than ideal, by all means save the peakbagging for another day and retreat back down the Crawford Path.

View Guide

Perhaps no summit on the Presidential Range offers a better perspective on its southern peaks than Eisenhower. Though the broad, flat summit area lacks the dramatic flair of other White Mountain peaks, its 360 degree view more than makes up for its shortcomings. Better perspectives S and N can be gained from spots a bit down either end of the Eisenhower Loop; please stay on the marked footway.

Mt. Washington's summit cone is the dominating feature close by to the NE, with the sharp crest of Mt. Monroe seen just below and to the R of its towering neighbor, and rounded Mt. Franklin in front of and below Monroe. The long flat ridge of Boott Spur extends E from Washington over deep Oakes Gulf, then descends R to the rounded bump of Slide Peak. The jumbled peaks of Rocky Branch Ridge (in back) and the long, flat Montalban Ridge (in front) stretch S from Boott Spur and Slide Peak, on the opposite side of the broad, remote Dry River Valley. To the R of Slide Peak and closer is North Isolation at the N end of Montalban Ridge, with Chandler Mtn. beyond. Next to the R, behind nameless bumps on Montalban Ridge, are the two highest summits of Rocky Branch Ridge, with the Doubleheads seen between them. Walter Mtn. is behind the Doubleheads on the L, and Mt. Shaw and The Gemini are behind them on the R, with Maine's Pleasant Mtn. beyond. Farther R is the prominent dome of Kearsarge North, with neighbors Rickers Knoll on its L and Bartlett Mtn. on its R. Part of Sebago Lake shimmers in the distance to the L of Kearsarge North, and Thorn Mtn. is seen in front.

Continuing to the R, the summit of Mt. Isolation is seen to the SE across the Dry River valley, with Black Cap (L) and Cranmore, Middle and Rattlesnake Mtns. (R) in the Green Hills of North Conway beyond. The low ranges of western Maine—Saddleback Hills, Burnt Meadows and Clark Mtn. group—are on the horizon beyond the Green Hills. To the R of Isolation is the flat summit of Mt. Davis, with Iron Mtn. peering over and Conway Lake beyond on its L and distant Ossipee Hill in Maine on its R. Farther R North Moat is seen above the S end of Mt. Davis, with South Moat just peering over on the L. In the distance beyond North Moat are Maine's Fort Ridge on the L and Green Mtn. in Effingham on the R. The long ridge of Little Attitash is down low between North Moat and Iron, with the tips of Mts. Stanton and Pickering visible beneath. Big Attitash is to the R of North Moat, with Mt. Langdon peering over below. Farther R, beyond the lower Dry River valley and a spur ridge of Mt. Davis, are the lower Montalban summits (L to R): Mt. Parker, Mt. Resolution peering over Stairs Mtn., Crawford Dome and Mt. Crawford. Table Mtn. is behind Parker, with Ossipee Lake in the distance to its L. The rocky crown of Chocorua rises in the back above Crawford Dome, with the distant Moose Mtns. and Copple Crown Mtn. on its L and the nearer Bear Mt. on its R. The tip of Mt. Hope pokes up off the R slope of Mt. Crawford, with Bartlett Haystack above. Mt. Paugus is behind and R of Bartlett Haystack, with Mt. Shaw in the Ossipees in the distance to its L and Faraway Mtn. (L) and Black Snout (R) behind it.

Next to the R, seen beyond a part of the Saco River valley, is humpy Mt. Tremont, with the Wonalancet Hedgehog and Nanamocomuck Peak above and beyond and Belknap and Gunstock Mtns. even more distant on the L. Now the view swings R across the high peaks of the Sandwich Range: Mt. Passaconaway, Mt. Whiteface, the Sleepers and Middle and North Tripyramid. The flat crest of Mt. Saunders is below Whiteface and the Sleepers, with Green's Cliff just peeking over under East Sleeper. Mt. Bemis and Mt. Nancy are in front of Tripyramid on the R, with Sandwich Dome in the distance. Mts. Lowell and Anderson are just R of Nancy with part of Mt. Kancamagus above; Jennings Peak sticks up between Nancy and Lowell. Next to the R are Signal Ridge and the looming mass of Mt. Carrigain rising above the sharp peak of Mt. Jackson and the ledgy ridge leading towards Mt. Pierce. Mt. Webster is just R of Jackson, with the sprawling Mt. Hancock beyond; South Hancock is on the L, the flattened dome of North Hancock is in the middle, and sharp NW Hancock is on the R. The two Osceola 4000-footers are between Carrigain and South Hancock, with Mt. Tecumseh peeking up between Osceola's East Peak and main summit. Osceola's West Peak juts up between South and North Hancock. Next to the R and close by is rounded Mt. Pierce, sporting a bald spot on top, with Mt. Willey rising beyond. Scar Ridge is seen farther away to the L of Willey, with Mt. Hitchcock below. From Willey the Willey Range extends R across Mt. Field and the lower Mt. Tom. Loon Mtn. is seen over the ridge running R from Willey, with (L to R) Carr Mtn., Mt. Kineo, Mt. Cushman and Smarts Mtn. beyond on the R. The E spur of Whaleback Mtn. is seen over the Field–Willey col (under Smarts), Whaleback Mtn. itself and the S spur of Bondcliff rear up just to the L of Field, and Bondcliff and the much higher Mt. Bond are just R of Field's summit nubble. Mt. Willard and Mt. Avalon can be seen down low in front under Field. Mt. Moosilauke hovers in the distance over the N (R) shoulder of Bond. Broad Mt. Guyot is to the R of Bond, over the Field–Tom col, and Mt. Liberty sticks out above the Bond–Guyot col. Zealand Mtn. can be seen under the col to the R of Guyot.

A long ridge runs across from Guyot to South Twin, with Mts. Lincoln (above Tom) and Lafayette (just L of South Twin) rising behind. North Twin is to the R of South Twin, with Mt. Hale farther R, lower and in front. The tip of Mt. Garfield is barely visible through the col between the Twins. Nubble Peak pokes up over Hale's summit on the R, with Vermont's Signal Range beyond to the R. Mts. Abraham and Ellen are on the horizon beyond the Signal Range. Next to the R, seen low down across the Bretton Woods valley, is Mt. Rosebrook with the Bretton Woods ski trails on its R slope. Above and beyond the ski trails are Middle and North Sugarloaf, then Mt. Cleveland and Mt. Agassiz, then Mt. Ethan Allen and the distinctive Camel's Hump on the horizon. A bit farther R, down in the valley, is the Mt. Washington Hotel complex, with the Worcester Range (L, above the hotel) and Mt. Mansfield (R, over Beech Hill, with the Sterling Range extending R) in the distance. Farther R on the horizon are Belvidere Mtn., Tillotson Peak and Haystack Mtn. with the Cold Hollow Mtns. peering over to the L of Belvidere. Next to the R, looking NW, is the long, rolling crest of Mt. Deception in the nearby Dartmouth Range, rising beyond the Bretton Woods plateau. Cherry Mtn. and its sharp spur, Owl's Head, are behind the L end of Mt. Deception, with Burke (L) and Umpire (R) Mtns. above. Distant Jay Peak is just L of Burke, and Willoughby Gap, flanked by Mts. Hor and Pisgah, is to the R of Umpire, above Owl's Head. On very clear days Round Top in Quebec can be seen through the gap. East Haven Mtn. and Bald Mtn. are farther R, over the middle of Deception's elongated crest. Over the R end of Deception is East Mtn., with Stone Mtn. and little Prospect Mtn. in front. To the R of Deception, beyond a deep col, is its neighbor, Mt. Dartmouth. Gore Mtn. is in the distance over the L end of Dartmouth. Over the R side of Mt. Dartmouth are Mt. Starr King (L) and Mt. Waumbek (R) in the Pliny Range, with Goback Mtn. seen through the col between them. The tip of Hutchins Mtn. is visible between the two summit knobs of Waumbek.

Bulky Mt. Cabot peers over the long, level E ridge of Waumbek, with Pliny Mtn. below in front, and Millen Hill even closer, just across the valley. Vermont's Monadnock Mtn. just peeks over to the L of Cabot. Farther R the sharp peak of The Horn rears above South Weeks. North Weeks is next to the R, with massive Long Mtn. in the distance just to its R, above Unknown Pond Ridge. North Whitcomb (Muise) Mtn. peers over the R end of Long. Farther R is the long, low Deer Ridge in Kilkenny with Mt. Bowman in front and broad Dixville Peak on the horizon. Cave and Rice Mtns. near Dixville Notch are seen in the distance to the R of Deer Ridge. Farther R is Mt. Randolph in the Crescent Range, seen over a low spur ridge of Mt. Jefferson, with Magalloway Mtn. poking up on the horizon. Then the view swings R to the rocky ridges of Mt. Jefferson, nearby to the NNE, with the Castles behind and above the Caps Ridge. Next comes the rock-strewn pyramid of Mt. Jefferson. Below Jefferson are the ridge followed by the Jewell Trail and then the nearer ridge that hosts the Cog Railway. To the R of Jefferson is the bare, double-humped summit of Mt. Clay, then the view swings back to Mt. Washington.

NO. OF 4000-FOOTERS VISIBLE: 32

Mount Isolation

ELEVATION: 4003 ft. / 1220 m   ORDER OF HEIGHT: 47 (tie)
LOCATION: Montalban Ridge, Townships of Sargents Purchase and
    Cutts Grant
USGS MAP: 7½′ Stairs Mtn.

Geography

Those who climb the 4000-footers are often pleasantly surprised by this remote and attractive little peak beside the historic Davis Path on Montalban Ridge. Hidden from civilization deep in the Presidential Range–Dry River Wilderness, the open summit of Isolation offers a unique and captivating view of Mt. Washington and the Southern Presidentials and a wonderful sense of, well, isolation.

The bare knob of Mt. Isolation is one of many small summits on the elongated, densely wooded Montalban Ridge, which stretches nearly 20 mi. S from Mt. Washington's Boott Spur, between the valleys of Dry River and Saco River on the W and the Rocky Branch of the Saco on the E. Isolation is towards the N end of this ridge. On the N side of Isolation is a minor hump with a ridge extending E towards the Rocky Branch, and farther N is a 4293-ft. knob sometimes called "North Isolation," one of the "Trailwrights 72" summits. To the S, beyond a 3660-ft. col, is Mt. Davis (3819 ft.), a long, flat crest bearing a series of minor peaks, some of them open and ledgy. Summits farther S along the main ridge include Stairs Mtn. (3463 ft.) and Mt. Resolution (3415 ft.), with Mt. Crawford (3119 ft.) capping Bemis Ridge, a SW branch.

On the E, Isolation overlooks the remote upper valley of the Rocky Branch, an area burned in forest fires from 1912–1914 and now supporting large areas of birch forest. A prominent bald crag juts E from the S end of Isolation's summit ridge on this side; along with the E ridge of the hump just N of Isolation, it encloses a small cirque-like basin on the NE side of the mountain. Across the valley to the E rises the mostly trailless Rocky Branch Ridge, a long subsidiary ridge extending S from Mt. Washington's Slide Peak. Directly across from Isolation are the two highest peaks of this ridge, 3921 ft. and 3633 ft. respectively. The Rocky Branch Trail, part of the most commonly used route to Mt. Isolation, passes through a col S of the 3633-ft. peak; on the S side of this col is South Engine Hill (3244 ft.). On the W of Mt. Isolation is the broad, secluded basin of the Dry River (also known as Mt. Washington River), draining down from Oakes Gulf on the S side of Mt. Washington. The high ridge of the Southern Presidentials, indented with several striking glacial cirques, walls in the Dry River valley on the W. A spur ridge runs SW from Isolation into this valley. Another spur ridge runs SW to Dry River from North Isolation; at the base of this ridge is the beautiful Dry River Falls.

The usual climbing route to Mt. Isolation is long—14.6 mi. round trip—but not overly strenuous and leads through the beautiful, secluded upper Rocky Branch valley. Because of its remoteness, many peakbaggers put this one off, and 4000-Footer Club records indicate that this is the most common "finishing peak" of the 48. It's well worth the wait.

Nomenclature

Isolation is an entirely appropriate name for this remote peak. It was bestowed by William H. Pickering, one of the most active of the early AMC explorers, and first appeared on his 1882 Contour Map of the Mount Washington Range. Pickering named Mt. Davis, Isolation's near neighbor to the S, for Nathaniel T. P. Davis, a Crawford Notch innkeeper who completed the daunting task of constructing a bridle path along this ridge in 1844–

Mount Isolation as it appears from a viewpoint along Rocky Branch Ridge.

45. The first *AMC Guide* (1907) noted that two higher wooded knobs along the ridge to the N of Isolation were known as "The Twins." The name "Montalban Ridge" was applied to the entire range by guidebook editor Moses Sweetser in 1876. This was a Latin version of "white mountain" and was originally rendered as "Mount Alban." Engine Hill on Rocky Branch Ridge was named for a mishap on the Rocky Branch logging railroad.

Historical Highlights

First Ascent: Unknown

1844–1845: Nathaniel T. P. Davis, son-in-law of Abel Crawford and manager of Mt. Crawford House in lower Crawford Notch, builds 16-mile bridle trail from Saco valley to Mt. Washington. Trail runs close by summit of Mt. Isolation. Because of length and comparatively monotonous wooded middle section, Davis Path is least popular of bridle paths to Mt. Washington and falls into disuse by 1853.

1871: Joshua H. Huntington, Assistant State Geologist, traverses Davis Path along Montalban Ridge. He also visits Dry River Valley and in published report for Charles H. Hitchcock's N.H. Geological Survey, he describes Dry River Falls as an "interesting series of falls on the river, 5 or 6 mi. above its junction with the Saco," with main part dropping 23 ft.

1881: AMC party led by William H. Pickering traverses Montalban Ridge from Boott Spur down past Mt. Davis, noting that Davis Path "has now ceased to exist, and the forests form an unbroken wilderness." They admire Isolation's "superb" view of Mt. Washington and Southern Presidentials.

1892–1898: Saco Valley Lumber Company builds logging railroad up Dry River to W base of Mt. Isolation and logs much of valley. Line has more than a dozen trestles over river. At peak 200–300 men are working in woods. River washes all trestles out within a few years of close of operation. Record is marred by 1896 accident in which brakes fail on train loaded with logs; engineer and brakeman are killed. RR grade later used for part of Dry River Trail.

1895: Tourist group makes summer excursion up valley on logging RR, riding in flatcar decorated with foliage and accompanied by the "Messrs. Garland" of Saco Valley Lumber Co. Some of party walk ¾ mi. from end of line to "The Falls," said to be "a scene resembling Glen Ellis, though on a smaller scale." Account of trip appears in the *White Mountain Echo*.

1896: AMC Snow-Shoe Section makes winter excursion into Dry River Valley.

1907: First edition of *AMC White Mountain Guide* cautions that three long days should be allocated for trip over Montalban Ridge to Washington since "the path no longer exists, and the way is exceedingly difficult on account of scrub." The book notes that Mt. Isolation can be climbed by following logging road and bridle path up Rocky Branch valley (latter cut ca. 1904 by owners of land to examine spruce timber in upper valley), then climbing up slope through virgin spruce with little undergrowth.

1910: Group from AMC Snow-Shoe section makes winter ascent of Mt. Isolation. Later in year Davis Path, then almost completely overgrown, is reopened as footpath by AMC. Party led by Warren W. Hart hires Maine woodsman Joe Bouchard to find route through the dense thickets, and spends twelve days cutting and blazing, including side paths to Mt. Isolation, Mt. Davis and Giant Stairs.

1908–1914: Logging railroad constructed by Conway Lumber Company up Rocky Branch to E base of Mt. Isolation and valley is heavily logged. Railroad bed is later resurrected as Rocky Branch Trail.

1912–1914: Fires sweep through upper valley of Rocky Branch in wake of logging, burning almost 5,000 acres.

1916: *AMC Guide* mentions view from ledge by Davis Path N of Mt. Isolation at edge of 1914 fire, giving "an impressive and desolate view." AMC has established Camp Isolation, shelter off Davis Path 1 mi. N of summit.

1923: Supplement to *AMC Guide* notes that rough blazed path leads up Dry River along old lumber RR, crossing stream 11 times. Trail ends at "Fork of Three Streams," 6½ mi. up valley at ca. 3400 ft.

1925: J. Brooks Atkinson (later to become drama critic for *New York Times* and Pulitzer Prize winner) describes journey with friend Pierre along Davis Path, including cold, rainy night spent at Camp Isolation, in quirky but engaging book, *Skyline Promenades*.

Ca. 1930: WMNF opens Rocky Branch Trail, following railroad grade up valley, then crossing Rocky Branch Ridge to NH 16. A few years later Rocky Branch Ridge Trail is marked, leading S from Rocky Branch Trail at height-of-land over South Engine Hill and on to Maple Mtn., but is abandoned shortly thereafter.

Early 1930s: Dry River Trail opened up that valley by WMNF; 5 mi. in it climbs W side of Montalban Ridge to meet Davis Path at Isolation Shelter. (This upper branch is later incorporated as part of W section of Isolation Trail.) E section of Isolation Trail built, connecting Isolation Shelter with Rocky Branch Trail in valley.

Ca. 1935: WMNF builds Rocky Branch Shelter #2 near jct. Rocky Branch and Isolation Trails.

1946: New USGS map raises elevation of Mt. Isolation to 4005 ft.; was previously measured at 3970 ft. on old 1896 quad.

1975: Presidential Range–Dry River Wilderness created by Congress, includes Mt. Isolation, Montalban Ridge and adjacent valleys of Dry River and Rocky Branch.

1981: Isolation Shelter removed; W part of Isolation Trail relocated.

Trail Approaches

East Approach from NH 16

Rocky Branch Trail, Isolation Trail, Davis Path
14.6 mi. round trip, 3600-ft. elevation gain

TRAILHEAD (1200 ft.): Parking area for NE end of Rocky Branch Trail is at end of short spur road off W side of NH 16, 5.5 mi. N of covered bridge in Jackson.

This is the most commonly used approach to Isolation, involving a climb over a col on Rocky Branch Ridge and a roundabout trek up the Rocky Branch valley to Montalban Ridge N of the summit. Grades are mostly easy after an initial steady climb. There are five crossings of Rocky Branch—difficult in high water, though some can be avoided.

From parking area, Rocky Branch Trail, partly blazed in orange, climbs by switchbacks through hardwoods and passes jcts. with Avalanche Brook Ski Trail on L at 0.5 mi. and on R at 0.7 mi. After approaching small brook on R at two L turns, trail makes steady, winding climb SW up hardwood slope—stiffest climbing of trip. At 1.8 mi. / 2900 ft. make sharp L onto old logging road and proceed at easy grade, slightly downhill, through lovely glades of white birch. At 2.3 mi. trail sweeps R and climbs moderately through mixed forest to Wilderness boundary, soon cresting broad height-of-land on Rocky Branch Ridge at 2.8 mi. / 3100 ft., just N of 3244-ft. knoll known as South Engine Hill. Follow short bypass L around boggy area and descend gradually, with glimpses of Montalban Ridge ahead. Farther down this gentle grade the footing becomes wet with tedious rock-hopping in bushy terrain. At 3.5 mi. trail angles L, crossing small brook, and descends to cross Rocky Branch at 3.7 mi. / 2800 ft.

On far side, up steep bank, is jct. R with Isolation Trail. (Rocky Branch Shelter #2 is short distance L down Rocky Branch Trail.) Turn R on Isolation Trail for easy stretch mostly on old RR grade, with one small brook crossing and occasional bypasses. Cross river at 4.1 mi., and climb up off RR grade at 4.3 mi., gaining old logging road at higher level. Footing is muddy at times through weedy meadows, though recent treadway work has alleviated problem. Next two crossings of river are close together and can be avoided by short bushwhack. In this area trail passes through fine open woods of birch and fir regenerated after 1912–14 fires. Last crossing is at 5.4 mi. / 3423 ft., high up in valley.

Trail now swings L away from river and climbs gradually on rocky footway through deep, mossy, wet fir woods with primeval feel. Blow-downs and soggy footing may be encountered on this section. At 6.1 mi. follow yellow blazes carefully through confusing area of campsites and side paths. Climb to jct. with Davis Path at 6.3 mi. / 3850 ft. Turn L (S) on Davis Path for 75-ft. descent to wet sag, then follow trail at easy grades along thickly wooded ridge, with occasional peeks ahead at summit of Isolation and R to Southern Presidentials beyond Dry River valley. After crossing col, at 7.0 mi., trail veers L and steepens, climbing around NE side of summit. Reach jct. R with side path to summit of Isolation at 7.2 mi. There is sometimes a sign here, but junction is easily missed. Turn R and scramble up ledgy pitch—steepest of day—emerging on open ledges with striking panorama of Mt. Washington and Southern Presidentials at 7.3 mi. High point is at cairn a few yards S from best viewing area, beyond gap in ledges.

Return trip involves 300-ft. climb from Rocky Branch back over Rocky Branch Ridge - grade is gentle, but climb comes near end of long day!

Northeast Approach from NH 16

Glen Boulder Trail, Davis Path
12.0 mi. round trip, 5050-ft. elevation gain

TRAILHEAD (1975 ft.): Glen Boulder Trail begins at S end of parking area for Glen Ellis Falls on W side of NH 16, 0.7 mi. S of AMC Pinkham Notch Camp.

This is a shorter but considerably more strenuous approach to Isolation, with spectacular above-treeline views en route and much exposure to weather. The downside is the grueling 1500-ft. climb over the shoulder of Boott Spur on the return trip. Longer but easier is the exit via the Isolation Trail / Rocky Branch Trail route to a spotted car at the Rocky Branch trailhead on NH 16, making a 13.3 mi. point-to-point hike with 3900-ft. elevation gain.

Glen Boulder Trail leaves S edge of Glen Ellis Falls parking area and ascends past restrooms into woods. After moderate start, climb steeply to R around cliff to meet Direttissima (1.0 mi. connecting route from NH 16 just S of Pinkham Notch Visitor Center) at 0.4 mi. / 2300 ft. Turn L here and traverse slope, then climb steadily, crossing Avalanche Brook Ski Trail at 0.8 mi. / 2600 ft. Cross two branches of brook, then commence stiff climb up rocky footway through dense conifers. After a couple of teaser views, break above trees with fairly difficult ledge scramble at 1.4 mi. and climb steadily in open to immense Glen Boulder, glacial erratic perched at edge of ridge, at 1.6 mi. / 3729 ft. Enjoy wide views N and S down valley and across to Wildcats and Carters.

Trail turns sharp R here and climbs steeply in open over rough ledges. Grade eases and trail re-enters scrub at top of ridge at 2.0 mi. / 4300 ft. Trail now climbs at mellow grade through high scrub, passing side trail R to spring at 2.3 mi / 4550 ft. Moderate ascent continues to small nub of Slide Peak at 2.6 mi. / 4806 ft., where trail emerges in open again. Here there is fine view S down Rocky Branch valley and Montalban Ridge (with summit of Isolation distinguishable as ledgy patch far below) and out to southern and western White Mountains, with Southern Presidentials to R. Trail now runs easily along rim of Gulf of Slides, with good views R into that cirque, then swings R (NW) and rises steadily through alpine meadows and patches of scrub to meet Davis Path at 3.2 mi. / 5175 ft.

Turn L and follow Davis Path on easy descent of broad, open S ridge of Boott Spur. Views are superb R into Dry River valley, L into Rocky Branch valley and ahead to Montalban Ridge and bare patch of Mt. Isolation. Pass fine rock perch on L and descend into scrub at 3.6 mi. / 4800 ft. Descent is steady through woods to col at 4.2 mi. / 4180 ft. Climb easily past knob of "North Isolation" (up on R) and down through blowdown area. Pass jct. R with W branch of Isolation Trail at 4.8 mi. / 4150 ft. and drop to jct. with E branch of Isolation Trail at 5.1 mi. / 3850 ft. Continue 0.9 mi. ahead on Davis Path to summit, as described above.

Other Approaches

Longer approaches, mainly used by backpackers, sometimes by strong day hikers, can also be made to Mt. Isolation. Consult the *AMC Guide* for full details.

Davis Path from US 302
9.8 mi. one-way with 4050-ft. elevation gain (plus 1050 ft. on return trip)

TRAILHEAD (1000 ft.) is at parking area for Davis Path on US 302 across from Notchland Inn, 5.6 mi. S of Willey House site in Crawford Notch. This is a long ridge walk through wild, varied forests with many ups and downs and little reliable water. Spectacular views can be enjoyed en route with short trips on side trails to Mt. Crawford (at 2.2 mi.; 0.6 mi. round trip, 220-ft. elevation gain, open peak with 360-degree view), Giant Stairs (at 4.4 mi.; 0.4 mi. round trip, 180-degree S view from clifftop) and Mt. Davis (at 8.5 mi.; 0.4 mi. round trip, 200-ft. elevation gain, flat open summit with best view on ridge, including stunning vista across Dry River valley to Southern Presidentials and Mt. Washington).

Dry River Trail and Isolation Trail from US 302
8.5 mi. one-way with 3400-ft. elevation gain (plus 600 ft. on return trip)

TRAILHEAD (1205 ft.) is roadside parking at start of Dry River Trail on US 302 in Crawford Notch State Park, 0.3 mi. N of Dry River Campground. This remote, lightly used approach begins with 4.9 mi. on the sometimes rough Dry River Trail through the deep, secluded Dry River valley (see Mt. Eisenhower or Mt. Monroe chapter for details). It then turns R on rough, muddy, overgrown W leg of Isolation Trail (may be hard to follow), which ascends steadily along Isolation Brook, then up spur ridge to Davis Path, 1.2 mi. N of summit of Isolation.

Rocky Branch Trail from Jericho Rd.
9.6 mi. one-way, 3050-ft. elevation gain

TRAILHEAD (1100 ft.) is S end of Rocky Branch Trail, at end of 4.4 mi.-long Jericho Rd., which leaves US 302 1 mi. W of the jct. with NH 16 in Glen. This approach features a long, easy and pleasant walk up the S section of Rocky Branch Trail, mostly on an old logging RR grade, with four potentially difficult crossings of river. At 6.1 mi. meet Isolation Trail just N of Rocky Branch Shelter #2 and follow it and Davis Path to summit (including 4 more river crossings). Return loop can be made via southbound Davis Path and Stairs Col Trail; total for loop is 19.1 mi. with 3900-ft. elevation gain.

Winter

One of the more difficult winter peaks due to its remoteness, especially if you're breaking trail the whole way through this little-used area. The trailhead parking area is usually plowed. The Rocky Branch Trail can be difficult to follow in the open hardwoods as it ascends to Rocky Branch

Ridge. Crossing the Rocky Branch is problematical if it's not well frozen. The Isolation Trail can also be hard to follow in the snow as it approaches the Davis Path near the ridgecrest. Some winter peakbaggers shorten the trip by bushwhacking NW from the Rocky Branch Trail, just over the height-of-land, down to the Isolation Trail beyond the first crossings. Additional bushwhack options involve a route from the Isolation Trail up to the Davis Path either N or S of Mt. Isolation. These bushwhack routes are suitable only for veteran snowshoers skilled at navigating off-trail with map and compass. The sense of remoteness on Isolation's snow-crusted peak is even greater in winter!

View Guide

The bare ledges atop the summit of Isolation offer spectacular views in several directions. The classic vista is looking N to nearby Mt. Washington thrusting above the craggy cirque of Oakes Gulf, buttressed by ledgy Boott Spur and the lower, wooded Slide Peak on the R and the sharp double peak of Mt. Monroe to the L. In the foreground are two wooded humps higher up on Montalban Ridge. To the L, across the remote Dry River valley, the long, high ridge of the Southern Presidentials extends L from Monroe to Mts. Franklin, Eisenhower, Pierce and Jackson, displaying their sharp E slopes, including two smaller bowl-shaped cirques below Monroe and Franklin. Beyond and between Pierce and Jackson are (R to L) Mt. Hale, then Mt. Tom with North Twin in back to its L, South Twin, and Mt. Field with Mt. Lafayette peering over in back. Mt. Lincoln is seen behind and just L of Jackson, with the double summit of Mt. Guyot a bit farther L. Next to the L and closer is Mt. Willey, with Mt. Bond rising in back to the R of Willey's summit. The tip of Mt. Webster can be seen under Bond and Willey's R shoulder. To the L of Willey are (R to L) Bondcliff, Mt. Flume, Mt. Moosilauke and Whaleback Mtn. Mt. Moosilauke's Blue Ridge extends across to Mt. Cushman behind Whaleback on the L. Smarts Mtn. just peers over the top of Cushman. Next to the L, looking SW, the great sprawl of Mt. Hancock rises beyond a S spur of Webster and the flat Ethan Ridge. Hancock's summits include the NW Peak on the R, the dome of North Hancock to the L of center, and South Hancock on the L end. Mt. Carrigain looms to the L of South Hancock, beyond the mouth of the Dry River Valley. Mt. Nancy is to the L of Carrigain, under Signal Ridge, with Mt. Bemis farther L and lower and Mt. Lowell peering over in back between them. Frankenstein Cliff can be seen down low in line with Nancy. Next to the L and farther back is the rolling crest of Mt. Kancamagus, with the gentle crest of Duck Pond Mtn. / Mt. Saunders in front.

The view SSW through SSE is somewhat limited by scrub, but by standing on the highest ledge and looking over the trees you can see the

Sandwich Range spreading beyond the nearby humps of Mt. Davis. Jennings Peak and Sandwich Dome are behind Mt. Kancamagus on the L, with Scaur Peak in front. Next to the L are North and Middle Tripyramid, with Green's Cliff below, then West and East Sleeper lead across to Mt. Whiteface, with its double summit, and Mt. Passaconaway with its spurs, Nanamocomuck and Wonalancet Hedgehog, descending in steps to its L. Mt. Tremont is below Whiteface and Passaconaway. Mt. Paugus is to the L of Passaconaway, with Bartlett Haystack in front on the R. In the foreground in this direction are the top of Stairs Mtn. (R) and Mt. Resolution (L). Black Snout and Faraway Mtn. are in the distance to the L of Paugus. Farther L and closer is Bear Mtn., with Mt. Shaw, highest of the Ossipees, behind on its L. Next to the L is Mt. Chocorua with its distinctive pointy crown, just E of S, with Copple Crown Mtn. and the Moose Mtns. beyond on its L. The partly restricted view continues across the humps of Big Attitash Mtn. to North Moat Mtn. with South Moat peering out in back on the L. Green Mtn. is in the distance to the L of the Moats. Farther L and much closer is Iron Mtn., with the bump of Ossipee Hill on the horizon just to its L and Conway Lake seen farther to the L. From here on the view is more open again.

Continuing to the L, the Green Hills of Conway, with their highest peak, Black Cap Mtn., on the L, are seen over nearby South Engine Hill. The Clark Mtn. range in Maine is on the horizon over the lower R end of the Green Hills, with the somewhat nearer Burnt Meadow Mtns. on its L. To the L of Black Cap is Bartlett Mtn., with Maine's Saddleback Hills beyond. Kearsarge North, Bartlett's parent peak, towers to its L, with Thorn Mtn. in front and below. Extending L from Kearsarge North are the lower Rickers Knoll, The Gemini and Mt. Shaw, with Maine's Pleasant Mtn. lurking beyond. Next to the L are South and North Doublehead, with Spruce Mtn. under South. To the L of the Doubleheads, close at hand across the Rocky Branch valley, is the 3633-ft. peak of Rocky Branch Ridge. Extending to the L behind this peak, looking due E, is the Baldface Range (R to L): Chandler Mtn., Sable Mtn., South Baldface and North Baldface, with the long ridge of Black Mtn. in front and below. The 3921-ft. peak of Rocky Branch Ridge is next to the L, and to its L, over the saddle joining it with the ridge from the much higher Slide Peak, are the high peaks of the Carters (R to L): Rainbow Ridge, Carter Dome with the Wildcats below in front, Mt. Hight, South Carter and Middle Carter.

NO. OF 4000-FOOTERS VISIBLE: 29

Mount Jackson

ELEVATION: 4052 ft./1235 m   ORDER OF HEIGHT: 39
LOCATION: Southern Presidential Range, Township of Beans Grant
USGS MAPS: 7½' Crawford Notch, 7½' Stairs Mtn.

Geography

Though it pokes only a couple hundred feet above the Southern Presidential ridgecrest, Mt. Jackson's small rocky cone is a distinctive and deservedly popular destination. The lowest 4000-footer among the Presidentials, it's flanked by Mt. Webster (3910 ft., forming the E wall of Crawford Notch) a mile away on the SW and Mt. Pierce (4312 ft.) 2 mi. to the N along a broad wooded ridge with an intermediate 3821-ft. hump. On the W it overlooks the upper portion of Crawford Notch, with the broad Bretton Woods valley to the NW. To the E is the large, wild valley of the Dry River in the Presidential Range–Dry River Wilderness. A broad spur ridge extends SE from Jackson into this valley, along with another from the ridge between Jackson and Webster. To the NE is a deep valley between Jackson and Pierce, drained by a major tributary of Dry River and traversed by the Mt. Clinton Trail.

Jackson's cone is girdled by steep ledges, and the view from its flat, rocky top is a fine reward for a short but rugged climb. Most of the mountain is cloaked in a beautiful coniferous forest, including old growth on the NW slopes along the Webster–Jackson Trail. On the lower NW slope are two prominent rock outcrops accessed by side trails—Bugle Cliff (2450 ft.) and the aptly-named Elephant Head (2050 ft.), which overlooks the "Gateway" at the top of Crawford Notch. Farther S are the long, thin waterfalls known as Flume Cascade and Silver Cascade, easily viewed from US 302 near the top of the Notch. Silver Cascade Brook extends far up on the W side of Mt. Jackson.

Another interesting natural feature of Mt. Jackson is the small Gray Jay population that seems to thrive in the summit area, ever ready to pluck a tasty morsel from a hiker's outstretched hand.

Nomenclature

Though it's often assumed that this Presidential Range peak was named for President Andrew Jackson, the appellation was actually given in honor of Charles T. Jackson, a Bostonian who supervised the first geological survey of New Hampshire in 1839–1841. The name was bestowed in 1848 by the botanist William Oakes, who reportedly had his guide light a bonfire on the summit to celebrate the occasion. Historian Frederick Kilbourne noted that Jackson's work in New Hampshire—authorized by the legis-lature with an appropriation of $9,000—was "primitive" in its methods and "accomplished little of real scientific value." The bulk of the field work was accomplished by assistants, among them Edward Everett Hale, whose name also lives on among the 4000-footers.

Historical Highlights

First Ascent: Unknown.

1771: Crawford Notch "discovered" by moose hunter Timothy Nash; he and friend Benjamin Sawyer maneuver horse down through pass and win land grant from governor. Within several years first crude road is built. Historians believe that before Nash's adventures, Native Americans had established their own rough path through Notch.

1803: Improved road through Notch, "Tenth New Hampshire Turnpike," is completed.

1828: Ethan and Abel Crawford build Notch House, a large inn, near base of Elephant Head. Henry D. Thoreau stays there in 1839.

1848: Botanist William Oakes names mountain after State Geologist Charles T. Jackson and sends his guide, Amasa Allen, to kindle bon-fire atop summit.

1870s: Charles H. Hitchcock's N.H. Geological Survey documents ledges and waterfalls in Dry River tributary valley between Mt. Jackson and Mt. Clinton (Pierce). Survey also includes ascent of Mt. Webster via Silver Cascade Brook.

1876: AMC stalwart William H. Pickering and friend ascend Webster via Silver Cascade Brook, then bushwhack across ridge to Jackson. He re-counts trip in March 1877 *Appalachia* and in Moses Sweetser's guide-book, noting that the summit "consists of a little cone of nearly bare rock, about 300 ft. in diameter at the base, and nearly 80 ft. in height. Only a few low bushes and some scanty grass grow upon it, and it has altogether a most lonely appearance." They stay 35 minutes on top, then bushwhack down to the Crawford Path. Sweetser himself notes that Mts. Jackson and Webster "are but rarely visited" and rec-ommends route along ridge from Mt. Clinton, though warning that "the transit is very laborious, the way being frequently obstructed by thickets of dwarf spruce."

Early 1890s: Path is cut to summits of Jackson and Webster for use by guests of Crawford House, grand hotel built in 1852 and rebuilt in 1859 on plateau just N of top of Notch. This is forerunner to today's Web-ster–Jackson Trail.

1892–1898: Saco Valley Lumber Company builds logging railroad up Dry River valley to E of Mt. Jackson and logs much of valley. In 1930s Dry River Trail is established along route of RR grade.

1895: Crawford House management cuts trail from Clinton (now Pierce) to Jackson, but it is soon abandoned.

1907: First edition of *AMC Guide* includes description of above-mentioned paths to Jackson and Webster, notes that a connecting path that once existed between the summits "is now overgrown with scrub and lost beyond discovery."

1911–1912: Webster-to-Jackson section of Webster Cliff Trail located and cut by Paul R. Jenks and Mrs. Jenks.

1913: Paul R. Jenks and Charles W. Blood cut Webster Cliff Trail from Jackson to Clinton, mainly following route of 1895 path.

1913: State of New Hampshire buys 5,975 acres in Crawford Notch for $62,000.

1914: Webster Cliff Trail is opened from Willey House Station along top of cliffs to summit of Webster by Jenks, Charles W. Blood, Nathaniel L. Goodrich and George Blaney. Quartet cuts trail in four days in August.

1917: Author Winthrop Packard pens chapter in his *White Mountain Trails* entitled "Up Mount Jackson—The Climb from Crawford's Through an Enchanting Forest."

1950: Crawford Notch State Park created from land originally acquired by state in 1913; lower W slopes of Jackson are included.

1975: E slopes of Jackson are included in new Presidential Range–Dry River Wilderness.

Trail Approaches

Northwest Approach from US 302 at top of Crawford Notch

Webster–Jackson Trail
5.2 mi. round trip, 2150-ft. elevation gain

TRAILHEAD (1900 ft.): Trail starts on E side of US 302 just N of Gateway of Crawford Notch, 0.1 mi. S of Crawford Depot. Parking is on W side of road. This is a relatively short but rough-and-tumble trail with some gnarly footing and a number of short, steep pitches. The lower section passes through old-growth spruce; the upper reaches traverse fine boreal forest.

From parking area, walk short distance N up road and cross carefully to trail sign and enter woods. Blue-blazed trail starts with moderate climb. At 0.1 mi. spur leads R 0.2 mi. to Elephant Head, open ledge with good view of Notch and area above Gateway. Main trail continues up bank above Elephant Head Brook, then turns R for section alternating easy traverses and steep, rocky pitches. At 0.6 mi. / 2450 ft., between second and third steep pitches, short side trail R leads up over knoll and down to top of Bugle Cliff and good view down into Notch; use caution if wet or icy.

Vista includes Willey and Rosebrook Ranges to W and Crawford's plateau, AMC Highland Center, Saco Lake, Mt. Washington Hotel, Cherry Mtn. and Mt. Deception to NW. Main trail continues climbing with rocky footing to crossing of Flume Cascade Brook on ledges at 0.9 mi. Trail now climbs easily, with occasional dips, to fork at 1.4 mi. / 2800 ft.

Bear L here on Mt. Jackson branch of trail (R fork leads to Mt. Webster) and climb at mostly moderate grade, with many twists and turns, crossing three small branches of Silver Cascade Brook at ca. 3250–3375 ft. Trail then pulls away from streams and ascends steadily through fine boreal forest. At 2.4 mi. / 3800 ft. swing L and climb beside open "fir wave" of dead trees, with partial views NW and of summit cone up ahead, then dip L past Tisdale Spring (unreliable and often muddy). Trail soon bears R and climbs steeply across and up W side of summit cone, with several fairly difficult hand-and-foot pitches, ending with scramble up open slabs. Reach jct. with Webster Cliff Trail on open ledgy summit at 2.6 mi / 4052 ft.; here there are excellent views W and S. Summit cairn and additional views to E and N are a few yds. L on Webster Cliff Trail.

LOOP OPTIONS

Several loop hikes over Mt. Jackson are possible using ridgetop Webster Cliff Trail (white-blazed, part of Appalachian Trail).

Mt. Jackson & Mt. Webster
6.5 mi., 2400-ft. elevation gain

From summit of Mt. Jackson, follow Webster Cliff Trail S. Drop steeply off cone with some down-scrambling, then meander gradually down along thickly wooded ridge, crossing several small, wet gullies. Cross 3740-ft. col at 1.0 mi. from Mt. Jackson, then climb moderately. At 1.3 mi., Webster–Jackson Trail splits R; continue 0.1 mi. ahead on Webster Cliff Trail, swinging L (S) for easy climb to craggy summit of Mt. Webster, with awesome view into Crawford Notch, across to Mt. Willey, and SW to more distant peaks. Retrace steps for 0.1 mi. and bear L on Webster branch of Webster–Jackson Trail for long, steady descent with wet and rough footing. Make steep down-and-up crossing of Silver Cascade Brook at foot of fine cascade just before reaching jct. with Jackson branch, 1.1 mi. from summit of Webster. From here descend 1.4 mi. to trailhead.

Mt. Jackson & Mizpah Spring Hut
6.9 mi., 2350-ft. elevation gain

From summit of Jackson, follow cairns marking Webster Cliff Trail N across open ledges, then swing R and L and negotiate two steep ledgy pitches off open cone. Trail continues very steeply down through woods, then grade eases at ca. 3800 ft. At 0.4 mi. from Jackson trail winds through two open alpine bogs with good views ahead to Mt. Washington and

Presidentials and back to nearby rocky crown of Jackson, then dips into woods and continues gradual descent N along ridge through nice fir forest with many plank walkways. Climb at mostly easy grades over 3821-ft. hump and descend easily, then rise gradually to jct. L with Mizpah Cutoff, 1.6 mi. from Jackson. To visit hut, continue 0.1 mi. ahead on Webster Cliff Trail, down and slightly up. To descend, return to Mizpah Cutoff and follow it 0.6 mi. to Crawford Path on easy, then moderate grade. Turn L here and proceed 1.7 mi. steadily downhill on Crawford Path to its terminus on US 302. Turn L for 0.4 mi. road walk past Saco Lake to Webster–Jackson trailhead (which can be varied by using scenic 0.3 mi. Saco Lake Trail along E shore).

To add loop over Mt. Pierce via Webster Cliff Trail and Crawford Path, totals are 8.5 mi. / 2900 ft. See Mt. Pierce chapter for details.

Southwest Approach from US 302 on floor of Crawford Notch

Webster Cliff Trail
9.4 mi. round trip, 3300-ft. elevation gain

TRAILHEAD (1275 ft.): Webster Cliff Trail, also marked as Appalachian Trail, starts from E side of US 302, 1 mi. S of Willey House site in Crawford Notch State Park. Parking is available on W side of highway by entrance to road leading to Ethan Pond Trail / Ripley Falls trailhead.

This is the longest and hardest but most scenic approach to Mt. Jackson, including a traverse of the spectacular Webster Cliffs and the summit of Mt. Webster, with numerous views over Crawford Notch. This section, combined with Mt. Jackson's outstanding views, makes for a classic hike on a clear day. For many years, the *AMC Guide* carried this endorsement for the Webster Cliff Trail: "The views along the cliffs of Mt. Webster are such that anyone with a normal appreciation of the grandeur of mountain scenery will add at least 2 hr. for their enjoyment. There is nothing finer in the White Mountains." With a carspot, the hike can be shortened by descending via a different route.

From parking area, where there is view up to S end of Webster Cliffs, cross US 302 to where Webster Cliff Trail enters woods. It runs level 0.1 mi. to crossing of Saco River on newly built (2007) footbridge, with view upstream (L) to Mt. Willey, then climbs moderately through fine hardwood forest. Saco River Trail comes in on L at 0.2 mi. and departs on R at 0.3 mi. Steady climb continues through hardwoods, slabbing across S slope of Webster's S ridge. At 0.8 mi. / 1825 ft. trail makes jogs to L and R, descends slightly across two small brooks, then traverses up across slope as large red spruces mix into forest. Pass partial vista on R and make sharp L turn past big boulders at 1.1 mi. / 2075 ft. Trail climbs at stiff grade through fine spruces, then levels for easy traverse along steep slope at 2300 ft. At end of traverse several short, rocky switchbacks lead up to tricky crossing of ledge atop old slide (2450 ft.), probably best negotiated across top. Here there is view S down Saco valley to Mt. Crawford, Mt. Chocorua and other peaks. Just beyond here, trail swings R for very steep climb to 2650 ft., then grade is less steep but still steady until abruptly leveling in ledgy terrain and leading out to large flat outcrop with expansive view of Crawford Notch and mountains to W at 1.8 mi./3025 ft. Most hikers take a long break here after the 1750-ft. ascent.

From this first major outlook, trail ducks back into woods, climbs easily and descends slightly, then makes fairly steep climb through eroded gully and up ledges to next viewpoint (3325 ft.), with good views W and S. Trail reenters woods, traverses mostly easy stretch, and beyond small col reaches next outlook, ledge with view straight down to Willey House site at 2.4 mi./3400 ft. Turn R here and scramble up steep ledges in open and soon reach expansive outcrops with large cairn on R. In addition to good view down into Notch, this inviting area provides vista N to Mt. Washington and Boott Spur. Trail turns L here, drops steeply for 50 ft. into col, then climbs to next viewpoint at 2.6 mi./3500 ft. This smaller ledge has widest S and E view along Webster Cliffs, including full panorama of Montalban Ridge.

Trail continues up ridge through woods, crossing another col, then emerges on next outlook ledge and proceeds in open for ca. 200 ft. to another outcrop with boulder perched on it. Dip beyond here, then scramble up very steep ledge requiring use of hands, and up more ledges beyond. Another down-and-up brings you to excellent perch at 3700 ft. Continue up ridge with more short rocky scrambles, occasional dips, and frequent wide views, with new perspectives looking into Notch and back down ridge to S. Clamber up steep pitch of rock, dirt and scree to still another vantage, then make final easier climb through woods and emerge on ledges at summit of Webster at 3.3 mi./3910 ft. Here there are good views to S, W and N.

Continue N on Webster Cliff Trail, descending briefly to jct. with Webster Branch of Webster–Jackson Trail at 3.4 mi. Turn R (E) on Webster Cliff Trail and descend moderately to 3740-ft. col at 3.7 mi. Trail now meanders gradually upward along thickly wooded ridge, crossing several small, wet gullies. Final short climb to summit of Mt. Jackson is quite steep with some ledge scrambling; reach jct. with Jackson Branch of Webster–Jackson Trail on open ledgy summit at 4.7 mi./4052 ft., with wide views here to W and S; for summit cairn and views to N and E, continue short distance ahead on Webster Cliff Trail.

With carspot, alternate descents after ascending Jackson via Webster Cliffs can be made via Webster–Jackson Trail from summit of Jackson to US 302 at top of Crawford Notch (total 7.3 mi., 3050-ft. elevation gain); via Webster Cliff Trail to Mizpah Spring Hut, then down via Mizpah Cutoff and Crawford Path to trailhead on Mt. Clinton Rd. (total 9.0 mi., 3250-

A signboard at the summit of Mount Jackson directs hikers along the Webster Cliff Trail.

ft. elevation gain); and via Webster Cliff Trail past Mizpah Spring Hut and over Mt. Pierce, with descent via Crawford Path to trailhead on Mt. Clinton Rd. (total 10.5 mi., 3800-ft. elevation gain).

Winter

Jackson is a popular winter peak with a snowshoe track much of the season. Snow-laden conifers make it an especially pretty climb. Steep pitches may be icy or crusty, and the final scramble up the ledges on the cone can be tricky and may require crampons. With deep, wind-drifted snow, the trail may be difficult and even impossible to follow in the open fir wave area near Tisdale Spring, even though the summit is in sight just above. Once past the steep pitches off the cone, the ridge walk along Webster Cliff Trail in either direction is winter wonderland material, although this trail, too, may be hard to follow.

View Guide

With exception of scrub on the E side, most of Jackson's summit is bare ledge with superb views all around. Jackson's placement on the southern extension of the ridge gives it an exceptionally fine perspective on the Southern Presidentials, Mt. Washington, Oakes Gulf and the Dry River valley. From the NE side you gaze up the winding ridge at an array of taller Presidential peaks: (L to R) the nearby wooded bulk of Pierce (with AMC's Mizpah Spring Hut at its base), the barren pyramid of Jefferson (with the Castles visible on its lower L slope), the bald dome of Eisenhower, the barren humps of Clay, Franklin's rounded swell, the dominant cone of Washington with Monroe's sharp peak below, and the broad, bare shoulder of Boott Spur rising above Oakes Gulf, at the head of the Dry River valley. Well to the R of Boott Spur is the lower nub of Slide Peak, and farther R are Carter Dome, the several Wildcat peaks, and the Dome's southern spur, Rainbow Ridge.

Across this expansive wilderness valley to the E is the long Montalban Ridge, bristling with dark forests, and including (L to R) Mt. Isolation, the several elongated summits of Mt. Davis, Stairs Mtn., Mt. Resolution (splotched with gravel slides), and rocky Mt. Crawford, anchoring the S (R) end. The tip of North Baldface just peeks over to the R of Isolation's summit, and South Baldface is seen farther to the R. Sable & Chandler Mtns. rise beyond Mt. Davis, and farther R are the Doubleheads, Mt. Shaw, the Gemini, Pleasant Mtn. in Maine, the prominent cone of Kearsarge North, North Moat (over Mt. Resolution), Big Attitash Mtn. and Table Mtn. (over Mt. Crawford). Iron Mtn. peers over through the broad gap between Davis and Stairs, with the Green Hills beyond. Black Cap, the highest of the Green Hills, is behind Iron on the L, and between Black Cap and Kearsarge North part of Sebago Lake can be seen in the distance. The distant Saddleback Hills of Maine are on the horizon beyond Black Cap, with the Burnt Meadow Mtns. a bit closer and farther R, and next to the R is Conway Lake with Maine's Clark Mtn. range in the distance. On the horizon to the L of Mt. Crawford is Green Mtn. in Effingham.

To the S the winding Saco River valley leads out to Mts. Chocorua and Tremont, with Bartlett Haystack between them and Bear Mtn. under Chocorua, with Mt. Hope still lower and in front. In line with Chocorua and nearby is a prominent S spur of Mt. Webster. Mt. Paugus is between the Haystack and Tremont, with Mt. Shaw in the Ossipees beyond to its L. Faraway Mtn. in the Ossipees is between Paugus and Tremont, and Black Snout pokes up to the R of Tremont. Part of the distant Belknap Range can be seen to the R of Black Snout. The high peaks of the Sandwich Range—Passaconaway (with its spurs, Nanamococmuck and Wonalancet Hedgehog, on its L), Whiteface, the rounded Sleepers, Tripyramid and Sandwich Dome—are to the R, above nearby Duck Pond Mtn. and Mts. Bemis (under West Sleeper) and Nancy (to the L of Sandwich Dome). Mts. Lowell and Anderson are just to the R of Sandwich Dome. Majestic Mt. Carrigain dominates to the SSW, with the far-flung ridges of Hancock (including the tip of South Hancock poking above Middle Hancock) just to the R and the Osceolas and the tip of Tecumseh popping up between them. Scar Ridge is to the R of Hancock's sharp NW Peak, and farther

R (SW), beyond nearby Mt. Webster and the Pemigewasset Wilderness, are distant Carr Mtn. with Loon Mtn. and North Hitchcock beneath, Mt. Kineo, Mt. Cushman and Smarts Mtn. The Willey Range looms large and close to the W across Crawford Notch, with Mt. Willey's talus slopes especially notable. The tops of Mts. Bond, Guyot, Lincoln, & Lafayette and the Twins (between Field and Tom) peer over the Willey Range, and Mt. Hale is to the R behind Tom. Mt. Avalon and the cliffs of Mt. Willard are seen below and in front of Tom. The lower Rosebrook Range extends to the R of Tom and Hale, with the bare dome of Middle Sugarloaf poking over behind. Vermont's Mt. Mansfield is seen on the horizon to the R of Hale, with a range extending R to Mt. Whiteface.

To the NW is the spacious Bretton Woods valley and Mount Washington Hotel, and distant northern Vermont peaks beyond, including Burke Mtn. with (L to R) Belvidere Mtn., Tillotson Mtn., Haystack Mtn. and the Jay Peaks on the horizon to its L and Umpire Mtn. (with Mt. Hor peering over its R slope), Mt. Pisgah, and Bald Mtn. above East Haven Mtn. to its R. To the NNW is the long, dark line of the Dartmouth Range (the several flattened peaks of Mt. Deception on the L, Mt. Dartmouth on the R), with Cherry Mtn. behind on the L and the Pliny Range (Mt. Starr King on the L and Mt. Waumbek on the R) beyond on the R. Goback Mtn. is to the L of Starr King, over the easternmost knob of Mt. Deception, and Vermont's Gore Mtn. is seen between the two westernmost Deception summits. East Mtn., also in Vermont, is to the R of Cherry, over the spur known as Owl's Head. Mt. Cabot peeks over the E ridge of Mt. Waumbek, and farther R are the rounded South and North Weeks with part of Long Mtn. in the distance to the R of North Weeks.

NO. OF 4000-FOOTERS VISIBLE: 30

Mount Jefferson

ELEVATION: 5716 ft. / 1742 m   ORDER OF HEIGHT: 3
LOCATION: Northern Presidential Range, Townships of Thompson and
    Meserves Purchase and Low and Burbanks Grant
USGS MAP: 7½′ Mount Washington

Geography

Mt. Jefferson is, like its neighboring Northern Presidential giants, Adams and Madison, a pyramid of broken rock whose upper slopes (above ca. 4500 ft.) are devoid of trees. The actual summit of the mountain is a small plateau festooned with three rocky peaklets, the middle and westernmost one being the highest.

Jefferson's nearest companions along the massive ridge of the Northern Presidentials are Mt. Clay (5533 ft.) to the S and Mt. Adams to the NE. On its S side Jefferson's summit cone descends to Monticello Lawn (ca. 5400 ft.), a gentle plateau carpeted with sedges. From here the ridgecrest narrows and descends to Sphinx Col (4959 ft.), the low point between Mts. Jefferson and Clay. On its NE side Jefferson's summit cone drops steadily to Edmands Col (4938 ft.), the wild, windswept saddle between Jefferson and Adams. On the N side of the col is Spaulding Spring, which, according to Moses Sweetser's 1876 guidebook, "discharges ten hogsheads of water an hour." On the S edge of the col is another water source, Gulfside Spring.

Several striking ridges and magnificent glacial cirques radiate from the summit mass of Mt. Jefferson; some of these are traversed by trails that are among the most rugged and exciting in the Whites. On the W is the Ridge of the Caps, marked by three rough, rocky knobs, "The Caps," at 4422 ft., 4691 ft. and 4830 ft. The lower, tree-clad part of this ridge rises from Jefferson Notch (3009 ft.), which divides Mt. Jefferson from the wooded, trailless Dartmouth Range to the W. Jefferson Notch is the highest point reached by a public road in New Hampshire. The slopes on the S side of the notch and the Ridge of the Caps are drained by one of the two Jefferson Brooks. Flowing from the N side of the notch and ridge is the South Branch of the Israel River.

Extending NW from the summit of Jefferson is the sharp, spectacular Castellated Ridge, which at ca. 4450 ft. narrows into wild, fin-like rock formations known as "The Castles." In his 1876 guidebook, Moses Sweetser wrote that the ridge's "vast crags resemble the walls of a battered fortress." At the lower end of this ridge is a broad wooded spur known as Mt. Bowman (3449 ft.). On the NE side of the Castellated Ridge is Castle Ravine, "wild, steep, rocky and well-watered," (Sweetser), one of the least-visited glacial cirques in the Whites. The talus-strewn headwall of this NW-facing bowl tops out at Edmands Col. Israel Ridge of Mt. Adams forms the other wall of the ravine. Castle Brook flows down the valley, uniting with Cascade Brook at the base of the Castellated and Israel Ridges to form the Israel River. There is a particularly fine view of Mt. Jefferson rising above the Castles and Castle Ravine from the trailhead for the Castle Trail at Bowman.

The E side of Mt. Jefferson, facing into the glacier-scoured abyss of the Great Gulf, is perhaps even more spectacular. On the NE the mountain's barren slopes drop precipitously into Jefferson Ravine, a deep cirque that opens E from Edmands Col, between Mts. Jefferson and Adams, and out to the main valley of the Great Gulf. This trailless basin is drained by another Jefferson Brook. High on the mountain's cone on this side, a snowfield often lingers into July. Dropping E into the Great Gulf from the upper slopes of Mt. Jefferson are two sharp, truncated ridges known as

Mount Washington and the head of the Great Gulf, as seen from the summit of Mount Jefferson.

"Jefferson's Knees." The northern of these ridges is a wildly steep and narrow arete, improbably traversed by the Six Husbands Trail.

On the SE side of Mt. Jefferson, opening E from Sphinx Col, is a smaller valley, sometimes called the "Ravine of the Sphinx," that drains into the Great Gulf; several waterfalls are found on the brook that flows down this valley. The Sphinx is a rock formation near a high meadow a short distance down to the E from Sphinx Col. All of Mt. Jefferson's eastern slopes eventually drain into the West Branch of the Peabody River, which flows NE through the main valley of the Great Gulf at the base of the mountain.

Nomenclature

Like several other Presidential summits, Mt. Jefferson was named by a group of explorers from nearby Lancaster who ascended Mt. Washington on July 31, 1820, under the guidance of the legendary Ethan Allen Crawford. The party, which included mapmaker Philip Carrigain, proceeded to name six of the surrounding peaks. This mountain was named for Thomas Jefferson (1743–1826), America's third President. Subsequently there was confusion among some mapmakers and guidebook writers, who transposed the names of Mts. Adams and Jefferson, but this was cleared up by the 1870s.

Jefferson's Knees and Jefferson Ravine were named by early AMC stalwart William H. Pickering in the late 1870s; a map which appeared in *Appalachia* showed the names "North Knee" and "South Knee." Monticello Lawn was named in 1876 by guidebook editor Moses F. Sweetser in reference to Thomas Jefferson's Virginia home. The name "Castellated Ridge" appeared in 1859 in Thomas Starr King's *The White Hills: Their Legends, Landscape and Poetry.* Sphinx Col takes its name from a nearby rock formation. The name of Edmands Col commemorates the great trailbuilder J. Rayner Edmands, who laid many graded paths across the Presidential Range from 1891–1909. Mt. Bowman was named either for Hon. Selwyn Z. Bowman, who was a student assistant on a mountain survey, or for John Bowman, an early innkeeper in nearby Randolph. The Six Husbands Trail was named to commemorate the sextet of husbands who, one after another, were wed to Weetamoo, a queen of the Wampanoag tribe in southern New England in the late 1600s. Spaulding Spring was named for Rev. H. G. Spaulding, a friend of Thomas Starr King's.

Historical Highlights

First Ascent: A month after the Weeks–Brackett party climbed Mt. Washington in 1820 and assigned names to the Presidential Range summits, three of its members (Adino Brackett, John W. Weeks and Charles J. Stuart), plus Richard Eastman, returned to the range for six more days of exploration. During this trip they climbed to the summits of all the Northern Peaks, including Mt. Jefferson, and are credited with the first recorded ascents of Mts. Adams, Madison and Jefferson.

1841: Boston minister and author Rev. Edward Everett Hale and W. F. Channing, on geological survey expedition, climb to summits of Mts. Jefferson (from the N) and Washington . Purpose of early September trip is to look for "large sheets of mica" purported to exist along south branch of Israel River.

1852: First trail on Northern Peaks—Stillings Path—is built under direction of John Stillings. Path begins at Jefferson Highlands and runs ca. 9 mi. up across slopes of Mts. Jefferson and Clay to Fabyan Path below summit of Mt. Washington. Path is used to haul lumber up to Mt. Washington for building of first Summit House.

1876: Moses Sweetser's guidebook describes "two lane-like tracks up the side of Jefferson from Storm Lake." One on R "passes dangerously near the verge of a line of high cliffs." The L route is said to follow old Gordon path (from ca. 1860), "which passed to the E. of (and not over) the peak of Jefferson."

1882: Eugene B. Cook and William H. Peek descend from Adams–Jefferson col down through Castle Ravine.

1883–1884: Castellated Ridge Trail (Castle Path) to summit from Bowman Station (Randolph) is built by Eugene B. Cook, Laban Watson,

George Sargent, Albert Matthews, Hubbard Hunt. Trail ascends by way of craggy Castellated Ridge.

Mid-1880s: Fred Crawford, brother of Ethan Allen Crawford, builds small cabin, Camp Crawford, at ca. 4000 ft. on W side of mountain. Cabin is accessed by Camp Crawford Path, starting from valley N of Jefferson Notch and climbing up onto Ridge of Caps. Later, obscure extension of path leads to Gulfside Trail SE of summit. Camp and trail disappear from maps in 1920s.

1892: J. Rayner Edmands begins multi-year project of extending Gulfside Trail from Airline on Mt. Adams to summit of Mt. Washington, including segment on Jefferson's E flank.

1893: Edmands oversees construction of Link across lower slopes of Mt. Adams, into Castle Ravine, and then up steep W wall of ravine to Castellated Ridge. Rough extension is made up ravine to Roof Rock.

Late 1890s: Early version of Cornice is marked between Castellated Ridge and Edmands Col.

1902: New Jefferson Notch Road from Crawford's to Jefferson Highlands opens. State road reaches elevation in excess of 3000 ft. in passing over height-of-land in Jefferson Notch.

1903: Lower section of Castellated Ridge Trail is blocked by ongoing lumbering operation. Lumbering devastates many trails on Northern Peaks from 1903–1907, including upper section of Link.

1907: First edition of *AMC Guide* makes note of trail running from Edmands Col to summit. So-called White Trail is approximately half-mile long and for most part follows series of white trail blazes painted onto rocks (1891) by Charles Lowe.

1909: One year after completing epic bushwhack descent over Jefferson's Knee into Great Gulf, AMC trailmaster Warren Hart oversees construction of Six Husbands Trail following same basic route. This is part of three-year trail-building spree in Great Gulf from 1908–1910.

1910: Randolph Mountain Club (RMC) is formed, begins restoring trails damaged by lumbering. Edmands Col Cutoff is built by Arthur Stanley Pease.

1913: Sphinx Trail from Clay–Jefferson col down into Great Gulf is built by RMC volunteers. Path serves as emergency route off ridge during stormy weather.

1915–1919: RMC members cut trail up Castle Ravine to Edmands Col. Upper portion of Link (called "Old Link") is restored.

1918: Maintenance of loop trail over summit from Gulfside Trail is taken over by AMC. Name of path is changed from New York University Trail to Mt. Jefferson Loop.

1920: Caps Ridge Trail from height-of-land at Jefferson Notch to summit is constructed by AMC crew.

1941: During October backpacking trip, Louis Haberland, 27, Roslindale,

Mass., dies on mountain from exhaustion, exposure. Haberland is second fatality on mountain in five years, another hiker having died of heart attack while ascending Caps Ridge Trail in July 1937.

Ca. 1948: Cornice Trail from Edmands Col and Randolph Path has been extended around N and W sides of summit cone, linking with Gulfside Trail near Monticello Lawn.

1955: Link trail is extended by RMC around NW side of Jefferson, connecting Castellated Ridge and Caps Ridge. Notoriously rough route is scouted by Robert and Miriam Underhill and Klaus Goetze, cut under supervision of Goetze. S end of trail is shortened in mid-1980s when Brad Washburn's Presidential Range map shows proximity of Link and Caps Ridge Trail near pothole ledge on latter.

1956: Forest Service erects Quonset-style survival shelter in Adams–Jefferson col, considered one of most potentially hazardous spots in White Mountains.

1960: Robert and Miriam Underhill, accompanied by Merle Whitcomb, make December 23 climb to summit and are first to complete Winter 4000-Footer list. Conditions at summit are less than ideal with temperature at -8 degrees and winds gusting over 70 mph.

1964: E slopes of Mt. Jefferson are included in new Great Gulf Wilderness created by Congress.

1982: Citing misuse of shelter by backpackers and increasing damage to local alpine vegetation, Forest Service removes Edmands Col emergency shelter.

Trail Approaches

As with the other high Presidentials, an ascent of Mt. Jefferson via any route, even the relatively short Caps Ridge Trail, requires caution as there is extensive above-treeline exposure and much scrambling over ledges and boulders. For safety's sake, and to enjoy the wide views, pick a clear day with a stable weather forecast for a climb of Jefferson.

West Approach from Jefferson Notch Rd.

Caps Ridge Trail
5.0 mi. round trip, 2700-ft. elevation gain

TRAILHEAD (3008 ft.): Caps Ridge Trail starts from a parking area at the high point of Jefferson Notch Rd., 3.4 mi. N of the Cog Railway Base Rd. near Bretton Woods and 5.5 mi. S of Valley Rd. in Jefferson (off NH 115 or US 2). This gravel road is not plowed in winter and may be muddy, icy or snowy early or late in the hiking season.

Due to the high elevation of the trailhead, the Caps Ridge Trail provides the shortest route and least elevation gain to a high Presidential peak and is, by a wide margin, the most popular route to Mt. Jefferson. However, this trail is far from easy as the traverse of the rocky Caps involves some fairly difficult ledge scrambling, and the upper half of the climb is fully exposed to wind and weather. Ledges on the Caps are very slippery when wet. Despite moderate statistics, the difficulty of this hike should not be underestimated.

From parking area, trail enters fir woods, crosses wet area and climbs at easy grade for about 0.3 mi. Pitch is steeper and rockier to ca. 3500 ft., then eases again in beautiful boreal forest. At 1.0 mi. / 3791 ft. large, whitish granite ledge on R provides view up to Caps and summit of Jefferson and out to Bretton Woods valley and Southern Presidentials, Willey Range and Twin Range; this outcrop is also notable for potholes scoured by glacial meltwater. At 1.1 mi. is jct. L with The Link.

Caps Ridge Trail continues up moderately, then becomes very steep, rocky and rough through scrub up to treeline. Ahead loom the Caps, tortured heaps of lichen-covered rock. Steep ledge scramble leads to top of first Cap at 1.5 mi. / 4422 ft. Climb remains sporty and very steep up ledgy ridge, with ever-expanding views, leading past second Cap (4691 ft.), then is a bit less steep up to highest Cap at 1.9 mi. / 4830 ft. Drop off end of last Cap outcrop, then climb moderately with bouldery summit mass looming ahead, to jct. with Cornice Trail at 2.1 mi. / 5025 ft. Now you slog steadily NE up summit cone over piles of broken rock (follow cairns and yellow blazes carefully), aiming for false summit, beyond which grade is easier, leading E to true summit several hundred yards beyond, reached at 2.5 mi. / 5716 ft. Summit knob is on L, while jct. with Castle Trail and Mt. Jefferson Loop is ca. 100 ft. ahead and slightly downhill, by tall cairn.

LOOP OPTIONS

For a scenic loop around S side of Jefferson's summit and back to Caps Ridge Trail, descend NE off summit on Mt. Jefferson Loop for 0.1 mi., then turn R on Six Husbands Trail and descend steadily E for 0.3 mi. over rocks to Gulfside Trail (5325 ft.). This side of summit opens striking views of Mt. Adams seen across depths of Jefferson Ravine. Turn R on Gulfside and slab along SE side of summit, with very slight climb, for 0.4 mi. to Monticello Lawn and jct. R with S end of Mt. Jefferson Loop (5375 ft.). Follow tall cairns of Gulfside across plateau, lushly grown with alpine sedges. In 0.1 mi. turn R on The Cornice and traverse SW side of summit cone, descending moderately over sedgy slopes and across fingers of talus. In 0.5 mi. reach Caps Ridge Trail (5025 ft.); turn L here for steep 2.1 mi. descent over Caps and down through woods to trailhead. Loop adds 1.0 mi. and 50 ft. of elevation gain to hike for total of 6.0 mi. / 2750 ft.

Other, more difficult loops are possible around NW side of summit back to Caps Ridge Trail via (1) Castle Trail and Cornice (adds 0.8 mi. to hike, entirely above treeline) and (2) Castle Trail and The Link (adds 1.7

Rugged Castellated Ridge, traversed by the Castle Trail, provides hikers with plenty of terrific viewpoints, but also many tough scrambles.

mi. and 150 ft. of elevation gain to hike, including traverse of spectacular Castles on Castellated Ridge). However, the 0.7 mi. section on Cornice or 1.7 mi. on Link are extremely rough and tiring, making for slow going, even though they involve little climbing. The Link, in particular, is noted for treacherous footing with rocks, roots and holes (with somewhat better going towards the Caps Ridge end), and is in woods except for crossing of slide with good view NW. The Cornice is a long, tedious rock-hop across sloping boulder fields on the side of the summit cone. Those who hike these trail sections don't often repeat them.

North Approaches from US 2 at Bowman

TRAILHEAD (1500 ft.): Two rugged approach routes are possible from trailhead for Castle Trail, located on S side of US 2, 3 mi. W of Appalachia parking and 4.2 mi. E of jct. with NH 115. Park in area on N side of old railroad grade, taking care not to block road / driveway.

Castle Trail
10.0 mi. round trip, 4200-ft. elevation gain

This is a long but highly rewarding approach up Castellated Ridge, with terrific views and some tough scrambling along the Castles, and the usual Northern Presidential rock-hop above treeline. The upper 1.2 mi. is fully exposed to weather and NW wind.

From parking area, follow railroad grade (Presidential Range Rail Trail) to R for 100 yds., then turn L into woods just past gate. Cross pipeline clearing and traverse on level through logged area to WMNF boundary at 0.3 mi. Cross powerline clearing and turn L along bank for 150 ft. to crossing of Israel River, at 0.4 mi.; not an easy crossing and very tough at high water. On far bank turn L and walk alongside stream for 100 yds., then bear R up bank and follow old logging road on easy climb through open hardwoods to jct. L with Israel Ridge Path at 1.3 mi. / 1900 ft. Bear R here with Castle Trail. At 1.5 mi. Castle Trail swings R and begins climb out of valley, up NE side of Mt. Bowman. Ascend steadily through hardwoods to ca. 2400 ft., then into white birches. At 2.2 mi. / 2750 ft. grade becomes quite steep and remains so until crest of ridge between Mt. Bowman and Castellated Ridge is attained at 2.5 mi. / 3350 ft. Blowdown area here gives partial views into Castle Ravine and up to Castles ahead.

Grade is easy along level shoulder, then you climb moderately with good footing through fine, lichen-draped fir forest. Trail steepens again as ridge narrows, and steady climb leads to jct. with The Link at 3.5 mi. / 4025 ft. Castle Trail now becomes steep and rough, with several fairly challenging scrambles up ledges and boulders and first open views. Reach first Castle at 3.8 mi. / 4450 ft.—exceptional viewpoint looking E into entire length of Castle Ravine, S to Ridge of Caps and Southern Presidentials, SW to Mt. Carrigain and Willey, Twin and Franconia Ranges, and N to Pliny Range and many distant ridges. Trail struggles up through rearing rocky plates of The Castles, at times skirting to R, where ridge is breathtakingly sharp and narrow. Continue steady, exposed climb as rocky ridge becomes less well-defined, enjoying continuous views, especially good to W and down into Castle Ravine. Pass jct. with The Cornice at 4.5 mi. / 5100 ft. and slog steadily up boulder-strewn slope to top of Jefferson and jct. with Mt. Jefferson Loop on L and then Caps Ridge Trail on R at 5.0 mi. / 5700 ft.; actual summit is ca. 100 ft. R (W) and slightly up on Caps Ridge Trail.

Castle Trail, Israel Ridge Path, Castle Ravine Trail, Randolph Path, Gulfside Trail, Mt. Jefferson Loop

5.2 mi. one way, 4250-ft. elevation gain

For strong and experienced hikers, the little-used ascent through Castle Ravine is one of the wildest and most beautiful trips in the Presidentials, and sees little hiker traffic. The many brook crossings can be difficult. The section up the headwall is a difficult scramble, and this route is not recommended for descent. With return to trailhead via Castle Trail, a spectacular 10.2 mi. loop is possible. Another option is to descend via Randolph Path and Israel Ridge Path on NE side of Castle Ravine, with short side trip to great views of ravine at Emerald Bluff. Including side trip, this is a 10.8 mi. loop.

From trailhead at Bowman, follow Castle Trail for gradual 1.3 mi. as described above. Bear L here onto Israel Ridge Trail and cross Israel River—may be tricky—at 1.4 mi. Proceed up along stream and turn R onto Castle Ravine Trail at 1.7 mi./2100 ft. Recross river at 1.9 mi. (again, not easy), pass the Forks of Israel (confluence of Castle and Cascade Brooks), and hop across Castle Brook by small cascades at 2.1 mi. and 2.2 mi. Cross brook again at 2.5 mi./2600 ft. Trail now climbs up above brook through birches, with glimpses up to Castles. At 3.2 mi./3125 ft. The Link comes in from L. Continue gradually up valley through wild, lush fir forest, passing jct. L with Emerald Trail at 3.4 mi. (This trail rises very steeply, but with no really difficult scrambling, for 0.5 mi./800 ft. to side path leading 50 yds. L to superb view of Castle Ravine and Castles at Emerald Bluff, then climbs gradually another 0.1 mi. to Israel Ridge Path.) Castle Ravine Trail crosses brook and just beyond Link splits R for very steep, rough 0.6 mi./900-ft. climb up sidewall to Castle Trail below Castles.

Castle Ravine Trail proceeds up floor of valley, crossing brook several times on mossy rocks. Clamber around boulders where stream gurgles beneath and begin steep ascent up headwall on narrow, rough, winding path, passing overhanging Roof Rock on L at 3.8 mi./3600 ft. Work up rugged trail to open boulders at ca. 4000 ft., offering fine view back down ravine and out to NW (including Pliny Range), and up to Castles. Scree-strewn headwall looms ahead. Above here is long, difficult scramble up loose and very steep talus. Follow markings carefully to top of headwall, where trail issues forth through sedgy draw to meet Randolph Path and Cornice at 4.5 mi./4900 ft.; Spaulding Spring is to R.

Turn R on Randolph Path for easy 0.1 mi. rise to Edmands Col, wind-swept saddle of glacier-scraped ledges, at 4.6 mi. Turn R here on Gulfside Trail as Edmands Col Cutoff continues ahead. (This rough sidehill trail quickly enters Great Gulf Wilderness, passes Gulfside Spring on R, and leads 0.5 mi. to Six Husbands Trail, climbing and then descending across numerous scrubby boulder fields. It provides spectacular views of Jefferson Ravine and Mt. Adams.) Gulfside Trail climbs steep, rough section past Dingmaul Rock, great rock perch with views L into Jefferson Ravine. At 4.8 mi./5125 ft. turn R onto Mt. Jefferson Loop and climb steeply up jumbled rocks, past jct. L with Six Husbands Trail at 5.1 mi., to jct. with Castle and Caps Ridge Trails near summit at 5.2 mi./5700 ft. High point is ca. 100 ft. ahead (W) and slightly up on Caps Ridge Trail.

North Approach from Lowe's Store (US 2)

Lowe's Path, Randolph Path, Gulfside Trail, Mt. Jefferson Loop
11.0 mi. round trip, 4200-ft. elevation gain

TRAILHEAD (1375 ft.): Park at Lowe's Store on US 2 in Randolph (check in at store to pay nominal parking fee, not covered by WMNF Parking

Pass) and walk 100 yds. W on US 2 to sign for Lowe's Path on S side of road.

This approach makes a long traversing climb along the flanks of Mt. Adams to Edmands Col, with an extended stretch of exposure to weather and many fine views of the Castellated Ridge and Castle Ravine from the upper Randolph Path. Before the opening of the Cog Railway Base Road in winter, this was the most commonly used route to Mt. Jefferson during that season.

From US 2, follow Lowe's Path on moderate, then steep climb up to jct. with Randolph Path at 2.7 mi. / 3600 ft.; see description in Mt. Adams chapter. Turn R on Randolph Path and climb moderately to S up W flank of Nowell Ridge, with rocky footing. Trail bends L (SSE) at 3.0 mi. / 3875 ft. and grade becomes easier, but footway is very rough with some occasional boulder scrambles. Trees diminish to scrub and good views W begin to appear at ca. 3.5 mi. / 4200 ft. Cross Perch Path at 3.7 mi. / 4325 ft. Randolph Path continues up at moderate grade through scrub. Gray Knob Trail comes in from L at 4.2 mi. / 4825 ft. From here on the route is completely exposed to weather. In another 200 ft. Israel Ridge Path comes up from R, and at 4.3 mi. it diverges L. Continue ahead (R) on Randolph Path as it contours on nearly level grade around head of Castle Ravine, with striking views into the ravine and across to Castellated Ridge. At 4.8 mi., near Spaulding Spring, Castle Ravine Trail and Cornice join from R. In another 0.1 mi. of easy climbing Randolph Path ends at Gulfside Trail in Edmands Col (4938 ft.). Here Edmands Col Cutoff leads ahead to Six Husbands Trail. Turn R on Gulfside and climb steeply past Dingmaul Rock (fine view into Jefferson Ravine) to Mt. Jefferson Loop at 5.1 mi. / 5125 ft. Turn R here and follow Mt. Jefferson Loop on stiff climb up boulder fields, past jct. L with Six Husbands Trail at 5.4 mi., to jct. with Castle and Caps Ridge Trails near summit at 5.5 mi. / 5700 ft. High point is ca. 100 ft. ahead (W) and slightly up on Caps Ridge Trail.

East Approaches from Great Gulf

Great Gulf Trail, Six Husbands Trail, Mt. Jefferson Loop
6.9 mi. one way, 4450-ft. elevation gain

TRAILHEAD (1350 ft.): This route starts at large parking area for Great Gulf Wilderness on W side of NH 16, 6.5 mi. S of US 2 in Gorham, and 4.1 mi. N of AMC's Pinkham Notch Camp.

Hikers who enjoy a challenging trip through wild, remote country will relish the rugged approach to Jefferson via the Six Husbands Trail. This audacious route scales the precipitous buttress of the northern Jefferson's Knee, with some difficult ledge scrambles and several nearly vertical ladders—not for the faint of heart! This trail is not recommended for descent. With a long car spot, a day trip can be made up Six Husbands with descent via Caps Ridge Trail to Jefferson Notch; total is 9.4 mi. Very strong day hikers, or, more reasonably, backpackers with a base camp in the Great Gulf, can make a 14.5 mi. loop with ascent via Six Husbands and descent back to Great Gulf on somewhat less difficult, but still very steep, Sphinx Trail from Sphinx Col (see below).

From parking area, walk N along old road for 0.1 mi., turn L and descend to cross Peabody River on suspension footbridge, then swing L and up to jct. with Great Gulf Link Trail (from Dolly Copp CG) at 0.3 mi. Bear L here at easy grade on wide trail (old logging road) through spruces along bank above West Branch of Peabody. At 0.6 mi. Great Gulf Trail splits L off road (a ski trail in winter), passes attractive ledgy pool in river, meanders through woods, then rejoins old road at 1.0 mi. Continue past more ski trail jcts. and over several brooks on bridges. At 1.6 mi. is jct. R with Hayes Copp Ski Trail. Enter Great Gulf Wilderness and reach jct. R with Osgood Trail at 1.8 mi. / 1850 ft.

Continue ahead on Great Gulf Trail, following West Branch of Peabody. Pass scenic view of stream at 2.4 mi., then climb steeper pitch to gravelly opening atop high bank known as The Bluff, reached at 2.7 mi. / 2278 ft. Here there are good views up to N side of Mt. Washington, Mt. Jefferson—including the Six Husbands "Knee"—and Mt. Adams. Just beyond, bear L on Great Gulf Trail where Osgood Cutoff veers R, and descend steep bank to cross Parapet Brook, then climb to hogback where Madison Gulf Trail splits R at 2.8 mi. Great Gulf Trail drops steeply to cross West Branch on suspension footbridge. Climb bank on far side and bear R on Great Gulf Trail as Madison Gulf Trail veers L towards Pinkham Notch. Great Gulf Trail now settles in for long, moderate stretch up along West Branch through deep fir forest, with rough, rocky footing in places. Pass Clam Rock on L at 3.1 mi. At 3.3 mi. rocks in riverbed provide another view ahead to Jefferson's Knee and route of Six Husbands Trail. Cross Chandler Brook at 3.9 mi. / 2800 ft.; on far bank Chandler Brook Trail departs L. Continue moderate climb up valley to four-way jct. at 4.5 mi. / 3100 ft.

Turn R here on Six Husbands Trail and drop to cross West Branch (difficult in high water) and climb easily over low ridge to bank above Jefferson Brook, where trail bears L to follow stream. Buttress Trail departs R at 5.0 mi. / 3350 ft. Here Six Husbands Trail turns sharp L and starts working up lower slope of Knee, passing two boulder caves. Very steep climbing leads to pair of almost-vertical ladders at 5.5 mi., the second scaling a sheer mossy ledge. Steep going continues to second pair of ladders; at top of upper ladder is dicey scramble up smooth ledge with steep dropoff on L. The way remains steep, with several views back down Great Gulf to Carters and across Jefferson Ravine to Mt. Adams.

Grade eases as top of Knee is approached, and open crest of ridge is reached at 5.8 mi. / ca. 4700 ft. Convenient crag provides well-deserved resting spot here, with stupendous broadside view of Mt. Adams. Traverse level shoulder, then wind up through scrub and bare patches to jct. R with Edmands Col Cutoff at 6.2 mi. / 4925 ft. Six Husbands Trail now climbs steeply over talus; snowfields may linger in this area into July. Cross Gulfside Trail at 6.5 mi. / 5325 ft. Continue climbing up broken rock to Mt. Jefferson Loop at 6.8 mi. / 5625 ft. Turn L for final short climb to jct. with Castle and Caps Ridge Trails near summit at 6.9 mi. / 5700 ft.; high point is ca. 100 ft. ahead (W) and slightly up on Caps Ridge Trail.

Great Gulf Trail, Sphinx Trail, Gulfside Trail, Mt. Jefferson Loop
7.6 mi. one-way, 4450-ft. elevation gain

Though quite steep in its own right (climbing 1350 ft. in 1.1 mi.), the Sphinx Trail is a less formidable option than the Six Husbands Trail for ascending Mt. Jefferson from the Great Gulf, and can also be used as a descent route to create a 14.5 mi. loop with Six Husbands. From Great Gulf trailhead, follow Great Gulf Trail 4.5 mi. to four-way jct. with Six Husbands and Wamsutta Trails, as described above. Continue up valley on Great Gulf Trail, first at easy grade, then climbing more steadily with rougher footing. Cross small brook and clamber up to nice cascade on West Branch on R at 5.2 mi. / 3400 ft. Trail climbs wet slab here with view back to Mt. Adams at top and continues up ledges past several more cascades, crossing another small brook. Above cascades grade is easier to crossing of West Branch (could be difficult in high water). Trail meanders through wet area, crosses brook coming from Sphinx Ravine, and reaches jct. R with Sphinx Trail at 5.6 mi. / 3625 ft. Turn R here and climb easily for 0.1 mi., cross brook to R and then back to L, then ascend steeply along brook with several cascades seen to R. At top of long narrow cascade trail climbs ledges at edge of small flume, then crosses back to R over brook. Ascend steeply past more cascades, then trail climbs up brookbed over slippery rocks for ca. 0.1 mi.

At top of this section, at 6.2 mi. / 4400 ft., trail turns L for short traverse at base of wet rock face, then R for more steep climbing under overhanging ledge, with two tricky scrambles and first views back down ravine. Stiff climb continues, with one brief leveling to cross small brook, to difficult scramble up rock chimney. Above this a ledge offers fine view back down valley to Great Gulf. Climb continues through mostly open terrain, then trail crests small rise and dips to scenic meadow where water can be found on boulders to R of trail. Scramble up boulders on far side of meadow, then up steep slabs past overhanging ledge on R. Trail dips slightly to cross small cut in ridge, then bears L through interesting level corridor with rock wall on R, leading to Sphinx Col and jct. with Gulfside Trail at 6.7 mi. / 4975 ft. Here there are wide western views. Turn R on Gulfside and ascend moderately to N along E side of open ridgecrest, passing jct. L with Cornice at 7.2 mi. / 5325 ft. In another 0.1 mi., on beautiful sedgy plateau of Monticello Lawn, bear L on Mt. Jefferson Loop and scramble up broken rock to jct. with Castle and Caps Ridge Trails near summit at 7.6 mi. / 5700 ft. High point is ca. 100 ft. L (W) and slightly up on Caps Ridge Trail.

Southwest Approach from Cog Railway Base Rd.

Jewell Trail, Gulfside Trail, Mt. Jefferson Loop
11.0 mi. round trip, 4200-ft.elevation gain (including 450 ft. on return trip)

TRAILHEAD (2500 ft.): A large hiker's parking lot is located on the R (S) side of the Cog Railway Base Rd., 1.1 mi. above the junction with Mt. Clinton Rd. and Jefferson Notch Rd., and 5.6 mi. from US 302.

Though the Jewell Trail is most often used as a western approach or descent route for Mt. Washington, it also provides a scenic and interesting approach to Mt. Jefferson, with 2.5 mi. of above-treeline walking. In recent years, with the plowing of the Cog Rd., it has also become a popular winter route to Jefferson, though it is exposed for a great distance to the prevailing NW winds. In summer / fall, with a relatively easy carspot, Jewell Trail approach can be combined with Caps Ridge Trail for an interesting 8 mi. traverse of Mt. Jefferson.

For description of 3.7 mi., mostly moderate climb on Jewell Trail, with last 0.7 mi. above treeline, see Mt. Washington chapter. At 3.7 mi. / 5400 ft., turn L on Gulfside Trail, which descends moderately N along W flank of Mt. Clay, passing loop path descending L to reliable Greenough Spring at 4.2 mi. / 5150 ft. and rejoining 100 yds. farther. Trail levels out at NW base of Mt. Clay, where N end of Mt. Clay Loop comes in from R at 4.5 mi. / 5025 ft. Gulfside Trail dips to Sphinx Col, a neat little corridor between rock walls, and jct. R with Sphinx Trail at 4.6 mi. / 4975 ft. Gulfside Trail now makes steady, rocky climb along E side of Jefferson's S shoulder. Cornice comes in on L at 5.1 mi. / 5325 ft. Gulfside Trail now traverses beautiful sedgy plateau of Monticello Lawn. At 5.2 mi. bear L on Mt. Jefferson Loop and hop rocks up at moderate grade to jct. with Castle and Caps Ridge Trails near summit of Mt. Jefferson at 5.5 mi. / 5700 ft. High point is ca. 100 ft. L (W) and slightly up on Caps Ridge Trail.

Winter

Mt. Jefferson is among the toughest of the winter peaks. Because Jefferson Notch Rd. is not plowed, Caps Ridge Trail is not a practical approach. Thus a climb of at least 5 mi. is required to reach the summit—longer than Washington or Adams. A commonly used winter route follows Lowe's Path (parking for fee at Lowe's Store) for 2.7 mi., then Randolph Path for 2.2 mi. to Edmands Col. The upper part of Randolph Path has great exposure to bitter NW winds. From Edmands Col winter peak-baggers must undertake a steep climb of 0.6 mi. up Gulfside Trail and Mt. Jefferson Loop, traversing a long, steeply sloping snowfield en route. Full winter gear, including crampons and ice axe, is required. In recent years, with the Cog Railway Base Rd. being plowed (parking for fee at Base Station), the Jewell Trail/Gulfside Trail approach has been used fairly frequently to approach Mt. Jefferson. This also has great exposure to weather and NW winds, with 2.5 mi. above treeline, but avoids the tricky snowfield. The Castle Trail is infrequently used in winter and has some difficult and potentially hazardous scrambling in the area below and around the Castles. The Castle Ravine approach is rarely used and is not recommended due to avalanche danger and ridiculously steep climbing on the headwall. Only experienced and properly equipped hikers should attempt Jefferson in winter, and then only on days with clear weather and relatively light winds.

View Guide

While certainly offering a view that is far better than average, Mt. Jefferson's summit vista is generally rated inferior to that of several other Presidential Range peaks, such as Mts. Adams, Madison, or Washington. Some would argue, in fact, that the mountain's best views are found not on its summit, but along its many rugged ridges and their varied approach trails. Still, there are fine vistas of Mts. Adams and Washington close by and of many other peaks further afield.

Close by to the NE is the sharp rocky crest of Mt. Adams, with Sam Adams prominent to its L and Adams 4 peering over a lower slope farther to the L. (More dramatic views of Adams rising from the cavernous Jefferson Ravine are obtained from trails on the E side of Jefferson's summit.) The flat crest of Cambridge Black Mtn. is seen under the skyline just L of Adams 4, with many peaks in NW Maine on the horizon. Between Adams 4 and Sam Adams is the mass of East Kennebago Mtn. on the horizon. Between Sam Adams and Adams are Mt. Bemis and Elephant Mtn. on the L and Crocker and Saddleback Mtns. in the Rangeley, Maine, area, seen over Old Blue Mtn., on the R. To the R of Adams are the eastern Mahoosucs (L to R): Lary Brook Mtn. (with the S end of Sunday River Whitecap behind on the L), then the higher Bear, Black and Wheeler Mtns. Puzzle Mtn. is seen over the gap between Lary Brook and Bear, with Hurricane Mtn. behind on its L and the pyramid of Mt. Blue to its R. The paired Bald and Saddleback Wind Mtns. are seen on the horizon over Wheeler. Closer in this direction part of Mt. Madison's Osgood Ridge is seen descending into the depths of the Great Gulf.

The E view out over the Great Gulf takes a wide spread of the peaks of the Carter–Moriah Range. On the far L end of the range is the ledgy hump of Shelburne Moriah Mtn., with Middle Moriah in front. Next to the R is Mt. Moriah, with its long S ridge sloping to its R. Peabody Mtn. peers over the middle of Moriah's S ridge. On the horizon over the Moriahs is an array of lower peaks S of Rumford, Maine, including (L to R) Mt. Zircon and Speckled, Black and Spruce Mtns. Cliff-faced Imp Mtn. can be seen under Moriah's rocky SE knob, and the Imp Face can be seen in front on a lower wooded slope. Farther R looms North Carter, with Gammon (L) and Caribou (R) Mtns. behind on the L. From North Carter the range extends R to Middle Carter and then South Carter. Speckled Mtn. near Evans Notch is seen over the slope descending R from Middle Carter, with Streaked Mtn. visible on the horizon. Continuing to the R, looking more to the ESE, Mt. Hight (L) and Carter Dome (R) are visible over a nearby jumble of rocks. To the R of Carter Dome can be seen Carter Notch and Wildcat Mtn., with Sable Mtn. over Wildcat A and Chandler Mtn. over Wildcat C; Maine's Pleasant Mtn. is beyond and farther to the R.

Mt. Washington's gray, bouldery mass rises out of the Great Gulf to the SE, blocking out everything in that direction. Portions of the auto road, clinging to the ridge on the lip of the Great Gulf, are visible below and L of Washington's summit, while the Cog Railway is seen attacking Washington on its W slopes. The headwall of the Great Gulf appears as a striking gouge in the side of the mountain.

Turning to the S, Mt. Clay and Monticello Lawn are close at hand in the foreground, with Mt. Monroe and Lakes of the Clouds Hut visible to the R of Mt. Clay. The rounded pair of Belknap and Gunstock Mtns. are in the distance just L of Monroe, with Mt. Paugus farther L and closer. The top of Bartlett Haystack can be seen under Paugus. Mt. Shaw in the Ossipee Range is seen in the distance over Clay, with broad Faraway Mtn. extending to its R, behind the L side of Paugus. A beautiful sweep of the southern Presidentials extends L to R from Monroe: Little Monroe, Mt. Franklin, Mt. Eisenhower, Mt. Jackson poking up in back, Mt. Pierce, and Mt. Webster. The Sandwich Range sprawls in the distance behind Little Monroe, Franklin and Eisenhower, starting on the L with Mt. Passaconaway (with its step-like spurs, Wonalancet Hedgehog and Nanmocomuck Peak on its L) and extending R across Mt. Whiteface, The Sleepers, the Tripyramids, and Sandwich Dome, with Jennings Peak on its R. Two peaks of Mt. Tremont are seen under Passaconaway and just L of Little Monroe, lowly Potash Mtn. is under the Passaconaway–Whiteface col just R of Little Monroe, and Green's Cliff is visible under East Sleeper, poking above the flat crest of Mt. Saunders. The Nancy Range (Mts. Bemis, Nancy, Lowell and Anderson, L to R) is under Sandwich Dome and behind Eisenhower. Mt. Carrigain in the Pemi Wilderness is visible to the SSW over Pierce, with Mt. Kancamagus seen behind Carrigain's Signal Ridge on the L; on very clear days Mt. Monadnock can be seen over Signal Ridge. To the R of Carrigain is the broad spread of Mt.

Hancock, with the four peaks of Mt. Osceola—East Peak, main summit (over South Hancock), Middle Peak and West Peak—beyond, sprawling between Carrigain and North Hancock. Mt. Tecumseh pops up in back just to the L of the main Osceola summit. Mt. Willey, anchoring the S end of the Willey Range, is seen under the long ridge between North Hancock's broad dome and the sharp NW Hancock. Above Willey, the double summit of East Scar Ridge peers over the Hancock ridge. Middle Scar Ridge's sharp peak is to the R of NW Hancock, with Mt. Cardigan beyond on the horizon.

The Willey Range continues from Mt. Willey across to Mt. Field, with the main Scar Ridge summit seen over the col between them. Mt. Hitchcock is seen in front of and below the L side of Scar Ridge. Down low in front in this direction is the Cog Railway Base Station. Loon Mtn. extends R from Scar Ridge above Field, with the higher and more distant Carr Mtn., Mt. Kineo and Mt. Cushman (L to R) spreading beyond to the R, across to the L slope of Mt. Bond. The lower, rounded Mt. Tom is to the R of Field, with Mt. Bond, anchoring the L end of the prominent Twin Range, above. The sharp nubble of West Bond peers over the R shoulder of Bond, and farther R is the rounded Mt. Guyot with Zealand Mtn. below in front and Mt. Flume peering over in back. Smarts Mtn. can be seen in the distance over West Bond. A long ridge extends R from Guyot to South Twin, with Mt. Liberty peering over on the L and Mt. Moosilauke hovering in back on the R. North Twin is to the R of South Twin, with Mts. Lincoln and Lafayette rising behind and between the Twins. Mt. Hale and then the lower Rosebrook Range are in front of the Twins. In the foreground looking in this WSW direction is the broad Bretton Woods plain, with the Mt. Washington Hotel nestled at the base of Mt. Rosebrook. To the R of Lafayette, over the shoulder of North Twin, can be seen the tips of North Kinsman, Mt. Garfield, and Cannon Mtn. The NW summit of Cannon is farther R, between North Twin and its spur, Nubble Peak. Mt. Oscar in the Rosebrook Range and the Bretton Woods ski slopes are seen down low in this direction. To the R of Nubble Peak are Big Bickford and Scarface Mtns., with Cooley and Cole Hills in Easton beyond on the R. A bit more to the R and very low and close by is Millen Hill, just across Jefferson Notch, and the Sugarloaves near Twin Mountain are seen above, behind and R of Mt. Oscar.

Farther R, looking W, the darkly wooded Dartmouth Range summits of Mts. Dartmouth (in front) and Deception (in back, with the two W peaks on the L) are close by on the opposite side of Jefferson Notch. Beyond is a vast view out towards Vermont, with the long chain of the Green Mtns. lining the horizon. The mountains in the Middlebury Gap area are to the L of the Dartmouth Range, leading R across to the Breadloaf Mtn. group. Over the W peaks of Deception is the lumpy Signal Mtn. range in the middle distance with the long ridge of Mts. Abraham and Ellen beyond. The little twin summits of Mts. Agassiz and Cleveland in Beth-lehem are closer in in this direction. To the R of the Dartmouth Range, looking almost due W over the lower S ridge of Cherry Mtn., is the un-mistakable Camel's Hump on the horizon. Farther R and a bit closer, over the upper S ridge of Cherry, is the Worcester Range. Next to the R is the summit of Cherry with its sharp spur, Owl's Head, on the R. Mt. Mans-field sprawls on the horizon over Cherry, with the nearer, long Dalton Ridge and the distant Sterling Range seen above Owl's Head. Down in front looking towards Owl's Head, little ledgy Currier Mtn. rises behind broad Mt. Mitten. Cherry Pond sparkles on the flats behind Owl's Head on the R, with the distant Laraway Mtn., the Cold Hollow Mtns., Belvi-dere Mtn., Tillotson Peak and Haystack Mtn. strung across the horizon. Next to the R and closer are the paired Burke and Umpire Mtns., with the sharp Jay Peaks beyond on the R. A bit farther R and much closer, seen over the flat Jefferson Meadows, is little, rounded Prospect Mtn. in Lan-caster. To the R of the Jay Peaks and closer is broad East Haven Mtn., with Mts. Hor and Pisgah around U-shaped Willoughby Gap in back on the L and Bald Mtn. behind on the R. On clear days some of Quebec's Sutton Mtns. can be seen on the horizon in this direction. To the R of Bald and closer are the great masses of East Mtn. (L) and Seneca Mtn. (R), with Burnside Mtn. in front of and below Seneca. Down below in this direc-tion Rt. 2 can be seen leading towards the village of Jefferson.

Next to the R, looking NNW, the Pliny Range rises abruptly from the lowlands of the Israel River valley, with Mt. Starr King on the L and Mt. Waumbek and its long, level E ridge on the R. Mt. Bowman, a spur of Mt. Jefferson, is seen down low in front of Starr King, while distant Gore Mtn. in Vermont's Northeast Kingdom is centered above Waumbek's double peak, with Black Mtn., Brousseau Mtn. and sharp Sable Mtn. strung out to its R. Conical Pliny Mtn. is seen under the middle of Waumbek's E ridge. The Pilot Range is behind and R of Waumbek's E ridge, with Hutchins Mtn. on the L, Mt. Cabot, the highest, in the middle, and The Bulge and the sharp Horn on the R. Rounded South Weeks is seen under the sad-dle between Hutchins and Cabot, and Goback Mtn. is seen behind and above the saddle. Terrace Mtn. can be picked out under and just in front of Cabot. North Weeks is seen under the Bulge–Horn col, with Middle Weeks in front. The Nash Stream mtns. extend behind the Pilots on the R, with West Peak at its L end, then Castle, Sugarloaf, Bunnell (in back) and Gore Mtns. Vermont's Monadnock Mtn. peers over the col to the R of West, and the bare Percy Peaks are noticeable under Bunnell. To the R and closer is Unknown Pond Ridge, an extension of the Pilot Range. Behind this on the R is the level crest of Long Mtn., with Rogers Ledge poking up under its middle and North Whitcomb (Muise) Mtn. behind its R end. Closer in and extending to the R is Deer Ridge, with Square Mtn. (L) and Greens Ledge (R) just barely peeking over in back. In close under the R end of Deer Ridge is Mt. Randolph at the W end of the Crescent Range, and on the horizon is the broad mass of Dixville Peak.

Extending R from Dixville are its North Country neighbors, Cave, Rice and Crystal Mtns. Just R of Crystal is the nearer Mt. Crescent with the L (NW) summit of Black Crescent Mtn. behind it and Magalloway Mtn. on the horizon. Just R of Black Crescent's NW summit is massive Stub Hill in the distance, with Rump Mtn. peeking over on the R. Farther R the double peak of Bosebuck Mtn. is seen over the main summit of Black Crescent. In the foreground under the Crescent Range is the long slope of Mt. Adams's Nowell Ridge. Seen over the R end of Black Crescent is the sharp peak of Mt. Dustan, and farther R and more distant, but under the skyline of far-off Maine–Quebec border peaks, is the double rounded summit of Aziscohos Mtn. More to the R is wavy West Kennebago Mtn. on the horizon, with little Jericho Mtn. near Berlin seen down low and much closer, then the view swings back to Mt. Adams.

NO. OF 4000-FOOTERS VISIBLE: 40

Mount Madison

ELEVATION: 5366 ft. / 1636 m   ORDER OF HEIGHT: 5
LOCATION: Northern Presidential Range, Townships of Thompson and
     Meserves Purchase and Low and Burbanks Grant, Town of Randolph
USGS MAPS: 7½′ Mount Washington, 7½′ Carter Dome

Geography

The rocky pyramid of Mt. Madison anchors the NE end of the Presidential Range, soaring 4000 ft. above the valleys of the Moose River to the N and the Peabody River to the E. Like its Northern Presidential neighbors, the upper cone of Madison is bare of trees and heaped with fragments of frost-broken rock. The summit itself is a narrow, rocky, wind-beaten crest. Thomas Starr King was enamored of Madison, calling it "beautiful, clear, symmetrical, proud, charming, gigantic."

Close by to the SW is Mt. Adams, which towers more than 400 ft. above Madison. In the flat, barren 4890-ft. col between the two peaks is tiny, rockbound Star Lake. To the S of Mt. Madison, with its headwall just below this col, is Madison Gulf, a wild glacial cirque that opens out into the lower valley of the Great Gulf. At the top of the headwall, just E of Star Lake, is a crag called The Parapet, which offers a magnificent view over Madison Gulf, the Great Gulf and the mountains beyond. Madison Gulf is drained by Parapet Brook.

Extending SE from Madison's summit cone is prominent Osgood Ridge, which stretches more than a mile above treeline over a series of small rocky peaks before broadening and descending steeply to the West Branch of the Peabody River. This ridge encloses Madison Gulf on the E. Partway down an eastern spur ridge drops over a 2586-ft. knob and down to the main branch of the Peabody River. On the NE side of Osgood Ridge is a broad basin drained by E-flowing Culhane Brook.

Extending NE from Madison's summit is the wild, curving Howker Ridge, which runs over a series of steep knobs known as "The Howks" (4315 ft. down to 3425 ft.) in its upper reaches. Below the Howks the ridge splits into two spurs, one dropping NE and the main crest N, then NW, with Town Line Brook draining the valley between them. (This stream runs across the town line between Randolph and Gorham, and drops over a trio of cascades—Proteus, Erebus and Evans Falls—known as Triple Falls.) At the base of the NE spur is the 1650-ft. col with Pine Mtn. (2405 ft.), a low, ledgy summit to the NE that offers outstanding views of Madison. To the W of Howker Ridge is Bumpus Basin, a trailless, wooded north-facing glacial cirque drained by Bumpus Brook. This bowl can be seen from US 2 and Randolph Hill to the N. Hitchcock Fall, Coosauk Fall and Stairs Fall are found on this stream's lower reaches.

Running N from Madison's summit is Gordon Ridge, which separates Bumpus Basin on the E from the long valley of Snyder Brook, flowing N from the Madison–Adams col, on the W. The lower NW spur of Gordon Ridge was burned in a 1921 fire, leaving bare ledges such as Dome Rock, Upper Inlook and The Overlook; this scenic ridgelet is traversed by the Inlook Trail. As described in the Mt. Adams chapter, Snyder Brook is home to Duck, Salmacis, Tama, Salroc and Gordon Falls and, in its lower reaches, a strip of old-growth hemlock and hardwood forest in the 36-acre Snyder Brook Scenic Area.

Nomenclature

Like several of its Presidential neighbors, Mt. Madison was named on July 31, 1820, by the Weeks–Brackett party from Lancaster, which was guided by Ethan Allen Crawford. James Madison (1751–1836) was the nation's fourth President.

Osgood Ridge was named for Benjamin F. Osgood, a well-known guide at the Glen House in the valley SE of the Northern Peaks; he opened a trail along his namesake ridge in 1878. Howker Ridge was named for James Howker, who had a farm in the valley at the base of the ridge. Gordon Ridge honors another guide, James Gordon of Gorham, who led Thomas Starr King on several adventures in the 1850s and built the earliest path up the mountain. Bumpus Basin and Brook were named for Silas Bumpus, an early settler in Randolph, while Culhane Brook commemorates another pioneer family in the Peabody valley to the E.

Historical Highlights

First Ascent: One month after the Weeks–Brackett climbed Mt. Washington and assigned names to the various Presidential Range summits, three of its members (Adino Brackett, John W. Weeks and Charles J. Stuart), along with Richard Eastman, returned to the range for six more days of exploration. During this trip they climbed to the summits of all the Northern Peaks, including Mt. Madison, and are credited with the first recorded ascents of Mts. Adams, Madison and Jefferson.

Ca. 1860: Gorham guide James Gordon builds short-lived trail to Mt. Madison, probably up Gordon Ridge, or possibly Howker Ridge.

1862: Inspired by writings of Rev. Thomas Starr King, group of trampers attempts ridge walk over Northern Presidentials to Mt. Washington. Clergyman Phillips Brooks of Philadelphia barely survives ordeal.

1875: Starting at Howker homestead at N base of mountain, E. C. Pickering traverses Mts. Madison, Adams, Jefferson and Clay and ends 12-hour trek at summit of Mt. Washington.

1876: Moses Sweetser's guidebook notes difficulty of ascending Madison, as there are no trails and, in the upper reaches, "almost impassable thickets." He recounts that his surveying party, which may have ascended via Howker Ridge, "encamped near Star Lake, on a still night in August, with watchers detailed to keep up a roaring fire all night; but at dawn the tent was incrusted with ice." He describes four other routes that have been used–from Great Gulf, up what are known today as Osgood Ridge (from the Copp homestead) and Gordon Ridge (from the Howker place), and from lower Bumpus Basin.

1877: Ravine House at northern base of mountain opens. Building, dating back to 1850s, was earlier known as Mt. Madison House.

1878: Benjamin Osgood opens path to summit from Glen House up what is today called Osgood Ridge. Laban Watson cuts trail (Madison Path) from Ravine House up valley of Snyder Brook to Salmacis Fall.

1882: Laban Watson completes work on Watson Path, cutting section from Salmacis Fall to Mt. Madison summit.

Mid-1880s: Marian Pychowska and other AMC explorers make three explorations of Howker Ridge.

1888–89: Stone hut (Madison Spring Hut) is built by AMC in Madison–Adams col.

1889: Watson, Rosewell Lawrence make first recorded winter ascent of peak. On previous day, pair had climbed up Mt. Adams, only second to do so. E. B. Cook builds Ridgeway Path up W side of Gordon Ridge, connecting with Watson Path; is abandoned by 1920.

1891: New path cut from Glen House to Mt. Madison—old path has been largely obliterated by logging.

1893–1899: J. R. Edmands builds long Randolph Path connecting lower Howker Ridge Trail with Adams–Jefferson col.

1894: E. B. Cook cuts path up Snyder Brook valley from Bruin Rock to Madison Hut, named Valley Way.

1895–1897: J. R. Edmands builds improved, graded Valley Way trail to hut, utilizing sections of existing trails previously built by E. B. Cook, Watson.

1902: Trail up Howker Ridge from Randolph (near train station) is finished, several years after first section was constructed. Primary builders are E. B. Cook and W. H. Peek. Lower part of path is subsequently relocated several times.

1903–1907: Northern Peaks ravaged by lumbering operations. In letter to *Among the Clouds* newspaper in August 1905, author laments condition of Valley Way, writing, "The path is rendered uncertain to strangers, inconvenient to all, and the beautiful forest, so distinctively an essential feature of the attractiveness of this path, has been sadly ruined for a long distance."

1904: Osgood Path reopened by summer camp group after some years of disuse; AMC adopts trail in 1907.

1906: Addition is built onto Madison Hut, doubling its overnight capacity.

1909: First of two steep, rough trails from Great Gulf to Adams–Madison col is built. Buttress Trail is laid out, maintained by E. H. Blood. The following year, Madison Gulf Trail from Great Gulf is blazed by Irving B. Crosby.

1910: Randolph Mountain Club is formed and begins restoring damaged trails on Northern Peaks.

1911: A separate stone hut (known as "Number 2") is built by AMC as cook house for nearby Madison Hut.

1912–1914: Summit is used intermittently as fire lookout station, with AMC hut caretaker making periodic checks and reporting via phone line to valley.

1918: Willard Helburn, Henry Chamberlain ascend Madison early on morning of Feb. 22 at start of first ever winter traverse of Presidentials.

1921: Gordon Ridge scene of forest fire. Local historian George Cross later writes: "It seemed as though all Madison . . . was on fire."

1922: Third building ("Number 3") is added to growing Madison Hut complex. New building serves as bunkhouse for up 60 guests.

1924–1926: Pine Link Trail connecting village of Gorham with Madison Spring Hut is constructed. Total length of trail, 8.1 miles.

1928: Southern terminus of Madison Gulf Trail relocated to Mt. Washington Auto Road.

1929: Hut operation is consolidated under one roof with addition built on to Madison "Number 3" and razing of original hut. Madison "2" converted to storage building.

1931: First winter ski traverse of Northern Presidentials is achieved by

Fritz Weissner, Milana Jank. Pair spend second night of three-day journey in Madison Hut.

1932: Inlook Trail to Dome Rock at lower end of Gordon Ridge cut by RMC. Trail follows course of former Inlook and Outlook Trail ravaged first by lumbering, then by 1921 forest fire. Osgood Cutoff is built.

1933: Daniel Webster–Scout Trail is constructed by New Hampshire Boy Scouts. It links Dolly Copp Campground with Osgood Trail at Osgood Jct., half-mile below summit. Kelton Trail on lower northern slopes is completed.

1938: Heavy rains from fall hurricane cause landslide to fall across portion of Daniel Webster–Scout Trail.

1940: Accidental fire guts Madison Hut. Madison "Number 2" is pressed into service until replacement hut is finished in 1941.

1940: *AMC Guide* describes WMNF Bumpus Basin Trail, connecting Bumpus Brook with Watson Path on Gordon Ridge; by 1946 edition, this trail has disappeared. Also abandoned during this period is rough trail leading from Triple Falls up Town Line Brook to Howker Ridge between first and second Howks. This trail had been shown on maps since 1914.

1948: Parapet Trail, linking Osgood Jct. with Madison Spring Hut, opens. Path provides rough but more sheltered route to hut by contouring along S side of summit cone.

1957: 21-year-old hiker Thomas Flint dies from fall, exposure halfway up to summit from hut.

1964: Congress creates Great Gulf Wilderness, including S slopes of Mt. Madison.

1998: January ice storm devastates hardwood forest on lower N slopes of Madison; yeoman effort by RMC clears fallen trees from trails.

Trail Approaches

Mt. Madison has a variety of possible trail approaches from several directions. This climb is only slightly less difficult than an ascent of Mt. Adams or Mt. Washington, with over 4000 ft. of elevation gain in about 4 mi. of steady climbing. The upper cone of the mountain is a jumble of broken rock, devoid of trees and any protection from the elements. The climb should only be undertaken in favorable weather conditions, and all above-treeline precautions that apply to Mt. Washington come into play when scaling Madison. Allow a full day for this very strenuous trip, which includes difficult boulder-hopping on the upper ridges.

North Approaches from US 2 at Appalachia

TRAILHEAD (1306 ft.): The large parking area at Appalachia is one of the major trailheads in the Whites. It's located on the S side of US 2, 5.5 mi. W of NH 16 in Gorham and 2 mi. E of Lowe's Store in Randolph.

The sharp summit cone of Mount Madison, seen here from the top of John Quincy Adams, rises high above Star Lake in the Madison–Adams col.

Valley Way, Osgood Trail
8.6 mi. round trip, 4100-ft. elevation gain

This relatively moderate route follows the steady and sheltered Valley Way—a wide, rocky trade route in places—to AMC's Madison Hut, from which the exposed boulder-climb up the summit cone is undertaken. If doing a loop, this is a preferred way to descend. From parking area, follow blue-blazed Valley Way across old RR grade and powerline (where Air Line forks R) and into woods. Climb moderately through hardwoods and then small area of old-growth hemlocks, passing several trail junctions: Maple Walk on L just into woods, Sylvan Way at 0.2 mi., and Fallsway on L at 0.5 mi. (Upper section of Fallsway parallels Valley Way and offer views of pretty Tama Fall on Snyder Brook.) Fallsway soon rejoins from L. Just beyond jct. R with Beechwood Way at 0.8 mi., Valley Way bears R (as Brookside diverges L) and climbs pitch to jct. with Randolph Path at 0.9 mi./1953 ft.

Valley Way now climbs steadily along slope high above Snyder Brook, bearing L (E), then R (S) into fine birch glade. Pass jct. with Scar Trail on R at 2.1 mi./2811 ft. and cross Watson Path at 2.4 mi./3175 ft. Long, steady climb continues up lower E slope of Durand Ridge, passing jct. L with Lower Bruin at 2.8 mi./3584 ft., side trail R to Valley Way Campsite (2 tent platforms) at 3.1 mi., and jct. R with Upper Bruin at 3.3 mi./4150 ft. Valley Way now climbs more steeply with rocky footing up headwall of ravine, with brook mostly close by on L except for one short loop out to R (W) at 4450 ft. Emerge from scrub and at 3.8 mi./4800 ft., just past jct. R with Air Line Cutoff, reach jct. with Gulfside and Star Lake Trails, 100 ft. below Madison Hut.

Continue up to hut (refreshments available in summer) and turn L on Osgood Trail. After passing jct. L with Pine Link, Osgood Trail quickly begins steep climb up N side of exposed W ridge of Madison, with scrambling over boulders and ledges. Views back to rock stack of Adams are impressive. At top of steep scramble, grade eases as trail angles along S side of ridge, then along narrow, rocky crest. Follow large cairns E to summit at 4.3 mi./5366 ft.

Valley Way, Watson Path
7.8 mi. round trip, 4050-ft. elevation gain

This is one of the shortest routes to Madison, but it is steep and rough for its upper 1.5 mi. with a long stretch of exposure to weather. Trail may be hard to follow with low visibility.

Follow Valley Way for 2.4 mi. as described above. Turn L here (3175 ft.) on Watson Path, which runs along W bank of Snyder Brook past large Bruin Rock. Pass jcts. with Brookside (L) and Lower Bruin (R) and cross brook at base of Duck Fall; follow signs and blazes carefully. Watson Path quickly commences relentlessly steep and rough climb up W side of Gordon Ridge through wild conifer forest, with poor footing on roots and rocks. At 3.2 mi./4400 ft. trail emerges from scrub and continues climb in open with long stretch of rock-hopping. Cross Pine Link on high, open shoulder where grade is briefly easier at 3.6 mi./4950 ft. Ascent becomes steeper again up N side of boulder-strewn cone, attaining summit at 3.9 mi./5366 ft.

Loop with ascent via Watson Path and descent via easier Osgood Trail/Valley Way route is 8.2 mi.

OPTIONS FROM APPALACHIA VIA LESS-USED TRAILS
The vast network of RMC trails makes possible some interesting variations for the lower half of the approach to Madison. One option, as described in the Mt. Adams chapter, is to take Valley Way for 0.9 mi., then the attractive Brookside, with fine birch forest in its lower half and Salmacis Fall above, for 1.7 mi., then a short stint on Watson Path and a steep 0.2 mi. climb up Lower Bruin back to Valley Way. Distance and elevation gain are the same as the direct approach on Valley Way.

The most scenic route is to take the Inlook and Kelton Trails. Follow Valley Way for 0.9 mi., then bear L on Brookside across Snyder Brook (no bridge) and continue straight on Inlook Trail as Randolph Path diverges L and Brookside bears R. Inlook Trail climbs steeply through woods for

0.3 mi., then emerges on first of series of open ledges with fine views "in" looking up Snyder Brook valley to Mt. Madison, and higher up to Mt. Adams, and "out" to the W and NW. Steep climb continues alternately through scrub and out on ledges,, then short level stretch leads to Dome Rock at 1.5 mi. / 2662 ft., glacially polished ledge with view N to Pliny, Crescent and Mahoosuc Ranges. Trail re-enters woods and climbs 0.1 mi. to Upper Inlook, ledge with view W back down Inlook Trail ridge and up to Madison and Adams. Just beyond turn R on Kelton Trail, which runs through conifer forest at mostly easy grades. Trail continues at mostly gentle grade, even on steep sidehill thanks to extensive trail work by RMC, then dips to cross Snyder Brook and climbs steep bank on far side to meet Brookside at 2.4 mi. / 2750 ft. Follow Brookside, Watson Path and Lower Bruin back to Valley Way at 3.1 mi. / 3584 ft. This is 0.3 mi. longer than direct approach up Valley Way, with 50 ft. more of climbing.

Both Brookside and Inlook / Kelton / Brookside routes can also be used in conjunction with Watson Path for ascent of Madison, with only slight differences in distance compared to Valley Way approach to Watson Path. Obviously, various loop options are possible using these routes as well.

OPTIONS FOR CLIMBING MADISON AND ADAMS TOGETHER
FROM APPALACHIA
Numerous possibilities exist using the extensive trail system on these peaks. These are two of many options:

1. Valley Way to Madison Hut; Gulfside Trail and Air Line to Mt. Adams, up-and-back; Osgood Trail to Mt. Madison, up-and-back; return from hut via Valley Way. Total: 10.4 mi., 5050-ft. elevation gain
2. Air Line to Mt. Adams; Air Line and Gulfside Trail to Madison Hut; Osgood Trail up-and-back to Mt. Madison; return from hut via Valley Way. Total: 10.0 mi., 5050-ft. elevation gain

North Approach from Pinkham B Rd. at Randolph East

Howker Ridge Trail, Osgood Trail
9.0 mi. round trip, 4750-ft. elevation gain (including 300 ft. on return)

TRAILHEAD (1225 ft.): Howker Ridge Trail begins at the Randolph East parking area on the Pinkham B (Dolly Copp) Rd., 0.2 mi. S of US 2. Pinkham B Rd. leaves US 2 about 1 mi. E of Appalachia parking area, at the foot of the steep climb up Gorham Hill.

Howker Ridge Trail is one of the wildest, least-used and most scenic routes to Madison, with waterfalls down low, beautiful forests, and several views from "The Howks" along the ridge. There are several significant ups and downs amidst the Howks, and a few fairly difficult short ledge scrambles. The lower 3 mi. has generally good footing by Northern Presidential standards, though the upper part is rough.

From parking area, trail crosses old railroad grade, bears L where Randolph Path splits R, crosses wet area, and rises gradually through logged areas—follow markings closely. At 0.4 mi. begin pleasant section alongside Bumpus Brook (on L), passing Stairs Fall, Devil's Kitchen (small rock chasm) and dried-up Coosauk Fall. Sylvan Way splits R at 0.7 mi, and at 0.8 mi. Howker Ridge Trail bears L as Kelton Trail continues straight. Cross Bumpus Brook at base of tumbling Hitchcock Fall at 1.0 mi. / 1875 ft.

Trail now ascends at much more serious grade through beautiful mossy spruce forest up NW spur of Howker Ridge; first pitch is very steep. About 0.1 mi. up from brook, trail turns L where signed side path descends short distance R to the "Bear Pit," a deep rock cleft. At ca. 2675 ft. trail levels on scrubby spruce shoulder once known as Blueberry Ledge (no views), then climbs steadily again, with occasional rough spots, passing limited N views between 3100 and 3200 ft. Trail then eases and meanders along narrow wooded crest, reaching summit of first Howk and limited view of Mt. Madison and upper Howks at 2.3 mi. / 3425 ft.. Descend 70 ft. and wander across level shoulder, then tackle stiff climb to second Howk at 3.0 mi. / 3951 ft.; open ledge provides dramatic view up to Mt. Madison beyond jumble of scrubby knobs, with Carters and Wildcats to E and Bumpus Basin and Pliny / Pilot Ranges to W. Drop steeply 125 ft. with one tricky ledge scramble to col, where Pine Link comes in from L at 3.1 mi., then climb to bare knob on next Howk and more views, especially to N; highest Howk looms close by to SW. Make short, steep 40-ft. drop down ledge crevice to pretty col and resume steep climb towards highest Howk, passing cave on R partway up. Pine Link splits R at 3.5 mi. / 4150 ft., and open climb with some scrambling leads to top of highest Howk at 3.6 mi. / 4315 ft. This bare peak has sweeping views of Madison, Carters, Mahoosucs and Pliny / Pilot Ranges. Steep 70-ft. drop is followed by more steep climbing through scrub and then completely in open, angling SW to top of Osgood Ridge. At 4.2 mi. / 5100 ft. reach Osgood Trail at crest of ridge just W of and above minor saddle. Turn R for steep, rocky, exposed climb, passing under overhanging ledges. After slight dip to flat spot, short final pitch leads to summit of Madison at 4.5 mi. / 5366 ft.

Various loops are possible for descent back to Randolph East, e.g. Watson Path (steep and rough), Brookside, Kelton Trail (lower half of Kelton Trail descends steeply from junction with Inlook Trail, soon passing excellent N view from ledge called The Overlook) and lower Howker Ridge Trail (4.8 mi.) or Osgood Trail, Valley Way and Randolph Path (4.9 mi.). Consult AMC or RMC guides for details.

Howker Ridge can also be climbed from Appalachia by following Valley Way, Maple Walk and Sylvan Way to Howker Ridge Trail 0.7 mi. from its start. One way distance to summit of Madison by this route is 5.0 mi. with 4400-ft. elevation gain. Various other, shorter routes can be used for a loop return to Appalachia.

Northeast Approach from Pinkham B Rd.

Pine Link, Watson Path

7.6 mi. round trip, 4150-ft. elevation gain (including 200 ft. on return)

TRAILHEAD (1650 ft.): Pine Link starts at height-of-land on Pinkham B (Dolly Copp) Rd., 1.9 mi. from NH 16 and 2.4 mi. from US 2. This is the shortest route to the summit, though the footing is often rough in its upper half, and offers several views at mid-elevations. From road, trail ascends NE spur of Howker Ridge at alternating steeper and easier grades, then climb eases on shoulder, where swampy flat is crossed. At 0.9 mi./2250 ft. trail begins steep climb up main part of spur. Higher up ascent continues at steady grade along wild, spruce-wooded crest of ridge. Pass limited outlook on L at 1.7 mi. At 1.9 mi./3650 ft. side path leads L to excellent ledge perch with view up to Madison and out to Carters on L and Pliny/Pilot Ranges on R. After slight dip, grades are easy/moderate, with one section in brookbed, to jct. with Howker Ridge Trail at 2.4 mi./3850 ft.

Bear L here as the trails coincide, climbing easily, then steeply to a bare Howk with good views, especially to N; highest Howk looms close by to SW. Make short, steep 40-ft. drop down ledge crevice to pretty col, then climb steeply again, passing cave on R partway up. At 2.8 mi./4150 ft. (a steep 0.1 mi. below highest Howk, an excellent viewpoint), Pine Link diverges R from Howker Ridge Trail and runs at easy grade across small plateau, crossing sphagnum moss area on bog bridges. Trail now climbs moderately, soon encountering section with several springs and small brooks with mossy, slippery rocks in footway. Steady climb continues through dense, dark conifers. At ca. 4500 ft. trail bends R and climbs more steeply through scrubby fir and birch, with some eroded sections and a couple of ledge scrambles. As treeline is approached, Howks can be seen looking back down over trees. Trail breaks above treeline at 3.3 mi./4750 ft. and grade becomes moderate to easy across beautiful lawn-like areas of sedge, diapensia and low scrub with occasional rough boulder fields; here there are wide views to N and E, and close-in looks down at Howks and part of Bumpus Basin. Continue up at moderate grade, with small craggy knobs downslope to R, and meet Watson Path at 3.5 mi./4950 ft. Turn L here for stiff, boulder-strewn climb up N side of Mt. Madison's cone, reaching summit at 3.8 mi./5366 ft. (Note: Section of Pine Link that continues 0.5 mi. SW from Watson Path jct. to Madison Hut is very rough sidehill scramble over nearly continuous jumble of large boulders. Despite relatively easy grade, it is slow and difficult going.)

Upper part of descent can be varied by looping back via Osgood Trail and Howker Ridge Trail; distance is same.

East Approach from Dolly Copp Campground

Daniel Webster–Scout Trail, Osgood Trail
8.0 mi. round trip, 4100-ft. elevation gain

TRAILHEAD (1250 ft.): From NH 16 S of Gorham, take Pinkham B (Dolly Copp Rd.) to W for 0.3 mi., then turn L (S) on entrance road to Dolly Copp Campground. Scout Trail leaves on R 0.9 mi. down this road.

This approach is relatively moderate for its first half, then quite steep and rough in the upper half, with the last mile fully exposed to weather. From campground, trail begins easy to moderate climb through hardwoods, crossing Hayes Copp Ski Trail at 0.2 mi. Trail angles NW, then at 0.7 mi. swings SW, working up S side of Culhane Brook basin at reasonable grades. At 2.0 mi. / 2800 ft. enter conifer forest and bear R to climb more steeply to top of 3175-ft. shoulder, then angle up NE side of Osgood Ridge. Trail bears L at 2.9 mi. / 3400 ft. to begin very steep and rocky ascent, with first views popping out.

Break out above treeline at 3.2 mi / 4100 ft. and continue relentless, rough climb up talus, swinging L and up to crest of ridge and Osgood Jct. at 3.5 mi. / 4822 ft. Turn R here on Osgood Trail and scramble up to small rocky peak (5086 ft.), dip slightly to saddle, then clamber steeply up E end of rocky summit ridge, passing jct. R with Howker Ridge Trail at 3.7 mi. / 5100 ft. Osgood Trail passes under overhanging ledges, dips slightly to flat spot, then climbs short final pitch to summit of Madison at 4.0 mi. / 5366 ft.

Southeast Approaches from Great Gulf Parking Area
TRAILHEAD (1350 ft.): These routes start at large parking area for Great Gulf Wilderness on W side of NH 16, 6.5 mi. S of US 2 in Gorham, and 4.1 mi. N of AMC's Pinkham Notch Camp.

Great Gulf Trail, Osgood Trail
10.2 mi. round trip, 4100-ft. elevation gain

This is a long but scenic approach with an easy valley warmup and the final 1.2 mi. along exposed Osgood Ridge. From parking area, walk N along old road for 0.1 mi., descend L and cross Peabody River on suspension footbridge, then swing L and up to jct. with Great Gulf Link Trail (from Dolly Copp CG) at 0.3 mi. Bear L here at easy grade on wide trail through spruces and hemlocks along bank above West Branch of Peabody. At 0.6 mi. Great Gulf Trail splits L off road (a ski trail in winter), passes scenic ledges and pool in river on L, then rejoins at 1.0 mi. Continue past more ski trail jcts. and over several brooks on bridges. At 1.6

mi. is jct. R with Hayes Copp Ski Trail. Enter Great Gulf Wilderness and reach jct. with Osgood Trail at 1.8 mi. / 1850 ft.

Turn R on Osgood Trail and ascend moderately through hardwoods. Osgood Cutoff comes in on L at 2.6 mi. / 2486 ft.; Osgood Tentsite is on side trail R. From here up Osgood Trail is part of Appalachian Trail. At 3.1 mi. / 3000 ft. trail becomes very steep and rocky through deep conifer forest. Climb is relentless for ca. 1000 ft., then pitch begins to ease off. Reach treeline at 3.9 mi. / 4300 ft. and traverse open rocky crest of curving ridge. Trail humps over long series of rocky nubbles and intervening terraces, with very rough footing. Views are magnificent, especially SW into Great Gulf surrounded by Mts. Washington, Clay, Jefferson and Adams, SE to Carter Range, and N over Culhane Brook basin to Howks.

Reach Osgood Jct. at 4.6 mi. / 4822 ft., where very rough, rocky, tedious Parapet Trail goes L to slab S side of summit and Scout Trail comes in from R. Continue up ridge over 5086-ft. double-peaked knob. Pass through minor saddle, then climb short distance to jct. R with Howker Ridge Trail at 4.9 mi. / 5100 ft. Osgood Trail clambers steeply up E end of rocky summit ridge, passing under overhanging ledges, dips slightly to flat spot, then climbs short final pitch to summit of Madison at 5.1 mi. / 5366 ft.

In addition to the loop with ascent via Madison Gulf Trail and descent via Osgood Trail described below, a long, strenuous loop out of the Great Gulf can be made using the Great Gulf Trail, Osgood Trail over the summit of Madison and down to Madison Hut, Star Lake Trail, Buttress Trail, lower Six Husbands Trail, and Great Gulf Trail again. This encompasses a tremendous variety of scenery, with stupendous views of Mt. Madison rising from Madison Gulf seen along the Buttress Trail. Buttress Trail route is described for ascent in Mt. Adams chapter. This loop is 12.8 mi. with 4250-ft. elevation gain.

Great Gulf Trail, Madison Gulf Trail, Parapet Trail, Star Lake Trail, Osgood Trail
6.3 mi. one way, 4150-ft. elevation gain

This is perhaps the most challenging and interesting route to Madison. The climb up the headwall of Madison Gulf is one of the steepest trail sections in the Whites and should not be attempted by hikers uncomfortable with ledge scrambling. It should be avoided in wet weather and is not recommended for descent. For a long, strenuous and very scenic loop of 11.4 mi. from Great Gulf trailhead, one could ascend via Madison Gulf Trail route and descend Osgood Trail.

Route begins on Great Gulf Trail as described above under Osgood Trail route. At 1.8 mi., where Osgood Trail branches R, continue ahead on Great Gulf Trail, following West Branch of Peabody. Pass scenic view of stream at 2.4 mi., then climb steeper pitch to gravelly opening atop high bank known as The Bluff, reached at 2.7 mi. / 2278 ft. Here there are good views up to N side of Mt. Washington, Mt. Jefferson and Mt. Adams. Just beyond, bear L on Great Gulf Trail where Osgood Cutoff veers R, and descend steep bank to cross Parapet Brook, then climb to hogback where Madison Gulf Trail splits R at 2.8 mi. Follow this trail up little ridge between Parapet Brook and West Branch and rejoin older route of trail at 3.2 mi. Rocky, rooty trail now climbs up wild valley of Parapet Brook through fir forest, crossing two forks of stream at 3.5 mi. and 3.6 mi. Route veers away from brook, then returns to cross tributary brook.

Ascending higher into Madison Gulf, trail crosses main brook three times starting at 4.2 mi. / 3500 ft. Reach Sylvan Cascade, split waterfall dropping over mossy ledge at 4.8 mi. / 3900 ft. Briefly traverse gentle upper floor of Gulf through wet, mossy fir forest, with walls looming above, then reach Mossy Slide and commence steep, rugged climb up headwall. This entails scrambles up boulders, several steep ledges, and a rock chimney; use of hands is required in places. A couple of spots are fairly difficult. After long pull, trail breaks above treeline and soon meets Parapet Trail atop headwall at 5.5 mi. / 4850 ft.

Turn L on Parapet Trail and climb to sharp R turn at 5.6 mi; side trail leads L to rocky battlement of The Parapet with dramatic view back down Madison Gulf and out to Mt. Washington and Carter Range. Parapet Trail runs across Adams–Madison col past rock-dotted Star Lake on L and meets Star Lake Trail at 5.7 mi. / 4900 ft. Turn R on Star Lake Trail and descend gently to AMC Madison Hut at 5.8 mi. / 4825 ft. Turn R here on Osgood Trail for steep, bouldery climb up W side of Madison summit cone. Grade eases along S side of ridge, then trail levels out on narrow crest and traverses to summit at 6.3 mi. / 5366 ft.

Winter

As with all the higher Presidentials, this is a serious undertaking in winter with great exposure to wind and weather, though less so than on Adams, Jefferson or Washington. It should only be attempted on fine winter days by experienced winter trampers fully equipped for above-treeline travel. By far the most popular route is up via Valley Way, which is sheltered almost to Madison Hut. This trail is well packed out for much of the winter. Crampons and caution are required on the steep climb from the hut (closed in winter) up the boulder-strewn summit cone. Other routes such as Watson Path, Howker Ridge and Osgood Trail receive much less use in winter and are exposed for much longer distances.

View Guide

The open, rocky crest of Madison combines nearby views of Mts. Washington and Adams, the Great Gulf and the Carter Range with distant prospects to the NW, N and NE.

The huge rocky bulk of Mt. Washington closes in the view to the S, beyond the lower Great Gulf. The Auto Road winds up the mountain's broad flank and past the little peak of Ball Crag to the L of the summit. To the R of Washington's summit is the gaping gouge of the upper Great Gulf, with Mt. Clay's double summit closing it in on the R. Close by to the SW is the giant rock-strewn pyramid of Adams, with the lesser peaks of Sam Adams and Adams 4 trailing out to the R. Below the creased crags of John Quincy Adams is Star Lake, sparkling on the flat col at the base of Adams' cone. On the L of the pond is the rocky battlement of The Parapet. Scar Ridge can be seen in the distance over the low point between Clay and Adams. (Mt. Jefferson is completely hidden by Adams.)

To the W and NW, beyond the great N ridges of Adams, there are distant views out to Vermont. On the far L are Signal and Spruce Mtns. near Groton, Vermont, with the long Mt. Abraham–Mt. Ellen ridge beyond. Farther R, looking due W, Camel's Hump is seen on the horizon over the nearer Cherry Mtn. The sharp spur of Owl's Head juts up on the R side of Cherry, with the Worcester Range beyond on its R. Farther R on the horizon is the long spread of Mt. Mansfield (L) and the Sterling Range (R). Closer in looking in this direction is the broad plain of the Israel River valley in the Jefferson–Whitefield area, with Cherry Pond visible under the R end of the Sterling Range. Down below on nearby Nowell Ridge, Crag Camp can be seen perched on the edge of King Ravine.

Continuing R on the Vermont horizon, one sees (L to R) Laraway Mtn. and then Belvidere Mtn., Tillotson Peak and Haystack Mtn., with the nearer pair of Burke and Umpire Mtns. in line with Haystack. Next to the R on the horizon are the prominent Jay Peaks. To the R of the Jays and closer is broad East Haven Mtn., with Mt. Hor peering over on its L and Mt. Pisgah on its R. To the NNW, beyond the Randolph valley at the foot of the mountain, are the wooded peaks of the Pliny Range — Mt. Starr King, Mt. Waumbek (with Pliny Mtn. in front) and the three rounded Weeks summits (L to R, South, Middle and North). Bald Mtn. in Vermont's Northeast Kingdom is on the horizon to the L of Starr King, with Quebec's Round Top peering over on its L. East Mtn. is seen above Starr King, Seneca Mtn. is over Waumbek, and the distant Sutton Mtns. in Quebec are visible over the long E ridge of Waumbek. The broad bulk of Mt. Cabot rises behind North Weeks, with its Pilot Range neighbors, The Bulge and The Horn, jutting out to the R. Vermont's Gore Mtn. is seen in the distance over the L slope of Cabot. Part of Terrace Mtn. can be seen tucked in behind North Weeks on the L, and down on a plateau in front of North Weeks is the Pond of Safety. Vermont's Black Mtn. is seen directly over Cabot, and Brousseau Mtn. is above The Bulge. Goback Mtn. near Stratford, New Hampshire, is above The Horn, with Sable Mtn. peering over its L shoulder and the broad mass of Vermont's Mt. Monadnock behind on its R.

The lower Unknown Pond Ridge extends the Pilot Range R from The Horn, with West Peak in the Nash Stream range above. The Nash Stream mountains continue to the R over Castle Mtn., with the bare Percy Peaks below, sharp Sugarloaf Mtn., Bunnell Mtn. in back, and Gore Mtn. Next to the R and a bit closer is the aptly-named Long Mtn., with Rogers Ledge under its L end and Square Mtn. and Greens Ledge peering over Deer Ridge under its R end. North Whitcomb (Muise) Mtn. rises behind Long on the R. Closer in under North Whitcomb is Mt. Randolph at the W end of the Crescent Range. Neighboring Mt. Crescent is to the R of Mt. Randolph, and next to the R, almost due N, is the double summit of Black Crescent Mtn. The broad hulk of Dixville Peak is on the horizon just L of Black Crescent, and other North Country ridges—Cave Mtn., Rice Mtn. and Crystal Mtn., are seen above Black Crescent leading across to Magalloway Mtn. Farther R Stub Hill dominates the distant skyline, with the truncated Rump Mtn. peering over in back on the R. A bit farther R is the double summit of Bosebuck Mtn.. Farther R and in the foreground is the little rounded, ledgy peak of Jericho Mtn. with the sharp peak of Mt. Dustan above and, a bit to the R, various high peaks along the Maine / Quebec border on the horizon.

Next to the R, in front of the border mountains, is the double summit of Aziscohos Mtn. with part of Umbagog Lake at its base. Farther R, looking NNE, the city of Berlin is prominent in the Androscoggin valley, with little Mt. Forist guarding it on the L and the flat Cambridge Black Mtn. looming behind. The wavy ridge of Maine's West Kennebago Mtn. is seen on the horizon over the L end of Cambridge Black. On the horizon to the R of Berlin is the long mass of East Kennebago Mtn. The nondescript Red Ridge is nearer and to the R of East Kennebago, and low down in this direction you look down on the first Howk of Howker Ridge. Farther R Bemis Mn. (L) and Elephant Mtn. (R) are seen well beyond the low ledgy ridges of Cascade Mtn. in the southern Mahoosucs. On clear days the sharp peak of Coburn Mtn. can be spotted in the distance between Red Ridge and Bemis / Elephant. The flat crest of Old Blue Mtn. extends R from Elephant beyond a col, with high peaks in the Rangeley Lakes region beyond, including (L to R) the Horns and West Peak of Bigelow Mtn., Crocker Mtn. and Saddleback Mtn. Next to the R is prominent Old Speck Mtn., highest of the Mahoosucs with The Trident and Mt. Hayes below. Baldpate Mtn. peers out just behind the R side of Old Speck, with Sugarloaf (L) and Spaulding (R) Mtns. in the distance. The vast sprawl of Mt. Abraham fills the skyline to the R of Spaulding; in the foreground are broad Bald Cap Mtn. and the ledgy Outlook on Mt. Success. Under the R end of Abraham are the North and East Peaks of Goose Eye Mtn., with the West Peak to the R; Mt. Success blends in below and in front of Goose Eye. Low down and close by in this direction is little ledgy Pine Mtn., and still closer are more of The Howks.

On the horizon to the R of Goose Eye are the Jackson Mtns. near Weld, Maine, with the bare summit of Sunday River Whitecap below; the Whitecap extends a long ridge to the R. Farther R you look down on Reflection Pond in the Androscoggin River beneath Lary Brook Mtn. in the Mahoosucs. Puzzle Mtn. rises behind Lary Brook, with Hurricane Mtn. behind on the L and Mt. Blue's prominent pyramid beyond on the R. Extending R from Lary Brook in the eastern Mahoosucs are the higher peaks of (L to R) Bear Mtn., Black Mtn. and Wheeler Mtn. The paired Bald and Saddleback Wind Mtns. are seen above Black and Wheeler. Next to the R, looking across the Peabody River valley, are the slopes of the Moriahs rising up to the ledgy hump of Shelburne Moriah with Middle Moriah in front. Mt. Zircon near Rumford, Maine, is seen in the distances over the ridges sloping L off Shelburne Moriah. Zircon's southern neighbors, Speckled (with a sharp dropoff), Black and Spruce, are seen above Shelburne Moriah. To the R of Shelburne Moriah, beyond a deep gap, Mt. Moriah rises above the Stony Brook valley. Peabody Mtn. (L) and Pickett Henry Mtn. (R) are seen through the gap. Gammon (L) and ledgy Caribou (R) Mtns. are seen over the long S slope of Mt. Moriah, and Caribou's southern spur, Haystack Mtn., is seen above Moriah's rocky SE knob, with ledgy Imp Mtn. just to the R.

The huge rounded mass of North Carter looms to the R of Imp, and between Imp and North Carter are East and West Royce, with Speckled Mtn. seen in back of West Royce on the R. The low crests of Butters and Redrock Mtns. can be spotted over the L slope of East Royce. Streaked Mtn. is on the horizon over the Royces, and on clear days the Camden Hills on the Maine coast can be seen to the L of Streaked. The Imp Face cliff is seen down low in line with the Royces. From North Carter the impressive broadside vista of the Carter–Moriah Range sweeps across Middle Carter, South Carter, Mt. Hight and Carter Dome, the latter with its NW slide well-displayed. In the foreground under the Carters is the sharp rocky spine of Osgood Ridge. The tip of North Baldface is seen through Zeta Pass, between South Carter and Hight, and the vast lowlands of Maine sprawl beyond the Carters. The Glen House clearing is seen under Little Wildcat Mtn. below the shoulder of Carter Dome. The great gap of Carter Notch is to the R of Carter Dome, with Wildcat A forming the R side of the pass. The summit of Jackson's Black Mtn. is seen right through Carter Notch, with the S slope of Chandler Mtn. behind on the L, Mt. Shaw over Walter Mtn. behind on the R, and Maine's Saddleback Hills, including Douglas Mtn., on the horizon.

The Wildcats carry the ridgeline on the R (W) side of Carter Notch, with the tip of the South Gemini visible between Wildcats A and B and Rickers Knoll peering over the L side of Wildcat C. The Burnt Meadow Mtns., Bill Merrill Mtn. group, and Clark Mtn. group are seen successively farther on the horizon over Wildcat C. Kearsarge North is prominent be-

hind and R of Wildcat C with its spur, Bartlett Mtn., extending R. Black
Cap Mtn. is seen in back between Kearsarge North and Bartlett. Maine's
distant Ossipee Hill can be seen on the skyline over Bartlett. Wildcats
D and E with their many ski trails are to the R of Bartlett, with sharp
little Middle Mtn. seen through the D/E col and many hills along the
Maine / New Hampshire border beyond. Over the R slope of Wildcat E is
double-humped Green Mtn. in Effingham. In the foreground to the R of
Green, White Horse Ledge peeks over the low ridge that leads down to
Humphreys Ledge.

Farther R, looking through Pinkham Notch, the Moat Range is seen,
with sharp South Moat on the L and lofty North Moat on the R. The
Moose Mtns. (L) and Copple Crown Mtn. (R) are on the horizon over
the Moats. Little Attitash Mtn. and the main Attitash ski slopes are under
North Moat, with Iron Mtn. seen closer and to the R. Big Attitash Mtn.
sprawls to the R of North Moat, with distant Blue Job Mtn. (L) and Parker
Mtn. (R) on the horizon in southeastern New Hampshire, and Attitash's
Bear Mtn. ski slopes in front. Two NE spurs of Mt. Chocorua are seen
just R of Big Attitash, then next to the R Table Mtn. is seen in front and
Mt. Flagg in the Ossipees is in the distance. Next to the R, above a prominent curve in the Auto Road on the shoulder of Mt. Washington, is the
pointy peak of Chocorua with the Three Sisters extending to the L and
Mt. Shaw in the Ossipee Range just to the R and behind. The Ossipees extend to the R over Faraway Mtn. (with a bit of the Belknap Range peering over in back) before disappearing behind the barren, rocky slope of
Mt. Washington.

NO. OF 4000-FOOTERS VISIBLE: 10

Mount Monroe

ELEVATION: 5372 ft. / 1637 m   ORDER OF HEIGHT: 4
LOCATION: Southern Presidential Range, Township of Sargents
   Purchase
USGS MAPS: 7½′ Mount Washington, 7½′ Stairs Mtn.

Geography

Though overshadowed by Mt. Washington, its giant neighbor to the NE,
craggy, treeless Mt. Monroe is one of the most distinctive peaks in the
Whites. It is the northernmost and tallest of the chain of peaks that poke
up from the ridgeline of the Southern Presidentials along the historic
Crawford Path. The bare, rocky mass of Monroe rises abruptly from

its 5108-ft. col with Mt. Washington to a short, level crest, with the high point on the S end. Monroe is a classic example of a glacially eroded peak known as a "sheepback" or "roche moutonee," with a moderate slope on the NW, where the continental ice sheet flowed uphill, and a steep, craggy face on the SE, where the glacier plucked rocks away as it moved downhill. This profile is easily seen from vantages on the slopes of Mt. Washington to the NE.

Just W of the summit is a small subsidiary peak known as Little Monroe (5225 ft.), from which the open ridgecrest descends gently towards the slight rounded swell on the ridge called Mt. Franklin (5001 ft.). From Franklin the ridge extends SW along a level shoulder, then descends sharply to a deep col with Mt. Eisenhower. Below the main summit of Monroe on the SSE is a broad, open, level shoulder traversed by the Crawford Path. This area is noted for its profusion of alpine flowers blooming in June. From here a sharp ridge descends steeply S into the remote upper valley of the Dry River, forming the boundary between two steep glacial cirques. The main bowl of Oakes Gulf, with a broad, flat floor, is to the E of this ridge, extending across to the high ridge of Boott Spur. To the W of Monroe's S ridge is a smaller cirque, enclosed by Monroe and Franklin, that has been called "Monroe Gulf." Yet another cirque is carved into the S side of the main ridge to the SW of Mt. Franklin; old maps show a tiny water body known as "Desolation Pond" on the floor of this basin, but it has long since filled in. The wild area around Oakes Gulf contains some of the finest scenery in the mountains. The steep headwall between Monroe and Franklin is especially impressive.

Among the famous features of the Mt. Monroe area are the Lakes of the Clouds, two tiny alpine tarns that lie NE of the summit below the Monroe–Washington col. The Upper Lake (5050 ft.) is 0.4 acre in area and 6.5 ft. deep, while the Lower Lake (5025 ft.) measures in at 1.2 acres in area and 8.5 ft. deep. They are the ultimate sources of the Ammonoosuc River. The scenery around these glacially scooped basins is a striking mosaic of water, tundra and rock, with Monroe's summit presiding above. Nearby is the AMC Lakes of the Clouds Hut. To the N of the Lakes is the broad Ammonoosuc Ravine on the W side of Mt. Washington, holding the headwaters of its namesake river and marked by numerous slides and scree slopes.

On the less dramatic NW side of Monroe a broad ridge descends from Little Monroe to the Cog Railway Base Station and the upper part of the Ammonoosuc River. Monroe Brook drains the basin to the E of this ridge, between Little Monroe and the main summit. This steep ravine is marked by a prominent slide. Franklin Brook flows down through the ravine to the W of Monroe's NW ridge. Two NW-facing ravines between Mt. Franklin and Mt. Eisnhower are drained by branches of Sokokis Brook.

Nomenclature

In 1820 the Weeks–Brackett party, including mapmaker Philip Carrigain and guided by Ethan Allen Crawford, ascended Mt. Washington and bestowed names on the surrounding Presidential peaks. This summit was named for James Monroe, our fifth President, who was in office at the time. Oakes Gulf to the E was named for William Oakes, a botanist who explored the White Mountains from 1825 until his untimely death in 1848, the same year in which his book, *Scenery of the White Mountains*, was published.

The Lakes of the Clouds were called the "Blue Ponds" by the Weeks–Brackett party, who drank the ice-cold water "until some of us became quite blue . . ." In earlier days they were also known as "Washington's Punch Bowl." Mt. Franklin was named for Benjamin Franklin (1706–1790) by the Weeks–Brackett party in 1820. Having exhausted the names of Presidents who had served up to that time, they chose one of America's most distinguished citizens of the era. The name "Ammonoosuc" River is derived from an Abenaki Indian word meaning "fish-place." In Crawford's time, Ammonoosuc Ravine was known as "Escape Glen."

Historical Highlights

First Ascent: It is generally thought that Darby Field and his Indian companions were the first persons to ascend Mt. Monroe during their epic journey up Mt. Washington in 1642. By all accounts, it is believed that Field at the very least passed by the two Lakes of the Clouds. A recently (1984) uncovered letter dating back to June 29, 1642, seems to indicate as well that Field and his party may have climbed over the summits of Mts. Eisenhower, Franklin and Monroe while on their way to Mt. Washington.

1642: Darby Field and Indian companions pass over summit en route to Mt. Washington.

1811: Norwich University founder Capt. Alden Partridge traverses Southern Presidentials with guide Ethan Allen Crawford. Walk more or less follows route of soon-to-be-built Crawford Path and includes ascent of then unnamed Mt. Monroe.

1819: Crawford Path over Southern Presidentials is constructed by Ethan Allen Crawford and Abel Crawford. Path probably passed over summit of Monroe at first, but was later rerouted around and below cone.

1820: Summit is christened Mt. Monroe by Lancastrian hikers guided to Mt. Washington by E. A. Crawford.

1823: Two trampers from Boston descend "Escape Glen" (Ammonoosuc Ravine) after climbing Mt. Washington; one falls after grabbing old root that gives way. Says Ethan Allen Crawford, "He was over a perpendicular precipice of fifty feet, but fortunately saved himself and returned safely home. He experienced no injury, save that of being frightened." In 1825 botanist William Oakes descends the ravine and calls it "the most villainous break-neck route of the Ammonoosuc. God help the poor wight who attempts that route, as we did."

1837: Nathaniel Hawthorne publishes short story, *The Great Carbuncle.* Tale, related to Hawthorne by Ethan Allen Crawford during 1832 visit, is based on Indian legend that great gem is hidden under remote cliff, supposedly at head of Dry River (probably in Oakes Gulf). Crawford recalled that some years earlier his father, Abel, had guided party of adventurers into Dry River Valley in fatiguing and fruitless multi-day search for carbuncle. Group had brought along "well-qualified" minister to ward off evil Indian spirit said to protect stone.

1876: Guidebook author M. F. Sweetser writes of mountain: "On account of its sharp and massive crags Monroe presents a fine alpine appearance to the distant observer. From points near at hand . . . Monroe has a formidable aspect, and the noble symmetry of its craggy walls excites the most lively interest."

1900: AMC members William B. Curtis and Allen Ormsbee perish on exposed Presidential Range when caught in fierce late June storm. Curtis dies near Crawford Path at base of Mt. Monroe; Ormsbee dies on summit cone of Mt. Washington.

1901: In aftermath of Curtis–Ormsbee deaths, AMC constructs small wood frame shelter in vicinity of Lakes of the Clouds.

1915: New stone refuge—Lakes of the Clouds Hut—is added to AMC hut chain and sees 272 visitors in first season of operation. Crawford Path is rerouted to pass by new hut, which is W of previously built wood shelter. For some time new section of trail is called MacGregor Cutoff after hutmaster Milton "Red Mac" MacGregor. Also, under direction of Councilor of Improvements Charles W. Blood, AMC opens new path, Ammonoosuc Ravine Trail, to Lakes of the Clouds from Cog Railway base station.

1916: Account of hikers snow-bound at Lakes of the Clouds Hut during Sept. 1915 snowstorm appears in *Appalachia.*

1918: AMC opens Camel Trail connecting Crawford Path just E of Lakes of Clouds with Davis Path NW of Boott Spur. Recently built Tuckerman Crossover is relocated.

1919: New loop path over summits of Monroe is "cairned" by AMC crews.

1922: Addition built on N side of Lakes of the Clouds hut for larger sleeping, kitchen facilities.

1927: Second addition to hut includes new women's bunkroom, kitchen and crew quarters.

Early 1930s: Dry River valley is added to WMNF. Dry River Trail opened

Mount Monroe provides the dramatic backdrop for the Lakes of the Clouds and their namesake hut.

by WMNF and CCC, leading up valley from end of old lumber RR to headwall of Oakes Gulf and thence up to Crawford Path on E side of Monroe. Upper part is called Oakes Gulf Trail.

1968: Hut at Lakes of the Clouds enlarged again. New dining room accommodating 90 guests added.

1972: Trail crews reconstruct path from hut to summit in effort to "harden" treadway.

1975: Presidential Range–Dry River Wilderness created by Congress, includes SE slopes of Monroe, Oakes Gulf and Dry River valley.

Ca. 1980: In effort to protect dwarf cinquefoil, rare alpine plant growing NE of Mt. Monroe, section of Crawford Path is rerouted away from fragile vegetation, as is upper portion of Dry River Trail, which now climbs over ridgecrest and descends past Lower Lake of Clouds.

Trail Approaches

North Approach from Cog Railway Base Road

Ammonoosuc Ravine Trail, Crawford Path, Mt. Monroe Loop
7.0 mi. round trip, 2900-ft. elevation gain

TRAILHEAD (2500 ft.): The Ammonoosuc Ravine Trail leaves from a large parking area on the S side of the Cog Railway Base Road, 1.1 mi. E of its jct. with Mt. Clinton Rd. and Jefferson Notch Rd.

The shortest and most often used route to Mt. Monroe follows the steep and scenic Ammonoosuc Ravine Trail up to Lakes of the Clouds Hut. In addition to an out-and-back journey to Monroe, this route can be used to create loops over Mt. Washington to the NE or other peaks of the Southern Presidentials to the SW (see below). The upper portion of this route is fully exposed to weather, though in-season (June to mid-September) shelter is available at the hut. Heed the usual above-treeline precautions. Note that the Ammonoosuc Ravine Trail holds snow late into the spring, and in late fall it can be very icy where water runs over the ledges. Even when merely wet the upper ledges are slippery, especially coming down.

From parking area, follow blue-blazed trail E at easy grades through open fir and birch woods, crossing Franklin Brook at 0.3 mi. Old route from Base Station (0.3 mi. long) comes in on L at 1.0 mi. Trail now climbs easily alongside Ammonoosuc River (on L) through fir forest, with rocky footing in places, passing memorial plaque for Herbert J. Young, Dartmouth student who perished here in December 1928. Cross Monroe Brook at 1.7 mi. / 3225 ft. Woods get scrubbier, with evidence of landslides. At 2.1 mi. / 3450 ft. cross tributary stream by Gem Pool, clear basin of water below small mossy cascade.

Trail turns R (SE) here and begins long, steep ascent up section of rock steps. At 2.3 mi. / 3750 ft. sign marks side trail R to the Gorge, where high perch provides great view of two long waterslides. Steep rocky climb continues to brook crossing and first view W over Bretton Woods valley at 2.5 mi. / 4175 ft. Ledgy scrambling leads up past series of cascades with more brook crossings. Trees shrink to scrub and views open out to NW, and L up to scree-splotched slopes of Mt. Washington. Ascent continues up rock slabs and through intermittent patches of scrub. Grade eases higher up, and near top of climb rocky pile of Monroe appears up to R. Reach AMC hut and jct. with Crawford Path at 3.1 mi. / 5012 ft. During season, refreshments are available at hut.

Now above treeline, follow Crawford Path S, climbing to jct. R with N end of Mt. Monroe Loop at 3.2 mi. / 5075 ft. Turn R on Monroe Loop and make winding climb up stone steps and over steep ledge scrambles to level ridgecrest. Proceed S 0.1 mi. and up to exposed summit outcrop at 3.5 mi. Views are excellent in all directions, especially down Southern Presidential ridge, out over Dry River Valley, and up to Mt. Washington.

SUMMIT LOOP OPTION

If climbing Monroe only, a short loop extension on Mt. Monroe Loop over Little Monroe and back via Crawford Path is rewarding. From main summit, follow Monroe Loop W on short, steep descent with rocky footing akin to that on Northern Presidentials. Cross small flat col and hop over small peak of Little Monroe, then swing S over boulders and descend to Crawford Path, 0.4 mi. from main summit. Turn L here for beautiful walk along barren slopes on S side of Monroe, with impressive views down into Dry River basin and back to steep E slopes of Mt. Franklin. On level shoulder, Crawford Path swings L (N) and leads back to jct. with N end of Monroe Loop; take extra care to remain on marked trail through this section to protect endangered dwarf cinquefoil. Loop from main summit of Monroe around to this jct. is 1.0 mi., compared to 0.3 mi. via direct return down Monroe Loop.

LOOP OPTION WITH MT. WASHINGTON

Because it is a relatively short side trip, Monroe is often combined with the classic loop over the W side of Mt. Washington, using the Ammonoosuc Ravine Trail, Crawford Path, Gulfside Trail and Jewell Trail. Including both summits, loop total is 10.4 mi. with 4200-ft. elevation gain. This is long, tiring day with great exposure to weather; for details see chapter on Mt. Washington.

SOUTHERN PRESIDENTIAL LOOP OPTIONS

With car spot, ascent of Monroe can be combined with Mt. Eisenhower and Mt. Pierce, using connecting link along Crawford Path.

Mt. Monroe and Mt. Eisenhower
9.1 mi., 3300-ft. elevation gain

Ascend Monroe via Ammonoosuc Ravine Trail, Crawford Path and Mt. Monroe Loop (3.5 mi.). Descend S on Monroe Loop over Little Monroe to Crawford Path at 3.9 mi. Turn R for beautiful open walk along gentle ridge, passing side path L to summit of Mt. Franklin at 4.2 mi.; this small peak offers fine view down into depths of Dry River basin. Walking continues easy on barren ridge, then at 4.7 mi. Crawford Path begins descent down steep, ledgy shoulder to Franklin–Eisenhower col, and rises to meet N end of Mt. Eisenhower Loop at 5.4 mi. / 4475 ft. Climb up Eisenhower Loop to summit at 5.8 mi., then retrace steps 0.4 mi. off peak and turn L on Edmands Path (just before reaching Crawford Path) and descend 2.9 mi. to trailhead on Mt. Clinton Rd.

Note: Edmands Path, short section of Mt. Eisenhower Loop, Crawford Path and S section of Mt. Monroe Loop can be used in reverse direction from that described above to make very scenic out-and-back climb of Mt. Monroe that is longer but less steep than Ammonoosuc Ravine Trail approach. Round trip to Monroe via this route from Edmands Path trailhead on Mt. Clinton Rd. (see Mt. Eisenhower chapter) is 9.6 mi. with 3400-ft. elevation gain. With side trip to Mt. Eisenhower included, it is 10.4 mi. / 3700 ft.

Mt. Monroe, Mt. Eisenhower and Mt. Pierce
10.7 mi., 3525-ft. elevation gain

From Ammonoosuc Ravine trailhead, ascend Monroe and Eisenhower as described above. From summit of Eisenhower (5.8 mi.), continue S on Eisenhower Loop, descending to Crawford Path at 6.2 mi./4425 ft. Follow Crawford Path S over open ledges and through patches of scrub down to Eisenhower/Clinton col at 6.7 mi./4060 ft. and up to jct. L with Webster Cliff Trail at 7.4 mi./4250 ft. Make side trip up and back to summit of Mt. Pierce (0.2 mi. round trip), then turn L on Crawford Path and descend 3.1 mi. to trailhead on Mt. Clinton Rd. via that trail and Crawford Connector.

ASCENT VIA DRY RIVER TRAIL

Backpackers and strong day hikers with a taste for remote country can make long trek through Dry River valley and up headwall of Oakes Gulf, emerging at Lakes of the Clouds Hut. One-way trip to Monroe via this route, which cuts through heart of Presidential Range–Dry River Wilderness, is 10.0 mi. with 4450-ft. elevation gain. Dry River Trail starts on US 302 in lower Crawford Notch. Trail partly follows old logging RR grade in first 5 mi., with some rough ups and downs and many looks at rockbound river. For description of this section, see Mt. Eisenhower Trail approach in Mt. Eisenhower chapter. Highlights include pool in river at 0.9 mi.; vista up valley to Mts. Monroe and Washington at 1.5 mi.; suspension bridge over Dry River at 1.7 mi. (damaged in 2005, scheduled for repair in 2008); jct. L with Mt. Clinton Trail at 2.9 mi.; jct. R with Isolation Trail at 4.9 mi.; and view up to Mt. Pierce at 5.0 mi. From jct. L with Mt. Eisenhower Trail at 5.2 mi./2650 ft., Dry River Trail continues up valley, passing obscure side path that drops steeply L to pool at base of beautiful Dry River Falls at 5.4 mi.; at top of main falls are smaller cascades and pothole ledge. After climbing over sprucey knoll, at 5.6 mi. main trail crosses to W side of Dry River (may be very difficult in high water) and continues generally easy climb up valley through mixed forest to Dry River Shelter #3 (only lean-to left in valley) on L at 6.3 mi./3125 ft. Cross tributary brook just beyond shelter, climb up rocky brookbed, then undertake long, gradual meander through mossy fir forest with primeval feel, heading NE. At ca. 7.4 mi./3650 ft. trail swings L (N); here, in upper valley, footway is rough and wet in places. Glimpses of walls of Oakes Gulf begin to appear as trail leads up W side of bowl below steep S spur of Mt. Monroe. Climb becomes steeper at ca. 4100 ft. as views open up more, with cliff and boulder field up to L.

After R turn and short, sharp descent, trail climbs steeply through scrub and then in open, with expanding vistas down to broad, fir-cloaked floor of gulf, across to Boott Spur, and back down the long Montalban Ridge. Trail winds up among crags and alpine flora—take care to stay on marked footway. At 8.9 mi. trail swings L, crosses small brook and follows it up, then at 9.1 mi./4925 ft. turns R off old route and angles up across slope on rim of bowl. It then swings L and ascends steadily to barren height-of-land at 9.4 mi./5175 ft. Here Dry River Trail turns L and, with beautiful views looking down at Lower Lake of the Clouds, descends in open to S shore of the tarn. It skirts edge of water, and after slight up meets Crawford Path by Lakes Hut. Turn L to reach summit of Monroe in 0.4 mi. With car spot, descent can be made via Ammonoosuc Ravine Trail (total 13.5 mi. point-to-point) or other access off Southern Presidential ridge.

East Approaches
Various approaches can be made to Monroe from Pinkham Notch to the E, but they are longer, more exposed, and involve much more elevation gain than the route from the Cog Base Road. From Tuckerman Jct. (5383 ft.) above headwall of Tuckerman Ravine (accessed by Tuckerman Ravine Trail, 3.6 mi. 3350-ft. climb from AMC Pinkham Notch Visitor Center, or by Tuckerman Ravine, Lion Head and Alpine Garden Trails, 3.9 mi. / 3400 ft.—see Mt. Washington chapter), completely exposed Tuckerman Crossover rises gradually SSW to crest of broad, open Bigelow Lawn, crossing Davis Path in 0.3 mi. (5475 ft.; 100-ft. ascent). It then descends moderately to Crawford Path at 0.8 mi. from Tuckerman Jct. Turn L on Crawford Path to reach Lakes of Clouds Hut in another 0.2 mi. From here it is 0.4 mi. to Monroe with 350-ft. elevation gain. There is 450-ft. elevation gain on return over Tuckerman Crossover. Round trip to Monroe from AMC Pinkham Notch Camp using Tuckerman Ravine Trail approach is 10.0 mi. with 4250-ft. elevation gain. Using Lion Head option adds 0.3 mi. each way.

Winter

With the opening of the Cog Railway Base Road in recent winters, access to Mt. Monroe has become easier, though still quite challenging. When the Cog Road was not open to public vehicular traffic (and there is no guarantee that access will remain in the future), Monroe was normally climbed from Pinkham Notch in winter, often in tandem with Mt. Washington. By this route Monroe is a very challenging winter peak that should only be attempted in good weather, by strong and experienced parties fully equipped for extended above-treeline travel. Full crampons are required. Possible approach routes from Pinkham include the lower Tuckerman Ravine Trail / Lion Head Trail winter route / Alpine Garden Trail / Tuckerman Jct. / Tuckerman Crossover (note that the area around Tuckerman Jct., above the Tuckerman headwall, can be unnerving and dangerous in icy conditions) or the lower Tuckerman Ravine Trail / Boott Spur Trail / Davis Path / Camel Trail. The Tuckerman Ravine Trail through the bowl and up the headwall has serious avalanche and other hazards and is suitable only for experienced technical climbers. The traverse of Bigelow Lawn is very exposed and dangerously confusing in cloud, as there are few terrain features to navigate by; over the years a number of winter trampers have become seriously disoriented in this area.

In recent winters hiker parking has been available for a fee at the Cog Railway Base Station; the summer trailhead parking lot for Ammonoosuc Ravine Trail is not plowed. The Ammonoosuc Ravine Trail is accessed by the connecting path from the Base Station, which actually shortens the hike by 0.7 mi. each way. The steep upper mile of Ammonoosuc Ravine Trail requires caution and, quite often, full crampons. The scramble up Monroe Loop on the NE side can be challenging in icy conditions.

With favorable weather and long enough daylight (e.g. late winter), it might be plausible for strong hikers to approach Monroe from Mt. Pierce and/or Mt. Eisenhower as an out-and-back trip along Crawford Path. Note that the section of Crawford Path on the S side of Monroe may present a difficult and dangerous slope of hard snow.

View Guide

Monroe's craggy peak is a superb viewpoint with especially fine views of the Southern Presidentials, the Dry River valley and its looming neighbor, Mt. Washington.

Washington is seen close by to the NE, beyond the level crest of Monroe's narrow summit ridge, with the two Lakes of the Clouds gleaming down to the R on the plateau between the two mountains. Mts. Clay and Jefferson extend to the L of Washington, with Sam Adams peeking up in back to the R of Clay. To the R of Washington (E) is Boott Spur beyond the sweeping, scrub-clad headwall of Oakes Gulf. Beyond these close-in vistas, off the ridge descending R from Boott Spur, the view expands out to the SE, with the Doubleheads in front of Mt. Shaw and The Gemini, and Maine's Pleasant Mtn. beyond. More to the R, beyond the wooded shoulder of Slide Peak, is Kearsarge North, flanked by its satellites Rickers Knoll on the L and Bartlett Mtn. on the R. Farther R and closer are the two rounded upper peaks of Rocky Branch Ridge, with Black Cap and the Green Hills beyond (behind and R of Bartlett Mtn.). In the distance beyond the Green Hills are the Burnt Meadow Mtns., Bill Merrill Mtn. and the Clark Mtn. group, all in western Maine. Conway Lake can be seen on the flats to the R of and beyond the Green Hills. Right below to the SSE is the broad, barren shoulder of Monroe, with the successive peaks of North Isolation (on Montalban Ridge), Engine Hill (on Rocky Branch Ridge) and Iron Mtn. beyond. The pointed peaks of South and North Moat are behind Iron on the R, with lowly Mt. Stanton and Mt. Pickering below them. Green Mtn. in Effingham can be seen in the distance to the L of the Moats. Big Attitash Mtn. spreads to the R of North Moat, with Mt. Langdon under its R end. Closer by in this direction, looking SSE, you gaze over the broad upper reaches of Dry River valley, clad in unbroken conifer forest, to the summit of Mt. Isolation, showing a bald patch on top. On the far horizon above Isolation are the Moose Mtns. and Copple Crown Mtn. The long crest of Mt. Davis stretches to the R from Isolation. Above the L end of Davis is Mt. Parker with the prominent sharp peak of Mt. Chocorua beyond. Table Mtn. can be seen under the lower L spurs of Chocorua. Bear Mtn. is to the R of Chocorua and closer, with Mt. Shaw and the Ossipee Range on the horizon. Stairs Mtn. and Mt. Resolution are nearer in this direction, above the middle of Mt. Davis. To the R of Resolution and farther is Bartlett Haystack with Mt. Paugus beyond; Black Snout and Faraway Mtn. in the Ossipees are over the L shoulder of Paugus. Farther R, closer and lower, is Mt. Crawford, and continuing to the R Mt. Passaconaway (with its spurs, Nanmocomuck and Wonalancet Hedgehog on its L) towers over Mt. Tremont, with the double summit of Mt. Whiteface to its R. The Belknap Range is in the distance through the gap between Paugus and Passaconaway.

The view now sweeps down through the sharp, winding cut of the lower Dry River valley to the Sleepers and Middle and North Tripyramid in the distance. Just beyond the mouth of the valley is flat-topped Mt. Saunders, with Greens Cliff peering over its L end, under the Sleepers. Sandwich Dome sprawls behind Tripyramid on the R. Mt. Bemis is seen closer in under Sandwich's sharp Jennings Peak, and farther R the broad crest of Mt. Kancamagus is seen over Mt. Nancy; on clear days Mt. Kearsarge can be picked out on the horizon above Kancamagus, with Mt. Monadnock just to its L and Ragged Mtn. to its R. To the R of the Dry River Valley, looking SSW, are majestic Mt. Carrigain and wide-spreading Mt. Hancock, with the four Osceola peaks in back between them. Mt. Tecumseh peers over between East Osceola and the main Osceola summit. Osceola's sharp West Peak is above South Hancock, the dome of North Hancock is father R, and NW Hancock is on the far R end of the mountain's ridge. Stinson Mtn. is seen in back between North and NW Hancock, and close by in this direction are Mt. Jackson (L) and Mt. Webster (R). Scar Ridge is behind NW Hancock on the R, with Mt. Hitchcock below. To the R of Webster, Mt. Willey rises beyond the nearer, rounded Mt. Pierce, with (L to R) Carr Mtn., Mt. Kineo and Mt. Cushman in the distance. Smarts Mtn. is still farther away, to the R of Cushman. East Whaleback is seen under Smarts, over the N ridge of Willey. Close by along the bare, twisting Southern Presidential ridge are the jutting face of Mt. Franklin, in line with Pierce, and the bald dome of Mt. Eisenhower, to the R of Pierce. Mt. Field is above Eisenhower, with Mt. Bond behind on its R. Whaleback Mtn., Bondcliff and the Blue Ridge are seen to the L of Bond, and Mt. Moosilauke looms behind on the R. Mt. Liberty pokes up over the col to the R of Bond, under the R slope of Moosilauke. Mt. Guyot is next to the R, with Zealand Mtn. above Mt. Tom in front to the R. A long ridge leads across from Guyot to South

Twin, with Mts. Lincoln and Lafayette (the latter over South Twin) rising behind. North Twin is to the R of South Twin, with the tip of Mt. Garfield just visible over the L shoulder of North Twin. Farther R and close at hand is the bare double hump of Little Monroe. Seen above Little Monroe is the S part of the Rosebrook Range with Mt. Hale beyond, under the N ridge of North Twin. The Breadloaf Mtn. range is seen on the Vermont horizon in this direction. Farther R is Mt. Rosebrook, striped with the ski trails of Bretton Woods, with the long ridge joining Mts. Abraham and Ellen in the distance beyond the Signal Mtn. range in central Vermont.

To the R of Mt. Rosebrook, ledgy Middle Sugarloaf rises behind Mt. Oscar, with lowly Mt. Cleveland and Mt. Agassiz behind on the R and the Mount Washington Hotel complex seen in the broad Bretton Woods valley below. The long view out over Bretton Woods extends to Vermont's Mt. Ethan Allen and Camel's Hump to the R of the hotel, just N of W. Next to the R the Worcester Range is seen over the low crests of Little Deception and Beech Hill, with Mt. Mansfield and the Sterling Range farther to the R beyond the lower spur ridges of Cherry Mtn. Swinging more to the R, the long crest of Mt. Deception, with several summits, rises across the Bretton Woods valley. Cherry Mtn. and its sharp spur, Owl's Head, are behind the middle part of Mt. Deception. In the distance over the R half of Deception and Cherry are (L to R) Belvidere Mtn., Tillotson Peak, Haystack Mtn. and the Jay Peaks behind the nearer Burke Mtn. Mt. Dartmouth is the Dartmouth Range neighbor to the R of Deception, with Mts. Hor and Pisgah around Willoughby Gap seen above the low point between them. Closer in, Cherry Pond is visible over the R slope of Deception. More Northeast Kingdom peaks are seen above Mt. Dartmouth, (L to R): East Haven Mtn., Bald Mtn. in back, and East Mtn. Little Prospect Mtn. in Lancaster can be seen closer in under Bald. The lower Mt. Mitten extends R from Mt. Dartmouth. Farther R, beyond Jefferson Notch, is Mt. Starr King at the L end of the Pliny Range, with Gore Mtn. on the horizon to its L. Mt. Waumbek is to the R of Starr King, with sharp Sable Mtn. seen right over its summit in the distance. A long level ridge extends R from Waumbek, with Goback Mtn. looming in the distance over Hutchins Mtn. South Weeks is to the R of Waumbek's E ridge, with Mt. Cabot rising behind. Extending R from Cabot are The Bulge and The Horn, the latter rearing up over North Weeks. The Nash Stream range is seen beyond Cabot/Bulge/Horn and North Weeks, with the bare Percy Peaks seen below, just R of The Horn. To the R of North Weeks are (L to R) Unknown Pond Ridge, the sharp peak of Rogers Ledge, and Deer Ridge, with the great mass of Long Mtn. beyond. North Whitcomb (Muise) Mtn. peers over the R end of Long, then the distant view is cut off by the rugged Ridge of the Caps leading up to Mt. Jefferson.

NO. OF 4000-FOOTERS VISIBLE: 32

Mount Pierce

ELEVATION: 4312 ft / 1314 m   ORDER OF HEIGHT: 27
LOCATION: Presidential Range, Townships of Beans Grant and
    Cutts Grant
USGS MAPS: 7½′ Stairs Mtn., 7½′ Crawford Notch

Geography

The rounded crest of Mt. Pierce rises about five miles SW of Mt. Washington, midway along the long ridgeline of the Southern Presidentials. It's flanked by the reddish-brown dome of Mt. Eisenhower to the N and the pointed crown of Mt. Jackson to the S. To the uninitiated Presidential Range tramper, the summit of Pierce—which is in the open alpine zone on its N side—affords a first close-up glimpse of life above the trees. For that reason, the mountain is perfect for hikers wishing to get a taste of above-treeline conditions without facing the perils of extensive exposure to the elements. From this open area there are excellent views N, especially up to the higher summits of the range. A ledge near Pierce's subsidiary, semi-open SW summit (4185 ft.) offers fine views S.

The mountain's long ridgeline, stretching NE to SW, is best viewed from the vicinity of Bretton Woods and the Mount Washington Hotel, which lie in a broad intervale to the NW. From this vantage point, Pierce rises gradually to the L (E) out of the narrow Crawford Notch. On closer inspection you will find that two separate ridges, split by tumbling Gibbs Brook, extend from the Notch and U.S Route 302 to a point near the summit ridge. Crawford Cliff is a small crag, accessible by a side trail and offering a view of the Willey Range, at the lower W end of the northerly of these ridges. At the base of these ridges is the Crawford's plateau, N of the top of Crawford Notch, with tiny Saco Lake nestled against the base of the southerly ridge and the AMC Highland Center situated across Route 302, on the former site of the grand hotel known as the Crawford House.

Deep Abenaki Ravine, with a recent and prominent slide scar near its head, lies just to the N of the summit and separates the mountain from Mt. Eisenhower's W ridge; it is drained, naturally, by Abenaki Brook. The NW slopes of Pierce are drained by Sebosis and Assaquam Brooks. The Gibbs Brook valley, on the W slope of the mountain, is noteworthy as the home to the Gibbs Brook Scenic Area. This 1,500-acre tract, through which the Crawford Path passes on its way up the mountain, is an old growth forest of unharvested red spruce and yellow birch. Studies here have found yellow birch as old as 261 years, red spruce at 323 years, and one hemlock over 500 years old. This dramatic section of forest is littered with ancient, moss-covered blowdowns which drape over both the trail

The summit of Mount Pierce is an excellent spot to gain a unique perspective on the snow-covered slopes of Mount Washington and the other peaks of the southern Presidentials.

and the brook valley. On the lower reaches of Gibbs Brook is the attractive Gibbs Falls in a small rocky gorge.

To the E and some 1500 ft. below the summit is the remote Dry River (or Mt. Washington River) valley, which drains out of Mount Washington's Oakes Gulf and flows S through the heart of the Presidential Range–Dry River Wilderness to meet up with the Saco River in the southern end of Crawford Notch. A nameless tributary of the Dry River flows SE down a long valley between the prominent ridge descending SE from Pierce's SW summit and a SE spur ridge of Mt. Jackson; this basin is the route of the Mt. Clinton Trail. Another stream drains a broad basin on the SE between Pierce and Eisenhower.

Beyond Pierce's SW summit, the ridge dips to a large, fairly level depression extending all the way to Mt. Jackson's sharp summit cone a mile and a half away. The summit of Jackson provides an excellent vantage point for seeing the layout of Mt. Pierce from the S. Particularly noteworthy is AMC's Mizpah Spring Hut, seen here tucked in the forest at the S base of the SW summit.

Nomenclature

The mountain has long endured an identity crisis of sorts as it has commonly been known as both Mt. Pierce and Mt. Clinton. As a result of an act of the New Hampshire legislature on April 13, 1913, the mountain's official name is Mt. Pierce, in honor of the nation's fourteenth President, New Hampshire native Franklin Pierce, "the only citizen or resident of New Hampshire who has been the incumbent of that exalted office." The peak's original name—in honor of former New York governor and senator DeWitt Clinton (1769–1828)—was applied as early as 1837 and has continued to live on, thanks in great part to the Appalachian Mountain Club, which for more than 70 years insisted on sticking with the Mt. Clinton name on its trail maps. It wasn't until the mid-1970s that AMC finally relented and tagged the summit with both names (with Mt. Clinton appearing in parentheses under Mt. Pierce). For the record, AMC maps now identify the mountain solely as Pierce.

Although it's been almost a century since the mountain's name was changed, the Mt. Clinton name continues to live on elsewhere in the vicinity. The Mt. Clinton Road connects US 302 with the Cog Railway Base Road, while the Mt. Clinton Trail leads hikers from the Dry River Valley up to AMC's Mizpah Spring Hut at the southern base of the mountain's summit ridge.

An earlier name for the mountain, used by Abel Crawford in the early 1800s, was the simple "Bald Hill."

Gibbs Brook is named after Joseph Gibb, proprietor of the Crawford House when it opened in the 1850s. Abenaki Ravine and Brook were named for the Abenaki Indians of northern New England; the name was applied by John Anderson, early manager of the Mt. Washington Hotel.

Historical Highlights

First Ascent: Unknown

1819: Crawford family members establish footpath from top of Crawford Notch to summit of Mt. Washington. The trail, known as the Crawford Path, passes near summit of Pierce.

1828: Notch House built by Crawford family on E side of Crawford's plateau; opens in 1829 under management of Thomas Crawford.

1839: Crawfords begin conversion of Crawford Path to bridle path.

1840: Abel Crawford, now 75 years old, is first to ride horse entire length of trail to Mt. Washington. He's accompanied by son, Tom, and state geologist Charles T. Jackson.

1852: Crawford House opens near base of Crawford Path.

1859: Original Crawford House burns in April, but new and larger hotel is quickly built and opens in time for summer tourist season.

Ca. 1870: Party from Charles H. Hitchcock's N.H. Geological Survey descends into Dry River valley via brook between Pierce and Jackson, notes several waterfalls.

1892–1898: Saco Valley Lumber Company builds logging RR up Dry River to SE of Mt. Pierce and logs much of valley. RR grade later used for part of Dry River Trail.

1895: Crawford House management cuts hiking trail from Pierce to Jackson, but path is soon abandoned.

1896: Large group from AMC Snow-Shoe Section makes all-day tramp up Dry River valley.

1902: Group of 54 AMC snowshoers ascends Mt. Pierce.

1913: Second permanent access route to summit is established with completion of trail from summit of Mt. Webster (to the S) to jct. with Crawford Path just beyond summit of Pierce. This section of trail becomes, a year later, a link in newly-cut Webster Cliff Trail from Willey House Station (at S end of Notch) to Mt. Pierce.

1913: New Hampshire legislature passes law renaming mountain in honor of fourteenth president, New Hampshire native Franklin Pierce.

1915: Mizpah Cut-off Trail, linking Crawford Path with recently established open log shelter at Mizpah Spring, is cut by AMC members. Shelter is situated approximately ¾ mi. from summit of Mt. Pierce.

1923: Rough blazed path leads up Dry River valley along old lumber railroad, making 11 crossings of river, and continues 1½ mi. past end of railroad to "Fork of Three Streams" (ca. 3400 ft.).

1932: Dry River valley is added to WMNF; soon official trail is opened up valley along route of rough old path.

1934: *AMC Guide* includes first mention of new path (Mt. Clinton Trail) connecting Dry River Trail with Mizpah Spring Shelter, providing approach from SE.

1961: Gibbs Brook Scenic Area designated by U.S. Forest Service.

1965: AMC dedicates Mizpah Spring Hut at S base of SW summit, newest addition to its chain of backcountry huts. It's first new hut to be built by club since completion of Zealand Falls Hut in 1932.

1966: Dry River Cutoff opened by AMC, connecting middle of Dry River valley with Mt. Clinton Trail.

1975: Ridges and valleys on E side of Mt. Pierce are included in new Presidential Range–Dry River Wilderness.

1976: Beset by financial problems attributed to energy crisis, Crawford House is shut down, contents are auctioned off.

1977: November fire levels Crawford House.

2003: AMC opens new 120-bed lodge, Highland Center at Crawford Notch, on former site of Crawford House.

Trail Approaches

West Approach from Mt. Clinton Rd.

Crawford Connector, Crawford Path, Webster Cliff Trail
6.4 mi. round trip, 2400-ft. elevation gain.

TRAILHEAD (1920 ft.): Though Crawford Path begins on E side of US 302 across from AMC Highland Center, 0.2 mi. N of Gateway of Notch, no parking is available here. Trail parking area is now found on W side of Mt. Clinton Rd. (signed), 0.1 mi. N of road's intersection with US 302. Mileages below are from Mt. Clinton Rd. parking area.

The Crawford Path, believed to be the longest continuously maintained hiking trail in America, provides the most direct route to the summit of Pierce. The grade of this ancient, well-worn, sometimes rocky path is mostly moderate, and rarely steep. Crawford Connector, built in 1991, leaves parking lot and crosses Mt. Clinton Rd. It climbs moderately, then gradually through spruces and at 0.4 mi., just after passing side trail L to Crawford Cliff, crosses bridge over Gibbs Brook, joining Crawford Path 0.2 mi. from its start at the highway. Turn L on Crawford Path, which climbs above and to R of Gibbs Brook through expansive old growth forest of red spruce, yellow birch and balsam fir. At 0.6 mi., short side path L leads to nice viewpoint overlooking Gibbs Falls in rocky ravine. Trail enters Gibbs Brook Scenic Area and continues ascending at moderate grade through fine open woods with occasional steeper or easier pitches. After about one mile of climbing, trail rises well above and to S of Gibbs Brook, and at 1.9 mi. / 3480 ft. reaches jct. with Mizpah Cutoff leading R to AMC's Mizpah Spring Hut.

Ascending now at various easy to moderate grades, Crawford Path continues for another 1.2 mi. along W slope of Mt. Pierce through fine boreal forest featuring many lichen-draped old firs, with wet footing in places, including one section of old corduroy. Higher up trees are considerably smaller, soon giving way to openings as summit area is approached. First glimpses are to NE, where Mt. Eisenhower and Mt. Washington dominate scene. Trail levels for ca. 0.1 mi. and emerges from scrub, reaching jct. R with Webster Cliff Trail at 3.1 mi. / 4250 ft. Crawford Path continues ahead to Mt. Washington; turn sharp R here on Webster Cliff Trail and climb SW through alpine zone to Pierce's mostly open summit at 3.2 mi. / 4312 ft. Please stay on marked and defined trail to protect fragile alpine vegetation.

MIZPAH HUT LOOP OPTIONS

There are several possible loop hikes available to Mt. Pierce-bound hikers, with the most popular including a SW-facing view ledge and a visit to AMC's Mizpah Spring Hut via the Webster Cliff Trail and Mizpah Cutoff. From summit of Pierce, descend gently S through high scrub along Webster Cliff Trail, soon passing outlook to N and E on L. After passing through shallow col, make short climb to partly open SW summit of Pierce at 0.6 mi., with view back (NE) to Mt. Washington and R (NW) to Cherry Mtn., the Dartmouth and Pliny Ranges, and out to Vermont. Here trail swings L and in short distance descends easily to broad ledge with wide view SW. From ledge, trail swings L again and descends two very steep pitches with switchback between, losing 350 ft. of elevation in a rocky 0.2 mi.; two ladders lead down over steep ledges. Reach Mizpah Spring Hut (water, snacks, restrooms available summer and fall) and nearby tent platforms at 0.8 mi./3800 ft. From NW edge of hut clearing follow Webster Cliff Trail another 0.1 mi., dipping and then ascending slightly, then bear R on Mizpah Cutoff. This trail, 0.6 mi. long, runs at easy grades through dark, wet fir forest, then descends moderately a short distance to meet Crawford Path, 1.5 mi. from summit of Pierce. Loop total is 6.6 mi. with little additional climbing.

More ambitious hikers can continue from hut S along Webster Cliff Trail to Mt. Jackson, which is reached in another 1.6 mi. past Mizpah Cutoff jct. This wooded ridge walk is at mostly easy grades, with several minor descents and ascents, including traverse of nameless 3821-ft. hump, but concludes with steep climb up cone of Jackson. Scenic highlight is two open alpine bogs crossed at 1.3 mi. from hut. For description of this route in reverse, see Mt. Jackson chapter. From Jackson's summit, follow Webster–Jackson Trail 2.6 mi. back to US 302. From here it's a 0.5 mi. walk back to trailhead parking on Mt. Clinton Rd. Loop total is 8.8 mi. with 2850-ft. elevation gain.

MT. EISENHOWER OPTIONS

Many peakbagging hikers choose to "bag" both Pierce and Mt. Eisenhower in a single day. This is usually accomplished by taking Crawford Connector, Crawford Path and Webster Cliff Trail to summit of Pierce, then returning to Crawford Path and following it N through scrub and over open ledge, descending to 4060-ft. col in 0.7 mi. from Webster Cliff Trail jct. At 1.2 mi./4425 ft. is jct. L with Mt. Eisenhower Loop. This trail climbs up bare dome, paralleling Crawford Path, and at 1.6 mi./4760 ft. reaches Eisenhower's bare, exposed summit. Hikers can retrace steps from here for 9.6 mi. round trip with 3200-ft. elevation gain. Or, follow Eisenhower Loop to its northern terminus, then bear L (W) on Edmands Path for 2.9 mi. descent to its trailhead on Mt. Clinton Rd., 2.3 mi. from US 302. Total loop distance (including road walk back to Crawford Path parking area) is 10.4 mi. with 3050-ft. elevation gain.

Southeast Approach from US 302 via Dry River Valley

Dry River Trail, Mt. Clinton Trail, Webster Cliff Trail
6.7 mi. one-way, 3200-ft. elevation gain

TRAILHEAD (1205 ft.): This approach starts on Dry River Trail on E side of US 302 in Crawford Notch State Park, 0.3 mi. N of Dry River Campground. There is roadside parking for several cars.

Another alternate, much longer approach to Mt. Pierce is via Dry

River and Mt. Clinton Trails from SE through Presidential Range–Dry River Wilderness. This is by far the least used and least crowded of Pierce approaches. Because of a potentially difficult and dangerous crossing of Dry River, this route should not be attempted in high water. Also, note that trails in this Wilderness area are maintained to a lower standard and may be rough and obscure. In return, the valley offers a real feeling of remoteness, quite different from the busy Crawford Path approach.

From trailhead, Dry River Trail follows old road at easy grade through fine hardwood forest for 0.5 mi., where Saco River Trail diverges L and path from Dry River Campground comes in on R. Here Dry River Trail joins old logging railroad grade and mostly follows it to edge of boulder-filled Dry River at 0.9 mi., where there is attractive pool downstream to R. Trail bears L here and climbs to bank, then descends back to riverside. Short steep sidehill climb leads to framed view of Mt. Washington at head of valley at 1.5 mi./1700 ft. Trail drops steeply to cross suspension footbridge at 1.7 mi. and continues up valley, with rough ups-and-downs, then nice section with easy walking on railroad grade. (*Note:* The suspension bridge was seriously damaged by a flood in 2005 and was closed at that time for safety reasons. It is scheduled to be repaired in summer of 2008. Without the bridge this crossing is difficult and possibly dangerous in high water. For update call Saco Ranger Station at 603–447–5448.) Reach jct. L with Mt. Clinton Trail at 2.9 mi./1900 ft. Bear L here onto Mt. Clinton Trail and cross river (very difficult at high water).

Bear R briefly on railroad grade, then L and climb at easy to moderate grades along tributary through hardwoods and mixed woods. At 3.4 mi. make first of seven crossings of brook. Trail is wet and eroded in places, and may be hard to follow, especially at crossings. However, there is some fine brook scenery. Last crossing is at 4.7 mi. Above here footing improves through beautiful, remote boreal forest. Pass jct. R with Dry River Cutoff (alternate access from central Dry River valley, climbing 1.7 mi. from Mt. Eisenhower Trail up small valley and across SE ridge of Pierce) at 5.4 mi./3425 ft. and climb moderately through deep fir woods to Mizpah Spring Hut at 5.9 mi./3800 ft. To reach Mt. Pierce, turn R on Webster Cliff Trail and climb steeply for 0.2 mi. to ledge with fine SW view and to SW summit just beyond, then continue another 0.6 mi. to main summit. With car spot at Crawford Path parking on Mt. Clinton Rd., one can make an interesting 9.9 mi. traverse.

Winter

Mt. Pierce is the easiest of the alpine summits to attain in winter since the distance above treeline is short, and the deep snows of late winter can transform the summit into a 360-degree viewpoint, with additional winter-only views down into the Dry River valley from snowfields a short distance NE. The Crawford Path is one of the most heavily used trails in winter, thus it's usually broken out soon after even the fiercest of winter storms. Its moderate grades are ideal for snowshoeing. The parking area off Mt. Clinton Rd. is reliably plowed. As the summit of Mt. Pierce lies on the fringe of the alpine zone, there's plenty of exposure near the summit, so all winter visitors to the mountain should be equipped with appropriate winter clothing and gear. At times crampons may be needed for the short stretch above treeline. Frequently, the scrubby upper section of the trail (near its jct. with the Webster Cliff Trail) is obscured by drifting snow and can be very difficult, if not impossible, to follow. When in doubt, especially in foul weather, retrace your steps and return the way you came. You can always make another attempt under more favorable conditions. The loop past Mizpah Spring Hut is fun in winter, but in deep snow the trail may be hard to follow in places between the main and SW summits, and caution may be needed on the steep section below the SW summit. The approach from the Dry River valley is very seldom used in winter.

View Guide

SUMMIT VIEW: Though views to the S and W are limited by high scrub (except in late winter, when deep snowpack may provide a 360-degree view), ledges just below the main summit area provide a spectacular close-up view of neighboring Presidential Range peaks and ranges to the N and E. Caps Ridge, rising out of Jefferson Notch, runs L to R up to the summit of Mt. Jefferson to the NNE, with The Castles peering over on the L. To Jefferson's R is the craggy double peak of Mt. Clay, with Mt. Adams poking up in back between Jefferson and Clay and the Jewell Trail ridge sweeping down to the L under Jefferson. Round-domed Mt. Eisenhower, Pierce's near neighbor to the NE, is flanked on the R by the massive summit cone of Mt. Washington. Just to the R of Eisenhower, and under Washington, with its E face sliced off as if with by a knife, is Mt. Monroe. More to the E is seen Oakes Gulf just under Boott Spur, while Slide Peak and the long, flat Montalban Ridge run to the S.

To the E, over the upper Montalban Ridge and Rocky Branch Ridge, are (L to R) South Baldface and Sable and Chandler Mtns. near Evans Notch. The upper, 3921-ft. peak of Rocky Branch Ridge is in front of and between Sable and Chandler. Farther R, looking ESE, is the humpy summit of Mt. Isolation across the Dry River valley, with North and South Doublehead peering over on the R. Mt. Shaw (L) and The Gemini (R) are behind South Doublehead on the R, over the col to the R of Isolation. Next to the R, seen over the N part of the long, flat crest of Mt. Davis, are Maine's elongated Pleasant Mtn. in back, and then the prominent dome of Mt. Kearsarge North, with satellites Rickers Knoll on its L and Bartlett Mtn. on its R. Part of Sebago Lake can be seen in the distance to the R of Kearsarge North. Farther R is the little hump of Hurricane Mtn. with Douglas Mtn. in Maine's Saddleback Hills on the horizon. On the far R Black Cap Mtn. and its lower Green Hills neighbors, Cranmore, Peaked, Middle and Rattlesnake Mtns., are seen over the middle part of Mt. Davis. The rest of the Saddleback Hills can be seen in the distance beyond Black Cap, while the Bill Merrill Mtn. group rises behind the Burnt Meadow Mtns. over Middle and Rattlesnake.

Good views to the N can be enjoyed a short distance in front of the actual summit (which is a clearing mostly surrrounded by scrub), and the view can be extended more to the NW by descending towards the Crawford Path junction. To the L of Mt. Jefferson's Caps Ridge, looking due N through Jefferson Notch, are distant peaks in New Hampshire's North Country. Just L of the Castles are the double summit of Bosebuck Mtn. and massive Stub Hill, with Rump Mtn. behind on its R. Farther L is Magalloway Mtn., with a sharp dropoff on its R. Mt. Randolph just peers over the lower Castellated Ridge to the L of Stub Hill, and sharp Mt. Dustan is seen under the skyline to the R of Magalloway. To the L of Magalloway and a bit closer are Crystal (R) and Rice (L) Mtns. seen over the flat crest of Mt. Bowman, a spur of Jefferson. Continuing to the L are Cave Mtn. and then Dixville Peak behind Mt. Kelsey, seen above the L half of the nearer low and sprawling Deer Ridge in the Kilkenny region. Next to the L, above nearby Millen Hill, is the E half of Long Mtn. with North Whitcomb (Muise) Mtn. peering over a col. The cliff of Rogers Ledge can be seen under the R end of Long. Farther L is nearby Mt. Dartmouth, with the long Pliny Range beyond. Mt. Waumbek's summit is right above Dartmouth's, with Starr King on its L, and the rounded South and North Weeks are at the R end of the range, with the W end of Long Mtn. seen in back between them. Bulky Mt. Cabot (L) and the jutting Horn (R) peer over between Waumbek and South Weeks, Hutchins Mtn. peeks above the Waumbek–Starr King col, and Goback Mtn. is just to the L of and behind Starr King.

Farther L, beyond the lower spurs of Starr King, is sharp Sable Mtn. in Vermont. Next to the L, looking NNW across the Bretton Woods valley, is the long, rolling crest of Mt. Deception. Gore Mtn. in northern Vermont is seen over the farthest R col on Deception, with its lower neighbors Black, Green and Brousseau Mtns. to its R, just L of Sable. Vermont's East Mtn., with a structure on top, is in the distance over the L end of Deception. To the L of Deception is Cherry Mtn., with the sharp peak of Owl's Head on its R. Bald Mtn. (R, in back) and East Haven Mtn. (L) are in the distance between Cherry and Owl's Head. Mt. Pisgah near Lake Willoughby is just L of Cherry's summit, and a bit farther L are Burke and Umpire Mtns., with Mt. Hor behind Umpire on the R. Part of Quebec's Sutton Mtns. can be seen through Willoughby Gap between Pisgah and Hor. The Jay Peaks are seen in the distance to the L of Burke, and continuing L on the horizon are Haystack Mtn., Tillotson Peak, the sharp cone of Belvidere Mtn. and the Cold Hollow Mtns. Farther down towards the Crawford Path one can look NW across the broad plain of Bretton Woods to the Mt. Washington Hotel complex, with the Rosebrook Range and Bretton Woods Ski Area to the L and Mt. Mansfield on the horizon over Mt. Oscar on the R end of the Rosebrooks. The Sterling Range is to the R of Mansfield. To the L of Mansfield, Middle Sugarloaf just pokes above the top of Mt. Rosebrook, with the Worcester Range in the distance. Farther L on the skyline are the distinctive, tilted Camel's Hump and its southern neighbor, Mt. Ethan Allen, and on the far L are the northern humps of Mt. Hale with Spruce Mtn. in Vermont's Signal Mtn. range beyond, and Mt. Hale itself above Mt. Echo and the L end of the Rosebrook Range.

SW LEDGE VIEW: This broad, flat ledge, located on the Webster Cliff Trail 0.6 mi. S of Pierce's summit and just S of the mountain's SW summit, offers an expansive view from the ESE around to the SW. This spot has a good sun exposure and is sheltered from the NW winds that often rake the main summit of Pierce.

On the far L is Mt. Isolation, with Chandler Mtn. to its L. Running to the R from Isolation is the long, flat, mostly wooded ridge of Mt. Davis. The twin Doubleheads peek over the L end of Davis, with Mt. Shaw to their R, and farther R Kearsarge North rises prominently over a saddle along the crest of Davis, with elongated Pleasant Mtn. behind to its L. The very top of Rickers Knoll is visible under the R end of Pleasant. Bartlett Mtn. extends R from Kearsarge, with part of Sebago Lake seen beyond. To the R of Bartlett, seen over more of Mt. Davis, are little Hurricane Mtn. and then prominent Black Cap Mtn., with Douglas Mtn. in Maine's Saddleback Hills seen in the distance between them. The rest of the Saddleback Hills are visible beyond Black Cap. To the R of Black Cap, through a col on Mt. Davis, is the sharp little peak of Middle Mtn. Seen in back from there to the R are Maine's Burnt Meadow Mtns. with the Bill Merrill Mtn. group beyond. Part of Conway Lake is seen over the far R end of Davis, with Maine's Clark Mtn. range on the horizon. Next to the R, seen above the Attitash ski trails, distant Ossipee Hill in Maine rises beyond Stewart Hill and other low ridges along the Maine–New Hampshire border.

Through the deep col to the R of Davis is the wild, jutting Back Stair with Little Attitash Mtn. behind. To the R of that col are the flat crests of Stairs Mtn. (L) and ledge-spotted Mt. Resolution (R), with Big Attitash Mtn. above them and the prominent cone of North Moat behind to the L. Green Mtn. in Effingham is on the horizon over the R end of Big Attitash. To the R of Resolution is Table Mtn. seen over Crawford Dome, with White Ledge peering over the Table–Big Attitash col. A bit farther R is rocky Mt. Crawford; seen in back between Crawford Dome and Mt. Crawford are Hobbs Mtn. (L) and Blue Mtn. (R), northern spurs of Mt. Chocorua. To the R of and behind Crawford is the distinctive ridge of Mt. Chocorua, with the Three Sisters extending to the L and Bear Mtn. beneath. The Moose Mtns. are seen over the ridge descending L from the Sisters. Farther R are Bartlett Haystack (L) and Mt. Tremont (R), with Mt. Paugus seen through the gap between them. Mt. Flagg (over Bartlett Haystack) and lofty Mt. Shaw in the distant Ossipee Range are to the L of Paugus, with distant Blue Job Mtn. seen between Flagg and the ridge descending R from Chocorua. Faraway Mtn. and Black Snout in the Ossipees are on the R of Paugus, and part of the Belknap Range is seen to the R of Tremont's main summit.

Behind Tremont on the R are the high peaks of the Sandwich Range (L to R): Wonalancet Hedgehog and Nanamocomuck Peak leading up to Mt. Passaconaway, Mt. Whiteface, East and West Sleeper, and Middle and North Tripyramid seen above the nearby peak of Mt. Jackson. Lowly Potash Mtn. is seen under and between Passaconaway and Whiteface. Closer in, Mt. Jackson is flanked by Mt. Bemis on the L, under West Sleeper (with flat Duck Pond and Saunders Mtns. extending L, under Whiteface), and Mts. Nancy, Lowell and Anderson on the R, with Sandwich Dome beyond between Nancy and Lowell. Next to the R Signal Ridge leads up to the massive Mt. Carrigain, rising behind and just L of nearby Mt. Webster, which is connected to Jackson by a level wooded ridge. The nubble of Jennings Peak is seen between Signal Ridge and Mt. Anderson. To the R of Carrigain is Mt. Hancock's long ridge, extending across its several peaks to the nearer Mt. Willey. The East Peak and main summit of Osceola, with the peak of Mt. Tecumseh between them, peer over to the L of South Hancock, above Webster. The broad rounded dome of North Hancock is farther R, then the sharp NW Hancock. Scar Ridge, with Mt. Hitchcock beneath, is seen between NW Hancock and the S (L) slope of Willey. On the far R and only a few miles away are Mt. Willey (L), striped with talus slopes, and Mt. Field (R), with Bondcliff jutting up just R of the col between them, and the top of Mt. Bond revealed just to the L of Field's summit. Through and over the scrub to the R one may catch glimpses of Mt. Guyot and South and North Twin with Mts. Lincoln and Lafayette peering over in back.

NO. OF 4000-FOOTERS VISIBLE: 30 (from main summit, partly through the trees)

Mount Washington

ELEVATION: 6288 ft. / 1916.6 m   ORDER OF HEIGHT: 1
LOCATION: Presidential Range, Townships of Sargents Purchase,
   Thompson and Meserves Purchase, Pinkhams Grant
USGS MAPS: 7½′ Mt. Washington, 7½′ Carter Dome, 7½′ Stairs Mtn.

Geography

At 6288 ft., Mt. Washington is the tallest of the New Hampshire 4000-Footers and the highest peak in all of New England and the Northeast. Though its summit elevation is puny compared to other great mountain ranges of the world, Mt. Washington is renowned worldwide for its fierce weather and frequent fatalities.

Lying as it does at the center of three storm tracks, the mountain is a magnet for severe weather at any time of the year. Typically, the mountain receives more than 250 inches of snow in a year, and snow has been known to fall in every calendar month, even July and August. One of the mountain's long-held claims to fame is that the highest land wind speed ever documented (231 mph) was recorded at the summit on April 12, 1934.

Mt. Washington's nearest "official" 4000-ft. neighbors along the Presidential Range are 5372-ft. Mt. Monroe to the SW and 5716-ft. Mt. Jefferson to the N. In between Washington and Jefferson is the 5533-ft. summit of Mt. Clay, essentially a NW shoulder of Washington. From the double summit of this rocky peak there are striking views down into the depths of the Great Gulf.

To the E of Mt. Washington is the great pass known as Pinkham Notch, across which rises Wildcat Ridge and, farther N, the Carter Range. From this height-of-land, traversed by NH 16, the Ellis River flows S and the Peabody River drains N.

The vast upper slopes of the mountain lie completely above timberline and are home to an abundance of rare and fragile alpine plants. Depending on the amount of exposure to the prevailing NW winds, timberline on Mt. Washington varies from ca. 4500 to 5000 ft. above sea level. As the summit cone is also littered with large boulders and loose rocks, for years the mountain has been appropriately dubbed "The Rock Pile." Though it is the highest peak in the Granite State, the mountain is composed not of igneous rock but instead of metamorphic rock, primarily mica schist and quartzite.

The massive bulk of Mt. Washington is flanked on practically all sides by deep and dramatic ravines featuring steep walls and broad, gentle floors. These were carved by ancient alpine glaciers. The best known of

Though seldom visited by summer hikers, Mount Washington's unique Gulf of Slides is a popular gathering spot during the busy spring backcountry ski season.

these cirques is Tuckerman Ravine, on the mountain's SE side. With its steep headwall and bowl-shaped rim, Tuckerman Ravine is probably the best example of a glacial cirque in all the White Mountains. The ravine is an especially busy place each spring as snow blown off the mountain's exposed ridges and into the bowl provides for exceptional backcountry ski possibilities. There are numerous famous ski runs in "Tucks," such as Hillman's Highway, Dodge's Drop, Left and Right Gullies, and the infamous plunge over The Lip. Some of the routes have pitches as steep as 50–55 degrees. Generally, the spring ski season runs through at least the month of May, and oftentimes well into June. Winter and spring visitors to the ravine must be cautious due to dangers from avalanches, icefall, steep icy slopes and hidden crevasses.

Looming high above Tuckerman Ravine to the N is the craggy 5033-ft. spur of Lion Head, while to the S lies 5500-ft. Boott Spur, the high point along Washington's rugged SE shoulder, with its picturesque Hanging Cliffs poised above the cirque. At the base of the ravine is delightful Hermit Lake, a 0.3-acre tarn with as dramatic a backdrop as any pond in the region. Close by are the Hermit Lake Shelters with 8 open-front shelters and 3 tent platforms.

Two other spectacular glacial ravines scarring the mountain's E face are Huntington Ravine and the Gulf of Slides. Huntington Ravine is NE of Tuckerman's and Lion Head, and its sheer face has long provided a challenging climb for summit-bound hikers (the Huntington Ravine Trail being generally considered the most difficult hiking trail in the Whites) and nimble rock climbers. For many winters it has also been a mecca for ice climbers. Among its prominent features are the craggy buttress known as The Pinnacle and several named gullies such as South, Odell's, Pinnacle, Central, Yale and Damnation. The less frequented Gulf of Slides lies to the S of Boott Spur, with Slide Peak (4806 ft., also known as Gulf Peak) and a bare spur ridge forming its S wall; just S of this spur another barren ridge bears the massive Glen Boulder, a glacial erratic. Although no officially maintained hiking trails lead up to its floor, a well defined ski trail (with wet footing in summer) starting at the Appalachian Mountain Club's Pinkham Notch Visitor Center can be followed 2.6 mi. to the base of the ravine's slide-raked headwall. This ravine is a favorite of some experienced backcountry skiers, though avalanche danger can be significant. In early spring its quiet, secluded bowl has an almost Western feel with its expansive snowfields and broad gullies.

Another lesser-known ravine on the Pinkham Notch side of the mountain is the Ravine of Raymond Cataract. This high, scalloped basin is sandwiched between Huntington and Tuckerman Ravines and is home to Raymond Cataract, a beautiful waterfall that, unfortunately, is no longer accessible by trail.

These great ravines on the E side of Washington are well-displayed in the views from Wildcat Ridge Trail and Wildcat Ski Area to the E, across Pinkham Notch.

On the lower E slopes of Washington N of Pinkham Notch are several low ledgy viewpoints accessed by trails. Brad's Bluff (2575 ft.) and nearby Lila's Ledge are along Liebeskind's Loop on a minor ridge partly encircled by the head of the Peabody River. Lows Bald Spot (2875 ft.) is a ledgy knob just N of the Auto Road and is accessed via a spur off the Madison Gulf Trail.

The White Mountains' largest glacial cirque, the Great Gulf, cuts into Mt. Washington's slopes on the N, culminating in an impressive 1600-ft. headwall. The huge gouge of the Great Gulf, several miles long, separates Mt. Washington and its massive NE shoulder, Chandler Ridge, from the various peaks of the Northern Presidentials and provides a dramatic foreground for camera-toting hikers and tourists aiming their lenses at the likes of Mts. Adams or Madison. On the floor near the head of the Great Gulf lies scenic Spaulding Lake (4228 ft.), a tiny, half-acre tarn deep in the federally-designated Great Gulf Wilderness. The Gulf and its tangled conifer forests are drained by the wild, boulder-filled West Branch of the Peabody River. Along its course are numerous cascades, including lovely, remote Weetamoo Falls.

On the mountain's W side are the non-glacial Ammonoosuc Ravine and Burt Ravine. The former is a broad basin cut into the mountainside nearly due W from the summit, while Burt Ravine lies more to the NW, between Mt. Washington and Mt. Clay. At the head of Ammonoosuc Ravine, at an elevation of just over 5000 ft., are the two Lakes of the Clouds and AMC's namesake Lakes of the Clouds Hut. The tiny alpine ponds are situated in the rocky, windswept, saddle between Mts. Washington and Monroe. The Upper Lake (5050 ft.) is 0.4 acre in size, while the Lower Lake (5025 ft.) is 1.2 acres. The hut, largest in the string of AMC's backcountry hut system, can accommodate 90 overnight guests, and is open from June to mid-September.

Between Ammonoosuc and Burt Ravines runs a narrow ridgeline on which the Mt. Washington Cog Railway ascends the mountain from Marshfield Station. Pioneer settler and trailbuilder Ethan Allen Crawford cut an early footpath to the summit up this same ridge nearly 200 years ago.

Directly S of the summit cone lies Oakes Gulf, a remote and little-visited glacial ravine bordered by Boott Spur to the E and Mts. Monroe and Franklin in the southern Presidential Range to the W. This gaping cirque at the head of the long, wild Dry River valley is a trademark feature of Mt. Washington when viewed from points to the S.

As rocky, steep, and craggy as Mt. Washington is, the mountain boasts several relatively "flat," but interesting areas at an elevation over 5000 ft. South of the summit cone on the divide between Tuckerman Ravine and Ammonoosuc Ravine is Bigelow Lawn, a broad alpine meadow featuring arctic grasses and a variety of flowering plants, best viewed in June and early July. Similarly, the Alpine Garden, E of the summit and upslope from Huntington Ravine and Ravine of Raymond Cataract, is a unique upland meadow best known for its assortment of alpine wildflowers.

The mountain's slopes are drained by several notable streams and rivers, the principal ones being the Ammonoosuc River, Dry River, Rocky Branch, New River, Cutler River, Peabody River and its West Branch, and Ellis River.

The Ammonoosuc River originates from the Lakes of the Clouds, flows in a westerly direction, and is eventually joined by Clay Brook (out of Burt Ravine), about a mile W of the Cog Railway base station. Dry River flows S out of Oakes Gulf for nearly 10 mi. down the wilderness valley between the Southern Presidentials on the W and Montalban Ridge on the E, joining the Saco River near the southern boundary of Crawford Notch State Park. To the S of Boott Spur and Slide Peak, the Rocky Branch flows S towards the Saco down another long valley, between Montalban Ridge to the W and the Rocky Branch Ridge on the E. These two wooded subsidiary ridges split from the main ridge S of Boott Spur and extend for miles southward through the 27,000-acre Presidential Range–Dry River Wilderness, which also encompasses Oakes Gulf and the Dry River valley. The Montalban Ridge is traversed by the Davis Path and includes the remote summits of Mt. Isolation (4003 ft.), Mt. Davis (3819 ft.) and Stairs Mtn. (3463 ft.), all excellent viewpoints. The Rocky Branch Ridge is trail-less except for one cross trail and features a series of nameless wooded humps descending gradually to 2601-ft. Maple Mtn. at its S end.

New River, on the mountain's SE slopes, drains out of the Gulf of Slides. The Cutler River flows from Tuckerman Ravine and is fed by branches from Raymond Cataract and Huntington Ravine as well as Nelson Brook from the SE slope of Nelson Crag. The New and Cutler Rivers merge in Pinkham Notch to form the Ellis River, which flows S from the pass. The Ellis River drops over spectacular Glen Ellis Falls just S of the notch, while the Cutler River plunges over Crystal Cascade just W of the notch. The course of the New River reportedly shifted during the great storm of 1826, stranding what was once said to be a fine waterfall near the notch road.

The main stem of the Peabody River originates on the mountain's eastern slopes and flows briefly S before wrapping around the Brad's Bluff ridge and heading N out of Pinkham Notch toward the Androscoggin River. The headwaters of the West Branch of Peabody River flow out of the Great Gulf and remote Spaulding Lake. The West Branch joins the main stem approximately 2 mi. N of the base of the Mt. Washington Auto Road.

Being the tallest of the peaks, it's no surprise that the mountain is among the most visited summits in New England. Besides attracting huge crowds of hikers each year, the summit is also frequented by swarms of tourists accessing it by either the Cog Railway or the Mt. Washington Auto Road. The Cog climbs 3.25 miles up the mountain from the W via tracks first laid more than 130 years ago. The average grade of the railway is 25% (1320 ft. per mile), with a maximum grade of 37.5% along Jacob's Ladder, the curving, 300-ft. trestle approximately two-thirds of the way up the mountain.

From the E, tourists can attain the summit by driving up the winding 7.6-mi. Auto Road from a location at the NE base of the mountain known as the Glen (by NH 16). The average grade of the road, which is part paved, part hard-packed gravel, is 12%. The upper part of the auto road traverses Chandler Ridge—the huge NE shoulder of the mountain—and skirts the rim of the Great Gulf to the N. Two notable landmarks along Chandler Ridge, both a little bit S of the auto road, are Nelson Crag (5635 ft.) and Ball Crag (6112 ft.). Both are accessible on foot by way of the Nelson Crag Trail.

The summit of Mt. Washington is like no other in the Whites, with a half dozen or more structures, towers and antennas occupying most of the mountaintop terrain. The Sherman Adams Summit Building serves as headquarters for Mt. Washington State Park, and is occupied year-round by staffers with the Mt. Washington Observatory.

Nomenclature

This peak, the highest in the Northeast, was named for Revolutionary War general and our nation's first President, George Washington, probably in 1784, during the so-called Belknap–Cutler expedition, the first scientific foray up the mountain. (At this time Washington was a recently retired general and not yet President.) The old Indian name for the mountain was "Agiochook," which has been translated to mean "Home of the Great Spirit," "The Place of the Spirit of the Forest," and "The Place of the Storm Spirit." The natives did not climb the mountain for fear of the Great Spirit which dwelled upon its summit. Another Indian name was "Waumbeket Methna," or "Mountain of the Snowy Forehead." Early explorers used the names "Sugarloaf" and "Christall Hill."

Tuckerman Ravine, the famous glacial cirque SE of the summit cone, is named for Dr. Edward Tuckerman, a botanist and longtime professor at Amherst College. Tuckerman was a frequent visitor to the White Mountains in the first half of the nineteenth century, devoting much of his time to studying and collecting plants, particularly in the Presidential Range.

Huntington Ravine, another of the mountain's well-known cirques, is named for Joshua H. Huntington, who was part of the team of observers to spend the winter of 1870–71 atop the mountain. Nelson Crag, the 5635-ft. sub-peak at the head of Huntington Ravine, is named for one of Joshua Huntington's fellow summit occupants, S. A. Nelson of Georgetown, Mass.

Boott Spur, a subsidiary peak SE of the main summit, is named for Dr. Francis Boott, an early nineteenth-century physician and botanist who was a member of Jacob Bigelow's 1816 scientific expedition on the mountain. Bigelow's name has been attached to the broad alpine meadow S of the summit and W of Tuckerman Ravine.

Mt. Washington's NE ridge, called Chandler Ridge, is named for Benjamin Chandler, the third person to die on the mountain. The 75-year-old Chandler disappeared on August 7, 1856, while ascending the peak. His body was found almost a year later under a ledge which he had crawled under, presumably to seek shelter.

Ball Crag, a sharp knob a short distance NE of the summit along the Nelson Crag Trail, is named for Dr. Benjamin Lincoln Ball, who in October 1855 got lost on the mountain during a winter-like storm, yet managed to survive the ordeal despite a lack of water, food, or sleep. Dr. Ball recounted his story in the book, *Three Days on the White Mountains*.

Mt. Clay is named for Henry Clay (1777–1852), the famous American senator and statesman. The name was applied by botanist William Oakes in the 1840s. Though not a President, Clay was a candidate for the office several times. Nearby Burt Ravine was named in 1901 for Henry M. Burt, the founder and first publisher of *Among the Clouds*, the newspaper published on the summit of Mt. Washington in the late 1800s and early 1900s.

The Great Gulf, the huge glacier-carved cirque N of the mountain, was originally called Gulf of Mexico, for reasons that have never been understood. It was first referred to by its present-day name by Ethan Allen Crawford, who made note of a "great gulf" which he and others stumbled upon while wandering around the mountain's fogged-in upper reaches.

Spaulding Lake, the remote half-acre tarn at the head of the Great Gulf, is named for John H. Spaulding, early manager of the hotels situated atop the mountain. Spaulding, who also authored the book, *Historical Relics of the White Mountains* (1855), first visited the lake named in his honor in 1853. The Lakes of the Clouds were called the "Blue Ponds" by the Weeks–Brackett party, who drank the ice-cold water "until some of us became quite blue . . ." In earlier days they were also known as "Washington's Punch Bowl." The name for once-secluded Hermit Lake in Tuckerman Ravine was applied in 1853 by S. B. Beckett, a guidebook publisher from Maine. The name Ammonoosuc River is derived from an Abenaki Indian word meaning "fish-place." In Crawford's time, Ammonoosuc Ravine was known as "Escape Glen."

Lion Head is named for its shape when seen from the floor of Pinkham Notch. It was originally called St. Anthony's Nose in Farmer and Moore's 1823 gazetteer of New Hampshire.

The Raymond Path is named for its builder, Major Curtis B. Raymond of Boston, as is the nearby Raymond Cataract.

Pinkham Notch, known as the Eastern Pass during Dr. Jeremy Belknap's expedition in 1784, was named for Daniel Pinkham, who came with his father, Col. Joseph Pinkham, to settle in the town of Jackson in 1789. In the 1820s and 1830s he toiled on building the first road through the pass, and homesteaded there for a few years. The origins of the names for the Peabody and Ellis Rivers are uncertain, but both were in use by the late 1700s; the Peabody may have been named after an early explorer of the region. The Cutler River was named to honor Manessah Cutler, a botanist who accompanied Jeremy Belknap's 1784 expedition to Mt. Washington.

Lows Bald Spot honors J. Herbert Low, an early twentieth-century visitor from Brooklyn who much admired the view from this perch. It was long thought that the knob was named after famed nineteenth-century guide Charles Lowe, but the correction was made and accepted by the U.S. Board on Geographic Names in 2003. Brad's Bluff was named for Bradford Swan, a prominent AMC member in the 1960s and 1970s.

Nearby Lila's Ledge was named for his wife, and Liebeskind's Loop honors AMC trail crew member Steve Liebeskind.

Historical Highlights

First Ascent: Darby Field and two Indian guides are credited with the first recorded ascent of the mountain back in June 1642. It has long been speculated that Field climbed the mountain from the SE, ascending by way of Boott Spur and Lakes of the Clouds. Documents uncovered within the last 30 years, however, seem to indicate that Field's route may actually have been over the peaks of the Southern Presidentials. Field made a second ascent of Mt. Washington a month later with five or six companions. Some historians speculate that Field's two climbs were motivated by the hope of finding precious stones on the mountain. In October, a third ascent of the peak was made by Thomas Gorges and Richard Vines.

1725: Visitors to mountain in late April report snow depth of four feet on its NW slopes and pond near top "frozen hard."

1774: June climbers find 13 feet of snow in deep gully on S side of mountain.

1784: Expedition led by Jeremy Belknap and Manasseh Cutler conducts first scientific research on Presidentials, taking various measurements and collecting rare alpine plants.

1792: Name "Mt. Washington" appears in print for first time in Vol. 3 of Jeremy Belknap's *History of New Hampshire*.

Ca. 1809: Col. George Gibbs, mineralogist who made several explorations here, cuts first crude trail on mountain, leading through scrub up on E side, possibly through Gulf of Slides to Boott Spur, then around rim of Tuckerman Ravine and up to summit.

1811: Capt. Alden Partridge from West Point military academy climbs mountain and measures its elevation at 6634 ft.

1816: Dr. Jacob Bigelow and party (including Dr. Francis Boott) tour the mountains. Barometric measurements made by party determine summit elevation to be close to 6250 ft.

1819: Abel and Ethan Allen Crawford construct footpath to summit from top of Crawford Notch over Southern Presidentials. Today Crawford Path is nation's oldest continuously maintained hiking trail.

1821: First women climbers, the Misses Austin of Portsmouth, N.H., guided by Ethan Allen Crawford, attain summit.

1821: The Crawfords cut second route (Fabyan Path) up mountain; this trail mostly follows route of today's Cog Railway.

1823: Ethan Allen Crawford builds three crude overnight shelters on summit; all fall victim to mountain weather within a year or so.

1823: John A. Lowell and John Lowell Jr. conduct first known exploration of Ammonoosuc Ravine on W side of mountain.

1827–1828: Hayes Copp, pioneer settler, establishes homestead in remote and wild area near Pinkham Notch.

1831: Daniel Webster, accompanied by Ethan Allen Crawford, ascends to summit on foggy day and makes oration at top, lamenting the "cold reception" granted him by the mountain.

1840: Abel Crawford, 75, is first to ride horse to summit over converted Crawford Path. Family patriarch is accompanied during Aug. 21 climb by Charles Jackson and two members of his geological survey team.

Ca. 1840: Path is built up E side of mountain from Elkins Farm to N of Pinkham Notch; by 1876 it has been "long forgotten."

1841: Members of geological survey team, including Edward Everett Hale, spend rainy night in rough shelter near summit after exploratory climb from Jefferson.

1844–1845: Nathaniel T. P. Davis, son-in-law of Abel Crawford, builds, opens new 15-mi. bridle path, the Davis Path, from lower Crawford Notch along Montalban Ridge to summit.

1849: Englishman Frederick Strickland is first person to die on the Presidential Range after losing his way in October snowstorm.

1850: First Glen House built in clearing E of mountain near Pinkham Notch; hotel burns to ground in 1884.

1852: First Summit House hotel is constructed atop mountain by Lancaster, Jefferson entrepreneurs. Stillings Path built from Jefferson Highlands up past Jefferson Notch and slopes of Mt. Clay to Fabyan Path near summit; is used to haul supplies by horse for construction of summit buildings.

1853: Second summit hotel, Tip-Top House, opens for business.

1853: Bridle path built from Glen House to summit. Mt. Washington Road Co. is chartered; it has plans to build carriage road to summit from the Glen House.

1854: Forty-ft. observatory is erected on summit. It proves to be economic failure and is demolished two years later.

1855: Lizzie Bourne, first woman to perish on mountain, succumbs to fatigue and weather just a few hundred yards from summit.

1855: Dr. Benjamin L. Ball survives three-night ordeal on mountain during October snowstorm, using his umbrella for shelter. He writes short book, *Three Days on the White Mountains*, about his misadventure.

1858: Deputy sheriff Lucius Hartshorn and local guide Benjamin Osgood make first winter ascent of summit. Purpose of trip is to make attachment of summit property in connection with ongoing litigation to title.

1858: Henry David Thoreau makes second visit to Mt. Washington, camping in Tuckerman Ravine. (His first visit was in 1839, via Crawford Path.) His guide starts accidental fire in scrub and Thoreau himself sprains ankle badly.

1861: Following failure of previous company to finish job, the Mt. Washington Summit Road Co. completes construction of Carriage Road.

1862: First overnight winter stay atop mountain is made by John Spaulding, Chapin Brooks, and Franklin White.

1869: Cog Railway, world's first mountain-climbing train, begins summer and fall passenger service to summit. Start up of operations vindicates Cog builder Sylvester Marsh, who 11 years earlier was chided by state legislators while applying for railway charter. One proposed amendment to charter facetiously suggested Marsh be granted permission to "extend the Railway to the moon."

1870–1871: Scientific team occupies summit for duration of winter. Team of four includes Joshua Huntington and photographer Amos Clough.

1871: U. S. Signal Service establishes year-round summit weather station; it operates continuously until 1877, then summers only until 1892.

1872–1873: Second Summit House is built. Construction is financed by Cog Railway and Boston and Maine Railroad interests.

1874: In February, Mrs. Orville Freeman and Mrs. Charles Durgin, both daughters of Ethan Allen Crawford, make first winter ascent of mountain by women. Route is via Cog Railway tracks.

1876: Moses Sweetser's White Mountain guidebook devotes 11 pages to description of summit view.

1877: *Among the Clouds*, unique mountaintop newspaper, publishes first issue.

1879: Raymond Path from Carriage Road to snow arch in Tuckerman Ravine is opened by Major Curtis B. Raymond of Boston. Route was originally blazed by Raymond in 1863.

1881: Frank H. Burt and others lay out new path from snow arch to summit. Benjamin F. Osgood builds new trail up Great Gulf to Spaulding Lake.

1884: Proposal by hotelier Asa Barron owner to build new road from Crawford Notch to summit appears in newspaper. Project, to cost close to $700,000, never comes to fruition.

1885: New carriage road linking Pinkham Notch road with summit carriage road two miles from its start is opened. Route is now known as Old Jackson Road and is link in Appalachian Trail.

1893: Second Glen House, built in 1885, succumbs to nighttime fire.

Mid-1890s: J. Rayner Edmands completes construction of Gulfside Trail, graded ridgecrest path connecting Mt. Washington with the Northern Peaks.

1895: AMC climber Herschel C. Parker makes first winter ascent of Tuckerman Ravine headwall.

1899: First engine-powered vehicle ascends mountain's Carriage Road.

Locomobile is driven by Freelan Stanley, with his wife, Flora, a passenger. Vehicle makes climb to summit in a little more than two hours.

1900: AMC cuts original Boott Spur Trail, leading up N side of ridge from Hermit Lake area.

1900: AMC members William B. Curtis and Allen Ormsbee perish on exposed Presidential Range when caught in fierce late June storm. Curtis dies near Crawford Path at base of Mt. Monroe; Ormsbee dies on summit cone of Mt. Washington.

1901: In aftermath of Curtis–Ormsbee deaths, AMC constructs small wood frame shelter in vicinity of Lakes of the Clouds.

1901: J. Rayner Edmands oversees construction of Westside Trail along W flank of summit cone.

1902: Two AMC climbers make first winter ascent through Huntington Ravine.

1902: Mount Washington Hotel, greatest of grand hotels on W side of mountain, opens in July.

1903: Account of two-day exploration of Dry River valley appears in pages of *Among the Clouds*. Author writes: "This is one of the wildest and most inaccessible ravines . . . and has been seldom traversed its whole length."

1904: First long-distance phone call from summit is made between Summit House and NE Telephone office in Burlington, Vermont.

1905: Three AMC climbers, including trail-builder Warren W. Hart, make first winter ascent of Great Gulf headwall. It takes trio 7½ hours to cut steps up icy headwall, after which they spend cold night in deserted stage-office.

1905: Norman H. Libby, assistant editor of *Among the Clouds*, climbs mountain from Cog base station and descends on skis.

1906: Glen Boulder Trail is completed. Another trail is cleared from Raymond Path to floor of Huntington Ravine.

1907: AMC Councillor of Improvements recommends line of cairns be placed up headwall of Huntington Ravine.

1908: Devastating fire sweeps over summit, destroying majority of buildings.

1908–1910: Under direction of Warren W. Hart, AMC builds series of bold, steep trails up from Great Gulf, including Great Gulf Trail up valley and headwall, and Wamsutta Trail and Chandler Brook Trail up N slope of Chandler Ridge.

1910: AMC rock climbers led by George Flagg make first ascent of exposed, difficult route up the Pinnacle in Huntington Ravine. Flagg documents feat with series of sketches.

1910: Alpine Garden Trail (originally part of Six Husbands Trail) is opened between Carriage Road and Tuckerman Ravine Trail.

1912: Grand plans for new summit hotel, and new electric train around mountain (including tunnel through Mt. Jefferson's Castellated Ridge), are announced. Survey teams are sent into field; one member of crew, John Keenan, disappears near summit in fog and is never found. By year's end, plans are scrapped due to financial difficulties.

1913: First ski ascent of mountain is made via Carriage Road by three members of Dartmouth Outing Club.

1915: Third Summit House opens; one week later, old Tip-Top House is gutted by fire.

1915: New stone refuge—Lakes of the Clouds Hut—is added to AMC hut chain and sees 272 visitors in first season of operation. Hut is expanded in 1922, 1927 and 1968. Crawford Path is rerouted to pass by new hut, which is W of previously built wood shelter. For some time new section of trail is called MacGregor Cutoff after hutmaster Milton "Red Mac" MacGregor. Also, under direction of Councilor of Improvements Charles W. Blood, AMC opens new path, Ammonoosuc Ravine Trail, to Lakes of the Clouds from Cog Railway base station.

1916: Account of hikers snow-bound at Lakes of the Clouds Hut during Sept. 1915 snowstorm appears in *Appalachia*.

1918: AMC opens Camel Trail connecting Crawford Path just E of Lakes of Clouds with Davis Path NW of Boott Spur. Recently built Tuckerman Crossover is relocated.

1919: Southside Trail built, connecting Crawford Path with Tuckerman Ravine Trail.

1920: Lion Head Trail constructed; AMC builds new Pinkham Notch Camp at E base of the mountain. Old Jackson Road is re-opened as trail.

1924: Huntington Ravine Trail blazed up headwall and on to Carriage Road, also extended on lower end to Tuckerman Ravine Trail.

1926: With help from friends, Arthur T. Walden, famed breeder of sled dogs, drives team of huskies to summit and back in 15 hours via Carriage Road.

1927: Major storm unleashes two large landslides on S side of Glen Boulder Trail ridge. For several editions, AMC guide includes description of climb up these slides and bushwhack above to Glen Boulder Trail, and tracks of slide are shown on trail map.

1928: Nelson Crag Trail built by AMC, ending at 7-mi. mark on Carriage Road.

1928–1930: Leading climbers of day, including Robert Underhill, Julian Whittlesey and Britain's Noel Odell, inaugurate ice climbing in Huntington Ravine with several notable first ascents.

1929: Peppersass, original Cog Railway engine, returns to mountain for one final ascent; on return trip, engine crashes; Boston photographer (Daniel Rossiter) is killed.

Early 1930s: Dry River valley is added to WMNF. Dry River Trail opened by WMNF and CCC, leading up valley from end of old lumber railroad to headwall of Oakes Gulf and thence up to Crawford Path on E side of Mt. Monroe. Upper part is called Oakes Gulf Trail.

1930s: Works Progress Administration (WPA) proposes scenic highway across Presidentials, but project is abandoned in face of strong opposition.

1931: John Carleton and Charles N. Proctor of DOC make first ski descent of Tuckerman Ravine headwall.

1932: Mrs. Florence Clark is first to drive dog sled team to summit unassisted.

1932: USFS and AMC construct Fire Trail from Pinkham Notch to Hermit Lake; this is lower 2.4 mi. of today's Tuckerman Ravine Trail.

1932–1933: Winter reoccupation of summit takes place by fledgling Mt. Washington Observatory.

1933: First Inferno race is held, starting at summit and running down through Tuckerman Ravine to Pinkham Notch.

1934: Highest land wind speed ever recorded (231 mph) occurs on summit, April 12.

1934: John Sherburne Ski Trail is cut from floor of Tuckerman Ravine to Pinkham Notch.

1934: WMNF and Civilian Conservation Corps workers cut Jewell Trail up W ridge of Mt. Clay; path is named for Sgt. Winfield S. Jewell, observer for Army Signal Corps on Mt. Washington who died on Greeley expedition in Arctic in 1884.

1935: CCC workers cut Gulf of Slides Ski Trail from Pinkham Notch to floor of ravine, following route laid out by Charles N. Proctor.

1937: Yankee Network establishes summit FM radio broadcasting facility.

1938: Powerful September hurricane blows across mountain, ripping up 2400 ft. of track on Cog Railway and heavily damaging two buildings at base station. Miraculously, Cog is back in operation by end of October.

1939: Toni Matt, 19, wins Inferno ski race down Tuckerman Ravine with legendary run, finishing in record time of 6:29.4 from summit to Pinkham Notch.

1942: U.S. military begins icing research and experiments on summit, to aid ongoing war effort.

1947: August forest fire burns 30–40 acres of hurricane-damaged timber one mile S of Cog base station.

1951: Longtime Cog owner Col. Henry Teague dies; wills railroad and his summit holdings to Dartmouth College.

1952: New trail up long E ridge of Boott Spur opens. Path leaves from Tuckerman Ravine Trail less than half-mile from NH 16 and AMC Pinkham Notch Camp.

1954: WMTW broadcasts its first television programming via summit transmitter.

1959: U.S. Dept. of Agriculture designates 5552 acres in Great Gulf as "wild" area to be preserved for future generations. Five years later, under Wilderness Act of 1964, Great Gulf is among tracts included in National Wilderness Preservation system.

1962: Arthur Teague purchases Cog Railway from Dartmouth College.

1964: State of New Hampshire buys summit property and buildings from Dartmouth.

1967: Cog engine and passenger car crash near summit; eight people are killed in worst ever disaster on Mt. Washington.

1968–1969: Record snowfall blankets summit during winter. Seasonal total tops 566 inches, with amazing 172.8 inches falling in Feb. 1969.

1971: Mt. Washington State Park is established at summit.

1972: Tuckerman Ravine warming hut is destroyed by fire.

1974: Network of short pleasure paths in vicinity of AMC camp in Pinkham Notch is constructed; includes George's Gorge Trail, Liebeskind's Loop.

1975: New Presidential Range–Dry River Wilderness is created by Congress; it includes Oakes Gulf, Dry River valley, Montalban Ridge and Rocky Branch Ridge to S of Mt. Washington. Additional land is added in 1984, expanding Wilderness to total of 27,000 acres.

1980: Sherman Adams Summit Building, built by state, opens. It serves as year-round home to Mt. Washington Observatory crews. To make room for new building, old Summit House is razed.

1980s: Nelson Crag Trail extended over Ball Crag to summit.

1987: Forest Service denies guiding permit to Cog Railway, which had hoped to ferry spring skiers up to summit, then lead them down to Tuckerman Ravine. Preserving traditional walk-in experience of skiers is cited by USFS as major reason for its decision.

1993: Forest Service completes purchase of 857 acres of land at E base of mountain. Land is purchased from Mt. Washington Summit Road Company, which retains minimal holdings in Glen House for eventual development of cross-country ski center (Great Glen Trails).

2000: Landmark Mt. Washington Hotel at Bretton Woods begins year-round operations over long Thanksgiving weekend. Grand resort hotel's first winter season is highlighted by gala New Year's Eve party welcoming in new millennium.

2003: February fire levels summit power generating facilities, forcing state park and Mt. Washington Observatory staffers to evacuate mountaintop. It marks first time in 70 years that summit is unoccupied.

2004: Cog Railway begins first-time winter operations, ferrying skiers and other joy riders part way up the mountain's western slopes.

2005: Cameron Shaw-Doran is first to ascend Auto Road via wheelchair.

He notes "incredible feeling of accomplishment" after grueling 14½-hour climb.

2007: New electric power line is laid alongside Cog Railway route to summit, ensuring permanent power source for top of mountain.

2008: In wake of heavy snows, large avalanches rake Hillman's Highway area in Tuckerman Ravine and upper end of Gulf of Slides ski trail.

Trail Approaches

As befits the Northeast's tallest mountain, there are a variety of trail approaches to Mt. Washington, some meandering across high, barren ridges, others shooting up through spectacular ravines. The scenery on these routes is among the finest in New England, though arrival at the top can be anti-climactic when, after several hours of exertion, you are greeted with an array of buildings and antennas and the noise and tourist bustle of the Auto Road and Cog Railway. Nevertheless, the summit of Washington is a fascinating place to visit, for its long and storied history as well as its horizon-stretching views. The best viewing spot may be the deck of the Sherman Adams Summit Building, the centerpiece of the Mt. Washington State Park. Food and souvenirs are available for purchase here during the season from Memorial Day to Columbus Day. The Mt. Washington Observatory's summit museum is well worth a visit. Note: No summit buildings are available for shelter from Columbus Day through Memorial Day.

Because every route involves extensive hiking above treeline, attention to safety and the mountain's notoriously fickle weather is of paramount importance in considering a climb of Washington. Only clear, mild days in summer and fall with relatively light wind are suitable. It is likely to be 20 to 30 degrees colder and much windier at the summit than at the trailhead, and the summit is in the clouds about 60 percent of the time. Above treeline the trails can be very difficult to follow when fog descends on the mountain; at such times hikers must carefully follow the cairns (piles of rocks) that mark the way. Be prepared to turn back if the weather deteriorates. Rain, fog, snow, icing, thunderstorms, high winds and other weather factors can make for extremely dangerous conditions above treeline, and the weather can change very quickly. Though this is a puny mountain compared to the giants out West or around the globe, it is one of the most dangerous of all peaks; as has been well documented, most notably in Nicholas Howe's book *Not Without Peril*, over 130 lives have been lost on the slopes of Mt. Washington and the Presidentials, many due to exposure.

In addition to safety precautions, hikers should note that the climb of Mt. Washington is an arduous trip, involving 3800–4300 ft. of elevation gain. Almost every approach has some steep, rough sections, and the jumbled rocks of the upper cone require a long stretch of tedious rock-hopping. Once at the top, the hiker must have enough energy and "legs" left for the long, knee-rattling descent.

West Approaches from Cog Railway Base Road

TRAILHEAD (2500 ft.): A large hiker's parking lot is located on the R (S) side of the Cog Railway Base Rd., 1.1 mi. above the junction with Mt. Clinton Rd. and Jefferson Notch Rd., and 5.6 mi. from US 302. This trailhead is nearly 500 ft. higher than Pinkham Notch on the E side of the mountain.

Ammonoosuc Ravine Trail, Crawford Path

9.2 mi. round trip, 3800-ft. elevation gain

This scenic and very popular route up the broad ravine SW of the summit passes by several waterfalls, the rock-rimmed Lakes of the Clouds, and the AMC hut of the same name. It is steep as it ascends to treeline and the hut.

Note that the Ammonoosuc Ravine Trail holds snow late into the spring, and in late fall it can be very icy where water runs over the ledges. Even when merely wet the upper ledges are slippery, especially coming down.

From parking area, follow blue-blazed trail E at easy grades through open fir and birch woods, crossing Franklin Brook at 0.3 mi., and old double water pipeline beyond. After short descent, old route from Base Station (0.3 mi. long) comes in on L at 1.0 mi. / 2875 ft. Trail bears R here and climbs easily alongside Ammonoosuc River (on L) through fir forest, with rocky footing in places, passing memorial plaque for Herbert J. Young, Dartmouth student who perished here in December 1928. Cross Monroe Brook at 1.7 mi. / 3225 ft. Woods get scrubbier, with evidence of landslides. At 2.1 mi. / 3450 ft. cross tributary stream by Gem Pool, clear basin of water below small mossy cascade.

Trail turns R (SE) here and begins long, steep ascent up section of rock steps. At 2.3 mi. / 3750 ft. sign marks side trail leading ca. 200 ft. R to The Gorge, where high perch provides great view of two long waterslides. Steep rocky climb continues to brook crossing and first view W over Bretton Woods valley at 2.5 mi. / 4175 ft. Ledgy scrambling leads up past series of cascades with more brook crossings. Trees shrink to scrub and views open out to NW, and L up to scree-strewn slopes of Mt. Washington. Ascent continues up rock slabs and through intermittent patches of scrub. Grade eases higher up, and near top of climb rocky pile of Mt. Monroe appears up to R. Reach AMC Lakes of the Clouds Hut and jct. with Crawford Path at 3.1 mi. / 5012 ft.

Turn L on Crawford Path and walk by hut, where water and toilets are available and refreshments may be purchased (in season, early June through mid-September). From here to summit route is completely above treeline, and is also part of Appalachian Trail. Dry River Trail splits R just past hut. Crawford Path passes between the two Lakes of the Clouds, with the larger Lower Lake on R and smaller Upper Lake on L. Climb to jct. just beyond at 3.3 mi. / 5125 ft., where Tuckerman Crossover continues straight and Camel Trail diverges R. Bear L on Crawford Path and begin moderate slabbing climb up rocky treadway, heading NE on L side of ridgecrest, with ever-expanding views back down to Lakes of Clouds, Southern Presidentials and horizons beyond.

At 4.0 mi. / 5625 ft. Davis Path comes in on R and in a few yards Westside Trail branches L. Crawford Path now zigzags more steeply up W side of Washington's summit cone. At flat spot at 4.4 mi. / 6150 ft., Gulfside Trail joins from L. Crawford Path turns R (ESE) and climbs last pitch up to summit area, where it swings L, passing by buildings and top of Cog Railway en route to highest outcrop, marked by sign and benchmark, up to L just past Tip-Top House, at 4.6 mi. / 6288 ft. Sherman Adams Summit Building is just beyond to NE.

Note: For side trip to Mt. Monroe from Lakes of Clouds Hut on Crawford Path and NE end of Mt. Monroe Loop, add 0.8 mi. round trip and 360-ft. elevation gain.

Jewell Trail, Gulfside Trail, Trinity Heights Connector
10.0 mi. round trip, 4000-ft. elevation gain

This western route is slightly longer and has less steep climbing than the Ammonoosuc Ravine approach, but is fully exposed to weather in the upper 2 mi. It ascends a westerly ridge of Mt. Clay, then follows the main ridge to Mt. Washington, with some spectacular views into the Great Gulf. Grades are mostly moderate with generally decent footing, though the upper section of Jewell Trail above treeline is rough and rocky.

From trailhead parking, cross Cog Railway Base Rd., enter woods, and cross Ammonoosuc River (here a mountain stream) on rocks at 0.1 mi. Climb at easy grades, passing jct. L with Boundary Line Trail at 0.4 mi. Climb moderately up small ridge, past jct. R with old trail route (0.4 mi. long) from Cog RR Base Station at 1.0 mi., then descend L, losing 50 ft. in elevation, to cross Clay Brook on footbridge at 1.1 mi. / 2850 ft.; nice cascade is seen to R from bridge. Trail now starts to ascend W ridge of Mt. Clay at moderate grades. After several switchbacks route ascends along L (NW) side of ridge, then swings sharp R across to S side and angles up to open blowdown area with impressive view of Southern Presidentials and partial view into Burt Ravine at 2.0 mi. / 3600 ft. Above opening trail turns sharp L and swings over to N side of ridge, climbing steadily but not steeply, keeping below crest. Ascent continues through high scrub with views starting to appear and a R turn leads to treeline at 3.0 mi. / 4575 ft. Here, where trail turns L, there are rocks with wide views of Southern

Presidentials, Bretton Woods valley, and ranges to W. Above here route is completely exposed rest of way to summit.

Trail now zigzags up slope of broken rock, with rough footing and continuous wide views to W. Follow cairns and blazes carefully. At 3.5 mi. / 5175 ft. swing R and angle up to Gulfside Trail on W side of Mt. Clay summit ridge at 3.7 mi. / 5400 ft. (From this junction, it is possible to scramble up the rocks a short distance E to Mt. Clay Loop near lower S summit of Clay; loop can then be followed S parallel to Gulfside Trail, meeting it in 0.3 mi. From cliffs of Clay there are stunning views down into Great Gulf.) Turn R here and head SSE along open ridge, with nearly level going and then slight descent to jct. L with Mt. Clay Loop at 4.0 mi. Gulfside Trail now begins climb up broad NW ridge of Mt. Washington, passing jct. R with Westside Trail at 4.1 mi. / 5500 ft. Gulfside bears L here and follows along rim of Great Gulf, with spectacular views L and down into that huge cirque and across to Mts. Jefferson, Adams and Madison. Cog Railway tracks are not far to R in this section. Higher up are more views into Great Gulf, with tiny Spaulding Lake nestling over 1500 ft. below on floor. These are some of finest views in White Mountains. At 4.6 mi. / 5925 ft. Great Gulf Trail enters on L. Gulfside Trail turns R here and ascends S up summit cone over broken rock, soon crossing Cog Railway tracks. At 4.8 mi. / 6100 ft. turn L on Trinity Heights Connector (part of Appalachian Trail loop over summit) and scramble fairly steeply up rocks to summit at 5.0 mi. / 6288 ft. (For slightly longer and easier alternative, continue 0.1 mi. ahead on Gulfside Trail to jct. with Crawford Path, then bear L for final moderate 0.2 mi. climb on Crawford Path.)

LOOP OPTION

Many hikers ascending Mt. Washington from the W go up via Ammonoosuc Ravine / Crawford Path approach and return by Gulfside / Jewell route, which is easier to descend (weather permitting). Total for loop is 9.6 mi. with 3900-ft. elevation gain.

East Approaches from NH 16 at Pinkham Notch

TRAILHEAD (2032 ft.): Several approaches to Mt. Washington begin at the AMC Pinkham Notch Visitor Center, located on the W side of NH 16 at the height-of-land in Pinkham Notch, 10.6 mi. S of US 2 in Gorham and 12 mi. N of US 302 in Glen. This is the busiest trailhead in the White Mountains. There is ample parking here, though at peak times you may have to use the overflow lots at Wildcat Ski Area, 0.7 mi. N along Rt. 16.

Tuckerman Ravine Trail
8.4 mi. round trip, 4250-ft. elevation gain

The trade route through Tuckerman Ravine is probably the most popular of all trails to Mt. Washington. On nice summer and fall weekend days there will be a steady parade of hikers ascending this way. Grades are relatively moderate and the scenery as you ascend through Tuckerman Ravine and up the headwall is magnificent. Snow and ice may linger in the famous bowl of Tuckerman well into spring and early summer, and at such times the portion of the trail up the headwall will be closed for safety reasons. Under ordinary conditions the ascent up the headwall is strenuous but not especially difficult; however, hikers should pay close attention to footing as fatal falls have occurred. From the bowl to the summit the trail is above treeline, though until you emerge above the headwall there is some protection from west winds.

From Pinkham Notch Visitor Center, follow footway to R behind Trading Post, passing avalanche warning signs (winter and spring only). In short distance bear L on Tuckerman Ravine Trail as Old Jackson Road splits R. Trail is wide and rocky tractor road in first 2.4 mi. to Hermit Lake area, with steady, moderate grade. After gentle start, at 0.3 mi. it swings L over bridge across ledgy Cutler River and climbs to viewpoint (up rock steps ahead) overlooking Crystal Cascade. Swing L to jct. L with Boott Spur Trail at 0.4 mi. / 2275 ft. After 3 more switchbacks, trail climbs steadily up rock-filled footway. Huntington Ravine Trail leaves on R at 1.3 mi. / 3031 ft. Tuckerman trail continues straight and steady, crossing brooks on bridges at 1.5 and 1.6 mi. Bear L at 1.7 mi. / 3425 ft. as Huntington Ravine Fire Road continues ahead. Catch occasional glimpses of Boott Spur as climb proceeds to jct. R with Raymond Path at 2.1 mi. / 3675 ft. Lion Head Trail (see below) leaves on R at 2.3 mi., and at 2.4 mi. / 3875 ft. Tuckerman trail reaches Hermit Lake complex on floor of ravine; here caretaker's building with deck is located in clearing. Hermit Lake, a tiny pond, and 8 shelters plus 3 tent platforms are to R; tickets for camping must be purchased at Pinkham Notch Visitor Center. Here also Boott Spur Link (see below) leaves L side of clearing. Views from clearing are magnificent: crags of Boott Spur up to L, Lion Head up to R, the great gray and green bowl of Tuckerman yawning ahead.

The Tuckerman trail continues ahead (W) toward the upper ravine, passing a tiny pond L and ascending fairly steeply via rock steps up the Little Headwall, passing cascade down to L. Look back for views to Wildcats and Carters. Beyond, you enter broad, open, upper floor of ravine at ca. 2.8 mi. / 4300 ft., with impressive views up to headwall. Grades are easier across floor through birch and alder scrub to foot of headwall. Here the "Lunch Rocks"—large boulders well-known as a hangout spot for spring skiers (though exposed to dangerous falling ice at that time of year)—provide perches for spectacular views up to the ravine headwall, Lion Head, and Boott Spur, and back down the valley. Here the trail angles steeply up to R, passing first aid cache on R; in early summer the Snow Arch, carved by running water, might be seen on L at 3.1 mi. / 4525 ft.; it is dangerous to approach too closely. Higher up trail swings L to traverse beneath cliffs high on headwall; watch footing carefully as there is serious dropoff to L. At top of headwall climb straight up slope to jct. R with Alpine Garden Trail at 3.4 mi. / 5125 ft. and on to multi-trail Tuckerman Jct. at 3.6 mi. / 5383 ft.; here Tuckerman Crossover comes in from L and Lawn Cutoff from sharp L.

Turn sharp R (N) here on Tuckerman Ravine Trail for tough slog up summit cone over broken rock. Lion Head Trail joins from R at 3.8 mi. / 5675 ft. Tuckerman trail continues steep, bouldery ascent to Auto Road by lower parking lot; from here, ascend wooden stairways to summit buildings and high point (located to R of Tip-Top House), marked by sign and benchmark, at 4.2 mi. / 6288 ft.

BOOT SPUR LINK

This trail offers chance to combine views from lower floor of Tuckerman Ravine near Hermit Lake with ascent of Boott Spur for great variety of scenery. From L (S) side of clearing at Hermit Lake, 2.4 mi. from trailhead, Boott Spur Link descends slightly to cross Cutler River on bridge and then John Sherburne Ski Trail, climbs slightly, then swings L and descends a short pitch. At 0.2 mi. from Hermit Lake it turns R across grassy spot and climbs very steeply through woods with rocky footing. At 0.4 mi. it bends R, breaks above treeline, and continues up steeply with superb views into Tuckerman Ravine and back to Nelson Crag. Grade moderates as crest of open shoulder is approached and trail meets Boott Spur Trail at 0.6 mi. / 4650 ft., with 850-ft. ascent from Hermit Lake area. From here Boott Spur Trail climbs W to Boott Spur, from where Davis Path and Crawford Path are followed to summit. Total distance one way to summit via this route is 5.7 mi.

LION HEAD TRAIL OPTION

Tuckerman Ravine Trail, Lion Head Trail, Tuckerman Ravine Trail
8.6 mi. round trip, 4250-ft. elevation gain

The route from Tuckerman Ravine Trail just below Hermit Lake up over the impressive crag of Lion Head makes an excellent loop in combination with an ascent or descent through Tuckerman Ravine. It is also the best option when the Tuckerman headwall is closed due to ice and snow. The views of the ravine from Lion Head are outstanding.

From trailhead at Pinkham Notch, follow Tuckerman Ravine Trail for 2.3 mi. Turn R on Lion Head Trail (3825 ft.), which runs at easy grade for short distance, crossing small outlet brook from Hermit Lake, then climbs steeply with rocky footing for 0.2 mi. At top of pitch it turns L and climbs by several switchbacks, ascending one ledge by a ladder and several more by short scrambles. Just after one R turn, flat ledge up on R offers views E and S. After level traverse, trail swings L and climbs short distance to treeline at 2.7 mi. / 4350 ft.; here winter route (not open for summer use) joins from R. Trail now climbs steadily in open over rocky footway, with good views N and E. Higher up trail has better footing with many rock steps. Reach "lower" Lion Head viewpoint on L at 4775 ft., with fine views down to floor of ravine, across to Boott Spur, and out to N and E. Lion Head crag looms close by to W. Continue up well-built trail, climbing steeply to R of impressive slab and cresting Lion Head at 3.2 mi. / 5033 ft. Ledges on L offer spectacular views down to floor of Tuckerman Ravine, across to cliffs of headwall and Boott Spur, and up to summit cone of Mt. Washington. To N are Nelson Crag and Mahoosucs and other distant ranges, and Carters and Wildcats are across valley to E. After slight dip, trail ascends gradually in open along gentle shoulder, crossing Alpine Garden Trail at 3.4 mi. / 5175 ft. Beyond junction Lion Head Trail climbs gradually through high scrub for ca. 0.2 mi., then emerges in open again and ascends steadily, steeply at times, over ledges and broken rock, with interesting views of Tuckerman's S wall and Bigelow Lawn. Higher up trail ascends through rugged crags, with several scrambles, turns L to pass through interesting crack, then angles L to meet Tuckerman Ravine Trail at 3.9 mi. / 5675 ft. Turn R here for steep slog up broken rock of cone, reaching summit at 4.3 mi. / 6288 ft.

Tuckerman Ravine Trail, Boott Spur Trail, Davis Path, Crawford Path
10.6 mi. round trip, 4300-ft. elevation gain

This longer route over the great shoulder of Boott Spur is very scenic, with miles of above-treeline walking (and exposure to weather), and sees far less hiking traffic than Tuckerman Ravine. Much of the trail has fairly rough footing. It can be combined with the Tuckerman Ravine or Lion Head route to make a very attractive loop of 9.5 or 9.6 mi.

From Pinkham Notch, follow Tuckerman Ravine Trail for 0.4 mi., passing Crystal Cascade up on R, and bear L onto Boott Spur Trail. Cross Sherburne Ski Trail and quickly swing R for start of climb. At 0.6 mi. trail uses 20-ft. ladder to scale steep ledge. At 0.9 mi., after crossing ledge with view of Huntington Ravine, trail turns sharp R where short spur L leads to very limited view E. After level muddy stretch, climb rough, rocky pitch up ridge, passing obscure side trail L to brook, and reach minor crest at 1.4 mi. / 3275 ft., where side path R leads to stand-up view of Huntington Ravine. Steady ascent with several short scrambles lifts you to short spur R to Harvard Rock (also known as Ravine Outlook) at 2.1 mi. / 4046 ft. Open rocky area here offers fine view into Tuckerman Ravine and out to Wildcats, Carters and Mahoosucs. Trail angles SW and steadily up through high scrub, breaks above treeline at 2.3 mi., and runs S at easy grade to aptly-named Split Rock at 2.4 mi. / 4337 ft.

Turn R (W) and ascend along S side of ridge, with views L into Gulf

The cliffs of Boott Spur loom ominously above Hermit Lake shelter at the base of Tuckerman Ravine.

of Slides. Boott Spur Link joins from R on flat shoulder at 2.6 mi. / 4650 ft.; here there is impressive view of Tuckerman headwall. After traversing shoulder, Boott Spur Trail proceeds up middle of open ridge, climbing steeply to short level terrace at 3.0 mi. / 5075 ft. Uphill march resumes over broken rock; near top of ridge swing L below shattered wall of rock, work up through it, and emerge by summit of Boott Spur, which is short distance to L. This satellite peak provides excellent views of Wildcats, Carters, Mahoosucs to E and NE, Nelson Crag and Mt. Washington's cone to N and NW, and many other White Mountain peaks to W and SW. Boott Spur Trail dips to meet Davis Path just beyond at 3.3 mi. / 5450 ft.

Turn R on Davis Path for long, gently graded walk in open, leading NW across ridge of Boott Spur and Bigelow Lawn beyond. This is grand stretch of hiking, with views of Carters and Maine mountains to R, Washington's great cone ahead, and Southern Presidentials and western Whites to L, all seen across expanses of alpine tundra. At 3.9 mi., where Lawn Cutoff diverges R, Davis Path begins traverse of broad plateau of Bigelow Lawn, following line of tall cairns. Camel Trail goes L at 4.0 mi., and Davis Path crosses Tuckerman Crossover at 4.3 mi. Southside Trail enters on R at 4.6 mi. / 5575 ft., and at 4.7 mi. Davis Path ends at Crawford Path. Turn R on Crawford Path for fairly steep climb up W side of summit cone, quickly passing jct. L with Westside Trail. Reach jct. L with

Gulfside Trail at 5.1 mi. / 6150 ft. Turn R for final climb on Crawford Path to summit at 5.3 mi. / 6288 ft.

Old Jackson Road, Nelson Crag Trail
10.6 mi. round trip, 4350-ft. elevation gain

This longer and less-used approach from Pinkham begins with a pleasant warmup on Old Jackson Road followed by a sustained steep climb up Nelson Crag Trail. The upper 2.5 mi. is above treeline with excellent views, especially into Huntington Ravine, and great exposure to weather.

Find start of Tuckerman Ravine Trail behind Trading Post at Pinkham; in 100 ft. or so Old Jackson Road (part of Appalachian Trail) diverges R at a sign. First 0.4 mi. is nearly level, passing several ski trail junctions. At jct. R with Crew Cut Trail, OJR begins steady climb through nice hardwood forest. Grade eases as you cross low divide, passing jct. R with George's Gorge Trail at 0.9 mi. / 2525 ft. Trail remains nearly level or slightly downhill until sharp L at 1.6 mi. After short, steep uphill pitch, pass jct. L with Raymond Path, cross small brook, and reach Nelson Crag Trail at 1.7 mi. / 2625 ft.

Turn L on Nelson Crag Trail and begin climbing through woods, moderate at first, then becoming steep, rough and relentless. Break above treeline at 2.8 mi. / 4350 ft. Trail is in open from here to summit, with inspiring views E, N and S. After crossing shoulder, climb at less steep grade to Cragway Spring beside curve on Auto Road at 3.4 mi. / 4825 ft. Trail bears L here and struggles up steep rocky terrain on upper Chandler Ridge. Grade eases as you approach Nelson Crag, which is reached at 4.1 mi. / 5635 ft. To L are eye-popping views into Huntington Ravine. After slight descent trail is nearly level to crossing of Alpine Garden Trail at 4.3 mi., then rises and swings L past minor crag on R to cross Huntington Ravine Trail at 4.5 mi. / 5725 ft. Steady climb over jumbled rocks leads to top of Ball Crag at 4.9 mi. / 6112 ft. After slight dip and flat stretch, cross Auto Road and Cog Railway tracks, bend L, and clamber up rocks to summit at 5.3 mi. / 6288 ft. Trail reaches summit area at L base of Sherman Adams Summit Building, where trail sign is located; follow along foundation to stairway leading up to building entrance. High point, with sign and benchmark, is up ahead on R.

Tuckerman Ravine Trail, Huntington Ravine Trail, Nelson Crag Trail
4.4 mi. one-way, 4250-ft. elevation gain

IMPORTANT NOTE: The notoriety of the Huntington Ravine Trail as the most difficult trail in the White Mountains is well-deserved. Although there are other trails that rival it in steepness, on no other route is there so much difficult rock scrambling with significant exposure. In several places on the headwall a slip and fall could have serious consequences.

Hikers carefully work their way up a slab on the Huntington Ravine Trail, long regarded as one of the most difficult hiking routes in the White Mountains.

This route should be attempted only by experienced hikers who are comfortable on steep ledges and are capable of maneuvering up tricky scrambles using handholds and footholds. The headwall should only be climbed on a dry day during the warm-weather hiking season. This section of trail is extremely dangerous if wet or icy. Descent of this trail at any time is emphatically discouraged.

All that being said, on a dry, warm day this is one of the most exciting and exhilarating climbs in the Whites. The scenery in this craggy ravine is magnificent. If you're up for the challenge, we recommend you take your time on the headwall and soak in the views—they are certainly "airy"! For those who are interested we provide a detailed description of this classic route.

From AMC Pinkham Notch Visitor Center, follow wide, rocky Tuckerman Ravine Trail on steady climb and at 1.3 mi. / 3031 ft. turn R onto Huntington Ravine Trail. Follow this narrow, darkly wooded path to NW, nearly level but rough, to crossing of Cutler River on rocks at 1.5 mi. At 1.6 mi. trail crosses nameless brook draining Huntington Ravine and climbs moderately on its N side, passing pretty cascade and pool. Ascent is then steeper to crossing of Raymond Path at 1.8 mi. / 3425 ft. Easier climbing leads past vista L to Boott Spur and crossing of Huntington Ravine Fire Road. Steadier pitch leads to L turn onto grassy, rocky Fire Road at 2.1 mi. / 3725 ft. Trail follows road for ca. 0.1 mi., with first views ahead to imposing "you gotta be kidding" headwall, then bears R off Fire Road. You cross and recross brook and at 2.3 mi. trail bears R onto Fire Road again and follows it along gentle floor of ravine, crossing brook again and passing Albert Dow Memorial first aid cache on L at 2.5 mi. / 4075 ft. Trail now climbs moderately in and out of small brookbed, ascends through dense scrub, and swings R and L into area of huge boulders. Easy scramble up first boulder on L provides tremendous view of ravine. Dark jagged crags of The Pinnacle are close by up on L, with narrow cut of Pinnacle Gully on its R. On R of this gully are higher crags forming L side of Central Gully; part of trail route up slabs at R base of Central Gully can be seen from here.

Trail now makes strenuous, fairly difficult scramble through the boulders, then climbs steeply through birch scrub and turns R, emerging in open at ca. 4300 ft. at base of large, steep talus slope known as The Fan. Trail route follows yellow blazes up through the big rocks a short way, then turns R to traverse across to R edge of Fan. Turn L here and ascend steeply through scrub along R (N) side of Fan. Scramble up open ledge with excellent view down over ravine and across to Wildcats. Here trail swings L and makes steep angling climb through alder scrub, with a couple of minor scrambles just before reaching open brookbed. It turns R up brookbed for 10 yds., then turns L out of it (easily missed), traverses a few yds., then bears R again for a scramble and continues up to L of brook on steep rocks; look for yellow, daisy-like blooms of arnica along brook in late summer. Reach open rocks at base of steep, wide, smooth slabs near bottom of Central Gully at 3.1 mi. / 4825 ft. This is good place for break as steepest and most difficult climbing begins with slabs directly in front across small brook; above here is point of no return!

Follow blazes carefully on the slabs—first ca. 20 ft. is friction climb, then low rock wall on R provides some handholds. A few yds. farther follow blazes up onto higher, easier ledge on R and continue up to comfortable shelf. Here trail swings R for brief traverse, then bends L to climb up somewhat easier but still steep slabs with impressive views L to crags on S side of Central Gully. Trail continues up very steeply and attacks series of difficult short scrambles up ledge crevices and chimneys. Proper use of handholds and footholds is essential for safe passage over these spots. One jutting ledge requires tricky swing move around its R (outer) edge. Farther up is daunting nearly sheer ledge where one must clamber up, then swing L along narrow lip of rock with some exposure. At top of this, trail exits up to R to spacious shelf with excellent flat ledge perch to R overlooking ravine. Above here is one more difficult move up rough, steep chimney, followed by one shorter scramble, then steps of broken rock lead up to moderate upper part of climb, marked by cairns up small ridge. Trail abruptly levels at edge of Alpine Garden plateau and meets Alpine Garden Trail at 3.4 mi. / 5475 ft. For summit, continue ahead on Huntington Ravine Trail, climbing steadily over open rocks. At 3.6 mi./5725 ft. turn L (SW) on Nelson Crag Trail and follow it on stiff climb up to Ball Crag at 4.0 mi./6112 ft. After short descent and flat stretch, cross Auto Road and Cog Railway tracks, bend L, and climb up boulders to summit, finishing along L base of Sherman Adams Summit Building. High point, marked by sign and benchmark, is past building up on R at 4.4 mi./6288 ft. Descend via one of other routes described above.

Southeast Approach from NH 16

Glen Boulder Trail, Davis Path, Crawford Path
11.4 mi. round trip, 4400-ft. elevation gain

TRAILHEAD (1975 ft.): Glen Boulder Trail starts at parking area for Glen Ellis Falls, on W side of NH 16, 0.7 mi. S of AMC Pinkham Notch Camp.

This route climbs past the landmark Glen Boulder and lofty Boott Spur, with views starting at just 1.4 mi. and nearly continuous vistas (and exposure) along the upper 3 mi.

Glen Boulder Trail leaves S edge of Glen Ellis Falls parking area and ascends past restrooms into woods. After moderate start, climb steeply to R around cliff to meet Diretissima (fairly rough 1.0 mi. connecting route, with several ups and downs, from NH 16 just S of Pinkham Notch Visitor Center, making various loop hikes possible.) at 0.4 mi./2300 ft. Turn L here and traverse slope, then climb steadily SW, crossing Avalanche Brook Ski Trail at 0.8 mi./2600 ft. Cross two branches of brook, then commence stiff climb up rocky footway through dense conifers. After a couple of teaser views, break above trees with fairly difficult ledge scramble at 1.4 mi. and climb steadily in open to immense Glen Boulder, glacial erratic perched at edge of ridge, at 1.6 mi./3729 ft. Enjoy wide views N and S down valley and across to Wildcats and Carters.

Trail turns sharp R (W) here and climbs steeply in open over rough ledges. Grade eases and trail re-enters scrub at top of pitch at 2.0 mi./4300 ft. Trail now climbs at mellow grade through high scrub, passing side trail descending ca. 200 ft. R to spring at 2.3 mi/4550 ft. Moderate ascent continues to small nub of Slide Peak at 2.6 mi./4806 ft., where trail emerges in open again. Here there is fine view S down Rocky Branch valley and Montalban Ridge and out to western and southern White Mountains, with Southern Presidentials to R. Trail now runs easily along rim of Gulf of Slides, with good views R into that cirque, then swings R (NNW) and rises steadily through alpine terrain and patches of scrub to meet Davis Path at 3.2 mi./5175 ft.

Turn R on Davis Path and climb moderately past craggy knob on L and up broad, open S ridge of Boott Spur. Look back for views down Rocky Branch and Dry River valleys. Pass just to L of summit of Boott Spur to jct. R with Boott Spur Trail at 3.7 mi. / 5450 ft. Continue on Davis Path across open, level ridge of Boott Spur and Bigelow Lawn, up to Crawford Path and on to summit of Washington as described above for Boott Spur Trail route. Reach summit at 5.7 mi. / 6288 ft.

Northeast Approach from Great Gulf

Great Gulf Trail, Gulfside Trail, Trinity Heights Connector
7.9 mi. one way, 5000-ft. elevation gain

TRAILHEAD (1350 ft.): This route starts at large parking area for Great Gulf Wilderness on W side of NH 16, 6.5 mi. S of US 2 in Gorham, and 4.1 mi. N of AMC's Pinkham Notch Camp.

One of the most dramatic ways to approach Washington is through the deep, secluded valley of the Great Gulf and up the great, rock-strewn headwall, emerging from the abyss just 0.4 mi. below the summit. This is a long, strenuous route recommended for ascent only, with descent via another, shorter route down the E side of the mountain to a car spotted at the base. The headwall can also be ascended by backpackers from a base camp in the gulf, but note that camping is prohibited above the Sphinx Trail jct. There are a number of marked, designated campsites along the Great Gulf Trail below this point.

From parking area, walk N along old road for 0.1 mi., turn L and dip to cross Peabody River on suspension footbridge, then swing L and up to jct. with Great Gulf Link Trail (from Dolly Copp CG) at 0.3 mi. Bear L here at easy grade on wide trail through spruces and hemlocks along West Branch of Peabody. At 0.6 mi. Great Gulf Trail splits L off road (a ski trail in winter), crosses small brook, passes ledgy cascade and pool in river, then rejoins road / ski trail at 1.0 mi. Continue past more ski trail jcts. On R and over several brooks on bridges. At 1.6 mi. is jct. R with Hayes Copp Ski Trail. Enter Great Gulf Wilderness and reach jct. R with Osgood Trail at 1.8 mi. / 1850 ft.

Continue ahead (W) on Great Gulf Trail, which mostly stays back in woods as it follows West Branch of Peabody. Pass scenic view of stream at 2.4 mi., where rocks provide view upstream to Mt. Jefferson, then climb steep rock staircase pitch and then moderate section through dense conifers to gravelly opening atop high bank known as The Bluff, reached at 2.7 mi. / 2278 ft. Here there are good views up to N side of Mt. Washington, Mt. Jefferson and Mt. Adams. Widest view is gained by scrambling up boulder on R.

Just beyond, bear L on Great Gulf Trail where Osgood Cutoff veers R, and descend steep bank to cross Parapet Brook (no bridge), then climb to hogback where Madison Gulf Trail splits R at 2.8 mi. Great Gulf Trail drops steeply to cross West Branch on suspension footbridge. Climb bank on far side and bear R on Great Gulf Trail as Madison Gulf Trail veers L towards Pinkham Notch. Great Gulf Trail now settles in for long, moderate stretch up along West Branch through deep fir forest, with rough, rocky footing in places. Pass Clam Rock on L at 3.1 mi. At 3.3 mi. rocks in riverbed provide view ahead to Jefferson's Knee. Cross Chandler Brook at 3.9 mi. / 2800 ft.; on far bank Chandler Brook Trail departs L. Continue moderate climb up valley,.and curve SW to jct. with Six Husbands (R) and Wamsutta (L) Trails at 4.5 mi. / 3100 ft. (See Wamsutta Trail option below.)

Beyond jct., Great Gulf Trail continues moderate climb up valley, with glimpses of Jefferson's Knees up to R. Pass by many fine cascades and pools, starting at 5.2 mi. and continuing for 0.2 mi., with some scrambling up wet ledges. Look back for views of Mts. Adams and Madison. Cross West Branch and tributary and in wet, mossy fir forest reach jct. R with Sphinx Trail, steep route up to Sphinx Col between Mts. Clay and Jefferson, at 5.6 mi. / 3625 ft. Recross West Branch and pass picturesque Weetamoo Falls at 5.7 mi. / 3675 ft. Continue climbing up bouldery footway into upper Gulf, obtaining occasional glimpses up to headwall. Last pitch up through stunted birch and fir lifts you to Spaulding Lake at 6.5 mi. / 4228 ft. Bordered by rock slides, this tiny tarn rests in one of most picturesque settings in East. Headwall of gulf is overpowering sight to S. Trail runs along E shore. From tall boulder at S end of lake, enjoy views N over water to Adams and Madison.

Beyond lake, Great Gulf Trail soon tackles arduous climb up 1600-ft. headwall. Scramble over huge boulders and along gurgling stream. Views open as you ascend—first back down gulf past Jefferson's Knees to Adams and Madison and Mahoosucs beyond. Continue clambering up broken rock; distant vistas start to appear over various cols and saddles on surrounding ridges. Look carefully for blazes and cairns as steep ascent continues in SSE direction. Watch footing on loose rocks. At top of headwall trail bears R and emerges to meet Gulfside Trail at 7.5 mi. / 5925 ft. Continue straight (S) on Gulfside Trail, easing up to jct. with Trinity Heights Connector at 7.7 mi. / 6100 ft. Turn L here for final 0.2 mi. climb over rocks to summit, reached at 7.9 mi. / 6288 ft.

WAMSUTTA TRAIL OPTION

Another option for climbing Washington from the Great Gulf is the route via the Wamsutta, Alpine Garden and Nelson Crag Trails. Wamsutta Trail is very steep and rugged in lower section, but offers unusual views. From Great Gulf trailhead, follow Great Gulf Trail for 4.5 mi. to four-way trail junction (elevation 3100 ft.), as described above. Turn L here on Wamsutta Trail, which leads S across floor of Gulf at easy grade for 0.1 mi., crossing small brook. It then climbs moderately for short distance but soon becomes very steep and rough, and just above R turn at 3500 ft. is difficult scramble up slippery rock chimney. At ca. 3800 ft. trail climbs very steeply through open scrubby area with several more scrambles and dramatic views across floor of Gulf to Mts. Jefferson, Adams and Madison. Trail re-enters woods and continues steep climb, then moderates and breaks out into open, scrubby, ledgy area, reaching first of several rocky knobs at 5.4 mi. / 4384 ft.; excellent views here. Above open area trail returns to woods and eases on shoulder, then climbs at mostly moderate grades through dense conifers. At ca. 5.9 mi. / 4950 ft. trail breaks above treeline and swings R. At 6.1 mi. it joins Auto Road Winter Cutoff (coming in from L) and follows this wide path to upper end of Wamsutta Trail at 6.2 mi. / 5305 ft. Cross main Auto Road to start of Alpine Garden Trail and climb moderately, then continue across level "lawn" to junction with Nelson Crag Trail at 6.6 mi. / 5575 ft. Turn R (W) on Nelson Crag Trail and climb in open over rocks, crossing Huntington Ravine Trail at 6.8 mi. and Ball Crag at 7.2 mi. / 6112 ft., and then Auto Road and Cog Railway tracks, reaching summit at 7.7 mi. / 6288 ft. Elevation gain from trailhead is 5000 ft.

Winter

Even though Mt. Washington experiences some of the worst weather in the world, especially during the winter months, the mountain is by no means off limits to winter climbing enthusiasts. Provided you are fully experienced in winter mountain travel and equipped with proper outerwear and appropriate gear, on the right day a winter ascent of the mountain can be a safe, enjoyable, and exhilarating experience.

Because much of the climb is above treeline, exposing hikers to cold winds and treacherous footing (featuring a mix of ice, snow and broken rock), only strong and experienced winter hikers, fully equipped for extended above-treeline travel, should attempt this climb. Even then, it should only be undertaken in clear weather with relatively light winds. The *average* winter wind speed on Mt. Washington's summit is 45 mph, and the average temperature in February is 5.6 degrees. Preventing frostbite and hypothermia is of critical concern on any winter venture on the mountain.

Among the essential items you'll need for a successful and safe climb are full crampons, snowshoes, ice axe, plenty of gloves and mittens, gaiters, extra hat, headlamps, map and compass, bivouac sack, sunglasses, abundant warm clothing layers and windproof outer garments.

Another potential hazard of any winter ascent of the mountain is the threat of avalanches, especially in Tuckerman and Huntington Ravines. Throughout the winter and the spring backcountry ski season, the U.S. Forest Service issues daily advisories concerning the threat of avalanches on the mountain. These bulletins are posted at the Pinkham

Notch Visitor Center, at Hermit Lake Shelter, and on the Internet at www
.tuckerman.org.

The most popular winter route up the mountain utilizes the Tuckerman Ravine and Lion Head Trails from Pinkham Notch (NH 16). The
winter route up Lion Head varies significantly from the Lion Head summer route in that it begins off the Huntington Ravine Fire Road, about
0.1 mi. from its junction with Tuckerman Ravine Trail (and 1.8 mi. from
AMC's Pinkham Notch Visitor Center.) The winter route, which is closed
to hikers during the summer and fall months, is less likely to be struck by
avalanches and joins the summer Lion Head route at treeline; it is somewhat shorter than the summer route. Other hiking routes from the E
side, such as the Glen Boulder Trail, Boott Spur Trail and Nelson Crag
Trail, are much less frequently used in winter and will likely involve extensive trail-breaking below treeline. The routes up through Tuckerman
and Huntington Ravines are suitable only for properly equipped technical
climbers with experience in assessing avalanche danger. The same holds
true for the remote route up through the Great Gulf.

In recent years the Cog Railway has run trains in the winter and the
plowing of the Base Road has made winter access to Mt. Washington
much more feasible from this side. The summer trailhead for the Ammonoosuc Ravine and Jewell Trails is not plowed, but parking (fee) may be
found at the Cog Base Station, from which connecting paths can be followed to either Jewell Trail or Ammonoosuc Ravine Trail. Parking at the
Cog shortens either route by over a half-mile each way. In good weather
the Jewell Trail / Gulfside Trail route is an attractive, moderately graded
option, but it has much exposure to NW winds and can be hard to follow on the upper Jewell Trail. In icy conditions caution is needed where
the Gulfside Trail skirts the rim of the Great Gulf. The Ammonoosuc
Ravine Trail / Crawford Path route is exposed for a shorter distance, but
the mile leading up to the Lakes of the Clouds Hut (closed in winter) is
very steep and has some potentially tricky spots. A long winter approach
from the Bretton Woods–Crawford Notch area is via the historic Crawford Path, but since this route involves more than five miles (one-way) of
above treeline travel, it should only be attempted in good weather and by
persons in excellent physical condition. Note that there is often a difficult
and possibly dangerous sidehill of hard snow along the Crawford Path on
the S side of Mt. Monroe, making it safer to go over the summit on the
Mt. Monroe Loop rather than around on the Crawford Path.

Take note that none of the summit buildings are open to the public
during the winter months and cannot be relied on as places to seek shelter in times of poor weather. If you have any doubts about the weather,
especially above timberline, do not hesitate to retrace your steps and save
the climb for another, better day.

A midwinter view of Mount Washington taken from Mount Lethe in the Carter Range.

View Guide

The view from Mt. Washington has been celebrated for centuries. In his 1876 guidebook, Moses Sweetser devoted eleven pages of very small print to describing its intricacies. Over the years several panoramic sketches identifying visible features have been produced, most recently by Brent Scudder in *Scudder's White Mountain Viewing Guide*. As the highest peak in the entire region, Mt. Washington naturally commands the most comprehensive view, in clear weather covering points in four states (New Hampshire, Maine, Vermont, New York) and the province of Quebec, plus the Atlantic Ocean. If you're lucky enough to have a clear day on top—and the summit is in cloud, on average, 60 percent of the time—you could spend hours scanning the horizons.

Over the years some observers have opined that Mt. Washington's superior height actually produces an inferior view, because everything around it is diminished in stature and effect. One nineteenth-century visitor deemed the Mt. Washington view "vast, but vague," preferring somewhat lower viewpoints such as Moosilauke or Lafayette. Inveterate peakbagger Gene Daniell places Washington 31st in his rankings of 4000-footer views, noting that "you can see forever, but forever's just too damn flat—Washington makes all the other peaks insignificant." Nevertheless, from Washington you can run your eye over a great deal of country, including the tops of 43 other New Hampshire 4000-footers—tying it with Mt. Carrigain in that regard. The observation deck of the Sherman Adams Summit Building is probably the best single place to take in the views. By scrambling around to various sides of the summit you can gain some better perspectives in several directions.

Perhaps the most dramatic view from Washington is that to the N, where the rocky peaks of the Northern Presidentials—Mts. Clay, Jefferson, Adams and Madison, L to R—rise in an orderly line from the abyss of the Great Gulf. Many mountains can be seen in the distance above the Northern Peaks.

Above the L (S) summit of Clay you look NW across the Israel River valley and the lowlands of Jefferson and Lancaster to East Mtn. (with a structure on top) in Vermont's Northeast Kingdom. Quebec's Owl's Head peers over in back to the L of East, with the nearer Stone Mtn. below in front. Seneca Mtn. is behind East on the R, with pyramidal Burnside Mtn. seen in closer. Farther R, looking between the summits of Clay, Mt. Orford in Quebec is visible on the horizon, with Vermont's Bluff Mtn. (in back) and West Mtn. (in front) to its L and closer. Down low and close by in this direction little Boy Mtn. in Jefferson is seen under the lower L slope of Mt. Starr King. Next to the R, seen beyond the main summit of Clay, are Mt. Starr King (L) and Mt. Waumbek (R) on the crest of the Pliny Range, with Vermont's Gore Mtn. on the horizon between them. A long, level ridge extends R from Waumbek, with Pliny Mtn. seen in front and (L to R) Black, Brousseau and sharp Sable Mtn. in Vermont on the horizon. Hutchins Mtn. in the Pilot Range is seen over the far R end of the Waumbek ridge, with the double peak of Goback Mtn. behind on its R. In the foreground in this direction is Mt. Jefferson's Ridge of the Caps. South Weeks (L) and North Weeks (R) are seen over Jefferson's summit with (L to R) Mt. Cabot, The Bulge and The Horn behind. Behind The Horn is more distant West Peak in the Nash Stream Range, which from there extends R across sharp Sugarloaf, Bunnell Mtn. (in back) and Gore Mtn. Vermont's Monadnock Mtn. (L) and Quebec's Hereford Mtn. (R) can be seen in the distance between West and Sugarloaf, while the bald Percy Peaks (long noted as "the most conspicuous mountains in the northern view from Mt. Washington" in the *AMC Guide*) are in front of and below Bunnell. Under the R end of Gore is Unknown Pond Ridge in the Kilkenny region. Behind this to the R is the elongated rolling crest of Long Mtn., with cliff-faced Rogers Ledge seen below and in front. North Whitcomb (Muise) Mtn. rises behind the R end of Long, and in closer and lower Square Mtn. (L) and Greens Ledge (R) peek over the gentle Deer Ridge. Farther R, looking due N, the broad mass of Dixville Peak (with Kelsey Mtn. in front) is seen over a shoulder of Mt. Sam Adams.

Farther R is the rocky pile of Sam Adams, with Dixville's neighbors (L to R) Cave, Rice and Crystal Mtns. beyond. The double summit of Deer Mtn. in Pittsburg can be seen between Cave and Rice, and on clear days massive Mt. Megantic in Quebec is visible between Rice and Crystal, 82 miles away. Mt. Magalloway's truncated summit can be picked out in the distance over the saddle to the R of Sam Adams. Next to the R and nearby is the great rocky pyramid of Mt. Adams, with distant Stub Hill on the horizon above it. Rump Mtn. on the Maine–New Hampshire border peers over Stub on the R. Countless ridges near the Maine–Quebec border can be seen between Adams and the lower Mt. Madison to its R, most prominently Mt. Gosford just L of Madison's summit. The sharp cone of Mt. Dustan can be seen closer in, under the skyline and above the Adams–Madison col. The double summit of Aziscohos Mtn. is seen over Madison, with Lake Umbagog in front to its R and more border mountains on the horizon, including White Cap Mtn. on the R. The flat crest of Cambridge Black Mtn. is in front of Lake Umbagog on the R, seen above Madison's Osgood Ridge and the city of Berlin. Over the L end of Cambridge Black is the wavy crest of West Kennebago Mtn., with Snow Mtn. near the Chain of Ponds peeking over behind. From West Kennebago many more remote border peaks lead R across to Spotted Mtn. and then the prominent mass of East Kennebago Mtn., with the nearer rounded Red Ridge seen in front above a western spur of Cascade Mtn. Cascade Mtn. itself, in the lower Mahoosuc Range, is seen down low over the lower R end of Osgood Ridge, with ledgy Pine Mtn. below it and closer.

Close by to the NE is the broad upper shoulder of Chandler Ridge, including the rock nubbles of Ball Crag (L) and Nelson Crag (R).(Ball Crag is just R of Pine Mtn.) In this direction are the many summits of the Mahoosuc Range, piled one upon another. The flat top of Mt. Hayes is above Ball Crag, with Cascade behind it on the L and the ledgy Trident above it. Elephant Mtn., dropping off sharply on the R, is in the distance above Hayes and The Trident, with Bemis Mtn. close behind on its L. On very clear days the distant spire of Maine's Coburn Mtn. might be spotted to the L of Elephant and Bemis. To the R of Hayes, Old Speck Mtn., highest of the Mahoosucs, rises in back above the broad crest of Bald Cap. Mahoosuc Arm is just in front of Old Speck on the L; on clear days the twin Horns of Bigelow Mtn. can be seen above it. The two main summits of Bigelow may be seen in back and just L of Old Speck's summit. Baldpate Mtn. is just behind Old Speck on the R, and Saddleback Mtn. is in the distance between them, with parts of the Redington–Crocker group peeking out behind it. Next to the R in the Mahoosucs are the three summits of Goose Eye Mtn., with Mt. Success (L) and Mt. Carlo (R) in front and below. On the horizon above Goose Eye are (L to R) Maine 4000-footers Sugarloaf Mtn., Spaulding Mtn. and sprawling Mt. Abraham, with the bare cone of Sunday River Whitecap under the R end of Abraham; closer in this direction is Reflection Pond in the Androscoggin River. Mt. Jackson near Weld, Maine, is seen above the ridge extending R from the Whitecap. Farther R and closer is the triple crest of Lary Brook Mtn. in the Mahoosucs. Next to the R, above and beyond Nelson Crag, the ledgy mass of Puzzle Mtn. rises behind Bear Mtn. (in the eastern Mahoosucs). The dark, rounded duo of Black (L) and Wheeler (R) Mtns. are to the R of Bear, seen above the NW ridge of Mt. Moriah. The prominent pyramid of Mt. Blue is on the skyline above Black, while lower Griffin Mtn. peeks over in back above Wheeler. Down low and close by the prominent cliff of the Imp Face is seen in this direction on a spur of the Carter Range.

Swinging to the ENE, the view now sweeps over the nearby Carter–Moriah Range across the Peabody River valley, starting on the L with Mt. Moriah (with lumpy Shelburne Moriah Mtn. seen over its summit and Middle Moriah Mtn. behind on its L) and running across North Carter, Mt. Lethe, Middle Carter and South Carter, dipping to Zeta Pass, then rising again to sharp-peaked Mt. Hight and the broad, rounded Carter Dome, seen due E. The distant view beyond the Carter–Moriah Range starts on the L with the paired Bald and Saddleback Wind Mtns. just R of Mt. Moriah's summit. Peabody Mtn., at the edge of the Caribou–Speckled Wilderness, peers over between North Carter and Lethe, with the sharp peak of Mt. Zircon near Rumford, Maine, in the distance. Pine and Pickett Henry Mtns. are seen right behind Middle Carter. Over the col between Middle and South Carter are the paired Gammon Mtn. (L) and ledgy, flat-topped Caribou Mtn. (R). The sharp knob of Speckled Mtn. in Peru, Maine, is prominent beyond Gammon, while Spruce Mtn. is seen above and just L of Caribou with Speckled's neighbor, Black Mtn., behind on its L. The lower Mt. Abram is somewhat closer behind Caribou on the R with Molly Ockett Mtn. behind it. Behind South Carter on the R are East Royce (L) and West Royce (R). Farther R, behind the L side of Mt. Hight, is the broad mass of Speckled Mtn. on the E side of Evans Notch. Down low under Mt. Hight is Little Wildcat Mtn. on the E side of Pinkham Notch. Next to the R Streaked Mtn. is seen in the distance over Carter Dome; on very clear days the bumpy outline of the Camden Hills on the Maine coast can be seen on the horizon above and to the L of Streaked.

To the R of Carter Dome and closer is the long spread of Wildcat Ridge with its five lettered summits and ski trails in front. The twin bare cones of North and South Baldface are over the highest Wildcat summits (A, B and C). Little Sabattus Mtn. can be seen behind a sliver of Kezar Lake to the R of South Baldface. Beyond the lower D and E summits of Wildcat are Jackson's Black Mtn., with a long ridge extending to the R, and the Baldface neighbors Sable Mtn. (L) and Chandler Mtn. (R) above. A bit farther to the R is the low, long profile of Maine's Pleasant Mtn. with Kezar Pond in front to its L and the nearer, twin Doubleheads to the R above the S ridge of Black Mtn. Another matched pair, the Gemini, are just above the Doubleheads, and their neighbor, Mt. Shaw, is seen to the L of North Doublehead with Sebago Lake beyond. The small double summit of Peaked Mtn. is seen at the edge of Sebago Lake, above Shaw.

In this direction, at mid-morning in summer, the glimmer of the Atlantic Ocean may be seen 75 mi. away on the Maine coast. On clear days the city of Portland on the Maine coast can be espied about in line with North Doublehead. Immediately to the R of Doublehead, looking SE, is the unmistakable pyramid of Kearsarge North near North Conway. Its low northern spur, Rickers Knoll, is on its L, with Lovewell Pond behind it and Maine's Saddleback Hills on the horizon. The Green Hills of North Conway extend behind Kearsarge on the R. Black Cap Mtn., highest of the Green Hills, is behind the shoulder of Kearsarge known as Bartlett Mtn., while Hurricane Mtn. peeks over the Kearsarge–Bartlett col. Thorn Mtn. in Jackson is in front in this direction, with Spruce Mtn. below, and behind Black Cap and successively farther are the Burnt Meadow Mtns., the Bill Merrill Mtn. group, and the Clark Mtn. Range, all in SW Maine. The lower Green Hills, including the sharp peak of Middle Mtn., trail away to the R of Black Cap. To their R is the town of North Conway in the broad Saco valley with Conway Lake beyond and little Ossipee Hill in Maine in the distance.

Farther R and close by down to the SSE is the great craggy side of Boott Spur, forming the S wall of Tuckerman Ravine. Little Mt. Agamenticus on the Maine coast is a bump on the horizon over the L side of Boott Spur. Farther R and closer are the double rounded humps of Green Mtn. in Effingham. Next to the R and nearer, seen over the R side of Boott Spur, is darkly wooded Iron Mtn. near Jackson, with part of Rocky Branch Ridge seen in front. The Moats rise prominently behind and R of Iron, with South Moat on the L and North Moat on the R. Little Attitash Mtn. and the ski slopes of Attitash, with lowly Mt. Stanton (L) and Mt. Pickering (R) below, are in front of the Moats. The several summits of Big Attitash Mtn. extend to the R of North Moat, with Silver Lake (front) and Ossipee Lake (back) seen beyond the L (highest) peak. The Moose Mtns. (L) and Copple Crown Mtn. (R) are in the distance above Big Attitash. Connected to Big Attitash on the R is Table Mtn., with Mt. Langdon's flattened dome in front on the L and Blue Job Mtn. in the distance, also on the L.

Farther R, almost due S, is the unmistakable rocky spire of Mt. Chocorua, with the Three Sisters on its L side. Mt. Parker in SE New Hampshire's Blue Hills is in the distance just L of the Sisters. Bear Mtn. is prominent to the R of Chocorua and closer, with Mt. Shaw in the distant Ossipee Range seen between them. The Mt. Parker on Montalban Ridge is seen in front under the L end of Bear. Faraway Mtn. and Black Snout, both in the Ossipee Range, are seen in the distance to the R of Bear, with the eastern part of the Belknap Range and the even more distant Fort Mtn. beyond on the horizon. Next to the R, just W of S, you look down the long, flattish Montalban Ridge. Mt. Isolation is seen under Mt. Davis in front, with Stairs Mtn. above and behind them. Mt. Crawford is behind

Stairs on the R and flat-topped Mt. Resolution is behind on the L. Bartlett Haystack is just behind Resolution on the R and Mt. Paugus is farther behind on the L.

Above Paugus in the distance are the paired Belknap Range peaks of Belknap Mtn. (L) and Gunstock Mtn. (R), with part of Lake Winnipesaukee seen through Paugus Pass to the R of Paugus. To the R of Bartlett Haystack and Mt. Crawford is triple-humped Mt. Tremont, with majestic Mt. Passaconaway looming behind. Passaconaway's shoulders, Nanamocomuck Peak and Wonalancet Hedgehog, descend in steps to the L, with little Hedgehog Mtn. seen below Nanamocomuck. On clear days the twin rounded bumps of the Uncanoonuc Mtns. are visible on the skyline to the L of Passaconaway. Mt. Whiteface rises just to the R of Passaconaway, with little far-off Joe English Hill visible over the deep gap between them and little Potash Mtn. down in front. To the R of Montalban Ridge is a nice view down the remote Dry River valley to (L to R) the rounded East and West Sleepers, the three peaks of Mt. Tripyramid, and the massive, double-summited bulk of Sandwich Dome, with Scaur Peak below, all in the Sandwich Range. On clear days North Pack Monadnock is visible above West Sleeper and Crotched Mtn. above Tripyramid. The Fool Killer and the lower Green's Cliff are seen under West Sleeper. On the skyline to the R of the Dome are far-off Mt. Monadnock (L, 105 mi. away, over Jennings Peak) and Mt. Kearsarge (R). Closer by in this direction is the Nancy Range, with low, flat Duck Pond Mtn. seen under Sandwich Dome, and Mt. Bemis (L) and Mt. Nancy (R), with rolling Mt. Kancamagus behind, looking towards Kearsarge. Peeking out behind Mt. Nancy on the R are Mt. Lowell (L) and Mt. Anderson (R).

Farther away, to the R of Kearsarge and above the middle of Kancamagus, is Ragged Mtn. Next to the R is the huge trademark profile of Mt. Carrigain with its Signal Ridge on the L. The rounded hump of Lovewell Mtn. is on the horizon between Signal Ridge and Ragged. Broad Forbes Mtn. is seen above Signal Ridge, and distant Sunapee Mtn. sprawls on the horizon right above Carrigain. East Osceola (L) and Mt. Osceola (R) are behind Carrigain on the R, with Mt. Tecumseh popping up between them, and farther R is the sprawling mass of Mt. Hancock, with South Hancock under the R end of Osceola, North Hancock's broad dome farther R, and the sharp peak of NW Hancock extending out to the R at the end of a long ridge. Close by between North Hancock and NW Hancock are Mt. Jackson, a small rocky peak (L), and Mt. Webster (R) in the Southern Presidentials. Mt. Cardigan is seen in the distance just L of North Hancock, with Cataloochee Mtn. just R of North Hancock. The several lower peaks of Scar Ridge peek over the ridge between North and NW Hancock, with Stinson Mtn. beyond. The main double summit of Scar Ridge is seen behind NW Hancock on the R, with Mt. Hitchcock in front and below and sharp Croydon Peak on the skyline.

Lest we forget—close by in this general direction, to the R of Hancock, is one of Mt. Washington's most striking vistas, looking SW down the barren, twisting ridge of the Southern Presidentials to the Willey Range and more distant peaks beyond. Especially notable are Mt. Monroe's sharp crags (L, in line with Mt. Webster, with the lower Mt. Franklin behind on the R) and Mt. Eisenhower's bald, rounded dome (R, under and just L of Mt. Field in the Willey Range). The Lakes of the Clouds and their namesake AMC hut are seen on the bare plateau in front of Monroe. The rounded swell of Mt. Pierce is seen between Monroe and Eisenhower, under the looming, rock-scarred hulk of Mt. Willey. Seen in the distance just R of Willey's summit are Carr Mtn. (L) and Mt. Kineo (R), with Vermont's Mt. Ascutney on the horizon above Carr; Stratton Mtn. peeks over the L side of Ascutney. Mt. Cushman is to the R of Kineo and closer. Farther R, on the horizon above the R side of Eisenhower's summit, is the broad bulk of Smarts Mtn., with flat-topped East Whaleback seen in front below it and Vermont's Okemo (Ludlow) Mtn. beyond on the R. Low down and close in this direction is Mt. Willard, a spur of Field, at the head of Crawford Notch. Slightly more to the R the sharp main peak of Whaleback Mtn. rises above Mt. Field. Just to the R and closer, under the ridge that rises R from Whaleback, and the Blue Ridge of Mt. Moosilauke beyond, is the craggy summit of Bondcliff; on the horizon in this direction Dorset Peak in SW Vermont can be spotted on very clear days. Next to the R, behind the Willey Range, is the lofty Mt. Bond, with Vermont's Salt Ash Mtn. above it on the skyline. Mt. Guyot is connected to Bond on the R, with Mt. Flume (L) and Mt. Liberty (R) peering over between them; the broad mass of Mt. Moosilauke rises in back. Only in just the right light, from the highest vantages on Washington, can the very tip of West Bond be spotted over the R shoulder of Bond. Sharp-eyed observers can also espy the rounded summit of Zealand Mtn. to the R of Guyot, lower and closer, and a slice of the long, low wooded crest of Owl's Head behind Guyot on the R. Vermont's sharp-peaked Coolidge Range (Killington Peak on the L, Pico Peak on the R) spreads in the distance over the R shoulder of Moosilauke, and closer in this direction is rounded Mt. Tom in the Willey Range.

Looking to the R of the Willey Range, a long ridge extends R from Guyot to the sharp little peak of South Twin and across to slide-marked North Twin, with Mt. Lincoln (L) and Mt. Lafayette (R) behind on either side of South Twin and the tip of Mt. Garfield to the L of North Twin. Various Vermont peaks in the Brandon Gap area are seen on the horizon above North Twin and to its R. Mt. Hale is to the R of the Twins and closer, beyond the nearer Rosebrook Range and the Bretton Woods valley. Behind Hale on the R is Nubble Peak, a spur of North Twin, with Cole Hill behind it. Farther R, looking beyond vast reaches of lower country, is the Breadloaf–Wilson–Grant range in the Green Mtns. Next to the R and closer, looking just S of W, is the lumpy Signal Mtn. range in west-central Vermont, with the long Mt. Abraham–Mt. Ellen ridge stretching above and beyond. Close in under the L end of these ranges are the ski trails of Bretton Woods, with rocky little Middle and North Sugarloaf just behind on the R. On exceptionally clear days Mt. Marcy, the highest of New York's Adirondacks, 130 mi. away, can be spotted slightly R of the red-and-white Mount Washington Hotel down in the valley, beyond the Signal Mtn. range and to the R of Mt. Ellen. Giant Mtn. in the Adirondacks may be spotted over the R end of the Mt. Ellen ridge, just L of sharp Spruce Mtn. in the Signal Mtn. range. Little Garnet Mtn., Mt. Cleveland and Mt. Agassiz (L to R) in Bethlehem can be seen under the R end of the Signal Mtn. range, with the village of Twin Mountain in front to the R.

Next to the R on the horizon is the distinctive tilted Camel's Hump, with the lower Mt. Ethan Allen joined on its L. On the clearest days New York's Mt. Whiteface (with Esther Mtn. on its R) may poke up as a dim blue pyramid just to the R of Camel's Hump. Low down in front in line with Ethan Allen / Camel's Hump is Little Mt. Deception, with the town of Bethlehem in the lowlands beyond. To the R of the Hump, close in and low down, is Beech Hill with the town of Littleton beyond. Next to the R, looking WNW, is the long, darkly-wooded crest of nearby Mt. Deception, featuring four summits, with Vermont's Worcester Range on the horizon over its lower L end (with Bolton Mtn. peeking up in back over a col) and sprawling Mt. Mansfield over its main summit, with the Sterling Range extending to the R. Cherry Mtn. rises behind the R end of Deception with its sharp spur, Owl's Head, on its R. The long, low Dalton Mtn. stretches behind Cherry, while Vermont's Laraway Mtn. pokes over on the horizon. Mt. Dartmouth in the Dartmouth Range is in front of Owl's Head on the R, and on the skyline is an array of summits in northern Vermont; L to R are the Cold Hollow Mtns., the sharp peak of Belvidere Mtn., Tillotson Peak, and Haystack Mtn. The lower Miles Mtn. is seen in front of these. Next to the R and closer are the paired Burke Mtn. (L) and Umpire Mtn. (R), with Cherry Pond seen down on the flats in line with Burke. The prominent Jay Peaks are beyond Umpire. To the R of the Jays are Mt. Hor (L) and Mt. Pisgah (R) framing Willoughby Gap in Vermont's Northeast Kingdom; in front of these is the low range of hills culminating on its R in Lancaster's tower-topped Mt. Prospect, and closer still is Mt. Mitten, a spur of the Dartmouth Range. To the R of and beyond Pisgah, in line with Prospect, is Sommet Rond in Quebec's Sutton Mtns. Next to the R is prominent Bald Mtn. in the Northeast Kingdom, with more of the Sutton Mtns. glimpsed in the distance to its R. From here the view swings around to the NW over more lowlands, coming back to nearby Mt. Clay and distant East Mtn.

NO. OF 4000-FOOTERS VISIBLE: 43

Carter Dome

ELEVATION: 4832 ft. / 1473 m   ORDER OF HEIGHT: 9
LOCATION: Carter Range, Township of Beans Purchase
USGS MAP: 7½′ Carter Dome

Geography

Carter Dome is the highest peak in the string of mountains which run more or less north-to-south on the E side of Pinkham Notch, which includes the Carter–Moriah Range and the peaks of Wildcat Ridge. This massive mountain is known for its round, symmetrical shape and its unique perspective on Mt. Washington, which lies directly across the way on the W side of Pinkham Notch.

The mountain's NW-facing slope is scarred by a huge landslide which stripped the mountain to its bedrock during a drenching October 1869 rainstorm. A major portion of the mountain, including the summit, has also never fully recovered from a devastating 1903 forest fire which severely scoured Carter Dome's broad, flat crest and denuded neighboring Mt. Hight of its vegetation.

On the SW side of the mountain is Carter Notch—the deep glacier-carved pass separating Carter Dome from Wildcat Ridge to the W. The U-shaped notch, with the rounded mass of the Dome towering on its E side, is a noted landmark visible from many distant points. Among the features of the notch are the Carter Lakes, two tiny tarns situated just S of the 3388-ft. height-of-land, and the nearby AMC Carter Notch Hut. On the SW flank of Carter Dome, overlooking the notch, is a remarkably steep and craggy face, with huge rocks strewn across the bowl beneath the cliffs. Pulpit Rock, an immense boulder jutting out above the notch high up on the Dome's side, is particularly prominent when viewed from the vicinity of the lakes and hut. Over the centuries, falling rocks and ledges from both Carter Dome and Wildcat Mountain have amassed into one gigantic boulder field S of the Carter Lakes. This barrier of rocks, known as the Rampart, is visited frequently by adventure seekers staying at the hut.

The main summit of Carter Dome is flanked by two major spur peaks. Bare-topped Mt. Hight (4675 ft.) is less than a mile NNE along the ridgecrest beyond a shallow col. This has probably the best view of any summit on the E side of Pinkham Notch. Just to the N of Hight, Zeta Pass (3890 ft.) separates the Carter Dome group from South Carter and the other Carter peaks.

The SE spur of Carter Dome, also bare on top, is sometimes called Rainbow Ridge (4274 ft.). To the SE its slopes descend steadily to Perkins Notch (2590 ft.), the broad, gentle gap between Carter Dome and Black Mtn. to the S. The Wild River takes its rise on the E side of Perkins Notch at tiny No-Ketchum Pond and surrounding bogs.

From the broad E side of the Carter Dome massif several ridges and valleys sprawl down to the upper Wild River valley. The lower slopes are largely cloaked in a paper birch forest that grew up after the great 1903 fire. Red Brook drains the slopes on the E side of Rainbow Ridge; several beaver ponds dot the plateau at the base of the ridge. The several branches of Spruce Brook drain the E side of Carter Dome itself and Mt. Hight. The main branch of the stream originates in a high cirque-like basin between the two peaks and flows down a long, curving valley. The ridge that borders this valley on the S sweeps down to a low but prominent rock peak (2930 ft.) that was bared by the fire. On the N side of the main Spruce Brook valley, Mt. Hight's E ridge splits into two massive wooded shoulders. To the E of Zeta Pass and N of Hight's NE ridge is the southern of two cirques at the head of the remote Cypress Brook valley; the flat floor of this bowl bears a large beaver meadow. This interesting E side of Carter Dome and its spurs can be studied from the barren Baldface summits across the Wild River valley.

The SW slopes of Carter Dome and Rainbow Ridge drain into the valley of Wildcat River. The NW slopes of the Dome and the W side of Mt. Hight are drained by tributaries of Nineteen-Mile Brook.

Nomenclature

The entire ridge from North Carter to Carter Dome was once known simply as "Mt. Carter," presumably for Dr. Ezra Carter, a physician who explored the Whites in the 1800s looking for medicinal herbs and roots. The name "Carter's Mt." appeared as early as 1823. Arnold Guyot's 1860 map listed "Carter, S. Peak and N. Peak." In 1876 the AMC adopted the name "Carter Dome" for the highest and southernmost peak. Mt. Hight, a 4675-ft. peak less than a mile north of the Dome, was originally called the N Peak of Carter Dome by AMC explorers and was later supposedly named for a frequent hiking companion of Dr. Carter, a Mr. Hight of Jefferson.

Other accounts, however, say the peaks were named for two local hunters (named Carter and Hight) who while passing through Carter Notch became separated, with each ascending the ridges on either side of the notch. As a result, one ridge was named Carter and the other Hight. Guidebook author Moses F. Sweetser wrote that it was uncertain which

The summit ridge of Carter Dome takes on the appearance of an island as it rises above an undercast as viewed here from the top of Mount Washington.

of the mountains assumed either of the names, but that the mountain W of Carter Notch was usually referred to as Mt. Hight, and the peak E of the notch, Mt. Carter. The western peak Sweetser refers to is today known as Wildcat Mtn., while the Mt. Hight was eventually assigned to Carter Dome's northern neighbor.

Historical Highlights

First Ascent: Unknown.

1852: First Glen House hotel built at western base of Carters.

Ca. 1853: Fisherman's path has been established from Jackson to Carter Notch.

1869: Heavy rains result in Oct. 4 landslide on Carter Dome that strips N and W slopes of mountain to its bedrock ledges for nearly one mile.

1876: William Nowell, Charles Lowe, and Dr. F. I. R. Stafford explore Carter Notch–Carter Dome area. Descent route is via steep NW slide. Jackson resident Jonathan "Jock" Davis builds path from Jackson to Carter Notch.

1877: Nowell and Lowe build Nineteen-Mile Brook Trail to Carter Notch from N; new lower part of trail is built in 1894.

1879: Jonathan Davis cuts trail from Carter Notch to summit of Carter Dome.

1881: AMC founders William Fenollosa and William Pickering climb to summit by way of Carter Notch and erect four-foot cairn atop mountain. In reporting on trip in *Appalachia*, Pickering writes of summit vista: "It may safely be said that there are few finer view-points for Mt. Washington than this."

1882: AMCer Randall Spaulding explores Wild River valley, passes through Perkins Notch. He notes pond there 30 rods long, 3–4 rods wide (today's No-Ketchum Pond?).

1883: AMC group, including Edith Cook, Eugene Cook, Charles Lowe, Thaddeus Lowe, Miss S. M. Barstow, and George Sargent, makes two-day trailless traverse of Carter Range from Gorham to Carter Notch. Edith Cook writes extensive description of journey in *Appalachia* (1884). Mt. Hight she calls "the crown jewel of the dark mountain brow . . . the pre-eminent grace of the Range." Also, trail from Carter Notch to Dome is extended to the "grand-viewing" north summit (Mt. Hight). Tripod observatory is erected on Dome.

1885: Under Nowell's direction, work is completed on extending ridge trail northward from Mt. Hight—today's Carter–Moriah Trail. Crude overnight camp is also established in Carter Notch.

1889: After failing in effort the previous year, group of AMC Snow-Shoe Section hikers make successful winter ascent of summit.

1893: *Among the Clouds*, published atop Mt. Washington, reports, "The fire in the forests on Carter Dome Mountain, only a short distance to the rear of the Glen House site, loomed up with renewed brilliancy last evening and was a grand sight when viewed from the Summit."

1891–1903: Major logging railroad operation in Wild River valley on E side of Carters, run by Wild River Lumber Company, then Hastings Lumber Company. Main line runs up valley beyond Red Brook, with short spurs up Cypress, Spruce and Red Brooks. Locomotive boiler explosion kills three workers near Spruce Brook in 1899.

1903: Fire sweeps over upper Wild River valley and portion of Carter Range, destroying viewing tripod at Carter Dome summit and forcing partial relocation of Jackson–Carter Notch path. Blaze puts end to Wild River logging operation. Burned area covers over 12,000 acres.

1904: N.H. Forestry Commission reports: "The forests of the Carter Range have been heavily lumbered. . . . The cutting on this range now extends up as far as there is merchantable growth, to 3,500 feet elevation on the average."

1904: AMC constructs log cabin in Carter Notch, on E shore of larger of two Carter Lakes; replaces previously built open shelter.

1907: Fire lookout tower erected on summit, replacing earlier observation tower built by local woodsmen. Station is used by N.H. Forestry Commission starting ca. 1913.

1914: Second hut, this one of stone, is built in Carter Notch. Original log cabin is given to Forest Service for use by fire lookouts working atop Carter Dome; it is evenually demolished in 1924.

Ca. 1915: WMNF acquires 35,000 acres in Wild River valley. Road is constructed up valley along old RR grade, with trail continuing up through upper valley and Perkins Notch.

1917: USFS completes cross trail that extends along lower slopes (at ca. 2000–2500 ft.) of Carters from Bull Brook near Mt. Moriah to Spruce Brook on E side of Hight and Carter Dome. Connecting links lead from main trail through Wild River Valley up Cypress and Spruce Brooks. New 11-mi. footway is called Boy Scout Trail.

1918: Fire lookout station is tranferred to USFS; new tower is built.

1921: Wildcat River Trail from Jackson is cut; replaces former Jackson–Carter Notch Path.

1923: USFS builds Carter Dome Trail up to Zeta Pass, then slabbing along W slope of Mt. Hight to Carter Dome; trail is described as "well-graded . . . constructed for the toting of supplies by saddle horse to Carter Dome Tower."

1924: New 30-ft. steel fire tower replaces older structure.

1928: *AMC Guide* notes that despite having been logged and burned, and now being wet and marshy, Perkins Notch "possesses a weird charm of its own." Book also notes that beavers have established colony at No-Ketchum Pond in 1927.

1929: Black Angel Trail from Wild River valley to ridge between Carter Dome, Mt. Hight, is built by USFS.

1933: Rainbow Trail from Wild River Trail in Perkins Notch to Carter Dome is built by USFS.

Mid-1940s: Boy Scout Trail abandoned.

1947: Summit fire lookout tower is removed.

1950s: Second major logging operation in Wild River valley is carried out by contractor Leo Nadeau of Berlin, using both horses and trucks.

1957: USFS builds Perkins Notch Shelter along Wild River Trail near No-Ketchum Pond, using site of cabin built ca. 20 years earlier.

1962: Lavatory building, bunkhouse added to Carter Notch facilities by AMC.

1963: USFS builds Spruce Brook Shelter along Wild River Trail by crossing of Spruce Brook.

1972: Carter Notch Hut opens for first time in winter on caretaker basis.

2006: Slopes and valleys on E side of Carter Dome and Hight are included in new 23,700-acre Wild River Wilderness.

Trail Approaches

West Approaches from NH 16

TRAILHEAD (1487 ft.): All approaches from W start at parking area for Nineteen-Mile Brook Trail, on E side of NH 16, 1.0 mi. N of Mt. Washington Auto Road and 2.3 mi. S of entrance to Dolly Copp Campground.

There are several ways to attack Carter Dome from Rt. 16 N of Pinkham Notch, including a rugged, but rewarding loop hike through spectacular Carter Notch and up and over the summit ridge. All involve elevation gain of ca. 3500 ft. The easiest route up the mountain is via the Carter Dome Trail, which leaves Nineteen-Mile Brook 1.9 mi. from its start. A series of switchbacks have tamed the steepest sections of the trail as it approaches the main ridge. This route is also convenient if you wish to loop over Mt. Hight via the Carter–Moriah Trail. The approach by way of Carter Notch is very scenic, but you pay for it with a very steep climb out of the Notch from Carter Lakes.

CARTER DOME ONLY OUT AND BACK

Nineteen-Mile Brook Trail (to Carter Notch), Carter–Moriah Trail
10.0 mi. round trip, 3550-ft. elevation gain

Nineteen-Mile Brook Trail provides a scenic brookside approach to Carter Notch. From parking area, trail follows old road at easy grades through hemlocks, then hardwoods, following Nineteen-Mile Brook (on R), passing several small cascades. At ca. 0.8 mi. traverse first of several rough spots along bank (tricky if icy). At 1.2 mi. pass small dam and pool in brook. Continue rolling, easy ascent through yellow birches, rocky for last 0.3 mi., to jct. L with Carter Dome Trail at 1.9 mi. / 2322 ft. Continue ahead on Nineteen-Mile Brook Trail, crossing two tributaries on footbridges and traversing more birch forest. Grade steepens through fir woods after small brook crossing at 3.1 mi. Stiff climb leads to height-of-land in Carter Notch and jct. R with Wildcat Ridge Trail at 3.6 mi. / 3388 ft. Continue ahead on Nineteen-Mile Brook Trail, descending L to shore of Upper Carter Lake, with view up to cliffs of Wildcat Mtn. At 3.8 mi. / 3300 ft. turn L on Carter–Moriah Trail by edge of pond. (Nineteen-Mile Brook Trail leads ahead, passing between Upper and Lower Carter Ponds, soon reaching AMC Carter Notch Hut.)

Trail soon begins very steep climb out of Notch on rock steps. At 4.1 mi. / 3900 ft. (0.3 mi. from Notch, and just after scrambling up exposed pitch with views W, including look NW to Northern Presidentials, and S), look for side path on R leading 30 yds. up to ledge with stunning vista. From this perch you overlook Carter Notch and Hut, with Wildcat Mtn. looming beyond, and gain view S down valley of Wildcat River to Kearsarge North, Moats, and Sandwich Range in distance. Pulpit Rock juts out close by on L. From outlook path, trail continues to climb, but on more moderate grades. At 4.5 mi. / 4300 ft. side path descends 60 yds. L to spring. Higher up grade eases, and at 5.0 mi. you swing R at small clearing; here ledges up on L provide very limited views S—this was once a fine viewpoint but trees have grown too high. Trail now ascends gently another 70 yds. to S end of large gravelly clearing atop broad, scrubby

4832-ft. summit. Here there are cairn and concrete footings from old fire tower, and Rainbow Trail comes in on R. View to NW and N, including Northern Presidentials and many distant ranges, is found by continuing 30 yds. N to other end of clearing, then descending 25 yds. L for most open perspective.

Nineteen-Mile Brook Trail, Carter Dome Trail

10.0 mi. round trip, 3450-ft. elevation gain (add 0.2 mi., 150-ft.
elevation gain for return loop over Mt. Hight on Carter–Moriah
Trail)

For approach via Carter Dome Trail, first 1.9 mi. is on Nineteen-Mile Brook Trail as described above. Turn L here (elevation 2322 ft.) on Carter Dome Trail and begin moderately-graded ascent E up N side of valley through yellow and white birch. Cross to S side of brook at 2.4 mi., traverse nice white birch glades, and cross back to N side at 2.7 mi. / 2800 ft. Trail now climbs by series of shorter, then longer switchbacks on N side of valley. Swing R at ca. 3400 ft. for steady sidehill climb through firs, with glimpses up to Carter Dome and one peek back at Gulf of Slides and Boott Spur. Reach deep woods of Zeta Pass at 3.8 mi. / 3890 ft. Turn R on combined Carter Dome and Carter–Moriah Trails and climb easily to where Carter–Moriah Trail splits L for Mt. Hight at 4.0 mi. / 4000 ft. Continue straight on Carter Dome Trail, which slabs at moderate grade up and across W slope of Hight. At 4.6 mi. / 4600 ft., just S of Hight–Carter Dome col, Carter–Moriah Trail re-enters from L. In another 25 yds. Black Angel Trail comes in on L. Carter Dome / Carter–Moriah Trails now climb at easy to moderate grades through high scrub, with occasional vistas. At 4.9 mi. side path leads 10 yds. R to spectacular viewpoint looking NW over Nineteen-Mile Brook valley to Presidentials and N to many distant ranges. Easy grades lead to large gravelly clearing at flat summit of Carter Dome at 5.0 mi. / 4832 ft. At N edge of clearing another viewpoint NW and N is 25 yds. down to R. Summit cairn, concrete footings for former firetower and jct. L with Rainbow Trail are another 30 yds. S across clearing. Here Carter–Moriah Trail continues ahead for descent to Carter Notch.

LOOP HIKE OVER CARTER DOME COMBINING
ABOVE TWO ROUTES

Nineteen-Mile Brook Trail (to Carter Notch), Carter–Moriah Trail, Carter Dome Trail

10.0 mi. loop, 3450-ft. elevation gain (add 0.2 mi., 150-ft. elevation gain
for loop over Mt. Hight)

LOOP OPTION OVER MT. HIGHT: If descending Carter Dome via Zeta Pass on either out-and-back via Carter Dome Trail, or loop up from Carter Notch, the short detour over Mt. Hight is highly recommended;

for extra 0.2 mile with just 150 additional ft. of climbing you can enjoy the best views on the Carter–Moriah Range. From summit of Carter Dome, descend gently N on combined Carter–Moriah / Carter Dome Trail. In 0.4 mi. Black Angel Trail diverges R for Wild River valley. In another 25 yds. keep straight on Carter–Moriah Trail where Carter Dome Trail splits L for Zeta Pass. Continue easy descent to Carter Dome–Hight col (4530 ft.). Mostly gradual climb lifts you to bare, rocky summit of Hight at 0.8 mi. from summit of Carter Dome. Panoramic view include great looks W to Presidentials, N and S along Carter Range, and E over Wild River valley to Baldface Range.

Atop summit, Carter–Moriah Trail makes sharp turn to L (NW) and drops into trees for very steep and rough descent for 0.4 mi., then more gradual as trail swings L to meet Carter Dome Trail at 1.2 mi. from Carter Dome summit. Turn R to reach Zeta Pass in an easy 0.2 mi.

Southeast Approach from Carter Notch Rd.

Bog Brook Trail, Wild River Trail, Rainbow Trail
12.0 mi. round trip, 3200-ft. elevation gain

TRAILHEAD (1810 ft.): Bog Brook Trail starts at a small, rough parking area on Carter Notch Rd. near its end, about 5.2 mi. from NH 16A in Jackson (the jct. is by Wentworth Hotel; road is paved until last 0.8 mi.). The USFS plans to relocate the trailhead nearby in conjunction with a logging operation, perhaps by 2008.

This is a remote, little-used but very scenic approach to Carter Dome. Brook crossings can be difficult in high water. From trailhead, follow Bog Brook Trail slightly downhill on old road, passing old camps on L, then bear R into woods and continue easy descent to cross Wildcat Brook at 0.4 mi. It runs over a low ridge, then crosses a nameless brook and Wildcat River (the most difficult of the three crossings) within a short distance. On far side of Wildcat River, at 0.7 mi., bear R on Bog Brook Trail as Wildcat River Trail goes L. Ascend gradually and cross gravel logging road at 1.0 mi. (This provides approach from end of Carter Notch Rd., where parking is available, that avoids previous three brook crossings, but is ca. 0.5 mi. longer.) Easy ascent continues N up valley through deep, varied forests of conifer and harwood. Footing is wet in places. At 1.9 mi. make first of five crossings of Bog Brook. Second and third crossings, at 2.1 mi., are close together. Fourth crossing is at 2.5 mi. In this upper part of valley trail passes through open spruce groves and skirts old beaver meadows. Just after last crossing (by beaver swamp; may need to detour L and cross on beaver dam) reach jct. with Wild River Trail at 2.8 mi. / 2417 ft. Turn R here and soon break out into beautiful birch glades. Climb easily and re-enter conifers just before reaching jct. with Rainbow Trail at 3.5 mi. / 2590 ft. in Perkins Notch.

Turn L on Rainbow Trail, climb over knoll and descend slightly, then ascend gradually at first. After crossing 2800-ft. plateau climb steadily through stunning white birch forest extending in all directions. At ca. 3200 ft., woods darken with conifers, and long stiff grade leads up through this mixed forest to open summit knob of Rainbow Ridge at 5.0 mi./4274 ft. Views are excellent from this unheralded vantage point: SW to great spread of southern and central White Mts., W to Wildcat Ridge and Mt. Washington, E to Baldface Range, NE to Evans Notch peaks and higher Mahoosucs. Carter Dome and Mt. Hight loom close at hand to N. From open area trail descends slightly to saddle, then climbs fairly steeply to 4600-ft. shoulder, with restricted view back down to knob. Route now climbs at easy to moderate grade through open fir forest, then swings L for steeper pitch to gravelly opening at summit of Carter Dome at 6.0 mi./4832 ft. For good view NW and N, walk 30 yds. N across clearing along Carter–Moriah Trail, then 25 yds. down to L.

LOOP OPTION

Descent can be made via Carter–Moriah Trail to Carter Notch (see description below), then back to Carter Notch Rd. via Wildcat River Trail and Bog Brook Trail (see Wildcat Mtn. chapter for details). This creates 11.5 mi. loop with great variety of scenery and much less hiker traffic than Nineteen-Mile Brook Trail approaches.

East Approach from Wild River Road

Wild River Trail, Black Angel Trail, Carter–Moriah Trail
8.0 mi. one-way, 3700-ft. elevation gain

TRAILHEAD (1150 ft.): Wild River Trail begins at end of gravel USFS Wild River Rd. (FR 12), 5.7 mi. from NH/ME 113 N of Evans Notch . Trailhead parking area is on L just before road enters Wild River Campground.

Backpackers and strong day hikers sometimes use this remote approach to climb Carter Dome from the beautiful Wild River valley. This route can be combined with other trails from Wild River (e.g. Rainbow Trail, Moriah Brook Trail, Shelburne Trail) and ridgecrest trails to create long day hikes or multi-day backpacks over Carter–Moriah Range. There are few views on Black Angel Trail route, but much fine forest walking through the newest Wilderness area in the WMNF.

From parking area, cross road and follow Wild River Trail to R of restrooms and across two small brooks. Trail bends L near Wild River, meanders through woods, then turns R on old road/RR grade at 0.2 mi. Easy walking leads past jct. R with Moriah Brook Trail at 0.4 mi. At 1.0 mi. trail crosses area of old slides along riverbank, then continues along grade with some washouts and stony footing. Occasional side paths lead down to ledgy pools in river. At 2.8 mi./1495 ft., shortly after passing site of Spider Bridge (washed out in 2005), Black Angel Trail joins from L. Bear R and descend 50 yds. to crossing of Wild River on rocks—very difficult and possibly dangerous at times of high water. On far bank follow recently cut path to four-way jct. where Wild River Trail turns L upstream and Highwater Trail comes in from R. (Alternate 3.4 mi. route to this point follows Moriah Brook Trail, with bridge over river, and Highwater Trail, but this has several ups and downs and includes crossings of Moriah and Cypress Brooks.)

Black Angel Trail continues straight (W) from intersection and makes long, easy to moderate ascent through fine hardwoods (including some large sugar maples), crossing occasional muddy spots and several old roads from 1950s logging operation. At 4.8 mi./2150 ft. trail crosses first of three N branches of Spruce Brook, this one usually dry. Climb moderately up hardwood slope, then through conifers, and at 5.2 mi./2400 ft. bear L aross second branch of Spruce Brook at nice mossy spot. Continue up L side of an eastern ridge of Mt. Hight through more hardwoods and birches, then re-enter spruces and cross small third branch of brook at 6.0 mi./3100 ft. Climb steadily and swing L to crest of shoulder at 6.6 mi./3700 ft., then wind easily through birch and fir, passing small spring. Footway becomes rockier and woods thicker, and at 7.2 mi./4150 ft. there is glimpse of Mt. Hight looming close ahead. Here trail swings L across flat area, then slabs up across very steep, rough SE slope of Hight—slow, difficult sidehill going with several tricky rock scrambles. In this section there are partial views out over Spruce Brook valley to Baldfaces and Sable and Chandler Mtns. Footing improves for last stretch angling up to jct. with Carter–Moriah Trail at 7.6 mi./4600 ft. Turn L for moderate climb through high scrub, passing fine NW outlook 10 yds. to R at 7.9 mi. and reaching gravelly summit clearing, with more views down 25 yds. to R, at 8.0 mi./4832 ft.

Winter

The western approaches from NH 16 are used almost exclusively for winter ascents of Carter Dome. Certainly the easiest route to the summit is via the Carter Dome Trail, but that's provided the trail is already broken out. Grades are moderate all the way, but the long sidehill along the W slope of Mt. Hight can be diificult in crusty conditions. The route over Hight involves a section of steep, difficult snowshoeing and a crossing of the exposed and possibly icy summit, where crampons may be needed. The approach along the scrubby N ridge of Carter Dome becomes an open ridge walk in late winter, with the small trees buried in snow and great views of the Presidentials. Since AMC Carter Notch Hut operates on a year-round caretaker basis, you'll almost always find Nineteen-Mile Brook Trail broken out to Carter Notch. The steep climb out of the notch by way of the Carter–Moriah Trail makes for a difficult, but not impossible ascent of the peak. Crampons may be needed if hikers have glissaded the steep pitch above the Notch.

View Guide

CARTER DOME: Not that many years ago extensive views were available in most directions from various points around the flat, scrubby summit. However, tree growth has completely obscured the eastern vista, and the southern view is almost gone as well, at least without substantial snow depth. There are still fine views to the NW and N from an opening at the NW side of the summit clearing and from another outook 0.1 mi. N on the Carter–Moriah Trail. The most striking part of this vista is directed across the Peabody River valley and Pinkham Notch toward Mt. Washington and the peaks of the Northern Presidential Range. As nineteenth-century author Julius Ward wrote, "The most impressive part of the view is the tremendous panorama of the Mount Washington Range, and in particular, the prospect into three of the great glacial ravines that lead toward the summit of the mountain. From no viewpoint can you gain a more comprehensive idea of the vast extent of the ravines."

Two of the glacial ravines Ward refers to—Tuckerman Ravine and Huntington Ravine—are best viewed from the outlook 0.1 mi. N on the Carter–Moriah Trail, as from the viewpoint by the summit clearing Washington's top can just be seen over the trees. More to the W, and just to the R of Mt. Washington, are seen (L–R) the craggy peaks of Jefferson, Adams and Madison, with the cirques of Jefferson Ravine and Madison Gulf in full view. From the more open outlook along the Carter–Moriah Trail, one can look down on Little Wildcat Mtn. and the Nineteen-Mile Brook valley below the Northern Presidentials. To the R of Madison, over the descending Howker Ridge, are the high peaks of the Pliny and Pilot Ranges, (L to R): the E ridge of Mt. Waumbek, the three peaks of Mt. Weeks, Mt. Cabot, The Bulge and The Horn. Vermont's West Mtn. is on the horizon between South and Middle Weeks. Mt. Crescent is seen in front under The Horn. Extending to the R of The Horn is Unknown Pond Peak with Goback Mtn. beyond. A nameless ridge in Vermont's Northeast Kingdom is to the R of Goback, then the view takes in the peaks of the Nash Stream region, with the Percy Peaks under West Peak and Sugarloaf, Bunnell and Gore to the R of West. Rogers Ledge is seen closer in under the Percys. To the R of the Nash Stream group and a bit closer is massive Long Mtn. with Black Crescent Mtn. in the foreground. The cliffs of Square Mtn. and Greens Ledge peer over Black Crescent. Farther R and close in is the low, ledgy Pine Mtn., with North Whitcomb (Muise) Mtn. on the horizon. Next to the R is little Jericho Mtn. on the W side of Berlin with broad Dixville Peak on the horizon. Close by in this direction the Imp Face peers over the descending W ridge of South Carter.

Farther R, almost due N, are Cave and Rice Mtns. and other ridges in the Dixville Notch area seen beyond the city of Berlin in the Androscoggin valley. The distant truncated peak of Magalloway Mtn. is visible over the R side of Berlin. Part of Cascade Mtn. is seen on the R side of Berlin, with Stub Hill in the distance on the R and Rump Mtn. to its R and still farther. The nearby wooded peak of South Carter is just to the R, under Rump Mtn. and blending in with the ridge leading to Middle Carter, the prominent peak looming to the R of South Carter. Cambridge Black Mtn.'s flat crest is visible off the L slope of Middle Carter, and the double peak of Aziscohos Mtn. is just L of Middle Carter's summit. The ledgy crest of Mt. Moriah is prominent to the R of and beyond Middle Carter; between them is Bald Cap in the Mahoosucs with Red Ridge behind and West Kennebago and other peaks in NW Maine on the horizon. Mt. Success, Mahoosuc Arm and Old Speck are seen in succession behind Moriah. Goose Eye Mtn. is to the R of Old Speck, with Elephant Mtn. above it and Baldpate Mtn. to its R. Farther R, behind the ledgy E ridge of Moriah, is the rocky hump of Shelburne Moriah Mtn. Over the R end of Shelburne Moriah, successively higher and more distant, are Lary Brook Mtn., Sunday River Whitecap, and Saddleback Mtn. Next to the R is the nearby sharp, ledgy peak of Mt. Hight. The Crockers/Redington group is on the horizon just L of Hight, and just to Hight's R are the far-off, prominent twin peaks of Sugarloaf and Spaulding. Next to the R the distant Mt. Abraham (L) and the nearer Jackson Mtn. group (R) are seen beyond the Bear Mtn. range in the eastern Mahoosucs. Howe Peak is seen under the R end of Bear, and farther R are Wheeler and Black Mtns. in the eastern Mahoosucs with Puzzle Mtn. rising behind. Farther R, looking NE, is the prominent pyramid of Mt. Blue seen beyond lower ridges in the Rumford, Maine, area, and on the far R edge of the view are Bald and Saddleback Wind Mtns.

Carter Dome's S view now consists of glimpses over the trees of the Moats, the Tripyramids, Mt. Tecumseh, the Osceolas, the Hancocks and Mt. Carrigain.

MT. HIGHT: The 360-degree panorama from this open rocky peak takes in many of the peaks mentioned above, and then some. Its perspective on Carter Dome's eastern slope is particularly impressive in autumn when the mountain's birch-covered landscape is transformed into a sea of yellows and golds.

The distant NW, N and NE views are essentially the same as those from Carter Dome, described above. The closer view W to the Presidentials is matchless and significantly better than that from the Dome. From here the full eastern spread of Mt. Washington is revealed, with Slide

Peak, the Gulf of Slides and Boott Spur on the L and Tuckerman and Huntington Ravines on either side of the main summit. The curving auto road to Washington's top is seen for nearly its entire eight-mile length. Additions to the view from Carter Dome are Mt. Clay peering over between Mts. Washington and Jefferson, the summits of Mts. Starr King and Waumbek over Mt. Madison's Howker Ridge, and the North Peak of Terrace Mtn. seen just to the R of North Weeks.

Looking N, South Carter is seen close at hand on the L above Zeta Pass, and on the R Middle Carter rears above the deep chasm of the Cypress Brook valley, with ledgy Mt. Moriah seen over the upper part of its long E ridge. Picking up the Carter Dome view on its R end, looking NE to Mt. Blue and Saddleback Wind, from Hight you see nearer Peabody Mtn. in line with Saddleback Wind. To the R of Peabody are Gammon (L) and Caribou (R) Mtns. in the Caribou–Speckled Mtn. Wilderness, with sharp Speckled (L) and broad Black (R) Mtns. beyond Caribou on the R, near Bryant Pond, Maine. To the R of Caribou and closer, seen across the middle Wild River valley, are the broad bulks of East Royce (L) and West Royce (R). Farther R the sprawling Speckled Mtn. on the E side of Evans Notch is seen above the truncated SE ridge of West Royce. Butters (L) and Red Rock (R) Mtns. are seen just behind Speckled on the L, with many low ridges in western Maine receding in the distance. Streaked Mtn. is prominent on the horizon to the R of Speckled. Next to the R Mt. Meader is seen across the valley beyond a nearby shoulder of Hight. The gentle Meader Ridge extends R from Mt. Meader to ledgy Eagle Crag and North and South Baldface, their rocky peaks rising across the upper Wild River valley beyond a humpy spur of Hight. A bit of Kezar Lake is seen to the L of North Baldface. A vast stretch of lower country is seen above the Baldfaces, with a bit of Long Lake glimpsed to the R of South Baldface. Eastman Mtn. peers over the col to the R of South Baldface, and farther R, looking SE, is flat-topped Sable Mtn. Over the L side of Sable is prominent Pleasant Mtn., with Kezar Pond in front of it and Sebago Lake behind its L end. Down in the Wild River valley in this direction are seen several beaver ponds and meadows along Red Brook.

To the R of Sable is its neighbor, Chandler Mtn., and through the broad gap between them are Major Mtn. (near) and the Saddleback Hills (far). Fryeburg's Lovewell Pond is seen right over the top of Chandler, and more bogs, including No-Ketchum Pond, are seen down in the Wild River valley in this direction. Behind Chandler on the R are Mt. Shaw, The Gemini (Twins) and Rickers Knoll leading across to the dominant cone of Kearsarge North. The low, rolling Burnt Meadow Mtn., Bill Merrill Mtn. and Clark Mtn. ranges are seen beyond Shaw and the Gemini, and Ossipee Hill is on the horizon between The Germini and Rickers Knoll. The shoulder of Bartlett Mtn. extends R from Kearsarge North, with the Doubleheads below. The high point of Black Mtn.'s long ridge is in front of the Doubleheads on the R. Thorn Mtn. is behind Black's summit on the R. In the distance beyond Black is Green Mtn. in Effingham, and on the horizon above Thorn are the Moose Mtns. and Copple Crown Mtn., with a bit of Ossipee Lake in front of Copple Crown. Farther R is a sliver of Silver Lake with White Horse and Cathedral Ledges below. Next to the R and close at hand is the bare summit of Rainbow Ridge, with South, Middle and North Moat above. Mt. Shaw crowns the distant Ossipee Range above North Moat. Extending R from North Moat is Big Attitash Mtn., with Faraway Mtn. in the Ossipees above. Mt. Chocorua's rocky cone is prominent above the R part of Big Attitash. Table Mtn. can be seen under the ridgeline extending R from Chocorua, and farther R you see Mt. Paugus rising in back with Bear Mtn. in front to its R. Through the wide gap between Chocorua and Paugus is distant Bean Hill in Northfield.

The view from Hight is now blocked by the impressive bulk of Carter Dome, rising just a mile away to the S and SW. Seen off the R slope of Carter Dome is Mt. Carrigain, with the sprawling ridge of Mt. Hancock to its R. The sharp peak of South Hancock is at the L end of the ridge, the broad dome of North Hancock is in the left-center, and NW Hancock is on the far R. Close at hand under NW Hancock is the summit of Wildcat Mtn. Just above and behind Wildcat are parts of Rocky Branch Ridge and Mt. Davis. In the distance to the R of NW Hancock is Mt. Cushman with Smarts Mtn. peering over in back. Farther R the double-humped Mt. Isolation peers over Rocky Branch Ridge, with Mt. Moosilauke's Blue Ridge on the horizon. Through the gap to the R of Isolation, Whaleback Mtn. is seen under the upper Blue Ridge, and farther R is the high, massive peak of Moosilauke itself. Just to the R of Moosilauke, Mt. Willey (L, with Bondcliff and Mt. Flume just peering over on its R) and Mt. Bond (R) poke above the ridge leading up to Mt. Washington's Slide Peak.

RAINBOW RIDGE: With a little moving around (taking care not to trample any alpine vegetation), this bare-topped SE spur of Carter Dome offers a fine near 360-degree panorama. Of particular note are the close-in views of Carter Dome (L) and Mt. Hight (R) rising close at hand to the N. Distant views extend from Old Speck, Goose Eye and more distant Maine peaks to the NNE, around through the Evans Notch mountains and the Baldface Range to the NE, E and SE; Kearsarge North, the Moats, and Mt. Chocorua to the S; and the central White Mtns. to the SW. Closer by to the W is an unusual view of Wildcat's craggy E face below Mt. Washington. The view S and SW is quite impressive as wave after wave of blue ridges extend to the horizon, with many 4000-footers visible, a sweep denied to those viewing from Carter Dome and Mt. Hight. Among the peaks clearly visible only here are Iron Mtn. under Bear Mtn. and Mt. Paugus, Mt. Passaconaway, Mt. Whiteface over Bartlett Haystack, the Tripyramids over Mt. Tremont and Mt. Parker, Mt. Kancamagus, Mt. Tecumseh over Mt. Resolution, and the Osceolas over Giant Stairs. Other peaks visible here include Mt. Carrigain, North Hancock, Mt. Moosilauke, Mt. Flume, Bondcliff over Mt. Isolation, Mt. Willey, Mt. Bond, Mt. Jackson, Mt. Guyot, Mt. Lincoln over Mt. Field, Mt. Lafayette and the lower Wildcat peaks.

NO. OF 4000-FOOTERS VISIBLE: 29 (from Carter Dome, some through the trees)

Middle and South Carter

Middle Carter

ELEVATION: 4610 ft. / 1405 m   ORDER OF HEIGHT: 15
LOCATION: Carter Range, Township of Beans Purchase
USGS MAP: 7½' Carter Dome

South Carter

ELEVATION: 4430 ft. / 1350 ft.   ORDER OF HEIGHT: 19
LOCATION: Carter Range, Township of Beans Purchase
USGS MAP: 7½' Carter Dome

Geography

The high, massive ridge that forms the heart of the Carter Range—from the Moriah–Imp col on the N to Zeta Pass on the S—rises to a pair of 4000-footers and several lesser summits in its four-mile expanse. The summits along the crest include trailless, cliff-faced Imp Mtn. (3730 ft.), North Carter (4530 ft.), a peak shown as Mt. Lethe on AMC maps (4584 ft.), Middle Carter (4610 ft.) and South Carter (4430 ft.). Only the latter two peaks show enough lift to be "official" 4000-footers. The entire ridge is densely wooded, but ledgy outcrops N and S of Middle Carter, and another just S of North Carter, provide excellent views. The summit of Middle Carter is narrow and scrubby, appearing as a small triangular peak jutting up from the ridge. Three ledgy knobs rise along the ridge just N of Middle Carter's summit; according to AMC maps, Mt. Lethe is the northernmost of these, and this is listed as one of the "Trailwrights 72" peaks. South Carter is a symmetrical wooded peak rising to the N of Zeta Pass (called "North Notch" by early AMC trail-builder William G. Nowell), across which looms rocky Mt. Hight.

The Carter ridge makes a steep 800-ft. drop on the N slope of North

Carter to a flat shoulder, a characteristic profile when seen from afar. Imp Mtn. rises just N of this shoulder, and Clay Brook drains NW through a steep ravine between Imp and North Carter. The Imp Face (3165 ft.) is a western spur of North Carter featuring a sheer cliff with spectacular views above the deep ravine of Imp Brook; a small ravine on the N side of the Imp Face is drained by Townline Brook. Cowboy Brook flows W through a deep valley below Mt. Lethe and Middle Carter, and another ravine between Middle and South Carter is drained by a branch of Nineteen-Mile Brook. All of these streams coming off the broad western slopes of the Carters empty into the Peabody River, which flows N along the W base of the ridge.

The E side of the Carter ridge is rugged and dramatic, presenting cirque-like basins and long valleys running out to the remote Wild River drainage. This aspect of the range can be studied from viewpoints on the Baldface–Royce Range to the E. Four cirques can be seen. Two are drained by SW branches of Moriah Brook—one E of North Carter and the other E of Middle Carter; they are separated by a high shoulder jutting E from Mt. Lethe. The twin cirques at the head of Cypress Brook (once known as Big Brook) are especially striking; one is between Middle and South Carter, the other, with beaver meadows on its flat floor, is below Zeta Pass. A short ridge descends E from South Carter between these cirques; beyond the confluence of its two branches Cypress Brook flows several miles farther E through a broad valley. A long gradual ridge extends four miles E from Middle Carter, dividing the drainages of Moriah Brook and Cypress Brook.

Nomenclature

The entire ridge from North Carter to Carter Dome was once known simply as "Mt. Carter," presumably named for Dr. Ezra Carter, a physician who explored the Whites in the 1800s looking for medicinal herbs and roots. The name "Carter's Mt." appeared as early as 1823 in *A New Hampshire Gazetteer* by John Farmer and Jacob B. Moore. George P. Bond's 1853 map showed "Mt. Carter 4900," while Arnold Guyot's 1860 map listed "Carter, S. Peak and N. Peak." In 1876 the AMC adopted the name "Carter Dome" for the highest and southernmost peak. William G. Nowell applied the names North, Middle and South Carter to the rest of the range. By the time the first *AMC Guide* came out in 1907, today's Middle Carter was called South Carter, and what is now known as South Carter was dubbed Middle Carter. This was due to an error on an 1893 USGS map. On the 1937 USGS map the order was reversed back to its original and more sensible arrangement, but this correction was not reflected in the *AMC Guide* until the 1950s.

The Imp Face was named for its "grotesque" appearance when viewed

The Carter Range peaks, including Middle and North Carter, as seen from the southern ledges of neighboring Mount Moriah.

from the Peabody River valley to the W, especially near the site of the Dolly Copp homestead. The name for Mt. Lethe, bestowed by an unknown person or party, has its origin in Greek mythology. The River Lethe was one of several rivers in the underground realm of Hades; its name means "forgetfulness," and those who drink from its waters would experience complete forgetfulness. This name has never appeared on USGS maps but made its way into the first *AMC Guide* in 1907 and has appeared on AMC maps to this day. There has been some controversy as to which of the several bumps just N of Middle Carter is entitled to the name "Mt. Lethe," and the matter may never be definitively resolved.

Historical Highlights

First Ascent: Unknown.

1827: Hayes Copp establishes homestead in Peabody River valley at W base of Carter Range. In 1831 he marries Dolly Copp and they operate farm, inn and tourist stand for many years. In 1881 they agree to go their separate ways. Says Dolly, "Hayes is well enough. But fifty years is long enough for a woman to live with any man."

1852: First Glen House hotel built at western base of Carters. Famous hotel is rebuilt several times after fires; last building burns in 1967.

1859: In his *The White Hills*, Thomas Starr King pays homage to Carter Range as rich scenic backdrop for Glen House, Gorham and Presidentials: "'The ballrooms of Saratoga could not outshine the splendors of color displayed in a season upon Mount Carter.'" Book includes two woodcut illustrations of Imp and North Carter, one by moonlight.

1870s: State Geologist Charles H. Hitchcock writes of the Carters: "It is the least known of all the mountain districts. I do not find any explorer of it anxious to continue his investigations therein."

1876: Moses Sweetser's guidebook notes that the Carter Range "has been but partially explored," possibly by the Hitchcock geological survey. "From people who have been over the range the Editor learns that there is a large area of dwarf spruce on its upper parts, through which it is very difficult to pass."

1877: Charles Lowe and William Nowell build Nineteen-Mile Brook Trail; lower section is cut in 1894, replacing original access from Glen House.

1883: AMC group, including Eugene Cook, Edith Cook, Charles Lowe and George Sargent, makes two-day trailless traverse of Carter Range from Gorham to Carter Notch. Edith Cook writes extensive account of trip for *Appalachia* (1884), noting excellent views from North Carter and cliffs on E side of Middle Carter.

1883: Miss S. M. Barstow and Laban Watson visit Imp Face as part of bushwhack loop around Imp Brook ravine. Barstow writes account for *Appalachia*.

1884: Under Nowell's direction, work begins on extending ridge trail northward from Carter Dome—today's Carter–Moriah Trail. Section from Mt. Hight to North Carter is completed in 1884, and that from Moriah to North Carter in 1885. Sweetser pronounces it a "magnificent mid-air promenade." Cost of building trail is $102. Imp Camp is also built in 1885.

1891–1903: Major logging railroad operation in Wild River valley on E side of Carters. Short spur is built from main line up Cypress Brook. Great 1903 fire puts operation out of business.

1906: New Imp Shelter built on ridge near Imp Mtn., described in 1907 *AMC Guide* as "a comfortable bark shelter." Obscure path leads to ledges near summit of Imp Mtn., where "the view is impressive, the summit weird and, off the path, dangerous."

Ca. 1915: WMNF acquires 35,000 acres in Wild River valley. Road is constructed up valley along old railroad grade, with trail continuing up through upper valley and Perkins Notch.

1917: USFS completes cross trail that extends along lower slopes (at ca. 2000–2500 ft.) of Carters from Bull Brook near Mt. Moriah to Spruce Brook on E side of Mt. Hight and Carter Dome. Connecting link leads from main trail through Wild River Valley up Cypress Brook. New 11-mi. footway is called Boy Scout Trail.

1923: USFS builds Carter Dome Trail up to Zeta Pass.

1929: Imp Trail built to Imp Face by USFS; Imp Trail loop soon completed.

1933: North Carter Trail built to connect Imp Trail with Carter–Moriah Trail.

1936: New Imp Shelter is built. Imp Shelter Cutoff is soon opened as shortcut from Stony Brook Trail. Highwater Trail is built along W side of Wild River, at E base of Carters.

1950s: Second major logging operation is carried out in Wild River valley by Leo Nadeau Co. of Berlin under USFS supervision. Scout Trail has been abandoned.

Late 1970s: Imp Shelter Cut-Off abandoned due to severe erosion.

1981: AMC rebuilds Imp Shelter with new partly enclosed A-frame design.

2006: Slopes and valleys E of Carters are included in new 23,700-acre Wild River Wilderness.

Trail Approaches

West Approaches from NH 16

North Imp Trail Approach
MIDDLE AND SOUTH CARTER LOOP HIKE

> **Imp Trail (N Branch), North Carter Trail, Carter–Moriah Trail, Carter Dome Trail, Nineteen-Mile Brook Trail, road walk on NH 16**
> 12.4 mi. loop, 3750-ft. elevation gain (subtract 1.6 mi. if car spotted at Nineteen-Mile Brook trailhead)

MIDDLE CARTER ONLY OUT AND BACK

> **Imp Trail (N Branch), North Carter Trail, Carter–Moriah Trail**
> 9.8 mi. round trip, 3600-ft. elevation gain

MIDDLE AND SOUTH CARTER OUT AND BACK

> **Imp Trail (N Branch), North Carter Trail, Carter–Moriah Trail**
> 12.4 mi. round trip, 4300-ft. elevation gain.

TRAILHEAD (1270 ft.): Start at the N end of Imp Trail on the E side of NH 16, 5.4 miles S of US 2 in Gorham; parking is on wide shoulder.

Many peakbaggers climb Middle and South Carter via the loop from NH 16 to the W—a long day with plenty of elevation gain. The loop can be done in either direction, and as noted above out-and-back options are also possible. The description below follows the loop over both summits from N to S, starting at the trailhead for the N branch of the Imp Trail. (Option for starting on S branch of Imp Trail is described below). For in-

Approaching the summit of Middle Carter on the Carter–Moriah Trail.

formation on loop and out-and-back options starting at Nineteen-Mile Brook trailhead, see below.

Starting on N branch of Imp Trail, climb gradually through hemlocks along S side of Imp Brook. Pass cascade and cross brook at 0.8 mi. / 1610 ft. Climb steadily through mixed woods, level on 1900-ft. hardwood plateau, then begin steeper ascent through conifers and birch (with one short ladder), skirting deep ravine to L. At 1.8 mi. / 2600 ft. bear R and wind steadily upward to open ledges atop Imp Face cliff at 2.2 mi. / 3165 ft., with spectacular view of Presidentials to SW and distant ranges to NW. From cliff, Imp Trail drops over ledge and passes vista over Imp Brook ravine, then swings L and contours roughly across slope, crossing small mossy brook (one of three) at 2.5 mi. Climb moderately, then bear R for gentle descent, crossing a fourth brook, then cross head of Imp Brook just before reaching jct. with North Carter Trail and S branch of Imp Trail at 3.1 mi. / 3270 ft. (S branch provides alternate 3.2 mi. approach to this point at moderate grades with no views. Trailhead is on NH 16, 0.3 mi. S of N branch. See description below.)

Turn L on North Carter Trail for moderate climb through fir and birch forest, bearing L at 3.6 mi. / 3650 ft. Steady climb continues, passing through many stands of dead firs in upper section and reaching ridgecrest and Carter–Moriah Trail at 4.3 mi. / 4470 ft. (From this jct., easy side trip L (N) along ridge on Carter–Moriah Trail is highly recommended in clear weather. Slight descent to ferny col is followed by short climb to ledge on North Carter with magnificent view E over Wild River valley—one of nicest spots on the range. Add 0.4 mi. for round trip with 100-ft. elevation gain.) From jct., route to Middle and South Carter follows Carter–Moriah Trail S (R) along high ridge. Hump over small ledgy knoll, climb to ledge with restricted view on second, higher knob, descend slightly and cross plank walkways, then wind easily up to W side of third knob (Mt. Lethe on AMC map; high point is to L through thick black spruce scrub), with glimpse of Middle Carter and nearer ledgy knob ahead. Descend slightly to cross planks over open black spruce bog, and climb ledges to open scrubby area on next knoll, with views to E, W and S. Short down-and-up leads to yet another knob, this one offering ledge perches with good views NE and NW. Make easy descent to minor col, then short climb to actual summit of Middle Carter leads past two outlooks with views from SW through N to NE. Ascend easily through high scrub to level wooded summit, marked by sign, at 4.9 mi. / 4610 ft. Views E into Wild River valley are available over trees.

From summit, Carter–Moriah Trail traverses level crest through high scrub, then descends to open area of ledge and low black spruce scrub with fine views of many mountains to N, Presidentials to W, and Wildcat, South Carter, Hight and Carter Dome to S. The Imp Face can be seen below to the NW. Going is nearly level along scrubby ridge with plank walkways and one short scramble to ledge with good view E to Baldface Range and S down ridge. Continue across terrace with more ledges, pass good E outlook up on R, then descend at varying grades through woods to Middle / South Carter col at 5.8 mi. / 4190 ft. Climb up towards South Carter is occasionally steep, with one narrow look back at Middle Carter, then eases on shoulder through beautiful boreal forest. Reach viewless summit of South Carter (sign) at 6.2 mi. / 4430 ft.; high point is on small rocky knob reached by 20-ft. path to R of trail.

Continuing S, drop steeply for ca. 0.2 mi. to shoulder, then descend at easy to moderate grades through fine fir forest, with two slight ascents and sections of plank walkways. Dip to low point at Zeta Pass and climb briefly to meet Carter Dome Trail at 7.0 mi. / 3890 ft. (No camping within ¼ mi.) Here joint Carter–Moriah/Carter Dome Trail continues ahead (S) to Mt. Hight and Carter Dome. (For strong hikers, out-and-back to Carter Dome from this point via Carter Dome Trail adds 2.4 mi. with 950-ft. elevation gain. Loop over Carter Dome and Mt. Hight via Carter Dome and Carter–Moriah Trails adds 2.6 mi. / 1100 ft.) To descend to NH 16, turn R (W) on Carter Dome Trail. Moderate grades lead down N side of valley with glimpses up to Carter Dome. Descend switchbacks to brook crossing at 8.1 mi. / 2800 ft., recrossing at 8.4 mi. Continue down through luxuriant forest of white and yellow birch to Nineteen-Mile Brook Trail at 8.9

mi. / 2322 ft. Turn R for rolling walk down along scenic stream, rocky at first, then with smoother footing, passing dam and pool at 9.6 mi. Reach trailhead for Nineteen-Mile Brook Trail at 10.8 mi. / 1487 ft. If no car spotted here, turn R for 1.6 mi. road walk, mostly downhill, to N trailhead for Imp Trail.

S BRANCH OF IMP TRAIL: As noted above, this provides alternate for lower part of loop, starting from NH 16 0.3 mi. S of trailhead for N Branch of Imp Trail. From trailhead, trail runs on level for short distance, then swings around to R and climbs SE at easy to moderate grade, traverses flat area to S, crosses logging road and brook, and swings L. It climbs moderately, then at 1.5 mi. / 1875 ft. makes major turn to L (NE), just before reaching Cowboy Brook. It now ascends steadily through hardwoods, then mixed forest of birch and conifer, with much rocky footing. Grade eases shortly before reaching jct. with North Carter Trail and N branch of Imp Trail at 3.2 mi. / 3270 ft. This is 0.1 mi. longer than N branch, though road walk for loop over Middle and South Carter is 0.3 mi. shorter.

Nineteen-Mile Brook Trail Approach

SOUTH AND MIDDLE CARTER LOOP HIKE

> **Nineteen-Mile Brook Trail, Carter Dome Trail, Carter–Moriah Trail, North Carter Trail, Imp Trail (N Branch)**
> 12.4 mi. loop, 3750-ft. elevation gain (subtract 1.6 mi., 200 ft. if car spotted at N Imp trailhead)

SOUTH CARTER ONLY OUT AND BACK

> **Nineteen-Mile Brook Trail, Carter Dome Trail, Carter–Moriah Trail**
> 9.2 mi. round trip, 2950-ft. elevation gain

SOUTH AND MIDDLE CARTER OUT AND BACK

> **Nineteen-Mile Brook Trail, Carter Dome Trail, Carter–Moriah Trail**
> 11.8 mi. round trip, 3650-ft. elevation gain

TRAILHEAD (1487 ft.): Parking area for Nineteen-Mile Brook Trail is on E side of NH 16, 1.0 mi. N of Mt. Washington Auto Road entrance and 2.3 mi. S of entrance to Dolly Copp Campground.

Both loop and out and back hikes to South and Middle Carter can be made from the Nineteen-Mile Brook trailhead. This is 200 ft. higher than either Imp trailhead, so if you are doing the loop with road walk you will be walking uphill back to your car. Trails used are same as those described for Imp Trail (N Branch) approach, only in reverse direction. (For full description in ascending direction up to Zeta Pass, see Carter Dome chapter.)

OTHER APPROACHES

Backpackers often approach the Carters via the Carter–Moriah Trail from S or N. For S approach see chapter on Carter Dome. The N approach comes up from 3127-ft. col between Mt. Moriah and Imp Mtn. (For routes to col via Stony Brook Trail from W or Moriah Brook Trail from E, see Mt. Moriah chapter.) Heading S, Carter–Moriah Trail skirts NW flank of nameless hump with several ups and downs, then swings L and ascends moderately to open ledgy area with views out to NW, back to Mt. Moriah, and ahead to nearby Imp Mtn. and the daunting North Carter. Trail turns L off ledges, descends over two more ledges with partial views, and drops to junction with side trail R to Imp Shelter and Campsite, 0.7 mi. from col (elevation 3350 ft.). This path descends moderately for 0.2 mi. to partly-enclosed A-frame shelter with water and extension of path in front to NW view. Main trail dips slightly, skirts E side of Imp Mtn., then climbs moderately to flat shoulder of North Carter, which it traverses with some ups and downs, passing through mossy fir forest and crossing wet areas on plank walkways. After dipping to low point, at 1.8 mi. from Moriah–Imp col begin climb to North Carter, first with steep pitch up to shoulder, then sustained steep, rough climb with several ledgy scrambles and occasional views N, including dramatic look down at cliffs of Imp Mtn. in front of Mt. Moriah. Reach gravelly summit clearing of North Carter, with limited views, at 2.3 mi and fine E outlook 0.1 mi. beyond. Elevation gain from Moriah–Imp col to North Carter is 1400 ft. From viewpoint North Carter Trail is reached in easy 0.2 mi., and Middle Carter is 0.6 mi. farther S along Carter–Moriah Trail, as described above.

Winter

If the snow is deep and unbroken, the trek over the Carters is a long slog. The loop route over the summits is good for snowshoeing with just an occasional ledgy scramble. (S branch of Imp Trail is easier snowshoeing than N branch, which has some sidehilling, but the view from Imp Face on N branch is especially stunning in winter.) The ledgy knolls N of Middle Carter are exposed to weather and may be icy in places. With deep snow views are improved along the scrubby ridgecrest on either side of Middle Carter, but even in the snowiest winters South Carter remains viewless. The section of Carter–Moriah Trail N of North Carter is seldom traversed in winter. The Nineteeen Mile Brook Trail parking area is plowed, and the shoulder along both Imp trailheads is also usually plowed wide for parking, though not recommended during a snowstorm!

View Guide

IMP FACE: The clifftop ledges open a huge vista SW across the Peabody River valley to Mt. Washington and an array of the Northern Presidentials, including a deep look into the Great Gulf. To the S is Pinkham Notch with Wildcat on the L. The upper Carter Range looms close by on the SE. The distant NW view takes in the Pliny and Pilot Ranges. The precipitous drop into Imp Brook ravine in front creates a dramatic effect.

NORTH CARTER VIEWPOINT: This flat SE-facing ledge has a magnificent outlook over the broad, remote valleys of Moriah Brook and Wild River, with the Royce–Baldface range and southern Maine lowlands to the E; occasionally the Atlantic Ocean is visible. Long wooded ridges extend E from the Carter Range into the valley below. Shelburne Moriah Mtn. and many distant Maine peaks can be seen to the N, Caribou Mtn. to the ENE, and Speckled Mtn. (over West Royce) to the ESE. Kearsarge North can be spotted to the S, and to the SSW, to the R of the nearby humps on the Carter ridge, are the distant Tripyramids, Mt. Tecumseh, Mt. Osceola, Mt. Carrigain and Mt. Hancock.

MIDDLE CARTER VIEWPOINTS: The best views from Middle Carter are found on several ledges along the Carter–Moriah Trail just N of the summit. Taken together, these offer views from SSW around to ESE; some of the panorama can be seen only if you stand. The best sitting perch is the lower of these ledges, on the E side, with a view from NW through NE. The upper ledge has a wider view to the SW and W. The views of the Northern Presidentials are especially good from Middle Carter. This part of the view is also well seen from the ledgy / scrubby opening along the ridge S of the summit.

To the S, the rounded hulk of Carter Dome can be seen over the trees. To the SSW is the distant Sandwich Range over the nearer summits of South Carter and Wildcat A. Mt. Paugus is seen off the lower R slope of Carter Dome, then Wonalancet Hedgehog and Nanamocomuck Peak are seen over South Carter. Next to the R are Mts. Passaconaway and White-face on the L, just L of Wildcat A. The Sleepers are seen over Wildcat A, and the Tripyramids are to the R. The lower Wildcats D and E, with ski trails on their slopes, are to the R of A, with Mt. Resolution seen through the gap between A and D and the Giant Stairs and Mt. Kancamagus above D and E. To the R of Kancamagus are Mt. Tecumseh; the East Peak and main summit of Osceola, with a deep gap between them; the dominant peak of Mt. Carrigain; and the long ridge of the Hancocks, with South Hancock on the L end, the dome of North Hancock in the middle, and NW Hancock on the R end. Mt. Nancy is directly under Carrigain. To the R of the Wildcat ski trails, under Carrigain and Hancock, is the upper

Rocky Branch Ridge with Mt. Davis (L) and humpy Mt. Isolation (R) behind, under Hancock.

To the SW the great rocky sprawl of Mt. Washington dominates. On the L of the summit are the bare Glen Boulder Ridge, Slide Peak (with Little Wildcat Mtn. seen down low in front), the Gulf of Slides, Boott Spur, Tuckerman Ravine and the shallow ravine of Raymond Cataract. The craggy headwall of Huntington Ravine is below the summit.

To the R of and behind Washington is Mt. Clay, at the head of the Great Gulf. Farther R, to the W, is the great trio of pyramidal Northern Presidentials: Mts. Jefferson, Adams and Madison. You look into the lower Great Gulf, which curves to the L below Jefferson. The headwall of Jefferson Ravine is between Jefferson and Adams, and part of Madison Gulf is below Adams. Madison's Howker Ridge runs out to the R, with Vermont's Burke and Umpire Mtns. beyond; Belvidere Mtn. is on the horizon to the L of Burke.

To the NW is the long ridgeline of the Pliny and Pilot Ranges—L to R, Mt. Starr King, Mt. Waumbek, the three rounded knobs of South, Middle and North Weeks, Mt. Cabot, The Bulge, The Horn, and Unknown Pond Ridge. The Jay Peaks in Vermont are in the distance to the L of Starr King, East Mtn. is visible between Waumbek's long E ridge and South Weeks, Seneca Mtn. rises beyond the South–Middle Weeks col, Gore Mtn. is seen through the gap between The Horn and Unknown Pond Ridge, and Goback Mtn. is behind Unknown Pond Ridge on the R. The Crescent Range is arrayed in front below the Pliny–Pilot ridge, with Mt. Randolph under Mt. Cabot and Mt. Crescent under Unknown Pond Ridge. Farther R Rogers Ledge (L) and Percy Peaks (R) are seen over Black Crescent Mtn. with Pine Mtn. below and in front. To the R of Black Crescent are (L to R) West Peak, Sugarloaf Mtn., and Long Mtn., with Bunnell Mtn. peering over its L end. North Whitcomb (Muise) Mtn. is farther R, then broad Dixville Peak is seen over little Jericho Mtn. near the city of Berlin. Other ridges in the Dixville Notch area are seen to the R of Dixville Peak.

The view due N, seen over the knobs just N of Middle Carter, takes in many peaks in northern New Hampshire, including Magalloway Mtn., and northwestern Maine. To the NNE is the ledgy mass of Mt. Moriah, with the higher Mahoosucs, including Old Speck and Goose Eye, beyond to the L. Mahoosuc Arm and Mt. Success are in front of Old Speck on the L. Elephant Mtn. is seen in the back between Old Speck and Goose Eye. Baldpate Mtn. is behind and to the R of Goose Eye, with the long ridge of Old Blue Mtn. farther to the R and in back. Lary Brook Mtn. and the bald Sunday River Whitecap are above and beyond the summit of Moriah. On clear days the 4000-footers of the Rangeley, Maine, region can be picked out to the R of the Mahoosucs and Baldpate, including Saddleback, Redington / Crocker, Sugarloaf, and Abraham. The ledgy hump of Shelburne Moriah rises over Mt. Moriah's gently sloping SE ridgecrest, with the Bear Mtn. range in the eastern Mahoosucs beyond and Jackson Mtn. near Weld, Maine, in the distance. Black and Wheeler Mtns. are to the R of the Bear Mtn. range, with Puzzle Mtn. in the distance. Farther R, over a prominent rock knob on Moriah's SE ridge, is the pyramidal Mt. Blue on the horizon, with Howe Peak, a spur of Shelburne Moriah, in closer to the R and Bald and Saddleback Wind Mtns. farther to the R in the distance. Next to the R, over a nearby spur of Mt. Lethe, is Peabody Mtn. at the N edge of the Caribou–Speckled Mtn. Wilderness. Next to the R are Gammon Mtn. and ledgy Caribou Mtn., with the lower Haystack Mtn. jutting to the R from Caribou.

In the distance beyond Peabody and Caribou are various mountains S of Rumford, Maine, including Mt. Zircon, Spruce Mtn., and Speckled and Black Mtns. To the R of Caribou / Haystack and closer, beyond the lower valleys of Moriah Brook and Wild River, are East (L) and West (R) Royce. Looking due E Speckled Mtn., on the E side of Evans Notch, peers over the long N ridge of West Royce. Streaked Mtn. is seen on the horizon over Speckled. Farther R and close in are parts of the long E ridge of Middle Carter.

The SE part of the view is best seen by standing and looking over the scrub near the summit of Middle Carter, or from outlooks along the ridge to the S and on knobs to the N, as mentioned in the trail description. To the R of the E ridge of Middle Carter, across the Wild River valley, is Mt. Meader, with the level, wooded Meader Ridge extending R across to ledgy Eagle Crag. The prominent rocky cones of North Baldface (L) and South Baldface (R) rise to the R of Eagle Crag, with Maine's Pleasant Mtn. beyond. Kezar Pond can be seen on the flats to the L of Pleasant. Extending R from the Baldfaces, seen over a spur ridge of Mt. Hight, are Sable Mtn. and Chandler Mtn. By peering down in this direction you may be able to spot the beaver meadows on the floor of the southern Cypress Brook cirque. Farther R is the dome of Kearsarge North, with Doublehead Mtn. to the R, under Bartlett Mtn., a spur of Kearsarge. Then the view is dominated by the nearby massive, steep-sided E shoulder of Mt. Hight, with the sharp, rocky summit up to the R, then the view swings back to Carter Dome.

NO. OF 4000-FOOTERS VISIBLE: from Middle Carter, 22; from South Carter: 19 (theoretical, through the trees)

Mount Moriah

ELEVATION: 4049 ft. / 1234 m   ORDER OF HEIGHT: 41
LOCATION: Carter–Moriah Range, Town of Shelburne, Township of
   Beans Purchase
USGS MAPS: 7½′ Carter Dome, 7½′ Wild River

Geography

Ledgy Mt. Moriah is the northeastern outpost of the White Mountain
high peaks, towering 3200 ft. above the town of Gorham. It's the king-
pin of three Moriah summits at the N end of the Carter–Moriah Range.
Major rivers enclose the mountain on three sides—the Peabody to the
W, the Androscoggin to the N, and the Wild to the E. Moriah is a sprawling mass of ledgy ridges with a small, knobby rock peak in the center.
Its proximity to town made it a popular destination—complete with bridle path and log shelter at the summit—as early as the mid-1800s. No
horse has set foot on Moriah's summit in many years, but today hikers
will find scenic trail approaches from several directions, with abundant
views from open ledges and a near 360-degree panorama at the top.

From the summit one ridge descends NW between Stony Brook and
Pea Brook towards Gorham, passing over a series of open ledges above
the low, rocky spur of Mt. Surprise (2194 ft.); this provides the route for
the N end of the Carter–Moriah Trail. This ridge sends out a ledgy SW
spur above Stony Brook. Another major ridge extends NE over Middle
Moriah Mtn. (3755 ft., no trail to the summit), dips to a saddle, then rises
to the broad, ledgy hump of Shelburne Moriah Mtn. (3735 ft.), with extensive subalpine bogs similar to those in the Mahoosuc Range. This ridge
is traversed by the Kenduskeag Trail. From Shelburne Moriah the ridge
descends E over Howe Peak (2965 ft.) and lesser summits to the Wild
River. The Rattle River flows N down a deep valley between Middle Moriah and Shelburne Moriah. On the E the three Moriah summits enclose
the long, trailless valley of Bull Brook, draining into the remote Wild
River. This basin features a steep headwall between Mt. Moriah and Middle Moriah.

The main ridgecrest of the range runs S from Mt. Moriah, descending 900 ft. to its 3100-ft. col with Imp Mtn. and the Carters. On the lower
part of this ridge is a line of S-facing cliffs overlooking the upper valley of
the long, twisting Moriah Brook, another tributary of Wild River; these
ledges are traversed by the Carter–Moriah Trail. A remarkable feature of
Mt. Moriah is the striking patches of bare rock on the upper part of its
great SE ridge, which rises for 4 mi. on the N side of Moriah Brook, and
on a minor southerly spur that descends from the top of the main SE

The southeast ridge of Mount Moriah and the distant Baldfaces in the Wild River valley as seen from the Carter–Moriah Trail.

ridge. This area was seared by a great forest fire about 1895; though much of the basin is revegetated with beautiful stands of paper birch, large areas of open rock persist. Below a prominent bare rock peak (3550 ft.), the main SE ridge is mostly wooded as it descends into the Wild River valley.

Nomenclature

It's believed that an early settler in the Androscoggin valley named Mt. Moriah after the hill of the same name in Jerusalem. Moriah in Hebrew means "provided by Jehovah." The name of the White Mountain Moriah appeared on Philip Carrigain's 1816 map of New Hampshire, and later on George P. Bond's 1853 map of the White Mountains. Arnold Guyot spelled it "Morijah" on his 1860 map. Over time the name was extended to other local features such as Middle Moriah and Shelburne Moriah Mtns., Moriah Brook and Moriah Gorge. The 1902 Scarborough map showed Moriah Brook as "Riley Brook" and Bull Brook as "Moriah Brook."

Historical Highlights

First Ascent: Unknown
1805: Stephen Messer establishes first homestead in Gorham, then part of Shelburne.

1852: Atlantic and St. Lawrence Railroad completed to nearby town of Gorham, spurring interest in tourism in region.

1854–1855: Bridle path built from Gorham to summit by John Hitchcock, proprietor of the Alpine House in Gorham. Log house, 13 × 16 feet, is built at top. Guests at Alpine House can rent ponies for ascent of mountain. Interest declines and path and house fall into disuse when Carriage Road opens on nearby Mt. Washington in 1861.

1859: Thomas Starr King rhapsodizes about the beauty of Mt. Surprise and Mt. Moriah in his classic *The White Hills: Their Legends, Landscape and Poetry:* "the long lines of its declivity towards the east, flow more softly than any others we can recall. They wave from the summit to the valley in curves as fluent and graceful as the fluttering of a long pennant from a masthead."

1860s: Samuel Eastman's guidebook recommends ascent of Mt. Surprise for ease of access and superb views, and touts Moriah as "a very charming excursion for those who care to undergo the fatigue . . . suddenly you are on the desolate and jagged peak. What a view! The whole region seems thrown into wildest confusion." Height of Moriah is given as 4700 ft.

1879: Old bridle path to summit cleared by Prof. E. T. Quimby of Dartmouth College, who occupies peak as station of U.S. Coast and Geodetic Survey. Moses Sweetser's guidebook makes note of large boulder ¾ mile below summit, dubbed "Quimby's Pillow."

1885: Carter–Moriah Trail built from Moriah S to North Carter under direction of AMC's William G. Nowell.

1890s: Heavy logging via railroad in Wild River valley to E. Spur lines are run up Bull Brook and Moriah Brook valleys, with trestle over Moriah Gorge in latter. Fire in ca. 1895 burns over much of Moriah Brook valley and SE ridge of Moriah. Damage from 4,000-acre blaze forces partial relocation of Carter–Moriah Trail to W.

1899: Irving E. Vernon and Warren W. Hart build section of Carter–Moriah Trail from Gorham to Mt. Surprise; from there to Mt. Moriah old bridle path is used.

1911: Fire burns for several days on slopes between Mt. Surprise and summit of Moriah.

Ca. 1915: WMNF acquires 35,000 acres in Wild River valley to E. Trail built up Moriah Brook valley to Moriah–Imp col, following old logging RR in lower part; this is precursor to present Moriah Brook Trail. In 1916–17 cross trail is built running N–S along lower E slopes of Moriah and Carters, connecting Bull, Moriah and Cypress Brooks. This is dubbed the "Scout Trail" and maintained into the 1940s.

1920s: Trail built from Pinkham Notch Rd. to Moriah–Imp col, is included under name of Moriah Brook Trail. AMC guidebooks describe arduous bushwhack route from Shelburne Moriah to Mt. Moriah.

Mid-1930s: Kenduskeag Trail opened from Wild River across Howe Peak, Shelburne Moriah and Middle Moriah to Mt. Moriah, and on to Pinkham Notch Rd. (W section of this trail abandoned mid-1940s; maintenance on E end over Howe Peak suspended mid-1950s.) Rattle River Trail opened from Androscoggin valley to col between Shelburne Moriah and Middle Moriah.

1950s: Leo Nadeau Co. of Berlin conducts second major logging operation in Wild River Valley, under supervision of USFS.

1960: W half of Moriah Brook Trail has been renamed Stony Brook Trail.

1979: Section of Carter–Moriah Trail N of Moriah–Imp col relocated to run along top of S cliffs.

2006: Slopes and valleys on E side of Moriah, including Moriah and Bull Brooks, are included in new 23,700-acre Wild River Wilderness.

Trail Approaches

Northwest Approach from Gorham

Carter–Moriah Trail
9.0 mi. round trip, 3550-ft. elevation gain

TRAILHEAD (800 ft.): From eastern jct. of US 2 and NH 16 in Gorham, drive 0.5 mi. E on US 2, turn R on Bangor St. and follow it 0.5 mi. to limited parking on L side at its end in residential area; do not block driveways or road. If no parking is available at trailhead, alternate access can be made by parking at available public areas in Gorham near the eastern jct. of NH 16 and US 2. Follow Washington St., which leaves the E side of NH 16 just S of the RR tracks, for 0.1 mi., then bear R on Mill St. and in another 0.1 mi. turn L onto a path that leads across a footbridge over the Peabody River. At the end of the path turn R on Bangor St. and follow it a short distance to its end, where the trailhead will be seen on the L.

The N end of the Carter–Moriah Trail provides a long, steady approach with views in its middle section from Mt. Surprise and from ledges above. There are several ups and downs in the upper half. From trailhead, trail climbs through private land at alternating moderate and easy grades on old logging road, passing logged areas, then grade steepens as trail narrows to footpath, entering WMNF at ca. 1.1 mi. Climb continues up through hardwood forest, then terrain gets ledgy and at 2.0 mi. / 2190 ft., near minor summit of Mt. Surprise, ledges offer good views R (SW) to Presidentials. By summit there is small flume beside trail on L. Beyond slight dip, ascent is gradual, then steeper across series of open ledges with good views W and N, and blueberries in season. Ledges extend from ca. 2400–2700 ft., with occasional ledgy spots to shoulder at ca. 3200 ft. From here trail makes meandering climb up Moriah's NW ridge through deep fir woods, with many little ups and downs and several disheartening false summits. At 4.2 mi. / 3700 ft., in fairly level section, summit is in view ahead. Final climb, fairly steep, leads to summit side path on R at 4.5 mi.; at this jct. is side path L to outlook with good view N. Side path on R leads to uplifted rock knob that is actual summit of mountain, with panoramic views.

Southwest Approach from NH 16

Stony Brook Trail, Carter–Moriah Trail
10.0 mi. round trip, 3150-ft. elevation gain

TRAILHEAD (930 ft.): From eastern jct. of US 2 and NH 16 in Gorham, drive 1.8 mi. S on NH 16 to parking area on L (marked by hiker symbol), just S of bridge over Peabody River.

This is a scenic approach up an attractive valley and across many open ledges on the ridge. From parking area, Stony Brook Trail crosses bridge over brook, then a second bridge over small flume, and ascends gently along E side of brook through hemlocks. Drop steeply R to cross brook at 1.0 mi. and soon turn L onto old logging road for long, gradual climb up valley through hardwood forest. Dip L to recross Stony Brook at 2.3 mi. / 1850 ft. Climb is now steadier up into open hardwood and birch forest, with a ledgy W ridge of Moriah and summit knob visible up to L. Continue moderately up through birch mixed with conifers, cross small brook at 3.1 mi., bear R at 3.4 mi., then quickly L for steeper pitch to Moriah–Imp col and jct. with Carter–Moriah Trail at 3.6 mi. / 3127 ft.

Turn L on Carter–Moriah Trail (part of Appalachian Trail), quickly passing jct. R with Moriah Brook Trail, and climb to ledge with view R into upper Moriah Brook valley and second viewpoint looking ahead to upper cliffs. Climb moderately through stunted woods to several tiers of open ledge atop cliffs at 4.1 mi. / 3500 ft. Perches to R offer stunning views SE of Moriah Brook valley enclosed by bare spur ridge of Moriah, with Meader–Baldface ridge beyond; S to Carter Range; SW to Presidentials; and NW to Pliny / Pilot Ranges. Beyond cliffs grade is mostly easier. Trail climbs alternately through woods and over ledges with views S, then meanders up through fine ridgecrest firs. It swings L, then R to ledges with good views W, with summit knob seen nearby. It then rises through woods to flat shoulder, swinging L and passing two good outlooks on R facing N to mountains of Maine. It crosses open top of knob, descends slightly, then wanders through woods to jct. R with Kenduskeag Trail at 5.0 mi. / 4000 ft.

Turn L with Carter–Moriah Trail for short, fairly difficult scramble up steep ledge. Side trail to summit of Moriah is short distance beyond on L; at this jct., less-used side path leads R to an outlook N.

Southeast Approach from Wild River Rd.

Wild River Trail, Moriah Brook Trail, Carter–Moriah Trail
14.6 mi. round trip, 2900-ft. elevation gain

TRAILHEAD (1150 ft.): From NH / ME 113 N of Evans Notch and 3.1 mi. S of US 2, follow USFS gravel Wild River Rd. (FR 12) 5.7 mi. SW along Wild River to parking area at end on L, just before Wild River Campground.

Strong hikers will enjoy this long, rewarding route that combines an approach through the new Wild River Wilderness up the secluded, beautiful Moriah Brook valley, rich in hardwood and birch forest, with views from S cliffs along ridge. From parking area, cross road and follow Wild River Trail to R of restrooms and across two small brooks. Trail bends L near Wild River, meanders through woods, then turns R on old road/RR grade at 0.2 mi. Easy walking leads to jct. R with Moriah Brook Trail at 0.4 mi. Turn R here and cross Wild River on suspension footbridge, then bear L upstream along W bank with large hemlocks and fine views of wide, rocky river. At 0.7 mi. bear R on Moriah Brook Trail as Highwater Trail stays L. Follow old logging RR grade through birch and hardwood. After rougher section high on slope, at 1.7 mi. / 1521 ft. cross Moriah Brook at head of Moriah Gorge, scenic rocky chasm downstream to L; difficult in high water. (Side path L leads down to gorge before reaching crossing.) Easy RR grade walking through hardwoods and birch and past beaver meadows on L leads to second crossing by ledges and pools at 3.1 mi. / 1750 ft. Now on N bank of brook, pass series of attractive cascades and pools. Cross tributary at ledgy spot at 3.5 mi. / 1950 ft. and continue up past more cascades into lovely white birch forest. Grades continue easy to moderate with four more crossings of dwindling brook, strewn with large gray boulders; last crossing is at 5.3 mi., high in winding upper valley. Continue up through birches, with S cliffs of Moriah looming ahead, cross swampy area on walkways, and make short, steep climb to Moriah–Imp col and Carter–Moriah Trail at 5.9 mi. / 3127 ft. Turn R to follow Carter–Moriah Trail for 1.4 mi. to summit, as described above under Stony Brook Trail approach.

North Approach from US 2

Rattle River Trail, Kenduskeag Trail, Carter–Moriah Trail
11.4 mi. round trip, 3500-ft. elevation gain

TRAILHEAD (760 ft.): Parking area for Rattle River Trail (part of Appalachian Trail) is on S side of US 2, 3.5 mi. E of its eastern jct. with NH 16 in Gorham.

This is a little-used, wooded approach, most often traversed as part of a backpacking route. From parking area Rattle River Trail follows old logging road at easy grade along E side of stream. Snowmobile trail joins on

R at 0.3 mi., trail enters WMNF, and snowmobile route leaves on L at 0.6 mi. Just beyond, Rattle River Trail crosses ledgy tributary, then continues easy, occasionally moderate ascent up valley through nice hemlock forest. Reach Rattle River Shelter on L at 1.7 mi./1250 ft.; down to R there are beautiful ledgy pools in stream. Trail soon crosses Rattle River (difficult in high water), climbs past lovely pool down to L, then crosses back over to E side of stream's western branch and climbs moderately on slope high above brook through hardwoods and hemlocks. Dip to recross river at 3.2 mi./ 2000 ft. and ascend steeply, with many rock staircases, angling up R (W) side of ravine. Woods change from hardwoods to birch and conifer at ca. 2500 ft. as steady ascent continues. Grade becomes quite steep at ca. 2800 ft. with more rock steps leading up through mossy conifer forest. After long pull, reach height-of-land, dip slightly, and traverse plank walkways to jct. with Kenduskeag Trail at 4.3 mi./3300 ft. (To L, or E, it is 1.3 mi./650 ft. climb to open, ledgy summit of Shelburne Moriah Mtn., with excellent views from ledges along way.) Turn R on Kenduskeag Trail and climb along S side of Middle Moriah Mtn., then traverse at easier grade with plank walkways and occasional minor descents. Trail climbs moderately, then steeply past outlook back towards Shelburne Moriah Mtn., crests knob with ledge at top, then descends slightly to meet Carter–Moriah Trail just below summit of Mt. Moriah at 5.7 mi./4000 ft. Turn R for short, steep scramble up ledge, then L on side path to summit ledge.

GRAND TOUR OF THE MORIAHS: Backpackers or strong day hikers can make a spectacular loop tour of the Moriah summits from the trailhead at the end of the Wild River Road, using the Wild River Trail, Moriah Brook Trail, Carter–Moriah Trail, Kenduskeag Trail, S half of Shelburne Trail, and a short walk on the Wild River Rd. This loop is 15.2 mi. with 3650-ft. elevation gain. The Shelburne Trail crosses the Wild River near the road; in high water, an alternate return to the trailhead, 1 mi. longer, can be made using the Highwater Trail and the lower Moriah Brook Trail with its suspension bridge over the river, and Wild River Trail; however, this still requires an unbridged crossing of Bull Brook on the Highwater Trail.

Winter

Choose from two approaches—Carter–Moriah Trail from the NW or Stony Brook Trail/Carter–Moriah Trail from the SW, which does have brook crossings that may be problematical if not well-frozen. Both have plowed parking (better at Stony Brook), moderate grades good for snowshoeing, and fine views from snowy ledges. In crusty or icy conditions good snowshoe crampons or boot crampons are required for the ledges, especially those atop the S cliffs. The trails may be hard to follow in the

Looking south towards the Carter Range from the summit of Mount Moriah.

ledgy areas, especially in deep snow winters. On the SW approach the ledge scramble just below the summit can be a challenge. The ledgy areas and summit knob are fully exposed to the wintry elements. The views from Moriah's ledges are especially dramatic in winter.

View Guide

The small rock knob at the summit provides a good panorama of mountains around the horizon. The full sweep is best seen standing, but much of the view to S, E and N can be seen while seated. To the N, on the L of nearby Middle Moriah, are the sprawling ridges of the Mahoosuc Range, starting on the lower L end, looking NNW, with ledgy Mt. Hayes (L) and Cascade Mtn. (R). Mt. Kelsey (L) and the broad mass of Dixville Peak (R) are seen in the distance over Hayes, and Cave Mtn., Rice Mtn., Crystal Mtn. (in back), Black Mtn. and other ridges to the E of Dixville Notch are seen beyond Cascade. The sharp Trident Col and The Trident are to the R of Cascade, with the truncated Magalloway Mtn. rising behind Mt. Tucker in the distance over Trident Col, and Stub Hill (L) and Rump Mtn. (R) seen far beyond the R peak of The Trident. Next to the R in the Mahoosucs is sprawling Bald Cap, with the broad, flat mass of Cambridge Black Mtn. behind on the L. Mt. Dustan's sharp peak is seen over the L end of Cambridge Black. The double summit of Aziscohos Mtn. is just L of the summit of Bald Cap, and distant ranges in NW Maine are on the horizon. To the R of Bald Cap is North Bald Cap with Red

Ridge under the distant West Kennebago Mtn. beyond on its L. Farther R
are the higher Mahoosucs, with Mt. Success seen under Mahoosuc Arm,
then Old Speck in the back, and then Goose Eye Mtn. with Mt. Carlo in
front and Baldpate Mtn. behind on its R. In the distance East Kennebago
is seen off the L slope of Mahoosuc Arm and part of Old Blue is behind
Baldpate on its R. Slide Mtn. (L) and Sunday River Whitecap (R, directly
over Middle Moriah) are seen to the R of Goose Eye. The nearer Lary
Brook Mtn. is under Sunday River Whitecap, and distant Saddleback Mtn.
is seen between Slide and the Whitecap. Other peaks in the Rangeley region are seen beyond and R of Saddleback. To the R of the Whitecap are
Bear Mtn. (L) and Black and Wheeler Mtns. (R) in the eastern Mahoosucs,
with Puzzle Mtn. peering over in back between them. The Jackson Mtns.
and far-off, sprawling Mt. Abraham (with Sugarloaf and Spaulding Mtns.
to its L) are visible beyond the L end of Bear. The pyramid of Mt. Blue
is seen on the horizon between Black and Wheeler. To the R of the eastern Mahoosucs and close at hand is the ledgy hump of Shelburne Moriah
Mtn., with the paired Bald and Saddleback Wind Mtns. seen above it on
the horizon. To the R of Shelburne Moriah, beyond its ledgy spurs, are
lower mountains S of Rumford, Maine, including Mt. Zircon. Farther R
and closer, Peabody Mtn. is seen above nearby Howe Peak, with Spruce,
Speckled and Black Mtns. beyond.

Farther R, looking due E beyond Evans Notch, are Gammon (L) and
ledgy Caribou (R) Mtns. Pine and Pickett Henry Mtns. are seen just behind and between Peabody and Gammon. The low Mt. Hastings is seen
in front of Caribou on the R, and a bit farther R is Caribou's low SW spur,
Haystack Mtn., overlooking Haystack Notch. Next to the R and a bit farther back is the low-lying Red Rock Mtn. range, with Albany Mtn. behind
and Streaked Mtn. on the skyline. Farther R and closer, looming large
across the Wild River valley, are East Royce (L) and the long crest of West
Royce (R). Durgin Mtn. is seen behind East Royce on the L, and Speckled Mtn. (on the E side of Evans Notch) rises between the Royces. To
the R of the Royces and the low gap of the Basin Rim, beyond a nearby
shoulder of Moriah, is the central and southern part of the Royce–Baldface Range, (L to R): Mt. Meader and Meader Ridge, Eagle Crag, the twin
bare cones of South and North Baldface, Sable Mtn. and Chandler Mtn..
The long, flat ridge of Maine's Pleasant Mtn. is over Meader with Kezar
Pond in front and Sebago Lake beyond on the L. In the back between
Pleasant Mtn. and the Baldfaces are lower ranges in SW Maine, including the Saddleback Hills, Bill Merrill Mtn., the Clark Mtn. group and part
of the Burnt Meadow Mtns. Black Cap Mtn. peers over in back between
Sable and Chandler, and the dome of Kearsarge North is behind Chan-
dler on the R. North Doublehead is to the R of Chandler, with Bartlett
Mtn. seen between them. The Moose Mtns. (L) and Copple Crown Mtn.
(R) are visible in the distance between Bartlett and North Doublehead. To
the R of Doublehead are the lower ends of the long E spur ridges of the

Carters running down to the Wild River Valley, with Thorn Mtn. peering over in back. Silver Lake can be seen in the distance between Doublehead and Thorn. Farther R the summit of Black Mtn. in Jackson is seen under South and Middle Moat, and continuing to the R North Moat rises above a shoulder of Mt. Hight. Mt. Shaw in the Ossipee Range is seen in the distance between Middle and North Moat, above Red Ridge. Faraway Mtn. in the Ossipees is to the R of North Moat. Then the view sweeps up to the high, wooded peaks of the Carter Range, just W of S. A long ridge rises to Mt. Hight, with Carter Dome peering over behind on its R. Farther R, with their own long ridges leading up to them, are (L to R) Middle Carter, Mt. Lethe and North Carter. The lower ridges of Imp Mtn. are seen below and in front of these three peaks. Starting off the R slope of North Carter, looking SW, is an impressive spread of the barren Presidentials; L to R are Mts. Washington, Clay, Jefferson, Adams and Madison. Under Clay and Jefferson you can peer into the depths of the Great Gulf. The great walls of the Carters and the Presidentials block out any views of the southern and western Whites, giving Moriah the lowest count of 4000-footers visible among the 48 high peaks.

To the R of the Presidentials, looking W, the view is obscured by scrub. Peering through the trees, you may be able to pick out the Worcester Range (L) and Mt. Mansfield (R) on the horizon. To the NW, standing and looking over the trees, one may see the long chain of peaks in the Pliny and Pilot Ranges, rising above the nearer Crescent Range. In the Pliny Range are (L to R) Mts. Starr King and Waumbek and South, Middle and North Weeks, with Mt. Crescent below South Weeks. To the R of the Weekses are the Pilots (L to R): Terrace Mtn., Mt. Cabot, The Bulge, The Horn, and Unknown Pond Ridge. Hutchins Mtn. just pokes up through the col between the Bulge and Horn. Black Crescent Mtn. is seen under the ridge between The Horn and Unknown Pond Ridge. To the R of Unknown Pond Ridge a plateau leads across to the ledgy peak of Rogers Ledge. Vermont's Gore Mtn. is seen in the distance to the L of Rogers Ledge. To the R of Rogers is the double peak of Goback Mtn., and farther R are the distinctive cones of the Percy Peaks, rising beyond Square Mtn.(with a large cliff face, and Sugar Mtn. in front and nearer) and Greens Ledge (with Round Mtn. below). To the R of the Percys is West Peak in the Nash Stream Range, and farther R is the great spread of Long Mtn., with Sugarloaf Mtn. poking over its L end. Bunnell Mtn. just peers over the middle of Long, and little Jericho Mtn. near the city of Berlin is seen under the R end of Long. Next to the R are two rounded summits of Whitcomb Mtn. and then the higher peak of North Whitcomb (Muise) Mtn., seen above lowly Mt. Forist in Berlin. Then the view swings back to Mt. Hayes and the Dixville mountains beyond. From the N outlook across from the summit side path one may see part of the town of Gorham down in the Androscoggin valley.

NO. OF 4000-FOOTERS VISIBLE: 8

Wildcat Mountain (A Peak) and Wildcat D

Wildcat Mountain (A Peak)

ELEVATION: 4422 ft. / 1348 m   ORDER OF HEIGHT: 20
LOCATION: Wildcat Ridge, Township of Beans Purchase,
Town of Jackson
USGS MAPS: 7½′ Carter Dome, 7½′ Jackson, 7½′ Stairs Mtn.

Wildcat D

ELEVATION: 4062 ft. / 1238 m   ORDER OF HEIGHT: 37
LOCATION: Wildcat Ridge, Township of Beans Purchase,
Town of Jackson
USGS MAPS: 7½′ Carter Dome, 7½′ Jackson, 7½′ Stairs Mtn.

Geography

Wildcat Ridge is a rugged mini-range extending about five miles from Pinkham Notch on the west to Carter Notch on the east. It bears a number of small peaks along its crest, five of which are lettered from "A" to "E", in order from east to west. Only two of these summits—D Peak and A Peak (the highest)—qualify for the 4000-footer list. D Peak replaced E Peak on the list only in the late 1980s, when Bradford Washburn's precise map of the Presidential Range established definitive elevations for the summits and showed D to be 16 ft. higher than E. The tough Wildcat Ridge Trail, with very steep climbing at either end, crosses all five peaks, with excellent views of Mt. Washington and Carter Notch from various ledges along the way.

Wildcat is renowned as a classic New England skiing mecca, with a skiing history dating back to the 1930s and a major ski area on the NW slopes of D and E Peaks. A gondola lift runs in both winter and summer/fall to the col between E Peak and D Peak.

At its west end the ridge rises very steeply out of Pinkham Notch, across from Mt. Washington and above the watery sliver of Lost Pond. (This great gap in the mountains is the divide between the Ellis River drainage on the south and the Peabody River drainage to the north.) Rough, ledgy terrain, with stunning views of the east side of Mt. Washington, swells up from the notch to wooded, viewless Wildcat E (4046 ft.). A shallow col separates E Peak from Wildcat D (4062 ft.), which sports an observation platform on top offering wide views to hikers and gondola-riding tourists. From here the ridge drops to deep Wildcat Col (3775 ft.), then rises, with occasional views, to Wildcat C (4298 ft.). Here the crest dips to another col and swings N over Wildcat B (4330 ft.) and up to the highest summit, Wildcat A (4422 ft.), where a ledge grants an excellent eastern outlook.

On its east side A Peak drops off precipitously into spectacular Carter Notch, which harbors the two tiny Carter Ponds just south of its 3388-ft. height-of-land. This craggy gap, with its opposite wall formed by massive Carter Dome, shows a classic glacier-carved U-shape when viewed from afar. Nineteen-Mile Brook flows north from the notch, while Wildcat River drains south through a long valley from the pass and the ponds. Over time a wild tumult of boulders has fallen from the cliffs of both Wildcat and Carter Dome, forming a rock barrier known as The Rampart on the floor of the notch a short distance south of the ponds and the AMC Carter Notch Hut.

A spur ridge runs north from A Peak to trailless Little Wildcat Mtn. (3350 ft.), forming the west side of the valley of Nineteen-Mile Brook. On the west side of this ridge is a minor ravine drained by Thompson Brook. Ridges also extend south from C Peak and E Peak, enclosing the deep valley of Wildcat Brook, a tributary of the Wildcat River. The upper part of this basin was once known as "The Hopper." At the south end of the ridge off E Peak is Hall's Ledge (2500 ft.), a spot once famous for its view of Mt. Washington. Though the ledge is overgrown, a cleared area nearby on the Hall's Ledge Trail provides a similar vista.

The corridors of the Wildcat River and its two major tributaries, Wildcat Brook on the west and Bog Brook on the east, are protected by the USFS under Wild and Scenic River designation.

Two waterfalls are found along the western base of Wildcat Ridge—the famous Glen Ellis Falls (on the Ellis River) and lesser-known Thompson Falls (on Thompson Brook). Both are accessed by short trails.

Nomenclature

On Jeremy Belknap's 1791 map this ridge was named East Mountain, as it is east of Pinkham Notch. For a time it was also called Mt. Hight, though the origin of the latter name is uncertain. Some accounts maintained that Hight was an early settler who accompanied Dr. Ezra Carter (for whom Carter Notch and the Carter Range were named) on his White Mountain explorations in search of medicinal plants in the early 1800s. Moses Sweetser's guidebook reported that Hight and Carter were two hunters who became lost around Carter Notch. Supposedly Hight climbed the mountain to the west (today's Wildcat) and Carter the peak to the east (now called Carter Dome). In any case, the "Wildcat" name was applied to the mountain in 1860 on geographer Arnold Guyot's map and

The Wildcat Mountain range as seen from Black Mountain in nearby Jackson.

it stuck, especially after being approved by the AMC committee on nomenclature in 1876. The name "Hight" was moved to the northern spur peak of Carter Dome. For some years the twin knobs of Wildcat E and Wildcat D were referred to as "The Wild Kittens." Thompson Brook and Falls were named for Col. J. M. Thompson, who was proprietor of the Glen House when it first opened in 1853. In addition to running the hotel, he built trails in the area for guests to use. Unfortunately he drowned in the Peabody River in 1869 during the same storm that unleashed a huge slide on Carter Dome. The name "Nineteen-Mile Brook" first appeared on George P. Bond's 1853 map of the Whites.

Historical Highlights

First Ascent: Unknown

1774: Captain John Evans starts building first road through Pinkham Notch.

1852: First Glen House is opened at NW base of Little Wildcat by Col. J. M. "Landlord" Thompson, using inn built several years earlier. Hostelry proves popular and is greatly enlarged in 1853, and again in 1866. Over years it gains renown as one of classic grand hotels in White Mtns. It is rebuilt several times after fires; last building burns in 1967.

1853: Famed intellectual Thomas Wentworth Higginson, an active mountain explorer, visits Carter Notch; meets local woodsman Bill Perkins, who recounts winter ascent of Wildcat on snowshoes. In *Forest and Crag*, Laura and Guy Waterman note that if true, this is first recorded winter ascent of 4000-ft. mountain in Northeast. Carter Ponds are called "Lakes of the Winds." Higginson's visit is described in article in *Putnam's Magazine.*

Mid-1800s: Sometime during his extensive explorations in the White Mtns., geographer Arnold Guyot probably climbs Wildcat. His 1860 map is the first to use the name "Wildcat Mt.," giving it elevation of 4350 ft.

1876: Moses Sweetser's guidebook notes that clearing has been made high on west side of Wildcat with "best view attainable of Mt. Washington and the great ravines on the E." Viewspot is reached by good 1½-mi. path from Glen House. Book gives description of view from clearing.

1876: Path built from Jackson to Carter Notch by Jonathan G. "Jock" Davis.

1877: Charles E. Lowe and William Nowell cut Nineteen-Mile Brook Trail for AMC, accessing Carter Notch from N. Lower part of trail built in 1894, replacing access from Glen House.

1883: Eugene B. Cook, Marian M. Pychowska and four other AMC members bushwhack up Wildcat from Carter Notch. They find viewpoint overlooking Carter Notch and another ledge (probably on C Peak) with view to Washington and western Whites. After making detailed view notes, they descend directly to Jackson–Carter Notch path. Trip is recounted in Dec. 1883 *Appalachia.*

1885: Crude shelter is built in Carter Notch, is rebuilt in 1893.

1901: Trail is cut from Carter Notch to main summit (A Peak) by AMC's Louis F. Cutter. Also, platform is erected to provide view east to Mt. Washington.

1903: Fire burns Wild River valley, Carter Dome, and area south of Carter Notch.

1903: Group from AMC Snow-Shoe Section makes winter ascent of Wildcat A. In 1904 E Peak is snowshoed, and both peaks are traversed in winter of 1905.

1904: AMC builds small log cabin in Carter Notch, replacing earlier open shelter.

1914: Stone hut, still in use today as part of Carter Notch Hut, is constructed by AMC in notch.

1917–1919: Wildcat Ridge Trail is built by AMC, connecting Pinkham Notch with Wildcat A; replaces very obscure footway described in 1916 *AMC Guide.* Path is laid out by Charles Blood, Paul Jenks and Nathaniel Goodrich. Blood observes that "considering its length, the route is much harder than would be expected."

1920: AMC builds first log cabins at Pinkham Notch Camp, opposite west base of Wildcat. The legendary Joe Dodge arrives in 1922 and expands camp over succeeding years.

1921: Wildcat River Trail built to replace original Jackson–Carter Notch path.

1924: Lost Pond Trail opened.

1920s: *AMC Guides* describe bushwhack route up south ridge of E Peak, passing over a 3655-ft. "F Peak" en route.

Early 1930s: USFS builds trail up valley of Wildcat Brook to Wildcat E, named Wildcat Brook Trail. Trail is abandoned in mid-1950s.

1933–1934: Several ski trails built by CCC on NW slope of Wildcats E and D. Katzensteig Ski Trail extends 1⅓ mi. from behind Glen House to summit of Little Wildcat. Wildcat E Ski Trail runs from NH 16 to top of Wildcat Ridge, with 2000-ft. elevation gain in 1½ mi.; rated for experts only with maximum grade of 33 degrees. Wildcat Col and Hopper Trails traverse lower slopes. Wildcat High Country Cabin, just over crest of ridge from top of Wildcat E Ski Trail, is built for day use by skiers, offering wood stove and benches.

1958: Wildcat Ski Area opens in January with first gondola lift in the country.

1972: Wildcat Valley Ski Trail is cut by Jackson Ski Touring Foundation, leading from top of gondola between E and D Peaks south to Jackson. In upper part trail traverses south ridge of E Peak, somewhat close to route of former Wildcat Brook Trail.

1972: AMC opens Carter Notch Hut for winter in first time, on caretaker basis.

Mid-1990s: Slide falls across Wildcat Ridge Trail in Carter Notch.

Trail Approaches

The rugged Wildcat Ridge Trail, a link in the Appalachian Trail, provides the only hiking trail access to the Wildcat peaks. Approaches can be made from west, north and south. A traverse combining the west and north approaches, both from NH 16, can be made with a car spot. The section climbing up the ridge from Pinkham Notch is very steep, with several ledge scrambles and traverses that can be dangerous if wet or icy. No matter what route you choose, you will sleep well after hiking the Wildcats. For those disinclined to negotiating steep trails, the ski trails of Wildcat offer an attractive option.

West Approach from NH 16 in Pinkham Notch

WILDCAT D ONLY OUT AND BACK

Wildcat Ridge Trail
4.4 mi. round trip, 2450-ft. elevation gain

WILDCAT D AND WILDCAT MTN. (A PEAK) OUT AND BACK

Wildcat Ridge Trail

8.4 mi. round trip, 3850-ft. elevation gain. (For optional approach via Lost Pond Trail, add 1.6 mi. round trip and 250 ft. of elevation gain to above totals.)

WILDCAT D AND WILDCAT MTN. (A PEAK), POINT-TO-POINT WITH CAR SPOT AND DESCENT TO NH 16 VIA NORTH APPROACH

Wildcat Ridge Trail, Nineteen-Mile Brook Trail

8.5 mi. traverse, 3150-ft. elevation gain. (For optional approach via Lost Pond Trail, add 0.8 mi. and 100 ft. of elevation gain to traverse total.)

TRAILHEAD (1960 ft.): Wildcat Ridge Trail starts on east side of NH 16 opposite parking area for Glen Ellis Falls (where hikers should park), 0.7 mi. south of AMC Pinkham Notch Camp. From parking lot, steep wooded wall of Wildcat Ridge looms dauntingly to east.

Cross under highway to trail sign, bear left on embankment, and immediately cross Ellis River, which can be very difficult in high water. (*Note:* This crossing can be avoided by starting hike at AMC Pinkham Notch Camp, on west side of NH 16 at height-of-land; ample parking; elevation 2030 ft. Cross highway to sign for Lost Pond Trail and cross infant Ellis River on bridge. Follow Lost Pond Trail south along river, then climb easily to Lost Pond at 0.5 mi. Trail runs along east shore with fine views across water to Mt. Washington, then passes through area of large boulders and descends to Wildcat Ridge Trail at 0.9 mi. This point is 0.1 mi. from start of Wildcat Ridge Trail.)

From jct. with Lost Pond Trail, Wildcat Ridge Trail quickly begins exceptionally steep, rocky, rugged climb up west end of ridge featuring rock steps and small ladder in lower part. L turn at base of ledge leads up to first outlook across Pinkham Notch at 2325 ft. Beyond, traverse along base of ledge with dropoff on L, then make fairly challenging scramble up through chimney, again with dropoff on L, and swing R up onto open ledge with superb view of east side of Mt. Washington. Climb continues very steep and rocky to another great outlook ledge at 2850 ft. Above this ledge, trail continues steeply a short way, then grade is easier along ridge, and short pitch leads up to another fine ledge perch with good view south down Ellis River valley at 0.9 mi. / 3050 ft. Several minor, though steep, ups and downs are followed by rocky, winding climb (with wooden pin steps and cut steps in places) to very steep, windswept ledge area at 1.5 mi. / 3750 ft. Here is spectacular view east to glacial cirques on Washington, plus view south to Moats, Sandwich Range and other peaks.

Grade eases considerably beyond here. Trail dips through three small cols, then one last fairly steep climb leads to densely wooded summit of Wildcat E, a former 4000-footer, at 1.9 mi. / 4046 ft. Descend to col and top of gondola station at 2.1 mi. / 3971 ft., with views north and south, then make short, steep climb to summit of Wildcat D at 2.2 mi. / 4062 ft. Observation platform provides fine views, though partly obscured in some directions; structure was roped off in 2007, possibly for repairs. (*AMC White Mountain Guide* notes that easiest descent via ski trails is 2.6 mi. from top of gondola, following Polecat ski trails on north side of area. The ski trails provide scenic, if at times tedious, walking with nearly constant views of Mt. Washington and the Presidentials and, in season, abundant wildflowers. Base of ski area is on NH 16 about one mile north of Pinkham Notch Camp.)

Continuing along ridge, trail makes alternately moderate and steep descent to deep, boggy Wildcat Col at 2.5 mi. / 3775 ft. Climb briefly, cross level area and dip slightly, then tackle steep, rough climb, with occasional breathers on level terraces (the first on a 4025-ft. shoulder), to Wildcat C, reached at 3.3 mi. / 4298 ft. At several points on climb up to C Peak there are vistas back (west) to Presidentials, D and E Peaks, and western White Mtn. peaks. The view east to Baldfaces from summit of C is now mostly grown up. Descend easily to narrow 4150-ft. col, swing to north and traverse level shoulder with small bog, then hop up to Wildcat B (4330 ft.). Short descent leads to final col on ridge (4270 ft.), then make easy to moderate ascent to summit of Wildcat A at 4.2 mi. / 4422 ft. Actual high point is rock just to R of trail; short spur path leads R to ledge with terrific view down into Carter Notch and across to Carter Range. For out-and-back option, retrace steps; for point-to-point traverse, descend steeply over switchbacks with many rock steps for 0.7 mi. on Wildcat Ridge Trail to height-of-land in Carter Notch, then turn left on Nineteen-Mile Brook Trail for 3.6 mi. descent to NH 16.

North Approach from NH 16

WILDCAT MTN. (A PEAK) ONLY OUT AND BACK

Nineteen-Mile Brook Trail, Wildcat Ridge Trail
8.6 mi. round trip, 2950-ft. elevation gain

WILDCAT MTN. (A PEAK) AND WILDCAT D OUT AND BACK

Nineteen-Mile Brook Trail, Wildcat Ridge Trail
12.6 mi. round trip, 4450-ft. elevation gain

WILDCAT MTN. (A PEAK) AND WILDCAT D POINT-TO-POINT WITH CAR SPOT AND DESCENT TO NH 16 VIA WEST APPROACH

Nineteen-Mile Brook Trail, Wildcat Ridge Trail
8.5 mi. traverse, 3650-ft. elevation gain

TRAILHEAD (1487 ft.): This route starts at parking area for Nineteen-Mile Brook Trail, on east side of NH 16, 1 mi. north of Mt. Washington Auto Road and 2.3 mi. south of entrance to Dolly Copp Campground.

The Nineteen-Mile Brook Trail provides a scenic brookside approach to Carter Notch. From parking area, trail follows old road at easy grades through hemlocks, then hardwoods, following Nineteen-Mile Brook (on R), passing several small cascades. At ca. 0.8 mi. traverse first of several rough spots along bank (tricky if icy). At 1.2 mi. pass small dam and pool in brook. Continue rolling, easy ascent, with rocky footing higher up, through yellow birches to jct. L with Carter Dome Trail at 1.9 mi. / 2322 ft. Continue ahead on Nineteen-Mile Brook Trail, crossing two tributaries on footbridges and traversing white birch forest. Grade steepens through fir woods after small brook crossing at 3.1 mi. Stiff climb leads to height-of-land in Carter Notch at 3.6 mi. / 3388 ft. (Carter Notch Hut is 0.2 mi. farther south and 100 ft. below via Nineteen-Mile Brook Trail.)

Turn R here on Wildcat Ridge Trail for steep ascent up side of Wildcat A via two long switchbacks (NW, then south), with many rock steps. At 3.8 mi. / 3600 ft., trail crosses open track of recent slide—use caution, dangerous if icy. From edge of slide there is nice view north down Nineteen-Mile Brook valley to Pine Mtn. and distant summits such as the Percy Peaks. At 4.0 mi. / 3900 ft. trail swings sharp L and climbs by shorter switchbacks. At top of this long rocky climb, trail bears L again and runs at easier grade for last 150 yds. to summit of Wildcat A at 4.3 mi. / 4422 ft.; east view is on short side path L. For out-and-back option, retrace steps. For point-to-point traverse, continue south, then west on rugged Wildcat Ridge Trail over B and C Peaks, down through Wildcat Col, and up to D Peak; route is described in reverse above. For traverse, slightly longer and much easier descent can be made via ski trails instead of west section of Wildcat Ridge Trail.

South Approach from Carter Notch Rd. in Jackson

WILDCAT MTN. (A PEAK) ONLY OUT AND BACK

Bog Brook Trail, Wildcat River Trail, Nineteen-Mile Brook Trail, Wildcat Ridge Trail
10.4 mi. round trip, 2750-ft. elevation gain

WILDCAT MTN. (A PEAK) AND WILDCAT D OUT AND BACK

Bog Brook Trail, Wildcat River Trail, Nineteen-Mile Brook Trail, Wildcat Ridge Trail
14.4 mi. round trip, 4250-ft. elevation gain

TRAILHEAD (1810 ft.): Bog Brook Trail starts at a small, rough parking area on Carter Notch Rd. near its end, about 5.2 mi. from NH 16A in

Jackson (the jct. is by Wentworth Hotel; road is paved until last 0.8 mi.). The USFS plans to relocate the trailhead nearby in conjunction with a logging operation, perhaps by 2008.

This route provides an attractive, less-used approach to Carter Notch up valley of Wildcat River. Brook crossings are tough in high water. From trailhead, follow Bog Brook Trail slightly downhill on old road, passing old camps on L, then bear R into woods and continue easy descent to cross Wildcat Brook at 0.4 mi. It runs over low ridge, then crosses nameless brook and Wildcat River (the most difficult of the three crossings) within short distance. On far side of Wildcat River, at 0.7 mi., turn L on Wildcat River Trail and follow east side of Wildcat River at gentle grade through mixed woods, close to stream at first, then high above and away from it. At 1.1 mi. cross gravel logging road (FR 233) that provides slightly longer approach from end of Carter Notch Rd. that avoids the three brook crossings. Trail climbs over rise and descends to cross Bog Brook at 1.7 mi. / 2050 ft. At 2.6 mi. / 2320 ft. reach jct. R with Wild River Trail. Continue ahead on Wildcat River Trail, soon crossing to west side of stream. Trail climbs up onto low ridge and ascends moderately high up on slope through fine hardwood and birch, with glimpses of Carter Dome. High up in valley grade becomes steep through conifers for ca. 0.2 mi., eases briefly on winding section, then a bit more climbing leads to south end of Carter Notch at 4.2 mi.; here side trail R leads out to wild boulders of Rampart, with views up to crags on Carter Dome and Wildcat and south down valley. Use caution exploring here as there are numerous crevices among the boulders. Carter Notch Hut is reached at 4.3 mi. / 3288 ft. Continue ahead on Nineteen-Mile Brook Trail, skirting small Lower Carter Pond on R and Upper Carter Pond on L; by Upper Pond is jct. R with Carter–Moriah Trail for Carter Dome. Shores of ponds provide wild views up to walls of notch. From Upper Pond, Nineteen-Mile Brook Trail swings L and climbs to height-of-land in notch at 4.5 mi. / 3388 ft. Turn L here on Wildcat Ridge Trail for steep climb to Wildcat A in 0.7 mi. and Wildcat D 2.0 mi. beyond, as described above.

Winter

The west approach up Wildcat Ridge Trail from Pinkham Notch is not recommended—some of the ledges can be very dangerous. The Nineteen-Mile Brook Trail is a good moderate and usually well-packed approach with plowed parking, but the climb up from Carter Notch is difficult and the crossing of the slide partway up is hazardous in icy conditions; crampons are essential for safety. The ridge walk between the peaks is a delight in winter, though there are some steep pitches in places. Winter peakbaggers often ascend or descend via the ski trails, usually Polecat; hikers should stay along the edge and be alert for fast-moving skiers and snowboarders.

View Guide

WILDCAT D: The viewing platform provides a good panorama, though in recent years tree growth has blotted out the southerly view, a communications antenna has further marred visibility, and the platform itself has deteriorated. In fact, it was roped off in 2007, hopefully for repair work. Even without the platform good views are found looking NW and south from open areas in the col between D and E Peaks, near the top of the gondola lift. The centerpiece is the spectacular view of the east side of Mt. Washington, with great looks into the Gulf of Slides (below Boott Spur on the L) and Tuckerman and Huntington Ravines (L and R of the main summit). This is Washington's most impressive aspect. Looking NW, the sharp, rocky peaks of Mt. Adams and the slightly lower Mt. Madison are seen in back, to the R of Washington, with a fine look into Madison Gulf. To the north, down the Peabody River valley, distant peaks are seen in northern NH and NW Maine beyond low, ledgy Pine Mtn. Long Mtn. is seen in the distance over the lower end of Madison's Howker Ridge, with Black Crescent Mtn. to the R and closer. Over Black Crescent are North Whitcomb (Muise) Mtn., and broad Dixville Peak, with Cave and Rice Mtns. farther R. Looking due north, Magalloway Mtn. pokes up on the horizon beyond Pine. Jericho Mtn. is to the L behind Pine, and Mt. Forist is on the R, overlooking the city of Berlin. To the R of Forist in the distance are Stub Hill (L) and massive Rump Mtn. (R). Mt. Dustan's pyramid is over the R side of Berlin. To the NNE the lower Mahoosucs and Imp Face are seen over nearby Little Wildcat. The long, flat crest of Cambridge Black Mtn. rises beyond the lower Mahoosuc peaks of Mt. Hayes (L) and Cascade Mtn. (R), with the double summit of Aziscohos Mtn. beyond on the L. The long, bumpy ridge of West Kennebago Mtn. in Maine is just L of the Imp Face, with even more distant Maine border mountains beyond on its L. The Trident is seen above the Imp, and to the R is sprawling Bald Cap in the Mahoosucs. Red Ridge is seen in the back between The Trident and Bald Cap, and East Kennebago Mtn. is in the distance to the R of Bald Cap.

The rounded crest of Wildcat A is seen close by to the NE, with Carter Dome peeking over, Middle and South Carter to the L, and Wildcats B and C to the R. (The portion of the view from ESE through SSW is now best seen from the clearing in the col between Wildcats D and E, or from the observation deck on the adjacent building.) Farther R, looking ESE, are South Baldface, Sable Mtn., Black Mtn., Chandler Mtn., and the more distant Pleasant Mtn. in Maine, with Kezar Pond in front on its L and Sebago Lake beyond on its R. Continuing to the R are Mt. Shaw, the twin Gemini, the nearer twin Doubleheads, and Kearsarge North. Black Cap Mtn. peers over between Kearsarge North and its R shoulder, Bartlett Mtn., and to the R of Bartlett, Middle and Rattlesnake Mtns. are seen over the nearer Thorn Mtn. Distant Ossipee Hill in Maine is on the horizon over Bartlett. The valley of North Conway is seen to the R of Thorn. Green Mtn. in Effingham is in the distance to the R of North Conway, and farther R Cathedral Ledge peers over a lower ridge of Little Attitash Mtn. Waves of peaks and ridges are seen to the south and SW. Next to the R are Spruce Mtn. in the foreground and the Moose Mtns. and Copple Crown Mtn. beyond Ossipee Lake in the distance. Farther R are South, Middle and North Moat, with the distant Blue Job Mtn. range over South and Middle. Big Attitash Mtn. is to the R of North Moat, with Mt. Shaw in the Ossipees in the distance. Next to the R is Mt. Chocorua, seen over the nearer Iron Mtn. Farther R, to the SSW, are (L to R) Bear Mtn. over Mt. Langdon, Mt. Passaconaway over Bartlett Haystack, Mt. Whiteface above Mt. Parker, the Sleepers above Mt. Tremont, and the Tripyramids. Mt. Resolution and the Giant Stairs are seen to the R of Tripyramid and closer, with Mt. Kancamagus above the Stairs. Farther R, to the SW, are Mt. Tecumseh, East Osceola and Mt. Osceola, Mt. Carrigain (with Mt. Nancy, the S part of Mt. Davis, and Rocky Branch Ridge in front) and wide-spreading Mt. Hancock, with South Hancock on the L, North Hancock's dome in the middle, and NW Hancock on the R. Nearby Wildcat E is just to the R of Hancock. Peering over to the R of Wildcat E are the double humps of Mt. Isolation, distant Mt. Moosilauke, Mt. Flume behind Bondcliff, Mt. Willey, and Mt. Bond; the summit of Mt. Webster can be seen under Willey.

WILDCAT MTN. (A PEAK): A small ledge on the east edge of the summit provides a startling view into Carter Notch, looking down on Lower Carter Pond and the roofs of the hut buildings and across to the massive Carter Dome with a huge rocky bowl gouged into its R flank. Mt. Hight is just to the L of the Dome, with South and Middle Carter (a pointed wooded peak) farther L. Seen through Zeta Pass, between South Carter and Hight, are Shelburne Moriah Mtn. (on the L, with a rock knob on Mt. Moriah's SE ridge in front of it on the R) and distant Maine peaks (L to R): Saddleback Mtn., Sugarloaf and Spaulding Mtns., Mt. Abraham, the nearer Sunday River Whitecap and Bear Mtn. in the eastern Mahoosucs, the Jackson Mtns. (near Weld), and part of Puzzle Mtn.

To the L of the Carters are the lower Mahoosucs, Imp Face and the city of Berlin. Red Ridge is seen off the L slope of the Carters. To the L and closer are (R to L) The Trident, Cascade Mtn. and Mt. Hayes. Deer Mtn. is in the distance over the L peak of The Trident. The long, level ridge of Cambridge Black Mtn. is over Cascade's main summit, with the double summit of Aziscohos Mtn. beyond. Mt. Dustan's pyramid rises beyond the Imp Face and the west peak of Cascade Mtn. The city of Berlin is seen to the L of the lower Mahoosucs. Magalloway Mtn., with a sharp dropoff on the R, is on the horizon over the L side of Berlin, with Stub

Hill and Rump Mtn. to the R and even farther. Little cliff-faced Mt. Forist overlooks Berlin on the L. On the far L is Jericho Mtn., with Rice and Cave Mtns. beyond in the distance.

To the R of the bouldery bowl on Carter Dome is the Dome's massive SE spur, Rainbow Ridge, with the bare cone of South Baldface seen off its descending ridge. Streaked Mtn. in Maine is visible in the distance through the Carter Dome–Rainbow Ridge col, and the tip of North Baldface peeks over the R shoulder of Rainbow Ridge. To the R of South Baldface are (L to R) Sable Mtn., Chandler Mtn., Mt. Shaw, The Gemini, Rickers Knoll, the Doubleheads, Kearsarge North, and Bartlett Mtn., all seen beyond the long ridge of Black Mtn. A wide spread of western Maine lowlands extends beyond the Baldface–Sable range, with Pleasant Mtn. seen over Chandler; Kezar Pond is in front of Pleasant on the L. In the distance over the Shaw–Gemini–Rickers Knoll group are the low ranges of western Maine, (L to R): the Saddleback Hills, the Bill Merrill Mtn. group, the Clark Mtn. range, and the Burnt Meadow Mtns. On the far R are Middle Mtn. in the Green Hills and the distant double peak of Green Mtn. in Effingham.

NO. OF 4000-FOOTERS VISIBLE: from Wildcat D, 24; from Wildcat Mtn. (A Peak), 26 (largely through the trees)

ZEALAND–CRAWFORD
REGION

Mount Field

ELEVATION: 4340 ft. / 1323 m   ORDER OF HEIGHT: 23 (tie)
LOCATION: Willey Range, Town of Bethlehem, Town of Hart's
    Location
USGS MAP: 7½′ Crawford Notch

Geography

The central and tallest of the three 4000-ft. summits comprising the Willey Range, Mt. Field towers to the W high above the floor of glacier-carved Crawford Notch and is flanked by imposing Mt. Willey to the SE and wooded Mt. Tom to the NW. The Willey Range parallels US 302 to the S and E as it passes through Crawford Notch. Field's summit is best seen from the highway as one approaches the Notch from the NW (Bretton Woods). The high point is a small, sharp wooded knob that rises from the main mass of the mountain. Because of its heavy tree cover, Field's summit offers only limited views.

Protruding from the NE flank of the mountain is Mt. Avalon, a 3442-ft. spur peak well-known for its craggy summit and excellent vista. A little to the E, and 600 feet lower, is Mt. Willard (2865 ft.), one of the best known and most visited peaks in the Whites, a rounded summit with a sheer cliff on its S face and a stunning view down Crawford Notch.

The W face of Mt. Field is very steep, with small cliffs and slides overlooking a high, hidden basin to the SW, from which a nameless brook flows S, then SW and empties into the North Fork of the Pemigewasset River's East Branch, to the W of Ethan Pond. Beyond the sharp dropoff, a long, broad, trailless ridge extends W over West Field (3691 ft., one of New Hampshire's 100 Highest peaks) and a nameless 3526-ft. knob before ending at Whitewall Mtn. (3405 ft.), whose ragged cliffs and talus slopes form the E wall of Zealand Notch. Two tiny ponds are hidden at the W base of West Field, and another boggy pond is sequestered in a valley on the NE side of Whitewall. This long, broad W ridge is bordered by the North Fork on the S.

Willey Brook, which flows into the Saco River in Crawford Notch, drains the high, steep SE slopes of Field. A 140-foot-long railroad trestle, seen high above US 302 when passing through the Notch, was built over Willey Brook in 1875. To the NE, Field shares the deep, cirque-like valley of Crawford Brook with Mt. Tom, which rises on the NW side of the ravine. On the lower reaches of Crawford Brook are the pretty Beecher and Pearl Cascades. On the NW slope of Field are the headwaters of Mt. Field Brook, which flows NW on the W side of Mt. Tom and down into the Zealand River.

Nomenclature

State geologist Charles H. Hitchcock is credited with naming this mountain in honor of Darby Field, the Englishman who led the first recorded ascent of Mt. Washington. For an untold number of years prior to Hitchcock's naming of the peak (in 1874), early stereoscopic views of the Crawford Notch region identified the mountain as Mt. Lincoln, for assassinated Civil War-era president, Abraham Lincoln. As Hitchcock noted in his *Geology of New Hampshire*, however, that name already existed on the 5089-ft. summit S of Mt. Lafayette on the Franconia Range. "I propose, therefore, the name of Mt. Field for the eminence near the Crawford House, in honor of the worthy gentleman (Darby Field) who first ascended Mt. Washington in 1642, and will use it upon the map and in the descriptions of this report," wrote Hitchcock.

Guidebook editor Moses F. Sweetser named the lower Mt. Avalon in 1876, "on account of its resemblance to certain bold hills in Avalon, the great S.E. peninsula of Newfoundland." Beecher Cascade was named for the Rev. Henry Ward Beecher (1813–1887), the famed preacher and abolitionist, who often summered in the area.

Historical Highlights

First Ascent: Unknown

1771: Moose hunter Timothy Nash reportedly discovers Crawford Notch, spotting gap from tree on Cherry Mountain to N. Nash and pal Benjamin Sawyer bring horse through Notch and receive land grant from governor. Soon Notch is established as part of trade route between coast and mountains.

1803: Road through Notch improved and becomes part of Tenth N.H. Turnpike.

1828: Notch House built by Crawford family on E side of plateau at top of Notch; opens in 1829 under management of Thomas Crawford.

1852: Crawford House opens at NE base of Mt. Tom.

1859: Crawford House burns in early spring, but new and larger hotel accommodating 400 guests is quickly built and opens in July. It becomes one of most fashionable grand hotels in White Mtns.; over the years guests include five U.S. Presidents.

1871: Party from Charles H. Hitchcock's geological survey traverses Willey Range, also ridge extending W towards Zealand Notch.

1874–1875: Portland & Ogdensburg Railroad constructs line through Crawford Notch along lower E slopes of Mts. Field and Willard, including high trestle over ravine of Willey Brook. This is one of most remarkable engineering feats of its time.

1874: Hitchcock names mountain for Darby Field; peak previously known as Mt. Lincoln.

1876: Guidebook author M. F. Sweetser says of mountain: "It is 4,400 ft. high, but possesses no interest for tourists, the top being covered with dense thickets which shut out the view." For those who venture onto the range, he advises, "Strong clothing should be worn during the exploration of this range, since any other would soon be riddled by the spruce boughs." He recommends Mt. Avalon as "a fine watch-tower from which to reconnoitre the main Mt.-Willey Range" and other scenery in the area.

1882: A. E. Scott, AMC Councilor of Improvements, leads groups of six mountain explorers over trailless peaks of Twin–Bond Range in epic week-long sojourn. On seventh day, Scott and two women members of group bushwhack up and over Mt. Field. They come up brook from North Fork, passing cascades, to swampy plateau at base of cliffs, then make steep and difficult climb to ridge over "immense fragments of rocks, covered with moss which treacherously conceals the pitfalls." From top of Field they descend precipitously NE to conclude journey atop Mt. Willard, where they meet a hundred visitors enjoying sunset views. Detailed account of journey appears in *Appalachia* in 1883.

Early 1880s: AMC proposal to build trail over mountain, linking Crawford's to Thoreau Falls region, is rejected by Crawford House management, owners of land on E side of mountain.

1886: *White Mountain Echo* reports, 'The trail to the summit of Mount Avalon and thence to the summit of Mount Field has been finally located , and men are now at work cutting it out."

1907: AMC Snow-Shoe Section hikers reach "bleak summit of Mt. Field" after arduous climb in "below zero" temperatures. "But the winter forest, vested with the charm and mystery of the white silence, was never more beautiful as our sinuous course wound in and out among the trees."

1909: First official trail to Field's wooded summit is established by Mr. and Mrs. J. A. Cruickshank. Trail leads from mountain's lower subsidiary summit, Mt. Avalon (to which trail had been built some years earlier), up to crest of Willey Range, over Field's summit, and south to Mt. Willey, where it connnects with existing trail up that peak from the S.

1919: Trail from Willey House Station in Crawford Notch, up and over Mts. Willey and Field, and down to Avalon Trail, is designated as Willey Range Trail.

1933: A–Z Trail over Field–Tom col, linking Crawford's with AMC's newly built Zealand Falls Hut, is constructed. Willey Range Trail is extended at N end from Mt. Field to Field–Tom col, while at S end, first 1.5 mi. from Willey House Station are designated as part of Ethan Pond Trail.

1938: September hurricane levels stand of virgin spruce on Crawford side of height-of-land between Mts. Field and Tom.

1941: Following outbreak of spruce bark beetle infestation, CCC crews, under direction of Forest Service, level affected trees near jct. of A–Z and Avalon Trails.

1950: November windstorm wreaks havoc on Willey Range Trail, closed until 1952.

1952: Crawford Notch State Park created.

1969: W slopes of Field are included by Forest Service in new Lincoln Woods Scenic Area.

1976: Crawford House closes doors, contents auctioned off.

1977: Crawford House destroyed in November fire.

1979: AMC acquires land around Crawford House site and develops hostel.

1984: Crawford Notch railroad line closed.

1995: Rail line reopened by Conway Scenic Railroad for tourist excursions.

2003: AMC opens new 120-bed lodge, Highland Center at Crawford Notch, on former site of Crawford House.

Trail Approaches

Northeast Approaches from US 302 at Crawford's

Avalon Trail, Willey Range Trail
5.8 mi. round trip, 2550-ft. elevation gain

TRAILHEAD (1900 ft.): The most direct ascent up Mt. Field is via the Avalon Trail, which climbs from the top of Crawford Notch to the summit in 2.8 mi. Mileage given above includes short side trip to summit of Mt. Avalon, highly recommended in clear weather. This approach starts at parking area by AMC's Highland Center on W side of US 302, 8.5 mi. E of stoplight in Twin Mountain and 0.1 mi. N of Gateway of Crawford Notch. Parking by AMC's Macomber Family Information Center (restored railroad depot that once served Crawford House) is short-term only; hikers should park nearby in the designated area.

Walk behind Macomber Family Information Center and cross railroad tracks (with caution) to start of Avalon Trail, which crosses brushy area and enters woods. At 0.1 mi. Mount Willard Trail diverges L by kiosk. Continue straight on Avalon Trail at easy grade to crossing of Crawford Brook at 0.2 mi. (potentially difficult at high water). Just beyond, loop path splits L, leading past Beecher and Pearl Cascades and rejoining main trail at 0.3 mi; this easy and scenic diversion is highly recommended on either ascent or descent. Main trail climbs moderately up wide, rocky old logging road, passing upper end of loop trail and then ledge on L with nice view of brook. Beyond, Avalon Trail swings R and up along relocated section, then dips L to cross brook at 0.8 mi. Climbing is easy to moderate, with glimpse of Mt. Avalon rearing up to L, then grade is steeper up to jct. with A–Z Trail at 1.3 mi. / 2700 ft.

Turn L here, staying with Avalon Trail. After moderate climb of 0.1 mi., trail cuts sharp L up steep scramble, then swings R for sustained steep and rocky climb through conifer forest. At top of this stiff ascent, grade eases to shallow col between two summits of Avalon. At 1.8 mi. / 3350 ft. Mount Avalon Spur Path splits L for summit, climbing steeply for ca. 0.1 mi., with ledgy scramble near top, emerging on open summit ledges with excellent views of Presidentials, Bretton Woods area, upper Willey Range, Crawford Notch and mountains to S. This side trip is highly recommended on clear day, and extra 0.2 mi. / 100 ft. is included in hike totals.

From col behind Mt. Avalon, trail runs through open flat, ledgy area with views up to Willey Range and across to Mts. Webster, Jackson and Pierce. Trail meanders into woods behind ledges, crosses tiny sag, ascends a short distance, then angles easily up to R and then to L. At ca. 3550 ft. it swings R and begins steep, rough climb up NE slope of Field with many slippery ledges and limited views back to NE. Higher up grade begins to moderate, and after obtaining partial view back to Mt. Washington, trail crosses level shoulder at 4060 ft. From here climb is at mostly easy grade to Willey Range Trail at 3.0 mi. / 4280 ft. From jct., turn L for summit, which is reached in less than 100 yds. at top of short, rocky climb. Look for views W and NW at top of steep pitch. From wooded summit clearing, marked by large cairn, short path leads to NE outlook. There is good chance of encountering gray jays here.

LOOP OPTIONS

Several loop hikes from Crawford's over Willey Range, with out-and-back jaunts to Tom and Willey, are popular with many peakbaggers. The loop over Tom and Field via Avalon Trail, A–Z Trail, Mt. Tom Spur, Willey Range Trail, and descent via Avalon Trail (with side trip to Mt. Avalon) is 7.4 mi., with a 2950-ft. elevation gain. For description of ascent to Mt. Tom via Avalon Trail, A–Z Trail and Mt. Tom Spur, see chapter on Mt. Tom. To continue to Mt. Field from jct. of A–Z Trail and Mt. Tom Spur at Field/Tom col (3700 ft.), continue 100 yards W and slightly downhill on

A–Z Trail and turn L on Willey Range Trail for easy to moderate climb up broad N ridge of Field through beautiful fir woods. Cross over flat subsidiary knob, descend easily to shallow sag, then climb a few yds. to jct. L with Avalon Trail at 0.9 mi. from A–Z Trail. Summit of Field is reached less than 100 yds. beyond, at top of short, steep pitch. The A–Z Trail approach is also a nice way to climb Field by itself: 6.4 mi. round trip, 2550-ft. elevation gain. With loop descent via Avalon Trail, including side trip to Avalon, 6.2 mi. loop, 2600-ft. elevation gain.

To reach Mt. Willey, continue S on Willey Range Trail, with three short, steep, rocky drops. Partway down, about 0.2 mi. from summit where trail hugs W side of ridge, look for nice partial SW view from blowdown patch over eastern Pemi Wilderness to Mts. Carrigain and Hancock. Reach Field–Willey col in 0.5 mi. and begin gradual, meandering ascent of Willey, passing over several knobs. Wooded summit of Willey is reached in 1.4 mi., shortly after trail swings L and up to fine W outlook over Pemi Wilderness. Excellent view to Presidentials and Crawford Notch is just beyond summit on short side path L. Return to Crawford's by way of Mts. Field and Avalon via northbound Willey Range Trail and then Avalon Trail. For loop over Tom and Field with side trip out-and-back to Mt. Willey, plus Mt. Avalon, distance is 10.2 mi. with 3550-ft. elevation gain. For Field and Willey only (plus Avalon), out-and-back hike from Crawford's is 8.6 mi. with 3200-ft. elevation gain.

South Approach off US 302 at Willey House Station

Ethan Pond Trail, Willey Range Trail
8.2 mi. round trip, 3500-ft. elevation gain

This approach includes ascent of Mt. Willey along the way, and on return trip. For trailhead directions and description of 2.7 mi. / 2850-ft. climb to Mt. Willey via Ethan Pond and Willey Range Trails, see Mt. Willey chapter. From summit of Mt. Willey, Willey Range Trail circles around past W outlook, then descends gradually N, meandering along broad wooded ridgecrest over several small knobs. Field–Willey col (3980 ft.) is reached 0.9 mi. from Willey, then trail climbs S side of Mt. Field with three short, steep pitches, passing partial view SW over Pemi Wilderness from blowdown area at ca. 1.2 mi., and attaining summit at 1.4 mi. from Willey.

Winter

A majority of winter hikers attack the summit from the N or NE from Crawford's, therefore avoiding the steep ascent of Mt. Willey from the S. Often Field is combined with Tom and / or Willey; with the increase in winter peakbagging and the opening of the Highland Center the trails on the Willey Range are frequently packed out. If ascending by way of the

Avalon Trail, take note that last half-mile of climbing up to spur trail to Mt. Avalon's summit is steep and sometimes icy. It is generally easier to ascend this stretch of trail then to descend it. The lower part of the climb up Field itself can also provide strenuous snowshoeing. Views around the summit area are improved by deep snow.

View Guide

MT. FIELD VIEW: Mt. Field's summit vista is increasingly being obscured by trees. The former view S and SW through a blowdown area is now grown up. However, as noted in trail descriptions, there is now a partial vista SW towards Mts. Carrigain and Hancock from a blowdown area along the Willey Range Trail ca. 0.2 mi. S of Mt. Field summit; this is similar to the W outlook from Mt. Willey, though from a more northerly perspective. From this area there are also peeks at Mt. Willey nearby and the Nancy and Sandwich Ranges to the S.

With a little work, a generous number of distant peaks can still be seen from two points around the summit of Field itself. From the Willey Range Trail at the top of the steep pitch a few yds. N of the summit clearing, one can see W and NW over the trees. To the W is the long spread of the Twin–Bond Range, with Mt. Bond on the L, then rounded Mt. Guyot with Mts. Lincoln and Lafayette seen over and beyond the ridgeline extending to its R. Farther R, looking W, are South and North Twin, the latter easily identified by the long slide scarring its E-facing slope. Closer in and lower, Zealand Ridge and the Zeacliffs are just S of W, under the Guyot–Twin ridge. South Hale is seen under North Twin. To the R of North Twin is its lower spur, Nubble Peak, with the Worcester Range on the horizon over Nubble Peak and Mt. Mansfield to the R. Farther R and closer is Mt. Hale, seen over the nearby N knob of Field. Mt. Tom's fir wave-striped summit is seen close by to the NNW. Between Hale and Tom is a distant view to the Jay Peaks, Burke, Umpire and Bald Mtns., and other ridges in Vermont's Northeast Kingdom, with East Haven Mtn. seen just L of Tom's summit. By moving around, you may be able to extend the view a bit to the L (SW) of Mt. Bond, spotting Bondcliff jutting off the L slope of Bond, with the Blue Ridge of Moosilauke, Whaleback Mtn., distant Smarts Mtn., and Mts. Cushman, Kineo and Carr farther to the L.

From the end of a short side trail found off the summit to the E is a nice viewpoint looking N and NE toward Bretton Woods and the mountains beyond. Mt. Tom is seen close by to the L. To the R of Tom is Cherry Mtn., with its spurs, Owl's Head and The Humps, on its R side. Vermont's East Mtn. is on the horizon between Tom and Cherry, and the sharp peak of Sable Mtn. is seen over The Humps. The long, prominent ridge of Mt. Deception sprawls to the R of Cherry, with several summits. Below the wide gap between Cherry and Deception, the red-roofed Mt. Washington Hotel and its golf course are seen down in the Bretton Woods valley. Goback Mtn. is seen in the distance in this direction, with Cape Horn much lower and in front, and farther R is West Peak in the Nash Stream region, seen over a prominent cliff in the Pilot Range and a low spur of Mt. Starr King. Next to the R is Bunnell Mtn. seen to the L of the nearer Hutchins Mtn. in the Pilot Range, with Gore Mtn. visible to the R of Hutchins. Next to the R and closer, Mts. Starr King and Waumbek rise above the L end of Mt. Deception. Mt. Cabot peers over just L of Waumbek's summit. Off the R end of Waumbek's long E ridge are Pliny Mtn. (L) and North Weeks (R). Mt. Dartmouth is to the R of Deception, with a broad gap between them, over which is seen Deer Mtn. in the Kilkenny area. On the horizon in this direction are Cave, Rice, Crystal and Tucker Mtns. and other ridges to the E of Dixville Notch. The Crescent Range, with double-humped Black Crescent Mtn. prominent, is seen behind and R of Dartmouth; Aziscohos Mtn. and other distant peaks in NE New Hampshire and NW Maine are beyond. Looking down, one can see ledge-spotted Mt. Avalon poking up from Field's NE slope. Over the gap to the R of Black Crescent is the flat Cambridge Black Mtn. Farther R, looking NE, and partly screened by trees, are the mighty Presidentials, including (L to R) Mts. Jefferson and Adams, Mt. Clay, Mt. Washington, Mt. Monroe above Mt. Eisenhower, and Boott Spur above Mt. Pierce.

MT. AVALON VIEW: The open ledges atop Avalon provide a near 360-degree view that features the Presidential Range, Crawford Notch and the nearby higher peaks of the Willey Range. You must stand and move around a bit to see the entire view. Close at hand is the looming wooded summit of Mt. Field to the SW, with Mt. Willey peeking out on the L. Mt. Tom's rounded peak is seen just a mile away to the NW. To the R of Tom is a distant view out to peaks in Vermont's Northeast Kingdom, including prominent East Mtn. with a building (an abandoned Air Force base) on top. To the NNW is Cherry Mtn., with the knobs of Owl's Head and The Humps to the R of the main summit. To the R of Cherry is the gap of Cherry Mountain Notch, with the red-roofed Mt. Washington Hotel and its golf course in front. Goback Mtn. in the Nash Stream region is seen in the distance on the R side of the notch. To the R of the notch is the long crest of Mt. Deception, with several rounded summits. Mt. Starr King is seen over the slope to the L of Deception's westernmost summit. To the R of Deception Mt. Dartmouth is seen beyond the broad intervale of Bretton Woods. Next to the R the view of the Presidentials begins with Mt. Jefferson, with the Castellated Ridge extending down to its L. The double summit of Mt. Clay is to the R of Jefferson, and farther R, to the NE, is the dominant summit of Mt. Washington. In this direction down on the plateau of Crawford's are the AMC's Highland

Center complex, Rt. 302 and Saco Lake. To the R of Washington is a foreshortened view of other Presidential peaks: the sharp crest of Monroe, Eisenhower's bald dome, Boott Spur peering over in back, and the double wooded hump of Pierce. Slide Peak is seen in back to the R of Pierce. Just S of E and less than three miles away across upper Crawford Notch is the small, bare peak of Mt. Jackson, topping a massive wooded ridge.

To the R of Jackson the ridge runs across to the craggy summit of Mt. Webster, with the low, rounded crest of Mt. Willard seen below. Extending R from Webster is the impressive line of the Webster Cliffs, forming the E wall of Crawford Notch. Over the R end of the cliffs are the tip of Stairs Mtn. and the broad mass of Mt. Resolution. Looking SE there is a striking view down into the depths of Crawford Notch, with several peaks arrayed beyond. From Mt. Resolution the Bemis Ridge extends R over Crawford Dome to the sharp rock peak of Mt. Crawford. North Moat Mtn. juts up behind and R of Mt. Crawford, with the several summits of Big Attitash Mtn. extending to its R. To the R of Big Attitash, Table Mtn. is seen above Mt. Hope, with the level wooded crest of Frankenstein Cliff underneath and closer, forcing the Notch to curve around to the L. Green Mtn. in Effingham is seen on the horizon to the R of Table, with White Ledge below, peering over the col to the R of Table. Next to the R is the high crest of Bear Mtn., and farther R, just off the L slope of the Willey Range, the Three Sisters and Mt. Chocorua's spiry peak are seen above the summit of Bartlett Haystack.

NO. OF 4000-FOOTERS VISIBLE: 28 (from Mt. Field, partly through the trees)

Mount Hale

ELEVATION: 4054 ft. / 1236 m   ORDER OF HEIGHT: 38
LOCATION: Little River Range, Town of Bethlehem
USGS MAPS: 7½′ South Twin Mtn., 7½′ Crawford Notch

Geography

At just over 4000 ft. in elevation, Mt. Hale is the highest of the peaks comprising the Little River Mountains, a minor range that extends N from Zealand Ridge to the three low Sugarloaves rising out of the Ammonoosuc River valley near the village of Twin Mountain. The Little River valley separates this range from the higher Twin Range to the W.

Hale's broad, flat summit, once the site of a firetower, is an open clearing, though surrounding tree growth has obscured what were once excellent views. Just to the N is a slightly lower secondary summit. Hale's sprawling mass features several other lower subsidiary summits, none, however, accessible by trail. From the main summit, these peaks extend to the N, E and S, along with lesser ridges extending NW and W.

The ridge connecting the three Sugarloaves—North (2310 ft.), Middle (2539 ft.) and South (3024 ft.)—leads progressively up to Hale's main summit ridge. North and Middle Sugarloaf are accessible by the Sugarloaf Trail and offer fine views, including Mt. Hale's N ridges, from their bare tops. South Sugarloaf is occasionally explored by trampers and its partially open summit offers unique views into the Zealand River and Mt. Tom Brook valleys. Hale's 3740-ft. North Peak sports several sets of small cliffs extending down towards South Sugarloaf. A massive, steep-sided east spur of Hale (3460 ft.) juts out toward the broad Zealand valley and features a bald, burned crown and talus slopes along its base. To the S, the mountain's ridge extends gradually downward to the heavily wooded valley at the northern base of Zealand Mtn. A long, flat S shoulder of Mt. Hale is crossed by the Lend-a-Hand Trail, a footpath connecting the main summit to the AMC's Zealand Falls Hut. Farther S a separate 3700-ft. spur, with three flattish summits, rises to the W of this trail, continuing the Little River Mountains towards the N spur of Zealand Mountain. This is one of New Hampshire's 100 Highest peaks, and is commonly known as "South Hale," "North Zealand," or "Zeale"—a hybrid of Mts. Zealand and Hale, but also perhaps a nod to ardent peakbaggers. Two other spur ridges of Hale extend NW and W towards the Little River valley.

Mt. Hale is surrounded on three sides by deep river valleys, including the Ammonoosuc River to the N, the Zealand River to the E and the Little River to the W. Both the Zealand and Little Rivers flow northward into the larger Ammonoosuc. Smaller streams draining the slopes of Hale include Tuttle Brook on the N, Hale Brook on the NE, and Hoxie Brook on the SE.

In the aftermath of two great forest fires that struck the Zealand area in 1886 and 1903, vast stands of white birch trees sprouted up on all flanks of the mountain. Today these mature birches constitute one of the largest and most spectacular such stands in all the Whites, and are particularly notable when ascending the mountain on either the Hale Brook Trail or the former firewarden's road. (This abandoned trail passes through an especially majestic birch stand and is ascended fairly frequently both by hikers in summer and backcountry skiers in winter. In the interest of preventing overuse, it will not be described here.)

As is the case with several 4000-footers, Hale's summit vista has deteriorated over the years, to the point that by 2007 there was virtually no view at all. Where once the summit offered nearly unobstructed views towards the majestic peaks of the Presidential Range and perfectly aligned Zealand and Carrigain Notches, trees now block nearly all of the view,

A hiker holding a compass checks out the magnetic rocks found at the summit of Mount Hale.

even from atop the five-foot high summit cairn. Ironically, all of Hale's major spur peaks and ridges feature fine outlooks, including one looking S just off the Lend-a-Hand Trail on the flat S shoulder. The rest of the spur viewpoints are accessible only to seasoned bushwackers. Of particular note are the views of Zealand and Carrigain Notches from the bald E spur, the vista up the Little River valley from ledges on the W and NW ridges, the Presidental Range panorama from the cliffs of the N peak, and views both E and W from clifftops on the edge of "Zeale."

In lieu of spectacular views, the summit does possess one unique feature among White Mountain peaks. Many of the volcanic rocks which litter the mountaintop are magnetic. A compass placed next to one of these stones will go haywire and no longer point N.

Nomenclature

The mountain is named in honor of Rev. Edward Everett Hale (1822–1909), a Boston Congregational minister, avid White Mountain explorer, writer, and author of the classic American short story, *A Man Without a Country*. Hale, who late in his life was a member of the fledgling conservation organization, the Society for the Protection of New Hampshire Forests, undertook many of his ventures into the White Mountains in the company of state geologist Dr. Charles T. Jackson. It was one of Jackson's successors, geologist Charles Hitchcock, who in 1874 chose to name the mountain after Rev. Hale. The Lend-a-Hand Trail was named after a journal for charitable organizations that was edited by Rev. Hale.

Historical Highlights

First Ascent: Unknown

1874: State Geologist Charles Hitchcock, in Vol. 1 of his massive three-volume *Geology of New Hampshire*, notes that the peak he has named Mt. Hale "is sometimes confounded with the Twin Mountains, because only one of the Twins is seen from the hotel named after them."

1881: Moses Sweetser's guidebook describes Hale as "fine wooded peak . . . usually called . . . one of the Twins."

1883: Eugene B. Cook, described by authors Laura and Guy Waterman as "one of the most indefatigable explorers of the 1870–1880's," makes "a solitary pilgrimage to the arcana of Mt. Hale" in late July, starting from Twin Mountain House. He follows woods roads through extensive logging on lower slopes, then ascends over several subsidiary summits. He finds summit wooded, but with some open spots that permit views, and measures elevation of 4198 ft. with his barometer. Cook writes account for December 1883 issue of *Appalachia*.

1885: Lumber baron J. E. Henry begins construction of logging rail line into Zealand River valley E of mountain.

1886: Sparks from passing train engine touch off devastating Zealand Valley forest fire that sweeps over Sugarloaves and nearby summits of Rosebrook Range.

1893: Nineteenth-century timber king George Van Dyke begins logging railroad operations in Little River valley, W of Mt. Hale.

1903: Second forest fire in Zealand area burns over 10,000 acres of forestland, including slopes of Mt. Hale.

1907: AMC guidebook describes Mt. Hale as "a desolate, burned wilderness."

1925: Though no description is provided, map in *AMC Guide* indicates existence of path from Little River to summit. Subsequent edition of guide says route is via old lumber road, and that "outlook from peak is unobstructed and includes remarkable view of Zealand Notch, and in line directly beyond, Carrigain Notch."

1928: U.S. Forest Service erects steel fire lookout tower on main summit. Becomes operational the following year, and remains in use through 1948. Tower is accessed by Mt. Hale Trail (aka Firewarden's Trail), 6–10 foot wide tractor road from Little River valley to NW.

1934: AMC blazes new Lend-a-Hand Trail up S ridge of Hale to provide interesting side trip for guests staying at recently opened Zealand Falls Hut. Trail is described in December 1934 *Appalachia* by Harland P. Sisk, Councillor of Trails. He notes that from cliffs at end of S shoulder "the tramper has one of the finest views in the mountains," including unusual angle on Zealand and Carrigain Notches "in perfect alignment." From there to summit trail is mostly in open. Sisk recommends trampers stay extra night at hut "to enjoy an easy and pleasant day on Mt. Hale."

1936: WMNF has opened Hale Brook Trail from Zealand Valley and Tuttle Brook Trail from Twin Mountain village; mountain is now accessible by four routes.

1940: *AMC Guide* notes that tractor road (Mt. Hale Tr.) from Little River affords "excellent ski run" for intermediate skiers.

Early 1960s: Tuttle Brook Trail and Mt. Hale Trail are now abandoned.

1972: Fire tower atop summit is dismantled by Forest Service. All that remains are concrete support piers, including one inscribed with the date 10–17–28.

Trail Approaches

Northeast Approach from Zealand Road (FR 16)

Hale Brook Trail
4.4 mi. round-trip, 2300-ft. elevation gain

TRAILHEAD (1770 ft.): Hale Brook Trail begins at small parking area on R (W) side of Zealand Road, 2.5 mi. from US 302; Zealand Rd. leaves S side of US 302 2.2 mi. E of stoplight in Twin Mountain. This trail provides the quickest and easiest ascent of Hale, which is considered one of the least difficult of the 4000-footers. Ascending on mostly moderate, steady grades, it climbs the mountain's NE slopes. Trail starts briefly on easy grade, soon crossing backcountry ski trail, then ascends moderately through hardwoods with recently logged areas noticeable on R. At ca. 0.6 mi. Hale Brook is heard on R. Trail then steepens and at 0.8 mi./2460 ft. stream is crossed just above smooth water chute, also on R.

Yellow-blazed trail climbs steadily up and away from stream. Passing through glade of white birches, grade lessens and trail narrows on steep sidehill high above brook. At 1.3 mi./3000 ft. trail makes rocky recrossing of Hale Brook. Following L turn at stream crossing, trail snakes its way up via series of switchbacks leading to plateau connecting main and east ridges. Trail is rockier and footing trickier for next 0.2 mi., then at R turn grade steepens for final 0.3 mi. march to summit through nice fir forest. At 2.0 mi. opening in blowdown area on L provides view SE to Mt. Willey, West Peak of Mt. Field, and distant North Moat Mtn., and summit clearing is reached at 2.2 mi./4054 ft.

South Approach from Zealand Falls Hut

Twinway, Lend-a-Hand Trail
5.6 mi. round-trip, 1300-ft elevation gain

Mt. Hale's alternative ascent route is the Lend-a-Hand Trail, which starts from the Twinway 0.1 mi. above AMC's Zealand Falls Hut and leads 2.7 mi. NW to the summit. This trail, in conjunction with the Hale Brook, Twinway and Zealand Trails, and Zealand Rd., provides a comfortable loop hike over Mt. Hale and through the scenic Zealand River valley. Grades on the Lend-a-Hand Trail are mostly easy with a few steeper pitches, though the footing is often fairly rough. It is an interesting, varied and remote trail with one nice view on a side path and other limited views from a ledgy area. Trail takes its name from journal for charitiable organizations that Rev. Hale (the mountain's namesake) once edited.

Lend-a-Hand Trail begins 0.1 mi. above hut, branching off from Twinway (link in Appalachian Trail) at 2730 ft. It ascends moderately to W, soon crosses tributary of Whitewall Brook, then ascends steadily through birch forest. Grade soon eases and trail crosses another brook. At ca. 0.6 mi. from hut trail swings more to N and begins gradual traverse through boggy conifer forest, with many plank walkways over wet areas. Open bog is passed on R, then trail returns to deeper mixed woods with continuing easy grades but rocky footing in places. Moderate climbing leads up to scrubby, ledgy plateau at 1.6 mi. / 3400 ft. Through and over the trees are limited views SE to Zealand Notch and Nancy Range and SW to Zealand Mtn. Better view can be obtained from top of large but slightly tippy boulder on L. Close by on L, but well off marked trail, is inviting crag on Hale's southernmost spur ridge, known as "South Hale" or "Zeale."

Following steeper and fairly rocky climb, second, higher set of semi-open ledges is reached at 2.0 mi. / 3720 ft. Short side path R (E) leads 15 yds. up to ledge with overgrown view, then drops off rock and leads another 15 yds. to opening with beautiful view of Zealand and Carrigain Notches and Mts. Anderson, Lowell and Carrigain. Short bushwhack down through scrub in front expands view to include Willey Range and Zealand Ridge. Next 0.5 mi. on main trail is on gentle grade, up at first, then with slight descent followed by level stretch leading along flat shoulder through scrubby growth of fir, spruce and birch. At 2.5 mi. trail pitches up again with rocky footing, passing interesting miniature birch forest. Trail then eases on another shoulder just S of summit and meanders gently upward through beautiful open fir forest. One short final pitch leads to summit clearing at 2.8 mi. / 4054 ft.

LOOP OPTION
8.7 mi. loop, 2300-ft. elevation gain
The Hale Brook / Lend-a-Hand loop hike usually begins with ascent of

mountain via Hale Brook Trail. From summit, it's 2.8 mi. down to AMC hut (2630 ft.), then steep 0.2 mile descent from hut to jct. of Ethan Pond and Zealand Trails (2460 ft.). Turn L onto Zealand Trail and follow it past series of beaver ponds and along former Zealand Valley Railroad grade. In 2.5 easy mi., trail ends at Zealand Trail parking lot. Follow unpaved Zealand Road 1.0 mi. downhill back to Hale Brook Trail parking area. For details on Zealand Trail, see chapter on Zealand Mtn.

Winter

While the hike up Hale is considered among the easiest in summer and fall, it is a different story in winter. Because Zealand Road is closed to motor vehicle traffic in winter, any effort to reach the mountain by the popular Hale Brook Trail means an additional 2.7 mi. of road walking each way. (Park at the large parking lot on the N side of US 302, 0.2 mi. E of Zealand Rd. Parking is not allowed at the base of Zealand Rd.) The cushy 2.2-mi. one-way summer jaunt is stretched to 4.9 mi. A 4.4 mi. round-trip hike is suddenly an epic 9.8 mi. battle.

Snowshoers can also expect some difficulty traversing the birch-lined quarter-mile section of the Hale Brook Trail approaching the second crossing of the stream. This steeply side-sloping stretch is particularly hazardous when the snow cover is crusty or hard-packed. Care must be taken not to lose one's footing and slide precariously down the steep slope into the brook valley.

Winter trampers who reach the summit do enjoy one advantage over summer trekkers. In a good snow year, a hiker on the mountaintop is elevated several feet higher than normal and is able to see over and above the growing trees which surround the summit area.

View Guide

SUMMIT VIEW: Not many years ago Hale was considered an excellent open viewpoint, with clear views of the Twin Range, Mts. Hancock and Carrigain, Zealand and Carrigain Notches, the Nancy Range, the Willey Range and the Presidentials. But over the last three decades tree growth around the fringes of the flat summit has been slowly choking off the panorama. Now you have to stand atop the summit cairn to get even a smidgen of a view. The one minor vista still available on the ground is found by following a narrow overgrown path 25 yds. from the W side of the summit clearing to a small opening with a framed view of the nearby massive peak of North Twin.

The view obtained by standing atop the summit cairn takes in the nearby and higher peaks of the Twin Range to the SW and part of the Willey Range to the ESE. Looking SW, North Twin is easy to identify with an impressive slide scarring its upper reaches. To the L of North Twin is massive South Twin, crowned with a tiny rock peak, and beyond that its connecting ridge with Mt. Guyot. Mt. Bond is just visible over the treetops behind and L of Guyot. The rest of the view to the S has been obscured by the trees save for a slight glimpse of Mt. Carrigain. To the ESE, pointed Mt. Willey and Mt. Field, Willey's near neighbor on the L, can be seen rising above the trees. The low rounded spur known as West Field is seen to the R of and below Willey, with the craggy little peak of Mt. Crawford jutting out behind its L slope. The Saddleback Hills in western Maine can be seen on the distant horizon beyond Crawford, and the Burnt Meadow Mtns. are visible in the distance to the R of West Field. To the L of Willey and Field the very tops of Mts. Tom, Jackson, Pierce and Washington are barely visible. In other directions, there are peeks through gaps in the trees at Mt. Deception and the Crescent Range to the NE and at East Mtn. and Burke Mtn. in Vermont to the NW. Enjoy what few views there are now—in 20 years even these may be gone.

VIEWPOINT OFF LEND-A-HAND TRAIL: For years this vista at the S end of the flat 3700-ft. S shoulder of Hale was obtained from a ledge on a side path 15 yds. E of the Lend-a-Hand Trail as it ascends through an area of semi-open ledges. The view from this rock is now mostly overgrown, but fortunately the path continues another 15 yds. E to an opening with a fine (though not panoramic) stand-up view S. The main feature of the view is a picturesque look at Carrigain Notch through the W side of Zealand Notch. On the L are the sharp wooded peaks of Mt. Anderson and Mt. Lowell, with Mt. Chocorua's rocky crest seen through the deep saddle between them. Carrigain Notch is to the R of Lowell, with northern spurs of Mt. Paugus seen beyond the U-shaped gap. Vose Spur forms the R side of Carrigain Notch, and to the R of the notch Mt. Carrigain's massive profile rises above the flat E end of Zealand Ridge, which drops steeply on the L to form the W wall of Zealand Notch. A short but fairly thick bushwhack of ca. 100 ft. down in front of this viewpoint expands the view to include all of Zealand Notch and the Nancy and Willey Ranges on the L. Whitewall Mtn. forms the L (E) wall of Zealand Notch, with Mts. Nancy and Bemis beyond on the L. Farther L Big Attitash Mtn. and North Moat are seen beyond the low, broad ridge that extends N from the Nancy Range. Next to the L Mt. Crawford and Crawford Dome rise beyond and between two western spurs of Mt. Field. The Saddleback Hills in Maine are seen in the distance to the R of Mt. Crawford. On the far L are the higher peaks of Mt. Willey and Mt. Field. By moving around one can also expand the view to the R to include all of Zealand Ridge and the nearby cliff-faced hump of South Hale.

NO. OF 4000-FOOTERS VISIBLE: 23 from summit (now partly theoretical)

Mount Tom

ELEVATION: 4051 ft./1235 m   ORDER OF HEIGHT: 40
LOCATION: Willey Range, Town of Bethlehem
USGS MAP: 7½′ Crawford Notch

Geography

Rounded and wooded to the top, Mt. Tom is the northernmost and lowest of the three high peaks of the Willey Range. It's one of the easier 4000-footers to climb, and its once limited views W and S into the Zealand and Pemigewasset Wilderness areas have been expanded in recent years by a summit fir wave blowdown patch. Another fir wave blowdown area now provides a view E and S towards the Presidentials and Crawford Notch.

To the S a 3700-ft. col separates Tom from neighboring Mt. Field. To the N the ridgecrest descends over two wooded humps, then continues several miles NNW as the rather level Rosebrook Range, which includes Mt. Echo (3084 ft.), Mt. Stickney (3043 ft.), Mt. Rosebrook (3004 ft.) and Mt. Oscar (2746 ft.). Other ridges run NW and NE from the summit.

To the W the mountain's slopes descend rather gently into the valley of the Zealand River. Mt. Tom Brook drains the area N of the summit, between Tom's NW ridge and the Rosebrook Range, while Mt. Field Brook flows from the broad basin on the W side of the mountain; both streams descend NW to the Zealand River. On the E is Crawford's, the small plateau just N of the gateway of Crawford Notch; tiny Ammonoosuc Lake is nestled here at the NE base of the mountain. From Crawford's Tom looms as a fairly impressive mountain, displaying a wooded cirque-like valley with a steep headwall beneath the Tom–Field col; this E-facing valley is drained by Crawford Brook, with the NE ridge of Tom bordering the basin on the N. On the lower part of this brook are the attractive Beecher and Pearl Cascades.

Nomenclature

The mountain was named for Thomas J. Crawford, one of the legendary family that opened up the Crawford Notch region to visitors in the early and mid 1800s. Thomas was one of Abel Crawford's six sons, and among his brothers was the famed "giant of the mountains," Ethan Allen Crawford. From 1829–1852 Thomas ran the Notch House, a hostelry on the plateau beneath his namesake mountain. Here he entertained famous guests such as Henry David Thoreau and Francis Parkman. He also improved the Crawford Path (originally built by Abel and Ethan in 1819) to a bridle path in 1840, and in 1846 he built a carriage road up Mt. Willard, a low spur of Mt. Field with a dramatic view of Crawford Notch. Thomas' name had actually been given to this mountain by Professor Edward Tuckerman, but Thomas himself renamed the lower peak after one of his guests. Thomas died in 1865, and in 1876 state geologist Charles H. Hitchcock bestowed Crawford's name on the 4000-footer in the Willey Range.

Historical Highlights

First Ascent: Unknown.

1828: Notch House built by Crawford family on E side of Crawford's plateau; opens in 1829 under management of Thomas Crawford.

1852: Crawford House opens at NE base of Mt. Tom.

1859: Crawford House burns in April, but new and larger hotel accommodating 400 guests is quickly built and opens in July. It becomes one of most fashionable grand hotels in White Mtns.; over the years guests include five U.S. Presidents.

Early 1870s: Charles H. Hitchcock ascends Mt. Tom three times during field work for state geological survey. Applies name, "Mt. Anadalusite," to a NE knob of mountain, after a rock found there by two Dartmouth student assistants. He also traverses Rosebrook Range to N. Names main peak "Mt. Tom" in final report.

1876: Moses Sweetser's guidebook describes route to summit of Tom roughly equivalent to today's trail route, and laments lack of view from top.

1885: Path is marked from Crawford House to summit, first following trail towards Mt. Avalon, then climbing up Tom's NE ridge. *White Mountain Echo* reports "many new views of great beauty are now obtainable from the mountain top. That of Carrigian Notch and the great wilderness of the Pemigewasset valley is particularly fine."

1890: Rev. Julius Ward's book, *The White Mountains: A Guide to Their Interpretation*, describes ascent of Mt. Tom. "It is here," writes Ward, "that one feels the richness of the touches of nature."

1890s: Trail network is developed on Rosebrook Range to NW, including connector trail leaving NE ridge of Tom, skirting slope at 3000-ft. level and passing Stump Spring, a col called Hunter's Hollow, and a knob known as San Juan Hill.

1907: First AMC trail guide describes Mt. Tom trail as "much neglected" above jct. with Rosebrook Range trail. By 1928 upper portion is deemed too obscure to follow.

1933: A–Z Trail built over Field–Tom col to connect Crawford's with AMC's newly built Zealand Falls Hut. Willey Range Trail is extended N from Mt. Field to Field–Tom col. 1934 AMC guide notes that Tom can be climbed without trail from col.

The Willey Range—including Mounts Willey, Field, and Tom—form the western wall of well-known Crawford Notch.

1938: Hurricane devastates trails on Rosebrook Range; they are soon abandoned. Stand of virgin spruce on E side of Field–Tom col is also leveled by hurricane.

Late 1950s: After creation of 4000-Footer Club, increased interest in climbing Tom leads to development of rough blazed trail to summit.

Late 1960s: Mt. Tom Spur is officially adopted as AMC trail.

Ca. 1970: Owners of Crawford House contemplate developing ski area on slopes of Tom, inviting Olympic skier Tom Corcoran (developer of Waterville Valley Ski Area) to look over site. Project never advances beyond speculative stage.

1976: Crawford House closes doors, contents auctioned off.

1977: Crawford House destroyed in November fire.

1979: AMC acquires land around Crawford House site and develops hostel.

2003: AMC opens new 120-bed lodge, Highland Center at Crawford Notch, on former site of Crawford House.

Trail Approaches

East Approach from US 302 at Crawford's

Avalon Trail, A–Z Trail, Mt. Tom Spur
5.8 mi. round trip, 2250-ft. elevation gain

TRAILHEAD (1900 ft.): This approach starts at parking area by AMC Highland Center on W side of US 302, 8.5 mi. E of stoplight in Twin Mountain and 0.1 mi. N of Gateway of Crawford Notch.

The usual approach to Mt. Tom is a moderate climb, much of it through open, attractive woods. Walk behind Macomber Family Information Center and cross railroad tracks (with caution) to start of Avalon Trail, which crosses brushy area and enters woods. At 0.1 mi. Mount Willard Trail diverges L by kiosk. Continue straight on Avalon Trail at easy grade to crossing of Crawford Brook at 0.2 mi. (potentially difficult at high water). Just beyond, loop path splits L, leading past Beecher and Pearl Cascades and rejoining main trail at 0.3 mi; this easy and scenic diversion is highly recommended on either ascent or descent. Main trail climbs moderately up wide, rocky old logging road, passing upper end of loop trail and then ledge on L with nice view of brook. Beyond, Avalon Trail swings R and up along relocated section, then dips L to cross brook at 0.8 mi. Climbing is easy to moderate, with glimpse of Mt. Avalon rearing up to L, then grade is steeper up to jct. with A–Z Trail at 1.3 mi. / 2700 ft.

Stay straight on yellow-blazed A–Z (Avalon–Zealand) Trail as Avalon Trail branches L. Cross down-and-up through steep stream gully and climb steadily, high up on S side of beautiful cirque-like valley through open mixed forest with large yellow birches. Mt. Tom's NE ridge is seen across valley to R. At 1.9 mi. / 3300 ft., just after sidehill section, trail dips to recross brook, now quite small, and turns sharp R to slab rather steeply up rock steps on headwall of valley through fir forest. Swing L for final easier climb to Field–Tom col and jct. with Mt. Tom Spur, reached at 2.3 mi. / 3700 ft.

Turn R on Mt. Tom Spur. (A–Z Trail continues 100 yds. ahead to Willey Range Trail, then begins descent to Zealand valley.) Climb is easy, then moderate, with one steep rocky pitch, along narrow, wild ridge trail, mostly along W side of crest. Look back for occasional views from open blowdown patches towards Mt. Field and Pemi Wilderness. Swing R and L and climb to small false summit, where side trail leads 250 ft. R to open blowdown area with bench and good views E and S. Main trail bears L here and in 200 ft. reaches clearing at true summit at 2.9 mi. / 4051 ft. Good view W and S from open blowdown area in front; highest point seems to be a short distance to R (N).

Loop hikes from Crawford's over the Willey Range, with out-and-back jaunts to Tom and Willey, are popular with many peakbaggers. These include: a loop over Tom and Field via Avalon Trail, A–Z Trail, Mt. Tom Spur, Willey Range Trail, and descent via Avalon Trail: 7.4 mi., 2950-ft. elevation gain; and a loop over Tom and Field with side trip to Willey on Willey Range Trail: 10.2 mi., 3550-ft. elevation gain. Both of these include short side trip to Mt. Avalon.

Another option for the three Willey Range peaks is a point-to-point hike with a car spot. The easier route is to start at Crawford's and use the Avalon Trail, A–Z Trail, Mt. Tom Spur, Willey Range Trail and Ethan Pond Trail down to its trailhead at the Willey House Station site: 8.5 mi., 3150-ft. elevation gain. In the reverse direction the hike is 8.5 mi. with 3600-ft. elevation gain.

West Approach from Zealand Rd. and Zealand Trail

Zealand Trail, A–Z Trail, Mt. Tom Spur

From Zealand Rd.: 11.2 mi. round trip, 2250-ft. elevation gain
  (including 100 ft. on return trip)
From Zealand Falls Hut: 7.6 mi. round trip, 2000-ft. elevation gain
  (including 300 ft. on return trip)

Mt. Tom can be climbed from the W via the A–Z Trail from its jct. with Zealand Trail, 2.3 mi. from end of Zealand Rd. This point is 0.5 mi. below AMC Zealand Falls Hut via Twinway and Zealand Trail. See chapter on Zealand Mtn. for details on Zealand Trail. From A–Z / Zealand jct. (2450 ft.), follow A–Z Trail to E as it skirts beaver pond with view across to ledgy E peak of Mt. Hale. Trail soon rises easily through forest of white birch and red maple. At 0.7 mi. from Zealand Trail it makes short descent to cross brook. On far side it rises steeply for short distance, then ascends moderately through beautiful birch forest, crossing several small brooks. At 1.3 mi. from Zealand Trail (2980 ft.), shortly after leaving birch forest, trail traverses semi-open bog on log bridges, with view back to South Twin, and crosses muddy snowmobile trail. You then enjoy long stretch of level to slightly downhill walking through open fir forest. At 1.9 mi. cross branch of Mt. Field Brook, and after 0.2 mi. through dense, blowdown-strewn woods, cross main brook. Trail soon recrosses snowmobile trail, climbs moderately to L turn where mossy cascade issues from ledges on R, then ascends steeply with rocky footing to reach Field–Tom col and jct. R with Willey Range Trail at 2.7 mi. / 3700 ft. Mt. Tom Spur is on L 100 yds. ahead on A–Z Trail; proceed to summit at 3.3 mi. / 4051 ft.

Strong hikers can use this route to climb all three Willey Range peaks in a day from the Zealand Trail trailhead. By following the Willey Range Trail out to Mt. Willey and then returning over Mt. Field to the A–Z Trail, the hike is 15.8 mi. round trip with 3550-ft. elevation gain. From Zealand Hut, this is 12.2 mi. round trip with 3300-ft. elevation gain.

For a very scenic loop returning through Zealand Notch, from Mt. Willey (8.5 mi.) follow the Willey Range Trail down to the Ethan Pond Trail at 9.6 mi. / 2680 ft. Turn R on the Ethan Pond Trail, climb over a height-of-land, and descend gently onto the vast spruce-wooded, boggy plateau in the upper basin of the Pemi East Branch's North Fork. At 10.6 mi. / 2860 ft. pass side trail R to Ethan Pond (extra 0.2 mi. round trip, but well worth it for the imposing view up to the looming Mt. Willey and distant view out to the Twin Range). Shoal Pond Trail diverges L at 12.6 mi. / 2500 ft. After crossing bridge over North Fork, pass jct. L with Thoreau Falls Trail at 13.1 mi. / 2460 ft. (0.2 mi. round trip side jaunt to broad ledge at top of Thoreau Falls is also very rewarding, with fine view of Mts. Bond and Guyot and Zealand Ridge.) From this jct., Ethan Pond Trail, following old grade of Zealand valley logging railroad, curves into Zealand Notch, breaking into open with great views of cliffs and talus slopes of notch along with Mts. Carrigan, Hancock and Hale. At 13.9 mi. pass jct. L with Zeacliff Trail, then enter birch woods and continue at easy grade to meet Zealand Trail and Twinway at 15.2 mi. Continue ahead on Zealand Trail back to trailhead. Total for loop is 17.7 mi. with 3350-ft. elevation gain, not including side trips to Ethan Pond and Thoreau Falls. From Zealand Hut, loop is 13.7 mi. with 3100-ft. elevation gain.

Winter

Mt. Tom is a fine winter climb with mostly moderate snowshoeing grades and little exposure to weather. Plenty of plowed parking is available near the AMC Highland Center or across from the Webster–Jackson trailhead a short distance further east on US 302, just before the Gateway to Crawford Notch. The most difficult spots are the steep down-and-up gully above the Avalon / A–Z junction, the sharp sidehill approaching the upper crossing of Crawford Brook, and the climb up the headwall of the valley. In deep unbroken snow both A–Z Trail and Mt. Tom Spur may be difficult to follow; the latter may require much branch-banging, but is a winter wonderland setting. With a deep snow platform the views from the blowdown areas along Mt. Tom Spur and the summit fir waves are even better.

View Guide

Tom has never been noted as an outstanding viewpoint, but in recent years the blowdown / fir wave areas at and near the summit have provided views W and S over the Zealand and Pemi Wilderness areas and E and S towards the Presidentials and Crawford Notch.

W/S VIEW FROM SUMMIT CLEARING: After being quite open for a number of years, the blowdown area by the summit clearing is starting to grow up with scrub in the natural process of fir wave regeneration. The views are still good, but require standing for the best perspective. On the far L nearby Mt. Field is seen through the trees. To the S, beyond Field's lower W spurs and the rolling uplands of the eastern Pemi, are (L to R) Mts. Nancy, Anderson and Lowell (with Mt. Shaw of the Ossipee Range in the distance through the Nancy–Anderson col), majestic Mt. Carrigain (above West Field, with Vose Spur and Carrigain Notch to its L), and the long ridges of Mt. Hancock, with its hidden N valleys well displayed, especially the Crystal Brook basin to the R of North Hancock's dome. Mts. Passaconaway (L, over Mt. Lowell) and Whiteface (R) are seen through Carrigain Notch, and Sandwich Dome peers over the E side of Mt. Kancamagus between Carrigain and Hancock. Mt. Osceola and its Middle and West Peaks poke above the ridge between North Hancock and NW Hancock, and farther R the various summits of Scar Ridge are seen on either side of Mt. Hitchcock, with Loon Mtn. to the R. Stinson Mtn. is seen in the distance to the R of the main Scar Ridge summit. The E ridge of Mt. Kineo and part of Mt. Cushman are seen behind Loon to the R.

To the SW, beyond the backside of Whitewall Mtn., is the great bulk of Mt. Bond, showing a bare E shoulder, with Mt. Guyot to the R above the Zeacliffs and Zealand Ridge. A long, high ridge runs from Guyot across to the small peak of South Twin and slide-scarred North Twin. On clear days Camel's Hump in Vermont can be spotted to the R of North Twin. The upper Zealand valley, including Zealand Falls and the nearby AMC hut, is seen below, and Mt. Hale is to the far R.

E/S VIEW FROM SPUR PATH: This path diverges off the Mt. Tom Spur a short distance before the viewpoint by the true summit. This is now probably Tom's best viewpoint. By moving up and down along the end of this path, views can be obtained from NE around to SW. On the far L, partly screened by snags, are the Presidentials, including Mts. Jefferson, Clay, Washington, Monroe and Eisenhower. Boott Spur rises in back to the R. Farther R are Mts. Pierce and Jackson, with Mt. Isolation (L) and Mt. Davis (R) seen between and behind them. A northern peak of Rocky Branch Ridge is visible behind Isolation on the L. To the R of Jackson are Mt. Webster and the great slabs of the Webster Cliffs. Kearsarge North pops out to the R of Webster's summit, with its spur, Bartlett Mtn., on the R, and close by Mt. Avalon's knob is seen, far below the ridge between Jackson and Webster. Part of Pleasant Mtn. is seen between Kearsarge North and Bartlett. Farther R and beyond the Webster Cliffs is the wooded peak of Stairs Mtn., with Black Cap Mtn. seen over its long L slope. Flat-topped Mt. Resolution is to the R of Stairs, and distant Douglas Mtn. in Maine is seen between them. From Resolution a ridge leads across to the sharp rock knob of Mt. Crawford, just off the L slope of nearby Mt. Field. Mt. Parker peers over the middle of the Resolution–Crawford ridge, and the Burnt Meadow Mtns. in Maine are in the distance, over the swell of Crawford Dome. Flat-topped Little Attitash Mtn. is seen beyond Mt. Crawford. To the R of Crawford and higher up the W slope of Field are a shoulder and the summit of North Moat. Field's great bulk rises close by to the S, and from there the view continues around through Mts. Anderson, Lowell, Carrigain, Hancock and Bond as described for the W / S viewpoint.

NO. OF 4000-FOOTERS VISIBLE: 21

Mount Willey

ELEVATION: 4285 ft. / 1306 m   ORDER OF HEIGHT: 29
LOCATION: Willey Range, Towns of Bethlehem and Hart's Location
USGS MAP: 7½' Crawford Notch

Geography

Forming the W wall of Crawford Notch, Mt. Willey is the southernmost and dominant peak of the Willey Range, though not quite the highest. A brooding hulk of a mountain, it's especially impressive when viewed from the depths of the Notch. Its steep sides are scarred by cliffs and rock slides, giving it a savage, ominous look. This aura was enhanced early on by the Willey Slide of 1826, which wiped out nine lives and captured the public imagination like no other episode in White Mountain history.

Willey's small conical summit is at the S end of a rolling crest about ¾ mi. long. On the N Mt. Willey is separated from the slightly higher Mt. Field by a shallow col. From the summit the mountain's slopes drop off steeply on three sides, giving the visitor a sense of lofty isolation.

On the E is a mile-long wall of scrub and broken rock that plummets nearly 3000 ft. to the floor of the Notch. A huge stretch of dark talus stretches across this face at ca. 3400 ft. This slope was steepened by the continental ice sheets; Crawford Notch is a textbook example of glacial geology, best viewed from the nearby summit of Mt. Willard. Well down on this face is the naked slab known as the Willey Slide, a favorite haunt of ice climbers (not to be confused with the 1826 slide, which has long since revegetated). Farther S on this E slope is steep-flowing Kedron Brook, which breaks into an area of scenic cascades at Kedron Flume. Lower down on the E slope is the cut of the Crawford Notch railroad, an engineering marvel when it was built in the 1870s, and still in use today as a tourist line.

On the S side the ridgeline plunges to a broad height-of-land, once dubbed Willey Notch, dividing Mt. Willey from a low trailless ridge (sometimes called Ethan Ridge) that extends S to the Nancy Range. On the SW side of the mountain, facing the Pemigewasset Wilderness, is another precipitous slope, marked with small talus fields just below the summit and a great slash of cliffs at ca. 3200–3400 ft. This side of the mountain overlooks beautiful Ethan Pond (formerly named Willey Pond) and the expansive spruce-wooded plateau that sprawls across the eastern Pemigewasset Wilderness. Ethan Pond has an impressive view up to Mt. Willey from its shore. The North Fork of the Pemigewasset River's East Branch takes its rise in Ethan Pond and flows W across the plateau to Thoreau Falls. A long cliff-faced ridge runs SW from the main ridge, enclosing Ethan Pond's basin on the N.

Hikers will find a steep and challenging climb up Willey from the S or a longer but easier ridgecrest approach from the N. Two outlooks near the summit offer dramatic views E to the Presidentials and Crawford Notch and W over the Pemigewasset Wilderness.

Nomenclature

For many years Mt. Willey was either nameless, or assigned some name lost to history. The name "Willey" was bestowed on the steep-faced peak in 1845 by the botanist Edward Tuckerman, who reportedly made the first ascent. It commemorates the notorious Willey Slide of 1826, which wiped out the family of settler Samuel Willey, Jr. According to Robert and Mary Julyan's *Place Names of the White Mountains*, Kedron Brook and Flume are named for a stream in the Bible, which rises on the east side of Jerusalem and flows into the Dead Sea. Ethan Pond (sometimes called Willey Pond) was named after its discoverer, the legendary pioneer Ethan Allen Crawford, who often guided fishing parties there.

Historical Highlights

First Ascent: It's believed that the first recorded ascent was made by the botanist Edward Tuckerman in 1845.

1771: Moose hunter Timothy Nash reportedly discovers Crawford Notch, spotting gap from tree on Cherry Mtn. to N. Nash and pal Benjamin Sawyer bring horse through Notch and receive land grant from governor. Soon Notch is established as part of trade route between coast and mountains.

Ca. 1792: First house built on floor of Notch below Mt. Willey by a Mr. Davis. Modest structure, known as "Notch House," serves as way station for those travelling through pass and is occupied by various tenants.

1803: Road through Notch improved and becomes part of Tenth N.H. Turnpike.

1825: Samuel Willey, Jr. settles in Notch House with wife, five children and two hired hands.

1826: After hot, dry summer, tremendous deluge on August 28 triggers massive landslide on E side of Mt. Willey. Willey family flees house for nearby shelter, but all are buried by slide and killed. Ironically, slide splits on rock upslope and house is unscathed. Three of nine bodies are never found. Storm leaves wake of flood and destruction through Saco valley. Arriving at the scene of the tragedy, Ethan Allen Crawford is so stricken by grief that his tongue "refuses utterance." Slide tragedy is later immortalized in Nathaniel Hawthorne short story, "The Ambitious Guest": *Down came the whole side of the mountain in a cataract of ruin.* This sad incident captures the public's imagination. Compelling accounts appear in Lucy Crawford's *History of the White Mountains* (1846) and in *Incidents in White Mountain History* (1856), by Benjamin G. Willey, the brother of Samuel Willey, Jr. Today the Willey Slide remains perhaps the single most notorious event in White Mountain history.

1829: Ethan Allen Crawford discovers Willey Pond, later named Ethan Pond, on wilderness plateau to SW of Mt. Willey. In following years he guides inn guests there on fishing trips.

1844: Hotelier Horace Fabyan repairs Notch House and builds Willey Hotel next to it.

1845: Botanist Edward Tuckerman ascends and names Mt. Willey.

1871: Party from Charles H. Hitchcock's geological survey traverses Willey Range, also ridge extending W towards Zealand Notch.

1874–1875: Portland & Ogdensburg Railroad constructs line through Crawford Notch along lower E slope of Willey, including high trestle over ravine of Willey Brook. This is one of most remarkable engineering feats of its time.

1876: On August 28, fiftieth anniversary of Willey Slide, group of AMC climbers makes trailless ascent of mountain from Willey House site via Kedron Brook and S slope. Group reaches summit in 2¾ hrs. from railroad. They leave record of their ascent in tin can at summit.

1878: Charles E. Lowe builds first trail up mountain, following same route. Branch trail is opened to Ethan Pond.

1881: Moses Sweetser's guidebook touts bushwhack route to Willey via Mts. Avalon and Field. He cautions, "Strong clothing should be worn during the exploration of this range, since any other would soon be riddled by the spruce boughs." He reports that path from S is well-marked and in good shape.

1906: AMC opens new trail to summit from Willey House RR station—route of today's Ethan Pond Trail; it meets original route near upper crossing of Kedron Brook. Trail is also opened from Ethan Pond past Thoreau Falls to North Fork Junction, with another leading S past Shoal Pond.

1909: Mr. & Mrs. J. A. Cruickshank blaze new trail from Mt. Avalon over Mt. Field to Mt. Willey.

1911–1916: J. E. Henry's crews are cutting timber in North Fork basin on

W side of Mt. Willey. Some crews are based at Camp 21-A between Shoal Pond and Ethan Pond.

1913: State of New Hampshire buys 5,975 acres in Crawford Notch for $62,000.

1918: AMC adopts ridgecrest path and names it Willey Range Trail.

1936: Kedron Flume Trail opened from Willey House site to S of original AMC route (now abandoned). Path is laid out by veteran AMC trailmen Charles W. Blood and Paul R. Jenks.

1950: Hurricane wreaks havoc on Willey Range Trail, closed until 1952. Crawford Notch State Park created.

1957: AMC builds Ethan Pond Shelter at SW base of Willey.

1969: Forest Service designates W slopes of Willey as part of Lincoln Woods Scenic Area.

1984: Crawford Notch railroad line closed. Lands to SW of Willey are included in new Pemigewasset Wilderness.

1995: Rail line reopened by Conway Scenic Railroad for tourist excursions.

Trail Approaches

Southeast Approach off US 302 in Crawford Notch

Ethan Pond Trail, Willey Range Trail
5.4 mi. round trip, 2850-ft. elevation gain

TRAILHEAD (1440 ft.): Take US 302 to Appalachian Trail crossing in Crawford Notch, 1 mi. S of Willey House site. At sign for Ripley Falls, drive 0.3 mi. S up paved side road (unplowed in winter) to kiosk and parking area at end.

This is shorter and steeper of two day-hike approaches to Willey; upper climb is very steep. From parking area follow Ethan Pond Trail (part of Appalachian Trail) across RR tracks and climb 0.2 mi. to jct. where Arethusa–Ripley Falls Trail bears L. Bear R here for stiff climb on Ethan Pond Trail through birch stand. Grade eases at 0.5 mi. / 1900 ft. and trail makes pleasant easy to moderate traverse through hardwood forest to jct. R with Kedron Flume Trail at 1.3 mi. / 2400 ft. Somewhat rougher climbing leads to jct. with Willey Range Trail at 1.6 mi. / 2600 ft.

Continue ahead on Willey Range Trail at easy grade, cross Kedron Brook (here small and rocky), and ascend at moderate grade. Trail swings L at 1.8 mi., crosses tiny brook, and quickly swings R. At 2.0 mi. / 3000 ft. climb becomes very steep, with some rough footing. At ca. 3400 ft. trail comes to base of impressive set of ladders built in 2004 by AMC trail crew, with 11 sections gaining ca. 100 ft. in elevation. Near top of ladders there is framed view back towards Mt. Resolution. Steep, relentless ascent continues, with another view back to S at ca. 3900 ft. Above here there is brief easing on shoulder, then stiff climbing is resumed, with several easy

The steepest section of the Willey Range Trail south of Mount Willey's summit requires hikers to negotiate this set of ladders.

scrambles, until reaching side path on R leading 20 yds. to superb E outlook at 2.7 mi. From this dark rock outcrop amidst low scrub there are outstanding views of Presidentials, Crawford Notch and mountains to S. Main trail bends L and climbs 40 yds. to true summit, marked by cairn on R, in scrubby firs. Descend 30 yds. along trail to W outlook just beyond, ledge shelf with panorama over eastern Pemigewasset Wilderness, best if standing. Here trail drops off ledge to R, rises slightly, and soon enters woods for ridge traverse N to Mt. Field.

KEDRON FLUME TRAIL OPTION

Kedron Flume Trail, interesting route with one steep section, is alternate approach for lower half of this hike. Beginning at hiker's parking area at Willey House site (1300 ft.) on US 302, it climbs into woods and makes long, gravelly switchbacks L and R to crossing of RR tracks at 0.4 mi., with view of Mt. Willard to R. It climbs steep bank above tracks, makes several more switchbacks, then angles L (S) across slope, becoming rougher and a bit steeper, but still moderate. At 1.0 mi. / 2000 ft. it descends short pitch to cross Kedron Brook at Kedron Flume; here there is waterfall on R with long, thin waterslide higher up. On L there is framed view across Notch to S end of Webster Cliffs; ledges at brink here are slippery and should be avoided. Above here climb is steep and rough for ca. 0.2 mi., then last section is at easier grade with better footing, meeting Ethan Pond Trail at 1.3 mi. / 2400 ft. Distance is same as lower approach via Ethan Pond Trail with additional 150 ft. of elevation gain.

North Approach from US 302 at Crawford's

Avalon Trail, Willey Range Trail
8.6 mi. round trip, 3100-ft. elevation gain

This approach includes ascent of Mt. Field along the way, and on return trip. For description of 2.8 mi. / 2450-ft. climb to Mt. Field via Avalon Trail, see Mt. Field chapter. (Add 0.2 mi. / 100 ft. for side trip to Mt. Avalon).

From summit of Field, Willey Range Trail descends S in three short, steep stages, passing partial view SW into Pemi Wilderness, with peek at Mt. Willey ahead, at ca. 3.0 mi., and reaching Field–Willey col at 3.3 mi. / 3980 ft. Trail climbs out of col and meanders along wooded ridgecrest, traversing several small knobs. Easy 0.2 mi. climb leads to pitch L up ledge to W outlook on Willey (with wide view over eastern Pemigewasset Wilderness, best if standing) and then to wooded summit, marked by cairn on L, 30 yds. beyond, at 4.2 mi. / 4285 ft. Continue another 40 yds. to side path leading 20 yds. L to fine E outlook with views of Presidentials, Crawford Notch and mountains to S.

For other loop and point-to-point options including Mt. Willey, see chapters for Mt. Tom and Mt. Field.

Winter

The approach via Avalon Trail over Mt. Field is most often used; a large plowed area for parking is available at the Crawford's trailhead. After initial steep pitches, snowshoeing is pleasant along the ridge between Field and Willey. Many peakbaggers also include Mt. Tom on the itinerary. The SE approach is much more difficult, and possibly dangerous if icy in the vicinity of the ladders. Plowed parking is available beside US 302 at entrance to the side road to summer trailhead; the walk up this road adds 0.6 mi. round trip and 200 ft. of elevation gain. Or, one can avoid the road walk and use the more difficult Kedron Flume Trail, where parking is available beside US 302. Deep snow improves the W outlook over the Pemi Wilderness.

View Guide

Taken together, the E and W outlooks provide a fine 270-degree view encompassing the Presidentials, Crawford Notch and the eastern half of the Pemigewasset Wilderness. Steep dropoffs on the E, S and W sides add a sense of drama and lofty isolation.

E OUTLOOK: This small area of open ledge amidst the scrub is a fine lunch spot. You can sit and enjoy nearly all the view, though standing will expand the fringes. The views of the Presidentials and Webster Cliffs are excellent.

On the far L, partly screened by the scrub, you can just see the long ridge of Mt. Waumbek with Mt. Cabot peering over on the L and the eastern knobs of Mt. Deception below. Farther R the open view begins with rounded North Weeks, with South Weeks in front on its L. In the distance to the R of North Weeks are Dixville Peak, Rice Mtn., and other peaks near Dixville Notch. Next to the R and closer is Mt. Dartmouth in the Dartmouth Range. More North Country ridges are on the horizon to the R of Dartmouth. Farther R is Millen Hill, a lower spur of Dartmouth, with the sharp peak of Mt. Dustan in the distance. The broad mass of Mt. Bowman, a spur of Mt. Jefferson, is behind Millen Hill on the R, with the two summits of Black Crescent Mtn. in back. The double rounded summit of Aziscohos Mtn. can be seen over the R summit of Black Crescent. Farther R, leading across to Jefferson's Castellated Ridge, is distant West Kennebago in Maine. To the NE is the great mountain wall of the Presidentials. On the L end of the range the sharp Castellated Ridge leads up to Mt. Jefferson. Mt. Adams is behind and to the R of Jefferson, with the double summit of Mt. Clay, rising above Burt Ravine, to the R. Mt. Washington looms to the R of Clay, with the foreshortened ridge of the Southern Peaks in front and below, including Pierce, Eisenhower, Franklin and jagged, double-peaked Monroe. To the R is the bare, level ridge of Boott Spur, ending in the wooded knob of Slide Peak.

ENE across Crawford Notch are the great granite slabs on the face of Mt. Webster, with a rocky outcrop marking the summit and the small rock peak of Mt. Jackson behind and to the L. Carter Dome rises in the distance over Webster, with Mt. Hight on its L and Rainbow Ridge on its R and the curving Wildcat Ridge beneath. To the R of the Dome are the dark, wooded ridges of Mt. Isolation and Mt. Davis on Montalban Ridge. Speckled Mtn. near Evans Notch is seen through the Isolation–Davis col. Over the long ridge of Mt. Davis are (L to R) North and South Baldface, Sable Mtn. and Chandler Mtn. The upper part of Black Mtn. in Jackson is visible over the Davis ridge and under South Baldface and Sable. Part of Maine's Streaked Mtn. is seen in the distance between Sable and Chandler. In the foreground the cliff-faced ridge of Webster slants southward; over its R end, through the broad gap between Mt. Davis and Stairs Mtn., are the Doubleheads, Walter Mtn., Mt. Shaw, The Gemini, and the shapely cone of Kearsarge North (just L of Stairs's summit). Part of Maine's Pleasant Mtn. is visible behind and R of Kearsarge North. Houses in the hills of Jackson can be seen under The Gemini.

To the SE is a magnificent view down to the winding floor of Crawford Notch, striped by the Saco River, US 302 and the Notch railroad.

Looking south down the Saco River valley from the summit of Mount Willey.

The Notch bends R beneath Stairs Mtn., shaggy, flat-topped Mt. Resolution, Crawford Dome, Mt. Parker (in back), and the rock-knob peak of Mt. Crawford. Beyond are the Green Hills in Conway, with Black Cap Mtn. (and distant Peaked Mtn. near Sebago Lake) over Resolution and sharp Middle Mtn. above Crawford Dome on the L, with Maine's Saddleback Hills on the horizon. The Attitash ski slopes and Little Attitash Mtn. are to the R of Mt. Crawford, with the Burnt Meadow and Bill Merrill Mtn. ranges beyond. Farther R is North Moat, with the distant Clark Mtn. range in southern Maine seen off its L side. Close by in this direction is the wooded backside of Frankenstein Cliff. Continuing to the R are the several summits of Big Attitash Mtn. (with Middle and South Moat seen over its L end), Table Mtn. and flat-topped Bear Mtn. Maine's Ossipee Hill is on the horizon between Big Attitash and Table, and Green Mtn. in Effingham is prominent between Table and Bear. To the R of Bear is distinctive Mt. Chocorua, with Bartlett Haystack below.

Closer in to the R, seen across a broad, forested plateau, is the notched summit of Mt. Bemis, with Mt. Tremont poking up behind and the Moose Mtns. and Copple Crown Mtn. on the horizon. Mt. Paugus and Mt. Shaw (Ossipee Range) are seen over the R shoulder of Bemis. Farther R, looking due S, are (L to R) Mt. Nancy, Mts. Passaconaway and Whiteface through the broad gap to the R of Nancy, and Mts. Anderson and Lowell. Faraway Mtn. in the Ossipee Range is over Nancy, and to the L of Passaconaway, Black Snout and Mt. Roberts peer over the Wonalancet Hedgehog, a spur of Passaconaway, with Nanamocomuck, another Passaconaway spur, just to the R. The two Sleepers (with the

Fool Killer beneath) and the three Tripyramids (with the North Slide visible) are spotted through the portal of Carrigain Notch. On the far R the view is closed in by the immense bulk of Mt. Carrigain, with Vose Spur jutting out below Signal Ridge on its L.

W OUTLOOK: This small tiered ledge right on the Willey Range Trail provides an expansive view over the eastern Pemi Wilderness and surrounding mountains. It's best taken in while standing, though the central part can be seen while seated. Wrote AMC climber J. B. Henck, Jr. in 1877, "There is perhaps no better point from which to study the East Branch of the Pemigewasset than here, for it is in full view from its source in Ethan's Pond to its confluence with the Pemigewasset near North Woodstock—the broad valley one unbroken stretch of forest." On the L (S) the view begins with the Nancy and Sandwich Range peaks as described above. Massive, dominant Mt. Carrigain is seen beyond a rolling, forested upland, with Vose Spur below Signal Ridge on the L. To the R of Carrigain the view sweeps across the broad Shoal Pond Brook basin to the wide-spreading ridges of Mt. Hancock. Part of Mt. Kancamagus is seen between Carrigain and the E ridge of Hancock. The tip of East Osceola pokes above Middle Hancock on its L side and the top of South Hancock is just seen over Middle Hancock's R side. Mt. Osceola peers over the Hancock ridge a bit farther R, and the rounded North Hancock is next to the R. Three are good looks into the two remote ravines of Carrigain Branch and that of Crystal Brook. The stripings of old logging roads can be seen on the flanks of Nancy, Carrigain and Hancock.

Farther R Scar Ridge and Mt. Hitchcock (below Scar and in front) are seen to the R of Hancock's pointed NW peak. The sharp Middle Scar Ridge and more distant Stinson Mtn. are seen between NW Hancock and the broad, massive main peak of Scar Ridge. You look almost straight down at the W part of Ethan Pond, with a broad spruce-covered plateau leading out to the low, rolling ridge of Shoal Pond Peak. A slice of Shoal Pond can be seen at the base of this ridge. To the L of Shoal Pond the East Branch valley opens out to the ski trails on Loon Mtn. North Hitchcock is to the L of Loon and closer, with East Kineo above on the horizon. Carr Mtn. lurks on the horizon just to the R of Loon, with Mts. Kineo and Cushman farther to the R. Bulky Smarts Mtn. is still farther away, behind and R of Cushman. In the middle distance in this SW direction, in line with Shoal Pond and the main summit of Shoal Pond Peak, and just R of Smarts, is the flat-topped ridge of East Whaleback. Next to the R is the abrupt rise of Whaleback Mtn. under Moosilauke's long Blue Ridge, with a level crest leading R across to Mt. Flume; Mt. Moosilauke rises behind this crest, and Bondcliff is in front of Flume, obscuring much of its summit.

To the R of Bondcliff the great bulk of Mt. Bond rears from the valley of the North Fork, showing a bare E ridge on its flank. Double-summited Mt. Guyot continues the ridge to the R of Bond, with Little Haystack and Mt. Lincoln peering over on its L. The serrated crest of Lafayette is on the R of Guyot, just S of W. Looking due W, in the foreground is the wooded backside of Whitewall Mtn. with the ledgy Zeacliffs and Zealand Ridge beyond, and South Twin to the R. Farther R is slide-marked North Twin, with South Hale below. Mt. Worcester in Vermont's Worcester Range can be seen off the lower R slope of North Twin. The ledgy spur of Nubble Peak extends to the R from North Twin, with Vermont's Mt. Mansfield on the horizon to its L and the Sterling Range to its R. On the far R is Mt. Hale, its flanks scarred by talus slopes and clearcuts. (The view to the R of North Twin is partly screened by trees.)

NO. OF 4000-FOOTERS VISIBLE: 33

Zealand Mountain

ELEVATION: 4260 ft. / 1298 m   ORDER OF HEIGHT: 31
LOCATION: N edge of Pemigewasset Wilderness, Township of
    Livermore
USGS MAP: 7½' South Twin

Geography

The flat, wooded, viewless summit of Zealand Mtn.—the highest swell on the elongated Zealand Ridge—is not an inspiring objective in itself. But there are sweet rewards on the long trek in, including brook and pond scenery in the Zealand valley, a spectacular wilderness vista from Zeacliff, and a ridge walk through boreal forest. Zealand is an interior ridge, far removed from major roads, and were it not for the USFS seasonal Zealand Rd. it would be very remote indeed.

The wooded crest extends for nearly two miles, from a high col with neighboring Mt. Guyot on the W to the lofty Zeacliffs (ca. 3600 ft.), overlooking rocky, glacier-carved Zealand Notch on the E. The true summit of Zealand Mtn. is 0.1 mi. N of the Twinway at the W end of the ridge. From here a spur ridge runs N, with a large talus slope on the W side above the isolated upper basin of Little River. These rock slides are prominent when viewed from the Twins across the valley. Hardy bushwhackers willing to battle dense scrub will find superb vistas of the Twins and the Little River valley from the top of this rock slide. This ridgeline is continued N for ca. 5 mi. as the "Little River Mountains," passing over an intermediate trailless peak known as "North Zealand," "South Hale" or "Zeale" (3700 ft., one of New Hampshire's "Hundred Highest" peaks) and culminating in Mt. Hale. On the W side of this ridge the Little River flows N through a long valley, with the high ridge of South and North Twin beyond.

Between Zealand's main summit and the Zeacliffs is a 4060-ft. knob known as "Zeacliff Pond Peak," with blocky cliffs overlooking tiny Zeacliff Pond (3700 ft.), which is tucked into a little bowl on the S side of the ridge. The outlet from Zeacliff Pond flows SE through a trailless basin overlooked by extensive cliffs on the S face of Zealand Ridge, larger than the Zeacliffs themselves. On its E side this valley is enclosed by a gentle birch-clad ridge extending S from the Zeacliffs; on the SE slope of this ridge a long, narrow beaver pond is snuggled into a small shelf. The Zeacliffs and this spur ridge form the W side of Zealand Notch; the E side is framed by the cliffs and talus slides of trailless Whitewall Mtn. (3405 ft.), the westernmost spur of the Willey Range.

In a broad basin on the NE side of Zealand Ridge are the headwaters of Whitewall Brook, which tumbles E past Zealand Falls Hut, then flows S through Zealand Notch. At the NE base of the ridge is beaver-dammed Zealand Pond, with outlets flowing both S into Whitewall Brook and N into Zealand River. From the pond the Zealand River flows 6 mi. N between the Little River Mtns. on the W and the Willey–Rosebrook Range on the E, emptying into the Ammonoosuc River W of Zealand Campground. There are numerous beaver ponds and meadows in its upper reaches.

On the S side of the western half of Zealand Ridge is a large basin drained by Jumping Brook into the North Fork of the Pemigewasset River's East Branch.

The Zealand region was ravaged by fires in 1886 and 1903, but has recovered from that devastation and is now a beautiful, peaceful country well worth exploring.

Nomenclature

Zealand Mtn. was originally included under the general title of "Little River Mtns.," referring to the ridge between Little River on the W and Zealand River on the E. This name was used in Charles H. Hitchcock's geological survey in the 1870s. "Mt. Thompson" was another early name, bestowed during an 1879 exploration led by veteran guide Allen "Old Man" Thompson. This name was still in use in 1888 when AMC stalwart Eugene B. Cook described his ascent of the mountain in *Appalachia*.

Sometime in the late 1800s the name "New Zealand" was applied to the general region W of the Willey–Rosebrook Range. It appeared in Sweetser's 1876 guidebook and on Walling's 1877 map. The origin is uncertain, but may have been a humorous reference to the area's remoteness. The "New" was apparently removed by the Zealand railroad and post office in the 1880s for convenience. Features bearing the Zealand name include a ridge, a mountain, a notch, a waterfall, a river, a pond, a valley, and a set of cliffs.

Historical Highlights

First Ascent: Unknown

1871: Members of Hitchcock's geological survey explore Zealand region, including Little River Mtns., Zealand Falls and Pond, and Zealand Notch; may have visited summit of Zealand.

1876: Moses Sweetser's guidebook warns of remoteness of eastern Pemigewasset region: "The inner solitudes should be entered only under the guidance of experienced foresters; and traveling will be found very slow and arduous." He notes that trek from Thoreau Falls N through New Zealand Notch to the Ammonoosuc River is "a good day's journey."

1879: Benjamin A. Macdonald and guide Allen "Old Man" Thompson traverse Zealand Notch; account of trip appears in Bethlehem (New Hampshire) paper, *The White Mountain Echo.* They follow deer paths through moss-grown primeval forests of spruce and birch, note the two outlets of Zealand Pond, and follow natural shelf in Zealand Notch that Thompson prophetically says could be used for railroad bed.

1884–1885: After purchasing Zealand valley acreage for $33,000, timber baron J. E. Henry begins construction of logging railroad up along Zealand River. Line eventually extends through Zealand Notch (high on E slope) to Shoal Pond. Ephemeral village of Zealand springs up near site of today's Zealand Campground. Several spur lines and side-tracks are built, including one on floor of Zealand Notch, possibly intended as eventual link to Lincoln to S. Logging operations continue until 1897.

1886: First Zealand fire ignited on July 8 in logging slash, possibly by sparks from woodburning locomotive; 12,000 acres are burned. The destruction horrifies conservation-minded citizens of the day. In 1891 speech, New Hampshire forest commissioner Joseph B. Walker notes "the two towering sentinels of fire-blasted rock which mark the opening of this valley," recalling Dante's famous hellish line, "All Hope Abandon Ye Who Enter Here."

1888: AMC explorers Eugene B. Cook and William H. Peek, guide Charles E. Lowe, and hired hand climb to high point of Zealand, coming across upper Little River valley from Twin Range. They measure summit at 4348 ft. and find initials "A.M.F." carved in tree in 1872.

1893–1900: Using J. E. Henry's equipment, George Van Dyke operates logging railroad in Little River valley, extending 6 mi. S to point even with N ridge of Zealand.

1903: After dry spring, second Zealand fire scorches 10,000 acres. Visitors call it "Death Valley," "the climax of desolation," and "a dull-brown waste of lifeless, fire-eaten soil and stark white boulders."

1907: First edition of *AMC Guide* describes walk along old RR bed through the "bare, fire-scarred walls of Zealand Notch." Second (1916) edition notes that area is "little visited except by fishermen and berry pickers."

1915: Zealand area added to WMNF, purchased for $6 / acre from Henry company.

1923: WMNF Zealand Trail opened along old RR bed into Zealand Notch from N. Zealand Ridge Trail opened by AMC into notch from S, and extended up to Zeacliffs and along Zealand Ridge past summit of Zealand Mtn. to Mt. Guyot. (Today this route is part of Ethan Pond Trail, Zeacliff Trail, and part of Twinway.) Short spur paths constructed to Zeacliff outlook and Zeacliff Pond; shelter built by pond.

1931: Under direction of legendary Joe Dodge, AMC builds Zealand Falls Hut at NE base of ridge. Frame is pre-cut at Vermont mill yard. Materials are packed halfway in by tractor, the rest of the way by burro. Workers dynamite ledge to make site for building. Hut opens in 1932. New section of trail links hut with Zeacliff outlook; this and rest of ridge trail is named Twinway.

Mid-1930s: Civilian Conservation Corps starts construction of Zealand Rd.

1948: Zealand Rd. completed; not open all the way for auto traffic until 1960.

Ca. 1960: Zeacliff Pond shelter removed. Short side path developed from Twinway to Zealand Mtn. summit for 4000-footer peakbaggers.

1973: Zealand Falls Hut begins opening in winter on caretaker basis.

Trail Approaches

Northeast Approach from Zealand Rd.

Zealand Trail, Twinway
11.4 mi. round trip, 2400-ft. elevation gain

TRAILHEAD (2000 ft.): From US 302, 2.2 mi. E of stoplight in Twin Mountain, follow USFS seasonal Zealand Rd. (paved for 1 mi., then gravel) 3.5 mi. to large parking area at end.

The usual approach to Zealand begins with a pleasant walk up the beaver-haunted Zealand valley, climbs past Zealand Falls Hut to the spectacular Zeacliff outlook, then follows the ridge to the wooded summit. From parking area, Zealand Trail starts up old logging railroad grade, then splits R on rough, bouldery, up-and-down bypass at 0.2 mi. After traversing rooty spruce grove, trail briefly rejoins grade, then makes R turn off it at 0.8 mi. where short spur L leads to ledges in Zealand River.

*The view towards Whitewall Mountain and Zealand Notch from atop
the Zeacliffs, an eastern spur of Zealand Mountain.*

Ascend gradually through conifers, then rejoin RR grade and follow it
through brushy, swampy area with several stream crossings. Footing is
mostly smooth on gravelly RR bed.

At ca. 1.8 mi. open swamp provides view of Zealand Ridge ahead.
Cross boardwalk (known as the "Z-bridge") and skirt long chain of
swamps and beaver meadows on L. At 2.1 mi. birch-lined aisle leads past
pond on L with view across to Mt. Tom. Pass jct. with A–Z Trail on L at
2.3 mi. / 2450 ft., cross N outlet of Zealand Pond on bridge and skirt shore
of pond on R. At 2.4 mi. short spur R leads to shore and view up to Zealand Ridge and Zealand Falls.

At 2.5 mi. turn R on Twinway (part of Appalachian Trail), cross southern outlet of pond, then make steep, rocky climb, passing side path L to
Zealand Falls, where Whitewall Brook spills over blocky granite ledges,
and reach AMC Zealand Falls Hut at 2.7 mi. / 2637 ft. Good view from

front of hut through Zealand Notch to Mt. Carrigain. Adjacent open ledges on Whitewall Brook have view down to Zealand Pond and out to Mt. Tom, excellent spot for break. Twinway bears R past hut, passing jct. R with Lend-a-Hand Trail to Mt. Hale at 2.8 mi. Cross small branch brook and pass side path to nice cascade on L, then cross main branch of Whitewall Brook. Trail soon begins long, steady climb, with rocky footing, through extensive white birch forest, mixing with conifers higher up. Reach crest of ridge at 3.9 mi./3600 ft. Here spur continues ca. 100 yds. ahead and slightly down to open ledges atop Zeacliff—one of finest viewpoints in White Mtns., with magnificent panorama over eastern Pemi Wilderness—and loops R back to main trail at mucky spot. Between loop jcts. Twinway runs over ledgy hump with view W to peaks of Twin Range.

Continuing up scrubby ridge, with glimpses of Mt. Hale and North Twin, pass jct. L with Zeacliff Trail at 4.0 mi. Gradual climb and descent through beautiful fir forest leads to side trail L to Zeacliff Pond at 4.4 mi. (This spur drops 0.1 mi./100 ft. to tiny, boggy pond, elev. 3700 ft. At bottom, path forks. L branch leads to open spot on shore with view to cliffs above pond. R fork, rough and obscure, leads around to sloping ledge with view across pond to Mt. Carrigain). Twinway makes steep, rocky climb in stages, with one ladder, to ledge atop "Zeacliff Pond Peak" at 4.7 mi./4060 ft., with standup view SE to Willey Range, southern Montalbans, Nancy Range and Mt. Carrigain. After slight descent, trail climbs at mostly easy grades up long ridge through boreal forest. This is good area to see rare and tame spruce grouse. At 5.6 mi. reach cairn just past high point of Twinway on Zealand Ridge; turn R on narrow, overgrown spur path and follow 0.1 mi. to small summit clearing and sign, just 20 ft. higher than main trail. No view here!

ZEACLIFF TRAIL LOOP OPTION
Strong hikers can make a longer and steeper loop through Zealand Notch to the Twinway near Zeacliff using Ethan Pond Trail and Zeacliff Trail. From three-way jct. below Zealand Falls Hut, follow Ethan Pond Trail S along gravelly old RR grade, high up on birch-clad slope, into Zealand Notch. Walking is mostly level with occasional washouts and boulder slides. At 1.3 mi. from jct. (elevation 2450 ft.) emerge on open rocks on side of Whitewall Mtn., with views S to Mt. Carrigain and Mt. Hancock and N to Mt. Hale and Zealand Falls Hut, with Zeacliffs looming across notch to W. Turn R here on Zeacliff Trail and descend W, then NW over open talus with good views, then bear L and drop very steeply through woods, losing 200 ft. in elevation. Cross Whitewall Brook at 1.5 mi. and climb steeply up E side of spur of Zealand Ridge, then bear R and ascend more moderately up birch-wooded crest. After short level stretch, trail makes scramble up past ledge and angles L, following winding, steep route up through wild, ledgy terrain. At 2.4 mi./3500 ft. trail turns R for

scramble up 6-ft. rock face; at top there is view of Mt. Bond. Trail now climbs moderately, then easily, reaching Twinway at 2.7 mi. / 3700 ft. Turn L for summit of Zealand Mtn. (1.7 mi. away) or R for Zeacliff outlook spur (0.1 mi.). Elevation gain on Zeacliff Trail is 1450 ft. from brook crossing. Loop is 1.2 mi. longer than direct route via hut, with extra 200-ft. elevation gain. Loop with ascent via Zealand Notch and Zeacliff Trail, out to Zealand Mtn. summit and back on Twinway, with return descent via Zealand Falls Hut, is 12.6 mi. with 2600-ft. elevation gain.

SOUTHWEST APPROACH FROM MT. GUYOT

Backpackers and hut-hoppers can climb Zealand as part of multi-day (or long point-to-point day hike) traverse of Twin Range. From jct. of Twinway and Bondcliff Trail, skirt open NE summit of Mt. Guyot (4580 ft.; fine views, but stay on trail to preserve fragile vegetation) and make long, gradual to moderate descent down NE ridge with rocky footing. Look for view of Zealand Mtn. talus partway down. In 0.4 mi., on 4400-ft. shoulder, trail swings R to continue long descent. Reach Zealand / Guyot col (4020 ft.) at 1.1 mi. from jct., then make steady, rocky climb of 0.2 mi. / 240 ft. to side path L to Zealand summit, 1.3 mi. from jct.

Winter

Zealand Rd. is gated in winter and not open to public vehicle travel, effectively isolating Zealand Mtn. as much as Owl's Head or the Bonds. Winter parking is in lot on N side of US 302, 0.2 mi. E of entrance to Zealand Rd. Road walking adds 3.7 mi. each way to trip, for a marathon 18.8 mi. round trip with 2950-ft. elevation gain. Some winter peakbaggers ski or snowshoe in to Zealand Falls Hut (open on caretaker basis in winter) and use that as a base to day hike Zealand Mtn. Expect deep, drifted snow up on Zealand Ridge; in places the white-blazed trail may be hard to follow. Experienced bushwhackers sometimes approach the mountain via the USFS Haystack Rd., North Twin Trail and the trailless upper Little River valley and N ridge of Zealand, an arduous but interesting route with possible views from the top of the Zealand talus slope.

View Guide

ZEACLIFF OUTLOOK: The S-facing outlook ledges on the spur loop off the Twinway are one of the great view spots in the White Mtns., sweeping over the eastern Pemi Wilderness and several mountain ranges. There is ample space for relaxing and enjoying the views. On the far L, looking NNE, is Mt. Dartmouth in the Dartmouth Range. To the E the Presidentials rise majestically beyond Mt. Tom, with Mt. Jefferson to the L and Mt. Clay right above Tom. Mt. Washington is to the R of Tom, with Monroe, Eisenhower, Boott Spur and the top of Pierce farther R. Mts. Field and

Willey are to the R of Washington; this is one of the best views of the Willey Range. To the ESE is an impressive view across Zealand Notch to the scarred face of Whitewall Mtn., with its cliffs, talus slopes and ledgy S knob. The Ethan Pond Trail, which follows the bed of the old Zealand Valley logging railroad, cuts a line across the lower slopes. The S ridge of Mt. Davis (with South Doublehead peering over in back), the Giant Stairs and Mt. Resolution are seen beyond Whitewall and the trailless ridge extending S from Mt. Willey. Walter Mtn. is seen in the distance through the Davis–Stairs col, with Mt. Shaw just peering over on the R. Kearsarge North pokes above the L end of Resolution. Farther R are Mt. Crawford, a sharp rock peak, and Mt. Parker (behind Crawford on the R), with Black Cap Mtn. between them. Mts. Bemis and Nancy rise prominently beyond the broad spruce-wooded plateau in the foreground. North Moat is in back off the L slope of Bemis, with the lower flat ridge of Little Attitash on its L.

On clear days two low ranges in western Maine can be seen: the Burnt Meadow Mtns. between North Moat and Little Attitash, and the Saddleback Hills to the L of Little Attitash. On the nearby plateau Shoal Pond is in line with North Moat, and Norcross Pond gleams at the R base of Mt. Nancy. The ledgy gash of Thoreau Falls can be seen below, in line with the Bemis–Nancy col.

To the SE is a classic vista of the spires of Mts. Anderson and Lowell, U-shaped Carrigain Notch, and massive, triple-humped Mt. Carrigain, seen across extensive rolling wildlands, including the long, trailless "Shoal Pond Ridge" between Shoal Pond Brook and the North Fork of the Pemigewasset River's East Branch. Duck Pond Mtn. (L) and Bear Mtn. (R) peer over the broad saddle between Anderson and Nancy, and sharp-peaked Mt. Tremont and Mt. Chocorua's Three Sisters Ridge are sighted through the gap between Anderson and Lowell. Part of Mt. Paugus is seen through Carrigain Notch. To the R of Carrigain is the low, flat-topped knob of The Captain, with Mt. Whiteface and East Sleeper in the distance. Farther R, almost due S, the sprawling ridges of Mt. Hancock fill a large section of the horizon, with the gaping valley of Crystal Brook (under the broad dome of North Hancock) revealed beyond the long valley of the North Fork. Hancock's sharp NW Peak is on the R side of Crystal Brook valley. To the R of Hancock are the four Osceola peaks, the West Peak of Mt. Tecumseh (behind the R end of Osceola), Mt. Hitchcock (with its S peak under Middle and West Osceola and the main summit just L of and in front of the double peak of East Scar Ridge), and the middle and main summits of Scar Ridge. To the SW and close by is the great mass of Mt. Bond, showing a bare spur ridge on the L. In the basin below the cliffs on the S is an interesting beaver meadow, a likely place to spot a moose.

NO. OF 4000-FOOTERS VISIBLE: from Zeacliff Outlook, 15; from Zealand Mtn. summit: 20 (theoretical, through the trees)

PEMIGEWASSET WILDERNESS

The Bonds

Mount Bond

ELEVATION: 4698 ft. / 1432 m   ORDER OF HEIGHT: 14
LOCATION: Twin Range, Town of Lincoln
USGS MAP: 7½′ South Twin Mtn.

West Bond

ELEVATION: 4540 ft. / 1384 m   ORDER OF HEIGHT: 16
LOCATION: Twin Range, Towns of Lincoln and Franconia
USGS MAP: 7½′ South Twin Mtn.

Bondcliff

ELEVATION: 4265 ft. / 1300 m   ORDER OF HEIGHT: 30
LOCATION: Twin Range, Town of Lincoln
USGS MAP: 7½′ South Twin Mtn.

Geography

The three peaks of the Bonds, situated at the S end of the Twin Range, are among the most remote, yet dramatic summits in all the White Mountains. Lying deep within the federally designated Pemigewasset Wilderness, the open summits of the Bonds offer unrivaled views of mountains, valleys and unbroken forests in every direction. Nowhere else in the Whites can the hiker find such a sense of removal from civilization. From many angles, the Bonds—West Bond and Bondcliff in particular—are impressive mountains to look *at* as well as *from*, with cliffs, slides and scree fields marking their steep slopes.

The Bonds rise sharply out of the Franconia Brook valley to the W and the valley of the North Fork of the East Branch to the E. The nearest neighbor to the W is the crouching mass of Owl's Head and to the E is the long, low Shoal Pond Ridge. Mt. Bond is the anchor peak of the range, lying 3 mi. S of the summit of South Twin. A bald area at the very summit permits panoramic views. To the N the ridge runs over a wooded sub-peak, then dips to a 4380-ft. col with Mt. Guyot (4580 ft.), whose bare, rounded double summits are 1 mi. N. Just S of this col a spur ridge extends SW to West Bond (see below). Two major ridges extend S from Mt. Bond, enclosing the valley of Black Brook. The SW ridge is dominated by Bondcliff (see below); the wooded SE ridge runs for 3 mi. out to the East Branch, curving to the SW at its lower end.

On the E Mt. Bond's huge mass slopes endlessly down toward the North Fork between Thoreau Falls and the main stem of the East Branch. Its NE slopes drain into the large basin of Jumping Brook, a major tributary of the North Fork that takes its rise below the col between Mt. Guyot and Zealand Mtn. High up on a shoulder of one of Bond's several E ridges, but not accessible by trail, is a unique alpine zone seen best from the area around Thoreau Falls. On its W side Bond drops steeply, with large scree slopes, into the upper valley of Hellgate Brook, a wild, twisting basin that is enclosed by all three Bond peaks.

The tiny rock peak of West Bond is perched atop a narrow, steep-sided ridgecrest running SW from the main ridgeline near the N end of Mt. Bond. The narrow crest is about 0.3 mi. long and bears three small knobs; the easternmost is considered the true summit. The deep, winding valley of Hellgate Brook separates West Bond from Bondcliff to the S. The steep S and SE slopes of West Bond are striped with five great slides that are seen to advantage from the nearby crags of Bondcliff and serve as landmarks from more distant southern viewpoints. The N side of the ridge is somewhat less steep, with several ridges and ravines extending into the long, hidden valley of Redrock Brook. These northern slopes are splotched with extensive talus fields. The horseshoe of ridges formed by West Bond on the S, Mt. Guyot on the E, and the SW ridge of South Twin on the N enclose a remote, trailless area at the head of Redrock Brook featuring two glacial cirques, several enormous slides and scree slopes, and a tiny tarn in the northern cirque, known as Bear Pond or Redrock Pond. To the W the ridge of West Bond broadens as it descends 2500 ft. to the Franconia Brook valley.

The summit of West Bond offers unparalleled views into the Redrock and Hellgate valleys and across the latter to Bondcliff, the fine series of crags and ledges SW of Mt. Bond. Bondcliff is probably best known for its ragged cliff face dropping off several hundred feet into Hellgate Brook valley on its NW flank. "Surely the best photo opportunity in the mountains is looking towards slide-scarred West Bond with the fractured cliffs in the foreground," wrote longtime AMC guide editor Gene Daniell of Bondcliff's summit vista. The great climber Robert Underhill wrote in 1929 that "no one within grasp of the opportunity should forego visiting it." N of the summit a bare ridge extends nearly a mile across a shallow col to the SW shoulder of Mt. Bond. To the E is the long valley of Black Brook. To the W a broad ridge runs over two wooded spurs (3314 ft. and 2889 ft.) before descending to the Franconia Brook valley; this ridge forms

The slide-scarred west-facing slopes of Bondcliff are best viewed from the summit of remote West Bond.

the S side of the Hellgate Brook basin. Another ridge leads S from Bondcliff, soon passing over a sharp, wooded 3900-ft. spur, then fanning out into three sub-ridges that drop away to the East Branch valley. To the SW of the summit is the broad basin drained by Camp 9 Brook.

Mt. Guyot, whose double rounded summit rises along the ridge just N of the Bonds, is a favorite peak of many who visit this remote area and would be a worthy addition to the 4000-footer list. A look at the USGS map shows that it *could* qualify under the rule of a 200-ft. rise from the cols on all sides, but uncertainty about the exact col depth to the N (with South Twin) and on the S (with Mt. Bond) has kept Guyot off the list. Guyot's NE summit, which is bare on the S and W and covered with scrub on the N and E, is slightly higher than the bald SW summit; the latter is the better viewpoint. From the NE summit a long shoulder descends NE to the 4020-ft. col with Zealand Mtn.; to the N of this col is the remote upper bowl of the lengthy Little River valley. A minor ridge descends E from NE Guyot into the broad, isolated Jumping Brook basin. To the NW from Guyot, beyond a broad 4380-ft. col, a wide, flat ridge, cloaked in high scrub, extends towards South Twin. Guyot's most dramatic aspect is its steep SW face, overlooking the southerly of the two cirques at the head of Redrock Brook. This slope is scarred by cliffs and vast talus fields, giving Guyot a distinctive craggy and crinkled appearance when viewed from Franconia Ridge to the W.

The Bonds are about as far away from civilization as one can get in the Whites. The closest trailhead to either Bond or West Bond (at the end of

Zealand Rd.) is 8.2 mi. away. For Bondcliff, the closest trailhead is 9.1 mi. away at the Lincoln Woods lot off the Kancamagus Highway.

Nomenclature

The three peaks of the Bond Range are named for Professor George P. Bond, an early mapmaker and geographer affiliated with Harvard University. Bond was responsible for producing the first highly respected map of the White Mountains area back in 1853. The name "Mt. Bond" was assigned to the "southernmost summit of the Twin Range" by the Appalachian Mountain Club in 1876. (At the same time, they named the next peak to the N after another noted geographer, Arnold Guyot, who produced his own map of the Whites in 1860.) For many years, Bondcliff was referred to as The Cliffs or The Cliffs of Bond. One group of early explorers of the peaks identified Mt. Bond as "Craggy Mtn.," and the AMC group that made the first ascent of the Bonds in 1871 originally proposed the name, "Mt. Percival," after a poet and geologist from Connecticut. West Bond was just known as a western spur of the range for many years; only after the 4000-Footer Club was formed in 1957 did it actually receive a name.

Early AMC maps, which used a system of letter-and-number notation for summits (similar to that which gave us "K2" in the Karakoram), assigned the letter "J" to the Twin–Bond Range. Mt. Bond was "J.3.1," the SW summit of Guyot "J.3.2," NE Guyot "J.3.3," West Bond's western and eastern knobs "J.3.4" and "J.3.4b" and Bondcliff "J.3.5."

Redrock Brook was presumably named for the red-tinted boulders in its bed. Early maps of the Pemi applied this name to the main stream flowing S between the Bonds and Owl's Head, what is now known as the Franconia Branch. Hellgate is presumably a logger's term referring to a constriction in a brook or valley and seems appropriate to the narrow, twisting brook valley to which it has been applied. The origin of Jumping Brook's name is unknown; perhaps it refers to its fast flow over countless boulders.

Historical Highlights

First Ascent: The first known ascent of at least one, and possibly all three Bonds, was made in 1871 by two members of Charles Hitchcock's geological survey team—Warren Upham and an unidentified Dartmouth College student. Working from a camp a mile up Franconia Brook in what was then true wilderness, four of the group climbed up the ridge of Owl's Head, then Upham and his companion dropped E into the valley and ascended the Bond ridge via "the western spur," noting "the almost perpendicular face of rock, like some castle wall . . . at the top of the south peak on its northwest side." In relating his findings in *Appalachia* in 1876, Upham said, "The view [from Mt. Bond] is wholly of forest-covered mountains on every side, and I think no evidence is seen of the works of man, except for the small settlement on the summit of Mt. Washington."

1882: A. E. Scott leads party of six on week-long bushwhack epic over Twin Range. Trip includes ascents of North Twin, South Twin, Mt. Guyot, Mt. Bond, Bondcliff, and Mt. Field (in Willey Range). Their descent to valley off Bondcliff is made via Black Brook valley. Account of adventure appears in April 1883 *Appalachia*. In article, Scott notes prominent boulder near summit of Mt. Bond and gateway leading up from Hellgate valley at edge of Bondcliff. He is particularly taken by the scene at the cliffs, which "rise almost vertically from the valley below, like the ruins of some enormous castle . . . the view from this crag surpasses everything we have ever beheld. Never before have we realized the extent of the Pemigewasset Forest, or the grandeur of the mountains which rise in and around it."

1883: Trail from South Twin to Mt. Bond is cut by Scott, others. Also, rough trail is spotted over Bondcliff and down to East Branch by way of Bear Brook (Black Brook).

1883: W. L. Hooper of AMC bushwhacks from Franconia Brook up W ridge of Bondcliff.

1900: AMC cuts new route from Mt. Bond down to North Fork Junction on East Branch, bypassing old route over Bondcliff.

1902: Overgrown and little-used path over Twins and Bond refurbished by AMC.

1903–1910: Working from Camps 9, 10 and 14 (the latter well up Redrock Brook valley) off Franconia Brook spur of logging railroad, J. E. Henry's crews strip timber from W slopes of Bonds.

1907: Great fire starts on Owl's Head and consumes much of remaining timber on W slopes of Bonds. Present birch forest in much of area is legacy of fire.

1907: First *AMC Guide* lists trail from Mt. Bond to North Fork.

1913: New log shelter, to be known as Guyot Shelter, is built near spring between Mts. Guyot and Bond.

1916: Charles Blood (AMC) proposes new path from Bond to Bondcliff.

1916–1931: Timber crews from Henry Co. and Parker-Young Co. advance up North Fork of East Branch along another railroad spur. Working from Camps 22, 22A, 23 and 23A, they ravage E slopes of Bonds.

1920: Lower portion of North Fork Trail from Mt. Bond is rerouted S to railroad nearer to North Fork Jct.

1920–21: Side trail cut from Bond to Bondcliff.

1923: AMC trail-builders complete Zealand Ridge Trail leading across Zealand Ridge from Zealand Notch to Mt. Guyot.

1924: Tireless AMC trail-builder Karl Harrington extends Twin Range Trail from summit of Mt. Bond down to Bondcliff, and then out to logging railroad line on East Branch of Pemi. Former trail from Bond to North Fork Jct. is abandoned.

1926: Original Guyot Shelter replaced by new log structure.

1929: Path over Twins–Bonds dubbed "Most Troublesome Trail in White Mountains" by Paul Jenks (AMC).

1934: Section of former Twin Range Trail between new Twinway trail near Mt. Guyot and logging rail line now called Bondcliff Trail.

1939: AMC crews construct third Guyot Shelter.

1960: For first time, *AMC Guide* describes bushwhack route to summit of West Bond, created by hikers pursuing new (1957) official 4000-footer list; hikers are cautioned to allow at least three hours for the short but arduous round trip. Description of route to West Bond first appeared in June 1958 issue of *Appalachia*.

1960: First known winter ascent of Bonds is made by party led by Bob Collin, via Zealand Ridge and Mt. Guyot. Feat is repeated next day by Robert and Miriam Underhill and Merle Whitcomb, from Galehead Hut.

1963: Group led by Collin makes spectacular winter traverse of West Bond, up from cirque in Redrock Brook valley and down W ridge to Franconia Brook. Trip is part of nine day backpacking epic in Pemi Wilderness, in era of unbroken trails.

1966: *AMC Guide* notes that side trail to West Bond is "well-worn" and takes just 25 min. each way. Path is soon officially adopted as "West Bond Spur."

1971: Tent platforms added at Guyot Shelter campsite.

1972: Camp 16 Shelter, built a few years earlier at bottom of Bondcliff Trail, burns in February fire.

Ca. 1980: Bondcliff is added to 4000-Footer list when it's determined that new USGS 7½′ South Twin quad shows elevation gain from Bond–Bondcliff col to summit exceeding requisite 200 feet. About this time lower mile of Bondcliff Trail is relocated along W side of Black Brook to avoid several stream crossings.

1984: Bonds are included in 45,000 acre Pemigewasset Wilderness created by Congress.

Trail Approaches

South Approach from Kancamagus Highway (NH 112)

BONDCLIFF ONLY

Lincoln Woods Trail, Wilderness Trail, Bondcliff Trail
18.2 mi. round trip, 3300-ft. elevation gain

BONDCLIFF AND MT. BOND

Lincoln Woods Trail, Wilderness Trail, Bondcliff Trail
20.6 mi. round trip, 4150-ft. elevation gain

BONDCLIFF, MT. BOND AND WEST BOND

Lincoln Woods Trail, Wilderness Trail, Bondcliff Trail, West Bond Spur
22.6 mi. round trip, 4800-ft. elevation gain

TRAILHEAD (1160 ft.): Large Lincoln Woods parking area on N side of Kancamagus Highway (NH 112), 5.6 mi. E of Exit 32 off I-93 in Lincoln. There is a staffed WMNF information station with restrooms here.

Though exceptionally long, the approach to the Bonds from the S is relatively easy as the trail (at least to Bondcliff) mostly follows either an old logging railroad grade or old logging roads. Only one steep section in the Black Brook valley, the last quarter-mile to Bondcliff's summit, the half-mile ascent of Bond from the S, and the short pitch to West Bond can be considered strenuous.

From Lincoln Woods parking area, drop down stairs in front of ranger cabin and cross large suspension footbridge over wide, rocky East Branch of Pemigewasset River, one of premier wilderness streams in region. On far side turn R on Lincoln Woods Trail for easy walking along wide, level bed of J.E. Henry's East Branch & Lincoln RR (1893–1948), with many hemlock ties still astride trail. At 0.4 mi. trail emerges on high bank with glimpses of river and ridges of Mt. Hitchcock beyond, then trail pulls away from river, crossing culvert over Osseo Brook at 0.8 mi. Long straightaway, with one section next to Osseo Brook, leads to jct. L with Osseo Trail at 1.4 mi. / 1300 ft. and Camp 8 clearing on L just beyond. Trail approaches river again at 1.6 mi. with picturesque view of Bondcliff upstream from rocks at water's edge. Trail soon crosses bridge over Birch Island Brook and enters mile-long straight section. At 2.6 mi. Black Pond Trail splits L. At 2.9 mi. / 1440 ft. is side trail L to scenic Franconia Falls (0.4 mi.).

Continue ahead across footbridge over Franconia Brook (rebuilt in 2007, view of Mt. Flume upstream to L), climb up bank, and bear R onto Wilderness Trail past boundary sign for Pemigewasset Wilderness as Franconia Brook Trail diverges L up onto high bank. After bypass of mucky area continue along railroad grade, mostly away from river, crossing "One-Mile Brook" at 3.9 mi.; approaching crossing, northern ridges of Mts. Hitchcock and Hancock can be seen through trees to R. Continue straight, nearly level walking, with many ties across trail in places, and reach extensive clearing on L at site of former Camp 16 tenting area, and jct. L with Bondcliff Trail just beyond at 4.7 mi. / 1600 ft. This part of walk is often accomplished in under two hours. (A short distance ahead on Wilderness Trail is remains of old railroad trestle over Black Brook, interesting to look at but unsafe to go on or under).

Bear L onto Bondcliff Trail on short stretch of spur railroad grade, with piece of rail visible, and in 100 yds. bear L up bank onto relocated section where trail formerly continued ahead across brook. Ascend moderately, then gradually N along relocated section of trail to W of and well above Black Brook, passing through nice hardwood forest. At 5.8 mi., after gradual descent and occasional wet footing, trail swings R and then turns L onto old logging road beside brook—former route of trail. Grade is easy to moderate, footing a bit rocky, through young conifers to first crossing of Black Brook (to E side) at 6.1 mi. / 2100 ft. Second crossing is at 6.6 mi / 2360 ft. Swing R and dip to third crossing, sometimes dry, at 7.2 mi. / 2780 ft. On far side of brook trail horseshoes around minor ridge, a confusing spot, first swinging R down dry brookbed for ca. 60 ft., then swinging L to climb long rock staircases. Trail levels on scrubby slope at 3000 ft. and crosses small gravel slide with view across and up to steep E flank of Bondcliff, crowned by rock peak. Just beyond is fourth crossing of brook, usually dry, in steep ravine. Trail loops around to R, bears L up tiny ridge, then at 7.9 mi. / 3360 ft. swings L again to pick up old logging road for slabbing ascent across steep slope. Spindly birches and young conifers crowd edges of footway.

At 8.4 mi. / 3650 ft. trail swings to R, with rocky footing. Reach crest of Bondcliff's S ridge at 8.8 mi. / 3960 ft. and bear R for steady climb. At 9.0 mi. you must negotiate short but difficult scramble up ledge (a 10-ft. high cliff), where it may be necessary to hand packs up, emerging at top to wide views S and W. Climb easily through scrub, with views L down into basin of Camp 9 Brook, then completely in open to flat, ledgy summit of Bondcliff at 9.1 mi. / 4265 ft. Here there are incomparable wilderness views in every direction. Craggy perch at edge of cliffs with West Bond in background is a hiker's favorite photo-op.

To continue to Mt. Bond, follow Bondcliff Trail to N along barren ridge. Trail is exposed for next mile and this section should not be traversed in bad weather. Follow markings carefully and keep back from W edge, which drops off in steep cliffs. In fair weather, this is one of most spectacular ridge walks in Whites. Trail descends steadily NE along side of barren ridge, then swings N at easy grade to long, level 4060-ft. col, with impressive views across to slides on West Bond. Trail continues in open as it begins ascent of SW slope of Mt. Bond, soon becoming steeper and rougher, with jumbled rocks. At ca. 10.0 mi. / 4400 ft., halfway up side of Bond, trail enters scrub and continues rugged, rocky climb, attaining open summit of Bond at 10.3 mi. / 4698 ft. Here trail makes sharp turn to L (N); high point is just to R of trail, with superb 360-degree view. Hiking in reverse direction, note that trail turns R (SW) as it leaves summit area en route to Bondcliff.

To proceed to West Bond, continue N on Bondcliff Trail, entering conifer woods and descending to minor col. Climb slightly over level-topped
N hump of Mt. Bond and drop easily, then more steeply to jct. L with
West Bond Spur at 10.8 mi. / 4500 ft. (Side trail R to Guyot Shelter, 0.2
mi. long, is 0.2 mi. farther N on Bondcliff Trail.) Turn L here and descend steadily on narrow trail through dense firs to col at 11.1 mi. / 4340
ft. Grade eases here as trail swings L and then quickly R to begin ascent
of West Bond. Climb is moderate at first, then quite steep up to E end
of summit crest, emerging in open and scrambling over rocks to top of
small, sharp peak of West Bond at 11.3 mi. / 4540 ft. Views are matchless,
especially across Hellgate valley to Bondcliff and over Redrock cirques to
South Twin.

Northeast Approach from Zealand Road (FR 16)
For options below, add 0.2 mi. for easy round trip to Zealand Mtn.
summit.

WEST BOND ONLY

Zealand Trail, Twinway, Bondcliff Trail, West Bond Spur
16.4 mi. round trip, 4050-ft. elevation gain

MT. BOND ONLY

Zealand Trail, Twinway, Bondcliff Trail
16.4 mi. round trip, 3900-ft. elevation gain

MT. BOND AND WEST BOND

Zealand Trail, Twinway, Bondcliff Trail, West Bond Spur
17.4 mi. round trip, 4250-ft. elevation gain

WEST BOND, MT. BOND AND BONDCLIFF

Zealand Trail, Twinway, Bondcliff Trail, West Bond Spur
19.8 mi. round trip, 5100-ft. elevation gain

ZEALAND TO LINCOLN WOODS TRAVERSE

Zealand Trail, Twinway, Bondcliff Trail, West Bond Spur,
Wilderness Trail, Lincoln Woods Trail
19.5 mi. one way, 3950-ft. elevation gain

With a long car spot, this traverse, which includes side trip to West Bond,
is probably the easiest way to do the Bonds! For Lincoln Woods to Zealand traverse, elevation gain is 4800 ft. due to lower starting point.

Standing atop the ragged cliff face of Bondcliff, with the scarred walls of West Bond in the background.

TRAILHEAD (2000 ft.): From US 302, 2.2 mi. E of stoplight in Twin Mountain, follow USFS seasonal Zealand Rd. (FR 16)—paved for 1 mi., then gravel—3.5 mi. to parking area at end.

A somewhat shorter alternative (especially for reaching Bond and West Bond) is the approach from the Zealand River valley by way of AMC's Zealand Falls Hut and Zealand Mtn. (another 4000-footer). Though shorter by a couple of miles, there's significantly more elevation gain with an out-and-back trip to all three Bonds since you'll be climbing the summit cones of Mt. Bond and Zealand Mtn. twice. The Zealand to Lincoln Woods traverse, with car spot, has become an increasingly popular option.

For description of route via Zealand Trail and Twinway as far as side trail to summit of Zealand Mtn. (5.6 mi.), see chapter on that mountain. From Zealand summit side trail, Twinway makes fairly steep, rocky descent to Zealand–Guyot col (4020 ft.) at 5.8 mi. Trail now begins moderate climb up long, heavily wooded NE ridge of Mt. Guyot. Grade eases on shoulder at 4200 ft., but footing is very rocky in places. Trail makes sharp L at 6.6 mi. / 4380 ft. and ascends steadily again, then gradually, to broad NE summit of Mt. Guyot at 6.8 mi. / 4580 ft. Here trail emerges into open; please stay on defined treadway to protect alpine vegetation. Descend to jct. L with Bondcliff Trail at 6.9 mi. / 4508 ft. Here the views open dramatically to the W over the wild Redrock Brook valley to Owl's Head, Franconia Range and SW ridge of South Twin, with two huge slides close by to the R.

Turn L here on Bondcliff Trail (Twinway bears R towards South Twin Mtn.) and traverse along W side of barren ridge to bald SW summit of Mt. Guyot at 7.1 mi. / 4580 ft. From this rounded alpine summit there are excellent views in all directions to the peaks in and around the Pemi Wilderness, including impressive broadside view of nearby West Bond ridge with its three small peaks. Continue S along Bondcliff Trail in open, then descend into woods, with rocky footing, to small col and pass over minor hump to main Guyot–Bond col at 7.5 mi. / 4380 ft. Here side trail leads L 0.2 mi., with 250-ft. elevation loss, to Guyot Shelter (accommodates 12) and Campsite (with 6 tent platforms). There is also a fine, reliable spring here that makes the down-and-up side trip well worthwhile for thirsty Bonds trekkers. As many hikers are not into torturing themselves with 20-mile-plus day-hikes, the Bonds are a popular destination with backpackers; though remote, this overnight destination is usually filled to capacity on summer / fall weekends. When full, campers are directed to overflow area near Bondcliff Trail on N shoulder of Mt. Bond.

From this jct., Bondcliff Trail ascends steadily to jct. R with West Bond Spur at 7.7 mi. / 4500 ft. West Bond is 0.5 mi. along spur; Mt. Bond is 0.5 mi. ahead on Bondcliff Trail, with Bondcliff 1.2 mi. beyond.

NORTH APPROACH

Another, lesser used approach to the Bonds, primarily for backpackers or guests staying at AMC Galehead Hut, is from the N, either from Galehead Hut (accessed from WMNF Gale River Loop Rd. via Gale River Trail and Garfield Ridge Trail) or from WMNF Haystack Rd. (North Twin Trail trailhead). One day traverses to Lincoln Woods are also possible with carspot. These entail ascents of South Twin (from Galehead Hut) or North and South Twin (from Haystack Rd.). For detailed descriptions of routes to these summits, see North and South Twin chapter. From South Twin, follow Twinway S steeply down off rocky summit cone and into woods. Trail continues on easy grades along high, broad ridge wooded with high scrub. At 0.9 mi. from South Twin pass over hump with limited views ahead to Guyot and Bond and back towards South Twin. After reaching South Twin–Guyot col (4380 ft.), trail climbs gently through scrub along W slope of Guyot and meets jct. with Bondcliff Trail (4508 ft.) 2.0 mi. S of South Twin summit. Follow Bondcliff Trail S over SW summit of Mt. Guyot and on to Bonds as described above.

ROUND-TRIP DISTANCES FROM GALEHEAD HUT

Twinway, Bondcliff Trail, West Bond Spur
(for options including West Bond)
    West Bond only: 8.2 mi., 2750-ft. elevation gain
    Mt. Bond only: 8.2 mi., 2600-ft. elevation gain
    West Bond and Mt. Bond: 9.2 mi., 2950-ft. elevation gain
    West Bond, Mt. Bond and Bondcliff: 11.6 mi., 3850-ft. elevation gain

TRAVERSE FROM WMNF HAYSTACK RD. (NORTH TWIN TRAIL TRAILHEAD) TO LINCOLN WOODS (INCLUDING SIDE TRIP TO WEST BOND)

North Twin Trail, North Twin Spur, Twinway, Bondcliff Trail, West Bond Spur, Wilderness Trail, Lincoln Woods Trail
20.2 mi. one-way, 4700-ft. elevation gain (5350 ft. in reverse direction)

TRAVERSE FROM WMNF GALE RIVER LOOP RD. TO LINCOLN WOODS (INCLUDING SIDE TRIP TO WEST BOND)

Gale River Trail, Garfield Ridge Trail, Twinway, Bondcliff Trail, West Bond Spur, Wilderness Trail, Lincoln Woods Trail
20.0 mi. one-way, 4650-ft. elevation gain (5100 ft. in reverse direction)
    (add 1.0 mi., 250 ft. for side trip to Galehead Mtn. on Frost Trail)

Winter

Due to their remoteness, the Bonds are among the hardest peaks to "bag" during the winter months. Although it makes for a grueling 20+ mile day, most hikers choose to ascend all three summits in a single day, rather than have to make one or two return trips. The best time of winter to tackle the Bonds is in February or March, owing to the extra hours of daylight available. It's best done on a clear, relatively calm day. As all three peaks are open (particularly Bondcliff), exposure to the winter wind and cold is always a concern on the Bonds; full winter clothing and gear are needed, and crampons may be required for the open ridge between Bondcliff and Bond.

The usual route taken is from the S (Kancamagus Highway) along the

Lincoln Woods, Wilderness and Bondcliff Trails. The first 4.7 mi. on Lincoln Woods and Wilderness Trails are usually well-tracked out and provide a quick approach. With unbroken snow, the remaining 4.4 mi. to Bondcliff can take many hours. It's easy to lose the trail as you climb into the scrub on the S side of Mt. Bond. The Bondcliff Trail N of Mt. Bond has some of the deepest snow in the Whites.

The out-and-back approach from Zealand is impractical as a day-hike as Zealand Rd. is closed to motor vehicle traffic. One possibility is to stay at Zealand Falls Hut (open on caretaker basis; winter-rated sleeping bag needed) and day-hike the Bonds from there, nabbing Zealand along the way. This would cut the trip to all three Bonds down to 14.6 mi. round trip with 4300-ft. elevation gain. Some peakbaggers opt for a longer winter version of the Zealand to Lincoln Woods traverse, parking at the large Zealand winter parking lot on US 302 and walking 0.2 mi. along Rt. 302 and 3.5 mi. up Zealand Rd. to the Zealand Trail. The winter traverse is 23.2 mi. with 4550-ft. elevation gain. The section between Zealand Mtn. and the West Bond Spur is less often broken out, and may be heavily drifted and in places hard to follow, and the section over Mt. Guyot is fully exposed to cold NW winds. The northern approaches from Galehead Hut (closed in winter) or the North Twin trailhead are both longer in winter due to unplowed roads and are rarely used to tackle the Bonds. The stretch of the Twinway between South Twin and Guyot can be a particularly difficult wallow through deep snow filled with spruce traps.

View Guide

All three Bonds are rated among the top viewing spots in the White Mountains for their expansive wilderness vistas. Warren Upham, along with a companion the first to climb the Bonds back in 1871, was captivated by what he saw: "From these summits, especially from Mt. Bond, which best overlooks the East Branch valley, the prospect is extensive and grand. As far as the view extends, we see only mountains and valleys and forest...All is silent untrodden forest, and all around are the lofty foreheads of our highest mountains." After a recovery from the rapacious logging of the early 1900s, these Pemi views are once again perhaps the finest in the mountains.

MT. BOND VIEW: The highest of the Bonds has the most comprehensive view, because Bond itself blocks out parts of the vistas from Bondcliff and West Bond. To the E Bond offers a great sweep over the eastern Pemi Wilderness. To the NE, beyond the basin of Jumping Brook, the mighty Presidentials tower above the Willey Range, with the prominent ledges of Whitewall Mtn. on the E side of Zealand Notch in front. Mt. Jefferson rises to the L of Mt. Tom, with Sam Adams poking up on its L and the summit of Mt. Adams just visible on its R. Mt. Clay is over the Tom–Field col, and Mt. Washington is just L of Mt. Field, with Mts. Monroe and Eisenhower below and in front on Washington's R and Mt. Pierce seen right above Field. Boott Spur rises in the back to the R of Field, with a ridge descending R to Slide Peak. Farther R Carter Dome pokes up, in back of and to the L of Mt. Willey, with Mt. Hight just poking up on its L and Rainbow Ridge on its R. The Wildcats can be seen in front of and under Carter Dome, but only if the light is just right. The tip of Mt. Jackson peeks over the ridge to the L of Willey, and Mt. Isolation is just behind Willey on the R. To the ENE the broad upper valley of the North Fork extends out to Ethan Pond at the base of Mt. Willey; the ledges of Thoreau Falls can be seen in line with the summit of Willey, as can the bare shoulder on the E ridge of Bond right below. To the R of Willey are the Webster Cliffs with the long ridge of Mt. Davis beyond. Peering over the Davis crest are (L to R) Speckled Mtn., North and South Baldface, Sable Mtn. and Chandler Mtn.

To the E the lower North Fork valley and the ridge informally known as "Shoal Pond Peak" are in the foreground; beyond, a spruce-clad plateau extends out to the trailless Ethan Ridge between Mt. Willey and the Nancy Range. Beyond this ridge are (L to R) North and South Doublehead (in back), the Giant Stairs, Mt. Resolution with Mt. Shaw behind, the twin Gemini, Mt. Crawford (in front), the dome of Kearsarge North, and Mt. Parker. The Nancy Range (L to R, Mts. Bemis, Nancy, Anderson and Lowell) is spread out to the ESE. Black Cap Mtn. is seen between Bemis and Nancy, with Maine's Pleasant Mtn. beyond to the L. Middle Mtn. (L, in back) and Little Attitash Mtn. (R) are seen above the Norcross Brook valley between Nancy and Anderson. North Moat Mtn. is behind Anderson, with Big Attitash Mtn. in front and Middle and South Moat extending to its R. Douglas Mtn. in Maine is seen in the distance to the L of North Moat, with Sebago Lake to its L, and the Burnt Meadow Mtns. are above Middle and South Moat. The Bill Merrill Mtn. range in Maine is on the horizon above Lowell. To the SE is the huge, shapely bulk of Mt. Carrigain, with Vose Spur on its L. Table Mtn. (L) and Bartlett Haystack (R) are seen through Carrigain Notch, between Mt. Lowell and Vose Spur, and Bear Mtn. pokes up between Vose Spur and Carrigain, with part of Mt. Tremont in front of it on the R. The Clark Mtn. range is in the distance to the L of Bear, and White Ledge is behind Bear on the R.

To the R of Carrigain is the sprawling mass of Mt. Hancock, with the great ravine of Crystal Brook carved into the S side of its rounded North Peak. The small nubble of The Captain rises from the deep gap between Carrigain and Hancock, with Mt. Paugus above it and Green's Cliff peering over on its L. The Nickerson Mtns. are seen under distant Bauneg Beg Mtn. over the saddle to the R of Paugus. Mt. Passaconaway (L) and Mt. Whiteface (R) pop out over the L shoulder of Hancock, with the tip of

Copple Crown Mtn. seen just R of Passaconaway and the top of Mt. Shaw in the Ossipee Range just L of Whiteface. Mt. Tripyramid is seen in back just to the R of North Hancock, with the sharp NW Hancock in front and below. To the R of Tripyramid Mt., Kancamagus is seen above Mt. Huntington, with a slice of the northern Flat Mtn. seen above and behind Kancamagus. A long spread of the Belknap Range can be seen in the distance over Kancamagus, with Belknap Mtn. prominent on its R end. Next to the R, looking S, Sandwich Dome is seen through Mad River Notch, with the four Osceola peaks rising beyond Mt. Hitchcock on the R. Mt. Tecumseh and its West Peak poke up in back to the R of the Osceolas. Next to the R are the various summits of Scar Ridge. North Pack Monadnock (L) and Crotched Mtn. (R) can be seen far away above and to the R of East Scar Ridge. Bridgewater Mtn. is in back to the L of the sharp Middle Scar. Mt. Kearsarge is seen in the distance between Middle Scar and the broad mass of the main Scar Ridge summit. Plymouth Mtn. is under and in front of Kearsarge, with Ragged Mtn. to their R. On clear days Mt. Monadnock can be seen peeking over to the R of Kearsarge.

Above the R end of the main Scar Ridge, the rounded Lovewell Mtn. peeks over a saddle between Forbes Mtn. and Tinkham Hill, and farther R Sunapee Mtn. stretches across the horizon above the nearer Tenney Mtn. range. Next to the R, looking SSW, you look down on the nearby, dramatic rearing crags of Bondcliff, with Loon Mtn. just above and Mt. Cardigan seen behind Stinson Mtn. in the distance. To the R of Bondcliff, seen over the nearby flat-topped E spur of Whaleback Mtn, is the broad mass of Carr Mtn. in the mid-distance. Mt. Kineo stretches in front of Carr, with Mt. Cushman to the R, over the sharp main peak of Whaleback. Croydon Peak is in the distance to the L of Carr, and Vermont's Mt. Ascutney is on the horizon above Cushman. On very clear days Stratton Mtn. can be spotted to the R of Ascutney. Farther R is massive Smarts Mtn. with Okemo Mtn. seen in the distance just to its R.

From Whaleback Mtn. a ridge extends R to Mt. Flume and Mt. Liberty with Mt. Moosilauke hovering beyond and between them. The rocky S peak of Owl's Head is in front of Liberty. The main mass of Owl's Head is in front of the central part of the Franconia Range. South Kinsman Mtn. peers over the ridge just L of Little Haystack Mtn., with distant ridges in the Brandon Gap area of Vermont's Green Mtns. seen farther L, over the broad saddle between Liberty and Little Haystack.

Due W and close by is the slide-scarred spine of West Bond, with Mts. Lincoln and Lafayette soaring behind. The sharp peak of Garfield is to the R of West Bond, and beyond the ridge joining Lafayette and Garfield the view extends out to Vermont's Green Mountains, including (L to R) the Worcester Range, Mt. Mansfield and the Sterling Range. In the foreground to the R of Garfield is the long SW ridge of South Twin Mtn., with more Green Mtns peaks on the horizon (L to R): Laraway Mtn., the

Cold Hollow Mtns., Belvidere and Haystack Mtns., the sharp Jay Peaks, and then Round Top in Quebec's Sutton Mtns.

Next to the R and close by, beyond the N shoulder of Bond, is the high rocky crown of South Twin Mtn. The tip of Burke Mtn. in Vermont can be seen through a col just L of South Twin, and part of North Twin Mtn. is seen off the R shoulder of South Twin. To the R of South Twin and closer are the two bald, rounded summits of Mt. Guyot, with a nameless hump above and just behind the L (SW) Guyot summit. Gore Mtn. in the Northeast Kingdom is seen on the horizon above the nameless hump, and Black and Brousseau Mtns. are in the distance above Burnside Mtn. (all in Vermont) through the little gap on the L side of Guyot's R (NE) summit. Sharp Sable Mtn. is over the L end of NE Guyot's broad summit, and over NE Guyot's R side, looking almost due N, is the double-peaked Goback Mtn. near Stratford, New Hampshire, with Quebec's Hereford Mtn. lurking on the horizon to the L. To the R of Goback is the Nash Stream range, including West Peak, Bunnell Mtn. (in back), Gore Mtn. and Sugarloaf. Next to the R Hutchins Mtn. and the Pilot Ridge are seen in the distance over Cherry Mtn., with Mt. Hale farther R and closer. Mt. Cabot is behind Hale on the R, and Long Mtn. can be seen in the back to the L of Cabot.

Stretching to the R of Hale and Cabot and closer is the long, wooded Zealand Ridge, with the summit of Zealand Mtn. on its L end (under Cabot) and the sharp Zeacliff Pond Peak to the R of center along the ridge. The Pliny Range is seen above Zealand, with Mt. Starr King in front of Cabot and Mt. Waumbek and its long E ridge to the R. To the R of Waumbek's E ridge is its low spur, Pond Hill, with Mt. Dustan's sharp peak seen over the gap between them and many far-off peaks in NW Maine on the horizon. In line with Pond Hill and lower, and just L of Zeacliff Pond peak, is the summit of Mt. Rosebrook. Mt. Deception in the Dartmouth Range is above Zeacliff Pond peak and extends to the R; West Kennebago Mtn. is in the distance over the L end of Deception. Mt. Dartmouth continues the range to the R of Deception, with the Crescent Range seen in back between them (Black Crescent Mtn. on the L, Mt. Crescent on the R). Cambridge Black Mtn. is seen behind and R of Black Crescent. Over the R shoulder of Mt. Dartmouth is Red Ridge with Metallak Mtn. behind on the L and Bemis Mtn. behind on the R; in this direction and lower and much closer is the flat ridge of Zeacliff. Then the view swings back to the Presidentials and the Willey Range.

WEST BOND VIEW: The tiny rock peak of West Bond is perhaps the penultimate wilderness viewpoint in the White Mountains, providing a splendid sense of lofty isolation amidst a maze of high ridges and deep valleys.

The most striking view is SSE across the wild, cavernous valley of Hellgate Brook to the arching crest of Bondcliff, with its ragged line of crags in full frontal view. Rising beyond Bondcliff and the scree-splotched ridge that extends L to Mt. Bond is a tumult of rumpled mountains. On the L between Bond and Bondcliff is the Moat Range. North Moat is on the L with Big Attitash Mtn. in front and Middle and South Moat are to the R. The Burnt Meadow Mtns. in Maine are beyond the R side of the Moats, then you see the scarred face of Mt. Lowell, forming the E side of Carrigain Notch with Vose Spur forming the other side to the R. Table Mtn. is seen through the notch with Maine's Bill Merrill Mtn. group on the horizon. Part of Bear Mtn. is seen through the col to the R of Vose Spur. Next to the R is the great bulk of Mt. Carrigain, with the sharp peak of Mt. Chocorua seen off its R slope. Part of Green Mtn. in Effingham is seen beyond Chocorua on the R. Farther R is Chocorua's neighbor, Mt. Paugus, with the flat top of The Captain seen under the lower N spurs of Paugus and several small peaks in SW Maine on the horizon. Green's Cliff can be seen through the little gap to the L of The Captain. Bauneg Beg Mtn. is in the distance just R of Paugus. Next to the R is the massive sprawl of Mt. Hancock, with Mt. Passaconaway peering over to the L of North Hancock's rounded dome, above the head of the Crystal Brook ravine. Behind the R side of North Hancock are Mt. Whiteface (L) and the Tripyramids (R, rising behind Mt. Huntington). Mt. Kancamagus is behind Huntington on the R, with the E end of the Belknap Range on the horizon just R of its sharp summit and the northern Flat Mtn. just seen over its R end.

Just L of Bondcliff's summit is Mad River Notch, with Belknap and Gunstock Mtns. on the horizon. Massive Sandwich Dome fills the R side of the notch, with the sharp peak of East Osceola just to its R. Next to the R is the main summit of Osceola, with its Middle and West Peaks on the R and Mt. Hitchcock below and in front. Mt. Tecumseh and its West Peak are seen behind and R of the Osceolas, with the East Peak of Scar Ridge in front of Tecumseh's West Peak. Hersey Mtn. is on the horizon to the R of West Tecumseh. The Bridgewater Mtns. can be spotted to the R of the sharp Middle Peak of Scar Ridge, and on a clear day North Pack Monadnock (L) and Crotched Mtn. (R) can be seen on the skyline above Middle Scar.

Farther R, over the lower W ridge of Bondcliff, sections of the wide, rocky East Branch can be seen winding out to the massive main summit of Scar Ridge, with the lower Loon Mtn. on its R. Mt. Kearsarge is on the distant horizon above the main Scar Ridge, with Ragged Mtn. to its R. On clear days Mt. Monadnock can be seen over Ragged. Forbes Mtn. (L) and Tinkham Hill (R) are over the saddle to the R of Scar Ridge, with Lovewell Mtn. behind, while Tenney Mtn. (L) and Mt. Crosby (R) are seen over Loon, with Sunapee Mtn. on the horizon between them. To the R of Loon, Mt. Cardigan is seen in the distance above Stinson Mtn. Farther R, the long E ridge of Mt. Kineo is seen over the flat E spur of Whaleback Mtn. Next to the R is the sharp main peak of Whaleback Mtn. Carr Mtn. is seen behind Mt. Kineo above Whaleback, with Mt. Cushman to their R. Croydon Peak is seen behind Carr on the L. A level ridge extends R from Whaleback, with Smarts Mtn. poking up in back and part of Mt. Moosilauke's Blue Ridge over its R end. Vermont's Mt. Ascutney can be seen in the distance to the L of Smarts, and on very clear days Stratton Mtn. is visible behind Ascutney on the R. Next to the R are the SW humps of West Bond rising close at hand, with the tip of Mt. Flume peeking over the top. To the R is the graceful peak of Mt. Liberty, with Mt. Moosilauke looming through the col between Flume and Liberty.

From Liberty a gentle ridge descends and rises on the R to the upper Franconia Range—Little Haystack Mtn., Mt. Lincoln and Mt. Lafayette, with the broad mass of Owl's Head below. The slash of Lincoln Slide is prominent to the R of Mt. Lincoln. Some of the Green Mtn. peaks in the Brandon Gap area can be seen over the saddle between Liberty and Little Haystack. From Lafayette the bumpy Garfield Ridge stretches across to the rocky pyramid of Mt. Garfield. Below these peaks is the remote forested basin at the headwaters of Franconia Brook. On the horizon between Lafayette and Garfield are (L to R) the Worcester Range, Mt. Mansfield (seen above the Garfield cliff and the bumpy hump on the ridge between Lafayette and Garfield) and the Sterling Range in Vermont. In the foreground in front of and to the R of Garfield, seen across the wild valley of Redrock Brook, a long ridge rises up over the wooded hump of SW Twin towards the main ridgecrest of the Twin Range, with the rocky crest of South Twin rising in back.

To the R of Garfield, the town of Littleton and part of Moore Reservoir are visible in the middle distance. Seen on the horizon between Garfield and SW Twin, beyond the eastern humps of Garfield Ridge, are distant mountains in northern Vermont, including (L to R) the Cold Hollow Mtns., the pyramid of Belvidere Mtn., Tillotson Peak, Haystack Mtn. and the prominent Jay Peaks. Through the saddle to the R of SW Twin are Burke and Umpire Mtns. with Bald Mtn. in Vermont's Northeast Kingdom behind on the R.

The view N across the wild cirques of Redrock Brook is unique to West Bond. The L, or northern of the bowls is under South Twin. Tiny Bear Pond can be glimpsed at the base of a talus slope on the floor of the ravine, and a great slide that fell ca. 1996 can be seen on the headwall of the cirque. The southern and closer of the glacial basins bears two more large slides facing towards West Bond. The L slide is long and narrow, the R is a huge, wide gash. Both fell in 1994. To the R is the nearby bald double dome of Mt. Guyot. Through the col to the L of Guyot are Mt. Cabot (L) and Mts. Starr King and Waumbek (R). Two lower Pilot Range peaks are seen to the L of Cabot, with Long Mtn. peering over in back. Mts. Jefferson and Clay are prominent through the col on Guyot's R.

Mt. Dartmouth is seen in closer on the L side of the col. In the distance between Dartmouth and Jefferson are (L to R) Red Ridge, Bemis Mtn. and Elephant Mtn. in Maine. Sam Adams peers over on the L side of Jefferson. To the R of Clay the tip of Mt. Washington just pokes over the N shoulder of Mt. Bond. The main mass of Bond shuts out any distant views to the E.

BONDCLIFF VIEW: The open flat ledges atop Bondcliff are one of the great hangout spots in the Whites. Some devotees maintain that this is the richest viewpoint of all among the Bonds. Most dramatic is the broadside view of West Bond's steep, slide-scored ridge, seen NNW across the deep valley of Hellgate Brook. Many a hiker has posed on a cliff-edge crag for a photo with this impressive backdrop.

Northward, the barren ridge stretches away towards the scrubby dome of Mt. Bond, with a nameless hump seen through the West Bond–Bond col and the SW summit of Mt. Guyot just peeking over the L shoulder of Bond. To the R of Bond, Mt. Clay, Mt. Washington and Boott Spur (L to R) loom impressively behind Mt. Field. Part of Mt. Jefferson can be seen to the L of Clay. Mts. Monroe and Eisenhower are seen above Field's summit and in front of Washington, and Mt. Pierce is seen over the R slope of Field. A long ridge descends from Boott Spur to wooded Slide Peak.

Closer by in this direction the broad valley of the upper North Fork leads out to Mt. Willey; Mt. Hight pops out between Slide Peak and Willey and Carter Dome rises in back just to the R of Willey with Rainbow Ridge on its R. With the right light the Wildcats can be seen under and in front of Carter Dome. Mt. Isolation is under Rainbow Ridge, and from it the Montalban Ridge stretches R across the long ridge of Mt. Davis, with the line of the Webster Cliffs below. North and South Baldface peer over the R end of Mt. Davis, with Sable and Chandler Mtn. to their R. Maine's Streaked Mtn. is seen on the horizon to the R of Chandler. Low down in front in this direction is the nearby ridge known as Shoal Pond Peak. Above it is the gentle Ethan Ridge between Willey and the Nancy Range. Beyond Ethan Ridge are the prominent Giant Stairs (L) and broad Mt. Resolution (R), with South Doublehead popping up between them and the tip of North Doublehead above Stairs. To the R of Resolution, looking about due E, is Mt. Crawford with Mt. Shaw and the twin Gemini beyond.

Just S of E, beyond the two S knobs of Shoal Pond Peak, are Mts. Bemis and Nancy, with the dome of Kearsarge North behind to the L of Bemis. Of special note is the vista SE across the broad, spruce-cloaked upper valley of the East Branch—known as the Desolation region—to Mts. Anderson and Lowell and mighty Mt. Carrigain, showing its distinctive three-humped profile. Black Cap Mtn. is seen in back between Nancy and Anderson, with part of Maine's Pleasant Mtn. behind on the L. Distant hills near Sebago Lake in Maine are seen between Anderson and Lowell. North Moat is seen over Lowell, with Big Attitash Mtn. in front of it and Middle Moat to the R seen through Carrigain Notch (between Lowell on the L and Vose Spur on the R). Parts of the Burnt Meadow Mtns. are glimpsed over Middle Moat and through the col to the R of Vose Spur. To the R of Carrigain is the great bulk of Mt. Hancock and its wild N ridges leading down to the East Branch. Mt. Chocorua is nicely framed between the two big peaks, with Green's Cliff in front on the R, above a spur ridge of Hancock, and Green Mtn. in Effingham behind on its R. The sharp NW Peak of Hancock is seen in front of and under North Hancock's broad dome.

To the R of Hancock, Mt. Whiteface (L) and Mt. Tripyramid (R) are seen in back above the nearer Mt. Huntington. The summit of Mt. Kancamagus pokes up over the R end of Huntington's broad W summit, and farther R the W knobs of Kancamagus are above Huntington's lower W spur and an eastern spur of Mt. Hitchcock. The northern Flat Mtn. peers over the R end of Kancamgus. To the R of Kancamagus is Mad River Notch; through the gap are the SW peak of Flat on the L and Sandwich Dome on the R. Looking due S are the Osceolas, with the sharp East Peak above the South Peak of Mt. Hitchcock and the main summit of Osceola seen above Hitchcock's main peak. Mt. Tecumseh (L) and West Tecumseh (R) are seen in back to the R of Osceola's Middle and West Peaks. Just W of S the sharp S spur of Bondcliff is seen close at hand, with the double East Peak and sharp Middle Peak of Scar Ridge rising beyond, above the West Peak of Hitchcock. Part of Hersey Mtn. is visible just R of East Scar, and on clear days North Pack Monadnock (L) and Crotched Mtn. (R) can be seen on the horizon between East and Middle Scar, with the Bridgewater Mtns. closer and just L of Middle Scar.

Next to the R the massive main summit of Scar Ridge is seen beyond the broad valley of the East Branch, with Mt. Kearsarge seen in the distance over its L end. Forbes Mtn. (L) and Tinkham Hill (R) are seen over the R shoulder of Scar Ridge, with Lovewell Mtn. popping up in back. The lower Loon Mtn. is to the R of Scar Ridge. Over the saddle between Scar Ridge and Loon, Sunapee Mtn. is seen in the distance beyond the Tenney Mtn. group. Mt. Cardigan is seen above Stinson Mtn. on the horizon over Loon. The long E ridge of Mt. Kineo is over the R side of Loon, and farther R, seen beyond the flat E spur of Whaleback Mtn., the broad Carr Mtn. rises above and behind Mt. Kineo. Croydon Peak is on the horizon to the L of Carr. Mt. Cushman is to the R of Carr and Kineo, with Vermont's Mt. Ascutney above it on the skyline; on clear days Stratton Mtn. can be seen just R of Ascutney. Farther R and closer is the sharp peak of Whaleback Mtn., truncated on its L end and on the R leading across a long ridge to Mt. Flume. Smarts Mtn. is seen in the distance just R of

Whaleback's summit, over a saddle between Mt. Cushman and the Blue Ridge of Mt. Moosilauke, with far-off Okemo Mtn. to its R.

Mt. Moosilauke is behind Flume on the L and the notched peak of Mt. Liberty is to the R of Flume above the remote basin of Lincoln Brook. The N ridge of Mt. Blue is seen over the R side of Flume. The Franconia Range continues across to Little Haystack Mtn.; South Kinsman pokes over the low point between Liberty and Little Haystack. To the W, you gaze down into the deep, winding valley of Hellgate Brook, which leads out to the Franconia Brook valley and a broadside view of the long, massive, wooded ridge of Owl's Head just beyond. Above the R (N) end of Owl's Head are Mt. Lincoln, with the Y-shaped Lincoln Slide to the R, and the high, serrated crest of Mt. Lafayette. To the NW is a wild view into the upper Franconia Brook basin. In this direction over the base of Lafayette's N ridge, part of Vermont's Sterling Range can be seen in the distance. From here the Garfield Ridge leads across and then up to the fine sharp peak of Mt. Garfield. Mountains in the Belvidere, Vermont, area are glimpsed over the low point to the L of Garfield. The prominent Jay Peaks are seen on the horizon to the R of Garfield, then the view swings back around to the nearby ridge of West Bond.

MT. GUYOT VIEW: Although space does not permit a full description, the view from the bare SW summit of Guyot is outstanding. Among the highlights are the spiny ridge of West Bond rearing up close by to the SSW, with Bondcliff peering over the L side of the West Bond–Bond col and Scar Ridge beyond; Mt. Bond looming nearby to the SSE; Mt. Carrigain and the Nancy Range sprawling to the SE beyond the wild ridges of the eastern Pemi; Montalban Ridge and peaks beyond to the ESE; the Presidentials beyond Mts. Willey and Field to the NE; the slide-scarred Twin Range ridge twisting NW to South Twin; Mt. Garfield to the WNW beyond the SW Twin ridge; a dramatic view of Mts. Lafayette and Lincoln to the W beyond the Redrock Brook valley and the N end of Owl's Head; the great mass of Owl's Head walling in the Franconia Brook valley at the lower end of Redrock Brook; and Mts. Liberty and Flume seen beyond the S end of Owl's Head. All told some 30 New Hampshire 4000-footers can be seen from SW Guyot. Additional perspectives can be gained from the NE summit, but scrub restricts the northerly views somewhat; please stay on the trail to protect fragile alpine vegetation.

NO. OF 4000-FOOTERS VISIBLE: from Mt. Bond, 38; from West Bond, 23; from Bondcliff, 28

Mount Carrigain

ELEVATION: 4700 ft. / 1433 m   ORDER OF HEIGHT: 13
LOCATION: SE Edge of Pemigewasset Wilderness, Town of Lincoln,
Township of Livermore
USGS MAP: 7½′ Mount Carrigain

Geography

Few peaks in the White Mountains can match the grandeur, spectacle and beauty of this towering mass, which for more than a century has been revered by climbers. Viewed from any angle, it is a dominant and easily identified landmark. Being the most centrally situated major peak, Mt. Carrigain offers a sweeping, unmatched view of the region, and in particular of the remote Pemigewasset Wilderness. It was once accurately described as the "great watch tower of the wilderness."

Mt. Carrigain lies in the SE corner of the federally-designated Pemigewasset Wilderness, with its main ridgeline serving as both the Wilderness boundary and the Lincoln–Livermore town line. Its summit rises 2650 ft. from the valley of the East Branch of the Pemi River at Stillwater Junction (to its N), and approximately 2060 ft. from the height-of-land in Carrigain Notch, just to its E.

As viewed from the N, Carrigain's main ridgeline descends sharply to the NE toward its namesake notch in a characteristic triple-humped profile. The ridge features two round subsidiary peaks, a nameless 4260-ft. knob and Vose Spur (3862 ft.), with cliffs overlooking Carrigain Notch along with talus slopes on its SE flank and in the col to its W. Vose Spur is one of New England's 100 highest summits and a frequent destination for bushwhacking peakbaggers. Carrigain Notch is a wild, remote pass separating Carrigain's sprawling mass from the rugged, inaccessible peaks of Mts. Lowell and Anderson to the E. From its height of land (2638 ft.) flow Carrigain Brook to the S, into the Sawyer River, and Notch Brook to the N, towards the headwaters of the East Branch.

To the SW, the main summit ridge drops 1500 ft. to a connecting ridge linking Carrigain with Mt. Hancock. The most prominent peak on this rough ridge, which is scarred on its S side by inviting cliffs and ledges, is 3520-ft. Carrigain Pond Peak (also known as The Captain), trailless and rarely visited by backcountry explorers. The Captain overlooks a long, remote valley drained by a northern tributary of the Sawyer River. On the NE side of this peak is secluded Carrigain Pond (3180 ft.), a deep four-acre tarn which forms the headwaters of the Carrigain Branch, flowing N down a long valley to the East Branch in the Stillwater area.

To the NW of Carrigain's summit a long wooded ridge drops steeply

The prominent mass of Mount Carrigain as seen from the shore of Shoal Pond in the Pemigewasset Wilderness.

down into the area known as Desolation. In the early part of the twentieth century this area was heavily logged by crews working for railroad lumber baron James E. Henry. For several years, a logging camp (Camp 20) was sited here. A short distance N of Desolation is the confluence of the East Branch of the Pemigewasset River and Carrigain Branch, called Stillwater. On the E side of the NW ridge is a deep, wild, N-facing ravine.

Just SE of the main summit, and only a few hundred feet lower, is the crest of Signal Ridge, Carrigain's open, knife-edged southeastern ridgeline that boasts as wild a view as any one spot in the mountains. Its perspective on Vose Spur, Carrigain Notch, and the slide-scarred wall of Mt. Lowell is exceptional. The precipitous E face of the upper Signal Ridge is especially impressive and encloses a steep ravine that was the site for several early ascents of the mountain. Beyond the crest, Signal Ridge descends for another 2 ½ mi. S and SE into the Sawyer River valley.

Nomenclature

The mountain is named for former New Hampshire Secretary of State Philip Carrigain (1772–1842), who served in that post from 1805 to 1810. Carrigain is best known for producing one of the state's earliest maps, published in 1816, which showed many of the northern mountains for the first time. The name of the mountain first appeared on George P. Bond's 1853 map of the White Mountains.

Signal Ridge was originally called "Burnt Hat Ridge," from an 1873 incident in which a storm overtook an exploring party atop the ridge and blew the hat of one of the climbers into their campfire. Its present name derives from surveying days in the late 1800s.

Vose Spur was named in 1876 for George L. Vose, an assistant in Charles H. Hitchcock's geological survey and an active member of the White Mountain Club of Portland, Maine, which specialized in exploring the Carrigain region.

Historical Highlights

First Ascent: Mt. Carrigain was first climbed by Arnold Henri Guyot (1807–1884) and his party of explorers in August 1857. It is thought that Guyot and his companions ascended the mountain from what is now known as Carrigain Notch, climbing over Vose Spur and another intermediary peak before reaching the summit. Despite "scratched face and hands, bruised feet and well-worn clothes," wrote S. Hasting Grant, one of the dozen adventurers accompanying Guyot, "I don't begrudge the pains taken in the least. Quite the contrary . . . the outlook was quite beyond anything yet seen."

Guyot was a Swiss scientist well-known for his study of glaciers, and was affiliated with Princeton University at the time of his Carrigain ascent. He roamed widely across the White Mountains and probably climbed more 4000-footers than anyone else before the 1870s. Guyot was also an early mapmaker and is credited with proving that New Hampshire's Mt. Washington was not the highest peak east of the Mississippi, as was previously believed. A 4580-ft. peak on the Twin–Bond Range is named in his honor.

1869: George Vose, local guide John C. Cobb, and artist George Morse, on geological survey expedition, attempt summit climb from Sawyer River valley by route known as "Cobb's Stairs." Group reaches Signal Ridge (later dubbed "Burnt Hat Ridge"), thinking it is summit; clouds obscure true summit, however, unbeknownst to group until descent is well under way.

1871: Geological survey party including Warren Upham reaches summit in what is likely second ascent of peak, ascending from East Branch up NW slope of mountain through open spruce woods. They measure summit elevation at 4678 ft.

1873: During expedition to mountain, group of climbers decide to form White Mountain Club of Portland, Maine, which devotes much of its time to visiting less-explored reaches of White Mountains. Over next couple of years, members climb Carrigain three more times, with

August 1875 trip featuring a descent from summit N into virgin forest of Pemi Wilderness. Member George F. Morse completes profile of view from Carrigain which is reproduced in atlas published by Hitchcock's New Hampshire geological survey.

1876: Town of Livermore, in which major portion of mountain lies, is chartered by state. Party led by guidebook editor Moses Sweetser climbs Carrigain from SW. Sweetser notes the "bold and remarkable architecture of this peak" and its view "overlooking many leagues of unbroken wilderness and stately mountains."

1877: Construction begins on Sawyer River Railroad, logging line owned by Saunders family of Lawrence, Massachusetts. Tracks are laid 8 mi. up Sawyer River valley to SE and S of Mt. Carrigain. Town of Livermore, incorporated in 1876 with hamlet established ca. 2½ mi. up valley, becomes center of operation and at its height has sawmill, school, post office, company store and some 150–200 residents. Saunders operation is noted for logging tactics that are selective and conservative for their time, allowing for several cuts on 30,000 acre tract over course of five decades.

1879: AMC cuts first trail up mountain, following for most part "Cobb's Stairs" route up steep E side of Signal Ridge. Path is called Mt. Carrigain Trail.

1880: Webster Wells, writing in *Appalachia*, describes August 1879 bushwhack excursion from Mt. Hancock to Mt. Carrigain, and then down to Carrigain Notch and up over Mts. Anderson and Lowell. Along tortuous ridge walk, group climbs over the "tremendously steep and craggy ridge" of The Captain and stumbles upon remote Carrigain Pond, where they spend 1½ hrs.; are probably first humans to ever visit pond.

1890: Julius Ward includes rhapsodic chapter about Carrigain in his book, *The White Mountains: A Guide to Their Interpretation*: "but I think that the sense of utter separation from humanity, the sense of utter lostness in the wilderness, the sense of complete abandonment of the soul to Nature was never realized as it was during my stay of a few hours on the topmost peak of Mount Carrigain."

1896: AMC Snow-Shoe Section members make probable first winter ascent of peak. Group includes Miss M. A. Furbish.

1898: Section of trail up mountain is relocated due to lumbering operations. New route follows more closely today's Signal Ridge Trail.

1906: AMC opens new path through Carrigain Notch. Trail runs from logging village of Livermore to North Fork Jct. on East Branch, a distance of 11.25 mi.

1910: New Hampshire Timberlands Owners Association funds construction of fire lookout on summit, one of first in state. Ownership is taken over by state in 1911, U.S. Forest Service in 1933–34.

1910–1914: Logging crews of J. E. Henry occupy Camp 20 in Desolation area. Twenty-five million board feet of timber are removed from Vose Spur, Mt. Carrigain and Mt. Hancock.

1912: Heavily logged-over area around Carrigain Pond is described thusly by Maurice Osborne: "Scarcely a green thing showed around its desolated shore. . . . Here was Carrigain Pond, now desecrated, profaned, and laid bare to the vulgar gaze."

1927: November flood washes out bridges, road bed of Sawyer River logging railroad. One year later, sawmill at Livermore village shuts down for good.

1932: New route up Carrigain from N is established by AMC to provide access from new Zealand Falls Hut. Desolation Trail begins from Stillwater area and climbs to summit first via old logging road, then through virgin forest at higher elevation. At about same time, Mt. Carrigain Trail is renamed Signal Ridge Trail.

1936: Due to fire danger created by softwood slash left over from lumber operations, Forest Service temporarily closes off major portion of East Branch drainage to public entry. Affected trails include Carrigain Notch and Desolation Trails.

1940: New 20-ft. steel fire lookout tower erected on summit by USFS.

Ca. 1940: Carrigain Notch Trail rerouted through Desolation area and former logging camp (Camp 20) site. Original portion of trail running to Shoal Pond Trail is listed in *AMC Guide* as Stillwater By-Pass.

1948: Summit fire lookout post placed on inactive status by USFS.

Ca. 1948: First 2.2 mi. of Carrigain Notch Trail from Livermore now designated as part of Signal Ridge Trail.

1949: New log shelter (Desolation) accommodating 12 campers is built near jct. of Carrigain Notch and Desolation Trails.

1955: Carrigain Notch Trail terminus now at Stillwater. Section of trail from there to North Fork Jct. designated part of Wilderness Trail from Lincoln.

1963: AMC group led by Bob Collin makes winter ascent of Carrigain from N as part of nine-day Pemi backpacking epic.

1966: *AMC Guide* lists recently built extension of Nancy Pond Trail from outlet of Norcross Pond to Carrigain Notch Trail, one mile E of Desolation Shelter.

1981: Old summit fire tower taken down; replacement observation tower erected by USFS, Young Adult Conservation Corps. Platform is 20 ft. from ground and measures 18 ft. × 14 ft.

1984: Forty-five-thousand-acre Pemigewasset Wilderness is added to National Wilderness Preservation System. N slope of Mt. Carrigain lies within Wilderness boundary.

Early 1990s: Bold 450-lb. black bear nicknamed "Brutus" terrorizes campers in Desolation region.

1995: Sawyer River Rd. washed out by major October storm, is not repaired for three years.

1997: Desolation Shelter is dismantled.

Trail Approaches

South Approach from Sawyer River Road (FR 34)

Signal Ridge Trail

10.0 mi. round-trip, 3300-ft. elevation gain

TRAILHEAD (1480 ft.): The Signal Ridge Trail begins off Sawyer River Road 2.0 mi. from its jct. with US 302, which is ca. 3.7 mi. from Bartlett village and just N of the bridge over Sawyer River. The trailhead parking lot is on the L just past bridge over Whiteface Brook.

This is the usual approach to Carrigain. After an easy 2-mi. start, there is a long, steady climb to the spectacular open crest of Signal Ridge, where excellent views are enjoyed before the final short push to the summit.

From parking area, walk back across road bridge to start of trail on L, which quickly joins old logging road. At 0.2 mi., small tributary and Whiteface Brook are crossed in quick succession. In times of high water, stream crossings can be difficult. They can be avoided by bushwhacking from Sawyer River Road along S bank of river to point where trail is met. Following along S bank of brook, trail climbs at easy grade past series of nice pools and cascades, then climbs away from stream at 0.8 mi. before leveling out as grade of another logging road is met. At 1.4 mi., unmaintained Carrigain Brook Road (FR 86) to end of Sawyer River Rd. is passed on L. At 1.7 mi./1900 ft. reach jct. R with Carrigain Notch Trail to Desolation/Stillwater area.

Signal Ridge Trail continues straight ahead, crossing Carrigain Brook almost immediately—may be dificult in high water. After passing through boggy area and crossing another stream, easy grade ends and long ascent of ridge begins with sharp L turn off logging road at 2.4 mi. After several switchbacks, trail takes sharp R at 2.8 mi./2650 ft. and begins mile-long traverse of old road angling its way up E side of ridge through small birch and conifer growth. Footing is rocky. Just above turn look for framed view R to cliffs and slides on Mt. Lowell. Pass first of two trailside springs at ca. 3.3 mi./3150 ft. Farther along is framed view R to Duck Pond Mtn. and peaks beyond. At 3.8 mi./3700 ft. trail turns sharp L off logging road and via series of twists and turns through thick growth (damaged by 1980 windstorm) makes steep ascent to S end of upper crest of Signal Ridge, reached at 4.5 mi./4420 ft. Trail passes over bare, level ridgecrest with steep dropoff on R. Here there are excellent views E and W and toward wooded mass of tower-topped summit just ahead to NW. Especially notable is view E across Carrigain Notch to gravelly slides, cliffs and talus on

Hikers push on across Signal Ridge as the main summit of Mount Carrigain rears up behind them.

W face of Mt. Lowell, with Vose Spur close by on L and Webster Cliffs, Willey Range and Presidentials beyond. To SW is wild view to lumpy ridges of Mt. Hancock, with profile of The Captain's cliffs below, and out to southern White Mtns.

From N end of open ridge, trail drops into sag, angles toward S slope of summit, and eventually reaches site of old firewarden's cabin. Water in old well here should not be imbibed without treatment. From clearing, trail continues on L, bears R and climbs more steeply to summit ridge, then steers R again to partly wooded main summit, with its clearing and observation tower, at 5.0 mi. / 4700 ft. From the ground, there are some views to N and S, but tower must be climbed for full panorama.

North Approach from Stillwater/Desolation

Desolation Trail
3.8 mi. round-trip, 2500-ft. elevation gain (from Carrigain
   Notch Trail)

TRAILHEAD (2180 ft.): One of the most remote and wild trails in the mountains, the Desolation Trail begins at the jct. with Carrigain Notch Trail near the site of the former Desolation Shelter. Mostly following old logging roads, this trail approaches the summit from the NW via a long wooded ridge E of Carrigain Branch valley. This approach is much steeper and rougher than the Signal Ridge approach, but is the most direct route up the mountain from the East Branch and Zealand areas. This is primarily backpacking country. For example, from Zealand Falls Hut the hike to the summit of Carrigain is 9.6 mi. one-way via Twinway, Ethan Pond Trail, Shoal Pond Trail, Carrigain Notch Trail and Desolation Trail. The shortest trail approach to bottom of Desolation Trail is 6.7 mi. from Sawyer River Rd. via the Signal Ridge and Carrigain Notch Trails, as described below under the loop option, which is feasible for strong day hikers.

Trail leaves Carrigain Notch Trail at sharp R turn near tributary of Carrigain Branch. It immediately crosses the brook, follows old logging railroad grade for 200 ft., then veers L onto ancient logging road which climbs at moderate grades. As nice stand of birches is met, trail merges onto long, straight road dug into W side of ridge. At ca. 3150 ft. trail follows this amazing road across to E side of ridge, where it is cut into side of steep slope. There are occasional glimpses into deep ravine on L. At 1.3 mi/3600 ft., trail leaves road and grade quickly becomes very steep, climbing over wet rocks and numerous stone steps while passing through shady stand of virgin spruce. Look back for occasional views N into Pemi Wilderness. Watch footing carefully through this steep, rugged section, where even J. E. Henry's bold loggers decided not to cut. Eventually, as trail climbs to crest of steep NW ridge, grade lessens and footway improves. At 1.8 mi./4600 ft. swing L for brief traverse before final sharp pitch leads to summit clearing and tower, 1.9 mi. from Carrigain Notch Trail.

LOOP OPTION

Signal Ridge Trail, Carrigain Notch Trail, Desolation Trail, Signal Ridge Trail
13.6 mi. loop, 3750-ft. elevation gain

A nice, but ambitious alternative to the traditional out-and-back ascent via Signal Ridge Trail is the loop hike through Carrigain Notch with the summit ascent via Desolation Trail. From Signal Ridge Trail, steer R onto Carrigain Notch Trail 1.7 mi. from Sawyer River Road and cross Carrigain Brook 60 yds. from jct. After passing beaver pond on L with view up to lower Signal Ridge, trail approaches notch at easy grades through fine open hardwood forest, crossing several dry stony brookbeds. At 3.3 mi./2200 ft. small gravelly opening in brook to R opens view up to Vose Spur. Trail soon steepens and works up W side of wild Carrigain Notch, offering tantalizing glimpses of Mt. Lowell cliffs and reaching height-of-land up on W slope (and Pemigewasset Wilderness boundary) at 4.0 mi./2637 ft. Trail now begins moderate descent on N side of notch, utilizing mostly old logging roads with occasional bypasses to L around muddy areas. In this area trail passes through deep conifer forest with wild, almost primeval feel. At 5.8 mi. / 2140 ft., trail turns L onto old logging railroad grade at jct. R with Nancy Pond Trail and follows easy grade for 0.8 mi., passing through old logging camp site (Camp 20) just before meeting Desolation Trail to Mt. Carrigain at 6.7 mi. / 2180 ft. Turn L here to continue loop hike, following Desolation Trail to summit, then descending via Signal Ridge Trail.

(Carrigain Notch Trail turns R at jct., passing by former Desolation Shelter site in 0.1 mi. and terminating in 0.7 mi. at 2050-ft. Stillwater Jct., where Wilderness Trail to Kancamagus Highway in Lincoln bears L and Shoal Pond Trail to Zealand area bears R and crosses East Branch of Pemigewasset River.)

Winter

Mt. Carrigain is a challenging peak to reach in winter, mainly because the access road to the Signal Ridge trailhead (Sawyer River Rd.) is gated at US 302. This adds 4 mi. to a round-trip hike, making it 14.0 mi. total from start to finish, with 3900-ft. elevation gain. Frequently, winter trampers will don cross country skis for the two-mile trek from the highway to the trailhead. The ski out is particularly nice as it's all downhill from the trailhead to US 302. If breaking trail, the mile-long slab up the E side of Signal Ridge is very tiresome. While most of the hike up Carrigain is in the sheltered woods along the road and trail, the traverse of treeless Signal Ridge may pose some problems for hikers, especially in times of stormy weather. Snow is often windpacked here. Fortunately, the summit mass of Carrigain frequently shelters Signal Ridge from the winter's often brutally cold NW winds. On a calm, sunny winter day, the crest of Signal Ridge is one of the finest spots in the hills. Use caution if climbing to the observation platform at the summit as the steps may be icy.

View Guide

Carrigain's isolated central position in the Whites gives it a commanding perspective on the region, and indeed the summits of 43 of its 4000-footer brethren can be seen from the observation tower, tying it with Mt. Washington for top honors in that regard. The all-encompassing view from Carrigain has extracted superlatives from hikers for more than a century. "From its central position a better idea of the arrangement of the White and Franconia Mts. is had than from any other point, perhaps, in the whole group," wrote George L. Vose, who visited the summit several times in the early 1870s. With unusual succinctness, guidebook editor Moses Sweetser noted that the view overlooks "many leagues of unbroken wilderness and stately mountains." Save this one for a clear day!

In addition to the nearly numberless summits visible from here, there is an unrivalled view over the vast (by New England standards) wild area of uplands in the eastern half of the Pemigewasset Wilderness. Ironically, these wilderness views would be limited by the dense fir growth atop the peak were it not for the observation tower that was renovated in 1981 for the benefit of Carrigain-climbers. As noted above, there are some N and S views from the ground at the summit, but only from the platform can the full, sweeping view be obtained.

The N view over the Pemi Wilderness overlooks a basin of unbroken forest thousands of acres in area drained by the North Fork, Shoal Pond Brook and the East Branch of the Pemigewasset itself. To the NW this region of long valleys and low, rolling ridges is closed in by the high peaks of the Bond–Twin Range. The rounded, ledgy crest of Bondcliff is almost due NW, with the sharp rocky peak of Garfield and slide-marked ridge of West Bond to its R. The distant peak of Vermont's Laraway Mtn. is seen just to the R of Bondcliff. Marching in quick succession along the Bond–Twin Range to the R of West Bond are the summits of Mt. Bond, Mt. Guyot, South Twin and North Twin, with the top of its E slide visible. In front of North Twin, elongated Zealand Ridge extends R and out to the deep scoop of Zealand Notch - this is one of the best places for viewing that rocky pass. The sharply cut valley of Jumping Brook is seen below the summit of Zealand Mtn., at the L end of Zealand Ridge. Bald Mtn. in Vermont's Northeast Kingdom is on the horizon to the R of Zealand's summit, with East Haven Mtn. to its R and closer. Mt. Hale is sighted through Zealand Notch, with Vermont's East Mtn. to its L and Gore Mtn. to its R, over Hale's prominent E ridge. In the foreground, below Zealand Ridge and Zealand Notch, are the broad, spruce-clad valley of Shoal Pond Brook and its long, low neighboring ridge on the L (W), known as Shoal Pond Mtn.

Ledgy Whitewall Mtn. forms the R (E) wall of Zealand Notch, and from that summit a long ridge extends R to the Willey Range. On the horizon over Whitewall are Black, Brousseau and sharp Sable Mtns. in Vermont. Little, ledgy Mt. Oscar is seen under shapely Cherry Mtn. through a gap on the R side of Whitewall. Goback Mtn. rises beyond Cherry on the R, with Mt. Rosebrook seen down low in front. A ridge extends R from Goback to the Nash Stream mtns. of West Peak and Sugarloaf Mtn., almost due N, with Vermont's Monadnock Mtn. peering over in back to the R of Goback. Hutchins Mtn. is seen to the R of Sugarloaf and closer, and next to the R and much closer is rounded Mt. Tom in the Willey Range. Higher neighbors Mt. Field and Mt. Willey are to the R of Tom. Mts. Starr King and Waumbek are seen to the L of Field, with Mt. Cabot peering over in back to the L of Waumbek. North Weeks is prominent over the Field–Willey col, with the E Peak of Mt. Deception poking up below, and farther R, over the N ridge of Willey, are Cave Mtn., Rice Mtn.

and other ridges near Dixville Notch. In the foreground the broad upper plateau of the eastern Pemi stretches out to the base of the Willey Range. The glimmer of Shoal Pond can be spotted on the tableland, in line with the W spur of Mt. Field. There's an unusual view into a hidden basin enclosed by the W spur of Field, Field itself, and Willey. Part of Mt. Dartmouth is seen behind Willey on the R; Stub Hill (with Rump Mtn. behind on its L) and other far-off North Country peaks are on the horizon. Little rounded Millen Hill is to the R of Dartmouth, with Mt. Randolph behind on its R. Mt. Bowman, a shoulder of Mt. Jefferson, is just R of Randolph, with distant peaks in NW Maine on the horizon.

To the NNE, beyond the 4260-ft. NE spur of Carrigain, is a striking vista to the gravel-gashed Webster Cliffs, forming the E side of Crawford Notch, with the peaks of the Presidentials piled beyond. On the L the sharp Castellated Ridge leads up to Mt. Jefferson, with Mt. Adams behind on the R. Mts. Jackson, Pierce and Eisenhower are seen in front and below. Mt. Clay is in front of and to the R of Adams, and next to the R Mt. Washington towers above Mt. Monroe, with Boott Spur extending out to the R and Oakes Gulf and the sprawling Dry River valley below. The lower Slide Peak is to the R of Boott Spur, with Mt. Isolation seen below. Farther R, looking NE, the high summits of the Carters rise above the Wildcats and upper Montalban Ridge, with Mts. Anderson, Nancy and Bemis in the foreground. Middle and South Carter are behind and L of the Wildcats, while Carter Dome is to the R. Farther R, beyond nearby Mt. Lowell, are the Giant Stairs and gravel-splotched Mt. Resolution. The long ridge of Jackson's Black Mtn. is seen behind Stairs and Resoultion, and West Royce Mtn. is seen farther back over Stairs. The sharp duo of Bald and Saddleback Wind Mtns. near Rumford, Maine, is in the distance just to the L of West Royce. The Baldface Range is seen over Resolution (L to R): North and South Baldface, Sable Mtn. and Chandler Mtn. Mt. Zircon and other peaks near Rumford are seen to the L of North Baldface. Mt. Crawford is in front of Resolution, below South Baldface. To the R of Chandler are North and South Doublehead, with Maine's little Mt. Tom beyond to the L of North Doublehead. Iron Mtn. and Mt. Parker are in front of and just R of South Doublehead, and in the foreground is the long flat crest of Duck Pond Mtn. Maine's Streaked Mtn. is on the horizon over the prominent S cliffs of Iron. Next to the R Mt. Hope (peering over Duck Pond's ridge) and Thorn Mtn. (in Jackson) are seen under the nondescript ridge of Walter Mtn. Extending R from Walter are Mt. Shaw, the two Gemini (with Mt. Langdon below), and then the great dome of Kearsarge North, with lowly Mt. Pickering and Mt. Stanton in front. On very clear days the bumpy outline of the Camden Hills on the Maine coast can be seen on the skyline to the L of Kearsarge North.

Farther R the town of Bartlett is seen in the Saco valley, guarded by Hart Ledge on the L and the ski slopes of Attitash Mtn. on the R.

Cranmore Mtn. and Black Cap (with Hurricane Mtn. to its L and Middle Mtn. to its R) in the Green Hills and Pleasant Mtn. in Maine are behind the Attitash slopes. Next to the R, looking ESE, graceful North Moat Mtn. rises behind Big Attitash Mtn. Middle and South Moat are to the R of North Moat, with Sebago Lake visible on the flats beyond the gap in the middle of the Moat Range. Table Mtn. is to the R of South Moat and lower. The Saddleback Hills in western Maine are on the horizon beyond South Moat, with the nearer Burnt Meadow Mtns., the Bill Merrill group and the Clark Mtn. range, all also in Maine, farther to the R. To the SE you look down on Signal Ridge, with the swath of the trail running across its crest. The jumbled peaks of Mt. Tremont and Owl Cliff (on the R) are beyond. Flat-topped Bear Mtn. is behind and above Tremont's summit, Bartlett Haystack is to the L, and hills along the Maine–New Hampshire border stretch out beyond. The city of Portland, Maine, on the Atlantic Ocean can sometimes be seen on the horizon to the L of Bear. Next to the R Mt. Chocorua is seen over the lower part of Signal Ridge, with its Three Sisters extending to the L. Maine's small Ossipee Hill is over the L end of the Sisters, Green Mtn. in Effingham peers over just L of Chocorua's summit, and Maine's Fort Ridge is prominent on the horizon to the R of Chocorua.

Farther R, Chocorua's western neighbor, Mt. Paugus, is seen over the flat crest of nearby Green's Cliff. Ossipee Lake shimmers over the wide saddle between Chocorua and Paugus. To the R of Paugus is another broad gap at Paugus Pass, with the Nickerson Mtns. and the Moose–Copple Crown range in succession beyond. Hedgehog Mtn. is seen in the foreground under Paugus Pass. Next to the R, just E of S, is a beautiful spread of the Sandwich Range high peaks, seen beyond the broad Albany Intervale. Graceful Mt. Passaconaway is on the L with its shoulder, Wonalancet Hedgehog on its L and little Potash Mtn. in front. Mt. Shaw in the Ossipees is seen in back just L of Passaconaway. Mt. Whiteface is to the R of Passaconaway, beyond a broad saddle; in the distance between them are Faraway Mtn. and Black Snout in the Ossipees (L) and the E end of the Belknap Range (R). From Whiteface the Sandwich Range extends R over East and West Sleeper to the three bunched peaks of Mt. Tripyramid. More of the Belknap Range is seen over saddles in the ridge, including Belknap and Gunstock Mtns. between the Sleepers. The flat-topped Fool Killer is seen under East Sleeper. Bulky Sandwich Dome is set back to the R of Tripyramid, beyond the eastern ridges of Mts. Huntington and Kancamagus. Red Hill peers over where the lower ridges of Tripyramid and the Dome converge. Just L of Sandwich the distant twin Uncanoonuc Mtns. are seen over the long crest of Bean Hill. On the R side of Sandwich, North Pack Monadnock is on the horizon above the sharp Jennings Peak, with Crotched Mtn. to its R, above the nearby summit of Mt. Kancamagus. Farther R, to the SSW, past the western part of Kancamagus, Mt. Kearsarge is seen on the horizon, with Mt. Monadnock peeping over on the L.

The Squam Range (L) and Campton Range (R) are seen in the middle distance over Kancamagus's rolling crest. To the R of Kancamagus are the Osceolas with Tecumseh popping up between East Peak and the main summit, and the two rounded summits of Mt. Huntington in front. Lovewell Mtn. is a bump on the horizon to the L of the eastern Huntington summit, above Mad River Notch and Plymouth Mtn. Sunapee Mtn. is seen in the distance just L of East Osceola, and the tip of Mt. Cardigan just peeks over the L side of Osceola's Middle Peak. Croydon Peak is seen in the distance above Stinson Mtn., to the R of Osceola's sharp West Peak. To the R of the Osceolas, across a deep gap, are the twin summits of East Scar Ridge, with the S spur of South Hancock close by in front and Vermont's Mt. Ascutney on the skyline. On very clear days Stratton Mtn. can be seen to the L of Ascutney, and Dorset Peak and its flat spur are visible to Ascutney's R. Farther R is the sharp peak of South Hancock, with Middle Scar Ridge just above it and Carr Mtn. behind on the L. The main Scar Ridge summit is to the R of South Hancock, with Smarts Mtn. beyond. Salt Ash Mtn. is in the distance to the R of Smarts. Mt. Cushman is behind Scar Ridge on the R. Mt. Cube rises over Cushman's R shoulder with Killington Peak on the horizon beyond. Shrewsbury Peak is close by Killington on the L and Pico Peak caps the long ridge to Killington's R. Ski-trailed Loon Mtn. is in front of Cube and the saddle to the R of Cushman. Close by to the WSW is the rounded hump of North Hancock, with massive Mt. Moosilauke rising beyond. Above the nearby W knob of Carrigain, one sees a long ridge extending R from North Hancock to the sharp peak of NW Hancock. Over the R half of this ridge are Big Coolidge Mtn. (L) and the truncated main peak of Whaleback Mtn. (R) with Mt. Wolf peering over behind. A long ridge rises to the R from Whaleback up to Mt. Flume. On the horizon between Wolf and Flume are the Breadloaf Mtn. range (L) and the Mt. Abraham–Ellen range (R) in the Green Mtns. On the very clearest of days Dix Mtn. in the Adirondacks can be espied to the L of Abraham. Mt. Liberty is just R of Flume with South Kinsman in back between them. North Kinsman peers over to the R of Liberty, and farther R Camel's Hump raises its distinctive profile over the saddle between Liberty and Little Haystack Mtn. To the R of Little Haystack, looking WNW, Mts. Lincoln and Lafayette dwarf the crouching ridge of Owl's Head beneath them. The V-shaped Lincoln Slide is especially prominent. From here the view swings back around to the Bonds.

NO. OF 4000-FOOTERS VISIBLE: 43

Galehead Mountain

ELEVATION: 4024 ft. / 1227 m   ORDER OF HEIGHT: 44
LOCATION: Garfield Ridge, Town of Franconia
USGS MAP: 7½′ South Twin Mountain

Geography

This mostly wooded mountain is situated on the E end of Garfield Ridge and appears as a rather inconspicuous hump from most perspectives. It sits at the head of the Gale River to the N and the Pemi Wilderness to the S, but is dwarfed by its higher, more spectacular neighbors to the E and W. To the E, 4902-ft. South Twin Mountain towers nearly 900 ft. above Galehead's summit, while to the W lies Mt. Garfield (4500 ft.) and several of its subordinate peaks (including East and West Garfield Ridge).

The North Branch of the Gale River flows off the mountain's lower slopes to the N, draining out through a long, deep mountain valley followed by the Gale River Trail. On the mountain's SE slope drains Twin Brook, which runs for nearly two mi. SW before converging with Franconia Brook near 13 Falls Campsite. This scenic mountain valley is traversed by the Twin Brook Trail, which passes through a stunning stand of white birches found on Galehead's lower south-facing slopes. Galehead forms the western wall of this valley, while South Twin and its 4357-ft. SW spur rise sharply on the opposite side of the stream. A long spur ridge runs SSW from Galehead's summit down to the 13 Falls area; a little more than halfway down this ridge is a flat-topped 2962-ft. knob fronted by small cliffs. To the W of Galehead's summit and this spur ridge is a secluded valley drained by the E fork of Franconia Brook.

Though Galehead's summit once offered views over the trees to Franconia Ridge and Mt. Garfield, the top is now completely wooded and viewless. However, there is a good outlook over the Twin Brook valley on the E side of the mountain along the Frost Trail, and additional views are available at the AMC's Galehead Hut, which is perched on a 3800-ft. hump at the NE base of the mountain.

Nomenclature

Galehead Mountain's name is tied directly to the river (Gale River) which originates on its N slopes and flows NW, eventually into the Ammonoosuc River. The headwaters of the North Branch of the Gale River flow off the slopes of Galehead and North and South Twin Mountains. According to *The History of Franconia* by Sarah N. Welch, Gale River is named for Susannah Gale, daughter of an early town resident on whose farm "the Gale Spring is located and across which the river flows."

Historical Highlights

First Ascent: Unknown

1880: Benjamin Macdonald and guide Allen Thompson spend six days exploring region around upper Gale River and Franconia Brook valleys. After ascending SW spur of South Twin, they climb over "a spur of Moose Mountain," which may have been today's Galehead Mtn. Account of trip appears in *White Mountain Echo*, tourist paper published in Bethlehem.

1903: Fire burns 3,000 acres in Gale River valley.

1904–1909: J. E. Henry's crews conduct intensive logging operations on S slopes of Galehead, working from Camp 13 at end of Franconia Brook spur line of East Branch & Lincoln Railroad. 1907 fire sears lower S slopes of mountain, where birch forest thrives today.

1914: Charles Blood leads week-long expedition over Garfield Ridge, scouting out proposed trail linking Twin Range with Mt. Lafayette.

1915: Trail is established between South Twin and Haystack Lake (Garfield Pond).

1916: Garfield Ridge Trail is completed.

1926: Galehead Shelter, accommodating 8 to 10 campers, is built by AMC in area known as Surveyor's Clearing.

1929–30: Galehead Trail, branch path from Gale River Trail (previously established route to Garfield Ridge Trail E of Mt. Garfield via Garfield Stream and Hawthorne Falls) opens. Path leaves trail 3 mi. from state highway, ascends steep ravine at head of North Branch of Gale River, and meets ridgeline near shelter site.

1932: Under direction of the legendary Joe Dodge, AMC completes construction of new Galehead Hut at cost of $10,527.98. Structure stands about 100 yards W of former shelter.

1938: In aftermath of September hurricane, hut is inaccessible as windthrown trees block every approach trail onto Garfield Ridge.

Ca. 1940: E end of Garfield Ridge Trail now coincides with upper portion of Galehead Trail.

1951: Hut visitors Jack and Ruth Frost begin effort to establish trail from hut to Galehead summit. Work is completed following July.

1952: AMC maps list Galehead Mtn. for first time.

1953: Trail to summit receives permanent name, Frost Trail.

1954: Heavy rains from two hurricanes cause landslide, flooding along Gale River Trail.

1960: Former Galehead Trail renamed Gale River Trail; old route up valley of Garfield Stream that once bore this name has been abandoned.

1962: AMC takes over maintenance of Frost Trail.

1968: AMC opens Twin Brook Trail from S, providing access to Galehead area from 13 Falls.

1975: Revised USGS maps elevate summit to 4000-ft. status. Previously, summit elevation was listed as 3948 ft.

1982: Fiftieth anniversary of Galehead and Zealand Huts opening is celebrated.

1999: Crews begin dismantling of original AMC hut and start construction of replacement facility.

2000: New Galehead Hut opens.

2005: Spring flood washes out footbridge on Gale River Trail.

Trail Approaches

North Approach from Gale River Loop Road (FR 92)

Gale River Trail, Garfield Ridge Trail, Frost Trail
10.2 mi. round trip, 2450-ft. elevation gain.

TRAILHEAD (1600 ft.): From jct. of US 3 and Trudeau Rd., between Franconia Notch and Twin Mountain, drive SE on USFS gravel Gale River Rd. (FR 25). Bear L at 0.6 mi. and turn sharp R at 1.3 mi. onto Gale River Loop Rd. (FR 92). Parking area for Gale River Trail is on L at 1.6 mi. This approach via the scenic Gale River valley is quickest, most direct approach to Galehead. It is also used by hikers headed up to South Twin or to hut. Many peakbaggers combine climb to Galehead with ascent of South Twin and sometimes North Twin as well. For details, see chapter on North and South Twin. (If Twins are climbed from Little River valley or as part of Twin Range traverse, Galehead is often ascended separately.)

From parking area, Gale River Trail soon drops over bank, crosses small brook, and then turns R on old logging road leading S at easy grades through hardwoods on W side of Gale River's North Branch, keeping well back from stream. Approach river at 1.4 mi. and cross to E side on rocks (former footbridge washed out in 2005) at 1.7 mi. Trail becomes rougher along bank, crosses tributary, then recrosses North Branch of Gale on large step stones at 2.5 mi. / 2250 ft., usually a fairly easy crossing. Grades continue easy through slide outwash areas to open gravel bank at 3.1 mi., with interesting view up to high ridges of Twins. Beyond, trail begins to steepen, and at 3.5 mi. / 3000 ft. commences stiff climb up rock staircases, reaching jct. with Garfield Ridge Trail at 4.0 mi. / 3390 ft.

Turn L here for easy to moderate, rocky traverse on Garfield Ridge Trail through deep, mossy coniferous forest. At 4.3 mi. pass view on L looking NNW down Gale River valley and across to cliffs on W ridge of North Twin. Trail soon turns R and climbs more steeply. Reach AMC Galehead Hut on side trail R at 4.6 mi. / 3780 ft. From hut clearing there are views E up to South Twin, S to Owl's Head, SW to nearby Galehead Mtn., and W to Mt. Garfield. From hut, Frost Trail drops into sag, passes through blowdown patch with view back to Twins, then at 0.1 mi. from hut passes jct. L with Twin Brook Trail to Pemi Wilderness. Trail soon jogs R and begins 250-ft. climb to summit, steep and rocky at first, then moderate. At 0.3 mi. from hut, side trail L leads to nice viewpoint S into Twin Brook valley and up to massive wall of South Twin. Easy climbing leads to sign and summit cairn at viewless clearing in woods, 0.5 mi. from hut.

OTHER APPROACHES
There are three additional ways to reach Galehead Hut and the Frost Trail, but all involve significantly more climbing and mileage.

The Twin Brook Trail provides the best access to Galehead from the S. It leaves from 13 Falls Campsite (2196 ft., nine tent pads, caretaker, fee) near Franconia Brook and climbs 2.6 mi. to its terminus at Frost Trail, 0.1 mi. from hut. The 13 Falls area is remote and beautiful, with numerous waterfalls and a nice open ledgy brookbed with view of Owl's Head on Lincoln Brook Trail just W of where its N end diverges from Franconia Brook Trail. The lower end of Twin Brook Trail begins near 13 Falls Campsite, 8.1 miles from Lincoln Woods parking area off Kancamagus Highway in Lincoln. It is reached via Lincoln Woods Trail (2.9 mi.) and Franconia Brook Trail (5.2 mi.), long easy walk along old railroad grades, with six brook crossings (three of Camp 9 Brook, the third after bypass R around beaver swamp, plus crossings of Hellgate, Redrock and Twin Brooks); some of these may be difficult at high water. Twin Brook Trail bears E and NE as it climbs out of Franconia Brook valley and enters splendid birch forest. About 1.2 mi. up from 13 Falls, trail traverses several minor ups and downs, then follows old logging road through fir and birch, climbing easily up side of steep slope. At 2.3 mi. / 3600 ft. trail turns L for brief level stretch, then R for fairly steep rocky climb to jct. with Frost Trail at 2.6 mi. / 3750 ft. Turn L to reach Galehead summit in 0.4 mi. Distance from 13 Falls to Galehead summit is 3.0 mi. (one-way) with 1850-ft. elevation gain.

From the W, Garfield Ridge Trail from Franconia Ridge and Mt. Garfield terminates at hut, 6.6 mi. from its start atop Mt. Lafayette. Garfield Ridge Trail, a link in the Appalachian Trail, is accessed by Garfield and Gale River Trails to N and Franconia Brook Trail from S. The distance between Mt. Garfield and Galehead Hut is 3.1 mi., with 700 ft. of elevation gain eastbound and 1400 ft. of elevation gain westbound. This trail is noted for its rough terrain and many ups and downs, especially the steep, wet 1000-ft. climb or descent on E slope of Mt. Garfield, and the climbs over the sides of two eastern subsidiary humps of Mt. Garfield (unofficially called West and East Garfield Ridge). Rugged loop can be made to both Mt. Garfield and Galehead Mtn. using Garfield Trail, Garfield Ridge Trail (including side trip to summit of Garfield), Frost Trail, and Gale River Trail, ending with 1.6 mi. road walk on Gale River

Loop Rd. Loop totals, including road walk, are 15.3 mi. with 3950-ft. elevation gain.

The Twinway, linking Galehead Hut with AMC's Zealand Falls Hut, is primary E approach to mountain. Twinway runs 7.0 mi. from hut to hut and along way passes near or over Mts. Zealand, Guyot and South Twin. The 0.8 mi. stretch from South Twin to Galehead Hut is exceedingly steep, dropping 1150 ft. in elevation.

Winter

The Gale River Loop Rd. is closed to auto travel in winter, adding 3.2 mi. round trip on snowmobile-packed road to approach via Gale River Trail (total 13.4 mi.). Parking is available on N side of US 3 by jct. with Trudeau Rd. Toughest snowshoeing is approach to Garfield Ridge Trail and isolated short, steep pitches on Frost Trail to summit. Few winter hikers will strike out only for Galehead; they'll usually add one or both of the nearby Twins, making for either a tiring out-and-back trip or a strenuous loop over No. Twin and down to Haystack Road. (See Twin Mountain chapter for mileage / distance.)

Note also that Galehead Hut is closed in winter.

View Guide

Back in the mid-1950s, when the trail to Galehead's summit was still quite new, visitors marveled at "a panorama that extends from Osceola and Tecumseh on the south through to Jay Peak on the Canadian border in Vermont—not to mention the unsurpassed view of nearby Franconia Ridge." Unfortunately, tree growth at the summit has now eliminated the views. However, there are two decent viewpoints available to the Galehead climber: the clearing at Galehead Hut and the outlook on the Frost Trail partway up the E side of the mountain.

GALEHEAD HUT VIEW: From the clearing around the hut, South Twin Mtn. looms close by and high above to the SE, with its massive SW ridge extending to the R over lesser peaks, including a prominent rocky knob. On the S, off the R slope of South Twin's SW ridge, the broad mass of Scar Ridge near the Kancamagus Highway is seen beyond the Twin and Franconia Brook valleys, with the much lower North Loon Mtn. (with its upper ski slopes visible) extending to its R. The flat-topped spur known as East Whaleback is seen in front of and below Loon on the R. The distant Bridgewater Mtns. can be seen over the saddle between Scar Ridge and Loon, and Plymouth Mtn. is just visible in the distance above Loon. On the horizon to the R of Loon and successively closer are (L to R) Mt. Kearsarge, Ragged Mtn. and Forbes Mtn., all in central New Hampshire.

Next to the R and much closer, Whaleback Mtn.'s summit pokes up over one of its spur ridges. Farther R the sharp S peak of Owl's Head is seen under the broad ridge that extends N from Whaleback, and farther R still is the upper ridge of Owl's Head Mtn., with Mt. Flume's pyramid peering over in back, just L of the steep E slope of Galehead Mtn. Close by to the SW is Galehead's rounded, wooded summit mass, and behind it to the R is the sharp peak of Mt. Garfield.

FROST TRAIL OUTLOOK: Views to the E and S are also gained from an open outlook L off the Frost Trail 0.3 mi. from the hut. The view is similar to that found at the hut, but from a vantage point 200 ft. higher. Most dramatic is the look almost straight down into the Twin Brook valley and across to massive South Twin and its great SW ridge. To the L (NE) you look down at Galehead Hut with North Twin's rounded bulk rising beyond. The S view here includes (L to R) Mt. Osceola and its sharp Middle and West Peaks, Mt. Tecumseh's cone rising behind the col to the R of the Osceolas, West Tecumseh's broad ridge above and behind East Scar Ridge, and the sharp peak of Middle Scar Ridge, all to the L of the broad, massive main summit of Scar Ridge. The long trough of the Franconia Brook and East Branch valleys leads out to Scar Ridge in the center of the view. The Bridgewater Mtns. are seen in the distance just R of Scar Ridge. Next to the R, adjacent to Scar Ridge, is North Loon Mtn. and its ski slopes, with distant Plymouth Mtn. rising behind it. The flat-topped spur known as East Whaleback is in front of and below Loon on the R. On the horizon to the R of Loon and successively closer are (L to R) Mt. Kearsarge, Ragged Mtn., and Forbes Mtn. Next to the R and much closer the peak of Whaleback Mtn. rears up over one of its spur ridges, and on the far R the sharp S peak of Owl's Head is seen under the high wooded ridge that extends N from Whaleback.

NO. OF 4000-FOOTERS VISIBLE: 11

Mount Garfield

ELEVATION: 4500 ft. / 1372 m   ORDER OF HEIGHT: 17
LOCATION: Garfield Ridge, Town of Franconia, Town of Bethlehem
USGS MAPS: 7½′ South Twin Mountain, 7½′ Franconia

Geography

The conical 4500-ft. peak of Mt. Garfield is one of the most dramatic and recognizable in the White Mountains. Lying midway between Mt. Lafayette and South Twin Mtn., the mountain is the culminating point of rugged Garfield Ridge, notorious among hikers for the many ups and downs along its 6-mi. length. Garfield's bare, pointed peak, standing at the head of the great mountain amphitheater that encircles the lush western Pemigewasset Wilderness, is its most striking attribute. The views of the Wilderness and the surrounding high ridges are among the finest in the White Mountains, amply rewarding the long (10 mi. round trip) but relatively easy hike to Garfield.

Garfield's long forested northern slopes sweep gracefully upward from the Gale River valley. On the NW side the slopes are drained by Burnt, Spruce, and Thompson Brooks, all draining into the South Branch of the Gale River. To the NE is cliff-faced Flat Top Mtn. (3248 ft.), a trailless spur overlooking Garfield Stream, a fork of the North Branch of the Gale River. This stream tumbles down over Hawthorne Falls and several unnamed cascades.

The mountain's steep, rocky S face presents a much more rugged aspect, overlooking the remote upper drainage of Franconia Brook, with Owl's Head Mtn. beyond to the S. When the continental glaciers ground their way S during the Ice Age, they gave Garfield a smooth N slope where the ice flowed uphill, and a rugged S face where the downward pull of the ice plucked chunks of rock away. The slopes on the SE side of the mountain are drained by several tributaries of the main branch of Franconia Brook.

Near the western base of the summit cone, about a half-mile distant, lies Garfield Pond, a small tarn nestled amidst the conifers at an elevation of 3800 ft. From the pond Garfield Ridge runs SW over a 3885-ft. hump, then rises to the North Peak of Mt. Lafayette. On the E the cone of Garfield drops precipitously to a 3420-ft. col, beyond which Garfield Ridge twists eastward over two unnamed knobs (3667 ft. and 3590 ft., sometimes called West Garfield Ridge and East Garfield Ridge or Mt. Pam, respectively) and continues on to Galehead Mtn.

Another prominent feature of Garfield is its long, gently sloping, densely wooded southern spur that abruptly ends in an impressive wall of cliffs overlooking the remote NW corner of the Pemi Wilderness. These inaccessible precipices are especially prominent when seen from the summit of Mt. Lafayette. At the SW base of the cliffs is a broad upland valley drained by the NW branch of Franconia Brook. Where this stream joins the main branch at the SE base of the mountain is a beautiful area of cascades and pools known as Thirteen Falls, named after Camp 13 from the logging days of the early 1900s.

Nomenclature

Originally known as the Haystack (for its symmetrical profile), the Franconia Haystack, and also Hooket, the mountain was renamed in August

1881 in honor of U.S. President James Garfield, who earlier in the year had been struck down by an assassin's bullet. The new name, proposed by Frances A. Willard, was officially bestowed upon the mountain by the selectmen of Franconia, in which a major portion of the mountain rests.

Historical Highlights

First Ascent: It is likely, though not absolutely certain, that a group of Dartmouth College students, all members of Prof. Charles H. Hitchcock's geological survey team, were the first to reach the summit of Garfield (then known as Mt. Haystack) early in the summer of 1871. C. H. Conant, Jonathan Smith, and (possibly) C. W. Hoitt are also credited with first discovering Garfield (Haystack) Pond during this same geological expedition.

1878: E. B. Cook of AMC leads five climbers on bushwhack trek across Garfield Ridge, starting atop Mt. Lafayette and proceeding E. At Haystack Lake, group meets three fishermen bound for trout streams in trackless wilds of Pemi Wilderness. On climb to summit, Cook reports "we soon came upon traces of previous visitors."

1880: Benjamin Macdonald and guide Allen Thompson ascend valley of Garfield Stream, stopping to admire and name Hawthorne Falls, as part of six-day journey through upper Gale River and Franconia Brook regions. They cross ridge between Mt. Garfield and next hump to E (which they call "Moose Mtn."), then descend branch of Franconia Brook to region now known as 13 Falls, passing "Moose Rapids" en route. Macdonald writes up account for *White Mountain Echo*, tourist paper published in Bethlehem.

1881: Moses Sweetser's guidebook describes trailless trek to mountain as "surpassingly difficult, leading through long unbroken thickets of dwarf spruce."

1881: Franconia selectmen officially change name of mountain to Garfield, in honor of President James Garfield.

1883: W. L. Hooper of AMC bushwhacks from Twins across Garfield Ridge to Mt. Garfield and on to Mt. Lafayette. Ascending steep E side of Garfield, it takes 3½ hrs. to climb 1½ mi.

1897: AMC's Franklin P. Clark cuts path starting at Profile & Franconia Notch RR bridge over Gale River and running up past Hawthorne Falls to summit of Garfield.

1902: Forest fire ravages N slopes of mountain.

1904–1909: J. E. Henry's men are logging S slopes of Mt. Garfield from Camp 13 and railroad line to SE. 1907 fire burns S slopes of mountain.

1914: Charles Blood leads week-long expedition on ridge, scouting out proposed route for new trail that will connect Twin Range with Mt. Lafayette.

1915: First trail is established between South Twin and Haystack Lake.

1916: *AMC Guide* lists two routes to summit. One (original 1897 trail) leaves from state highway (today's Route 3), follows North Branch of Gale River and Garfield Stream, passes by picturesque Hawthorne Falls on NE slope of mountain, then climbs to new Garfield Ridge Trail in low col E of Mt. Garfield. This is later named Gale River Trail. Second route (Garfield Trail, recently cut by USFS), follows South Branch of Gale River, then steers SE through forested area burned over in 1902.

1916: Garfield Ridge Trail is finally completed. First Garfield Pond shelter constructed; rebuilt in 1925.

1918: AMC votes to officially change name of Haystack Lake to Garfield Pond.

1940: 14-foot square forest fire lookout cabin is constructed on summit by CCC crews. Materials hauled up by tractor road. It remains in operation through 1948. Cement foundation is all that remains of cabin today. Franconia Brook Trail opened to Garfield Ridge from 13 Falls in valley to S.

Late 1950s: Trail past Hawthorne Falls disappears from hiking guides.

1971: Garfield Ridge Campsite is established 0.4 mi. E of summit. It serves as replacement for Garfield Pond Shelter, closed that same year due to overuse and lack of reliable water source. Garfield Pond Cut-Off abandoned.

1984: S slopes of Garfield and Franconia Brook drainage are included in new 45,000-acre Pemigewasset Wilderness.

Trail Approaches

North Approach from Gale River Loop Rd. (FR 92) in Bethlehem

Garfield Trail, Garfield Ridge Trail
10.0 mi. round-trip, 3000-ft. elevation gain

TRAILHEAD (1500 ft.): Garfield Trail starts from Gale River Loop Road (FR 92), 1.2 mi. from US 3. To reach trailhead, leave US 3 0.3 mi. W of intersection with Trudeau Road. Avoid R fork, and continue until road turns sharp L and crosses bridge over South Branch of Gale River. Parking lot is on R after bridge.

Although a lengthy walk with 3000-ft. elevation gain, this hike is mellow as the trail mostly follows old logging roads and the tractor road that once serviced the summit fire lookout cabin.

Initial section of trail, relocated by Forest Service in 1991, climbs short pitch, then leads over narrow, bumpy embankment through fine hemlock woods, with much blowdown from 2007 storm evident. At 0.7 mi. trail makes short descent to R, then turns L onto original route, following old logging road at easy grade. Cross Thompson Brook at 1.0 mi. and Spruce

Brook just beyond, then cross snowmobile trail and recross Spruce Brook at 1.2 mi. / 1850 ft. (Snowmobile trail has bridges over both brooks, so in high water one can avoid all three crossings by bushwhacking up E side of Thompson Brook to snowmobile trail, turning R and crossing both brooks on bridges, then bushwhacking up W side of Spruce Brook back to trail.) Trail continues long climb at mostly easy, occasionally moderate grades through hardwood forest. After level stretch at ca. 2500 ft., trail passes large flat rock, bends R, and ascends into fine white birch forest. At 2.8 mi. / 2750 ft. climb over low ridgecrest and descend briefly in nice forest of birch and conifer; this is known as Burnt Knoll from 1902 forest fire. Rocky section ascends through more white birches, then at 3.1 mi. turns sharp L on first of seven switchbacks leading up through increasingly coniferous forest. First three switchbacks are fairly long, upper four are shorter. At top of last switchback, ca. 3900 ft., trail bends R with partial views NW through trees to L. Trail angles up at easy to moderate grade across N and then NE side of summit cone with additional restricted views to L and meets Garfield Ridge Trail at 4.8 mi. / 4180 ft. Turn R for steep, rocky 0.2 mi. stretch, with a couple of easy scrambles, to open, ledgy summit, located a few yards S (left) of trail at 5.0 mi. / 4500 ft. Highest point bears old foundation of lookout cabin; best viewing spots into Pemi Wilderness are on S side. (Note: From Garfield Ridge Trail jct., steep 0.2 mi. descent to E leads to Garfield Ridge Campsite, elevation 3900 ft., which features 12-person log lean-to and seven four-person tent platforms and reliable water source. Campsite is staffed and maintained by AMC; fee is charged in summer and fall.)

OPTIONAL APPROACHES

While there are approaches to the summit from all four points of the compass, only the N approach from US 3 is popular with day-hikers. The others, such as the E and W approaches via the rocky Garfield Ridge Trail, are used primarily by backpackers.

From Mt. Lafayette and Franconia Ridge, it's a rugged 3.5 mi. walk to Garfield's summit, with many ups and downs totaling 1000 ft. of elevation gain. From summit of Mt. Lafayette, Garfield Ridge Trail runs across bare N ridge, over beautiful North Peak, and descends steeply in open to jct. L with Skookumchuck Trail at 0.8 mi. / 4680 ft. Ledges to R here offer beautiful views over NW part of Pemi Wilderness. Trail continues down steeply to treeline and drops steadily through mossy fir woods to col at 1.7 mi. / 3740 ft. Climb over 3885-ft. hump, passing obscure side path R leading to wild outlook towards Owl's Head Mtn. Trail meanders along ridge, climbs easily to tiny Garfield Pond at 3.0 mi. / 3860 ft. (Side path L leads to S shore of lily-dotted pond.) From here climb is steep and rocky to summit of Garfield at 3.5 mi. from Mt. Lafayette.

From AMC's Galehead Hut to E, it's a 3.1-mi. trek to Garfield summit, with 1400 ft. of elevation gain. From hut (3780 ft.), Garfield Ridge Trail descends moderately with rocky footing, passing outlook to N, to jct. R with Gale River Trail at 0.6 mi. / 3390 ft. Ridge trail then traverses series of humps with several short, steep ups and downs, passing partial outlook S to Owl's Head Mtn. near top of first major hump. Catching glimpses of daunting steep side of Garfield ahead, drop to deep col and jct. L with Franconia Brook Trail at 2.2 mi. / 3420 ft. Climb from here is very steep and rocky, wet in places, with one especially tricky scramble up wet ledges, rising nearly 1100 ft. in 0.9 mi. Pass jct. R with spur to Garfield Ridge Campsite (water and view) at 2.7 mi. / 3900 ft., and jct. R with Garfield Trail at 2.9 mi. / 4180 ft. Last pitch is steep and rocky to summit at 3.1 mi. / 4500 ft.

From the S, hikers can join Garfield Ridge from deep recesses of Pemi Wilderness via Franconia Brook Trail from 13 Falls Campsite (2196 ft.). This scenic spot with numerous cascades and pools is reached from Lincoln Woods trailhead (1160 ft.) off Kanacamgus Highway via long but easy 8.1 mi. walk almost entirely on old railroad grades, starting with 2.9 mi. on Lincoln Woods Trail to crossing of Franconia Brook on bridge, then on Franconia Brook Trail. Latter trail makes three crossings of Camp 9 Brook (the last, at 4.1 mi. from trailhead, after a detour R around a beaver swamp), and single crossings of the larger Hellgate Brook at 5.5 mi., Redrock Brook at 6.5 mi., and Twin Brook at 7.6 mi. From 13 Falls, Franconia Brook Trail climbs moderately N up valley of main branch of Franconia Brook, crossing E branch of brook 1.0 mi. up from 13 Falls, then continues more steeply up with rough footing at times, to Garfield Ridge Trail in deep col E of Mt. Garfield, 2.2 mi. from 13 Falls, elevation 3420 ft. Turn L here for steep 0.9 mi. climb to summit as described above. From Lincoln Woods trailhead, ascent is 11.2 mi. one-way with 3340-ft. elevation gain. From 13 Falls Campsite, one-way climb is 3.1 mi. with 2300-ft. elevation gain.

Rugged loop can be made to both Mt. Garfield and Galehead Mtn. using Garfield Trail, Garfield Ridge Trail (including side trip to summit of Garfield), Frost Trail, and Gale River Trail, ending with 1.6 mi. road walk on Gale River Loop Rd. Loop totals, including road walk, are 15.3 mi. with 3950-ft. elevation gain.

Winter

Winter on Garfield tends to be long and brutal. As the summit area is treeless and exposed, it can be quite inhospitable, especially during a snowstorm, or when bone-rattling winds are ripping across the mountaintop from the NW.

The access road to the Garfield Trail is not open in winter, so any ascent of the mountain from US 3 will require a 1.2-mi. road walk each

The summit view from Mount Garfield takes in much of the central and western Pemi Wilderness, including the remote summits of the Bond Range.

way. Plowed parking is usually available by the entrance of the west loop of the Gale River Loop Rd. Although the grade is never steep along the Garfield Trail, the snow accumulates to a great depth on the mountain's N-facing slope and snowshoes may be needed from the end of November until early May. The comfortable grade makes it a good snowshoeing trail. The final quarter-mile pitch to the summit along the Garfield Ridge Trail can be very icy, and caution is required on both the ascent and descent of this steep, ledgy section of trail.

View Guide

Garfield's sharp, ledgy summit is one of the premier viewing perches in the Whites, especially on the S side looking down into the remote, mountain-ringed valleys of the western Pemigewasset Wilderness. To the NW and N there are sweeping views across extensive lowlands into northern New Hampshire and Vermont, though these are hard-pressed to compete with the compelling wilderness vistas to the S. This summit deserves a long visit on a clear day.

Looking L, to the E, the high, massive summits of North and South Twin loom just 3 mi. away. A high shoulder, striped with fir waves, extends to the L from North Twin, with Mts. Adams and Jefferson poking above and distant Goose Eye and Old Speck in the Mahoosucs to the L.

The top of Mt. Washington peers over just to the R of North Twin's summit, and the tip of Mt. Eisenhower is seen through the col between the Twins. Under North Twin and its shoulder is the nearby broad hump on Garfield Ridge called West Garfield Ridge. Farther away, the Garfield Ridge bump known as East Garfield Ridge is seen below the col between the Twins. The low hump of Galehead is seen in front of the great, scree-streaked bulk of South Twin. Galehead Hut can be spotted on the level col between these peaks. To the SE, beyond the broad, birch-wooded upper basin of Franconia Brook, are the other peaks of the Twin–Bond Range: bald Mt. Guyot, scarred with many rock slides, peering over the great SW ridge of South Twin; Mt. Bond rising behind and to the L of the sharp peak of West Bond; and the craggy face of Bondcliff. The tip of Mt. Chocorua just peeks over the R side of Bondcliff. Mt. Carrigain's dome rises in the back between West Bond and Bondcliff, and North (L) and South (R) Hancock rise massively to the R of Bondcliff. To the R of the Hancocks, looking SSE down the Franconia Brook valley, (L to R) Mts. Passaconaway, Whiteface, Tripyramid and Kancamagus (with its summit under South Tripyramid) are seen in the back above the nearer peaks of Mt. Huntington (L, flat-topped, under Whiteface) and Mt. Hitchcock (R, two summits under the R end of Mt. Kancamagus). Over the R slope of Hitchcock the northern Flat Mtn. can be sighted through Mad River Notch.

Close by to the S the rounded, wooded mass of Owl's Head dominates the interior of the western Pemi Wilderness. The Osceolas rise beyond Owl's Head on the L, with East Osceola forming the R side of Mad River Notch and a prominent slide marking the main Osceola peak. Part of Sandwich Dome can be seen to the R of West Osceola's knobby peak. The broad, double main summit of Scar Ridge is directly over Owl's Head. Mt. Tecumseh (L) and West Tecumseh (R) rise prominently in back between the Osceolas and Scar Ridge. To the R of Owl's Head, looking SSW, the graceful pyramids of Mts. Flume and Liberty rise beyond the remote valley of Lincoln Brook. Various spurs of Whaleback Mtn. are seen to the L of Flume. Loon Mtn. peers over these low spurs, with Prospect Mtn. behind it on the L and Hersey Mtn. above it on the horizon. The Bridgewater Mtns. are seen over the slope just to the L of Flume's summit. Mt. Kearsarge is in the distance over the sweeping ridge that joins Flume and Liberty, with Ragged Mtn. and Forbes Mtn. in front of Kearsarge on its R. Down below, in line with Liberty, is the long, spruce-clad ridge that extends S from Garfield. Mt. Cardigan (L) and its spur, Cataloochee Mtn. (R) can be seen over the ridge joining Liberty wth Little Haystack on the R, with distant Sunapee Mtn. visible behind Cardigan on the L. Nearby to the SW looms the great wall of Franconia Ridge, with Mt. Lafayette impressively revealed from base to serrated crest. The tips of North Kinsman and Cannon Mtn. can be seen over the R shoulder of Lafayette. The NW Peak of Cannon pops out farther R off the R slope of

Lafayette, with Cooley (L) and Cole (R) Hills behind on the R and Moody Ledge (L) and Green Mtn. (R) behind them. On the horizon in this direction is the Breadloaf–Wilson range in the Green Mountains.

Farther R, tiny Bald Mtn.and Artists Bluff at the top of Franconia Notch are seen down low, with the long ridge of Mts. Abraham and Ellen on the horizon. Next to the R is the prominent, humpy Signal Mtn. range in west-central Vermont, with Mt. Ethan Allen and Camel's Hump seen beyond to the R of sharp Spruce Mtn. at the R end of the range. Next to the R, Big Bickford Mtn., a low spur of Mt. Lafayette, is seen nearby, with Vermont's Worcester Range on the horizon. To the R of Big Bickford is its lower neighbor, Scarface Mtn., above which are Mt. Mansfield (L) and the Sterling Range (R) on the horizon. Part of I-93 and the village of Franconia can be seen in line with Mansfield. Farther R on the horizon is the sharp peak of Belvidere Mtn. with part of the Moore Dam reservoir seen in line with it. Tillotson Peak and Haystack Mtn. are seen to the R of Belvidere, and farther R are the two prominent Jay Peaks, all in northern Vermont. The town of Littleton can be seen in the middle distance to the L of the Jay Peaks. Next to the R lowly Mt. Agassiz is in the foreground with Vermont's Mt. Hor seen above Kirby Peak beyond. Next to the R is the prominent pyramid of Burke Mtn. with Mt. Pisgah poking off its L side. Umpire Mtn. is on the R of Burke with Bald Mtn. behind. Continuing to the R are East Haven Mtn. and broad East Mtn., with distant Gore Mtn. behind on its R. Part of Forest Lake (Dalton) is seen in line with the L end of East Mtn. Next to the R is the Burnside/Stone Mtn. group with sharp Sable Mtn. beyond. Farther R, looking just E of N, is the range of peaks in the Nash Stream Forest region. This starts on the L with Goback Mtn., with Vermont's Mt. Monadnock behind Goback's sharp L peak. The pass between little Mt. Pleasant (L) and Prospect Mtn. (R), along with the Mountain View House, can be seen in front under Goback. The Nash Stream range extends R to the sharp peak of Sugarloaf Mtn. and rounded Gore Mtn. To the R of the Nash Stream range are the bare Percy Peaks with North Whitcomb behind on their R. Farther R the crest of Long Mtn. is seen over the ridge comprised of Hutchins Mtn. and its Pilot Range neighbors.

Close by and below, in line with the Nash Stream range, is the wild-looking Flat Top Mtn., the nothern spur of Garfield, with the low, level-topped Beech Hill behind it. To the R of the Pilots is the bulky mass of Mt. Cabot, and next to the R, looking NNE, is the long ridge of Mts. Starr King (with North Terrace behind on its L) and Waumbek in the Pliny Range, seen beyond Cherry Mtn. The summit of Cherry is almost directly under the summit of Waumbek. Cherry Pond can be seen on the flats to the L of Cherry Mtn., and the fields of Jefferson are seen by the lower L end of Starr King. Part of the village of Twin Mountain is at the base of Cherry Mtn. Looking below Cherry's summit, the rocky Nubble can be spotted peering over a nearer low ridge. A long ridgecrest extends R from Waumbek's summit, with Pliny Mtn. under its R end, and a similar ridge extends R from Cherry Mtn. To the R of Pliny are the lower Pond Hill and the double rounded summit of Black Crescent Mtn. The flat crest of Cambridge Black Mtn. is seen in the back between Pliny and Black Crescent. Nubble Peak, a spur of North Twin on the New England 100 Highest list, is seen under the R summit of Black Crescent. In the distance behind Black Crescent on the R are Maine's Mt. Bemis, Red Ridge and Elephant Mtn. Next to the R is the prominent knob of Mt. Crescent, with the broad mass of Old Blue Mtn. beyond on the R. Farther R Mt. Deception pokes above the L slope of North Twin, with Old Speck Mtn. on the horizon on its L. Just to the R the tip of Mt. Dartmouth peers over a flat shoulder of North Twin, with Goose Eye Mtn. in the distance. Then the view continues across to Mts. Adams and Jefferson and North Twin.

NO. OF 4000-FOOTERS VISIBLE: 30

North and South Hancock

North Hancock

ELEVATION: 4420 ft. / 1347 m   ORDER OF HEIGHT: 21
LOCATION: S edge of Pemigewasset Wilderness, Town of Lincoln
USGS MAPS: 7½' Mount Carrigain, 7½' Mount Osceola

South Hancock

ELEVATION: 4319 ft. / 1316 m   ORDER OF HEIGHT: 26
LOCATION: S edge of Pemigewasset Wilderness, Town of Lincoln,
    Township of Livermore
USGS MAPS: 7½' Mount Carrigain, 7½' Mount Osceola

Geography

The sprawling mass of Mt. Hancock dominates the south-central region of the Pemigewasset Wilderness. Though its ridges are densely wooded and its summit views are partly restricted, upon closer inspection this turns out to be a very interesting mountain. It has long held an aura of mystery and inaccessibility and offers a wilderness flavor not found on the more popular White Mountain ridges.

Hikers on the Hancock Loop Trail—the only path on the mountain—traverse only a small central section of an entire range of Hancock peaks and ridges. The trail makes a loop over the two 4000-footer summits: the broad, flattened dome of North Hancock, with an outlook ledge featuring a fine view S, and the sharp peak of South Hancock, with partial outlooks SE and NW near the top.

The main Hancock ridge stretches over 4 mi. from N to S. At its N end it rises steeply from the East Branch of the Pemigewasset River to a 3420-ft. knob, from which a narrow ridge leads up to the trailless NW Peak (4020 ft.), a sharp knob with extensive cliffs on the E side of its NE ridge. This peak bore a fire tower for a few years after the 1938 hurricane. Around 1970 it was briefly on the list of New England's Hundred Highest peaks, but was removed after a new USGS survey showed that it was over 4000 ft. but lacking the required 200-ft. rise above its col with North Hancock. In recent years this peak has been added to the "Trailwrights 72" list of 4000-footers. A long, narrow ridge connects the NW Peak with North Hancock; to the W of this ridge is the long, isolated valley of Cedar Brook. On the W flank of the ridge is a prominent gravelly slide that fell in 1927. On the S face of North Hancock is the Arrow Slide, a great Y-shaped gash that identifies the peak from afar and once served as the climbing route to the summit. On the W a 3100-ft. saddle joins North Hancock with the E spurs of trailless Mt. Hitchcock (3620 ft.).

A high, curving ridge joins North Hancock with South Hancock, which has a precipitous E face and appears as a sharp wooded pyramid from some angles. Partway along this ridge is a subsidiary summit, traversed by the loop trail, sometimes referred to as "Middle Hancock." On the SW this central ridge encloses a wooded bowl that forms the headwaters of the Hancock Branch, North Fork. The ridge continues S from South Hancock to a bold, trailless spur (3940 ft.) that overlooks Hancock Notch and the headwaters of Sawyer River. Across Hancock Notch to the S rises trailless Mt. Huntington (3700 ft.)

From Middle Hancock a rough, tangled ridge runs E towards Mt. Carrigain, dropping steeply at the E end to its col with the rock-faced nubble known as "The Captain" (3520 ft.), hidden between Hancock and Carrigain. On the S side of Hancock's E ridge are two small glacial cirques that drain into the Sawyer River; the eastern of these holds two beaver ponds on its floor. In addition to its main N–S ridge, Hancock throws out two more prominent ridges to the N. Between the main ridge, which bears the NW Peak, and the middle northerly ridge is the supremely wild valley of Crystal Brook, with a steep headwall on the N side of North Hancock. This slide-scarred basin is well-seen from Zeacliff to the N. The middle and eastern of Hancock's three N ridges enclose the valley of the W fork of Carrigain Branch, one of the most remote nooks in the mountains. The main stem of Carrigain Branch flows down from Carrigain Pond at the NE base of The Captain. This valley is enclosed by Mt. Carrigain and the easternmost of Hancock's N ridges.

Although it is now relatively easy to climb, Hancock remains an untamed and mysterious mountain, a place of deep fir woods and untrodden ridges, of savage slides and hidden ravines.

Nomenclature

The original name for the mountain was "Pemigewasset Peak," as coined by geographer Arnold Guyot on his 1860 map of the White Mountains, for its proximity to the East Branch of the Pemigewasset River. The current name was applied in the 1870s by state geologist Charles H. Hitchcock in honor of John Hancock, the first patriot to sign the Declaration of Independence, though Dr. Edward Tuckerman contended that the name in fact honored a nineteenth-century lumberman.

Historical Highlights

First Ascent: Unknown.

Mid-1840s: Nicholas G. Norcross, earliest lumber baron in White Mtns., logs large white pines along upper reaches of East Branch; logs are floated down Pemigewasset and Merrimack Rivers to Lowell, Massachusetts.

1876: Moses Sweetser's guidebook notes of Hancock that "its extent and shape are vaguely represented on the maps because much of the adjacent country is still unexplored."

1878: AMC trampers are exploring the region; cylinder placed on summit for hikers to register in.

1879: Party led by AMC explorer Webster Wells climbs Hancock from North Fork, spends two hours on summit, then traverses ridge from Hancock to Carrigain, climbing over The Captain and discovering Carrigain Pond. Three-day expedition also includes ascents of Mts. Anderson and Lowell. Trip described in July 1880 *Appalachia*.

1894–1904: Lumber baron J. E. Henry builds logging railroad up Hancock Branch and on into North Fork drainage to SW of Hancocks. Slopes are heavily cut over.

1907: First edition of AMC guidebook recommends that pathless Hancock be ascended from East Branch via long N ridge.

1908: Party of 30, "many of them ladies," is recorded in summit cylinder. Crude, short-lived trail cut from S using logging roads and Arrow Slide.

1908–1909: J. E. Henry's logging crews extend East Branch & Lincoln RR along East Branch of Pemigewasset at N base of Hancock. Camp 17 is established along river at base of NW ridge, and Camp 18 is occupied to E of Crystal Brook. N slopes of Hancock are mostly clearcut, and cutting in large Crystal Brook basin continues into early 1930s.

The moss-carpeted and lush Hancock Loop Trail meanders along the connecting ridge between the North and South summits.

1927: AMC *Bulletin* lists club trip from town of Lincoln via train to Parker–Young lumber camp. Itinerary includes climb of Hancock and dinner at lumber camp.

1932–1945: Parker Young Co. logs Cedar Brook valley on NW side of Hancock, mainly from Camp 24 on spur logging RR extended southward from main line along East Branch. Slash from logging and blowdown from 1938 hurricane creates fire hazard. Firetower is erected on NW Peak and is operated ca. 1936–1941 by CCC, then USFS employees; for several years around 1940 area is off limits to hikers, patrolled by WMNF rangers.

1936: Parker–Young Co. sells 69,969 acres in East Branch watershed, including Hancocks, to U.S. Forest Service for $2.50 per acre, retaining cutting rights for 20 years.

1949: In *Appalachia* article, peakbagger Francis "Mully" Parsons describes ascent of Hancock via remote W fork of Carrigain Branch.

1955: *AMC Guide* cautions that ascent of Hancock is "a stunt to be undertaken only by strong trampers with knowledge of woodcraft who should be prepared to camp overnight." Various approach routes are used for bushwhack climbs, with Arrow Slide a favorite. About this time Kancamagus Highway is extended to hairpin turn (present-day trailhead), eliminating long walk from Lincoln and making Hancock more accessible. Highway is linked with Conway in 1959.

1957: Interest in Hancock surges with creation of 4000-Footer Club. AMC trip in May places 46 trampers on North Hancock, and 41 ascend South Hancock on September jaunt.

1960: AMC group including Robert and Miriam Underhill make first winter circuit of Hancock peaks. As recounted in Miriam's *Give Me the Hills*, this is multi-day epic with many miles of trail-breaking.

1965–1966: AMC's Worcester Chapter cuts Hancock Loop Trail. As reported in *Appalachia*, first hiker to traverse the trail upon completion in 1966 is "a Mr. Waterman of the New York Chapter." For many years thereafter Hancock is one of Guy Waterman's favorite peaks.

1984: Northern ridges and valleys of Hancock are included in new 45,000-acre Pemigewasset Wilderness.

Trail Approaches

South Approach from Kancamagus Highway (NH 112):

Hancock Notch Trail, Cedar Brook Trail, Hancock Loop Trail

North and South Hancock: 9.8 mi. round trip, 2700-ft. elevation gain
North Hancock only: 8.6 mi. round trip, 2500-ft. elevation gain
South Hancock only: 8.2 mi. round trip, 2200-ft. elevation gain

TRAILHEAD (2129 ft.): Parking is at the Hancock Overlook on the Kancamagus Highway, just E of the hairpin turn and 4.7 mi. E of the Lincoln Woods parking area. Parking at trail's start at hairpin turn is strictly prohibited. Hike to Hancocks features gentle approach through the wild, remote valley of the North Fork of Hancock Branch, with many stream crossings, followed by steep climb to top of either peak. The two summits are linked by an attractive and generally easy wooded ridge trail; most hikers do the loop over both Hancocks.

From N end of overlook parking, descend path past kiosk and carefully cross highway at hairpin turn to sign for Hancock Notch Trail. Trail follows old railroad grade built by J. E. Henry's logging crews in 1890s. Walking is easy through mixed woods, with occasional dips at washouts. Pass large boulder on R, then cross small brook at 0.6 mi. and continue up grade through spruces, passing spot with view over North Fork of Hancock Branch at 1.2 mi. Turn R up bank at 1.4 mi. (where RR grade continues ahead across North Fork), heading NE along S side of North Fork. From high bank look L through opening for glimpse of high, sharp wooded peak of South Hancock rising over trees. Trail weaves across three small brooks and swings R to jct. with Cedar Brook Trail at 1.8 mi. / 2520 ft.

Turn L on Cedar Brook Trail and climb moderately with rocky footing for 0.2 mi., then make first of five crossings of North Fork (potentially difficult in high water) interspersed with easy stretches through spruce woods and along boggy openings. First two crossings are only 100 ft. apart and are easily bypassed via well-beaten path through woods on R. Other crossings can be bypassed with longer, less-used paths. After fifth crossing reach jct. with Hancock Loop Trail at 2.5 mi. / 2720 ft. Turn R on Loop Trail and quickly make final crossing of North Fork, ascend across rough, rocky side stream, then climb moderately through conifers and birch with sometimes rocky footing; higher up there are glimpses L through trees to North Hancock and Arrow Slide. Reach Loop Jct. at 3.6 mi. / 3400 ft. Loop will be described from North Peak to South Peak.

Turn L on North Link and descend steadily for 0.1 mi. / 100 ft. to dry brook outwash in flat hollow. From here trail ascends moderately at first but soon shoots up very steeply, parallel to but away from Arrow Slide, which is off to L. Grade is relentless for most of climb to North Peak, with recently built rock staircases partway up and loose rock underfoot in places higher up. At ca. 4100 ft. there is view back to South Hancock from open area. Nearing top trail angles L and moderates, passes by fir waves, and reaches broad wooded summit at 4.2 mi. / 4420 ft. Here Ridge Link to South Peak goes R and side path descends 50 yds. L to outlook ledges with good view S over scrub to Osceolas and Sandwich Range.

From jct., wild, winding Ridge Link meanders across summit plateau through nice fir woods, then descends steadily to dense fir wave and 4180-ft. col. Trail climbs minor bump, descends briefly, and ascends easily, then steadily to flat wooded top of Middle Hancock at 5.1 mi. / 4300 ft. Dip to another 4180-ft. col, with one muddy stretch, then climb easily up narrow ridge. At 5.4 mi. rock on R offers partial views to W: (L to R) Mt. Hitchcock with Big Coolidge Mtn. and Mt. Wolf beyond, Whaleback Mtn., the Signal Mtn. range in Vermont, South Kinsman with North Hitchcock below, Mts. Flume and Liberty, Mts. Lincoln and Lafayette with Owl's Head below, and nearby North Hancock with the Arrow Slide prominently displayed. After final moderate climb attain wooded summit of South Hancock at 5.6 mi. / 4319 ft. Short side path drops sharply L to small ledge with restricted view SE over Sawyer River valley.

From summit, South Link begins steep descent NW back to Loop Jct. A short distance down, trail offers framed view across Pemi Wilderness to Owl's Head and Franconia Range with North Hancock and its Arrow Slide nearby to the R; Mt. Garfield can be seen off the L slope of North Hancock. Upper part of descent is very steep and eroded; partway down, at ca. 3850 ft., look for traces of old logging road cutting across trail. Grade moderates and footing improves below 3700 ft., and after bend to L, Loop Jct. is reached at 6.1 mi. / 3400 ft. From here it is 3.6 generally easy mi. back to trailhead.

There are no other day-hike trail approaches to the Hancocks. Backpackers can make long approaches through remote valleys via Hancock

Notch Trail from Sawyer River valley to E, passing through Hancock Notch, or via Cedar Brook Trail from East Branch valley in Pemigewasset Wilderness to N, walking up long valley of Cedar Brook and climbing over pass between Mts. Hancock and Hitchcock; consult *AMC White Mountain Guide* for details.

Winter

A challenging but fun winter trip, relatively easy up to Loop Jct. if North Fork crossings have good snow bridges. The climb up either peak is steep and difficult snowshoeing, requiring vigorous step-kicking or crampon-clawing. Snow piles deep on the ridge, and the Ridge Link may be very hard to follow. Along the way it offers neat winter-only views into various nooks and crannies of the Pemi Wilderness. In late winter, with a deep platform of snow, South Hancock can become a wonderful wilderness watchtower with views over the trees in several directions. Parking area at Hancock Overlook is plowed.

View Guide

NORTH HANCOCK OUTLOOK: This sunny granite outcrop has a 180-degree panorama to the S. The view is good sitting, but you must stand to see over the scrub for the full panorama. To the far L is North Moat with Big Attitash Mtn. below. Farther R South Moat is seen over Mt. Tremont, with parts of Table Mtn. behind Tremont. Next to the R Bear Mtn. is seen over Owl's Cliff. On the horizon over Bear, in southern Maine, are the lumpy Burnt Meadow Mtns, with the Saddleback Hills beyond and the Bill Merrill Mtn. group farther R. Continuing to the R, the low hills in the Madison / Eaton area along the New Hampshire / Maine border and the distant Clark Mtn. range in Maine are seen beyond the spur of Mt. Chocorua known as Blue Mtn. Close by to SE is the wooded ridge leading over to South Hancock; rising beyond are the high peaks of the Sandwich Range. Mt. Chocorua is seen above Middle Hancock, Mts. Paugus and Passaconaway are between Middle and South Hancock, and Mts. Whiteface and Tripyramid are over the R side of South Hancock. Green Mtn. in Effingham is seen over the long N (L) ridge of Paugus, and Hedgehog Mtn. is seen under and to the R of Paugus. The Nickerson Mtns. are seen over Paugus Pass (the gap between Paugus and Passaconaway), with Square Ledge and Potash Mtn. below and in front. Flagg Mtn. in the Ossipee Range peers over the col between Passaconaway and Whiteface, with the distant Moose Mtns. behind on its L. Part of Copple Crown Mtn. can be seen behind Flagg on the R. The tip of Mt. Shaw, highest of the Ossipees, pokes over a hump on the N ridge of Whiteface. West Sleeper is seen off the L slope of North Tripyramid, Scaur Peak is under Tripyramid's North Slide, and the tip of Middle Tripyramid just peers over North on the R. Farther R, looking nearby to the S, are the two broad, dark summits of Mt. Huntington, the R (W) one scarred with scree slopes, with the rolling crest of Mt. Kancamagus above and behind. The southern Flat Mtn. is seen through the cut of Lost Pass over the E (L) hump of Kancamagus. The long ridge of the northern Flat Mtn. sprawls over the two middle humps of Kancamagus, and Sandwich Dome rises to the R, over the W hump of Kancamagus. Extending R from the Dome is its SW shoulder, Black Mtn., with Jennings Peak below and Sachem Peak and the smaller Black Mtn. lower down and to the R. On the horizon between Tripyramid and Sandwich Dome is the long ridge of the Belknap Range, with Mt. Major on its L end and Belknap and Gunstock Mtns. over the summits of Kancamagus and the northern Flat. The tip of Red Hill pokes up over the col between the northern Flat and Sandwich.

Perhaps the most striking view from North Hancock is S down the North Fork basin to the rippled, slide-marked ridge of Osceola, with the East Peak on the L, the main summit in the middle, and the Middle and West Peaks to the R. The many summits of Scar Ridge extend to the R of Osceola, with low spurs of Mt. Hitchcock in front. Mt. Cardigan can be spotted over the notch between Osceola and Scar Ridge, with Cataloochee Mtn. to its R, over the double-summit East Scar Ridge, and the nearer Tenney Mtn. range and the more distant Mt. Sunapee to its L. Stinson Mtn. is to the R of East Scar Ridge, with Croydon Peak to its R and farther away, while Vermont's Mt. Ascutney is to the R of the sharp peak of Middle Scar Ridge. Carr Mtn. (L) and Mt. Kineo (R) are seen over the main Scar Ridge summit, with distant Smarts Mtn. and then Mt. Cushman to the R. The ski trails of Loon Mtn. are farther R and closer. Mt. Cube is beyond Loon and Vermont's Killington and Pico are on the horizon to the R. Mt. Moosilauke anchors the view on the far R, with the sharp nearby peak of Mt. Hitchcock in front and below.

SOUTH HANCOCK OUTLOOK: This small ledge, with a steep dropoff in front, offers a narrow but unusual view to the E and SE, best seen standing. Through the branches Mt. Carrigain can be glimpsed close by to the L, with Signal Ridge trailing to the R. The open view starts on the L with the high dome of Kearsarge North, with The Gemini and Mt. Shaw extending to its L and the town of Bartlett in the Saco valley below. The Attitash ski slopes are to the R of Kearsarge North, with Hurricane Mtn. in the Green Hills beyond. The broad Sawyer River valley leads out to lumpy Mt. Tremont (L) and Owl's Cliff (R), with Sawyer Pond at their base. North Moat is beyond Tremont, with Black Cap Mtn. and Pleasant Mtn. in Maine to the L and farther away. Bear Mtn. rises over Owl's Cliff, with Middle and South Moat behind to the L. Table Mtn. is seen under Middle and South Moat. On the horizon to the R of Bear are the

Burnt Meadow Mtns. in western Maine with the Saddleback Hills beyond and the Bill Merrill Mtn. range to the R. On the R of the Sawyer River valley is the wooded backside of Green's Cliff. Blue Mtn. and nameless lower spurs of Mt. Chocorua are seen over the L slope of Green's Cliff, with hills along the New Hampshire / Maine border beyond and Maine's Clark Mtn. range farther R. The rocky spire of Mt. Chocorua is seen behind Green's Cliff on the R, with the Three Sisters on its L. To the R of Chocorua are its Sandwich Range neighbors, Mt. Paugus and dark, cone-shaped Mt. Passaconaway. Green Mtn. in Effingham is seen in the distance over the L (N) ridge of Paugus, and Hedgehog (L) and Potash (R) Mtns. are seen below and between Paugus and Passaconaway. The wooded crest of Square Ledge can be discerned above Potash, with the Nickerson Mtns. near Ossipee Lake beyond.

NO. OF 4000-FOOTERS VISIBLE: from North Hancock summit, 41 (theoretically / through the trees); from North Hancock outlook, 8; from South Hancock summit (through the trees or in late winter), 37

Owl's Head Mountain

ELEVATION: 4025 ft. / 1227 m   ORDER OF HEIGHT: 43
LOCATION: Western Pemigewasset Wilderness, Town of Franconia
USGS MAP: 7½′ South Twin

Geography

Rising aloof and remote deep in the Pemigewasset Wilderness, Owl's Head Mtn. suffers from a terrible reputation among peakbaggers. Nine miles by trail from the Kancamagus Highway, its flat, wooded summit offers a quintessential non-view. "Owl's Head is everything a mountain should not be," lamented one weary hiker after completing the trek. "It is a mountain that has much to be modest about," wrote another.

But Owl's Head does have its rewards. The approach up the Lincoln Brook Trail brings you through a deep valley with a wonderful sense of isolation. The views of that valley and the "back side" of the Franconia Range from the mountain's western slide are one-of-a-kind. The committing length, potentially difficult stream crossings, and steep scrambling at the end make this one of the most memorable of all the 4000-footer hikes.

The wooded ridge of Owl's Head sprawls several miles N and S in the center of the western Pemigewasset Wilderness. On the W, N, and E it is surrounded by a great horseshoe of higher mountains: the Franconia

The wooded mass of Owl's Head Mountain as seen from Franconia Ridge.

Range, Garfield Ridge, and the Twin–Bond Range. Deep valleys separate the long, squat mass of Owl's Head from its taller neighbors. On the W and S is the sharply cut valley of Lincoln Brook, while on the N and E the mountain is bounded by the broad trough of Franconia Brook. The two brooks join near the SE base of the mountain.

At the NW end of Owl's Head a broad, boggy saddle (3180 ft.) divides the headwaters of Lincoln and Franconia Brooks and links the mountain with the E side of Mt. Lafayette. From here the Owl's Head ridge rises SE to the narrow N–S crest, which is nearly level at the 3800–4000 ft. tier for a mile. The 4025-ft. summit is about in the middle of the long ridgecrest.

Finding this highest point proved mettlesome for early Owl's Head peakbaggers, and in 2005 it came to light that there was, in fact, a slightly higher knob 0.2 mi. N of where the summit had been marked for many years. According to measurements made by several hikers equipped with GPS and/or reliable altimeters, the "new" summit is apparently 10–20 ft. higher than the "old" summit, where the unofficial path has long ended. On the USGS quad, the "new" summit is at the "4025" mark, within a fairly large area inside a 4000-ft. contour, while the "old" summit seems to be within a much smaller 4000-ft. contour area farther S along the ridgecrest. As of 2007, a discontinuous path had developed from the "old" to the "new" summit, but it was still partly a bushwhack, with blowdown and dense growth in places. As of this writing, the 4000-Footer Committee continues to recognize ascents to the "old" summit and is likely to continue doing so in the foreseeable future.

A half-mile S of the summit the ridge dips to a col before rising to the sharp 3660-ft. cone at the S end—the true "Owl's Head"—with a double summit, the northern bump being slightly higher. Seen from the S, this peak is a wooded spire. On its SE side the "Owl's Head" thrusts out a flat-topped 3060-ft. spur that ends in a prominent set of cliffs. On the W flank of the mountain, between the summit and the "Owl's Head," is a steep slide of broken rock that plunges into Lincoln Brook valley and provides part of the climbing route to the peak.

The E side of the mountain is broken by several truncated ridges and three brook ravines. A series of four prominent talus fields is strung along the lower E slopes towards the N end. These and the SE cliffs offer outstanding views to experienced bushwhackers. Although its ridgecrest is thickly wooded with conifers, the sides of Owl's Head are largely cloaked in a paper birch forest that grew up after a forest fire devastated the region in 1907.

Owl's Head is the only New Hampshire 4000-footer reached exclusively by an unofficial, unmaintained path. USFS Wilderness rules preclude marking and maintenance of unmaintained trails, and this has engendered some controversy in recent years, especially after an unknown party blazed the path. Hikers should be aware that cairns, signs and other markings may not be present at the bottom of the path, along its route, or at either the "old" or "new" summit. This contributes to the unique nature of the Owl's Head experience!

Nomenclature

Owl's Head Mtn. takes its name from the sharp peak at the S end of the ridge (though at least one veteran hiker contends that it refers to the cliffs on the lower SE spur). This local name was used in Moses Sweetser's guidebook as early as 1881, and it appeared on the AMC's 1887 map of the White Mountains. This moniker has also been applied to two other summits in the White Mountains, one a cliff-faced knob at the south end of the Benton Range, the other a spur of Cherry Mountain. In all three cases the summit was thought to resemble the shape of the wise bird's head. The Owl's Head in the Pemigewasset Wilderness has also been called the "Franconia Owl" for its location in the SE corner of the town of Franconia. The name "Wilderness Mountain" was proposed by a climber in the 1930s, but never caught on.

In early accounts, and on AMC maps into the 1920s, today's Lincoln Brook (on the W side of Owl's Head) was called Lafayette Brook or Franconia Branch or Brook, while what is now Franconia Brook (on the E side of Owl's Head) was known as Redrock Branch or Brook. The latter name now belongs to an eastern tributary of Franconia Brook.

Historical Highlights

First Ascent: Probably 1871, by a small party of Dartmouth College students working for Charles H. Hitchcock's geological survey. After setting up camp near Franconia Brook, four members bushwhacked N to the confluence of Franconia and Lincoln Brooks and headed up: "There we climbed the steep north and south ridge which lies between these brooks, being about 1500 feet above them, and separated by them and by a hollow at its north end from the surrounding higher mountain ranges." From the top of the ridge two members descended the E slope, crossed the Franconia Brook valley, and climbed to the Bonds, while the other two continued N along the crest of Owl's Head, possibly crossing the actual summit. The trip was described by Warren Upham in the first issue of *Appalachia*, 1876. In his *Geology of New Hampshire*, Hitchcock described the mountain as an "isolated ridge of no great dimensions," beginning the time-honored tradition of disrespecting Owl's Head.

1903–1910: J. E. Henry's crews push branches of East Branch & Lincoln logging railroad up valleys of Franconia and Lincoln Brooks, with latter line curving around S side of Owl's Head, and cut virgin forest off much of mountain. Logging camps are established along both brooks: Camps 9, 10, 12 and 13 along Franconia Brook, and Camps 11 and 12 along Lincoln Brook.

1907: Huge fire kindled by lightning strike in dry slash high on E side of mountain rages for two weeks in August and burns over Owl's Head and surrounding ridges, over 10,000 acres in all. Fire receives almost daily coverage in Mt. Washington summit newspaper, *Among the Clouds*. "Large force of men" is sent out to fight blaze, with limited results. In 1908 hikers on Lafayette observe "a country of charred stumps and dry stream beds."

1931: AMC trailman Nathaniel Goodrich publishes list of 4000-footers in *Appalachia*. Owl's Head, given elevation of 4023 ft. by recently issued USGS Franconia 15' quadrangle, is included on list as one of "three strangers . . . dwarfed by their neighbors, remote, featureless, but dragged up to fame by the new maps." Goodrich proceeds to climb Owl's Head "in one not too long day from Greenleaf Hut," scrambling up two trees along the ridge to make sure he hit highest spot.

1936: *AMC Guide* describes route to Owl's Head, descending from Franconia Ridge via Lincoln Slide, then bushwhacking up to summit from Lincoln Brook; est. 9 hrs. round trip from Greenleaf Hut. Hiker Murray H. Stevens writes up bushwhack route from Galehead Hut, down valley of Twin Brook and up N ridge of Owl's Head, following old woods roads much of way.

Late 1930s: Franconia Brook Trail and Lincoln Brook Trail opened along old logging RR beds by WMNF.

1949: Blazed trail laid out from Lincoln Brook up N end of ridge, but is short-lived.

1953: Writing in *Appalachia*, peakbagger Dana Converse Backus describes rough bushwhacking on Owl's Head: "My clothing was ripped to ribbons. Scarcely enough was left of my shirt to flag a wheelbarrow, but I had at last reached the top of Owl's Head."

Late 1950s: With formation of 4000-Footer Club in 1957, route up W slide becomes standard approach, first described in 1960 *AMC Guide*. It is reportedly marked with "yellow crayon and a few blazes."

1959: First recorded "sporting" winter ascents made by two parties on March 8, one group of four led by Robert Collin, other consisting of Robert and Miriam Underhill and Merle Whitcomb. Starting at dam on East Branch above Lincoln, ascent is two-day, 24-mile winter epic. Only Underhill group reaches "true" summit, a fact revealed later when Miriam shows slides at Boston gathering displaying spectacular views E to Bonds.

1960: Large AMC group led by Al Robertson scouts entire ridge and marks new summit location.

1963: Bob Collin returns with five-man group and traverses entire ridge in winter—final ascent of nine-day Pemi winter epic in era of unbroken trails. Says Collin, "Well, Miriam Underhill, sometime, somewhere today—I don't know just when, I don't know just where—we stood on the summit of Owl's Head."

1969: *AMC Guide* reports that club is considering building trail from Franconia Ridge down to Lincoln Brook, but project never comes to fruition.

1984: Owl's Head and surrounding valleys included in new Pemigewasset Wilderness.

2005: Hikers discover and measure slightly higher "new" summit ca. 0.2 mi. N along ridge from traditional "old" summit.

Trail Approaches

South Approach from Kancamagus Highway (NH 112)

Lincoln Woods Trail, Franconia Brook Trail, Lincoln Brook Trail, Owl's Head Path

18.0 mi. round trip, 2900-ft. elevation gain (add 0.4 mi. round trip for "new" summit)

TRAILHEAD (1160 ft.): The long walk to this remote summit starts from the large Lincoln Woods parking area, with ranger cabin and restrooms, on the N side of the Kancamagus Highway (NH 112), 5.6 mi. E of Exit 32 off I-93 in Lincoln.

The lengthy walk to Owl's Head features 8 mi. of pleasant valley trekking, largely on old logging railroad grades, and one mile of steep climbing, including a scramble up a very steep slide. The crossings of Franconia and Lincoln Brooks are very difficult in high water, and will often require getting wet feet. There are also three lesser crossings to contend with both before and after the two big ones.

From parking lot, drop down stairs in front of ranger cabin, and cross large suspension footbridge over wide, rocky East Branch of Pemigewasset River, one of premier wilderness streams in region. On far side turn R on Lincoln Woods Trail for easy walking along wide, level bed of J. E. Henry's East Branch & Lincoln Railroad (1893–1948), with many hemlock ties still astride trail. At 0.4 mi. trail emerges on high bank with glimpses of river and ridges of Mt. Hitchcock beyond, then trail pulls away from river, crossing culvert over Osseo Brook at 0.8 mi. Long straightaway, with one section next to Osseo Brook, leads to jct. L with Osseo Trail at 1.4 mi./1300 ft. and Camp 8 clearing on L just beyond. Trail approaches river again at 1.6 mi. with picturesque view of Bondcliff upstream from rocks at water's edge. Trail soon crosses bridge over Birch Island Brook and enters mile-long straight section. At 2.6 mi. Black Pond Trail splits L (offering bushwhacking alternative to avoid the two biggest stream crossings; see below). At 2.9 mi./1440 ft. is side trail L to scenic Franconia Falls (0.4 mi. to falls and start of "fisherman's path" route to avoid stream crossings; see below).

Continue ahead across footbridge over Franconia Brook (rebuilt in 2007; view of Mt. Flume upstream to L) and bear L and up bank on Franconia Brook Trail. Follow another, narrower RR grade N, crossing Camp 9 Brook twice. At 3.9 mi. follow muddy detour R around beaver swamp with glimpses L to cliffs and sharp S peak of Owl's Head from edge of open area. Cross Camp 9 Brook again, bear L and up muddy slope, then descend slightly and turn R back onto railroad grade at 4.2 mi. (note L turn off grade and R turn across brook for return trip). At 4.6 mi./1760 ft. turn L on Lincoln Brook Trail. (Ca. 100 yds. ahead on Franconia Brook Trail is open beaver pond with interesting views of lower ridges of Bonds and South Twin.) Follow Lincoln Brook Trail on traverse SW through blowdown area, then descend easily, turn R on RR grade, and quickly cross very wide Franconia Brook at 5.1 mi.—easiest route is to L. Cross Lincoln Brook—also a large stream that is difficult at high water—at 5.5 mi. Follow gradually rising trail W along S base of Owl's Head, with glimpses up to SE cliffs and sharp, wooded S peak up to R. Trail then begins long curve to N up deep valley through yellow birches with fine brook scenery, including several ledgy cascades and pools. Trail is occasionally rough along streambank. Cross tributary at 6.8 mi., join old logging RR grade, and enjoy section of easy walking away from brook, heading N through birch and conifer. Cross Liberty Brook at 7.4 mi., then

A hiker picks his way up the infamous Owl's Head slide on the mountain's west-facing slope.

swing L through Camp 12 clearing and up and over short relocation. At 7.6 mi. bear R to cross Lincoln Brook—possibly difficult—and continue up E side of stream, bearing R away from dry brookbed and reaching base of Owl's Head slide and jct. with unmaintained path—possibly indicated by small cairns or other markings—at 8.0 mi. / 2560 ft. (About 30 yds. past this junction there is a mossy rock slide in woods to R.)

Turn R on narrow, unsigned path and ascend stony outwash through dense conifers. In 0.1 mi. swing L to ascend steep slope of gravel and loose rock, with first views back to Franconia Ridge. Assortment of cairns have usually marked main, winding route up slide, but hikers may need to choose route that looks best to them. Footing is treacherous, with mix of loose rock, gravel and ledge—caution is required both ascending and descending. Take care not to dislodge loose rocks that could endanger hikers below. At 2800 ft. route angles up to R and ascends very steep pitch though scrub, emerging on widest, most open section of slide at ca. 2900 ft. Flat ledges on L (N) side offer viewing perch with impressive vista of Franconia Range. From here ascend through belt of scrub and emerge in open again for more steep scrambling. Reach top of open slide at 8.3 mi. / 3200 ft. Route now struggles up very steep, ledgy gully in woods, usually wet with tricky footing, soon passing spring bubbling out from crack in ledge. Path bears L for brief traverse at 3350 ft., then R to resume steep climb, but with somewhat better footing. Rough, well-trodden path now angles steadily up to L (NE) with many twists and turns; this section requires clambering over many old blowdowns. At 8.8 mi. path reaches top of ridge, curves around to L, and heads N along crest at nearly level grade through nice fir forest, making one R turn that could be missed. After skirting to R of one knob, veer L, then R and up to small clearing on heavily wooded "old summit" at 9.0 mi. / ca. 4010 ft. Paths diverge L and R leading N towards "new summit"; as of 2007 there was no continuous path between the summits, and some bushwhacking may be required to cover the ca. 0.2 mi. between them. The "new summit" may or may not be marked by a cairn and / or sign.

HIGH WATER ROUTE

To avoid difficult crossings of Franconia and Lincoln Brooks, experienced hikers can follow a rough, unmaintained and sometimes obscure path starting at end of side trail to Franconia Falls, a beautiful area of ledges, cascades and pools on Franconia Brook (0.4 mi. from Lincoln Woods Trail and 3.3 mi. from parking lot). This path leads ca. 1.5 mi. along W bank of Franconia Brook and S bank of Lincoln Brook, meeting Lincoln Brook Trail just beyond its first crossing of Lincoln Brook, 0.9 mi. from its S jct. with Franconia Brook Trail. Path is fairly continuous, but requires searching to pick up where it crosses various small tributary brooks and brookbeds, and is overgrown and strewn with blowdown in places. It mostly stays near Franconia and Lincoln Brooks and provides many views of these wild, rocky streams.

Another high water option is to follow Lincoln Woods Trail for 2.6 mi., then bear L on Black Pond Trail and follow it 0.8 mi. to shore of scenic, secluded Black Pond, with view of Owls Head spire by outlet of pond and vista of Bonds from rock on SW shore. Follow herd path around L (W) side of pond, then bushwhack NNW for ca. 1 mi. (skirting beaver swamp to NW of pond) through mostly open woods to Lincoln Brook Trail just W of first crossing of Lincoln Brook. This route is more difficult to navigate on return as you can overshoot pond to W or E.

North Approach from 13 Falls Campsite

Backpackers can also approach Owl's Head via little-used N end of Lincoln Brook Trail from 13 Falls Campsite (2180 ft.), located at N jct. of Franconia Brook and Lincoln Brook Trails (8.1 easy mi. from Kancamagus Highway via Lincoln Woods Trail and Franconia Brook Trail, though with major crossings of Hellgate, Redrock and Twin Brooks). This is highly scenic area with multiple cascades at site of logging Camp 13. From jct. by campsite, follow Lincoln Brook Trail across broad, open ledgy brookbed with view up to N ridge of Owl's Head—an idyllic spot for a rest break. Trail climbs along N side of W fork of Franconia Brook, passing several scenic cascades, then at 0.3 mi. from 13 Falls Campsite crosses stream to L with cascade and gorge down to L. Trail now climbs S for 0.2 mi., then turns sharp R (W) and ascends steadily on old logging road. At 1.5 mi. swing L (S) and climb rocky stretch, reaching flat, boggy height-of-land between Owl's Head and Mt. Lafayette at 1.8 mi. / 3180 ft. Trail is obscure and quite wet as it traverses this broad saddle and may be very hard to follow, and markings are scarce; use caution as hikers have gotten lost in this remote area. There are occasional glimpses of Franconia Ridge and Mt. Garfield. Trail skirts to L of boggy area and swings R (SW), crosses a small headwater of Lincoln Brook, then swings S and descends moderately along W side of upper Lincoln Brook. It crosses to E side at 2.6 mi. / 2950 ft. Descend along slope above brook, with cascades audible down to R, and reach jct. L with Owl's Head Path at 3.5 mi. / 2560 ft. Turn L for 1.0 mi. / 1500-ft. climb to summit.

Circuit around Owl's Head from Kancamagus Highway via Lincoln Woods Trail, Franconia Brook Trail and Lincoln Brook Trail, including side trip to summit, is 21.6 mi. with 3500-ft. elevation gain.

A strenuous N approach can also be made from AMC Galehead Hut by descending 0.1 mi. on Frost Trail and a steady, moderate 2.6 mi. on Twin Brook Trail to 13 Falls Campsite, with beautiful white birch forest in lower half. Round trip to Owl's Head summit from Galehead Hut is 14.4 mi. with 4800-ft. elevation gain.

Winter

One of the most challenging winter peaks. The two large brook crossings on Lincoln Brook Trail can be quite difficult unless very well frozen. Many peakbaggers opt for the Black Pond bushwhack, and in recent years there has often been a well-established snowshoe track on this route. The W slide is often icy and dangerous, requiring crampons, ice axe and great caution. Years ago many winter climbers opted for a bushwhack ascent up the E side of the mountain from Franconia Brook Trail near Hellgate Brook, starting with a potentially dicey crossing of Franconia Brook. This 2200-ft. climb to the ridge is steep and arduous, with hardwood and birch on the lower slopes and thick conifers in the upper part. Lucky climbers may find a ledge with a fine view E to the Twin–Bond Range. This eastern route seems to be less-used recently, replaced by a different bushwhack route up the W side (coined the "Brutus Bushwhack," after the famous winter peakbagging Newfoundland), starting some distance S of the slide route. Any of these ascent routes are for fully-equipped snowshoers with solid winter experience.

View Guide

Summit views are nonexistent on the ground, though Eugene Daniell III (who has climbed Owl's Head ca. 20 times) notes in the *AMC White*

Mountain Guide that "excellent views are sometimes obtained from the summit area by ambitious tree-climbers." It was not always thus, for up through the early 1970s the guide mentioned vistas of the Franconias and Bonds near the summit. Miriam Underhill took spectacular photos of the Twin–Bond Range from Owls' Head on the March 1959 ascent mentioned above; one was printed in her autobiography, *Give Me the Hills*.

The W slide does offer unique views across the remote Lincoln Brook valley to the "back" (E) side of the Franconia Range. The best viewing spot, ideal for an extended break, is a set of gently sloping ledges on the N side of the slide at ca. 3000 ft. Here there is an impressive base-to-crest panorama of nearly the entire E side of the range. On the far L, looking SSW, is the graceful peak of Mt. Flume. Next to the R is the notched rock summit of Mt. Liberty, rising above the secluded basin of Liberty Brook. To the NW across the valley are the craggy peaks of upper Franconia Ridge—Little Haystack, Lincoln, Lafayette—and the great V-shaped gravel gash of Lincoln Slide. Up the valley to the R (N) are the headwaters of Lincoln Brook and humps on the W end of Garfield Ridge beyond; from points lower on the S side of the slide a slice of Mt. Garfield itself can be seen.

NO. OF 4000-FOOTERS VISIBLE: 22 (theoretical, through the trees)

North and South Twin Mountain

North Twin

ELEVATION: 4761 ft. / 1451 m   ORDER OF HEIGHT: 11
LOCATION: Twin Range, Towns of Bethlehem and Franconia
USGS MAP: 7½′ South Twin

South Twin

4902 ft. / 1494 m   ORDER OF HEIGHT: 8
LOCATION: Twin Range, Town of Franconia
USGS MAP: 7½′ South Twin

Geography

North Twin and South Twin are the two highest peaks of the Twin Range, the loftiest ridge between the Presidentials and the Franconias. Both offer superb views of the Pemigewasset Wilderness and surrounding mountains and out to distant horizons.

North Twin is massive, rounded and thickly wooded to the top, but ledgy outlooks near the summit provide wide views E and W. Three ridges run out on its NE side to the long, deep valley of the Little River, a major tributary of the Ammonoosuc River; the North Twin Trail ascends the upper part of the middle ridge. To the W and NW several steep wooded buttresses drop into the basin drained by the North Branch of Gale River. Between the Little River and North Branch valleys a high ridge with many gray "fir waves" extends NW from the summit, swinging down over an intermediate peak, then NE to the wooded eminence known as Nubble Peak or Peak Above the Nubble (3813 ft.). This trailless peak is one of New England's "Hundred Highest" and is guarded by steep ledges on its E flank. Its N side bears the distinctive "check-mark" slide, prominently seen from US 3 in the village of Twin Mountain, which lies in the Ammonoosuc River valley N of North Twin. Haystack Brook flows down from the bottom of this slide. On the NW slope of Nubble Peak is a striking little rock cone known as Haystack Mtn. or The Nubble (2712 ft.), thought by geologists to be the core of an ancient volcano. On the W side of The Nubble is a branch of Haystack Brook that drains from another slide on Nubble Peak. On the E side of North Twin, at the head of a deep valley draining into Little River between the summits of North and South Twin, is a great slide with its top starting just below North Twin's summit. Another long, prominent slide fell on the N side of North Twin in an October 1995 rainstorm, at the head of a hidden valley that drains N, then NE between the main summit and Nubble Peak. Southward the summit ridge runs over a small rock knob before dropping to the 4460-ft. col between the Twins.

The summit of South Twin is a small rocky peak rising from a long, massive, heavily wooded ridge. The top is quite open and is marked by two rock knobs just a few yards apart. A broad, semi-open shoulder extends N to the col with North Twin, and from this shoulder a ridge descends NE to the Little River valley. To the SE the high, flat, densely wooded main crest of the Twin Range extends for 2 mi., running over two wooded humps and eventually dipping to a 4380-ft. col and rising to the rounded double summit of Mt. Guyot. Midway along this ridge a broad buttress spreads NE to the Little River valley; between it and the summit of South Twin is a two-pronged ravine scored with several slides.

On the W the scree-scarred slopes of South Twin drop steeply to a 3740-ft. col with Galehead Mtn. and down into the deep valley of Twin Brook. Just S of the summit is a 4723-ft. spur; from this a prominent ridge runs SW for several miles between the valleys of Twin Brook and Redrock Brook, ending at the deep trough of Franconia Brook in the heart of the western Pemigewasset Wilderness. Two trailless knobs crown the upper end of this ridge; the first (4580 ft.) is bare and rocky on top; the second (4357 ft.) is wooded and sometimes referred to as SW Twin, one

The view from the summit of South Twin takes in Mounts Galehead and Garfield, plus the peaks of Franconia Ridge.

of the "Trailwrights 72" peaks. On the S side of this ridge is the wild, picturesque valley of Redrock Brook with its two glacial cirques and numerous slides and talus slopes. The upper part of this SW ridge overlooks the northern cirque, which bears a tiny tarn, Bear Pond, on its floor. In addition to the SW ridge of South Twin, the Redrock valley is enclosed by the main ridgecrest between South Twin and Mt. Guyot, Guyot itself, and West Bond.

Nomenclature

The name "Twin Mts." was originally applied to these neighboring peaks by geographer George P. Bond on his 1853 map of the White Mountains. Charles H. Hitchcock added the "North" and "South" in his 1870s *Geology of New Hampshire*. The nearby town to the north shares the name of Twin Mountain. North Twin looms large in the view from the town, but the summit of South Twin is hidden.

Historical Highlights

First Ascent: Probably 1871, by New Hampshire state geologist Charles H. Hitchcock and a Dartmouth student, who ascended both North Twin and South Twin as part of the state geological survey. "Scarcely any mountains are more difficult to reach than these, on account of the stunted growth near their tops," lamented the intrepid geologist.

Hitchcock's report on the survey included a profile of the view from North Twin.

1876: Moses Sweetser's guidebook describes an 8-mile route to South Twin via Little River and a W branch near its head, based on information provided by Assistant State Geologist Joshua H. Huntington. Dwarf conifers atop ridge are again noted as impediment: "Frequently the most rapid mode of advance is found by lying flat on the ground and crawling under the bristling boughs."

1880: Benjamin MacDonald and guide Allen Thompson undertake six-day journey through upper Gale River and Franconia Brook regions. Trip includes grueling ascent of 4580-ft. SW spur of South Twin, which is christened "Mt. MacDonald." Account of trip appears in *White Mountain Echo*, tourist paper published in Bethlehem.

1882: In August, A. E. Scott leads AMC party of six—three men, three women—on week-long bushwhack epic over Twin Range. They spend first night high on N slope of North Twin and battle to summit on second day, bivouacing in rain beside slide, then proceed over South Twin on third day, where they spend two hours marveling at the view, calling it "grand beyond description." Trip continues over Mt. Bond and Mt. Field before ending in Crawford Notch. Scott writes up adventure in April 1883 *Appalachia*.

1883: AMC cuts Twin Range Trail, leading from Twin Mtn. House into Little River valley, up North Twin, then over South Twin and Bond. Path is dedicated during outing of 30–40 trampers led by A. E. Scott; group spends night at camp on slope of North Twin built by Charles E. Lowe.

1883: After traversing Bond–Twin Range (including bushwhack ascent of Bondcliff from W), solo AMC adventurer W. L. Hooper descends off-trail from col between Twins into Gale River valley to W, then ascends to ridge between South Twin and Garfield. Here he camps and dines on partridge shot with his revolver. The next day he continues over Mt. Garfield through very difficult terrain and concludes bushwhack epic with ascent of Mt. Lafayette.

1893–1900: Timber mogul George Van Dyke logs Little River valley, hauling wood out via railroad.

1895: Four women, guided by Mr. F. B. Rosebrook of Twin Mountain, ascend North Twin after hitching ride to base of mountain on logging train operating in Little River valley. *White Mountain Echo* reports AMC path to summit is found "in good condition."

1903: Fire burns 3,000 acres in Gale River valley.

1903–1909: Logging crews employed by J. E. Henry cut slopes of SW ridge of South Twin from Camps 12 and 13 along Franconia Brook and Camp 14 by Redrock Brook, all on spurs of East Branch & Lincoln logging railroad. Lower spurs of SW ridge of South Twin are burned in the large 1907 Owl's Head fire.

1915: AMC trailmasters Paul Jenks, Charles Blood, Nathaniel Goodrich and others cut Garfield Ridge Trail from South Twin summit to Garfield Pond. Trail is completed in 1916, connecting Twin and Franconia Ranges.

1922: Jenks laments that logging operation has ruined face of North Twin.

1926: AMC builds Galehead Shelter in col at W base of South Twin summit cone.

1929: Portion of Twin Range Trail from Little River valley abandoned. AMC cuts new 2½-mile North Twin Loop, ascending from Gale River valley on W. Part of trail follows slide.

1932: AMC builds Galehead Hut on small hump near site of shelter. Trail from hut to South Twin and across ridge to Guyot and Zealand is renamed "Twinway" and connects Galehead and Zealand Falls Huts. New Galehead Trail provides approach to hut and South Twin from N via Gale River valley.

Ca. 1935: Trail from Little River valley up North Twin re-opened by WMNF as North Twin Trail. New Little River Trail opened by WMNF leading 6½ mi. up Little River valley, connecting with Twinway at South Twin–Guyot col. This trail abandoned in late 1950s.

1938: W side of North Twin Loop from Gale River valley obliterated by hurricane. Portion of trail between Twins retains this name until ca. 1950, then re-named North Twin Spur.

1968: Twin Brook Trail from S opened by AMC, providing access to Galehead Hut and South Twin from Pemi Wilderness.

1975: WMNF opens gravel Haystack Rd. from US 3, shortening approach hike to North Twin.

1984: 45,000-acre Pemigewasset Wilderness created by Congress, includes SW ridge of South Twin and Twin and Redrock Brook valleys.

Trail Approaches

Northeast Approach from USFS Haystack Rd. (FR 304)

NORTH TWIN ONLY

North Twin Trail
8.6 mi. round trip, 2950-ft. elevation gain

NORTH AND SOUTH TWIN

North Twin Trail, North Twin Spur
11.2 mi. round trip, 3700-ft. elevation gain

TRAILHEAD (1800 ft.): From US 3, 2.3 mi. W of stoplight in Twin Mountain, drive 2.5 mi. S on gravel Haystack Rd. (FR 304) to parking area and sign for North Twin Trail at end.

The hike up North Twin is two trips in one—an easy ramble along the Little River followed by a grinding climb up a NE ridge. The trail starts at easy grade through hardwoods mostly on bed of old logging railroad, following along E side of boulder-filled river. There are three crossings of river that are very difficult in high water. This river is a public water supply, so hikers should take extra care not to pollute it. First crossing is at 0.8 mi. and second is at 1.3 mi.; these crossings can be avoided by following rough beaten path along E bank, with several ups and downs and crossing of tributary brook. After second crossing, trail climbs up bank away from river and railroad grade, meanders through mixed woods with minor ups and downs, then rejoins grade before reaching third crossing at 1.9 mi. / 2350 ft.

Now back on W side of river, trail briefly climbs, traverses parallel to river, crossing a brook, then swings R away from river and climbs moderately into birch and fir forest, crossing another brook. At 2850 ft. trail swings R across dry brookbed and climbs steadily up eroded section with loose rock. Swing L on old logging road at 3600 ft., then R at 3.5 mi. / 3750 ft., where ascent becomes quite steep over eroded footway. At 4.0 mi. / 4500 ft. is first view N and E from outcrop. Grade soon eases through high scrub to magnificent outlook ledge on L at 4.2 mi. / 4700 ft., with wide view E. Continue gently up ridge to junction with North Twin Spur at 4.3 mi. / 4750 ft. Here 200-ft. side path leads R over actual summit of North Twin (wooded) to open ledge with fine view W.

From junction near summit, North Twin Spur continues ahead (S), descending easily, then moderately, leading down S ridge of North Twin. One ledgy scramble leads to passage through rock cut. There are several views of South Twin rising ahead, and two fir waves offer partial vistas to L (E). Reach broad, ferny col between Twins at 4.8 mi. / 4460 ft. Trail now climbs at easy to moderate grade to broad N shoulder of South Twin, where trail runs level through high scrub and crosses open area with wide views E; rocky crown of South Twin looms close ahead. Re-enter scrub for final short climb to open rocky summit at E knob, and junction with Twinway by W knob at 5.6 mi. / 4902 ft.

Northwest Approach from Gale River Loop Road (FR 92)

SOUTH TWIN ONLY OUT AND BACK

Gale River Trail, Garfield Ridge Trail, Twinway
10.8 mi. round trip, 3400-ft. elevation gain

SOUTH AND NORTH TWIN OUT AND BACK

Gale River Trail, Garfield Ridge Trail, Twinway, North Twin Spur
13.4 mi. round trip, 4150-ft. elevation gain

LOOP OVER SOUTH AND NORTH TWIN WITH CARSPOT
AT NORTH TWIN TRAIL TRAILHEAD

Gale River Trail, Garfield Ridge Trail, Twinway, North Twin Spur, North Twin Trail

11.0 mi., 3650-ft. elevation gain
(For all options, add 1.0 mi. / 250 ft. for round trip
to Galehead Mtn. summit)

TRAILHEAD (1600 ft.): From jct. of US 3 and Trudeau Rd., between Franconia Notch and Twin Mountain, drive SE on USFS gravel Gale River Rd. (FR 25). Bear L at 0.6 mi. and turn sharp R at 1.3 mi. onto Gale River Loop Rd. (FR 92). Parking area for Gale River Trail is on L at 1.6 mi.

This approach via Gale River valley is often used to climb South Twin alone, or in combination with Galehead Mtn. If two cars are available, a loop hike over both Twins is an excellent option.

From parking area, Gale River Trail soon drops over bank, crosses small brook, and then turns R on old logging road leading S at easy grades through hardwoods on W side of Gale River's North Branch, keeping well back from stream. Approach river at 1.4 mi. and cross to E side on large rocks (former footbridge washed out in 2005; may be difficult in high water) at 1.7 mi. Trail becomes rougher along bank, crosses tributary, then recrosses North Branch of Gale on large step stones at 2.5 mi. / 2250 ft., usually a fairly easy crossing. Grades continue easy through slide outwash areas to open gravel bank at 3.1 mi. / 2580 ft., with interesting view up to high ridges of Twins. Beyond, trail begins to steepen, and at 3.5 mi. / 3000 ft. commences stiff climb up rock staircases, reaching jct. with Garfield Ridge Trail at 4.0 mi. / 3390 ft.

Turn L here for easy to moderate, rocky traverse on Garfield Ridge Trail through deep, mossy coniferous forest. At 4.3 mi. pass view on L looking NNW down Gale River valley and across to cliffs on W ridge of North Twin. Trail soon turns R and climbs more steeply. Reach AMC Galehead Hut on side trail R at 4.6 mi. / 3780 ft. From hut clearing there are views E up to South Twin, S to Owl's Head, SW to nearby Galehead Mtn., and W to Mt. Garfield. (From hut, Frost Trail leads 0.5 mi R to summit of Galehead Mtn. with 250-ft. climb.) Continue ahead on Twinway. After short, steep drop into col, begin long, grueling climb up well-constructed rocky footway, rising 1100 ft. in 0.8 mi. Trees shrink to scrub and views open back to W as you approach top of climb. Reach open rocky summit of South Twin and jct. with North Twin Spur at 5.4 mi. / 4902 ft. by W knob. Here Twinway turns R (S) for Mt. Guyot. For North Twin, turn L (N) on North Twin Spur, cross E knob of South Twin summit, and continue down and up to summit of North Twin at 6.7 mi. / 4769 ft.

South Approach via Twinway

Backpackers and hut-hoppers can approach South Twin via Twinway from Mt. Guyot to S. From open area at jct. of Twinway and Bondcliff Trail near NE summit of Guyot (good views W here towards Owl's Head and Mt. Lafayette), Twinway rambles easily along broad ridge thickly wooded with high fir scrub, leading towards South Twin. Cross knob with limited views 1.1 mi. from jct. Grades continue easy/moderate until fairly steep 0.3 mi. climb to summit of South Twin at 2.0 mi.

Winter

Because the access roads are not plowed, the approaches to the Twins are longer in winter. Haystack Rd. is closed, adding 5.0 mi. round trip to that approach via the North Twin Trail (total 13.6 mi. / 3400 ft. for North Twin, 16.2 mi. / 4150 ft. for both Twins). Parking is tight off US 3 at the entrance to Haystack Rd.; you may need to shovel out a space. Recently a better option has been to park at the Seven Dwarfs Motel on Little River Rd., which leaves US 3 ca. 1.2 mi. E of Haystack Rd. The Seven Dwarfs is 1.0 mi. from US 3. For the past few years the owner has allowed parking here for a small fee (for current status, call the Seven Dwarfs at 603–846–5535.) From the motel, walk 0.2 mi. S to the end of Little River Rd. and turn R to cross Little River on a snowmobile bridge. Here there are two options. You can turn L on the W side of the river and follow the somewhat overgrown bed of the old Little River logging railroad for ca. 1 mi. to the trailhead at the S end of the Haystack Rd. (11.0 mi. / 3150 ft. for North Twin only, 13.6 mi. / 3900 ft. for both Twins). Or, you can continue ahead on the snowmobile trail to the Haystack Rd. and turn L to follow it to the trailhead; this route is slightly longer. The Little River crossings on the North Twin Trail are the biggest obstacles to a winter ascent; hope for good snow bridges. The bypass that avoids the first two crossings is often well broken out but can be a tricky sidehill in crusty conditions. The upper part of the North Twin Trail is a grind-it-out snowshoe climb. The high wooded col between the Twins has some of the deepest snowpack in the mountains.

The Gale River Rd. is also closed to auto travel in winter, adding 3.2 mi. round trip on the snowmobile-packed road to approach via the Gale River Trail (total 14.0 mi. / 3650 ft. for South Twin, 16.6 mi. / 4400 ft. for both Twins out-and-back, 13.8 mi. / 3900 ft. for loop over both Twins with car-spot at Seven Dwarfs; add 1.0 mi. / 250 ft. for side trip to Galehead Mtn.) Parking is available on the N side of US 3 by the jct. with Trudeau Rd. Some winter peakbaggers shorten the road walk by parking at the Beaver Brook Ski Trail on US 3 (ca. 1 mi. E of the Trudeau Rd. jct.) and snowshoeing S on the W section of the Badger Loop X-C Trail for ca. 0.5 mi. Where that trail turns sharp L to head back to the NE, a short bushwhack R (SW) leads to the Gale River Rd. Hikers using this route should take care not to trample ski tracks, and at times the longer, snowmobile-packed road walk may be easier. The toughest snowshoeing on the Gale River Trail route is the final approach to Garfield Ridge Trail and the steep climb from Galehead Hut (closed in winter) to South Twin on the Twinway; crampons may be needed on the exposed upper cone in crusty or icy conditions.

View Guide

NORTH TWIN, E OUTLOOK: This is a premier ledge perch jutting above the scrub, offering a 180-degree panorama which features a fine view of the Presidentials.

On the far R (S) the massive rock-crowned summit of South Twin looms close at hand, with distant Mt. Kearsarge seen beyond Loon Mtn. to its R; Plymouth Mtn. can be spotted under Kearsarge. Seen over the slope descending to the L from South Twin are (R to L): the top of Mt. Bond with the bare SW summit of Mt. Guyot below, the more distant crest of North Hancock with the top of Mt. Whiteface peering over its L side, and the flat dome of Guyot's NE summit rising over a nearer spur. The dark cone of Mt. Passaconaway rises over the L end of NE Guyot. Farther L the great mass of Mt. Carrigain rises over the sloping NE ridge of Guyot. Vose Spur, forming the W side of Carrigain Notch, juts out off the L side of Carrigain, above the Guyot–Zealand col. The Three Sisters (L) and Mt. Chocorua (R) are above Vose Spur.

To the SE the view opens out to the sprawling mass of Zealand Mtn., scarred by an extensive talus slope, with the summit on its R end and the Nancy Range beyond. Mt. Lowell, forming the E side of Carrigain Notch, is above Zealand's summit, with pointed Mt. Tremont sighted to its R through Carrigain Notch. Southern Maine's Ossipee Hill is a little bump on the horizon to the L of Tremont. Mt. Anderson is to the L of Lowell, with Bear Mtn. seen between them. A broad gap separates Anderson from Mt. Nancy, highest of the Nancy Range, to its L. Through this gap Table Mtn. peers over the L end of flat Duck Pond Mtn. On the horizon above these are various hills along the New Hampshire–Maine border on the R and Maine's more distant Clark Mtn. range on the L, above Table. South and Middle Moat Mtns. are seen off the L slope of Nancy; Maine's Bill Merrill Mtn. pokes up in back to the L of Middle Moat. Next to the L North Moat rises above Mt. Bemis, with Little Attitash Mtn. and the Attitash ski slopes to the L. Maine's Saddleback Hills stretch across the horizon above Little Attitash.

Continuing to the L, one sees Mt. Parker on the lower Montalban Ridge with ledgy Mt. Crawford in front on the L, Black Cap Mtn. behind on its L and the lower Green Hills behind on the R; in the distance over the R shoulder of Black Cap is the double knob of Peaked Mtn. near Sebago Lake. Along the ridge to the L of Parker are flat-topped Mt. Resolution and the distinctive Giant Stairs. Maine's Pleasant Mtn. is on the horizon above Resolution, while under Resolution, beyond the col in the long ridge joining Zealand Mtn. with Mt. Hale, is Whitewall Mtn. The dome of Kearsarge North rises above the col between Resolution and Stairs, while the lower Rickers Knoll peers over just L of the Stairs. Next to the L, looking E, the three peaks of the Willey Range—R to L, Mt. Willey, Mt. Field and the lower, rounded Mt. Tom—are seen beyond the deep Little River valley and the long ridge that connects Zealand Ridge with Mt. Hale. North Doublehead Mtn. in Jackson pops up over the col between Willey and Field. Over the saddle between Field and Tom are (R to L) Mt. Jackson with the flat crest of Mt. Davis behind and Chandler Mtn. just peeking over in back; Sable Mtn., also in back; Mt. Isolation; and South Baldface in back above the upper Rocky Branch Ridge. North Baldface peers over to the L of Tom, then the view swings NE to the chain of Southern Presidential peaks—R to L, Mt. Pierce (with Slide Peak behind), and Mts. Eisenhower, Franklin and Monroe with the rocky shoulder of Boott Spur above—leading up to Mt. Washington, which rises high above the S ridge of Mt. Hale and the Rosebrook Range just beyond.

To the L of Washington are the two summits of Mt. Clay, then the high sharp peaks of Mt. Jefferson and Mt. Adams, rising beyond nearby Mt. Hale. Farther L the darkly wooded Dartmouth Range, with Mt. Dartmouth on the R and Mt. Deception on the L, rises above the N humps of Hale. The North Peak of Goose Eye Mtn. (R) and Old Speck Mtn. (L) in the Mahoosucs are seen in the distance beyond Mt. Dartmouth. The flat crest of Old Blue Mtn. is seen over Deception, with Elephant Mtn. to its L, and on clear days Saddleback Mtn. can be spotted between them. The Crescent Range is behind Deception on the L, with Mt. Crescent on the R and the double humps of Black Crescent Mtn. on the L. The flat top of Cambridge Black Mtn. is seen over the L end of Black Crescent. On clear days far-off East Kennebago Mtn. can be seen to the L of Cambridge Black, with more peaks in NW Maine extending to its L across to the wavy West Kennebago. Closer in this direction is the R end of the Pliny Range, with Pliny Mtn. sticking up in front. The double summit of Aziscohos Mtn. is seen above Pliny, just L of West Kennebago. To the L of Pliny a long level ridge leads across to Mt. Waumbek, with a lower ridge of Cherry Mtn. in front. The low rocky knobs of Middle Sugarloaf (R) and North Sugarloaf (L) are seen low down in this direction over a lower shoulder of Mt. Hale. Mt. Starr King is to the L of Waumbek, with humpy Mt. Cabot behind on its L. The sharp peak of Cherry Mtn. is seen in front of Cabot on the L.

The several peaks of the Pilot Ridge extend L from Cabot, with the rolling crest of Long Mtn. behind; North Whitcomb (Muise) Mtn. peeks over the L end of Long, just R of the sharp knob of Hutchins Mtn. in the

Pilots. To the L of the Pilots extends the more distant Nash Stream Range, seen beyond the village of Twin Mountain and the plains of Whitefield and Jefferson. Seen in this range are (R to L) the sharp Sugarloaf, Gore Mtn., Bunnell Mtn. in back, and West Peak. The double hump of Goback Mtn. is seen farther to the L, looking due N. Seen down in the lowlands to the L of and in front of Goback is little tower-topped Prospect Mtn. in Lancaster. On clear days Quebec's Hereford Mtn. can be espied on the horizon above Prospect. Next to the L is a broad nameless ridge leading L across to sharp Sable Mtn. in Vermont's Northeast Kingdom. To the L of Sable, Brousseau Mtn. (with pyramidal Burnside Mtn. in front) and Black Mtn. lead across to the prominent mass of Vermont's Gore Mtn. In front of and to the R of Gore, West Mtn. is seen above Stone Mtn. Low down and close by in this direction is Beech Hill. In the foreground in this direction is nearby Nubble Peak, with rough ledges spotting its flank. Continuing across the northern Vermont horizon to the L of Gore one sees massive East Mtn., with a structure on top, then East Haven Mtn. (with some of Quebec's Sutton Mtns. in the distance to its R), and Bald Mtn. On the far L, if you stand, you can see the paired Umpire Mtn. (R) and Burke Mtn. (L, with Miles Mtn. beneath); Mt. Pisgah can be seen over the R slope of Burke.

NORTH TWIN, W OUTLOOK: This open, sun-struck ledge is just a few yards W of the true summit and affords a superb vista of the Franconia Range and the Pemigewasset Wilderness. On the far L (S) is the nearby rocky crown of South Twin, with Mt. Passaconaway to the L. Off the R slope of South Twin is the sharp peak of Mt. Tecumseh, with West Tecumseh to its R, above East Scar Ridge. To the R of West Tecumseh is the low, sharp Middle Scar Ridge, with wooded SW Twin below, and farther R is the main mass of Scar Ridge. In the distance between West Tecumseh and the main Scar Ridge are the bump of Joe English Hill (L) and wavy Hersey Mtn. (R). On clear days, North Pack Monadnock (L) and Crotched Mtn. (R) can be seen over the R shoulder of the main Scar Ridge. Loon Mtn. is just R of Scar Ridge, with Mt. Kearsarge prominent on the horizon; Ragged Mtn. sprawls in front of Kearsarge on the R and Plymouth Mtn. can be seen in front of and L of Kearsarge. On very clear days Mt. Monadnock can be seen on the horizon over the R end of Ragged. To the R of Ragged and closer are the paired Forbes Mtn. (L) and Tinkham Hill (R), with Rumney's Bald Mtn. in front between them.

To the SSW is a dramatic view, down past Galehead Mtn. and its namesake hut, into the deep, remote valley of Franconia Brook, guarded on the R by the rib-like ridges of Owl's Head. Whaleback Mtn.'s knob sticks up to the L of the S peak of Owl's Head, with the lower flat-topped East Whaleback down to its L. The rounded bump of Lovewell Mtn. is on the horizon to the L of Whaleback, just R of Tinkham Hill. From

Whaleback a ridge leads R across to the shapely pyramid of Mt. Flume, which rises above the N end of the main crest of Owl's Head. Seen in the distance over the ridge between Whaleback and Flume are (L to R) Sunapee Mtn. in back, the closer Stinson Mtn., and the mid-distance Mt. Cardigan. A long, graceful ridge connects Flume with Mt. Liberty to its R, with the rounded hump of Galehead in the foreground; Galehead Hut is nestled at its L base. Seen over the Flume–Liberty saddle are Mt. Kineo (in front), Carr Mtn. (in back) and far-off, sharp Croydon Peak (in back to the R of Carr).

From Liberty a long, gentle ridge leads R across to Little Haystack Mtn; over the R half of this are seen Mt. Braley (L) and Mt. Waternomee (R) on Mt. Moosilauke's Blue Ridge, with Smarts Mtn. peering over between them. To the R of Galehead Mtn. you look SW across the broad, remote uplands at the head of Franconia and Lincoln Brooks to the high, sharp-edged crests of Mts. Lincoln and Lafayette—perhaps the finest single vista from North Twin. From Lafayette a ridge descends sharply to the R, with the tip of Cannon Mtn. peeking over. Shapely Mt. Garfield rises to the R of Lafayette, lower and closer, beyond the wooded humps of Garfield Ridge. On the horizon in this direction are distant Green Mountain ridges in the Brandon Gap area. Off the R slope of Garfield are Cobble Hill (L) and Moody Ledge (R), then the nearer Cooley Hill (L) and Cole Hill (R), with Green Mtn. in Landaff between them. The broad hump of Breadloaf Mtn. is on the horizon above Cole Hill, with Mt. Wilson and shapely Mt. Grant to its R. Farther R, down low and close in, are Big Bickford Mtn. (L) and Scarface Mtn. (R), low rounded spurs of Mt. Lafayette, and closer still, looking down into the Gale River valley, are the cliffs and slide on Flat Top Mtn., a NE spur of Mt. Garfield. Above these peaks in the middle distance is Vermont's lumpy Signal Mtn. range, with the long Mt. Abraham–Mt. Ellen ridge seen on the horizon over its L half, above Knox and Butterfield Mtns., just L of Signal Mtn., highest in that range. Spruce Mtn. is the sharp peak on the R end of the Signal Range. Farther R and more distant are Mt. Ethan Allen and then the distinctively tilted Camel's Hump.

Continuing to the R, the view sweeps across a vast expanse of lower country to the wavy Worcester Range near Stowe, Vermont. Farther R, looking NW, is the sprawling ridge of Mt. Mansfield, with the Sterling Range extending to its R; little Garnet Mtn. can be seen down low and nearby in this direction. Farther R in the low foreground are the paired Mt. Cleveland (L) and Mt. Agassiz (R). Beyond Cleveland is seen the town of Littleton and part of Moore Reservoir, with Laraway Mtn. on the horizon. The Cold Hollow Mtns. are on the skyline above Agassiz, and to their R are the sharp Belvidere Mtn., Tillotson Peak and Haystack Mtn. Farther R, looking NW, are the distant but prominent Jay Peaks. From here the view continues R to Burke and Umpire Mtns., Bald Mtn., East

Haven Mtn. and East Mtn. (all in Vermont's Northeast Kingdom), as described under the E Outlook; standing, one may extend the view around to the Nash Stream range.

SOUTH TWIN SUMMIT: This open rock peak affords an impressive panorama of peaks and ridges, with an especially good vantage on the western Pemigewasset Wilderness and the high crest of the Twin Range twisting S to the Bonds. Fine perches can be found around either of the adjacent rocky knobs at the summit. The broad mass of North Twin, spotted with ledges and with fir waves and twin slides on its W ridge, is close by just W of N, with long vistas on either side. The sharp Sable Mtn. in NE Vermont is seen on the horizon just R of North Twin's summit, with a broad nameless ridge extending to its R. Farther R little Prospect Mtn. in Lancaster just pokes above the R shoulder of North Twin; on clear days Quebec's Hereford Mtn. can be seen on the horizon directly above. Next to the R on the horizon is the double peak of Goback Mtn. The Nash Stream range stretches to the R of Goback, including (L to R) West Peak, Bunnell Mtn. (in back) Gore Mtn. and Sugarloaf. Continuing to the R, looking over the broad N shoulder of South Twin, the several peaks of the Pilot Ridge lead R across to bulky Mt. Cabot. The rolling crest of Long Mtn. is seen behind the Pilots, with North Whitcomb (Muise) Mtn. peeking over its L end, and Dixville Peak is seen behind on the R. Down in front between the Pilots and Cabot is the shapely peak of Cherry Mtn. Mt. Starr King is just R of Cabot and closer, and from it the Pliny Range extends R across Mt. Waumbek and Waumbek's long E ridge. The top of North Weeks is seen over the middle of the E ridge, and Pliny Mtn.'s cone sticks up in front of the R end of the ridge. On the horizon to the R of Pliny, beyond a northern spur of Mt. Hale (in front and below) and the low summit of Pond Hill, are various peaks in NW Maine near the Canadian border, leading R across to the mass of East Kennebago Mtn. To the R of East Kennebago and closer is the Crescent Range near Randolph, with the double summit of Black Crescent Mtn. on the L and Mt. Crescent on the R. In front of Mt. Crescent are Mt. Deception in the Dartmouth Range and then the nearby Mt. Hale, seen across the Little River valley. Cambridge Black Mtn. is seen behind Black Crescent and Red Ridge is visible over the R end of Deception. Elephant Mtn. is seen in the distance to the R of Red Ridge.

Looking NE, neighboring Mt. Dartmouth is to the R of Deception, with Old Speck Mtn. in the Mahoosucs prominent behind it. On clear days Saddleback Mtn. can be seen above Old Blue Mtn. to the L of Old Speck. To the R of Dartmouth and Old Speck the eye is drawn to a magnificent view of the Presidentials. Mts. Adams and Jefferson are on the L, then Mt. Clay and lofty Mt. Washington; in the foreground below these peaks is the long ridge of the Little River Mtns. extending S from

Mt. Hale with the Rosebrook Range behind. To the R of Washington, Boott Spur presides above the upper Southern Presidential peaks of (L to R) Mt. Monroe, Mt. Franklin and Mt. Eisenhower. Farther R Mt. Pierce is seen above Mt. Tom, with Slide Peak behind on the R. To the R of Tom the Willey Range extends across to Mts. Field and Willey, looking due E. Mt. Isolation is seen behind and L of Field, with North Baldface behind on its L, above a peak on Rocky Branch Ridge, and South Baldface on its R. The tip of Mt. Jackson just peeks over to the R of South Baldface. Cliff-faced Mt. Webster is seen over the Field–Willey col, with Sable Mtn. (L) and Chandler Mtn. (R) behind. The Doubleheads are prominent off the R slope of Willey, and Ethan Pond can be seen sparkling at Willey's base.

Next to the R and close at hand, seen across the heart of the Little River valley, is the scree-splotched mass of Zealand Mtn. Seen above the L side of Zealand is the long sloping crest of Stairs Mtn., with the Giant Stairs on its R end. Mt. Shaw (L) and the twin Gemini (R) are seen beyond Stairs. Over the R half of Zealand is the ledge-splotched bulk of Mt. Resolution, from which a long ridge leads R to Mt. Parker; the rocky peak of Mt. Crawford can be seen in front of Parker on the L. Kearsarge North rises behind Resolution with its spurs Rickers Knoll on the L and Bartlett Mtn. on the R. Maine's Pleasant Mtn. sprawls behind Kearsarge on the R, with Hurricane Mtn. under its R end. Black Cap Mtn. is behind Parker on the R, with Mt. Langdon below and in front. The lower Green Hills descend to the R from Black Cap above a flat spur of Little Attitash Mtn. Next to the R, looking SSE, are Mt. Bemis (L) and Mt. Nancy (R) in the Nancy Range with North Moat rising behind Nancy and Maine's Saddleback Hills on the horizon. A wide plateau holding Norcross Pond extends R from Mt. Nancy across to Mt. Anderson; above this are Middle and South Moat on the L (with Maine's Burnt Meadow Mtns. and Bill Merrill Mtn. beyond) and Table Mtn. on the R, just L of Anderson. Maine's Clark Mtn. range is on the horizon above Anderson.

To the R of Anderson is Mt. Lowell, with Bartlett Haystack seen between them. Carrigain Notch is to the R of Lowell, with Vose Spur forming its other side, and through this gap are sighted flat-topped Bear Mtn. (L) and pointed Mt. Tremont (R). To the R of Vose Spur rises the mighty Mt. Carrigan, seen over the broad NE summit of nearby Mt. Guyot. Part of Mt. Chocorua's Three Sisters ridge is seen to the L of Carrigain. Mt. Paugus is seen through the deep gap to the R of Carrigain. Rising from the R side of the gap is the low, flat-topped knob of The Captain, with the Nickerson Mtns. in the distance. In front of and just R of The Captain is the bald SW summit of Guyot; the faces of both Guyot summits are scarred by rock slides. The pyramid of Mt. Bond rises prominently to the R of Guyot, with cone-shaped Passaconaway behind Bond on the L, over the E ridge of Mt. Hancock. North Hancock is in back of Bond on the R, with Mt. Whiteface peering over its top and Mt. Tripyramid to its R. The tip of Mt. Shaw in the Ossipee Range can just be seen to the L of Whiteface. The ridge of West Bond sweeps out to the R from Bond; over the saddle between them are Mt. Huntington (L, in front of North Hancock and Tripyramid) and Mt. Kancamagus (R and farther back). The nubby summit of West Bond is under the R end of Kancamagus while the northern Flat Mtn. is above and behind, and Sandwich Dome rises over the R end of West Bond's crest. The Belknap Range, with Belknap and Gunstock Mtns. prominent on its R end, stretches in the distance to the L of Sandwich Dome, above the gap of Mad River Notch. East Osceola is in front of Sandwich on the R, with the main summit of Osceola seen farther R. Black Mtn., a shoulder of Sandwich, peeks over the col between the Osceolas, Mt. Hitchcock is seen below and in front of that col, over the lower W ridge of West Bond. Mt. Tecumseh's sharp peak is seen over Osceola's R shoulder, due S, with its broad West Peak on its R above the East Peak of Scar Ridge. From East Scar that ridge extends R over sharp Middle Scar to the bulky main summits of Scar Ridge, with the lower, ski-trailed Loon Mtn. to its R.

In the foreground in this direction are two wild SW spurs of South Twin, with the broad East Branch valley leading out to the main Scar Ridge. Wavy Hersey Mtn. is on the horizon to the L of the main Scar Ridge, with Mt. Prospect in Holderness in front of and below it. North Pack Monadnock (L) and Crotched Mtn. (R) are in the distance above the main Scar. On the skyline between the main Scar and Loon is the prominent Mt. Kearsarge, with Ragged Mtn. in front of it on the R; Plymouth Mtn. is seen in front of Kearsarge and closer. On clear days Mt. Monadnock can be spotted in the distance to the R of Kearsarge. In the distance to the R of Loon, the broad, paired Forbes Mtn. (L) and Tinkham Hill (R) are seen beyond Bald Mtn., a spur of Stinson Mtn. The hump of Lovewell Mtn. is seen over the R side of Tinkham, and Tenney Mtn. is seen in front of Tinkham. Closer in this direction the South Peak of Loon is seen above the flat-topped E spur of Whaleback Mtn. Next to the R Sunapee Mtn. sprawls on the horizon. Continuing to the R, Stinson Mtn. is seen above the sharp peak of Whaleback Mtn., with Mt. Cardigan behind on the R. From Whaleback a long gentle ridge extends R to the pyramid of Mt. Flume, with the S peak of Owl's Head seen below and the long E ridge of Mt. Kineo above, with the northern spurs of Cardigan beyond. Mt. Kineo (L) and broad Carr Mtn. (R) are seen above and behind Flume, while Mt. Cushman is seen through the wide saddle to the R of Flume, which leads across to Mt. Liberty. The indistinct main summit of Owl's Head is seen under this saddle. On clear days Vermont's Mt. Ascutney can be seen beyond Mt. Liberty. From Liberty a long ridge runs R to Little Haystack, and above this another ridge rises R over Mt. Braley, Mt. Waternomee and Mt. Jim to the bald crest of Mt. Moosilauke. Smarts Mtn. peers over in back to the R of Braley.

To the WSW is a fine broadside look at the upper Franconia Range, viewed across the rolling wildlands of the western Pemigewasset Wilderness, with Mt. Lincoln on the L and Mt. Lafayette on the R, presenting its characteristic long, serrated profile. In the distance to the R of Lafayette is the Breadloaf–Wilson–Grant range in the Green Mtns., S of Lincoln Gap. In the foreground under Mt. Grant is Cole Hill in Easton. Looking in this direction from the W edge of the summit, where the Twin-way begins its steep descent to Galehead Hut, you can see down to the hump of Galehead Mtn. Next to the R and close at hand, looking due W, is Mt. Garfield's pointed peak. The lumpy Signal Mtn. range in west-central Vermont sprawls above and beyond Garfield, and over the L end of that range is the long, distant ridge that joins Vermont 4000-footers Mt. Abraham and Mt. Ellen. Over Garfield's lower R shoulder are Big Bickford (L) and Scarface (R) Mtns., rounded northern spurs of Lafayette, and over Big Bickford on the skyline are Mt. Ethan Allen (L) and the tilted Camel's Hump (R). In the foreground in this direction are various wooded humps on Garfield Ridge. Extending R from these humps is Flat Top Mtn., scarred by cliffs and a curving slide. Above Flat Top are expansive lowlands, including the village of Franconia, and Mt. Mansfield on the horizon, with the Sterling Range extending to its R. The nearer Worcester Range stretches across to the L of Mansfield. Farther R, to the NW, are the low, twin humps of Mts. Cleveland (L) and Agassiz (R) near Bethlehem, with the town of Littleton behind on the L. On the horizon in this direction in northern Vermont are (L to R) the Cold Hollow Mtns., the pyramid of Belvidere Mtn., Tillotson Peak and Haystack Mtn. Farther R are the prominent Jay Peaks.

Continuing to the R, looking beyond a spur ridge of North Twin marked by twin slides, the view sweeps over more lowlands out to many peaks in Vermont's Northeast Kingdom; L to R are Mt. Hor (with Round-top in Quebec's Sutton Mtns. peering over a ridge to its L); the nearer Burke Mtn. (L) and Umpire Mtn. (R), with Miles Mtn. in front, Quebec's Owl's Head peeking over between them and Whitefield's Forest Lake seen in front of Umpire; Bald Mtn. behind and R of Umpire; East Haven Mtn. with low Dalton Mtn. in front and Mt. Orford in Quebec behind on the R; the massive East Mtn. with a structure visible on top; and Gore Mtn., seen just L of North Twin's summit, with the lower and closer Stone Mtn.–Burnside Mtn. range to its R.

NO. OF 4000-FOOTERS VISIBLE: from North Twin, 27 from summit, 2 additional from E outlook; from South Twin, 35

FRANCONIA RANGE

Mount Flume

ELEVATION: 4328 ft. / 1319 m   ORDER OF HEIGHT: 25
LOCATION: Franconia Range, Town of Lincoln
USGS MAPS: 7½' Lincoln, 7½' Mt. Osceola

Geography

Mt. Flume is the southernmost 4000-footer in the Franconia Range, and is distinguished by its slide-scarred western face and its ledgy, knife-edged summit. Travelers on I-93 and US 3 in the Lincoln area can't help but notice the great slides which scar the mountain from summit to base. These slides came down in 1883, as did the smaller, more grown-up slides seen on Mount Liberty's south-facing slope. When viewed from Mount Liberty's 4459-ft. summit, Flume's impressive slides angle down and away from the summit at a grade seemingly impossible to negotiate. Seen from more distant vantage points to the S, Flume presents a sharp, triangular peak much like its Franconia Range neighbors.

The mountain's narrow summit ridgecrest, no more than 8–10 ft. wide, drops off steeply on both its E and W flanks and the view directly down the length of the W-facing slides can be dizzying. Looking E from the summit, over and through the trees which line that side of the peak, one sees the Pemigewasset Wilderness and its jumble of remote peaks and twisting valleys.

Mt. Liberty, Flume's closest 4000-ft. neighbor, is to the NW, separated by a deep col some 450 ft. lower than Flume's summit. To the S a long, flat, heavily wooded ridge connects Flume with Whaleback Mtn. (3586 ft., also known as Osseo Peak), a prominent summit that rears impressively over the town of Lincoln. From Whaleback several lower knobby spurs extend S and E.

Two spur ridges run to the E off the main summit ridge of Flume. The Osseo Trail from the East Branch valley follows the upper portion of the southernmost of these ridges, which begins at the flat shoulder S of Flume's summit. Its upper end is steeply truncated and scored by slides, and its lower end bears a prominent 2779-ft. knob. Between this ridge and the NE spurs of Whaleback is the valley of Osseo Brook. The more northerly ridge starts a short distance N of the summit and descends

343

several miles toward tranquil Black Pond, a tiny four-acre tarn bordering the southern reaches of the Pemi Wilderness. The Lincoln Brook valley is to the N of this ridge. Between Flume's two E ridges is the spacious, remote valley of Birch Island Brook.

On the opposite side of Mt. Flume, Flume Brook runs several miles WSW from the base of the slides through a broad, deep valley to the famous Flume Gorge, the Pemigewasset River, and US 3. The Flume Gorge is some 700 ft. long with walls 70 to 90 ft. high and 12 to 20 ft. apart. At the head of The Flume, Flume Brook plunges over beautiful Avalanche Falls. From May through October there is a boardwalk through The Flume and an admission is charged; during the off-season there is no charge and though the boardwlk is taken up paths lead to interesting views of The Flume from the bottom and top of the gorge.

Extending W from an unnamed 3834-ft. summit less than a mile SSW of Mt. Flume is Hardwood Ridge, a long, wooded spur bordering Flume Brook valley on the S. Another ridge runs SW off the 3834-ft. knob, dipping to a col and then rising to steep-sided, trailless Big Coolidge Mtn. (3294 ft.), then dropping to the long, low SW extension known as Little Coolidge Mtn. (2421 ft.), the southernmost peak of the Franconia Range.

Nomenclature

The mountain borrows its name from the famous 700-ft. natural granite gorge near the mouth of Flume Brook. According to legend, The Flume was discovered in 1808 by "Aunt Jessie" Guernsey while the 93-year-old woman was fishing in the remote wilds of the Pemigewasset watershed. Flume Brook, which passes through the gorge, originates on the lower slopes of Mt. Flume and provides the link between the mountain and the much-visited gorge, which is owned by the State of New Hampshire. Whaleback Mtn. was presumably a name locally bestowed upon the ridge S of Mt. Flume. In 1887 AMC explorer Frank O. Carpenter recommended that the name "Osseo Peak," meaning "Son of the Evening Star," be applied to the sharp peak at the S end of the ridge; this name had been suggested by visitors a few years earlier. Birch Island Brook was named for a long, high-water island on the East Branch near where the stream issues into the river. This island was mentioned in an 1876 article in *Appalachia* by AMC explorer Warren Upham.

Historical Highlights

First Ascent: Unknown

1808: While on a fishing trip into the unexplored wilds just S of Franconia Notch, 93-year-old "Aunt Jess" Guernsey discovers Flume Gorge.

1813: First road is built through Franconia Notch; in 1820 this is incorporated as Pemigewasset Turnpike.

1835: English writer Harriet Martineau visits Franconia Notch, Flume. A description of region and narrative of her journey appears three years later in Vol. II of book, *Retrospect of Western Travel.*

1847–1848: First Flume House, near present-day entrance to Flume Reservation and Gorge, is built, probably by William Kenney and Ira Coffin. Building is then sold to Richard Taft, who opens hotel for business in 1849.

1866: Flume Covered Bridge is built over Pemigewasset River.

1871: Flume House burns to ground.

1872: Second Flume House, built on foundation of original hotel, opens.

1876: Moses F. Sweetser's guidebook describes trailless route to summit by way of Flume Brook. "The journey is arduous, the choice being given of the rolling stones of the brook or the thickets at its side." He notes the "very beautiful and extensive views."

1883: Landslides come crashing down off Mts. Flume, Liberty, dislodging suspended, egg-shaped boulder in Flume Gorge.

1886: AMC stalwart J. Rayner Edmands climbs Flume from Flume House, accompanied by axeman, hired to clear summit for observation. They ascend through The Flume and up loose, treacherous slide. From summit, Edmands proceeds northward along ridge but, lacking compass, strays off course and ends up descending into Lincoln Brook valley to E. He spends night with several campers in birchbark camp near Franconia Branch and walks out via Lincoln next morning. Edmands's misadventure, which triggered one of first nighttime search missions in White Mtns., is written up for *Appalachia.*

1887: AMC Councillor of Exploration Frank O. Carpenter explores "Whale-back" ridge S of Mt. Flume.

1896: Branch of Boston & Maine Railroad is extended N from North Woodstock towards Flume House.

1901–1907: Lower E slopes of Whaleback Mtn. and Mt. Flume are logged by J. E. Henry's crews, working from Camps 7 and 8 on East Branch & Lincoln Railroad. Operation includes incline, narrow-gauge railway built in 1901 on N side of Osseo Brook. This gravity-powered, switchbacking line is operated for only two years and is abandoned after train loaded with logs jumps the tracks, resulting in death of brakeman.

1904: Lumberman George L. Johnson sets up shop in North Lincoln with sawmill and logging railroad operation. Over next several years his crews log W slopes of Franconia Range. Short extension of railroad is built towards base of Hardwood Ridge.

1905: With assistance from AMC, North Woodstock Improvement Association completes Franconia Ridge Trail, extending it from logging railroad by East Branch up Osseo Peak and across to Mts. Flume and Liberty.

1908: Fire burns 423 acres on W slopes of Mts. Flume and Liberty.

1917: AMC establishes new trail to summit from Flume Gorge by way of old slide. Path is initially known as Mt. Flume Trail, but by 1928 is listed in guidebooks as Flume Slide Trail.

1918: Fire claims second Flume House.

1928: After extensive fundraising and publicity campaign spearheaded by Society for Protection of N.H. Forests and Federation of Women's Clubs, Franconia Notch becomes Forest Reservation and State Park.

1948: Ownership of Flume Gorge and southern part of Franconia Notch is transferred from SPNHF to state of New Hampshire and becomes part of state park.

1949: Section of Franconia Ridge Trail from upper terminus of Flume Slide Trail to Kancamagus Highway in Lincoln is renamed Osseo Trail.

Early 1970s: Bottom of Flume Slide Trail relocated to N of The Flume; now branches off Liberty Spring Trail.

1983: Due to condominium construction, Osseo Trail is relocated. Path now begins off Wilderness Trail (1.4 mi. from Kanc Highway) and ascends ridge from SE.

1984: Eastern slopes of Mt. Flume, including valley of Birch Island Brook, are included in new Pemigewasset Wilderness.

1988: After nearly two decades of controversy, new Franconia Notch Parkway, scaled-down section of I-93, is opened through Franconia Notch. New Flume Visitor Center is built as part of Parkway project.

Trail Approaches

Southeast Approach from Lincoln Woods Trail

Lincoln Woods Trail, Osseo Trail, Franconia Ridge Trail
11.2 mi. round trip, 3150-ft. elevation gain

TRAILHEAD (1160 ft.): Large Lincoln Woods parking area, with ranger cabin and restrooms, is on N side of Kancamagus Highway (NH 112), 5.6 mi. E of Exit 32 off I-93 in Lincoln.

This is the lone approach to Mt. Flume and the Franconia Range from the valley of the East Branch of the Pemigewasset River. It starts off on an old logging railroad, then follows a relatively new and well-engineered path (1983) that ascends the mountain via a SE spur ridge. Upper sections of trail are steep and are negotiated by several wooden staircases—it has been reported that there are 396 rock and wooden steps on Osseo Trail.

From parking lot, drop down stairs in front of ranger cabin, and cross large suspension footbridge over wide, rocky East Branch of Pemigewasset River, one of premier wilderness streams in region. On far side turn R on Lincoln Woods Trail for easy walking along wide, level bed of J. E. Henry's East Branch & Lincoln Railroad (1893–1948), with many hemlock ties still astride trail. At 0.4 mi. trail emerges on high bank with glimpses

Slides scar the western face of Mount Flume from base to summit and are best viewed from the summit of Mount Liberty.

of river and ridges of Mt. Hitchcock beyond, then trail pulls away from river, crossing culvert over Osseo Brook at 0.8 mi. Long straightaway, with one section next to Osseo Brook, leads to jct. L with Osseo Trail at 1.4 mi. / 1300 ft. Osseo Trail starts out in W direction, meandering at level grade in hardwood glade beside Osseo Brook for 0.2 mi. It then climbs short, steep pitch, traverses sidehill though hemlocks on steep bank high above stream, then settles into long, easy to moderate climb up N side of valley with good footing. For short distance it follows one switchback of 1901 incline logging railroad built by J. E. Henry, then follows old logging roads for long, pleasant stretch of walking with open hardwood corridors. During leafless seasons there are views through trees of various spurs of Whaleback Mtn. on S side of valley. At 3.5 mi. / 2400 ft., trail swings R up rock steps and begins steeper ascent of ridge by switchbacks through birch and conifer forest. Look back for glimpses of huge rock slab on flank of spur across valley. Trail reaches top of ridge at 3.8 mi. and swings L, meandering moderately up through conifers and birch. Higher up it begins bold zig-zag climb up steep nose of ridge, with partial views SE and NE from various switchback turns. Three short switchbacks lead to first of several sets of wood ladders and staircases. At 4.6 mi. / 3475 ft., at top of long ladder, look for signed viewpoint ("Down-Look") up on R. Here there is memorable view NE and E into Pemi Wilderness, including (L to R) Mt. Flume's summit close by on L, Mt. Garfield over the NE ridge of Flume, the great crouching mass of Owl's Head, Galehead Mtn. under North Twin between the summit and sharp S spur of Owl's Head, South Twin, Mt. Guyot, West Bond, Mt. Bond, the great craggy Bondcliff, Mt. Davis and Stairs Mtn. in the distance, and Mt. Nancy, Mt. Anderson and Mt. Carrigan up long valley of East Branch. Especially fine is view into slide-marked cirques at head of Redrock Brook, between South Twin and Guyot.

After rock steps, a long wooden staircase (at top of which you jog R to another view into Pemi), and several more shorter staircases, main ridge is attained and trail levels out. You now meander through black spruce scrub, with some muddy footing, and view of Flume summit to R, then open fir forest. At 5.1 mi. / 3800 ft., in large flat area, trail heads R toward Flume's narrow ridgecrest. Steady climb begins at 5.2 mi., and Flume Slide Trail comes in on L at 5.5 mi. / 4220 ft. For summit, go straight on Franconia Ridge Trail for final 0.1 mi. climb, ending with scramble up jagged rock outcrops along W edge of narrow summit ridge. Along this stretch there are dramatic views across face of crags to upper Franconia Ridge peaks and impressive look down scree-filled gully. Use caution as there are steep drops to L. High point is open ledge at N end of crest, reached at 5.6 mi. / 4328 ft.

West Approaches from US 3

Whitehouse Trail, Liberty Spring Trail, Flume Slide Trail, Franconia Ridge Trail
4.8 mi. one way, 3100-ft. elevation gain

MTS. FLUME AND LIBERTY LOOP OPTION

Whitehouse Trail, Liberty Spring Trail, Flume Slide Trail, Franconia Ridge Trail, descent via Liberty Spring Trail, Whitehouse Trail
9.9 mi. loop, 3750-ft. elevation gain

MTS. LIBERTY AND FLUME OUT AND BACK

Via Whitehouse Trail, Liberty Spring Trail, Franconia Ridge Trail ascent
10.2 mi. round trip, 4250-ft. elevation gain

TRAILHEAD (1400 ft.): These routes begin in a hiker's parking area on the E side of US 3, 0.1 mi. N of the parking area for Flume Visitor Center. If driving N on I-93, take Exit 34A off Franconia Notch Parkway and proceed 0.5 mi. N on US 3 to exit on R for hiker's parking. Coming S on I-93, parking area is on L, 0.2 mi. S of Exit 34A.

The ascent via Flume Slide Trail is the most direct approach to the summit from the W, and though the lower portion is a pleasant woods walk, the trail is extremely steep and difficult in its upper section as it follows the route of one of the mountain's old slides (which is almost completely revegetated with limited views, and is well to the S of the open slides on the W face of Mt. Flume). Because many of the rock slabs which the route passes over are extremely dangerous when wet, this route is not recommended in times of wet weather. Hikers will also encounter difficulties while descending via this trail, therefore it is not generally used as a descent route. Hikers not comfortable with such steep terrain are advised to use the Osseo Trail route to Mt. Flume, or ascend Mt. Liberty via Liberty Spring Trail, go out-and-back to Mt. Flume on Franconia Ridge Trail, and descend from Mt. Liberty. See Mt. Liberty chapter for details.

From parking area, follow Whitehouse Trail up onto hardwood plateau and N along rolling course parallel to parkway. Descend to paved Franconia Notch Recreation Trail (the bike path) at 0.6 mi. (Alternatively, one may park in northernmost lot of Flume Visitor Center and walk bike path 0.8 mi. to this point, longer but with smooth footing.) Turn L on bike path and follow it over bridges across minor brook and Pemigewasset River, passing jct. L with Cascade Brook Trail at W side of second bridge. From here to jct. with Flume Slide Trail, the route is part of Appalachian Trail. On far side of bridge, at 0.8 mi., turn R off bike path onto white-blazed Liberty Spring Trail.

Trail traverses northward at moderate grade across hardwood slope for 0.4 mi., then swings back to R on route of very old logging road that once served mill at Whitehouse Bridge, and climbs to jct. R with Flume Slide Trail at 1.4 mi. / 1800 ft. Flume Slide Trail initially runs at easy grade on old logging road, then soon veers L (E) off the road and climbs at easy to moderate grade across lower slopes of Mt. Liberty. Trail crosses small brook at 1.7 mi., then descends by short switchbacks to cross larger brook at 1.8 mi. (down the slope this stream flows through Liberty Gorge near The Pool). Moderate climb continues through fine hardwoods to another brook crossing at 2.5 mi. On far side trail angles up to R, then swings L for easy traverse followed by descent to another brook crossing at 2.9 mi. On far side trail winds R and L, then continues SE up valley, entering conifers as it approaches Flume Brook and then crosses it at 3.3 mi. / 2300 ft. It now follows Flume Brook ENE up the valley, recrossing to N side in ca. 0.1 mi. It climbs along N branch of brook, skirts a beautiful birch forest on the lower S slope of Mt. Liberty to the L, and crosses the N branch in a flat area at 3.7 mi., with a glimpse up to Mt. Flume just beyond. On the far side it meanders up through conifer forest, then starts to climb moderately along gravel outwash of slide.

Steeper climb up old slide track begins at 4.0 mi. / 2800 ft., and grade soon becomes very steep over wet ledges and loose rocks, with occasional limited views to WSW available. If hiking with or near someone else, be aware of rocks dislodged by hiker above you or by your footwork. Much of climb is over smooth ledges that are slick when wet; frequent use of hands is required. Some hikers may be driven to woods along edges of trail, where beaten paths bypass some of the trickiest spots. Care is required to follow the trail in places. After half-mile of unrelieved brutal climbing, trail steers L at ca. 3800 ft. for final steep, rocky ascent of ridgecrest. Atop ridge, at 4.7 mi. / 4240 ft., Flume Slide Trail ends at T-junction where Franconia Ridge Trail to summit leaves L and Osseo Trail to East Branch valley leaves R. Turn L and follow Franconia Ridge Trail 0.1 mi. N to summit ledges, ending with scramble up jagged rock outcrops along W edge of narrow summit ridge. Along this stretch there are dramatic views across face of crags to upper Franconia Ridge peaks and impressive look down scree-filled gully. Use caution as there are steep drops to L. High point is open ledge at N end of crest, reached at 4.8 mi. / 4328 ft.

LOOP OPTION

From the W, a loop over Mts. Flume and Liberty can be made via the Flume Slide, Franconia Ridge and Liberty Spring Trails. Since it is inadvisable to descend the Flume Slide Trail, most hikers will instead take that trail *up* Mt. Flume, follow Franconia Ridge Trail 1.1 mi. N to Mt. Liberty, then continue N on ridge to terminus of Liberty Spring Trail 0.3 mi. from summit. From there, Liberty Spring Trail is taken 2.9 mi. back to Whitehouse Trail.

From Mt. Flume, Franconia Ridge Trail descends to knob N of summit, then drops down to Liberty–Flume col (3900 ft.). From col, trail begins stiff 550-ft climb up Liberty, heading mostly in westerly direction; upper part of climb is steep and rough over large rocks. From open summit of Mt. Liberty, head N down and over ledges and into woods until Liberty Spring Trail is reached. (For detailed description of Liberty Spring Trail see Mt. Liberty chapter.)

By spotting vehicles, one at Lincoln Woods and one at the lot above Flume Visitors Center, it's also possible to do a point-to-point traverse over Mt. Flume or Mt. Liberty and Mt. Flume, using Flume Slide Trail or Liberty Spring Trail for ascent and Osseo Trail for descent. Total mileage for Mt. Flume-only traverse is 10.4 mi. / 3100 ft. For Flume / Liberty traverse mileage is 10.7 mi. / 3600 ft.

Winter

The most popular (and therefore mostly likely to be beaten out) route to Mt. Flume is via Mt. Liberty, which is usually climbed in conjunction with the former. Be aware that the trail between the two summits may be hard to follow in places, especially in the open, windswept woods in the col between Liberty and Flume. Use caution on the summit ledges, especially if icy. Due to its steepness, the Flume Slide Trail is not recommended for winter travel. The Osseo Trail from the East Branch valley is another option, but it does not see anywhere near the winter use of the Mt. Liberty approach and features some steep, difficult snowshoeing (or cramponing, depending on conditions) in the vicinity of the staircases. The rest of the Osseo Trail route is good for snowshoeing, but caution is needed on the final exposed approach along summit ledges, especially on windy days. Summit views to the E are better in winter with a deep snow platform.

View Guide

Unlike the other Franconia Ridge peaks, the summit of Mt. Flume is partially wooded, thus there is not a full 360-degree view from any one spot. But Flume's ledges have excellent open views W, S and N, and by standing atop the highest ledges one can also gain a good view E into the Pemigewasset Wilderness.

Because the mountain is set off to the SE from the taller peaks of Franconia Ridge, Flume offers a unique perspective looking N up the range. Close by to the NW is the shapely peak of Mt. Liberty, displaying a prominent talus patch on its side. The tip of Cannon Mtn. is seen over the ridge descending R from Liberty's summit. To the R of Liberty is a fine view of the bare peaks of Little Haystack, Mt. Lincoln and Mt. Lafayette, the latter looking especially sharp from this angle. Far to the NW, through the broad gap between Liberty and Little Haystack, are the Jay Peaks in northern Vermont.

To the R of the Franconias, looking just E of N, is a beautiful look up the remote valley of Lincoln Brook to the sentinel of Mt. Garfield standing guard at its head. The distinctive double peak of Goback Mtn. is seen in the distance to the L of Garfield. (From here around to the SE you must stand to get the full view over the scrub.) To the R of Garfield is the Pilot Range on the horizon, leading across to Mt. Cabot on its R end. North Percy Peak pokes up over the L end of the Pilots. Close in, the Lincoln Brook valley is walled in on the R by the long, level-topped ridge of Owl's Head, with a sharp wooded peak prominent at its S end. To the NNE, over the "summit" of Owl's Head, Galehead Mtn. can be spotted, with North Twin looming behind on its R. Swinging around through the ENE you gain a sweeping view of the other peaks of the Twin–Bond Range with their many slides and cliffs. South Twin is to the R of North Twin, then a long ridge leads across to rounded Mt. Guyot. Mt. Jefferson is seen over Mt. Guyot, with Sam Adams on its L and Mt. Clay over the col to the R of Guyot. Next to the R on the Twin Range skyline is Mt. Bond, with Mt. Washington rising beyond on its L and Boott Spur on its R. West Bond is seen in front of Mt. Bond on the L. The crags of Bondcliff rear impressively to the R of Bond. Mt. Willey is just R of Bondcliff's summit, with Mt. Hight behind to the L and Carter Dome to the R and beyond; Wildcat is beneath the Dome and hard to spot.

A bit farther R and closer in Mt. Isolation can be picked out along the upper Montalban Ridge, with Carter Dome's Rainbow Ridge beyond on the R. Part of the Webster Cliffs can be seen under Isolation. Farther R is elongated Mt. Davis, with North Baldface above its R end, then South Baldface, Sable Mtn. and Chandler Mtn. Next to the R, looking ENE, are the Giant Stairs and Mt. Resolution. Peering over the scrub to the E, you can gain a beautiful perspective of the East Branch valley leading for miles out to Mt. Nancy at its head. Mt. Anderson is to the R of Nancy, with The Gemini (Twins) peeking over between them. Kearsarge North pops out to the R of Anderson. On the R the East Branch valley is closed in by the great bulk of Mt. Carrigain (on the L, in back, with the lower Vose Spur on its L) and the sprawling ridges of Mt. Hancock (R). Hancock's NW Peak is in front of Carrigain on the R, and from it a ridge, marked by a prominent slide, leads across to the rounded peak of North Hancock, then on to South Hancock and its bold S spur. By peering down in this direction, one can spot the dark water of Black Pond in the valley E of Mt. Flume. Hancock Notch is to the R of the S spur, with little Bill Merrill Mtn. in western Maine seen in the distance. Farther R are the wooded ridges of Mt. Hitchcock (in front) and Mt. Huntington (in back), occupying a large area to the ESE. Mt. Chocorua is seen over the summit of Huntington, with the Three Sisters to its L. To the R of Huntington are Mt. Paugus (L) and the great dome of Mt. Passaconaway (R), with Green Mtn. in Effingham seen between them. Next to the R and closer is Mt. Kancamagus, with the three peaks of Tripyramid behind it on the R, due SE. The summit crest of Mt. Whiteface can be spotted between Middle and South Tripyramid. Next to the R the Osceolas are prominent, with the East Peak on the L and the main, Middle and West Peaks to the R. From there the ridge runs across various lesser peaks to the main, massive summit of Scar Ridge, with Sandwich Dome (L) and Mt. Tecumseh (R) beyond. Close in in this direction are various spurs between Mt. Flume and Whaleback Mtn.

Over the R shoulder of Scar Ridge are Dickey and Fisher Mtns. with the more distant Campton and Squam Ranges beyond. To the R of Scar Ridge, almost due S, is Loon Mtn.'s North Peak and its ski trails, with Bean Hill on the horizon on the L and the even more distant twin Uncanoonuc Mtns. on the R, above flat-topped Prospect Mtn. in Holderness. Farther R is the South Peak of Loon with part of Loon Pond visible below and wavy Hersey Mtn. in the distance. Next to the R is low Russell Mtn., with Mt. Kearsarge on the horizon; Plymouth Mtn. can be seen in front of Kearsarge on the L and Ragged Mtn. on the R. On clear days Mt. Monadnock is visible to the R of Ragged. Next to the R and close in is the lowly hump of Big Coolidge Mtn. peering over Hardwood Ridge, with portions of the Pemigewasset River valley beyond, including part of the town of North Woodstock. In the middle distance Tenney Mtn. is visible over Big Coolidge. Farther R is Stinson Mtn., with Lovewell Mtn. in the distance to its L and Sunapee Mtn. just to its R. To the R of Sunapee and closer, looking SSW, is the prominent dome of Mt. Cardigan. Farther R is little Grandview Mtn. outside of North Woodstock, then the long, low profile of Little Coolidge Mtn.; beyond are Mt. Kineo under Carr Mtn. with Mt. Cushman closer and to the R. Farther R on the horizon are Mt. Ascutney in Vermont (L, over the saddle to the R of Cushman) and Smarts Mtn. (R, over the slope of Mt. Moosilauke's Blue Ridge). On very clear days Stratton Mtn. can be seen just R of Ascutney. Close by in this SW direction is the high wooded shoulder of Hardwood Ridge, forming the S wall of the Flume Brook basin; Mt. Liberty closes the valley in on the R. The view in this westerly direction is especially dramatic, as these ridges form a wide portal through which you gaze out at mountains near and far, starting with the Mt. Moosilauke massif, (L to R): Blue Ridge, Mt. Waternomee, Mt. Jim, South Peak, the main summit, and Mt. Blue, with its long N ridge trailing off to the R. To the R of and in front of Blue's N ridge is Mt. Wolf, with its own long N ridge descending to the R. Bloodroot Mtn. and other peaks in the central Green Mtns. can be seen on the horizon beyond Wolf. The Benton Range summits of (L to R) Jeffers Mtn. and The Hogsback (both broad, level crests), knobby Sugarloaf Mtn. and prominent Black Mtn. extend to the R behind Wolf. Mt. Pemigewasset is seen down low and in close in line with Sugarloaf. The Flume Visitor Center, Indian Head Resort, and a long stretch of I-93 and US 3 can be seen in the Pemigewasset River valley down under and to the L of Mt. Pemigewasset.

The most exciting aspect of the SW view is the dizzying look down the steep slides into the great wooded bowl of Flume Brook. On the horizon to the R of Black Mtn. are the Breadloaf Mtn. range, then the long ridge of Mts. Abraham and Ellen farther to the R, almost due W. On very clear days Dix Mtn. in the Adirondacks can be espied through Lincoln Gap to the L of Mt. Abraham. Farther R and just 6 mi. away across Franconia Notch are the two Kinsman peaks, with South Kinsman on the L and North Kinsman on the R. Camel's Hump juts up in the distance over the col between the Kinsmans. Farther R, just L of the slope descending L off Mt. Liberty, Mt. Mansfield can be seen rising behind and R of the Worcester Range.

NO. OF 4000-FOOTERS VISIBLE: 33

Mount Lafayette

ELEVATION: 5260 ft. / 1603 m   ORDER OF HEIGHT: 6
LOCATION: Franconia Range, Town of Franconia
USGS MAP: 7½′ Franconia

Geography

With an elevation of 5260 ft., Mt Lafayette stands as the highest mountain in the Franconia Range and the tallest peak in the White Mountains outside of the Presidential Range. Besides its lofty ranking, it also possesses a summit view rivaled by few mountains anywhere in the East—especially the broad prospect E into the remote backcountry of the Pemigewasset Wilderness. The entire upper portion of the mountain lies above timberline and is home to rare and fragile alpine plants. Visitors to this unique mountain environment are urged to remain on the marked trails at all times to protect the alpine vegetation.

Mt. Lafayette is the northernmost 4000-footer along the Franconia Range, which rises out of Franconia Notch to the W and the Gale River drainage to the N. The Pemigewasset River takes its rise in Profile Lake at the NW base of Lafayette and flows S through the Notch. Just N of Profile Lake is Echo Lake, which drains northward into the Gale River watershed.

A mile to Lafayette's S along the bare, narrow, rocky ridgecrest, beyond an intermediate 5020-ft. hump sometimes called Truman Peak, lies its craggy neighbor, 5089-ft. Mt. Lincoln. From Lafayette's high point the open summit ridge extends one half-mile N over several rocky knobs to the rounded North Peak (5060 ft.), giving the mountain a characteristic serrated, sloping profile when seen from E or W. From here the main ridge swings NE, descends below treeline, and runs 3 mi. over several rough, wooded humps to Mt. Garfield. From the North Peak another ridge descends NW, then splits into two spurs, one extending N and then W for several miles over Big Bickford Mtn. (3261 ft.), Scarface Mtn. (2802 ft.) and Bickford Mtn. (2380 ft.), the other dropping NW towards I-93.

Several spur ridges running W and NW from the main summit form the eastern wall of Franconia Notch. From the summit a broad ridge descends a mile W to a 4200-ft. shoulder. Here, just below treeline, are the two boggy Eagle Lakes (once called Lakes of the Clouds), tiny alpine tarns at the western base of Lafayette's exposed summit cone. On a nearby shelf is the Appalachian Mountain Club's Greenleaf Hut. From this shoulder the high, sweeping Agony Ridge descends SW between Franconia Notch and Walker Brook, forming the route of Old Bridle Path and providing spectacular views of Walker Ravine and the upper ridge from its ledgy brink. The broad, steep W face of this ridge walls in the Notch across from the great Cannon Cliffs. This slope is littered with landslides, some of which fell as recently as 1959.

From the W shoulder of Lafayette another, shorter ridge descends NW to the wild, rocky cleft of Eagle Pass (2980 ft.); on the far side of this gap is craggy Eagle Cliff (3420 ft.), a ragged line of precipices directly across I-93 from the NE slopes of Cannon Mtn. that is a frequent nesting site for, not eagles, but peregrine falcons

Several deep ravines guard the main summit mass to the NW and SW. Lafayette Brook drains out of the seldom-visited ravine to the NW. This deep basin is flanked by Eagle Cliff ridge on one side and the un-named ridge running NW from the North Peak on the other. Much of this drainage, which is best seen from I-93 about one mi. N of Cannon Mtn., is a part of the Lafayette Brook Scenic Area; several slides scar its upper slopes. In the latter part of the nineteenth century, doctored photographs and postcards frequently depicted an exaggerated "snow cross" that would appear high in Lafayette Brook ravine in the spring. The cross was apparently inspired by William Henry Johnson's famous 1873 photograph, "Mountain of the Holy Cross," which also depicted a snow cross, but this one on a mountain in Colorado.

To the N of the above-mentioned unnamed ridge, in the valley between it and Big Bickford Mtn., flows Skookumchuck Brook, which drains in a westerly direction, eventually merging with Lafayette Brook. E of the Big Bickford ridge is the valley drained by the South Branch of Gale River. The N slopes of Scarface Mtn. are drained by Scarface Brook, and Jordan Brook flows W out of a small valley between Bickford, Scarface and Big Bickford Mtns.

SW of the summit is the deep, sharply carved Walker Ravine, out of which flows the northern branch of Walker Brook. Hikers ascending the mountain via the Old Bridle Path gain an excellent perspective on this ravine while traversing the heights of Agony Ridge. The southern branch of Walker Brook flows out of a second ravine cut into Franconia Ridge halfway between Mts. Lafayette and Lincoln. The two ravines of Walker Brook are separated by a short spur ridge running up to the main ridge and culminating in the 5020-ft sub-peak between Mts. Lafayette and Lincoln.

The E slopes of Lafayette drop 2000 ft. along a broad front into the NW corner of the Pemigewasset Wilderness, drained by the deep, broad Lincoln Brook valley and the upper NW part of the Franconia Brook valley. This remote area is guarded to its N by sphinx-like Mt. Garfield and to the E and SE by the forested mass of Owl's Head Mountain. A broad, boggy height-of-land (3180 ft.) links Owl's Head to Lafayette and divides the Lincoln Brook and Franconia Brook headwaters. In contrast to its busy western slopes, this E side of Lafayette is one of the wildest and most remote places in the mountains.

Nomenclature

The peak is named after the French solider, statesman and American Revolutionary War hero, Marquis de Lafayette (1757–1834), who was hailed as a hero during a stay in the United States in 1824–25. The mountain was previously identified on maps as "Great Haystack," initially by Philip Carrigain on his 1816 map of New Hampshire. It was renamed Mt. Lafayette on October 19, 1825, the forty-fourth anniversary of the famous Battle of Yorktown, which ended the Revolutionary War. According to White Mountain historian Frederick Kilbourne, Yale University president Timothy Dwight, who twice visited the White Mountains (in 1797 and 1803), at one time proposed the mountain be called Wentworth Mountain, presumably for Governor Benning Wentworth.

Greenleaf Hut and Trail were named for Col. C. H. Greenleaf, former proprietor of the Profile House in Franconia Notch. The unofficial names "Agony Ridge" and "The Agonies" refer to the steep humps along the upper Old Bridle Path, particularly discouraging to hut crews carrying heavy loads. Curiously, the name for Skookumchuck Trail and Brook has its origins in the Chinook Indian language from the Northwest, with a meaning of "dashing water" or "rapids." The origins of the names for Walker Brook and Ravine and the Bickford Mtns. are uncertain.

Historical Highlights

First Ascent: While it is not known for certain who was first to reach the summit, the first "recorded" ascents took place in 1826, a year after the first trail up the mountain was built. One early account of a climb to the summit appeared in the *Concord Register* and the *New Hampshire Statesman*, both in September 1826. The following year, the *American Journal of Science and Arts* published "Notice of an Ascent up Mt. Lafayette and of Irised Shadows" by Forrest Shepard. This article chronicled an August 7, 1826 ascent by the author, a Mr. Sparhawk of Dartmouth College, and a local guide.

1813: First road is built through Franconia Notch; previously there had reportedly been a rough trail through the pass. An early traveler over this road, Thomas Boise, is caught in blizzard in Notch. Desperate to stay warm, he skins his horse and uses hide to keep warm, taking shelter under overhanging rock at W base of Lafayette. This becomes known as Boise Rock. Road is incorporated as Pemigewasset Turnpike in 1820.

1825: First trail up mountain (forerunner of today's Greenleaf Trail) is constructed under supervision of Stephen C. Gibb with help from his son Joseph L. Gibb (later to become owner of Crawford House in Crawford Notch). Path, one of earliest built in White Mtns., ascends by way of Eagle Pass.

Mount Lafayette and Eagle Cliff Ridge as seen from Artist's Bluff in Franconia Notch.

1835: Lafayette House tavern is built near Echo Lake in Franconia Notch by Stephen and Joseph Gibb.

1837: Norwich University founder Capt. Alden Partridge leads excursion of student cadets to summit.

1840: Geological survey team led by Charles T. Jackson climbs mountain and ascertains summit to be 5067 feet above sea level.

1850: Landslide crashes down mountain at head of Walker Brook ravine.

1852: New bridle path up mountain from Lafayette Place to Eagle Lake is opened. Path was probably used as footpath previously.

1853: 110-room Profile House opens in Notch. Lafayette House is moved and incorporated into Profile House complex. Also, old trail through Eagle Pass is widened for use as bridle path to summit.

Ca. 1855: Mt. Lafayette Summit House, crude structure at top of mountain, is built. Building falls into disrepair sometime around 1865, though exact date remains unknown.

Late 1850s: Mount Lafayette House, a small hotel, is built near site of present-day Lafayette Campground. It is destroyed by fire in spring of 1861.

1858: Henry David Thoreau, on second visit to White Mtns., camps out at base of Lafayette, climbs summit the following day via Old Bridle Path in "fine weather." He makes detailed notes on flora, notes "wild mountain and forest scene from south-southeast round eastwardly to north-northeast," and builds fire near Eagle Lake to boil tea for dinner.

1858: Sylvester Marsh (who later builds Cog Railway up Mt. Washington) receives charter from state legislature to build steam railway up Lafayette, but financial difficulties and Civil War scuttle plans.

1859: In his classic *The White Hills*, Thomas Starr King calls Lafayette "the Duke of Western Coos" and says "the view from its upper shoulders and summit has an entirely different character from that which Mount Washington commands. It is the lowlands that are the glory of the spectacle which Lafayette shows his guests."

1876: Moses Sweetser's classic guidebook *The White Mountains* praises Lafayette for "the sharpness and decision of its lines, and the thin, keen profile of the summit ridge." He offers detailed description of summit view and notes that toll for pedestrians on bridle path is 50 cents, while a "sure footed horse" and guide can be hired for $3.50.

Mid-1880s: Trail route is opened across ridge from Lafayette to Lincoln and Little Haystack.

1897: Old path up mountain from Lafayette Place (Old Bridle Path) is reopened, but because of logging in area, quickly falls into disrepair. Second attempt to reopen trail takes place in 1901, but again, trail is quickly obliterated.

1903: Forest fire burns 3,000 acres in Jordan Brook area to NW of Lafayette.

1905: Original Profile House is torn down to make way for new structure.

1904–1907: J. E. Henry Co. of Lincoln logs E slopes of Lafayette, working from Camp 12 on Lincoln Brook. In wake of extensive clearcutting, the 1907 "Owl's Head fire" burns vast area in Pemigwasset Wilderness, including lower E side of Lafayette.

1914: Charles Blood leads week-long expedition along Garfield Ridge, scouting out proposed route for new trail that will connect Twin Range with Mt. Lafayette. Trail is ultimately completed in 1917.

1915–1920: Poet Robert Frost climbs Lafayette several times while living in nearby Franconia.

1923: Second Profile House leveled by major fire. Soon afterwards, hotel baron Karl Abbott sells Franconia Notch holdings (including Old Man of Mountain) to state of New Hampshire.

1928: After extensive fundraising and publicity campaign spearheaded by Society for Protection of N.H. Forests and Federation of Women's Clubs, Franconia Notch becomes Forest Reservation and State Park. This includes western slopes of Lafayette.

1929: Old Bridle Path reopened by AMC.

1930: Greenleaf Hut, built on W spur ridge near Eagle Lake, opens.

Ca. 1937: Skookumchuck Trail from US 3 to Garfield Ridge Trail, just N of Lafayette's North Peak, is built.

1938: September hurricane strikes New England. Greenleaf Trail "obliterated by fallen trees and more than half a dozen slides," reports *Ap-*

palachia in June 1939 issue. Upper section of Old Bridle Path "is a blind mess of churned-up vegetation."

1948: Heavy rain on June 24 touches off landslide which blocks Franconia Notch highway.

1954: Account of early overnight stay on summit in 1827 appears in December issue of *Appalachia*. Includes description of crude stone shelter atop mountain.

1956: Plane crash-lands on mountain 150 yards off Old Bridle Path. Pilot, one passenger walk away with minor injuries.

1958: Longtime state worker Clyde Smith lays out Falling Waters Trail from Lafayette Campground to ridge near summit of Little Haystack Mountain. Also, October 24 landslide buries Notch highway in 27 feet of debris.

1961: U.S. Forest Service designates 990 acres as Lafayette Brook Scenic Area.

Late 1970s: In effort to protect trampled alpine vegetation, AMC and WMNF crews build scree walls defining trail across Franconia Ridge.

1980: Laura and Guy Waterman adopt Franconia Ridge Trail; during nearly two decades of their stewardship trail is carefully improved and vegetation recovers.

1984: E slopes of Lafayette are included in new 45,000-acre Pemigewasset Wilderness designated by Congress.

2002: Group of disabled hikers makes wheelchair ascent of Lafayette, spending night at Greenleaf Hut. With support from friends and volunteers from Northeast Passage program, Geoff Krill and Khrista Matthews summit on second day of adventure.

Trail Approaches

West Approach from Franconia Notch Parkway (I-93) at Lafayette Place

MT. LAFAYETTE ONLY OUT AND BACK

Old Bridle Path, Greenleaf Trail
8.0 mi. round trip, 3600-ft. elevation gain

LOOP OVER MT. LAFAYETTE AND MT. LINCOLN

Old Bridle Path, Greenleaf Trail, Franconia Ridge Trail, Falling Waters Trail
8.9 mi. loop, 3900-ft. elevation gain

TRAILHEAD (1780 ft.): Old Bridle Path starts at large hiker's parking area on E side of Franconia Notch Parkway, across from Lafayette Place Campground. Parking is also available on W side of road, with 0.1 mi. paved path leading under road to E side.

The scenic, heavily used Old Bridle Path, combined with the Greenleaf Trail from Greenleaf Hut to the summit, is the most popular ascent route for hikers bound solely for Mt. Lafayette. The last 0.6 mi. of the route is completely in the open and should be avoided in bad weather. Because the ridge is exposed and narrow, it's a dangerous place in a thunderstorm and should be avoided when boomers are predicted. While above treeline, hikers should walk only on the marked footpaths to protect the delicate alpine vegetation on the ridge.

From parking area, Old Bridle Path and Falling Waters Trail coincide at first, starting up paved walkway past restrooms on R and entering hardwood forest. Easy climbing brings trail alongside Walker Brook, and at 0.2 mi. Falling Waters Trail diverges R, crossing Walker Brook on footbridge. Old Bridle Path continues along brook for 50 yds., turns L and begins easy traverse to N through beautiful hardwood forest, then swings R at 0.6 mi. and climbs more steadily to E and then to SE into extensive stand of white birch. Grade eases and at 1.1 mi./2400 ft. yellow-blazed trail crosses WMNF boundary, makes slight dip, then veers sharply L on bank above Walker Brook. Trail soon swings away from stream and climbs steadily with rocky footing through open conifer and birch forest. Returning to edge of ravine, at 1.6 mi./3020 ft. trail makes another sharp L turn and begins steeper climb up to S end of Agony Ridge. Where trail turns L, look for partial view on R across Walker Brook valley and up to Mt. Lincoln.

After steady, ledgy climb of 0.3 mi., at 1.9 mi./3325 ft. reach first of three spectacular open ledge viewpoints on brink of steep drop, looking across Walker Brook ravine and up to huge barren crest of Franconia Ridge crowned by soaring peaks of Lafayette and Lincoln, and out to SW. (These ledges are an excellent destination in their own right for a shorter hike.) Beyond viewpoints path continues at easier grade through scrub up spine of ridge. First (and steepest) of three humps along Agony Ridge is soon reached, with steep scramble up eroded, slippery basalt dike (sometimes referred to as "red rocks"). This is probably trickiest spot on Old Bridle Path, especially when wet. At top of this scramble, ledges on R of trail offer great views down Agony Ridge to Kinsmans beyond, and R to Cannon Cliffs. Ascents of remaining humps are somewhat easier, but still have steep rocky sections interspersed with short breathers. Look for occasional viewing spots from path or on either side (including views W to Cannon, Kinsmans and Moosilauke). Trail jogs to L and R at ca. 4000 ft., makes rocky climb to crest of knob in fir wave, dips slightly to grassy col, then climbs moderately again before leveling and dipping to meet Greenleaf Trail next to Greenleaf Hut at 2.9 mi./4220 ft. From open area around hut, summit crest of Lafayette looms close at hand beyond boggy Eagle Lake.

From hut, pick up Greenleaf Trail and descend pitch down into scrub, cross flat area with Eagle Lake to L, and ascend moderately through scrub. Path passes over several minor knobs, with occasional views back toward hut and Cannon Mtn. At 3.4 mi. / 4500 ft. swing R for short level traverse past gravelly area on R, then bear L and soon R again and break above treeline. Trail now climbs more steeply with many rock steps, following cairns on well-defined, winding route. At 4850 ft. trail angles L and ascends towards prominent large ledge, passing to L of it at 3.8 mi. / 5000 ft. Here trail angles to R for final climb to summit at 4.0 mi. / 5260 ft., where Garfield Ridge Trail enters on L and Franconia Ridge Trail on R. Highest point, near low rock walls remaining from 1850s summit building, is a few yds. to R (S).

South Approach from Mt. Lincoln
If traversing open ridge from Mt. Lincoln (see that chapter for its approaches), follow Franconia Ridge Trail N off summit, descending easily over a small knob. After level stretch, descend steeper ledgy pitch to 4900-ft. saddle before climbing moderately to top of rocky 5020-ft. hump ("Truman Peak") at 0.5 mi. from Mt. Lincoln. From atop this knob, look for Lincoln Slide on slope to E, with Pemi Wilderness beyond. Trail then drops moderately to second saddle, where patch of scrub is found in 4900-ft. col. Trail now climbs easy to moderate grade through scrub, crosses level shoulder in low scrub, then climbs more steeply in open, passing to L of some crags. Trail swings R, more out to E side of ridge, then quickly L with easy scrambling up ledges to summit of Lafayette, 1.0 mi. from Mt. Lincoln.

West Approach from Franconia Notch Parkway (1–93) at Cannon Mtn. Tramway parking area

Greenleaf Trail
7.6 mi. round trip, 3400-ft. elevation gain

TRAILHEAD (1980 ft.): The Greenleaf Trail begins on the northbound entrance ramp of the Franconia Notch Parkway (I-93) at Exit 34B, the Cannon Mtn. Aerial Tramway exit. While the trail begins on the E side of the highway, designated hiker parking is found near the S end of the Tramway parking lot on the W side of the highway.

The Greenleaf Trail is the shortest and oldest route to the summit, but because it lacks the fine views of some of the other approaches, it is the least used of those originating in Franconia Notch. The trail starts from the Cannon Mountain Aerial Tramway parking lot and climbs to Greenleaf Hut by way of Eagle Pass, the narrow cleft on the ridge running NW from the summit. The way is almost completely in the woods. From the hut, however, much of the route to the summit is above treeline and thus exposed to the weather.

From S end of parking lot, follow paved sidewalk E through underpass below Parkway, turn L and follow northbound entrance ramp for 25 yds., then bear R across ditch and into woods where sign marks start of footpath. At first, path climbs at easy grade, but with rocky footing, and parallels highway (below and on R) with several minor ups and downs. After passing outwash of slide below Eagle Cliff at 0.7 mi., it turns L and begins climbing steadily. Short switchbacks lead to R turn at 2200 ft. near edge of slide and longer angling climb, with one squeeze between boulders, then at 1.0 mi. trail swings L near edge of ravine, makes several more switchbacks, and ascends into dramatic Eagle Pass, reaching height of land at 1.5 mi. / 2980 ft. Trail levels as it enters boulder-strewn pass, emerging in open at base of sheer cliff looming up to L, with partial view back to SW. Partway through pass a scramble up large boulder on R rewards with view back to Cannon Cliffs, SE ridge of South Kinsman, and Mt. Kineo and Carr Mtn. in distance. Beyond, you enter woods and soon swing around to R and head more S, beginning steady zigzag ascent of NW shoulder on trail frequently littered with loose and slippery rocks. Use care ascending or descending rocks during wet weather. As height of shoulder is reached, grade moderates for final approach to hut, where Old Bridle Path from Lafayette Place comes in on R. A short distance before reaching hut, side trail on R descends 100 yds. to ledge with standup view NW to Cannon ski slopes and beyond. See Old Bridle Path approach above for description of Greenleaf Trail from hut to summit.

Northwest Approach from US 3

Skookumchuck Trail, Garfield Ridge Trail
10.2 mi. round trip, 3550-ft. elevation gain

TRAILHEAD (1700 ft.): Skookumchuck Trail begins at parking lot off US 3 just N of its split with I-93, 2 mi. past Cannon Mountain Ski Area and 0.3 mi. S of the US 3 / NH 141 jct. The lot doubles as parking area for N end of Franconia Notch bike path, which leaves from S end of lot.

Probably the least used of the various approaches to Mt. Lafayette, the Skookumchuck Trail route is a pleasant, albeit longer alternative, with attractive woods and nearly a mile of above treeline walking over the relatively less-visited N ridge of Lafayette along the Garfield Ridge Trail.

Leaving NE corner of parking lot, trail climbs moderately up through recently logged area, crossing grassy logging road/snowmobile trail at 0.1 mi. and swinging R (S), parallel to and well above highway. Grades are mostly easy, with several minor ups and downs, along this traverse, with crossing of Jordan Brook at 0.5 mi. At 1.1 mi. / 2000 ft., former section of trail from old Rt. 3 comes in on R just as Skookumchuck Brook is reached. Path swings L and follows course of stream E, climbing on mostly easy grades with occasionally wet footing until small tributary is crossed at 1.8

mi. / 2400 ft. Trail then steers L and climbs steeply away from brook on long set of stone steps and continues walk up valley through attractive birch forest, spectacular at fall foliage time. Moderate climb continues up slope until crest of ridge connecting Lafayette with Big Bickford Mtn. is attained at ca. 2.9 mi. / 3350 ft. Here trail swings R and meanders moderately up ridge through open forest of birch and fir.

At 3.6 mi. / 4200 ft., after attaining flat, densely wooded NW shoulder, summit of North Lafayette is glimpsed ahead. Trail drops slightly, then climbs again, swings L (E) at easier grade, then dips before swinging R for final climb to ridgeline over rocky, rougher treadway, with one slippery tilted slab, emerging above treeline a short distance before meeting with Garfield Ridge Trail at 4.3 mi. / 4680 ft. Ledges on E side of jct. offer striking view down into remote NW corner of Pemi Wilderness, with Owl's Head and Bond Range beyond to SE, Mt. Garfield to NE, Sandwich Range to S, and many distant ranges to N and W.

Turn R (S) at jct. and begin short, steep, rocky climb in open up to rounded peak of North Lafayette at 4.6 mi. / 5080 ft. This is superb viewpoint in its own right, with far fewer visitors than main summit. After slight descent into sag, trail follows open ridgecrest S, ascending over several little knobs to reach main summit at 5.1 mi. / 5260 ft., where Franconia Ridge Trail continues straight ahead along ridge and Greenleaf Trail diverges R to Greenleaf Hut.

Winter

A winter ascent of Mt. Lafayette, no matter which approach you choose, is a serious undertaking with extensive exposure to wind, storms, whiteouts, and a possible mix of snow, ice and rock on the exposed summit cone and ridge. The potential dangers of this trip in bad weather should not be underestimated; there have been several tragedies on this ridge in recent winters. Full winter clothing and gear, including crampons, are required. The Old Bridle Path is by far the most popular winter ascent route. It is a good snowshoeing route, though it's usually packed out shortly after any snowfall. One steep pitch on the Greenleaf Trail as it curves around a rock buttress just below the summit is particularly tricky if coated in ice or hard snow. It's always wise to carry snowshoes on any ascent of Lafayette as it is easy to get turned around while traveling above treeline during stormy weather. Over the years a number of winter adventurers have inadvertently ended up in one of the mountain's trailless ravines, where great amounts of snow can collect, even in the mildest of winters. In particular, several parties heading north along the ridge to Lafayette in bad weather have missed the L turn onto Greenleaf Trail and ended up in trouble. Many winter trampers will, of course, be tempted to complete the loop in the other direction over Mt. Lincoln and Little

Haystack Mtn. and descend the Falling Waters Trail. This is a spectacular trip on a fine winter day, but potentially dangerous in bad weather with over two miles of exposure. As noted under the Mt. Lincoln chapter, the Falling Waters Trail can be hard to locate where it enters the trees on the descent, and may be tricky if icy in the area around the waterfalls.

The Greenleaf Trail and Skookumchuck Trail approaches are used much less frequently than Old Bridle Path in winter, so extensive trail-breaking may be required. Both are good snowshoeing routes below treeline and thus present pleasant alternatives. The Skookumchuck approach has a long exposed stretch along the mountain's N ridge.

View Guide

Few visitors to Mt. Lafayette will dispute the notion that its summit is among the finest in the White Mountain range. And even though some observers rate its view inferior to that of several of its sister peaks along Franconia Ridge, the mountain's overall perspective of the surrounding country is unsurpassed. Of special note are the views S down the open ridge, E over the vast Pemigewasset Wilderness, and W across Franconia Notch.

Looking S down the barren, rocky spine of Franconia Ridge is the slightly lower summit of Mt. Lincoln, while just over Lincoln's E slope can be seen the tip of Mt. Liberty. On the horizon over Lincoln, Joe English Hill pokes up over the broad Hersey Mtn. with the twin Uncanoonucs in Goffstown to the L. Prospect Mtn. in Holderness is just L of the Uncanoonucs and closer, above the tip of Liberty, with the Campton Range extending to its L in front. Bean Hill is on the horizon between Prospect and the Camptons, and the ski trails of Loon Mtn. are seen in front, with little Cone Mtn. just behind on the R. Fisher Mtn. is seen behind Loon on the L. The unmistakable pyramid-shaped peak of Mt. Flume is seen a bit further to the L, with the slide-marked main summit of Scar Ridge on its L and Fort Mtn. on the horizon. In back of and L of Scar Ridge are Waterville Valley's Mt. Tecumseh (R) and Sandwich Dome (L), with Belknap and Gunstock Mtns. seen in the distance just R of Tecumseh. The several peaks of Mt. Osceola are farther L, extending E from the lower summits of Scar Ridge. Caverly Mtn. in New Durham peeks up over the gap between Osceola's main summit and its sharp East Peak, and Faraway Mtn. (R) and Mt. Shaw (L) in the Ossipee Range are seen in the distance to the L of East Osceola, over Mad River Notch.

To the SE, beyond the lower valley of Lincoln Brook, the sprawling, wooded mass of Mt. Hitchcock rears up out of the southern Pemigewasset Wilderness, a little E of the Osceolas. Above Hitchcock are slide-scarred Mt. Tripyramid (R) and the dark cone of Mt. Passaconaway (L). The summit crest of Mt. Whiteface can just be seen between North and

Middle Tripyramid. Mt. Kancamagus is in front of Tripyramid and flat-topped Mt. Huntington is below Passaconaway, with Mt. Paugus behind to the L. Fort Ridge and other distant hills in southern Maine can be seen through the broad gap between Passaconaway and Paugus. Green Mtn. in Effingham is seen over the L side of Paugus, with Ossipee Hill in Maine seen farther off to the L.

The long, flat mass of Owl's Head Mtn. dominates the nearby Lincoln Brook valley landscape to the E and SE, with its sharp S peak directly under Mt. Paugus and the Cedar Brook valley, and its notable W slide a bit farther L. Above the S (R) end of the main Owl's Head ridge is the great mass of Mt. Hancock, with the lower Juno Peak on the R and the South and North Peaks higher and to the L. Mt. Chocorua rises directly over South Hancock, with the Three Sisters over the col between the Hancocks. The majestic Mt. Carrigain, with its distinctive three-humped profile, rises to the L of Hancock. In the distance between Hancock and Carrigain are lower ranges in SW Maine, including the Clark Mtn. group on the R. Bear Mtn. juts out behind the R side of Carrigain. On the L side of Carrigain, North Moat is seen over Vose Spur, with slide-scarred Mt. Lowell just to the L. Mt. Anderson is to the L of Lowell, with Little Attitash Mtn. seen between them and low hills near Maine's Sebago Lake on the horizon. To the L of Anderson and closer are the dramatic crags of Bondcliff, with Mts. Nancy (R) and Bemis (L) behind on the L. Black Cap Mtn. is seen through the broad gap between Anderson and Nancy, and Maine's sprawling Pleasant Mtn. is behind Nancy and Bemis. The prominent dome of Kearsarge North is behind and L of Bemis, with Mt. Parker seen in front.

To the E and NE is a dramatic view across the broad, remote valleys of the upper Franconia and Lincoln Brook drainages to the Twin–Bond Range and the Presidentials beyond. In late September this rolling birch-clad upland is carpeted in gold. Mt. Bond is just S of E over the lower N end of the Owl's Head ridge, with West Bond in front. To the L are Mt. Guyot's two rounded alpine summits, with many rock slides in front and Little Singepole Mtn. in Maine on the far horizon. Stairs Mtn. (R) and the Doubleheads (L) in Jackson are seen above the connecting ridge between Guyot and Mt. Bond. Parts of Walter Mtn. can be seen in back on either side of Stairs. Chandler Mtn. peers over the L summit of Guyot, with the S ridge of Mt. Davis in front. Mt. Willey, near Crawford Notch, peers up just to the L of Guyot, with Sable Mtn. behind it. Mt. Field is to the L of Willey, and South and North Baldface are in back between Willey and Field. Mt. Jackson peers over just R of Field, and Mt. Isolation is seen behind Field and just L of and in front of North Baldface. Farther to the L, Mt. Washington and the Presidentials rise up behind the Twins. From the R a ridge rises up over Slide Peak to Boott Spur, and thence up to Washington, which is behind and just to the L of South Twin. The tip of Carter

Dome is visible just L of Slide Peak. Mt. Monroe is over South Twin, with Mt. Eisenhower and Mt. Pierce lower and to the R, under Boott Spur. Mt. Clay is on the L of Washington, and farther L Mt. Jefferson (R) and Mt. Adams (L) rise behind and just R of North Twin, while the round hump of Galehead Mtn. huddles below and between the Twins.

Swinging around more to the L, Mt. Garfield and its long connecting ridge with Lafayette are seen to the NE. The cliffs at the end of Garfield's long, wooded S arm are in full view. Old Speck (L) and Goose Eye (R) in the Mahoosuc Range are seen on the horizon in the direction of these cliffs. Bemis, Elephant and Old Blue Mtns. (L to R) are seen behind Old Speck on the L. Mt. Abraham can be seen in the distance between Old Speck and Old Blue, and Saddleback Mtn. pokes up in back between Old Blue and Elephant. Mt. Crescent in the Crescent Range is seen under Saddleback, and the double summit of Black Crescent Mtn. is visible under Bemis Mtn. and directly above the summit of Garfield and North Twin's Nubble Peak. On clear days the West Peak (R) and Horns (L) of Bigelow Mtn. peek over the L side of Bemis. The broad mass of Cambridge Black Mtn. is behind Black Crescent on the L. Next to the L is the distant mass of East Kennebago Mtn. on the horizon. Farther L, beyond the village of Twin Mountain, Cherry Mtn. runs diagonally above Garfield Ridge, with the Pliny Range behind. Pliny Mtn. is at the R end of the Pliny Range, then it extends L across a long, level ridge to Mt. Waumbek, seen directly over the summit of Cherry. Mt. Starr King is just L of Waumbek. In the distance are West Kennebago Mtn. above Waumbek and the boundary mountains of NW Maine above and on either side of Starr King. Bulky Mt. Cabot is seen behind and L of Starr King, with the Pilot Range trailing off to its L, including pointed Hutchins Mtn. towards the L end, with lowly Beech Hill in the foreground. Cherry Pond can be seen on the flats below and just L of Cabot. The mass of Long Mtn. sprawls behind Hutchins, with Dixville Peak just peeking over the col between its two main summits. In the distance between the R end of Long and the L slope of Cabot are (L to R) Rump Mtn., Stub Hill and Rice Mtn. Just L of Long are the Percy Peaks with North Whitcomb (Muise) Mtn. rising beyond. On very clear days Quebec's Mt. Megantic can be glimpsed to the L of North Whitcomb.

Farther L the foreground is dominated by a nearby rocky knob (R) and the North Peak of Lafayette (L). In the distance to the R of the rocky knob are the town of Whitefield on the flats and the peaks of the Nash Stream range beyond (R to L): Sugarloaf, Gore Mtn., Bunnell Mtn. (in back) and West Peak. The double summit of Goback Mtn. is L of the Nash Streams, with Vermont's Monadnock Mtn. behind on its L. Directly over Lafayette's rocky knob, beyond a vast sweep of lowlands, is the distant hulk of Hereford Mtn. in Quebec. Extending to its L is a long ridge that runs over sharp Sable Mtn. (with Stone Mtn. in front), Brousseau

Mtn. and Black Mtn., then rises to Gore Mtn directly above Lafayette's North Peak. Dalton Mtn. is in the middle distance in this direction, with Forest Lake at its base. Just to the L of North Peak, just a few miles away, are the low twin summits of Mts. Agassiz (in back) and Cleveland (in front) in Bethlehem, with massive East Mtn. beyond in Vermont. Both Agassiz and East bear prominent mountaintop structures. Next to the L on the horizon is East Haven Mtn. Farther L are the prominent pair of Umpire Mtn. (R, with Miles Mtn. in front) and Burke Mtn. (L), with Bald Mtn. centered in back between them. Quebec's Mt. Orford can be seen in the distance to the R of Umpire. To the L of Burke, Willoughby Gap is framed by Mt. Pisgah (L) and Mt. Hor (R), with the hump of Quebec's Owl's Head seen behind Hor. Over the ridge extending L from Hor are more summits in the Sutton Mtns. of Quebec, including Round Top at the L end. The town of Littleton can be seen in the foreground in this direction. Farther L, looking NW, I-93 snakes its way along the Gale River valley and through Franconia village.

In the distance, above the waters of the Connecticut River and Moore Reservoir, is northern Vermont's Jay Peaks. Continuing across the horizon to the L of the Jays, beyond Franconia village, one sees Haystack Mtn., Tillotson Peak, sharp Belvidere Mtn., the Cold Hollow Mtns. and the top of Laraway Mtn. Next to the L you look down on Echo Lake and rocky little Bald Mtn. in Franconia Notch State Park. On the horizon above them, beyond many miles of lower country (including the long crest of Gardner Mtn.), spreads Mt. Mansfield, Vermont's highest peak, with the Sterling Range extending to its R and the slightly nearer Worcester Range to its L. Continuing to the L on the Vermont skyline are Bolton Mtn. and then the distinctive Camel's Hump to the WNW, with Ethan Allen Mtn. attached on its L. Next to the L and closer is the lumpy Signal Mtn. range in west-central Vermont, with Spruce Mtn., the sharp peak at the R end of the range, seen under Ethan Allen, and Signal Mtn., the highest, in the center. The view now swings L to the nearby bulk of Cannon Mtn., seen due W, with its precipitous cliffs dropping off sharply into the Notch and ski trails on the slopes to the R under its NW Peak. The long ridge joining Mt. Abraham (L) and Mt. Ellen (R) is on the horizon between Cannon's NW Peak and main summit, with Cooley Hill (L) and Cole Hill (R, under Signal Mtn.) seen much closer and just behind the Cannon peaks. On exceptionally clear days several peaks are visible in New York's Adirondacks, over 100 mi. away: Saddleback Mtn. in the Jay Range (just R of Signal Mtn.), Hurricane Mtn. (a dim pyramid seen through Appalachian Gap, to the R of Mt. Ellen, and L of Signal Mtn.) and Macomb Mtn. (sighted through Lincoln Gap, to the L of Abraham). The Mt. Grant–Mt. Wilson–Breadloaf Mtn. Range is to the L of Lincoln Gap, with Green Mtn. (R, behind Cooley Hill) and Moody Ledge (L) seen in the middle distance. The Cannon Balls extend S (L) from Cannon Mtn.

along Kinsman Ridge, with Green Mountain peaks on either side of Brandon Gap strung along the horizon.

To the L of the Cannon Balls, looking WSW across Franconia Notch, are the two summits of Kinsman Mtn., North on the R and South on the L, with Lonesome Lake nestled on a plateau below them. Black (R) and Sugarloaf (L) Mtns. in the Benton Range are seen in back between the Kinsmans. The Killington Range is seen in the distance to the L of South Kinsman, with sharp Pico Peak on the R, Killington Peak in the middle, and Shrewsbury Peak on the L. Farther L, Mt. Moosilauke is seen to the SW over the lower end of Kinsman Ridge, with Mt. Wolf in front and the low mass of Mt. Clough behind on the R. In the distance are more Vermont peaks: Salt Ash Mtn. (R) and Dorset Peak (L, with a flat-topped spur on its R) over Clough, and Okemo Mtn. over the R slope of Moosilauke. Smarts Mtn. is seen behind Moosilauke on the L, with Stratton Mtn.'s double flattened dome in the distance to its R and Mt. Ascutney on its L. On very clear days Mt. Snow (R) and pointed Haystack Mtn. (L) in southern Vermont can be seen L of Ascutney. Pond-lovers will enjoy the glimpse of little Mud Pond at the base of South Kinsman's SE ridge, in line with Ascutney. Farther L, Croydon Peak is seen on the horizon with Mt. Pemigewasset (Indian Head) seen low down in front. Next to the L is bulky Carr Mtn. with Mt. Kineo and Mt. Cushman in front on the L. Farther L, over Kineo's long E ridge with the Pemigewasset River valley in the foreground, are seen (R to L) Mt. Cardigan, Sunapee Mtn., the little bump of Lovewell Mtn., and the dim bulk of Mt. Monadnock, 94 mi. away. Stinson Mtn. is seen in front between Lovewell and Monadnock, with Tenney Mtn. behind on its L, under Monadnock. Farther L Mt. Kearsarge is prominent on the horizon, with Ragged Mtn. in front on the R and North Woodstock village in the foreground over the R slope of Mt. Lincoln. To the L of Kearsarge and closer are Plymouth Mtn. (R) and the Bridgewater Mtns. (L). On clear days Crotched Mtn. (R) and North Pack Monadnock (L) can be seen over Plymouth, and the Lyndeboro Mtns. appear to the R of the Bridgewaters. Then the view swings back to Mt. Lincoln to the S.

NO. OF 4000-FOOTERS VISIBLE: 38

Mount Liberty

ELEVATION: 4459 ft. / 1359 m   ORDER OF HEIGHT: 18
LOCATION: Franconia Range, Town of Lincoln
USGS MAP: 7½′ Lincoln

Geography

The sharp rock peak of Mt. Liberty is a distinctive landmark towering above lower Franconia Notch near the S end of the Franconia Range. Seen from the vicinity of the Flume Visitor Center, Liberty is a massive pyramid of a mountain, wooded except for its craggy crown, the shape of which has been likened to "Washington lying in state." From the summit ledges the hiker is rewarded with a magnificent 360-degree view over Franconia Notch, the Pemigewasset Wilderness and dozens of peaks.

Liberty's near neighbor to the S is slide-scarred Mt. Flume, which is set back to the SE and separated by a deep, broad 3900-ft. col. Flume Brook drains the broad basin S of Mt. Liberty and W of Mt. Flume and flows down through the famous Flume Gorge at the SW base of Liberty. A short, sharp ridge descends S from the summit into this valley. To the N a long, gentle, wooded ridge joins Liberty with Little Haystack Mtn. two miles up the range.

On the W the slopes of Liberty sweep gracefully upward from the Pemigewasset River valley at the S end of Franconia Notch. The Pool, a deep rock-walled pothole in the river, is a notable landmark at the foot of the mountain. It is accessible by paths leading from the Flume Visitor Center (admission charged May–October); the Sentinel Pine Covered Bridge spans the river at the N end of The Pool. The W slope of the mountain forms a very broad ridge between a northern tributary of Flume Brook and a nameless brook that begins in two branches in ravines on the NW side of Liberty, then flows SW to the Pemigewasset River at The Pool. This latter stream drops over the Liberty Gorge Cascades just before reaching the river; this feature is also accessible by paths from The Flume Visitor Center. A long slide scars the SW face of Liberty near the top of another northern tributary of Flume Brook.

To the E of Mt. Liberty is the remote valley of Lincoln Brook, deep in the Pemigewasset Wilderness; on the other side of this drainage is Owl's Head Mtn. A broad spur ridge extends ENE from Liberty into the Pemi; on the N side of this ridge is the main valley of the three-pronged basin of Liberty Brook, a major tributary of Lincoln Brook. On the E side of the Liberty–Flume col is a cirque-like valley that also drains into Lincoln Brook via a nameless stream.

Nomenclature

In the early 1800s Mt. Liberty was known as one of the Franconia Haystacks, for when seen from the S the peaks of Flume, Liberty, Little Haystack, Lincoln and Lafayette appear as a chain of sharp, pyramidal peaks. No one is sure who bestowed the name of Liberty on this particular mountain, but it appeared as early as 1852 in a *Harper's Magazine* article, "Scenery of the Franconia Mountains," by William Macleod.

Historical Highlights

First Ascent: Unknown.

1813: Improved road through Franconia Notch completed; in 1820 this becomes Pemigewasset Turnpike.

Late 1800s: Sawmill in operation at Whitehouse Bridge on Pemigewasset River, at W base of Mt. Liberty. Settlement of 20 families develops here, with all buildings painted drab red.

1876: E. C. Pickering of AMC and B. P. Moore of Baltimore ascend Liberty from Flume House (hotel near The Flume). Last hundred yards through scrub is "slow and laborious," taking ½ hour. They spend 3 hours making observations at summit and leave AMC register bottle at top. Account appears in March 1877 *Appalachia*.

1880s: Moses Sweetser's guidebook says of Mt. Liberty: "A long day is needed for the exploration of this summit; and a skillful guide should be taken."

1883: Major landslides occur on W slopes of Mts. Liberty and Flume.

1889: Under direction of Frank O. Carpenter and Franklin Clark, steep trail, dubbed "The Air Line," is built from Flume House to summit of Liberty. Path is extended along ridge to Little Haystack. Route up to Liberty is soon devastated by logging.

1901: AMC opens new path to Mt. Liberty, with lower branches beginning at Flume and at Johnson's Mills, 2 mi. S of Flume House.

1903–1907: J. E. Henry's crews are logging in Lincoln Brook valley on E side of Liberty, operating from Camp 11 along spur line of East Branch & Lincoln Railroad.

1904: Logger George L. Johnson sets up shop with sawmill and logging railroad operation in North Lincoln; over next few years his crews log extensively on W slopes of Franconia Range.

1905: In cooperation with AMC, Karl P. Harrington and R. J. Jackman of North Woodstock Improvment Association open S section of Franconia Ridge Trail, extending from J. E. Henry's logging railway on East Branch across Osseo Peak and Mt. Flume to Mt. Liberty. Liberty Camp, open shelter accommodating six, is built at site of spring high up on AMC trail ascending Mt. Liberty from W.

1908: Fire burns 423 acres on W slopes of Mt. Liberty and Mt. Flume. Evidence of blaze remains today in birch forest on lower slope of Liberty's S ridge, above Flume Brook.

1912–1913: George L. Johnson has crews log 2.5 million board feet in Liberty Brook valley on E side of mountain; he makes arrangement for cut timber to be transported to North Woodstock on J. E. Henry's

East Branch & Lincoln Railroad at fee of $5 per car. Johnson builds RR spur into Liberty Brook valley and establishes camp for loggers well into basin.

1916: Second edition of *AMC Guide* describes the AMC path up Mt. Liberty, leaving from upper end of The Flume. Trail crosses burned area partway up, threading among "huge rocks and luxuriant raspberry bushes." Upper part of Carpenter's old path is "nearly impassable" due to logging and fire.

1921: Whitehouse Bridge Trail completed, extending from Kinsman Pond near North Kinsman Mtn. down to Whitehouse Bridge over Pemigewasset River, then following old logging road from former Whitehouse mill up W slope of Liberty to meet AMC path about 2 mi. above The Flume.

1922: New, larger shelter built at Liberty Spring, accommodates 12.

1939: Another new shelter with space for 25 is constructed to replace former lean-to, which was destroyed by 1938 hurricane. Covered bridge is built over Pemigewasset River by The Pool using huge pine felled by hurricane as base.

1970: AMC removes Liberty Spring Shelter and establishes tent platforms and caretaker at site.

1972: Section of trail between The Flume and Whitehouse Trail has been closed; Liberty Spring Trail now starts at Whitehouse Bridge.

1984: Ridges and valleys on E side of Mt. Liberty are included in new 45,000-acre Pemigewasset Wilderness.

1987: Whitehouse Bridge trailhead now closed due to construction of Franconia Notch Parkway; new Whitehouse Trail opened from parking area near recently built Flume Visitor Center. This lengthens hike to Mt. Liberty by 0.8 mi. each way.

Trail Approaches

West Approach from US 3

MT. LIBERTY ONLY

Whitehouse Trail, Liberty Spring Trail, Franconia Ridge Trail
8.0 mi. round trip, 3250-ft. elevation gain

MTS. LIBERTY AND FLUME OUT AND BACK

Whitehouse Trail, Liberty Spring Trail, Franconia Ridge Trail
10.2 mi. round trip, 4250-ft. elevation gain

TRAILHEAD (1400 ft.): This route, the usual way to ascend Mt. Liberty, begins in a hiker's parking area on the E side of US 3, 0.1 mi. N of the parking area for Flume Visitor Center. If driving N on I-93, take Exit 34A off Franconia Notch Parkway and proceed 0.5 mi. N on US 3 to exit on R for hiker's parking. Coming S on I-93, parking area is on L, 0.2 mi. S of Exit 34A.

After a warm-up approach, this climb to Liberty entails a long, steady slog up the W slope of mountain followed by a short ridge walk to the summit. From parking area, follow Whitehouse Trail up onto hardwood plateau and N along rolling course parallel to parkway. Descend to paved Franconia Notch Recreation Trail (the bike path) at 0.6 mi. (Alternative is to park at Flume Visitor Center and walk 0.8 mi. up bike path to this point, longer but with smoother footing.) Turn L on bike path and follow it over bridges across minor brook and Pemigewasset River, passing jct. L with Cascade Brook Trail at W side of second bridge. From here to top of ridge route is part of Appalachian Trail. On far side of bridge, at 0.8 mi., turn R off bike path onto white-blazed Liberty Spring Trail.

Trail traverses northward at moderate grade across hardwood slope for 0.4 mi., then swings back to R on route of very old logging road that once served mill at Whitehouse Bridge, and climbs to jct. R with Flume Slide Trail at 1.4 mi. / 1800 ft. Stay ahead on Liberty Spring Trail at easy grade in hardwoods, crossing two small brooks. At 1.9 mi. / 2050 ft. trail crosses larger brook flowing down from ravine on NW side of mountain. After short steep pitch cross a couple of smaller brooks and climb moderately to sharp L turn at 2.2 mi. / 2350 ft. Trail now traverses up across slope to R turn at ca. 2525 ft. marking start of long, relentless climb through white birch and conifer forest. Footing is rocky in places. Straight, steady grade continues, then at 3.0 mi. trail bends R for more winding climb. Pass through open grove of firs just before reaching Liberty Spring Campsite at 3.4 mi. / 3870 ft. Ten tent platforms are to L; caretaker and fee in summer. Side path R leads to spring and limited view W. Liberty Spring Trail continues up at stiff grade, reaching jct. with Franconia Ridge Trail at 3.7 mi. / 4260 ft. Turn R on ridge trail and wind moderately up through conifers, traverse nice level stretch through open firs, then climb steeply to emerge on level crest of small, open, ledgy ridge, with summit crags looming fortress-like just ahead. Traverse spine of open rock with views W and N and swing L, then R to scramble up open ledges to flat perches with panoramic views on summit at 4.0 mi. / 4459 ft.

To continue to Mt. Flume, follow southbound Franconia Ridge Trail off summit, which actually descends E at first, dropping steeply over ledges and large rocks. Grade then moderates and trail swings SE to broad 3900-ft. col. Continue SE, then S on climb up N ridge of Mt. Flume and reach knife-edged summit at 5.1 mi. / 4328 ft. Retrace steps to return to Mt. Liberty and then trailhead; descent via Flume Slide Trail is not recommended. Climb back up Liberty entails 550-ft. elevation gain.

North Approach from upper Franconia Ridge
Strong day hikers or backpackers can fashion long loops over Franconia Ridge peaks with car spots at Lafayette Place and Liberty Spring trailheads. (These locations are 3.6 mi. apart.) Franconia Ridge Trail provides connection to Mt. Liberty from jct. with Falling Waters Trail (4760 ft.) near summit of Little Haystack Mtn. (See Mt. Lincoln and Mt. Lafayette chapters for descriptions of Falling Waters Trail and upper Franconia Ridge Trail.) From jct. with Falling Waters Trail, southbound Franconia Ridge Trail runs gradually down for 0.3 mi. out to S end of summit ridge of Little Haystack, then descends steeply over ledges into scrub; here there is fine view S down long, wooded ridge to Mts. Liberty and Flume. Grade soon eases and trail provides pleasant ridge walk through fine fir forest. Reach 4060-ft. col between Little Haystack and Liberty ca. 1.2 mi. from Falling Waters Trail. Rise is gradual to jct. R with Liberty Spring Trail at 1.8 mi./4260 ft. Summit of Mt. Liberty is 0.3 mi. ahead on Franconia Ridge Trail.

OTHER OPTIONS
Really ambitious hikers can do a loop walk over Mts. Lafayette, Lincoln and Liberty. This loop entails an ascent from Lafayette Place via Old Bridle Path and Greenleaf Trail, a ridge walk on Franconia Ridge Trail, and a descent via Liberty Spring Trail and Whitehouse Trail to car spotted at Liberty Spring hiker's parking area. Total distance is 11.8 mi., with a 4350-ft. elevation gain. Hikers adding an out-and-back to Mt. Flume on this loop will increase the round-trip distance to 14.0 mi. with 5350-ft. elevation gain.

The option to walk uphill back to Lafayette Place from jct. of Liberty Spring Trail/Whitehouse Trail (via Pemi Trail or bike path) will add 2.1 mi. to hike distance, so for Lafayette, Lincoln and Liberty it's 13.9 mi. with 4720-ft. elevation gain; adding Mt. Flume out-and-back 16.1 mi. with 5720-ft. elevation gain.

Winter

Mt. Liberty is a popular and moderately difficult winter 4000-footer. The Liberty Spring Trail is a long, uphill snowshoe slog but often has a good packed track. The last short climb over ledges at the summit may be crusty or icy; good snowshoe crampons or boot crampons may be required. Winter peakbaggers often include an out-and-back to Mt. Flume in the itinerary. The trail may be hard to follow in the open, windswept woods in the col between Liberty and Flume. Descent via the steep and difficult Flume Slide trail is definitely not recommended. Both the Liberty Spring trailhead and Flume Visitor Center parking lots are plowed.

The open summit of Mount Liberty provides an unobstructed view into the Pemigewasset Wilderness just to the east.

Watch out for snowmobiles along the bike path, which is a major snowmobile corridor trail.

View Guide

The open summit ledges provide one of the best 360-degree panoramas in the White Mountains. Perhaps the finest vista is eastward into the vast Pemigewasset Wilderness, but there are also fine vistas of the southern White Mountains, the Pemigewasset River valley, Franconia Notch and neighboring Franconia Range peaks.

Up the ridge to the N, beyond the rocky shoulder of Liberty, rises the bare peak of Mt. Lincoln, with Little Haystack below in front and the top of Lafayette just peering over in back on the R. To the R of the Franconias, looking NNE, you gaze up the big, remote valley of Lincoln Brook to the pyramid of Mt. Garfield, fronted with S-facing cliffs, at its head. Between the E slopes of the Franconias and Mt. Garfield is the distant range of mountains in the Nash Stream Forest, with West Peak on the L, the sharp peak of Sugarloaf on the R, and Bunnell and Gore Mtns. peering over in back in the middle. The tip of North Percy Peak pops out over the L slope of Garfield, with a spur of North Whitcomb (Muise) Mtn. behind on its L. Seen through the broad gap to the R of Garfield, beyond the lower eastern humps of Garfield Ridge, are Mt. Cabot (L) and Mts. Starr King and Waumbek (R). Cherry Mtn. is seen under Starr King. Next to the R is the great mass of North Twin, with Galehead Mtn. and the lower

N slope of Owl's Head Mtn. below and in front. Farther R the sharp little peak of South Twin soars above the long flat crest of Owl's Head, which itself rises impressively from the Lincoln Brook valley in the foreground. The western slide which forms part of the climbing route to Owl's Head can be seen farther R along the side of its ridge.

Continuing to the R, looking beyond a nearby flat NE spur of Liberty, the two slide-gashed cirques of Redrock Brook rise above the S end of the main Owl's Head ridgecrest; the rounded summit of Mt. Guyot is just to the R of the R cirque. Beyond the cirques and Guyot rise the high Presidentials: Mt. Adams and Mt. Jefferson (between the cirques), Mt. Clay (above the R cirque), Mt. Washington (just R of Guyot), and Mts. Eisenhower, Franklin and Monroe over the col to the R of Guyot, with Boott Spur beyond on the R. The Twin Range continues R across from Guyot to Mt. Bond, which rises above the sharp S peak of Owl's Head. West Bond can be seen in front of Bond to the L. The great craggy face of Bondcliff is to the R of Bond and lower, with Mt. Isolation (L) and Mt. Davis (R) seen over the col between them. To the R of Bondcliff, North and South Baldface peer over the S ridge of Davis, with Sable Mtn. and Chandler Mtn. farther R over the wide gap to the R of Davis, above the wooded S peak of Bondcliff. The tip of Eastman Mtn. peers over the Sable–Chandler col.

Next to the R are the distinctive Giant Stairs and the gravel-splotched mass of Mt. Resolution. North Doublehead peeks over the L end of Resolution, and in the distance between Stairs and North Doublehead is Maine's Streaked Mtn. Farther R, looking due E, is a beautiful long view up the remote East Branch valley to Mt. Nancy at its head, with Mt. Bemis peering over in back on the L. The tip of South Gemini just pokes up over the R slope of Nancy. To the R of Nancy is Mt. Anderson with Kearsarge North rearing up behind. Part of Mt. Lowell is seen to the R of Anderson, then Vose Spur and a nameless hump pile up to the dominant, hulking mass of Mt. Carrigain, which towers above lower northern spurs of Mt. Hancock. In the lower foreground in this direction is a NE spur ridge of Mt. Flume. The NW Peak of Hancock is just R of Carrigain in front, then the Hancock ridge, marked by a prominent slide, extends across to the rounded North and South Hancock and the lower, bold S spur overlooking Hancock Notch. The N peak of Mt. Hitchcock can be seen under South Hancock. Part of Green's Cliff is seen through the L side of Hancock Notch, and through the middle of the gap is Blue Mtn., a spur of Mt. Chocorua, with low hills in western Maine beyond. Mt. Huntington is to the R of Hancock Notch, with Mt. Chocorua and the Three Sisters beyond. Mt. Hitchcock is seen in closer, under the Three Sisters and the ridgeline of Huntington. Next to the R and close at hand to the SE is the great slide-streaked face of Mt. Flume, one of the outstanding features of the view from Liberty. Mt. Paugus is seen in the distance above Flume's summit crest, with little Potash Mtn. and the West Peak of Mt. Huntington below in front.

To the R of Flume is a jumble of peaks in the southern Whites. First comes Mt. Kancamagus in front with Mt. Passaconaway behind on the L and the three Tripyramids behind on the R. Distant Green Mtn. in Effingham is visible through the gap between Paugus and Passaconaway, and there's a glimpse of the summit crest of Mt. Whiteface between Middle and South Tripyramid. Next to the R and closer are the impressive Osceolas, seen over a lower S spur of Mt. Flume, with East Peak on the L and the main, Middle and West Peaks on the R. Sandwich Dome is behind the Osceolas on the R, with Whaleback Mtn. seen below and closer. The SW peak of the northern Flat Mtn. is seen over the ridge descending R from West Osceola. Next to the R is slide-marked Scar Ridge with Mt. Tecumseh rising behind. Belknap, Gunstock and Piper Mtns. (L to R) in the Belknap Range are seen over the ridge descending R from Tecumseh's spurs. Farther R is the ski-trailed North Peak of Loon Mtn. Behind North Loon on the L are ledgy Dickey (L) and Fisher (R) Mtns. and then the more distant Squam (L) and Campton (R) Ranges. Just to the R of the Loon ski trails is the mountain's South Peak, with part of Loon Pond visible below and flat-topped Prospect Mtn. in Holderness beyond. Bean Hill is on the horizon between the Loon peaks. The twin rounded Uncanoonuc Mtns. are on the horizon to the R of Prospect. Next to the R and close in, looking due S, is the wild hump of Big Coolidge Mtn. with wavy Hersey Mtn. in the distance. Joe English Hill can be spotted over the L side of Hersey. Russell Mtn. is behind Big Coolidge on the R, with the Bridgewater Mtns. in the middle distance and the Lyndeborough Mtns. on the skyline. Plymouth Mtn., also mid-distance, is to the R of the Bridgewaters, with Pack Monadnock Mtn. (L) and Crotched Mtn. (R) beyond.

A bit farther R, looking SSW, you look down on the town of Lincoln with a long view through the Pemigewasset River valley beyond and Mt. Kearsarge rising behind Ragged Mtn. on the horizon. To the R of Kearsarge, Tenney Mtn. is seen in the mid-distance with Forbes Mtn. (L) and Tinkham Hill (R) just behind it and Mt. Monadnock on the horizon. Lovewell Mtn. pops up behind Tinkham Hill on the R. To the R of Lovewell and closer is Stinson Mtn., with the prominent bald dome of Mt. Cardigan behind on the R, rising over the E spur of Mt. Kineo. Sunapee Mtn. is seen in the distance between Stinson and Cardigan. Down in front in this direction is Little Coolidge Mtn. with North Woodstock village beyond. A long ridge runs to the R from Cardigan above the long E ridges of Kineo and Mt. Cushman. Next to the R is the prominent bulk of Carr Mtn., with Mt. Kineo (L) and Mt. Cushman (R) in front. Croydon Peak rises in the distance to the R of Carr. To the R of Croydon is a broad gap separating Carr and Cushman from the Mt. Moosilauke massif; through this are seen Thompson Hill and associated ridges in Dorchester. Mt. Ascutney is seen in the distance over the R side of this gap, and next to the R is Smarts Mtn. peering over Moosilauke's Blue Ridge. On clear days Stratton Mtn. can be seen in the far distance between Ascutney and Smarts. Low down in this direction are the lower valley of Flume Brook and the strip of North Lincoln along US 3 and I-93. Vermont's Okemo Mtn. is in the distance to the R of Smarts. The Blue Ridge rises R to Mt. Waternomee and Mt. Jim, then Mt. Moosilauke itself rises impressively in the back, with Mt. Blue in front on the R. The Flume Visitor Center is seen down on the floor of the valley, in line with Moosilauke. Pico Peak in Vermont pokes up over the ridge descending R from Mt. Blue.

Farther R, lower and closer, is Mt. Wolf, with Bog Pond and Mt. Pemigewasset seen below its N ridge. Behind the N ridge of Wolf and the lower N ridge of Mt. Blue is the N ridge of Mt. Clough with the Benton Range rising just beyond, including (L to R) the flat crests of Jeffers Mtn. and The Hogsback, the bump of Sugarloaf Mtn. and the more prominent Black Mtn. A long chain of Green Mountain peaks is seen on the horizon in this WSW direction, including the ridges around Brandon and Middlebury Gaps over the Benton Range and the Breadloaf Mtn. group to the R of Black Mtn. Farther R, looking just N of W across lower Franconia Notch, is the great bulk of South Kinsman, with the long Mt. Abraham– Mt. Ellen ridge on the horizon to its L. Ledgy North Kinsman is next to the R, with Camel's Hump seen over its L side, and through the col between the Kinsmans is part of Vermont's Signal Mtn. range. To the R of North Kinsman the distant Worcester Range is seen over a nameless hump on Kinsman Ridge, and farther R Mt. Mansfield is seen over the West Cannon Ball and the Sterling Range above the Middle Cannon Ball. Lonesome Lake can be seen resting at the base of the Middle Cannon Ball. Next to the R the great bulk of Cannon Mtn. looms across the notch, with its cliffs and talus slopes mostly revealed. Northern Vermont's Cold Hollow Mtns. are seen on the horizon to the L of Cannon's summit, the Belvidere Mtn. range is just R of the summit, and the Jay Peaks are visible over the R side of Cannon's ledgy East Peak. Farther R, looking over the lower part of Mt. Lafayette's Old Bridle Path ridge, which closes in Franconia Notch on the R, are seen several peaks in Vermont's Northeast Kingdom (L to R): Mts. Hor and Pisgah around Willoughby Gap, Burke Mtn., Bald Mtn. and Umpire Mtn. Part of Greenleaf Hut is visible on the shoulder of Lafayette, off the L slope of Little Haystack.

NO. OF 4000-FOOTERS VISIBLE: 32

Mount Lincoln

ELEVATION: 5089 ft. / 1551 m   ORDER OF HEIGHT: 7
LOCATION: Franconia Range, Town of Franconia
USGS MAP: 7½' Franconia

Geography

Mt. Lincoln and Mt. Lafayette, its slightly higher neighbor to the N, are the two major summits along the narrow, barren, steep-sided crest of the upper Franconia Range. Lincoln's craggy top presents views just as stunning as those from Lafayette, and with over two miles of continuous views the loop hike over the two summits is one of the most popular treks in the White Mountains. Because of the heavy use in this area, hikers should take extra care to remain on the trail to protect the fragile vegetation of the alpine zone.

From many angles Mt. Lincoln presents a sharp, rocky peak rising from the ridgeline. The clearing by Lafayette Place Campground provides a dramatic view up to the pinnacle of Lincoln. The summit is actually an elongated crest with small knobs at either end; the S knob is the true summit, with the high point being a ledge marked by a large cairn on the W side of the trail. To the N the open ridge dips to a col, passes over a ledgy intermediate 5020-ft. peak (sometimes called Truman Peak), then rises to 5260-ft. Mt. Lafayette. To the S the ridge forms a knife edge with interesting rock formations as it descends from the summit of Lincoln, then it runs nearly level, still above treeline, to the small bare peak of Little Haystack Mtn. (4780 ft.) To the S of Little Haystack the ridgecrest is gentle for a short distance farther to a minor wooded peak, then descends sharply into the woods and extends 2 mi. across a broad forested saddle to its next summit, Mt. Liberty.

To the W the slopes of Mt. Lincoln plunge steeply into Franconia Notch. The upper slopes are impressively craggy and are scarred with numerous slides and naked rock slabs. Among these is a gully that has been referred to as "Lincoln's Throat." Nearby slabs were dubbed "Lincoln's Shaving Nicks" by the late Guy Waterman, who was conversant with every nook and cranny of Franconia Ridge. A sharp ridge, with a rocky arete near the top, drops westward right off the summit, then bends SW, dividing the ravine of Dry Brook on the S from that of the S branch of Walker Brook on the N. Another ridge descends W from the S end of the minor peak just N of Mt. Lincoln, splitting the two branches of Walker Brook. Two other westerly ridges come off Little Haystack Mtn., with the wet rock slab known as Shining Rock Cliff between them.

Looking north up the ridge toward Mount Lafayette from a point near the summit of Mount Lincoln.

To the E the slopes of Lincoln drop sharply into the valley of Lincoln Brook in the Pemigewasset Wilderness, with Owl's Head Mtn. rising beyond. A short rocky ridge descends directly E off the summit. Between the base of Mt. Lincoln and Lincoln Brook is a remote 3000-ft. plateau holding two beaver ponds. On this side of the ridge, between Lincoln and the small peak to the N, is the Lincoln Slide, a huge Y-shaped gash of gravel that is a distinctive landmark from distant points.

Nomenclature

In early days this sharp peak was included under the general term of the Franconia Haystacks, in reference to the array of pyramidal peaks presented by the Franconia Range when viewed from the S. The mountain was once called Mt. Pleasant, a name that appeared in Thomas Starr King's *The White Mountains: Their Legends, Landscape and Poetry*. (Not to be confused with Mt. Eisenhower, another former Mt. Pleasant.) Its current name honors President Abraham Lincoln. This name was apparently bestowed by a Mr. Fifield in the late 1800s. Little Haystack Mtn. was named for its similar but less imposing appearance near the Great Haystack (Mt. Lafayette). At an AMC field meeting in 1877, Professors Clarke and Cross recommended the name "Mt. Samoset" for the summit S of Mt. Lincoln (Little Haystack Mtn.), but the appellation did not stick. In his 1876 guidebook, Moses Sweetser referred to the peaks S of Mt. Lafayette as Mt. Lincoln (named after the "Matryr-President"), the "South Peak" (presumably today's Little Haystack) and then a wooded peak known as "The Haystack."

Historical Highlights

First Ascent: Unknown. Geographer Arnold Guyot is presumed to have climbed it sometime during his extensive explorations in the White Mountains in the mid / late 1800s.

Late 1850s: Small hotel, Mt. Lafayette House, is built near site of today's Lafayette Place Campground. Path for hotel guests is built to "Walker's Falls" on lower Dry Brook—precursor to lower part of today's Falling Waters Trail.

1876: Moses Sweetser's guidebook notes that from Mt. Lincoln "the views to the E., W. and S. are broad and beautiful." The walk from Lafayette over to Lincoln and the "South Peak" (today's Little Haystack) "takes about 2 hrs., and is comparatively easy" save for one belt of scrub. Much of the ridge is traversed by a "singular path-like trench, 1–2 ft. wide, which some people think has been made by countless generations of animals passing along the summit." For two-day traverse of Franconia Range, Sweetser recommends Levi E. Guernsey as "competent guide." His guidebook also extols beauty of cascades on Dry Brook.

1880: Charles E. Fay and a companion climb Mt. Lafayette, then cross the ridge to Mt. Lincoln and descend partway along its W ridge before plunging down a "sunless gorge," negotiating a precipitous drop into the ravine of Walker Brook without benefit of ropes. They bushwhack out to road in Franconia Notch, emerging after dark. Trip is written up in May 1881 *Appalachia*.

Mid-1880s: Trail route is opened across ridge from Lafayette to Lincoln and Little Haystack.

1889: Trail built from Mt. Liberty N to Little Haystack.

1897: Frank O. Carpenter cuts trail up steep W ridge of Lincoln, but it is soon rendered impassable by logging. "This new path cut in 1897 makes this splendid peak accessible to climbers with strong muscles and cool heads," writes Carpenter in his 1898 *Guide Book to the Franconia Notch and the Pemigewasset Valley*.

1903–1907: Lower E slopes of Mt. Lincoln are cut over by J. E. Henry's loggers, working from Camps 12 and 13 on Lincoln Brook spur of East Branch & Lincoln Railroad. In 1907, "Owl's Head fire" devastates large area, including lower E side of Mt. Lincoln.

1936: *AMC Guide* describes route to Owl's Head Mtn. that includes descent from Franconia Ridge via Lincoln Slide.

1958: Working for N.H. Dept. of Parks, Clyde Smith builds cascade-rich Falling Waters Trail from Lafayette Place to Little Haystack Mtn.

Late 1960s: AMC considers building trail from upper Franconia Ridge down to Lincoln Brook Trail in valley to E, but route is never laid out.

Late 1970s: To help trampled alpine vegetation recover, AMC and WMNF crew builds scree wall defining trail across Franconia Ridge. Also, Falling Waters Trail is relocated away from Shining Rock Cliff, which is now reached by spur path.

1980: Laura and Guy Waterman adopt Franconia Ridge Trail; during nearly two decades of their stewardship trail is carefully improved and vegetation recovers.

1984: E slopes of Lincoln are included in new 45,000-acre Pemigewasset Wilderness.

Trail Approaches

West Approach from Franconia Notch Parkway (I-93) at Lafayette Place

MT. LINCOLN ONLY, OUT AND BACK

Falling Waters Trail, Franconia Ridge Trail
7.8 mi. round trip, 3450-ft. elevation gain

LOOP OVER MT. LINCOLN AND MT. LAFAYETTE

Falling Waters Trail, Franconia Ridge Trail, Greenleaf Trail,
Old Bridle Path
8.9 mi. loop, 3900-ft. elevation gain

TRAILHEAD (1780 ft.): Falling Waters Trail starts at large hiker's parking area on E side of Franconia Notch Parkway, across from Lafayette Place Campground. Parking also available on W side of road, with 0.1 mi. paved path leading under road to E side.

The steep but scenic Falling Waters Trail provides the shortest access to Mt. Lincoln. The last 0.8 mi. of this route is completely in the open and should be avoided in bad weather. Because the ridge is exposed and narrow, it's a dangerous place in a thunderstorm. Hikers should be sure to walk only on the marked footpath to protect the delicate alpine vegetation on the ridge Also, caution is advised, especially descending, on wet ledges in area of the waterfalls.

From parking area, Falling Waters Trail and Old Bridle Path coincide at first, starting up paved walkway past restrooms on R and entering hardwood forest. Easy climbing brings trail alongside Walker Brook, and at 0.2 mi. Falling Waters Trail diverges R, crossing Walker Brook on footbridge. Trail climbs parallel to brook, then swings R at easy grade, traversing southward through hardwoods across base of Lincoln's W ridge. After slight descent, at 0.7 mi. / 2000 ft. Dry Brook is crossed (difficult in high water). Trail scrambles up S bank and turns sharp L to follow rough course along brook past Stairs Falls (small but pretty) and Sawteeth Ledges. At 0.9 mi. recross brook at base of twisting Swiftwater Falls. Walk up slippery ledges by base of falls, then climb rock staircase up steep bank beyond, and swing R across washout with peek back to South Kinsman. Trail ascends along brook past several small cascades, then picks up old logging road and climbs moderately up narrow valley. Rougher stretch leads to base of lacy, 80-ft. Cloudland Falls at 1.3 mi / 2500 ft. Steep, rocky climb—with dropoff on R and fairly difficult scramble up through crevice at upper end—leads to top of falls, where a few yards R ledge at brink offers view SW to Mt. Moosilauke, Mt. Wolf and SE spur of South Kinsman. Just above are two small waterfalls where two branches of Dry Brook converge.

Trail follows L side of brook, soon crosses brook to R, scrambles up through slippery, ledgy area, then crosses stream back to L and climbs steadily with numerous rock steps. At 1.6 mi. / 2860 ft. it crosses brook back to R and follows old logging road up to SE at easy grade. Trail swings L on another old logging road, then bears L again and begins long, fairly steep ascent through firs over rocky footway, with several short switchbacks. At 2.8 mi. / 4130 ft. side path R descends 100 yds. / 75 ft. to base of Shining Rock Cliff, large, wet rock slab that is dangerous to ascend. Here there is view W to Kinsmans and Mt. Moosilauke. Main trail bears L at this jct., then soon swings R and climbs steep, rough, rocky section directly up slope. Trees diminish in size and views W start to appear, and trail emerges from scrub just below jct. with Franconia Ridge Trail at 3.2 mi. / 4760 ft., by bare nubble summit of Little Haystack. (If returning this way, note carefully where trail emerges from scrub.)

Turn L (N) on Franconia Ridge Trail and traverse open, nearly level ridge on treadway well-defined by low rock walls. Views are spectacular to E and W; ahead Mt. Lincoln looms as impressive rocky pyramid. Cross small rocky hump, then at 3.7 mi. traverse ledges on E side of wild knife edge section of ridge with jutting crags and climb steadily up cone of Mt. Lincoln. Open rocky summit is reached at 3.9 mi. / 5089 ft.

North Approach from Mt. Lafayette

If traversing open ridge from Mt. Lafayette (see that chapter for its approaches), follow Franconia Ridge Trail S off summit, descending moderately over ledges, then swinging R and L in open on footway lined with scree walls. Descend past crags (on L), level out on shoulder in low scrub, then continue down to 4900-ft. col, where there is patch of scrub, at 0.4 mi. Climb moderately to top of rocky 5020-ft. hump ("Truman Peak") at 0.5 mi.; in this area huge, gravelly Lincoln Slide can be seen down on slope to E (L), with Pemi Wilderness beyond. Trail descends moderately to second 4900-ft. saddle, climbs fairly steep ledgy pitch, briefly levels, then proceeds up at easy grade, passing over small knob and reaching summit of Mt. Lincoln, 1.0 mi. from Lafayette. Beyond, it is 0.7 mi. in open to jct. with Falling Waters Trail by summit of Little Haystack.

South Approach from Liberty Spring Trail
Franconia Ridge Trail can be followed from top of Liberty Spring Trail along wooded, mostly gentle ridge to jct. with Falling Waters Trail. This is most lightly used section of ridge trail. From Liberty Spring jct. (4260 ft.), Franconia Ridge Trail descends gradually for 0.7 mi. to 4060-ft. col between Liberty and Little Haystack. Ridge walk continues pleasant through nice fir forest until moderate, then steep climb leads to S end of Little Haystack ridge. Near top, ledge provides fine view S down ridge to Liberty and Flume. Trail levels through scrub, then emerges above treeline and reaches jct. L with Falling Waters Trail at 1.8 mi. from Liberty Spring jct.

Winter

By White Mountain standards, Mt. Lincoln is a serious winter mountaineering destination with great exposure to wind and storms and a possible mix of snow, ice and rock on the ridge. It should be attempted only in clear weather as whiteout conditions can make the trails very hard to follow. A hiker fatality on Little Haystack in the winter of 2008 underscores that this can be a very dangerous ridge in severe conditions. Full winter clothing and gear, including crampons, are required. Falling Waters Trail is often packed out, but is a fairly difficult winter trail, especially if icy around the waterfalls. If descending Falling Waters after a ridge traverse, note that the trail may be hard to locate where it enters the scrub if it's not broken out. If attempting the Lincoln–Lafayette loop, see additional cautionary notes in Winter section of Mt. Lafayette chapter.

View Guide

Mt. Lincoln's sharp, open summit is a premier vantage for reconnoitering the Pemigewasset Wilderness to the E, Franconia Notch and mountains beyond to the W, and the Sandwich and Osceola groups to the S. Though smaller than the spacious summit of Lafayette, it is likely to be much less crowded. There is a fine ledge perch on the E side of the summit.

To the N, up the ridge, is the nearby rocky pyramid of Mt. Lafayette, with the winding route of the Franconia Ridge Trail clearly visible, leading over the intermediate Truman Peak. Part of distant Goback Mtn. juts out off the R slope of Lafayette, and farther R is the Nash Stream range, including (L to R) West Peak, Bunnell Mtn. (in back), Gore Mtn. and Sugarloaf. To the R of the Nash Streams and farther is a ridge leading R up to North Whitcomb (Muise) Mtn., with the Percy Peaks in front. Next to the R the Pilot Ridge, including sharp Hutchins Mtn., is seen in front with Long Mtn.'s rolling crest beyond. To the R of the Pilots is the broad bulk of Mt. Cabot, then the view swings R and in to the distinctive cone of Mt. Garfield with its S cliffs well-displayed, seen nearby to the NE across the broad forested basins of Lincoln and Franconia Brooks in the Pemigewasset Wilderness. In succession behind Garfield are Cherry Mtn. and the Pliny Range, the latter with Mt. Starr King on its L end, just R of Mt. Cabot, Mt. Waumbek and its long E ridge in the center, and Pliny Mtn. on its R end. Farther R and closer a long ridge leads up over Nubble Peak and a high shoulder to the rounded summit of North Twin. The flat Cambridge Black Mtn. is seen in the distance over Nubble Peak, with East Kennebago Mtn. on the horizon to the L.

The Crescent Range (Black Crescent Mtn. on the L, Mt. Crescent on the R) is seen above the North Twin shoulder, with Bemis Mtn. (L) and Elephant Mtn. (R) seen in the distance over Mt. Crescent. The long ridge of Old Blue Mtn. extends R of Elephant. Old Speck Mtn. in the Mahoosucs is seen right over North Twin. South Twin's sharp little cone is to the R of North Twin, with the bare pyramids of Mts. Adams (L) and Jefferson (R) rising majestically behind and between them and Galehead Mtn. huddled low down in front. Mt. Clay is seen in back and just R of South Twin, and Mt. Washington rises next to the R. In the foreground leading across to the Twins are the broad, remote wooded upper basin of Franconia Brook (under North Twin) and the sharply cut valley of Twin Brook (under South Twin).

Barren Boott Spur extends to the R from Mt. Washington, with Mts. Monroe, Eisenhower and Pierce (L to R) seen underneath. Wooded Slide Peak is to the R of Boott Spur, with the top of Carter Dome peeking over on its L and Rainbow Ridge seen over Wildcat C on its R. Mt. Field is seen under Rainbow Ridge and above a col in the Twin Range; just R of that col is the rounded double summit of Mt. Guyot rising above the slide-scarred S cirque of Redrock Brook. In the foreground is the low N ridge of Owl's Head. Mt. Isolation is behind Field on the R, with Mt. Jackson just poking up between them. Mt. Willey peers over the R summit of Guyot, with North Baldface behind on its L and South Baldface on its R. Over the saddle to the R of Guyot, Sable Mtn. (L) and Chandler Mtn. (R) rise behind the level crest of Mt. Davis. Maine's Streaked Mtn. is visible in the distance just R of Chandler. Next to the R is massive Mt. Bond with West Bond seen in front. Lurking beyond the Lincoln Brook valley, close by to the E and SE down in the Pemi Wilderness, is the long, level, wooded ridge of Owl's Head, with the slide that provides part of the route to its summit seen towards the R (S) end of the ridge. Seen over the N end of the main crest of Owl's Head, to the R of Mt. Bond, is the craggy face of Bondcliff.

Between Bond and Bondcliff in the back are (L to R) Mt. Resolution with Mt. Shaw peering over its R side, the twin Gemini, and Rickers Knoll. Above and beyond Bondcliff, the blue dome of Kearsarge North rises behind Mt. Bemis. Mt. Nancy is seen behind Bondcliff on the R, with Mts. Anderson and Lowell farther R across a wide gap. Through that gap is seen Hurricane Mtn. with Maine's Pleasant Mtn. lurking behind, and Black Cap Mtn. is seen above Mt. Anderson. In the distance over Lowell and Vose Spur are small, distant hills near Sebago Lake in Maine. Farther R, seen over the S end of Owl's Head's summit crest, is massive Mt. Carrigain, with Vose Spur on its L facing across Carrigain Notch to Mt. Lowell. Part of North Moat Mtn. is seen through the gap to the R of Vose Spur. Through the gap to the R of Mt. Carrigain are Mt. Tremont (L) and Bear Mtn. (R), with the Bill Merrill Mtn. group in the distance to the R of Bear. Farther R North Hancock bulks large above the sharp S peak of Owl's Head, with South Hancock and the lower Juno Peak to its R. Mt. Chocorua's sharp peak is above Juno. Farther R Mt. Paugus rises beyond Mt. Huntington, with small hills along the Maine / New Hampshire border (in the Madison–Parsonfield area) in the distance between Chocorua and Paugus.

The great pyramid of Mt. Passaconaway is next to the R, rising beyond the lower Lincoln Brook valley and the sprawling ridges of Mt. Hitchcock. Green Mtn. in Effingham is seen between Paugus and Passaconaway. Mt. Tripyramid is to the R of Passaconaway, with Mt. Whiteface peering over in back and Mt. Kancamagus in front. Next to the R Mt. Shaw in the Ossipee Range is seen through Mad River Notch, with East Osceola on the R side of the gap. Farther R is the main summit of Osceola, with Mt. Roberts in the Ossipees poking over the col to its L. Sandwich Dome's double summit is behind Osceola on the R. Continuing to the R, Mt. Tecumseh (in back) and Scar Ridge are seen over the sharp summit of Mt. Flume rising from the S end of Franconia Ridge. Belknap, Gunstock and Piper Mtns. (L to R) in the Belknap Range are in the distance over the R shoulder of Tecumseh. Looking due S and close in, the barren crest of Franconia Ridge twists southward to the bare nubble of Little Haystack Mtn., with Mt. Liberty's rocky pyramid behind. The ski trails of Loon Mtn. are behind Liberty on the L, with the Campton Range sprawling beyond. Bean Hill is in the distance over the R end of the Campton Range, and Prospect Mtn. in Holderness is directly above Liberty, with the twin Uncanoonuc Mtns. on the horizon a bit to the R. Off the R slope of Liberty is part of Big Coolidge Mtn. with Russell Mtn. seen above and wavy Hersey Mtn. on the horizon. Farther R is the lower wooded peak of Little Haystack with Little Coolidge just above and the Pemigewasset River valley leading out to many distant hills. The Bridgewater Mtns. are above the rock peak of Little Haystack, with Plymouth Mtn. to their R.

On clear days, North Pack Monadnock (L) and Crotched Mtn. (R) are visible on the horizon over Plymouth Mtn., with the Lyndeborough Mtns. seen over the Bridgewaters. Prominent on the horizon over the wooded Little Haystack peak is Mt. Kearsarge. Ragged Mtn. is seen in front of Kearsarge on the R, and a bit farther R Forbes Mtn. is seen behind Tenney Mtn. Tinkham Hill is behind and R of Tenney, with Mt. Monadnock on the skyline to its L. Next to the R and closer is Stinson Mtn., seen behind the long E ridge of Mt. Kineo. The round hump of Lovewell Mtn. is on the horizon just R of Stinson. Farther R is prominent Mt. Cardigan behind more of Kineo's E ridge, with sprawling Sunapee Mtn. behind it on the L. Farther R, beyond spur ridges of Cardigan, Carr Mtn. looms behind the nearer Mt. Cushman and Mt. Kineo. Through the gap to the R of Carr, Croydon Peak rises sharply above Thompson Hill.

Next to the R and closer the long Blue Ridge leads R up to Mt. Moosilauke, which dominates the SW view, rising beyond Mt. Wolf. The humpbacked Smarts Mtn. is seen in back over the Blue Ridge, with Mt. Ascutney on the horizon to its L. On very clear days Stratton Mtn. is visible over the R side of Smarts.

Down low in the direction of the Blue Ridge, Mt. Pemigewasset rises above I-93, with a cliff-faced northern spur to its R. The broad Mt. Clough is behind Moosilauke on the R, with part of Piermont Mtn. seen just to its L. To the R of Clough are the long, flat Benton Range summits of Jeffers Mtn. and The Hogsback, punctuated by the knob of Sugarloaf Mtn. on the R. Killington and Pico Peaks are on the Vermont horizon above Jeffers. Next to the R are South Kinsman (L) and North Kinsman (R), seen to the WSW across Franconia Notch, with Lonesome Lake nestling on a plateau in front of North Kinsman. Peering down to the floor of the Notch, one can see the Lafayette Place parking area. Black Mtn. in the Benton Range peeks over the R side of South Kinsman. On clear days a long chain of Green Mountain ridges in the Brandon and Middlebury Gap areas can be seen across the horizon above the Kinsmans. The lower ridge of the Cannon Balls extends R from North Kinsman, with the Cobble Hill–Moody Ledge–Green Mtn. ridge just beyond. The Breadloaf Mtn. group is on the Vermont skyline over the L end of the Cannon Balls ridge and the long Mt. Abraham–Mt. Ellen ridge is over the R side. Just N of W, across the ravine of Walker Brook and the ledgy, lower Agony Ridge followed by Old Bridle Path, is the great bulk of Cannon Mt. fronted by its huge cliffs and talus slopes. Behind and between the Cannon Balls and Cannon are Cooley Hill (L) and Cole Hill (R), with Vermont's lumpy Signal Mtn. range beyond. The distinctive Camel's Hump is on the horizon above Cannon, with Ethan Allen Mtn. on its L. Cannon's NW Peak is behind the main summit on the R. In the distance to the R of NW Cannon, seen over vast lowlands and long, low ridges, is the Worcester Range near Stowe, Vermont, and farther R are Mt. Mansfield and the Sterling Range.

Looking NW out to the horizon over the upper Agony Ridge and the shoulder of Lafayette, and little Bald Mtn. down at the N end of Franconia Notch, one sees more peaks in the northern Green Mountains (L to R): Laraway Mtn., the Cold Hollow Mtns., the pyramid of Belvidere Mtn. above Greenleaf Hut and a winding section of I-93, Tillotson Peak, Haystack Mtn. above Franconia village, and the prominent, sharp Jay Peaks. To the R of the Jays one can spot some of the Sutton Mtns. in Quebec. Farther R, beyond the town of Littleton and Moore Reservoir, Mt. Hor (L) and Mt. Pisgah (R) frame Willoughby Gap. Next to the R are the paired Burke (L) and Umpire (R, over Miles Mtn.) Mtns., with the Northeast Kingdom's Bald Mtn. seen in back between them. To the R of these is East Haven Mtn., then the view comes back to the L slope of Mt. Lafayette.

NO. OF 4000-FOOTERS VISIBLE: 38

KINSMAN–MOOSILAUKE
REGION

Cannon Mountain

ELEVATION: 4100 ft. / 1250 m   ORDER OF HEIGHT: 36
LOCATION: Kinsman Ridge, Town of Franconia
USGS MAP: 7½′ Franconia

Geography

A sprawling, bulky and very rugged mountain at the N end of Kinsman Ridge, Cannon (or Profile) Mountain is one of the most visited peaks in the region, and the reasons for that are mutli-fold.

Besides being a mountain that tops the 4000-ft. mark in elevation, Cannon was long the home of the most recognizable face in the state—New Hampshire's granite symbol, the Old Man of the Mountain, also known as The Profile and the Great Stone Face. It also boasts the largest cliff face in the East and some of the state's most challenging downhill ski terrain at the Cannon Mountain Ski Area on the N slopes. And, lest we forget, its summit is serviced year-round by the famous Cannon Mountain Aerial Tramway, erected on the mountain in 1937 and put into service the following year.

Cannon Mountain's massive girth forms the W wall of scenic Franconia Notch. The peak rests solely in the town of Franconia, from which the notch below gained its name. Kinsman Ridge, of which Cannon is the northernmost peak, runs more than 10 miles S to N from Kinsman Notch to Franconia Notch. Mt. Wolf, the summits of North and South Kinsman Mtns., and the three intervening rounded ridgeline humps known as the Cannon Balls (3693 ft., 3660 ft. and 3769 ft., W to E) are all southern ridgemates of Cannon. The Northeast Cannon Ball is one of New England's Hundred Highest peaks and is separated from the main mass of Cannon by the deep, U-shaped Coppermine Col. The S slopes of the Cannon Balls are drained by several branches of Cascade Brook.

The valley of the main stem of the Pemigewasset River separates Cannon Mountain and the other peaks of Kinsman Ridge from the craggy heights of Mt. Lafayette and the Franconia Range on the opposite side of the Notch. To the N, the minor mountain ridge connecting the low summits of Bald Mountain and Artist's Bluff (both 2340 ft.) serves as a natural barrier between Cannon's lower slopes and the deep valley in which lies Franconia village. Meadow Brook flows NNW from the little gap that divides Cannon and Bald Mtns. To the W of the mountain lies the broad, flat Easton Valley, traversed by the Ham Branch of the Gale River, into which flows Coppermine Brook, a scenic mountain stream draining a deep, secluded ravine enclosed by Cannon and the Cannon Balls. The beautiful Bridal Veil Falls, accessible via the Coppermine Trail, is tucked into this basin. Farther up the brook are the little-known Holden Falls and Noble Falls.

Cannon itself is composed of three main masses, stretching out, more or less, in an E-to-W pattern. The main summit, in the middle, houses the Aerial Tramway summit building, most of the ski lifts and trails, and, on the actual high point, a new (1995) observation tower and deck. A broad, level shoulder extends S from the summit, ending abruptly in cliffs overlooking Lonesome Lake, a 14-acre pond nestled on a high plateau to the S.

Cannon's flat-topped East Peak (3860 ft.) was home to the Old Man of the Mountain and rises above the sheared-off walls which form the spectacular Cannon Cliffs—at 1000 ft. the biggest rock face in the East and a renowned venue for rock and ice climbing. The Old Man had long been storied in prose and poetry, with perhaps the most famous quote being that from New Hampshire native Daniel Webster: "Up in the Franconia Mountains God Almighty has hung out a sign to show that in New England He makes men." Below the cliffs is a vast, steep slope of large talus, also unrivalled in the eastern mountains. This is an active cliff, where huge rock chunks occasionally break off to join the thousands of blocks jumbled below. Between the S side of the East Peak and the E side of the main summit's S ridge is an impressive steep-sided bowl, with additional talus slopes.

Slightly NW from the main summit is an open 3620-ft. foot sub-peak, with fine views, which formerly hosted the Mittersill ski resort and is sometimes called Mt. Mittersill or Mittersill Peak. Cannon's main summit and the Mittersill summit are connected by the 1¾-mile long Taft Ski Trail, New Hampshire's first ski racing trail. Two ridges descend NW from the Mittersill peak, with Tucker Brook flowing between them, and another drops to the N.

Some 2000 ft. below Cannon's true summit, on the floor of the great mountain pass of Franconia Notch, lie two of the region's most scenic tarns—Echo and Profile Lakes. Between the two is the base terminal of the Aerial Tramway, which in just seven minutes can whisk as many as eighty passengers from the relative comfort of the notch floor to the oftimes cold and clammy mountaintop.

Trail routes to Cannon's summit are short but quite steep, rocky and rugged. There are good views at several points on the mountain's flanks and a 360-degree panorama from the summit tower. Please note that hiking is not allowed on the ski trails.

Nomenclature

The peak which we all know as Cannon Mtn. has been known alternately over the years by several different names. Its present name is derived from an oblong rock near the East Peak, which from a distance resembles the outline of a cannon. This name appeared on George P. Bond's 1853 map of the White Mtns. As early as 1827 the mountain was known as Profile Mountain or Old Man's Mountain, in deference to the "Great Stone Face" which until 2003 jutted out from the mountain's easternmost shoulder. The Profile Mtn. name has received widespread use over the years, but the Cannon Mtn. name was officially adopted by the U.S. Board on Geographic Names in 1972. Philip Carrigain's 1816 map of New Hampshire, the most complete map of the state at that time, identified the peak as Freak Mtn. On one map from the early 1900s, the NW peak of Cannon was named Mt. Jackson, presumably for President Andrew Jackson, and this name was at one time also applied to the main summit. Profile Lake was originally called "Ferrin's Pond." Lonesome Lake was named by William C. Prime, the famed angler and author who built a camp on its shore in the late 1800s. Previously the pond had been known as Tamarack Pond and Moran Lake. The rounded Cannon Balls were obviously named for their resemblance to the type of shot used in the artillery of the 1800s. Coppermine Brook was so named due to copper mines in the area, the ore from which was processed at foundries in nearby Franconia village.

Historical Highlights

First Ascent: Unknown

1773: First settlers arrive in town of Franconia to N of Cannon. Town is incorporated in 1782. Rough wagon road is established through Franconia Notch.

1805: Luke Brooks and Francis Whitcomb, two workers on survey crew laboring in Franconia Notch, are first to "discover" Old Man of the Mountain while stopping for break at present-day Profile Lake. They declare it to be likeness of then-President Thomas Jefferson.

1813: State of New Hampshire builds upgraded road through Franconia Notch; is incorporated as "Pemigewasset Turnpike" in 1820.

1828: First printed account of Old Man appears in the *American Journal of Science and Arts*, drawing more visitors to Franconia Notch. Also in this year, artist Thomas Cole is first to document use of name, "Old Man of the Mountain."

1835: Lafayette House tavern is built in Franconia Notch near Echo Lake by Stephen and Joseph Gibbs.

1841: First photograph of Old Man is taken by Dr. Samuel Bemis, Boston dentist and habitue of Crawford Notch.

1850: Nathaniel Hawthorne immortalizes Old Man in epic short story, *The Great Stone Face*.

1853: 110-room Profile House opens at base of mountain, approximately 500 ft. SE of present day tramway station. Lafayette House is moved and incorporated into Profile House complex. Hostelry is expanded over years and rebuilt in 1905, and gains renown as one of great grand hotels in White Mtns. In later years bridle path to Lonesome Lake is developed for use of guests.

1855: John Spaulding, in tourist guide *Historical Relics of the White Mountains*, writes, "A footpath from the Lafayette House leads directly over the top of the old man's head and sometimes a mortal may be seen standing mong the bristly hair (bushes) of the old man's foretop."

1859: Writer and fishing enthusiast William C. Prime discovers Lonesome Lake on plateau just S of Cannon; on first visit he catches 45 trout. Seventeen years later (1876) he and William Bridges would build cabin on E side of pond, hosting famous guests such as General George B. McClellan, Union commander during Civil War.

1859: In his classic *The White Hills: Their Legends, Landscape and Poetry*, Thomas Starr King writes of Cannon: "The whole mountain from which the Profile starts is one of the noblest specimens of majestic rock that can be seen in New Hampshire."

1864: Edward Roth publishes *Christus Judex, A Traveller's Tale*, a romantic story about the Old Man.

1867: *Eastman's White Mountain Guide* makes reference to trail "which seems to lead almost directly from the front of the [Profile House] to the summit."

1869: President Ulysses S. Grant is guest at Profile House.

1871: State Geologist Charles H. Hitchcock notes that only the lower E summit of the mountain is generally visited, the apex being still covered by trees. He cites measurements showing Old Man ledges to be 36–40 ft. in height, at an elevation 1200 ft. above Profile Lake.

1874: Under direction of Dartmouth professor E. T. Quimby, U.S. Coast Survey sets up observation station on summit, marked by bolt and triangle.

1876: Moses Sweetser's *The White Mountains: A Handbook for Travellers* calls the Old Man "the most remarkable phenomenon of the kind in the world." He notes that profile may not last much longer due to "rapid decomposition of the granite" and cites Charles H. Hitchcock's warning: "I would advise any persons who are anxious to see the Profile for themselves, to hasten to the spot, for fear of disappointment."

Sweetser's guide mentions "rude path" leading from Profile House up to ledges of East Peak.

Ca. 1877: Professors Cross and Clarke ascend to true summit from path's end on East Peak, then bushwhack down to Lonesome Lake, where they "were almost stopped by the precipitous face which fronts toward the lake."

1879: Profile and Franconia Notch Railroad Co. constructs narrow-gauge RR from Bethlehem to Profile House.

1881: Trail built by AMC up Coppermine Brook valley to Bridal Veil Falls.

1916: Rev. Guy Roberts of Whitefield and stone quarry superintendent Edward Geddes of Quincy, Mass. climb to top of Old Man and install turnbuckles in effort to prevent rocks which comprise profile from breaking off mountain. Second edition of *AMC Guide* notes that path from Profile House only goes to E summit; main summit "can be reached only by a hard scramble of about 1 hr. through dense scrub."

1917: AMC trail crews begin construction of Kinsman Ridge Trail, linking Kinsman Notch to the S with Kinsmans, Cannon Balls, Cannon Mtn. and Franconia Notch. Route is completed in 1919.

1918: AMC crews build trail from Lonesome Lake to Kinsman Ridge Trail in Coppermine Col.

1923: Second Profile House (built after original hotel was torn down in 1905) is leveled by major fire. Soon afterwards, following extensive fund-raising drive led by Society for Protection of N.H. Forests and N.H. Federation of Women's Clubs, hotel baron Karl Abbott sells Franconia Notch holdings (including Old Man) to state of New Hampshire. Franconia Notch becomes state park in 1928.

1928: Climbers Robert L. M. Underhill and Lincoln O'Brien make first ascent of Cannon Cliff.

1929: Hassler Whitney and Bradley Gilman climb exposed arete on Cannon Cliff, establishing famed Whitney–Gilman route.

1929: AMC leases, renovates former William C. Prime cabin on Lonesome Lake and opens it to use by campers in following year.

1932: Civilian Conservation Corps cuts first ski racing trail (Richard Taft Trail) on mountain, over NW summit. "A wide variety of turns lends excitement," notes a ski guidebook of the era. First descent is made in February 1933 by Austrian Sig Buchmayr, who is ski instructor at Peckett's inn at nearby Sugar Hill. In subsequent years Coppermine Ski Trail is cut, leading from Taft Trail down to Bridal Veil Falls and NH 116, along with adjacent Tucker Brook Ski Trail descending from Coppermine Trail into next valley to N.

Ca. 1935: Shelter built near Bridal Veil Falls. Rough trail can be followed from there up to Kinsman Ridge between Middle and West Cannon Balls.

1938: America's first Aerial Tramway, whisking visitors from floor of Notch to Cannon summit in minutes, opens for first summer season.

1939: Actress Bette Davis, staying in nearby Sugar Hill, becomes lost on hike along Coppermine Brook and is rescued by Arthur Farnsworth, whom she marries in 1940.

1945: Old Man of Mountain becomes official state symbol of New Hampshire.

1946: Mittersill Ski Area is opened on N slopes of NW Peak by Austrian baron Hubert von Pantz. Accompanying alpine-style village is developed at base.

1951: After first being on display at Eastern States Exposition in Springfield, Mass., steel fire lookout tower is erected on summit.

1955: President Dwight D. Eisenhower visits Notch as part of celebration of 150th Anniversary of Old Man's discovery. U.S. Postal Service issues 3-cent Old Man stamp.

1955: State park worker Clyde Smith locates and cuts new Hi-Cannon Trail, linking lower Lonesome Lake Trail to Kinsman Ridge Trail and thence the summit.

1958: State of New Hampshire oversees extensive reinforcement of ledges forming Old Man, including installation of four turnbuckles.

1964: State builds, leases new structures at SW corner of Lonesome Lake. Is later purchased outright by AMC and operated as Lonesome Lake Hut.

1965: Niels Nielsen takes over annual maintenance of Old Man.

1967: Northeast Cannon Ball is included on new list of New England Hundred Highest Peaks compiled by AMC.

1967: World Cup ski races held at Cannon; French skier Jean Claude Killy sweeps downhill, slalom and giant slalom.

1971: Ice climber John Bouchard makes legendary solo ascent of Black Dike on Cannon Cliff.

1980: New tramway with 80-passenger cars replaces original lift from 1938.

1981: Summit fire tower is taken out of service.

1988: Unique stretch of I-93, Franconia Notch Parkway, is opened through Notch after years of controversy and negotiations. U.S. Postal Service releases another Old Man stamp.

1991: Niels F. Nielsen retires after several decades of service as caretaker of Old Man; tradition is carried on by his son, David.

1995: New observation tower built on summit.

1997: Major rockfall on Cannon Cliff, scar easily visible from Franconia Notch Parkway. Among debris is mammoth boulder weighing an estimated 20 to 30 tons, which comes to rest a short distance above bike path through Notch.

2000: Old Man is featured on New Hampshire Quarter issued by U.S. Mint, ninth in series of fifty States Commemorative Quarters.

2002: Lonesome Lake Hut opens in winter for first time.

2003: In early morning hours on May 3, following heavy rainstorm, ledges

The Kinsman Ridge Trail works its way through a boulder-strewn, semi-open stretch before attaining the main summit ridge and the state-maintained Rim Trail.

forming Old Man collapse and tumble to talus slope below Cannon Cliffs. Rumble is heard by two rock climbers sleeping in van near Profile Lake. State Park workers on litter cleanup duty discover fall of Old Man at 7:30 that morning.

Trail Approaches

Northeast Approach from Cannon Mtn. Tramway parking area off Franconia Notch Parkway (I-93)

Kinsman Ridge Trail
4.4 mi. round trip, 2200-ft. elevation gain

TRAILHEAD (1980 ft.): Parking for the N end of Kinsman Ridge Trail is at Cannon Mountain Aerial Tramway parking lot, off Exit 34B from Franconia Notch Parkway (I-93). Hiker parking is indicated at S end of parking lots.

This trail provides the most direct ascent of the mountain, reaching the top of the Cannon Cliffs, where there are magnificent views, in just 1.5 mi. and the main summit in 2.2 mi. Like all the routes on Cannon, it is steep and rough and generally takes longer than the distance would suggest.

From S end of Tramway parking lot, follow gravel road ca. 150 yds. to picnic area, turn R and walk 80 yds. across grassy area at base of ski slope, and turn L into woods at sign for Kinsman Ridge Trail. After traversing L for ca. 0.1 mi, trail swings R and begins rather steep, winding climb, with gravelly footing, through hardwood forest. At 0.4 mi. / 2400 ft. trail bends L and climbs a badly eroded gravelly section with poor footing; in places the trail has been worn down to a deep trench. Trail continues winding steeply upward through more eroded sections, now in dense birch and conifer forest. At ca. 2700 ft. trail gets rockier, and at 0.8 mi. / 2800 ft. it enters area that has been partly cleared for ski trail known as"Kinsman Glade". (On descent, look for hiking trail entering woods ahead where brushy ski route angles down to L.) Trail now becomes quite rocky, with some slippery ledges, as it swings back and forth across ski glade four times (R, L, R, and L again), while climbing steeply. At third crossing there is partial view to NW; above here it climbs slippery slabs, parallel to the ski glade. After fourth crossing trail angles R up to L edge of brushy ski trail, bends L and follows it, then runs along upper edge of open ski glade with views out to N and NW to peaks in northern New Hampshire and Vermont. From here hiking trail runs along L edge of ski trail (used by skiers to access Kinsman Glade). At 1.2 mi. / 3450 ft. Kinsman Ridge Trail turns L off ski trail (signs) and enters conifer forest; ahead, in summer, ski trail is roped off. Hiking trail now climbs steadily to SE with rocky footing, easing off as broad crest of Cannon's East Peak is attained. Trail runs level through high scrub for some distance, and at 1.5 mi. / 3800 ft., where main trail turns sharp R (WSW), spur path, marked by sign, "OUTLOOK," continues ahead (SE) through scrub and descends gradually for 200 ft. to broad open ledges with spectacular views of Franconia Notch, Franconia Range and distant mountains to N and S. This is fine lunch and viewing spot and is well worth short side trip.

From jct. with spur path to top of cliffs, Kinsman Ridge Trail climbs gently over wooded summit of East Peak, descends moderately past viewpoint S to flat, muddy col, then winds up through scrub with partial views back. You now climb to open slab where trail swings R; here there is wide view to E and S. Trail climbs through scrub with more views, then angles L in open across jumbled talus boulders with views down into bowl to SE. Several more switchbacks through scrubby, rocky, semi-alpine terrain lift you to gravel Rim Trail at 2.0 mi. / 4050 ft. Kinsman Ridge Trail turns L onto Rim Trail and follows it along steep E edge of summit area, with excellent views. Gravel path then swings R into woods and at 2.2 mi., where Kinsman Ridge Trail bears L on narrower footway to continue southward, signed gravel path on R ("Short Path") leads 100 yds. up to summit and observation tower deck, reached by climbing several sets of stairs. Gravel path continues ahead past tower, descending to summit Tramway station, where other end of Rim Trail is met. (Tramway station and then summit can also be accessed by turning R on Rim Trail where Kinsman Ridge Trail first joins it after it climbs from col with East Peak.)

Southeast Approaches from Lafayette Place
on Franconia Notch Parkway/I-93

TRAILHEAD (1770 ft.): These approaches to Cannon start at parking area for Lonesome Lake Trail at Lafayette Place Campground on W side of Franconia Notch Parkway/I-93. Access is from southbound side of Parkway; from exit ramp for campground, bear L for Lonesome Lake parking area. Additonal parking is found by continuing on exit ramp and bearing R where road diverges L into campground. Still more parking is available on northbound (E) side of Parkway at Old Bridle Path/Falling Waters trailhead; access is provided by pedestrian underpass. Two major approaches from this trailhead, both with challenging steep sections, are described below, along with various loop options and other variations.

Lonesome Lake Trail, Hi-Cannon Trail, Kinsman Ridge Trail
5.6 mi. round-trip, 2350-ft. elevation gain

The ascent of Cannon via the Hi-Cannon Trail is scenic and rugged, with fine views overlooking Franconia Notch and Lonesome Lake en route, and a steep ladder to negotiate. Yellow-blazed Lonesome Lake Trail, marked by sign, begins at wooden bridge over Pemigewasset River and immediately passes through section of state park campground, crossing three gravel roads and passing by several campsites. It then ascends moderately through hardwoods, swinging L (S), crossing two small brooks on bridges and reaching jct. R with Hi-Cannon Trail at 0.4 mi./1925 ft. Turn R on Hi-Cannon Trail, which soon begins steady ascent via numerous short switchbacks, some of which are badly eroded with poor, gravelly footing. Note important turn to R at 0.5 mi. where old logging road continues ahead. Reach jct. L with Dodge Cutoff (from Lonesome Lake) at 1.2 mi./2850 ft. Here Hi-Cannon Trail swings R (N) and climbs at alternately moderate and steep grades, then makes rough, rocky traverse of steep slope. Use caution at gravelly washout where there is view of Little Haystack Mtn. and Mt. Liberty. Just beyond, at 1.6 mi./3350 ft., nice outlook across floor of Franconia Notch to Mts. Lafayette and Lincoln is reached. Trail turns L here for very steep, rocky climb.

A hundred yards further, Cliff House, natural rock shelter, is passed on R. Just above, ascend steep ledgy area on long wooden ladder (difficult for small children and dogs, dangerous if icy), with tricky traverse L across narrow ledge at top, where 2x4 is bolted to edge for foothold. Trail traverses up and across steep S face of Cannon's S ridge and soon passes series of three rock outcroppings on L (ca. 3500 ft.) with stunning bird's eye views of Lonesome Lake and S down Pemigewasset valley. View extends to Franconia Range on L and Kinsmans on R. Use caution on these sloping ledges if wet or icy. At last viewpoint trail turns R to resume steady ascent. Follow narrow path on fairly rough climb, with occasional leveling and dips, to jct. with Kinsman Ridge Trail at 2.4 mi./3850 ft. Turn R on Kinsman Ridge Trail and climb at mostly easy grades along wooded S ridge, with occasional glimpses of distant peaks from blowdown patches, and rise to meet gravel Rim Trail at 2.8 mi. / 4050 ft. Here Kinsman Ridge Trail turns R to join Rim Trail; for summit and observation tower continue straight ahead and uphill on gravel path for 100 yds.

LONESOME LAKE/DODGE CUTOFF OPTION
For slightly longer option of Hi-Cannon route that includes visit to shore of scenic Lonesome Lake, continue on Lonesome Lake Trail past Hi-Cannon Trail jct. and, as described below, ascend steadily by long switchbacks to four-way junction by E shore of Lonesome Lake at 1.2 mi. / 2740 ft. A few yds. ahead on spur path there is beautiful view of South and North Kinsman seen across water. From four-way junction, take lightly used Dodge Cutoff, which cuts back sharply to NNE and may be poorly marked and somewhat difficult to follow. Dodge Cutoff crests small rise and traverses through fine woods, dips to cross wet low spot, then climbs fairly steeply by switchbacks before dipping slightly to meet Hi-Cannon Trail at 1.5 mi. / 2850 ft. This route is just 0.3 mi. longer than direct route via lower Hi-Cannon Trail and makes a nice loop for either ascent or descent.

Lonesome Lake Trail, Kinsman Ridge Trail
6.4 mi. round trip, 2350-ft. elevation gain

This route follows Lonesome Lake Trail past the scenic lake and all the way up to its end at Coppermine Col, then follows Kinsman Ridge Trail up a very steep, rugged section to the mountain's S ridge, from which the final ascent is easy. Yellow-blazed Lonesome Lake Trail, marked by sign, begins at wooden bridge over Pemigewasset River and immediately passes through section of state park campground, crossing three gravel roads and passing by several campsites. It then ascends moderately through hardwoods, swinging L (S), crossing two small brooks on bridges and passing jct. R with Hi-Cannon Trail at 0.4 mi. / 1925 ft. Trail now climbs steadily up side of steep slope by two long switchbacks, first to S, then, after sharp R turn, to NE. At 0.9 mi. you swing L for short stiff climb, then grade eases on high plateau of conifer and birch to S of Cannon Mtn. Short descent leads to four-way junction at NE corner of Lonesome Lake at 1.2 mi. / 2740 ft. Here side path leads a few yds. ahead to shore of lake and beautiful view across water to South and North Kinsman.

Route now follows coinciding Lonesome Lake and Around-Lonesome-Lake Trails to NNW along NE shore of lake, passing grassy clearing where original Lonesome Lake Hut once stood, then traversing series of bog bridges through wet area. At 1.4 mi. bear R on Lonesome Lake Trail as Around-Lonesome-Lake Trail diverges L to continue around shore through open bogs. Lonesome Lake Trail continues across flat, boggy terrain for another 0.2 mi. At 1.6 mi. trail begins to climb, easily at first, then at increasingly steep grade with rough and eroded footway. Ascent remains steep until trail eases at 2.1 mi. / 3300 ft. and slabs through dense firs along W side of Coppermine Col. Slight dip leads to junction with Kinsman Ridge Trail at 2.3 mi. / 3400 ft. Bear R at intersection onto northbound Kinsman Ridge Trail and, after easy stretch across low point of col, climb very steeply up boulder-strewn W slope of Cannon. One pitch requires use of hands, and this section of trail should be avoided if icy. Along this stretch look for vista L over Coppermine Brook valley. Trail eases abruptly just before meeting Hi-Cannon Trail on R at 2.7 mi. / 3850 ft. Bear L here, following northbound Kinsman Ridge Trail at mostly easy grade along S ridge of Cannon. Meet gravel Rim Trail at 3.1 mi. / 4050 ft. For summit and observation tower, continue ahead and uphill on gravel path for 100 yds.

Attractive 6.0 mi. loop trip can be made by descending via Hi-Cannon Trail route, though this requires down-climb of ladder below Lonesome Lake outlooks.

SIDE TRIP TO NORTHEAST CANNON BALL

New England Hundred Highest peakbaggers can nab the Northeast Cannon Ball with a short, steep side trip L (W) along Kinsman Ridge Trail from jct. with Lonesome Lake Trail in Coppermine Col. From col, climb steep pitch, then ascend moderately for a time, with two short trench-like sections. Trail then becomes very steep and ledgy, with one scramble up through rocky slot; at top look back for views to steep W flank of Cannon Mtn. and down to Coppermine Col. Above here grade soon slackens and trail meanders up to crest of Northeast Cannon Ball, reaching ledge on R side of trail at 0.2 from col / 3760 ft. Scramble up onto this rock for view E to Mts. Lafayette and Lincoln rising over S ridge of Cannon, and SE to Mt. Liberty and more distant peaks. Kinsman Ridge Trail wanders across flat summit, with high point a short distance to R in dense scrub. For a partial view of Kinsmans, continue 0.1 mi. farther on southbound Kinsman Ridge Trail, descending easily, passing through semi-open blow-down patch and reaching vista at top of sharp drop. Round trip to summit of Northeast Cannon Ball from Coppermine Col is 0.4 mi. with 370-ft. elevation gain; add 0.2 mi. for Kinsmans vista.

Southwest Approach via The Cannon Balls

A much longer approach can be made to Cannon Mtn. by traversing the Kinsman Ridge Trail across the Cannon Balls and then ascending to Cannon's summit from Coppermine Col. This approach is sometimes used by overnighting backpackers, or by super-strong day hikers traversing the entire Kinsman Ridge Trail. Cannon is the final obstacle on this 16.9 mi.

traverse (with 6200-ft. elevation gain) from NH 112 in Kinsman Notch to I-93/Franconia Notch Parkway at N base of Cannon. The first 11.5 mi. from NH 112 are a link in the Appalachian Trail. Kinsman Ridge Trail passes over numerous summits, including Mt. Wolf, North and South Kinsman, the Cannon Balls, and Cannon Mtn.

This approach may also be used by day hikers looking for a long and interesting loop hike from the Lafayette Place trailhead. This involves ascending 3.5 mi. to Kinsman Junction (3750 ft.) via Lonesome Lake, Cascade Brook and Fishin' Jimmy Trails, as described in Kinsmans chapter. (Scenic view of steep E face of North Kinsman from shore of Kinsman Pond can be enjoyed with easy 0.2 mi. round trip to L on Kinsman Pond Trail.) For traverse of Cannon Balls, turn R (N) onto northbound Kinsman Ridge Trail. Descend slightly, cross flat area, then ascend steeply up SW slope of nameless 3812-ft. hump; look back for view of rocky spine of North Kinsman. Trail traverses narrow, level crest of hump, with restricted vistas from blowdown areas, then descends steadily to shoulder at far end of which ledge on R offers partial view E, then descends again to 3580-ft. saddle.

After level stretch, trail climbs over small knoll, then swings R (E) and makes fairly steep climb to flat, viewless top of West Cannon Ball, clad in scrawny black spruce scrub, at 4.5 mi./3693 ft. Descend easily at first, then steeply with several sharp, ledgy pitches and glimpses ahead to Middle Cannon Ball, to darkly-wooded 3250-ft. col with small brook running through it. Next you climb partway up Middle Cannon Ball, then slab along its N side, passing partial vista to N. Trail now descends easily, losing only 75 ft. in elevation, into broad col, passing through beautiful open fir glade. From low point trail ascends steadily up Northeast Cannon Ball, passing blowdown patch with partial view of Pemigewasset valley and peaks to S at 5.5 mi. and vista back to Kinsmans at 5.6 mi. Grade now eases, and trail crosses flat, scrubby summit of Northeast Cannon Ball at 5.7 mi./3769 ft. At E end of summit plateau rock on L offers interesting standing view ahead to Cannon Mtn. and Franconia Range beyond. Kinsman Ridge Trail now makes steep, rough descent of 370 ft. in just 0.2 mi., including scramble down ledgy slot, to jct. R with Lonesome Lake Trail in Coppermine Col at 5.9 mi./3400 ft. Continue ahead on Kinsman Ridge Trail for very steep, rugged climb to jct. R with Hi-Cannon Trail at 6.3 mi./3850 ft. Bear L here and continue at mostly easy grade on Kinsman Ridge Trail along S ridge of Cannon to meet gravel Rim Trail at 6.7 mi./4050 ft. Summit and observation tower are 100 yds. ahead. Descend via Kinsman Ridge, Hi-Cannon and Lonesome Lake Trails to complete 9.5 mi. loop with 3550-ft. elevation gain. With side trip from Kinsman Junction to North Kinsman, trip is 10.7 mi./4100 ft.; adding South Kinsman brings totals to 12.5 mi./4750 ft.—a full day on the Kinsman Ridge!

Winter

Windy conditions frequently prevail atop Cannon, especially in winter. Expect bitter cold winds, and plenty of snow (150 inches a year, on average). There are no easy winter ascent routes up Cannon. If ascending via Kinsman Ridge Trail from Tramway parking lot, watch out for fast-moving skiers in Kinsman Glade section, where you may be snowshoeing over steep, hardpacked moguls, and on narrow ski trail above. The trail may be hard to follow in the glade. Also, use caution for final, partly exposed half-mile from the top of Cannon Cliffs to summit ridge as deeply drifted and blowing snow frequently obscure the trail. On Hi-Cannon route, beware of tricky ascent of ladder near Cliff House, a natural rock shelter about halfway up the mountain; traverse of narrow ledge at top of ladder is also dicey in winter. Although the Lonesome Lake Trail is generally a good snowshoeing route, the steep, rough section of the Kinsman Ridge Trail from Coppermine Col to the jct. with Hi-Cannon Trail is very difficult in winter and may be dangerously icy. Thus this is normally not recommended as a winter ascent route. Please note that the ski area does not allow hiking on ski trails.

View Guide

SUMMIT OBSERVATION TOWER: The summit observation deck offers a 360-degree view; a neighboring old fire tower (now dismantled) had long marred the vista to the N. A tabletop panorama with pointer helps you pick out the peaks. Most impressive, perhaps, is the broadside view E across Franconia Notch to barren, slide-scarred Franconia Ridge, with Mt. Lafayette to the L and Mt. Lincoln to the R. The massive, rounded East Peak of Cannon is seen below Lafayette. The sheer rocky face of Eagle Cliff is seen under the ridge descending L from Lafayette, and over this ridge peer the tops of (L to R) Mt. Adams, Mt. Jefferson, Mt. Garfield and North Twin. The summit of Mt. Washington is just visible to the R of North Twin from the tower, but can't be seen at ground level from the summit (though it is visible from the upper Tramway station). The ridge followed by the Old Bridle Path sweeps down in front of Mt. Lincoln. The less prominent peak of Little Haystack Mtn. adorns Franconia Ridge to the R of Mt. Lincoln, then the now-wooded ridge leads down and up across to the pointed, rocky peak of Mt. Liberty, seen to the SE high above the winding Franconia Notch Parkway. The tip of Mt. Flume is just visible over a little notch in the ridge descending L from Liberty.

To the R of Liberty, East Osceola (L) and Mt. Osceola (R) are seen over Hardwood Ridge. The top of Whaleback Mtn. just peers over the R slope of Hardwood Ridge. To the R of Osceola are the lower East and Middle Peaks of Scar Ridge, with the SW peak of the northern Flat Mtn.

peeking over between them, then the view swings R to the slide-marked mass of the main Scar Ridge summits, with the double summit of Sandwich Dome looking over in back. Mt. Tecumseh is to the R of Sandwich and closer, over the R shoulder of Scar Ridge, with Big Coolidge Mtn. below and in front. Loon Mtn. and its ski trails are seen behind and R of Big Coolidge, with the S spurs of Tecumseh above. Farther R the Belknap Range is on the horizon, with Dickey Mtn. (L, peering over a nearer ridge) and ledgy Fisher Mtn. (R, above Loon's South Peak) in front. The highest peaks of the Belknap Range—Belknap, Gunstock and Piper Mtns.—are seen above Fisher. The Campton Range spreads to the R of Fisher, with Little Coolidge Mtn. (front) and Russell Mtn. (back) seen under its R end. Farther R, just L of the broad swath of the Pemigewasset River valley, is flat-topped Mt. Prospect in Holderness, with Bean Hill in the distance to its R. The North Lincoln strip can be seen in the valley foreground, with part of North Woodstock beyond, on the R side of I-93.

In the distance over the R side of the Pemigewasset valley, nearly due S, is the wavy crest of Hersey Mtn. Next to the R, close by and low down, Mt. Pemigewasset is seen rising behind its nameless northern neighbor, with the Bridgewater Mtns. on the horizon. Plymouth Mtn. is to the R of the Bridgewaters. Farther R and closer, seen beyond the broad S ridge of Cannon, is the long E ridge of Mt. Kineo, with Stinson Mtn. stretching across behind its center. To the L of Stinson, Mt. Kearsarge is seen in the distance over Ragged Mtn. with part of Tenney Mtn. just visble over the Kineo E ridge. On clear days (L to R) the Lyndeboro Mtns., North Pack Monadnock and Crotched Mtn. can be seen on the horizon to the L of Kearsarge. Closer in this direction, Mud Pond can be glimpsed on the plateau behind Mt. Pemigewasset. To the R of Stinson, Mt. Crosby rises beyond a deep gap in the Kineo ridge. Farther R, beyond a double-humped spur of South Kinsman, is the main summit of Mt. Kineo with Mt. Cushman in front on the L and Mt. Cardigan behind and just L of Kineo's peak. Rounded Lovewell Mtn. can be seen over a col well to the L of Cardigan, and on clear days Mt. Monadnock can be seen over the far L end of Kineo's main ridge. Part of Sunapee Mtn. can be seen behind Kineo on the R. Farther R Carr Mtn. rises prominently through a deep gap. Next to the R, the Blue Ridge of Mt. Moosilauke rises to the R across Mt. Braley, Mt. Waternomee and Mt. Jim, above the great SE ridge of South Kinsman. Mt. Wolf peers over the Kinsman ridge under Braley.

The view now swings R to the great mass of South Kinsman rising nearby beyond Coppermine Col, spur ridges of the Cannon Balls, and the wild basin of Cascade Brook. Mt. Moosilauke peers over to the L of South Kinsman's summit. The ledgy face of North Kinsman is next to the R, rising far above the Northeast and Middle Cannon Balls. The flat top of the West Cannon Ball is to the R of North Kinsman, with Sugarloaf Mtn. (L) and Black Mtn. (R) in the Benton Range beyond. On clear days the Killington Range can be seen on the horizon between the R slope of North Kinsman and Sugarloaf, while Green Mountain peaks in the Brandon and Middlebury Gap areas stretch across the horizon to the R of Black. This wild view towards the Kinsmans and Cannon Balls is unique to Cannon's summit. To the R of the Cannon Balls there is a beautiful view down into the backcountry valley of Coppermine Brook, closed in on the R by a lower spur of Cannon's NW Peak. In the mid-distance, seen over the lower end of the long slope that descends R from the West Cannon Ball, are (L to R) Cobble Hill, Moody Ledge, and Green Mtn. Cooley Hill is in front of Green Mtn. on the R, due W, with its higher neighbor, Cole Hill, farther R. The Breadloaf–Wilson–Grant range is on the horizon over Moody Ledge and Green Mtn. The lumpy Signal Mtn. range in west-central Vermont is seen behind Cooley and Cole Hills, with the Mt. Abraham–Mt. Ellen range behind on the L, over Cooley. The distinctive Camel's Hump rises over the lower R end of the Signal Range, with its neighbor, Mt. Ethan Allen on its L, above pointed Spruce Mtn.

Farther R the Worcester Range near Stowe, Vermont, is seen on the horizon over nearby, lowly Bronson Hill. Next to the R and farther is sprawling Mt. Mansfield, with the Sterling Range to its R. Continuing to the R on the horizon, looking across a vast reach of lowlands, one sees Laraway Mtn., the Cold Hollow Mtns., and the sharp peak of Belvidere Mtn., the latter seen looking due NW above the nearby ledgy NW Peak of Cannon, which is marked by the swath of the Taft Ski Trail. To the R of Belvidere are its neighbors, Tillotson Peak and Haystack Mtn., and farther R are the prominent Jay Peaks. To the R of the Jays some of the Sutton Mtns. in Quebec can be seen on clear days. Next to the R and somewhat closer are the mountains around Willoughby Gap, with Mt. Hor on the L and Mt. Pisgah on the R. The round hump of Owls Head in Quebec peeks over to the L of Hor. Looking down in the valley below, to the L of Mt. Hor, the village of Franconia can be seen by a curve in I-93. To the R of Mt. Pisgah are the prominent duo of Burke (L) and Umpire (R) Mtns., with Bald Mtn. peering over just L of Burke's summit. The town of Littleton can be seen below and in line with Burke. To the R of Umpire are East Haven Mtn. and then the massive East Mtn. with a structure on top; close by in this direction is lowly Garnet Mtn. Gore Mtn. in northern Vermont peers over to the R of East.

Continuing to the R, one sees the nearby low range consisting of (L to R) Lewis Hill, Mt. Agassiz (with a building on top, and seen over the Tramway upper station) and Mt. Cleveland. Behind and above Lewis Hill and the col to its R are, in succession, the long, low ridge of Dalton Mtn., then Stone (L) and Burnside (R) Mtns., and, on the horizon, the sharp Sable Mtn. at the L end of a long, nameless ridge (which is above Stone and Burnside); West Mtn. is to the L of Sable and closer. Above Mts. Agassiz and Cleveland are Vermont's Monadnock Mtn. (L, in back) and the double-peaked Goback Mtn. (R). The Nash Stream range extends to the R of Goback, with the sharp peak of Sugarloaf towards its R end. Lowly Propsect Mtn. in Lancaster and Cape Horn in Groveton can be seen down low to the R of Sugarloaf and closer. The Nash Stream valley is to the R of Sugarloaf, and farther R are the bare Percy Peaks with North Whitcomb (Muise) Mtn. behind on their L and Long Mtn. stretching to their R. To the R of Long and closer is the Pilot Ridge, with sharp Hutchins Mtn. prominent among its several peaks. Bulky Mt. Cabot anchors the R end of the Pilots, with nearby Scarface Mtn., a spur of Mt. Lafayette, below. To the R of Cabot is the Pliny Range with Mt. Starr King on the L and Mt. Waumbek on the R, with its long, level E ridge. Under the R end of that E ridge is the summit of Cherry Mtn., with its own long ridge extending to the R. Jefferson village spreads at the base of Mt. Starr King, and part of Twin Mountain village is seen below Cherry Mtn. Pliny Mtn. peers over just R of Cherry's summit, and down low in this direction is Big Bickford Mtn. Peering over the middle of the ridge extending R from Cherry is the flat crest of Cambridge Black Mtn. Next to the R is the double summit of Black Crescent Mtn., with Bemis Mtn. (L, over the L summit) and Elephant Mtn. (R, between the summits) in Maine visible beyond. Mt. Crescent is to the R of Black Crescent, with Old Blue Mtn. visible between them. Next to the R is prominent Old Speck Mtn. in the Mahoosucs, with Goose Eye Mtn. to the R and slightly closer, seen over Mt. Deception. Nubble Peak, a spur of North Twin, is next to the R, with Mt. Dartmouth to its R, then the view swings back to Mts. Adams and Jefferson seen over the shoulder of Mt. Lafayette.

CANNON CLIFFS (EAST PEAK) VIEW: These flat, open ledges provide a stunning view E across the floor of Franconia Notch to the high peaks of Franconia Ridge, including barren 5000-footers Mts. Lafayette and Lincoln. In the words of nineteenth-century guidebook editor Moses Sweetser, this view is "very noble and satisfactory." To the L of the Franconias the view sweeps out to the NE and N, including (R to L) the Crescent Range, Cherry Mtn., the Pliny Range over Big Bickford Mtn., Mt. Cabot and the Pilot Ridge with Hutchins Mtn. above Scarface Mtn., Long Mtn., the Percy Peaks, North Whitcomb (Muise) Mtn., and the Nash Stream range leading across to Goback Mtn. To the R of the high Franconias is the pointed peak of Mt. Liberty. Seen to the R of Liberty, looking from L to R, are Mt. Osceola peering over Hardwood Ridge, Scar Ridge with Sandwich Dome behind and Whaleback Mtn. in front, Mt. Tecumseh, the distant Belknap Range beyond ledgy spurs of Tecumseh, the Campton Range over South Loon and Russell Mtn. Farther R, looking S, the winding Pemigewasset River valley dominates the view landscape, striped by I-93 with parts of North Lincoln and North Woodstock visible and the wavy ridge of Hersey Mtn. far to the S. Of this vista, Moses Sweetser

wrote, "This view is the great attraction of Mt. Cannon, and is of remarkable beauty and variety." To the R of the Pemi valley are (L to R)
the Bridgewater Mtns., Plymouth Mtn., nearby Mt. Pemigewasset and its
nameless northern neighbor, distant Mt. Kearsarge above Ragged Mtn.,
the long E ridge of Mt. Kineo with Stinson Mtn. behind, the long main
ridge of Kineo with Mt. Cushman in front and Mt. Cardigan beyond, the
summit of Kineo, Carr Mtn., Mts. Braley, Waternomee and Jim over the
SE ridge of South Kinsman, the shoulder of Mt. Moosilauke, the summit of South Kinsman over Cannon's S ridge, and the summit of Cannon
with its tower.

NO. OF 4000-FOOTERS VISIBLE: 16 (from summit observation deck)

North and South Kinsman

North Kinsman

ELEVATION: 4293 ft. / 1309 m   ORDER OF HEIGHT: 28
LOCATION: Kinsman Ridge, Towns of Lincoln and Easton
USGS MAP: 7½′ Franconia

South Kinsman

ELEVATION: 4358 ft. / 1328 m   ORDER OF HEIGHT: 22
LOCATION: Kinsman Ridge, Towns of Lincoln and Easton
USGS MAPS: 7½′ Franconia, 7½′ Lincoln

Geography

The double peaks of Kinsman Mtn. are the culminating points of the long
ridge running S to N from Kinsman Notch (NH 112) to Franconia Notch
(I-93), with South Kinsman's 4358-ft. elevation topping its sister peak by
just 65 ft. They form an impressive wooded wall when viewed from the
broad Easton valley to the W.

North Kinsman's peak, mostly wooded at the top, has a distinctive pro-
file with a moderate slope on the W and a precipitous, ledgy face on the
E, which drops off sharply to a flat narrow shelf on which rests remote
Kinsman Pond (3740 ft.). This scenic five-acre tarn has long been a favor-
ite destination of backpackers. To the NE along Kinsman Ridge, North
Kinsman is flanked by a nameless 3812-ft. hump and then the three Can-
non Balls, wooded humps leading across to Cannon Mtn. A ledge on the
E side of North Kinsman's summit opens a spectacular view out to the
Franconia Range.

South Kinsman's summit, which is actually comprised of two readily apparent knobs, is flatter and less defined than the narrow north peak. There is some dispute over which of the two summit knobs is higher. The U.S. Geological Survey map shows the northernmost knob as being the higher of the two. Trampers who have visited the mountaintop know, however, that the summit cairn has been built on the southernmost of the knobs. In any event, South Kinsman's summit is fairly open (due to a ridgetop forest fire sometime around 1870), and from different locations scattered around both summit knobs, but especially the southern one, fine views are obtained in all directions.

While Kinsman Pond lies at the base of North Kinsman's summit cone, South Kinsman has a watery neighbor of its own, scenic Harrington Pond, named after AMC trailbuilder Karl Harrington, who discovered the pond while laying out the proposed Kinsman Ridge Trail in 1917. This tiny acre and a half pond, overlooked by cliffs and surrounded by wet, boggy terrain, rests on a 3400-ft. shoulder a mile S of the peak alongside the Kinsman Ridge Trail. For hikers headed N along the trail, the view of the mountain from the shore of Harrington Pond is quite daunting as the peak's steep S slope forms a formidable wall ahead.

Several long, lower ridges extend off the main mountain mass of the Kinsmans. Most prominent, perhaps, is the great SE ridge of South Kinsman, especially when the mountain is viewed from the S and E. This runs over a 4220-ft. shoulder, from which a lower, 3340-ft. shoulder extends due E to the Pemigewasset valley, then descends to a 3655-ft. knob. On the E side of this knob the slope drops precipitously to tiny, secluded Mud Pond on a 2420-ft. plateau. Just E of Mud Pond is a nameless 2615-ft. spur with a prominent rock slab overlooking I-93, and S of this spur is Mt. Pemigewasset (2557 ft.), home to the famous Indian Head profile on its large S cliff and a popular objective for a short day hike. From the 3655-ft. knob another spur ridge runs S down to a broad, swampy plateau that holds 43-acre Bog Pond (2317 ft.). Set between the gloomy ridges of South Kinsman and Mt. Wolf, Bog Pond is a scene of "utter desolation and loneliness," in the words of Karl Harrington, though a powerline built across the area in the 1950s took away some of the wildness.

After dropping over a steep and rocky slope to Harrington Pond, the scrubby, rocky main ridgeline from South Kinsman extends a mile or so farther to the SSW, terminating where crags look down upon the floor of the original Kinsman Notch (the mountain pass which the powerline runs through), with Mt. Wolf (3500 ft.) across to the S.

Cascade Brook—with branches draining out of Kinsman Pond and off the S slopes of the Cannon Balls ridge—flows down through a broad, wild basin E of the Kinsman peaks and empties into the main branch of the Pemigewasset River. In its lower reaches it drops over Rocky Glen Falls, Kinsman Falls and other cascades. Eliza Brook, rich in mossy cascades,

A bird's-eye view of Kinsman Pond is available to hikers from a set of ledges just below the true summit of North Kinsman.

drains the valley between the S (main) and SE ridges of South Kinsman and flows into Bog Pond, the large swamp farther E known as Bog Eddy, Harvard Brook (home to Harvard and Georgiana Falls) and eventually the Pemigewasset River. Whitehouse Brook drains the lower E slopes of South Kinsman, between the main SE ridge and its eastern shoulder.

On the NW flank of North Kinsman, 2470-ft. Bald Peak, accessible to hikers along the Mt. Kinsman Trail, protrudes from the mountainside and provides a bird's eye view of the wide and flat Easton Valley, drained by the Ham Branch of Gale River. This sharp little peak, which is open on the top, is quite prominent as one travels along NH 116 through Franconia and Easton. Nearby also is steep-walled Kinsman Flume, a narrow, 400-ft. long gorge on Flume Brook that writer John Jerome once mused "seems almost gaudy," lying as it does in the middle of an otherwise serene mountainside forest. Kendall Brook drains the slope below the flume. Judd Brook drains the next basin to the S, and farther S Slide Brook flows down from a deep W-facing ravine between North and South Kinsman. A W spur ridge of North Kinsman, bordering the N side of the Slide Brook basin, bears an extensive set of bare ledges that are prominent from the Easton valley. Reel Brook flows NW from the notch between South Kinsman and Mt. Wolf, and its various eastern tributaries drain the broad SW slopes of South Kinsman. All of these brooks coming off the W slopes of the Kinsmans are tributaries of the Ham Branch.

Nomenclature

The mountain, its namesake pond, and the narrow mountain passageway (Kinsman Notch) dividing Mt. Wolf and Kinsman Ridge from Mt. Moosilauke are named for early Easton settler and farmer Nathan Kinsman (1741–1822). He, his wife, and several children arrived in the unpopulated valley W of the mountain in 1782 after relocating north from the Ipswich, Massachusetts area. Their journey through the mountain wilderness, with an ox-drawn cart hauling all their worldly possessions, is one of legendary status in the White Mountains. It is uncertain whether they came from the Pemigewasset valley across the notch between South Kinsman and Mt. Wolf (which was originally called Kinsman Notch, the notch which now bears that name then being known as Moosilauke Notch) or from Haverhill to the W. The family made their homestead near Slide Brook in what was then part of the town of Lincoln, and Kinsman became a widely respected citizen. Among his many skills he was a doctor and served as Grafton County coroner.

Kendall and Judd Brooks were named for other early Easton families. The Fishin' Jimmy Trail was named for a lovable local character (real name James Whitcher) featured in a story by regional author Annie Trumbull Slosson. Harrington Pond was named for AMC trail-builder Karl P. Harrington, who discovered it while laying out the Kinsman Ridge Trail in 1917. "It was to this little Harrington Pond that a frog piping his nightly serenade guided the writer through the dense darkness, when first a trail was roughly blazed along this hitherto inaccessible ridge," wrote Harrington in his 1926 book, *Walks & Climbs in the White Mountains.*

Historical Highlights

First Ascent: Probably Dartmouth College graduates A. A. Abott and A. M. Bacheler, members of Prof. Charles H. Hitchcock's 1871 geological survey team which explored many heretofore unreached areas of the White Mountains. Hitchcock himself acknowledges that Abbott and Bacheler were the first to discover Kinsman Pond, which at an elevation of 3740 ft. rests just 553 ft. below North Kinsman's summit. One can only surmise that these two nineteenth-century explorers eventually made their way to the mountaintop as well.

1782: Nathan Kinsman and family arrive in Easton valley and become first permanent settlers in area that is now Town of Easton.

1816: Name of Kinsman Mountain first appears on map produced by N.H. secretary of state Philip Carrigain.

Ca. 1870: Summit of South Kinsman is burned over in forest fire.

1876: Town of Easton is officially established per state legislative action. Previously, land was part of Town of Landaff, and before that, Lincoln.

1876: Guidebook editor Moses Sweetser writes: "The ascent of this formidable peak is rarely undertaken, so great is the labor in comparison with the reward." His guidebook party had been forced to turn back ½ mi. below summit due to approaching nightfall.

1878: AMC party including George A. Sargent, Marian Pychowska, Lucia Pychowska, Eugene B. Cook and Rev. Henry G. Spaulding, ascend South Kinsman from Easton via Slide Brook and slide on S side of ravine. On top they find a "magnificent view" and a U.S. Coast Survey signal used for surveying.

1879: AMC explorer Prof. Gaetano Lanza ascends South Kinsman via Slide Brook route, above slide battling through "as bad scrubs, rotten and fallen timber and moss-covered rocks as one often meets with." He writes report for *Appalachia*.

1880: Benjamin Macdonald, in piece appearing in tourist paper, *The White Mountain Echo and Tourists' Register*, describes visit to recently discovered Kinsman Flume and Bald Peak on mountain's W slopes.

1884: First crude trail is built to North Kinsman from Easton valley. About this time path is also cut from Easton valley to Bog Pond.

1897: Trail to Kinsman is spotted by AMC, but not used.

1910: First official trail to North Kinsman is established by Frederick Tuckerman and A. B. Hubbard. "Trail commences at Cecil Bowles farm in Easton . . . and is about three and a half miles in length," reports *Appalachia*.

1911: Tuckerman and Hubbard extend trail to South Kinsman.

1917–1919: AMC crews cut Kinsman Ridge Trail, linking Kinsman Notch with Franconia Notch and leading over both Kinsman summits. Future N.H. governor Sherman Adams is among workers on trail crew. Decsription in *AMC Guide* notes that trail passes over "Stetson Cave" as it ascends South Kinsman from S.

1920: Karl Harrington oversees work on trail from Whitehouse Bridge to Kinsman Pond. Route (called Whitehouse Bridge Trail; upper part later becomes Kinsman Pond Trail, lower part Cascade Brook Trail) was cut several years earlier by Forest Service, but was not maintained. Same trail is also extended E to shelter on Mt. Liberty.

1921: Open log shelter accomodating 12 backpackers is constructed at Kinsman Pond.

1924: AMC builds small log shelter near Eliza Brook, several miles S of Kinsmans along ridge trail.

1926: Harrington writes of Kinsman traverse in book, *Walks & Climbs in the White Mountains*.

1928: *AMC Guide* notes WMNF trail leading from Easton valley to Bog Pond. Western part of this trail later becomes Reel Brook Trail.

1930: Fishin' Jimmy Trail from Lonesome Lake to Kinsman Pond is cut by AMC. Eliminates tedious climb over Cannon Balls to terminus of Lonesome Lake Trail in Coppermine Col.

Mid-1930s: Kinsman Cabin is built along Mt. Kinsman Trail to accommodate growing number of skiers frequenting White Mountains.

1934: *AMC Guide* provides brief description of Kinsman Ski Trail which runs three miles from Mt. Kinsman Trail to col between S. and Middle Cannon Balls.

1939: Ski guide to Eastern US describes Kinsman Ski Trail as "sporty with many sudden pitches which keep the skier on the alert."

1950s: Powerline is built from North Woodstock to Easton, crossing over Bog Pond and through notch between South Kinsman and Mt. Wolf. In 1970s this corridor is considered but rejected as alternative route for I-93 instead of Franconia Notch.

Late 1950s: Basin–Cascades Trail built by state park workers.

1965: Veteran AMC trail-builder Charles Blood recalls construction of Kinsman Ridge Trail in *Appalachia* article titled, "Evolution of a Trailman."

1966: AMC builds new shelter at Kinsman Pond.

1982: Forest Service decides to remove Kinsman Cabin and rehabilitate site.

2007: Kinsman Pond Shelter is rebuilt by AMC.

Trail Approaches

West Approach from NH 116 in Easton Valley

NORTH KINSMAN ONLY

Mt. Kinsman Trail, Kinsman Ridge Trail
8.2 mi. round trip, 3300-ft. elevation gain.

NORTH AND SOUTH KINSMAN

Mt. Kinsman Trail, Kinsman Ridge Trail
10.0 mi. round trip, 3950-ft. elevation gain.

TRAILHEAD (1030 ft.): Mt. Kinsman Trail begins on NH 116 a few yds. S of Franconia–Easton town line and runs 3.7 mi. to Kinsman Ridge Trail, intersecting the latter 0.4 mi. from North Kinsman's summit. Parking is sparse at trailhead and is limited to immediate roadside; do not block driveways of nearby residences. The trailhead is 4.4 mi. S of NH 18 in Franconia village; it is 0.2 mi. S of Kinsman Lodge and 0.2 mi. N of Tamarack Camp. Trail entrance is marked by prominent stone pillars with chain between them.

The ascent via the Mt. Kinsman Trail from Easton Valley is the primary western approach to the Kinsmans. As South Kinsman is much tougher to reach from points S (on either the E or W side of the range), most peakbaggers opt to hit both peaks on a single hike. Backpackers traversing the Kinsman Ridge Trail are the exception, as are hikers who might have spotted vehicles at the Reel Brook and Mt. Kinsman trailheads, both off NH 116 (see below). Though it starts at a lower elevation than other Kinsman approaches, the Mt. Kinsman Trail has the virtues of moderate grades and, with the exception of a few rough spots, generally good footing. It is also a quiet, lightly used route. Lower 1.1 mi. is on private land. From gate, blue-blazed trail heads SE and follows sandy logging road, climbing moderately under tall pines. In first 0.2 mi. four older roads fork to L; in each case stay R on main road. Watch for directional arrow at 0.5 mi. indicating where trail bears R again at grassy logging yard. Swing L at 0.6 mi. / 1400 ft. past old sugarhouse on L, then bear R again. At 0.9 mi. short loop on L bypasses wet section. At 1.1 mi., trail crosses WMNF boundary and turns R off old road, then in 30 yds. turns L (watch for arrows, blazes and cairns) and climbs moderately to former site of Kinsman Cabin at 1.5 mi. / 1900 ft. Turn R to cross stream on flat ledges, climb steadily S across slope to cross another brook (called Mossy Falls Brook in early *AMC Guides*) at 1.8 mi., and at 2.1 mi. / 2400 ft. reach Flume Brook. Just after brook is crossed, look for side path R (sign) leading 150 yds. and 75 ft. down to edge of Kinsman Flume, deep eroded dike several hundred feet long (use caution).

Less than 100 yds. past side trail to flume, another path branches R, this one leading 0.2 mi. (with short descent and easy climb) to bare, flat summit of Bald Peak (2470 ft.), prominent spur of North Kinsman. Here there are good views W over Easton valley, SW to Mt. Moosilauke, Benton Range and mountains in Vermont, E to looming wooded wall of North Kinsman, and N to peaks of northern New Hampshire and Vermont.

At Bald Peak spur jct., Mt. Kinsman Trail turns L and runs at easy grade across plateau, passing through blowdown area. Soon it begins to meander upward at varying easy to moderate grades, with occasional steeper pitch, crossing two small brooks in flat areas. In this section it makes several twists and turns. Higher up the grade steepens and the woods darken with dense conifers. At 3.2 mi. / 3300 ft. trail swings R, then L on relocation around steep ledge (where trail formerly ascended ladder). At 3.5 mi. / 3600 ft. swing R and climb up across slope, then bear L and ascend ledge swath through stunted growth to meet Kinsman Ridge Trail at 3.7 mi. / 3850 ft. Turn R here and climb moderately at first, then steeply at times, with several short scrambles up ledges and slabs (slippery when wet), passing view NW over fir wave partway up. At 4.1 mi. / 4293 ft. reach summit of North Kinsman; high point is steep-sided boulder just L of trail. A few yds. farther side trail L, marked by sign, drops over two ledge steps and leads 20 yds. to large flat ledge offering 180-degree view to E, including stunning panorama of Franconia Ridge. From L end of this ledge, path leads 10 yds. N, then turns R to drop down steep 6-ft. ledge and continues easily down another 25 yds. through scrubby trees and muddy area to expansive open ledges with dizzying view down to Kinsman Pond and broad Cascade Brook basin.

To reach South Kinsman, continue S on Kinsman Ridge Trail, descending moderately for 0.1 mi., with one steep ledgy pitch, to ledges with good view S to Mt. Moosilauke and SW to Vermont. Drop steeply down these ledges, cross open area with good view E, then clamber down another rocky pitch and meander down to flat wooded col at 4.5 mi. (270-ft. descent). Trail now climbs moderately, levels on shoulder in beautiful mossy fir forest, then climbs steady rocky pitch to scrubby N knob of South Kinsman summit at 4.9 mi.; ledgy high point, with standing views in most directions, is 20 yds. to L. Main trail descends short pitch, then ascends gradually in open and 0.1 mi. from N knob, at 5.0 mi. / 4358 ft., it reaches open S knob with large cairn and near-360 degree views, though not all from one spot. Right by high point there are good views W and N; better views E are obtained by following ledgy path 30 yds. E to standup view over scrub. Take care not to trample fragile vegetation in mini-alpine zone here. For best views S and SE, including dramatic look down to Eliza Brook valley and Bog Pond, follow Kinsman Ridge Trail S, descending gadually in open with fine views, crossing small wooded col, and rising slightly to fine open ledges ca. 150 yds. from summit.

To return to trailhead, reverse direction and climb back up North Kinsman. After passing over summit, descend steeply and bear L at point where Mt. Kinsman Trail to NH 116 enters.

Northeast Approach from Lafayette Place
on Franconia Notch Parkway/I-93

NORTH KINSMAN ONLY

Lonesome Lake Trail, Cascade Brook Trail, Fishin' Jimmy Trail,
Kinsman Ridge Trail
8.2 mi. round trip, 2900-ft. elevation gain.

NORTH AND SOUTH KINSMAN

Lonesome Lake Trail, Cascade Brook Trail, Fishin' Jimmy Trail,
Kinsman Ridge Trail
10.0 mi. round trip, 3550-ft. elevation gain

TRAILHEAD (1770 ft.): This approach starts at parking area for Lonesome Lake Trail at Lafayette Place Campground on W side of Franconia Notch Parkway / I-93. Access is from southbound side of Parkway; from exit ramp for campground, bear L for Lonesome Lake parking area. Additonal parking is found by continuing on exit ramp and bearing R where road diverges L into campground. Still more parking is available on northbound (E) side of Parkway at Old Bridle Path / Falling Waters trailhead; access is provided by pedestrian underpass.

Of the several eastern approaches to the Kinsmans from Franconia Notch State Park, the most popular is the route described here starting at

Lafayette Place, which reaches the summit of North Kinsman in 4.1 mi. and the summit of South Kinsman in 5.0 mi. It passes scenic Lonesome Lake and close to picturesque Kinsman Pond, and presents some steep and rough climbing along the Fishin' Jimmy Trail.

Yellow-blazed Lonesome Lake Trail, marked by sign, begins at wooden bridge over Pemigewasset River and immediately passes through section of state park campground, crossing three gravel roads and passing by several campsites. It then ascends moderately through hardwoods, swinging L (S), crossing two small brooks on bridges and passing jct. R with Hi-Cannon Trail at 0.4 mi. / 1925 ft. Trail now climbs steadily up side of steep slope by two long switchbacks, first to S, then after sharp R turn, to NE. At 0.9 mi. you swing L for short stiff climb, then grade eases on high plateau to S of Cannon Mtn. Short descent leads to four-way junction at NE corner of Lonesome Lake at 1.2 mi. / 2740 ft. Here side path leads a few yds. ahead to shore of lake and beautiful view across water to South and North Kinsman. Main route turns L (S) here along shoreline and follows Cascade Brook Trail around E and S sides of pond to jct. with Fishin' Jimmy Trail at 1.5 mi. Continue ahead on Fishin' Jimmy Trail (Cascade Brook Trail diverges L) and cross Lonesome Lake's outlet on bridge, with view R to Northeast Cannon Ball and S side of Cannon Mtn., then bear L where there is beach and dock area on R (from which magnificent view of Franconia Range across water is obtained; here also Around-Lonesome-Lake Trail leads N along W shore).

Fishin' Jimmy Trail climbs up past AMC's Lonesome Lake Hut on R, eases before another short climb, then runs on mostly level terrain through open fir and birch forest. After minor ups and downs it climbs over small crest on S ridge of Middle Cannon Ball at 2.1 mi. More ups and downs follow; some of these undulations feature short, sharp pitches. At 2.6 mi. / 2825 ft., after short descent, cross N branch of Cascade Brook on floor of ravine, then begin main ascent towards Kinsman Ridge. Climb is moderate at first with crossings of several small brooks, then route is steep and winding, rough and ledgy in places, to crest of knoll. Here trail eases and then descends to cross small brook on mossy 3180-ft. plateau. Rugged climb soon resumes, with wooden steps pinned to ledges aiding passage on steepest pitches. Brief breather at ca. 3450 ft. precedes last sharp climb. As trail nears crest of ridge, it levels out and passes through wet area of sphagnum moss on bog bridges, crests a rise, and dips to Kinsman Junction, four-way trail intersection near N end of Kinsman Pond, at 3.5 mi. / 3750 ft. (If time permits, easy side trip L on Kinsman Pond Trail to shore of Kinsman Pond, 0.1 mi. each way, is well worthwhile for fine view up to steep face of North Kinsman.)

Take Kinsman Ridge Trail ahead (W, then S), climbing up ledges with occasional views to N. At 3.7 mi. / 3850 ft. Mt. Kinsman Trail comes in from R. Steep, rocky way continues up Kinsman Ridge Trail to North Kinsman summit at 4.1 mi. / 4293 ft. Follow Kinsman Ridge Trail S additional 0.9 mi. for South Kinsman (See Mt. Kinsman Trail description above).

East Approach from Basin Parking Area
on Franconia Notch Parkway/I-93

NORTH KINSMAN ONLY

Basin–Cascades Trail, Cascade Brook Trail, Kinsman Pond Trail, Kinsman Ridge Trail
9.6 mi. round trip, 2800-ft. elevation gain.

NORTH AND SOUTH KINSMAN

Basin–Cascades Trail, Cascade Brook Trail, Kinsman Pond Trail, Kinsman Ridge Trail
11.4 mi. round trip, 3450-ft. elevation gain

TRAILHEAD (1520 ft.): This route starts at the large Basin parking area on W (southbound) side of Franconia Notch Parkway/I-93. Additional parking is found on E (northbound) side of Parkway, with pedestrian underpass providing access.

This is a scenic, longer and less-used route to the Kinsmans, with fine waterfall scenery along Cascade Brook, cascades and beautiful boreal forest on Kinsman Pond Trail, and spectacular shoreline views at Kinsman Pond. However, parts of the Basin–Cascades Trail are rough, and the upper mile of Kinsman Pond Trail has very rough, wet footing, often in a brookbed, which is particularly tedious on the descent.

From southbound Basin parking area, follow path down across paved bike path, then navigate maze of paths around The Basin, bearing R and crossing two bridges, and find start of scenic (but rough) Basin–Cascades Trail, marked by sign, ca. 0.2 mi. down from parking area, and to W of The Basin itself. (This remarkable pothole in the Pemigewasset River is certainly worth the short side trip required to see it.) Basin–Cascades Trail climbs easily, soon comes alongside Cascade Brook, then ascends steadily past open ledges and cascades along brook, some with views across the valley (use caution as ledges on brookbed may be slippery). Trail then climbs high up on bank above brook, passing Kinsman Falls in gorge down to L at 0.6 mi.; steep and rough path leads down to base. Trail crosses brook to L at 0.7 mi., traverses rough section up on bank, then climbs along scenic section of brook to viewpoint up on R overlooking Rocky Glen Falls at 1.1 mi. Trail swings L through small flume-like formation and ascends easily to meet Cascade Brook Trail at 1.2 mi. / 2084 ft. Turn R here on Cascade Brook Trail and cross stream on sturdy, recently constructed footbridge, climb easily along NE bank of brook, then meet Kinsman Pond Trail 1.7 mi. / 2294 ft.

Bear L here on Kinsman Pond Trail (Cascade Brook Trail bears R and follows rocky old logging road 0.8 mi. / 450 ft. up to Lonesome Lake and Fishin' Jimmy Trail). Kinsman Pond Trail immediately crosses Cascade Brook and ascends at easy grade along stream on old logging road. After crossing tributary at 2.0 mi., trail swings more to L (SW) and ascends moderately along this brook through fine mixed forest of yellow and white birch, spruce and fir, with good footing. Several cascades can be heard and seen down to L. Trail gets rougher and woods darker as more cascades are passed, including one with easily accessible ledge perch at top just L of trail. Trail soon enters deep, mossy boreal forest and is rough and eroded in spots, with more glimpses of brook. After crossing the small mossy stream at 3.0 mi. / 3100 ft., trail runs in and out of brookbed, with rough, rocky and wet footing. It swings to N and continues rough ascent, steadily at times, in and out of brookbed, then grade eases at 3.3 mi., though footing remains wet and difficult. Outlet brook from pond is crossed at 3.6 mi. and S end of pond is reached at 3.8 mi. Trail then traverses ledgy E shore of pond, with rough ups and downs and impressive views up to ledgy wall of North Kinsman. Fine shoreside sitting rocks are passed on L just before reaching newly rebuilt (2007) Kinsman Pond Shelter (and tentsites) in woods behind NE end of pond at 4.1 mi. Easy walking leads to Kinsman Junction at 4.2 mi. / 3750 ft. Turn L here on Kinsman Ridge Trail to reach North Kinsman at 4.8 mi. and South Kinsman at 5.7 mi. as described above.

After ascending Kinsmans, it is possible to make loop descent from Kinsman Junction by following Fishin' Jimmy Trail to Lonesome Lake and then Cascade Brook Trail down to lower end of Kinsman Pond Trail. With ascent via Kinsman Pond Trail and loop return, trip is 9.9 mi. / 2950 ft. for North Kinsman only and 11.7 mi. / 3600 ft. for North and South Kinsman.

Southwest Approach from Reel Brook Rd. off NH 116 in Easton

SOUTH KINSMAN ONLY

Reel Brook Trail, Kinsman Ridge Trail
12.8 mi. round trip, 3450-ft. elevation gain

SOUTH AND NORTH KINSMAN OUT AND BACK

Reel Brook Trail, Kinsman Ridge Trail
14.6 mi. round trip, 4100-ft. elevation gain

TRAVERSE OF SOUTH AND NORTH KINSMAN
WITH DESCENT VIA MT. KINSMAN TRAIL

Reel Brook Trail, Kinsman Ridge Trail, Mt. Kinsman Trail
11.5 mi. point-to-point, 3500-ft. elevation gain

TRAILHEAD (1400 ft.): Turn S onto gravel Reel Brook Rd. (marked by hiker symbol) off NH 116 in Easton, 3.7 mi. N of its eastern junction with NH 112. Drive 0.6 mi. up this narrow road to fork with hiker symbol on post and bear L into rough, rocky field to park.

Perhaps the most scenic, interesting and difficult route to the Kinsmans comes up via the very rugged section of the Kinsman Ridge Trail S of the Kinsmans. Highlights include a powerline view, cascades on Eliza Brook, remote Harrington Pond, and rock scrambles interspersed with fine views on the S side of South Kinsman. The approach to the ridge is made via the Reel Brook Trail, a moderate trail with several brook crossings and a muddy, unpleasant section where it is used for maintenance access to the Easton–North Woodstock powerline. With a car spot, the traverse across the Kinsmans and descent via Mt. Kinsman Trail makes for a superb day.

From parking area, follow Reel Brook Trail into woods along old logging road, heading ESE at easy grades and crossing several tributaries of Reel Brook. At 1.2 mi. trail swings R and dips, then bears L across a brook and at 1.3 mi. turns L again onto wide road (be sure to bear R off road here on descent.) Trail soon angles up across open powerline swath at 1.4 mi. / 1800 ft. and re-enters woods on far side. Follow road across tributary and then two crossings of Reel Brook itself, and at 1.9 mi. / 2025 ft. join newer road coming in from L and cross Reel Brook again. On far side follow road to R, away from stream, and climb steadily with muddy, uncertain footing. At 2.4 mi. / 2475 ft. bear R off road (which veers L to powerline) onto older road with better footing. Trail soon bears R off this road and ascends gently to meet Kinsman Ridge Trail on S side of Wolf–South Kinsman col at 2.9 mi. / 2600 ft.

Turn L here on Kinsman Ridge Trail and follow it N along crest, ascending slightly to cross under powerline at 3.4 mi. From this manmade opening there are wide views E over Bog Pond and its broad, swampy basin and out to the SE ridge of South Kinsman, Scar Ridge, Mt. Osceola and Mt. Tecumseh. Look for trail sign on far side of powerline, where trail swings R up a knoll, then descends through open hardwoods, reaching spur trail leading 50 yds. L to Eliza Brook Shelter at 3.9 mi. / 2400 ft. Trail immediately crosses Eliza Brook, continues 50 yds. ahead, then turns L on old logging road. At 4.2 mi. trail bears L off old road and ascends through mossy fir forest along Eliza Brook, passing series of lovely cascades and pools. At 5.0 mi. Kinsman Ridge Trail crosses the dwindled brook to L and climbs moderately, then, after a L turn, steeply, emerging through a ledgy portal to the boggy shore of Harrington Pond at 5.3 mi. / 3400 ft. The small pond is surrounded by extensive shrub mat and overlooked by low cliffs, with rugged ridge of South Kinsman looming to N.

Trail swings R at edge of pond, crossing boggy area on wooden walkways, then begins rugged, rocky climb to South Kinsman, noted as one of tougher stretches of Appalachian Trail in New Hampshire. Grade is moderate at first, with scattered ledge scrambles, then becomes steeper with more frequent scrambling. At ca. 5.8 mi. / 4000 ft., at top of shoulder, there is excellent view rock overlooking Eliza Brook valley. Trail winds along shoulder, then resumes steep climb with some fairly difficult ledge scrambles and several good views to S and E. At top of this long pitch grade eases and trail winds up through scrub to excellent outlook down Eliza Brook valley to Bog Pond, with Harrington Pond visible down on its shelf, in AMC trailman Karl Harrington's words "a wee mirror of water set in its little cup far below, reflecting over the treetops a shimmering glint." From here trail descends slightly to small col, then ascends gradually in open to S summit knob of South Kinsman at 6.4 mi. / 4358 ft. North Kinsman is 0.9 mi. ahead on Kinsman Ridge Trail.

Winter

As is usually the case with summer hikers headed to the Kinsmans, winter trampers tend to "bag" both summits in the same trip rather than make a second separate trip for the one they didn't get the first time around. Space for cars is limited alongside NH 116, so it may be difficult in winter to find adequate parking near the Mt. Kinsman Trail at the Easton–Franconia town line—bring a shovel! This trail has good, mostly moderate grades for snowshoeing. Parking is not a problem for hikers bound for the Kinsmans from the E, however, as the parking lots in Franconia Notch at both Lafayette Campground and The Basin are regularly plowed.

The Lonesome Lake Trail/Fishin' Jimmy Trail route is often packed out, the more so in recent years with Lonesome Lake Hut open in winter. The steeper sections of Fishin' Jimmy tend to ice up quickly and can be decidedly treacherous in winter. Although broken out less often, the hike up to Kinsman Pond via the Kinsman Pond Trail tends to be a more pleasant experience than in summer as the rocky stream bed over which upper portions of the trail run is usually blanketed under several feet of snow. The upper part of the trail can, however, be difficult to follow in deep snow.

The parking area for the Reel Brook trailhead on Reel Brook Rd. off NH 116 is not plowed and the trail itself receives little, if any, use in winter, thus plans including this trail are not recommended.

View Guide

The views from the Kinsmans have long been hiker's favorites, especially the vista E to the Franconia Range, which the 1916 *AMC Guide* praised as "unsurpassed, as Mt. Kinsman is at the proper distance and angle to fully appreciate its lines and proportions. The range is seen entire from the horn of Mt. Garfield to Mt. Whaleback (Osseo Peak)." One other item of

The sheer east-facing slopes of North Kinsman drop off to hidden Kinsman Pond.

note on the Kinsman views: often you will see silent gliders from a nearby airport in Franconia plying the skies around the summits.

NORTH KINSMAN, E VIEW: The E outlook is a roomy table-flat ledge with a spectacular view across Franconia Notch to the barren, slide-scarred Franconia Range (L to R, Mt. Lafayette, Mt. Lincoln and Little Haystack Mtn.), with Lonesome Lake nestled on a plateau in the foreground in line with Mt. Lincoln. This is one of the finest of all views to Lafayette and Lincoln. The ridge followed by Old Bridle Path sweeps down below the peaks. The tip of Mt. Garfield pokes over the L shoulder of Lafayette, with (L to R) Mts. Sam Adams, Adams and Jefferson rising in back. (In a departure from our usual view guide procedure, the rest of the view will be described to the L of the centerpiece Franconia Range and then to the R of the range.)

Cannon Mtn. with its prominent tower rises nearby to the L of Lafayette, with the Middle and Northeast Cannon Balls in front and below. Distant Old Speck Mtn. is to the R of Cannon, and to the R of Old Speck part of Mt. Deception (L) and the peaks of Goose Eye Mtn. (R) peer over the lower L slope of Lafayette. Mt. Crescent is seen directly over the summit of Cannon, with Black Crescent Mtn. to its L and Maine's Old Blue Mtn. seen over the saddle between them. Distant Elephant Mtn. pokes up between the two summits of Black Crescent, and Bemis Mtn. pokes above the L Black Crescent summit. Next to the L Cherry Mtn. is seen above rounded Big Bickford Mtn. Cambridge Black Mtn. is seen over the middle of the long ridge descending R from Cherry (in line with Big Bickford's summit), and Pliny Mtn. in the Pliny Range is right above Cherry's summit. Mt. Waumbek (R, with its long, level E ridge) and Mt. Starr King (L) are seen behind and L of Cherry, with the ridge leading L across to Cannon's rounded NW Peak in the foreground. Scarface Mtn., Big Bickford's lower neighbor, peers over just R of NW Cannon, and lowly Beech Hill is seen above the NW Peak.

On the horizon above and just L of the NW Peak is Mt. Cabot, with North Terrace Mtn. just peeking over on its R and the several peaks, including sharp Hutchins Mtn., of the Pilot Ridge trailing off on the L. Part of the West Cannon Ball can be seen in front of NW Cannon on the L. To the L of NW Cannon, in the middle distance, are the low rounded summits of Mt. Cleveland (R) and Mt. Agassiz (L, with structure on top). The Mountain View House in Whitefield and rounded little Mt. Prospect in Lancaster are seen above Cleveland. The small, sharp Cape Horn in Groveton is seen through the gap to the L of Prospect, and through the wide gap of the Nash Stream valley on the horizon, one can spot the double summit of remote Deer Mtn. in Pittsburg. In the distance above Cleveland and Agassiz are the mountains of the Nash Stream region. Long Mtn. is behind and L of the Pilot Ridge, and next to the L are the bald Percy Peaks, with North Whitcomb (Muise) Mtn. behind on their L. Farther L, across the Nash Stream valley, sharp Sugarloaf Mtn. is seen over Agassiz, with Gore Mtn. just to its L and Bunnell Mtn. peering over West Peak farther L along the ridge. Next to the L is the double summit of Goback Mtn., with Vermont's broad Monadnock Mtn. behind on its L. To the L of Monadnock and closer are the pyramidal Burnside (R) and Stone (L) Mtns., with a long nameless ridge behind on the L leading across to sharp Sable Mtn. Just L of Sable and closer is West Mtn., and on the far L, seen over the scrub, is the broad mass of East Mtn. in Vermont's Northeast Kingdom.

From Little Haystack Mtn. on the R end of the upper Franconia Range, a long gentle wooded ridge sweeps across to the R. Partway along this ridge the tip of Mt. Nancy pokes up, in line with a prominent slide in the basin to the R of Little Haystack. Farther R, just R of the low point in the ridge, are the tops of Mt. Lowell (L) and Vose Spur (R), then the looming mass of Mt. Carrigain rises above the ascending ridge. To the R of Carrigain the Franconia Range sweeps up to the rocky peak of Mt. Liberty, with slide-streaked Mt. Flume immediately behind to its R. North Hancock pops up between Liberty and Flume, and South Hancock barely peers over just R of Flume, with prominent Juno Peak a bit farther R. The pointy top of Mt. Hitchcock protrudes above the flat shoulder to the R of Flume, and farther R is the lumpy mass of Mt. Huntington with Mt. Chocorua behind on its R. The top of Whaleback Mtn. is seen under the lower W peak of Mt. Huntington just R of Chocorua. Mt. Paugus, Chocorua's neighbor, is next to the R. To the R of Paugus and closer is Mt. Kancamagus, with Mt. Passaconaway's symmetrical cone behind on its R.

North and Middle Tripyramid are R of Passaconaway, then come East Osceola and Mt. Osceola, with Big Coolidge Mtn. below and in front. The S summit of Mt. Whiteface just peeks over the R side of East Osceola. To the R of Osceola is the slide-marked Scar Ridge, with the crest of the northern Flat Mtn. above its R shoulder. Mt. Shaw in the Ossipee Range is seen over the R end of Flat, with Loon Mtn. and its ski trails in front. Next to the R Mt. Tecumseh rises behind Loon's S peak, with Sandwich Dome and its heavy Black Mtn. shoulder lurking behind on the R. Sandwich's lower Black Mtn. is down to the R, with Chesley Mtn. in the distant Blue Hills Range on its L. The central part of the Blue Hills Range, including Blue Job Mtn., spreads to the R of the lower Black. Fisher (front) and Dickey (back) Mtns. are under the R end of the Blue Hills Range, with Red Hill poking up behind. Mt. Major is behind Red Hill, and from it the Belknap Range extends R across the horizon to Belknap, Gunstock and Piper Mtns. and then farther R to Whiteface Mtn. and other lesser hills. Part of the Squam Range is seen under the L (Mt. Major) end of the Belknaps, while the Campton Range sprawls in front of the rest of the Belknaps. On the far R and close at hand are the great wooded SE spurs of South Kinsman.

As noted in the description for the Mt. Kinsman Trail route, from the main outlook ledge one can drop down a rough path on the L to an expansive lower perch with a dramatic view down to Kinsman Pond and out over the broad, wild basin of Cascade Brook. From here you can also look R to the great mass of South Kinsman rising beyond the col between the peaks.

NORTH KINSMAN, SW VIEW: About 0.1 mi. S of North Kinsman's summit along the Kinsman Ridge Trail, ledges on the trail offer a good view to the S and SW. The broad wooded mass of South Kinsman looms close by to the S. Mt. Moosilauke is seen to the R of the slope of South Kinsman, with the lower Mt. Clough stretching out to its R. Mt. Cube pops up in back between Moosilauke and Clough, with distant Stratton Mtn. in Vermont seen over its L end. Okemo Mtn. is seen to the R of Clough's summit, and farther R Piermont Mtn. (L, peeking over in back) and long, flat Jeffers Mtn. (R) are seen over Clough's N ridge. In the distance over the L end of Jeffers are Dorset Peak (L) and Salt Ash Mtn. (R). The equally flat Hogsback extends R from Jeffers, with the Killington Range above it on the horizon. The knob of Sugarloaf and the prominent cone of Black Mtn. are to the R of the Hogsback, with many more Green Mtn. peaks in the Brandon Gap–Middlebury Gap area strung across the skyline.

SOUTH KINSMAN VIEW: The best views are from the more open S knob, where from various ledges around the plateau you can cobble together a

360-degree panorama. The best E views are from the end of a 30-yd. side path leading in that direction from the top of the S knob. The most open S views, including the looks down at Harrington and Bog Ponds, are from the ledges 150 yds. S of the S knob along the Kinsman Ridge Trail; this may be the single best spot in the summit area. Good views in most directions can also be found on the N knob when standing at the open high spot 20 yds. E of the trail.

To the NE the upper Franconia Ridge—Mt. Lafayette, Mt. Lincoln, and Little Haystack Mtn. (L to R)—rises above the nearby scrubby N knob (though not as dramatically as from North Kinsman). A long ridge sweeps to the R, down and up, from Little Haystack to the rocky peak of Mt. Liberty; over this ridge Mt. Bond (L) and Bondcliff (R) peek over to the R of Little Haystack. Farther R, over the low point in the ridge, is the sharp S spur of Bondcliff, with Mt. Resolution behind on the R. To the R of the col the tops of Mt. Bemis and Mt. Nancy are seen. The slide-scarred Mt. Flume is just R of Mt. Liberty, with Mt. Carrigain rising in back between them. From here to the R, the humps along the great wooded SE ridge of South Kinsman occupy the foreground. North and South Hancock and Juno Peak are seen over the gentle ridge to the R of Flume. Next to the R and lower are the main and S peaks of Mt. Hitchcock, with Stone Mtn. in Maine's Burnt Meadow Mtns. in the distance between them. To the R the squat Mt. Huntington rises over the level top of Whaleback Mtn. The Three Sisters and Mt. Chocorua are next to the R, over the W spur of Huntington.

To the R of Chocorua Mt. Kancamagus rises above Big Coolidge Mtn. Part of Mt. Paugus is seen off the L slope of Kancamagus, and down low Potash Knob pokes over the saddle between Whaleback and Big Coolidge. The symmetrical cones of Mt. Passaconaway (L) and North Tripyramid (R, marked by the North Slide) are to the R of Kancamagus. Next to the R is East Osceola, with Middle Tripyramid just peering over its L side and the main summit of Osceola to its R. In back between the Osceolas are South Tripyramid (L) and the summit of Mt. Whiteface (R). To the R of Osceola, looking SE, is slide-marked Scar Ridge, with the lower, ski-trailed Loon Mtn. on its R. The long, low crest of Little Coolidge Mtn. stretches under the Loon ski slopes. Rising beyond the R end of Loon are Mt. Tecumseh (L) and Sandwich Dome (R, with its bulky Black Mtn. shoulder on its R). The long crest of the northern Flat Mtn. stretches in back between Osceola and Tecumseh, with Mt. Shaw in the Ossipee Range over its R end, just L of Tecumseh. Farther R is Sandwich Dome's lower Black Mtn. spur with distant Chesley Mtn. in the Blue Hills Range to its L and the central part of the Blue Hills, including Blue Job Mtn., extending to its R, with Dinsmore Mtn. visible below, just R of Black. Fisher (front) and Dickey (back) Mtns. are in front and R of the lower Black, with Red Hill behind and R of Dickey. Low down in this direction one looks down at the town of Lincoln and part of I-93 below the W slope of Loon (L) and Russell Mtn. (R).

Farther R, beyond the Pemigewasset River valley and I-93, are two long, sprawling ranges—the Campton Range in front and the Belknap Range in back, the latter with Mt. Major at its L end and the prominent trio of Belknap, Gunstock and Piper Mtns. to the R of center. Down in front one can see part of North Woodstock village, on the W (R) side of I-93. The N end of the Squam Range can be seen behind the L end of the Campton Range, and other parts of the Squams are seen peeking over the Camptons. Farther R, looking SSE under the skyline, is flat-topped Mt. Prospect in Holderness. Bean Hill is seen as a long ridge on the horizon to the R of Prospect. Farther R and nearer than Bean Hill is the wavy crest of Hersey Mtn., with the distant twin, rounded Uncanoonuc Mtns. seen over its R slope; the similar Joe English Hill is seen a bit more to the R. Next to the R and closer are the Bridgewater Mtns. (L) and Plymouth Mtn. (R), seen beyond nearer ridges. In the foreground in this direction is the trailless mountain called "The Wolf Cub" by 3000-footer peakbaggers. When looking down from the ledges along the Kinsman Ridge Trail 150 yds. S of the S summit knob, one gains a dramatic, gaping view down the Eliza Brook valley to Bog Pond, with its accompanying powerline cut, sprawling in front of The Wolf Cub.

Starting above the summit of The Wolf Cub and extending well to the R is the long E ridge of Mt. Kineo, with Stinson Mtn. rising behind a gap in its middle. The Lyndeboro Mtns. are seen in the distance over the L end of Kineo's E ridge, with North Pack Monadnock Mtn. glimpsed a bit farther to the R. Mt. Kearsarge is prominent to the R of and beyond Stinson, with Ragged Mtn. and then Forbes Mtn. in front of Kearsarge; Tinkham Hill is seen to the R of Ragged. Farther R and close by, walling in the basin of Bog Pond, is the ominous-looking mass of Mt. Wolf, with three distinct summits. Mt. Cushman is seen above the L end of Wolf and Mt. Kineo's pointed peak rises above the middle peak of Wolf. On clear days Mt. Monadnock is visible just L of Kineo's summit. Carr Mtn.'s broad summit is to the R of Kineo, with Mt. Cardigan (L) and Sunapee Mtn. (R) in the distance between them.

On the R side of Carr a great ridge rises R across Mt. Waternomee, Mt. Jim and Mt. Blue, with Mt. Moosilauke's lofty summit seen behind Blue on the R. From the viewpoint to the S along the trail, in this direction you look down at the scrubby S ridge of South Kinsman and tiny, boggy Harrington Pond nestled on its small plateau. Route 112 can be seen winding through rugged Kinsman Notch at the base of Moosilauke. The broad mass of Mt. Clough is to the R of Moosilauke and considerably lower. Mt. Cube is seen through the Tunnel Brook Notch between Moosilauke and Clough, with Vermont's Stratton Mtn. on the far horizon to its L. Terrible Mtn. is visible between Cube and Clough, and Okemo

Mtn.'s double summits are seen in the distance over Clough. Piermont Mtn. peers over the R shoulder of Clough, with Dorset Peak beyond on the skyline; Salt Ash Mtn. is seen to the R of Dorset. Extending to the R of and just behind Clough is the Benton Range, starting with the long, flat crests of Jeffers Mtn. (L) and The Hogsback (R). The Killington Range is on the horizon above Jeffers and the Hogsback, with Shrewsbury Peak on the L, Killington Peak in the middle, and Pico Peak on the R. From the Hogsback the Benton Range continues R over the nubble of Sugarloaf Mtn. and then the prominent cone of Black Mtn. The Green Mtns. in the vicinity of Brandon and Middlebury Gaps are seen on the horizon in this direction. Farther R, looking W across the Connecticut River valley and a vast expanse of lowlands and lesser ridges, more Green Mountain ridges are strung across the skyline, including the Breadloaf Mtn.–Mt. Wilson–Mt. Grant range on the L and the long Mt. Abraham–Mt. Ellen crest on the R. On exceptionally clear days Dix Mtn. in New York's Adirondacks may be spotted to the L of Mt. Abraham, with the lower Mt. Hough to its L.

To the R of the Abraham–Ellen ridge, the lumpy Signal Mtn. range in west-central Vermont is seen in the mid-distance over the nearer Cobble Hill (L, with Moody Ledge behind) and Green Mtn. (R). Mt. Ethan Allen (L) and the distinctive, tilted Camel's Hump (R) are seen through a broad gap on the R side of the Signal Mtn. range, between Signal Mtn. (L) and sharp Spruce Mtn. (R). Farther R the wavy Worcester Range near Stowe, Vermont, is prominent on the horizon, and to its R and farther away is Mt. Mansfield, with the Sterling Range extending to its R. Cooley Hill is seen in the foreground under Mansfield. Flat-topped Cole Hill is connected to Cooley Hill on the R, with low, rounded Bronson Hill out to its R. Above Cole and Bronson Hills in the middle distance is the Gardner Mtn. range in Bath and Monroe. On the horizon above these are several prominent ridges in the northern Green Mountains (L to R): Laraway Mtn., the Cold Hollow Mtns., and, due NW, the sharp peak of Belvidere Mtn. On the horizon to the R of Belvidere are (L to R) Tillotson Peak, Haystack Mtn., and then the prominent, sharp Jay Peaks. The line of distant ridges is continued farther R with the long, bumpy outline of the Sutton Mtns. in Quebec. Next to the R, a long nearer ridge extends R to Mt. Hor on the L side of U-shaped Willoughby Gap. More Quebec peaks can be seen peering over this ridge. Very low in the foreground in this direction are Ore Hill (L, in front) and Garnet Hill (R, in back, with the town of Sugar Hill at its base). Mt. Pisgah is on the R side of Willoughby Gap, and from it a ridge extends R to the higher Bald Mtn. Pyramidal Burke Mtn. is just R of Bald and closer, with Umpire Mtn. on its R. The town of Littleton's Meadow St. shopping complex is seen in line with Burke. Flat-topped East Haven Mtn. is to the R of Umpire, with Miles Mtn. in front; part of downtown Littleton can be seen closer in this direction.

Next to the R on the horizon are Seneca Mtn. (L) and massive East Mtn. (R, with a prominent summit structure); seen in front are Towns Mtn. (L) and Mann Hill (R) in Littleton. Next to the R, rising sharply and just a mile away to the N, is the striking peak of North Kinsman. From certain spots along the Kinsman Ridge Trail you can also see Kinsman Pond at the base of North Kinsman. Seen in the distance to the L of North Kinsman's summit, between it and East Mtn., are (L to R) Black and Brousseau Mtns. in back, then the nearer West Mtn. with sharp Sable Mtn. peering over on its R and Harris Mtn. in front. A broad nameless ridge E of Sable is seen just L of North Kinsman's summit. To the R of North Kinsman's peak are the symmetrical Stone (L) and Burnside (R) Mtns. Next to the R and more distant is the broad mass of Vermont's Monadnock Mtn. Continuing to the R you see the double peak of Goback Mtn., then the Nash Stream range (L to R, West Peak, Bunnell Mtn. in back, Gore Mtn. and sharp Sugarloaf Mtn.). Closer in the direction of the R end of the Nash Stream range, and much lower, are the top of the West Cannon Ball, and the paired Mts. Agassiz (L) and Cleveland (R), with Mts. Pleasant (L) and Prospect (R, with a tower) behind.

Cape Horn in Groveton is seen through the gap between Pleasant and Prospect, and on the horizon is the double peak of Deer Mtn. in Pittsburg. Next to the R on the skyline is North Whitcomb (Muise) Mtn., with the bare Percy Peaks in front to its R. Part of Long Mtn. is to the R of the Percys, then the nearer Pilot Ridge extends farther to the R over sharp Hutchins Mtn. and several other peaks. The ledgy, rounded NW peak of Cannon Mtn. is seen nearby under the R end of the Pilots. Bulky Mt. Cabot rises to the R of the Pilots, and to its R is the lower rounded North Terrace Mtn. Low down in this direction, over the ridge extending R from NW Cannon, is Beech Hill near the town of Twin Mountain. Next to the R and slightly closer is the Pliny Range, with Mt. Starr King on the L and Mt. Waumbek and its long E ridge on the R. To the R of Waumbek and close by is Cannon Mtn. with its prominent tower. The summit of Cherry Mtn. is directly over the top of Cannon Mtn., with symmetrical Pliny Mtn. above to the R. Flat-topped Cambridge Black Mtn. is seen over the middle of the long ridge that descends R from Cherry. Continuing to the R one sees the distant twin peaks of Metallak Mtn. in Maine, then the nearer double broad summit of Black Crescent Mtn. In the distance between the Black Crescent summits are Bemis Mtn. (L) and Elephant Mtn. (R). Next to the R is Mt. Crescent with the long crest of Old Blue Mtn. above it in the distance. Then the view swings back to the Franconia Range.

NO. OF 4000-FOOTERS VISIBLE: from North Kinsman, 22; from South Kinsman, 21

Mount Moosilauke

ELEVATION: 4802 ft. / 1464 m   ORDER OF HEIGHT: 10
LOCATION: Towns of Benton, Woodstock and Warren
USGS MAPS: 7½′ Mt. Moosilauke, 7½′ Mount Kineo

Geography

Since the mid-1800s Mt. Moosilauke has had a large and devoted follow-ing among White Mountain hikers. This massive, bald-topped giant has it all: horizon-stretching views, a grassy alpine zone, beautiful forests, wild ravines, waterfalls, and a network of varied and interesting trails. It also has as fascinating a history as any 4000-footer save Mt. Washington. In the twentieth century it has become known as "Dartmouth's mountain," for the Hanover college has had a long association with Moosilauke, and in fact owns 4,500 acres on the E side of the mountain.

Located SW of Franconia Notch, Moosilauke dominates the coun-tryside for miles around. It is a large mountain mass with several sub-sidiary summits and ridges. The main summit is a broad, gently sloping dome crowned with an alpine zone of about 100 acres, home to high-land rush, Bigelow sedge, mountain sandwort, mountain cranberry and other alpine flora. A narrow, scrubby ridge leads a mile southward over a minor hump sometimes called "Middle Peak" to the prominent South Peak (4523 ft.), which is bare on top and offers excellent views, especially to the W. From South Peak a long ridge runs S over the minor summits of Hurricane Mtn. (3015 ft.), Chokecherry Hill (2971 ft.) and Bald Hill (2397 ft.), then the low knobs of Clement Hill (1489 ft.) and Foote Hill (1371 ft.). The E slopes of this ridge are drained into the Baker River by Big Brook, Little Brook and Merrill Brook; on the W side of the ridge is Berry Brook, which is impounded by Hildreth Dam near its S end.

To the W the deep Tunnel Brook Notch, drained northward by Tunnel Brook, divides the main summit of Moosilauke from its trailless neighbor, Mt. Clough (3561 ft.). Many slides have scarred the E face of Clough, and a chain of beaver ponds is strung along the floor of the notch, the south-ernmost being called Mud Pond. On the W slope of Moosilauke between the main summit and South Peak is a deep, slide-scarred ravine carved out by SW-flowing Slide Brook, which drains into Oliverian Brook. There is an excellent view of Slide Brook ravine and its necklace of gravelly slides from ledges on Blueberry Mtn. to the W.

NW of the main summit is a cirque-like valley known as Benton Ra-vine or Tunnel Ravine, marked by a large slide on its E wall and narrow slides on its headwall. A Dartmouth Outing Club (DOC) trail and cabin were once located in this basin. A good view of this cirque is found at the ledgy summit of Black Mtn. to the W. A major ridge runs N from the main summit to the broad wooded dome of Mt. Blue (4529 ft., a "Trailwrights 72" 4000-footer), with a spur ridge splitting off to the NW; the latter ridge carries the Benton Trail and forms the E side of Benton Ravine. From Mt. Blue another spur ridge, this one trailless, continues N over several nameless wooded humps before descending to the Wild Ammonoosuc River near a location called Wildwood. Between this ridge and the Benton Trail ridge is the deep, wild, ravine of Little Tunnel Brook, which flows NW and is laced with hidden waterfalls, once known as the Nine Cascades. An outlook on the Benton Trail peers down into this ravine.

From Mt. Blue the heavily wooded main ridge curves SE to Mt. Jim (4172 ft., another "Trailwrights 72" peak) and Mt. Waternomee (3940 ft.), enclosing the magnificent cirque known as Jobildunk Ravine, where the Baker River takes its rise. This now-trailless glacial basin has a cliffy headwall and a broad, flat floor dotted with beaver ponds and meadows. On the marshy shelf above the headwall is a small bog that was once a tiny pond known as Deer Lake.

To the NE the steep slopes of Mts. Blue and Jim form one wall of glacier-carved Kinsman Notch, site of the famed Lost River caverns. This spectacular series of caves, boulders, potholes, gorges and waterfalls, formed by glacial meltwater, is one of the region's premier tourist attractions. Another scenic highlight of Kinsman Notch is picturesque Beaver Pond (once known as Beaver Meadow, but later ponded by a small dam) along NH 112. Kinsman Ridge rises on the far side of the pass. The precipitous drop of Beaver Brook has created a long series of scenic cascades on the slope NE of Mt. Blue, accessible along the Beaver Brook Trail. There are more cascades on trailless Stark Falls Brook to the N. To the N the Notch is drained by the Wild Ammonoosuc River, flowing from Beaver Pond down to the Ammonoosuc River; to the E the Notch and the NE slopes of Waternomee are drained by Lost River (called Moosilauke Brook below its confluence with Walker Brook and Jackman Brook), which flows into the Pemigewasset River at North Woodstock.

The high Blue Ridge continues several miles S from Mt. Waternomee, enclosing the upper valley of Baker River; the E slopes of Moosilauke itself form the other wall of this valley. The DOC has named several of the minor knobs on Blue Ridge after prominent club members: Mt. Braley (3770 ft.), Mt. Kirkham (3341 ft.) and Sayre Peak (3157 ft.). The E slopes of the Blue Ridge are drained by Walker Brook and tributaries of Jackman Brook. From Kirkham a spur ridge runs S to a 2531-ft. saddle that divides the Moosilauke massif from trailless Mt. Cushman (3221 ft.) to the S; NH 118 crosses this height-of-land.

On the SE side of Moosilauke's main summit a flat spur ridge runs across the barely discernible East Peak (4660 ft.). Though once mostly open, this spur is now largely grown to scrub conifers. Between the South

The less-visited South Peak of Mount Moosilauke is a fine place to gain a different perspective on the mountain's main summit ridge.

and East Peaks is the ravine of Gorge Brook, a partially formed cirque striped with slides on its SW side. In the steep upper part of this ravine are waterfalls once known as The Pleiades or Seven Cascades. Gorge Brook is the first major tributary of the Baker River as it flows S and E to Plymouth; the two streams meet in a broad valley close by the DOC's Ravine Lodge, location of the major trailhead on the SE side of the mountain. Hatch Brook drains a minor ravine just E of Gorge Brook and also flows S into the Baker.

Nomenclature

It's believed that the name "Moosilauke" derives from the Abenaki Indian words "moosi" and "auke," which mean "bald place." A version of this name, "Mooselauk," appeared in print as early as 1755, and various other spellings were used over the next hundred years. Philip Carrigain's 1816 map of New Hampshire used the term, "Moosehillock," and this variant gained wide acceptance for many years. The present spelling of "Moosilauke" first appeared in an 1852 article on "The Mountains of New Hampshire" by C. E. Potter. Within a few years this became the standard name for the mountain. Sentiment appears evenly divided as to whether the name should be pronounced "moos-i-lawk" or "moos-i-lawk-ee."

Mt. Waternomee was named for a chief of the Abenaki tribe (see below). This spur was originally named Blue Mtn., and today's Mt. Blue was once called Waternomee. The name switch took place in 1876. In 1884 AMC explorer Isabella Stone wrote that "Mt. Jim" was a local name which she hoped would "soon be changed for the better." Chances are it was named for James "Jim" Clement, who was one of the builders and a longtime proprietor of the Prospect House and the Carriage Road, and was an enthusiastic explorer of the mountain. On some older maps the Mt. Blue–Mt. Jim crest was simply called Blue Ridge. Jobildunk Ravine (sometimes spelled Jobildunc) was supposedly named for three early explorers or loggers in the area—Joe, Bill and Duncan. The Baker River was named for Capt. Thomas Baker, a militia leader from Massachusetts who in 1712 led an attack on an Indian village near the present-day town of Plymouth. The Abenaki name for this river was Asquamachumauke, which has been translated to mean "salmon spawning place" or "water of the mountain place."

Historical Highlights

First Ascent: Although local legend avers that earlier climbs were made by the Indian chief Waternomee in 1685 and two of Rogers' Rangers in 1759, a more widely accepted (though still not certain) first ascent was by local moose hunter Chase Whitcher in ca. 1773.

1685: According to legend, Waternomee, an Abenaki sachem, crosses the mountain with a group of his men en route from the Pemigewasset River valley to the Connecticut River valley. They are driven off summit by fierce storm brewed by Gitche Manitou, the great spirit dwelling atop peak.

1712: Lt. Thomas Baker leads thirty troops along river that would later bear his name, then called Asquamchumauke. They ambush Indian encampment by river near present-day Plymouth and kill Waternomee.

1759: Two of the famed Rogers' Rangers are said to wander onto Moosilauke during retreat from raid on St. Francis in Quebec. Story goes that Robert Pomeroy dies at summit; other Ranger, in state of delirium, is found by old trapper at foot of Pleiades Cascades in Gorge Brook ravine and is nursed back to health.

1767: First settlers arrive in nearby town of Warren.

Ca. 1773: Moose hunter Chase Whitcher reportedly makes ascent of mountain, calls it "a cold place."

Ca. 1800: Scientific expedition including Dr. Ezra Bartlett and Samuel Knight explores mountain.

1817: Champion walker Alden Partridge climbs South Peak, writes article for *American Monthly Magazine.*

1834: Nathaniel Merrill builds farmhouse at S base of mountain at location that becomes known as Breezy Point.

Ca. 1840: First trail on mountain, from Glencliff on SW, is cut by local residents led by innkeeper Benjamin Little, who supplies ample libations as incentive; this later becomes bridle path. Today's Glencliff Trail follows part of route.

Ca. 1840: Mrs. Daniel Patch becomes first woman to climb Moosilauke; she fixes cup of tea at summit.

1844: In document titled *Final Report of the Geology and Mineralogy of the State of New Hampshire*, geologist Charles T. Jackson describes Moosilauke's physical features, including Jobildunk Ravine.

1851: Boston, Concord & Montreal Railroad is extended into Warren, launching era of logging in Moosilauke area. Small logging operations and sawmills spring up in surrounding towns.

1852: While fishing near head of Lost River, young Lyman Jackman falls into boulder cave. His brother, Royal, hauls him out, and Lost River caverns are discovered. In 1890s, Royal begins giving tours of caverns.

1858: Bridle path is built to summit from Breezy Point to S.

1859: Bridle path built up Moosilauke from NW—precursor to present Benton Trail.

1860: Six-room hotel, 30 ft. × 15 ft. and made of stone, is built on S side of summit by local entrepreneurs. Opens for business on July 4 with brass band entertaining throng of 1,000 visitors. Building, variously known as Prospect House, Summit House and Tip-Top House, is expanded in 1872, 1881, 1901. In 1880 rates are $3 per day.

1860: Merrill family converts farmhouse at Breezy Point into inn known as Merrill's Mountain Home.

1860: Ninety-year-old Philip Hadley walks from Bradford, Vermont, to Moosilauke summit.

1869–1870: Geologist Joshua H. Huntington and photographer Amos F. Clough occupy Summit House for January and February, establishing precedent for winter occupation of Mt. Washington following year. Their pioneering observations on Moosilauke include measurements of fierce storms and then-record wind of 100 mph. Clough also makes wild sliding descent into Jobildunk Ravine. Summit occupation is written up in Charles H. Hitchcock's book, *Mount Washington in Winter.*

1870: Moosilauke Mountain Road Co. incorporated, upgrades bridle path from Breezy Point into Carriage Road, charges tolls. In 1881 tolls are 2 cents for pedestrians, 3 cents for horseback riders, 5 cents for persons riding in carriage, plus 2 cents for horses drawing the carriage. Road is operated into early 1900s; last toll is collected in 1919.

1870: William Little publishes lengthy, colorful *History of Warren*, including many tales of Moosilauke.

Early 1870s: Under direction of Dartmouth professor E. T. Quimby, U.S. Coastal Survey occupies survey station on summit.

Ca. 1876: Jim and Daniel Clement, builders of Carriage Road, spend full year living in Summit House. Daniel keeps journal of their sojourn. Jim serves as host at Summit House for many years.

1877: Breezy Point House built at Breezy Point near bottom of Carriage Road, accommodates 50 guests.

1880: Thomas Wentworth Higginson writes article for *Atlantic Monthly* magazine describing bushwhack exploration of Gorge Brook ravine in search of Pleiades Cascades.

1880: James Garfield visits Summit House during Presidential campaign, a year before his assassination.

1882–1883: Warren historian William Little helps scout and build trail from North Woodstock to Moosilauke, later named Little's Path. Trail follows route of earlier path cut about 1860, but later abandoned, skirting Mts. Waternomee, Jim and Blue. Little's Path is obliterated by logging after turn of century.

1884: Current edition of Moses Sweetser's guidebook devotes five pages to description of view from Moosilauke. Mentions great slide 2000 ft. long on W slope, with recently constructed path leading to it from Summit House.

1884: Breezy Point House destroyed by fire.

1884: AMC explorer Isabella Stone and innkeeper George F. Russell ascend trailless Mt. Waternomee, taking bearing off path from North Woodstock. On another trip they descend from Moosilauke summit along North Woodstock path, then bushwhack over summits of Mts. Jim and Waternomee, painting their initials and date on trees atop both peaks. Later that year AMCers E. B. Cook and W. M. Sargent make short bushwhack to Mt. Blue from path, and "by sitting ten feet aloft in a tree-top, an unobstructed circular view was gained." All three of these trips are written up in Dec. 1884 *Appalachia*.

1885–1886: Moosilauke Inn is built at Breezy Point to replace Breezy Point House. New hostelry accommodates 100 guests.

1887: Julius and Grace Woodworth of Concord, N.H., ages 9 and 7 respectively, climb to summit, thus becoming "youngest party who have ever ascended the mountain alone," reports *White Mountain Echo*.

1889: Charter is secured for "Moosilauke Railroad Company" to build railway from Warren to summit, but plans never come to fruition.

1891–1892: Poet Lucy Larcom, for whom Moosilauke is favorite mountain, spends parts of summers at summit. There, on September 7, 1892, the day after death of fellow poet and lifelong friend John Greenleaf Whittier, she composes one of her best-known poems, "The Mountaineer's Prayer."

1895: New path is established up mountain from Beaver Meadows in Kinsman Notch. *White Mountain Echo* reports "Miss C. Cummings was the first to go over the new trail."

1899–1914: Fall Mountain Paper Co. strips softwood timber off slopes of

Moosilauke in Kinsman Notch area and in drainages of Tunnel Brook and Little Tunnel Brook; logs are driven down Wild Ammonoosuc River. Logging village develops at Wildwood, with school, post office, boardinghouse and several sawmills. In same period G. L. Johnson operation logs extensively on S side of Kinsman Notch, on side of Mt. Waternomee, and in inaccessible basin of Stark Falls Brook (where woods boss James McGraw devises method of snubbing logs down precipitous slope). Johnson, said to be a "shrewd old cuss" and "so crooked he could stand behind a corkscrew," builds Gordon Pond Railroad to haul lumber back to sawmill in North Lincoln; spur lines extend up Lost River towards Kinsman Notch and up Walker Brook, with additional sawmill located on Lost River 2 mi. S of notch.

1901: Logger William R. Park, Jr. builds gravity railroad to serve logging operation in upper Baker River valley, starting at junction with Gorge Brook. Upon Park's death his daughter, Ruth Park, the "Lumber Queen," takes over operation. Land is sold to Parker–Young Co. in 1923.

1904: Parker House is built on Tunnel Stream at NW base of mountain, accommodates 40 guests at rate of $8 to $12 per week. Hotel burns ca. 1932.

1909: Dartmouth Outing Club (DOC) is formed.

1910–ca. 1913: Summit House is used as fire lookout station, with funding from N.H. Timberland Owners Association.

1912: DOC members Carl E. Shumway and G. S. Foster make first ski ascent of Moosilauke, skiing all the way from Hanover and back in five-day epic.

1912: Society for the Protection of N.H. Forests purchases 152 acres around Lost River caverns and continues to manage Lost River as natural attraction today.

1914: DOC builds Great Bear Cabin at SW base of mountain near bottom of Glencliff Trail. Structure burns in 1926 but new cabin is built at site later that year.

1914–1917: U.S. Forest Service purchases substantial acreage in Moosilauke area.

1915: Tunnel Brook Trail established through valley at W base of Moosilauke. Glencliff Trail taken over by DOC.

1915: Merrill's Mountain Home is destroyed by fire.

1916–1924: Champlain Realty Co. logs International Paper Co. land on E side of upper Baker River valley, using Camp 2 (from earlier Park cutting) near confluence of Gorge Brook and Baker River and establishing new Camp 3 a mile farther up valley. Land is then sold to Parker–Young Co.

1916: DOC adopts and rehabilitates Beaver Brook Trail (also called Beaver Falls Trail) from Kinsman Notch to summit, following cascades on Beaver Brook. This section partly follows old trail built perhaps as early as 1850s and for a time reportedly maintained by AMC, but in recent years badly damaged by lumbering. Upper part follows old route of Little's Path. In this year Benton Trail is also adopted by DOC.

1920: Dartmouth alumni Charles and E. K. Woodworth purchase 100 acres on summit, including Summit House, and donate to college. DOC takes over management of Summit House and renames it Summit Camp, operates it as AMC-style high mountain hut with meals and lodging. Hut crew members pack supplies up Glencliff Trail. In 1930s rate is $2.85 per night for lodging, supper and breakfast. Over 1,300 overnight guests are hosted per season, many from summer camp groups. Highlight of stay is telling of "Doc Benton" story, about country doctor driven mad by search for Elixir of Eternal Life and whose malevolent spirit haunts Moosilauke. Oral tradition of Doc Benton story continues today at Ravine Lodge.

1924: Model T Ford makes first automobile ascent of mountain—takes 3 hours to top. Feat is repeated by another Model T in 1926 or 1927, and third auto climb is made with jeep in 1949. On latter ascent, which takes 4 hours from Warren, wheels spin so much on rough road that odometer measures 30 mi. for trip up and only 10 mi. for trip down.

1927: First downhill skiing race in U.S., the Moosilauke Down Mountain Race, is held on Carriage Road in April with 15 entrants; Charles Proctor wins with time of 21 minutes. Winter cabin is built at summit.

1927: Major storm causes slides in Gorge Brook ravine and Tunnel Brook Notch.

1930: Tunnel Ravine Trail cut through Tunnel (Benton) Ravine up to Benton Trail; shelter is built in lower part of ravine. Trail is abandoned in late 1940s.

1930–1931: USFS acquires International Paper Co. lands in upper Wild Ammonoosuc drainage and adds to WMNF.

1931: Cabin built in Jobildunk Ravine by DOC; abandoned after 1938 hurricane.

1932: Shelter built by Beaver Pond in Kinsman Notch. Short-lived trail built from Jobildunk Ravine up over East Peak to summit. Shelter named Camp Misery is built along lower part of Carriage Road near crossing of Big Brook; this is abandoned in early 1940s.

1933: Under guidance of legendary ski coach Otto Schniebs, DOC cuts classic Hell's Highway Ski Trail down W side of Gorge Brook ravine, described as "the steepest and most difficult trail in New England, requiring expert technique." Section called "Rock Garden" has 38-degree pitch. That year first National Downhill Championship Race is held on Carriage Road. DOC skier Henry Woods wins with time of 8 minutes; Harry Hillman, for whom Hillman's Highway in Tuckerman Ravine is named, comes in second.

1933: Dartmouth purchases 933 acres from Parker–Young Co. and converts horse stable from Champlain Realty's Camp 2 into Ravine Camp; this burns in 1935.

1933: First Civilian Conservation Corps camp authorized in New Hampshire is established at Wildwood at N base of mountain. Camp is operated in two sessions: 1933–1937, during which crews work on constructing N part of Rt. 118 joining Woodstock and Warren, and 1939–1941, with emphasis on cleaning up blowdown from 1938 hurricane. Another CCC camp is established at S base of mountain in East Warren. From 1933–1937, these crews work on S part of Rt. 118, and from 1938–1941 they also participate in hurricane cleanup.

1934: DOC cuts short ski trails near Ravine Camp–Go-Back Trail and Bieten–Boten Trail—plus 3-acre practice slope.

1934: Mt. Blue is one of two sites (along with Cannon Mtn.) considered for construction of aerial tramway for skiers. Cost estimate for Mt. Blue location by American Steel & Wire Co. is $180,000 for tramway with vertical descent of 2470 ft. On map of proposal, valley station is shown at S end of Beaver Pond and mountain station on summit of Mt. Blue, with cable passing over Beaver Brook Trail and cascades.

1935: DOC builds Hurricane Trail over S slope of Moosilauke. Short-lived Pleiades Trail built up Gorge Brook headwall. Wadchu ("Great Mountain") Shelter constructed along Carriage Road near top of Hell's Highway. After two successful winters, Ravine Camp burns in September fire.

1935: Tradition of Dartmouth freshman hiking trips is started and, under direction of DOC, is expanded through the years. Today over 85% of freshmen take part, with base at Ravine Lodge.

1936: Official opening of Rt. 118 joining Woodstock and Warren over saddle between Blue Ridge and Mt. Cushman.

1937–1938: Under direction of Ross McKenney, large new Ravine Lodge is built at base of Gorge Brook from large virgin spruce cut nearby. Lodge opens for business in 1939.

1938: Hurricane devastates old growth in Jobildunk Ravine and wipes out Hell's Highway with slides (though trail was reopened for two years in 1941), isolates Jobildunc Cabin, and flattens Wadchu Shelter.

1939: DOC cuts Dipper and Snapper ski trails.

1942: Summit Camp burns in October, presumably struck by lightning. Four Dartmouth students climbing up Slide Ravine discover remains of structure, with only chimney still standing. Some blame fire on Moosilauke's legendary malevolent spirit, Doc Benton. Foundation is still in place today, providing hikers with shelter from west winds.

1942: On night of January 14, B-18 bomber on anti-submarine patrol along coast wanders off course in snow squalls and crashes into E side of Mt. Waternomee. Two crewmen are killed; despite darkness, cold, wind and deep snow, five are miraculously rescued by teams quickly asssembled in nearby town of Lincoln. This story is compellingly told in Floyd Ramsey's *The Night the Bomber Crashed*. Site is marked by memorial today.

1943–1946: Under direction of Sherman Adams, Parker–Young Co. logs slopes in upper Baker River valley and Jobildunk Ravine, salvaging much timber felled by 1938 hurricane.

Ca. 1946: Gorge Brook Trail cut by DOC.

1949: DOC builds Ridge Trail over Mts. Waternomee and Jim, and Asquamchumauke Trail cut up through Jobildunk Ravine; latter is abandoned ca. 1973. Club also installs 1,500-ft. rope tow and cuts several ski trails on W slope of Sayre Peak. This mini-ski area is operated until 1953.

1953: Moosilauke Inn at Breezy Point burns after closing for season. Smaller inn is built at site next year and operates into 1980s.

1957: Second winter cabin built below summit, original winter cabin is dismantled. DOC officials drive up Carriage Road to inspect work—last visit to summit by automobile. New shelter is constructed at base of Beaver Brook Trail.

1963: Ravine Lodge closed as overnight lodging property. Is offered to AMC for $1.00 per year lease, but AMC turns offer down because too many repairs needed.

1965: Dartmouth acquires another 1,179 acres on E side of mountain thanks to generosity of alumnus J. Pennington Haile, includes upper Jobildunk Ravine, East Peak, NE side of Gorge Brook valley and area S of South Peak. Plaque honoring Haile is later placed on South Peak.

1966: Very steep Slide Trail opened up old 1927 landslide in Gorge Brook ravine, offering steep scrambling and good views over valley. It is "intended to be used in only one direction—uphill." Route is abandoned ca. 1980.

1970: Newly appointed DOC Director of Outdoor Affairs Al Merrill evicts "hippie" commune that had taken up residence in Ravine Lodge bunkhouse.

1970: Two developers form Waternomee Glen Corp., seeking to acquire land from Franconia Paper Co. for possible ski area development in Jobildunk Ravine, but plans fail to materialize.

1972: Gorge Brook watershed is dedicated as Ross McKenney Forest in honor of Dartmouth's longtime Woodcraft Advisor; plaque placed on Gorge Brook Trail in 1985.

1974–1975: Under direction of Al Merrill, Ravine Lodge undergoes major renovations; resumes operation for paying overnight guests in 1976.

Late 1970s: USFS crew sets ca. 100 wooden pin steps on steep ledges of Beaver Brook Trail.

1978: DOC Environmental Studies Division publishes guidebook to Moosilauke.

1979: Dartmouth acquires remainder of land in Jobildunk Ravine and Ravine Lodge area; total ownership is 4,500 acres. Winter Cabin is removed from summit.

1983: Al Merrill Ski Trail opened on slopes of Blue Ridge. John Rand Cabin built.

1988: Second Great Bear Cabin burns, is rebuilt in 1990; one log used for post in new cabin was found to have horseshoe embedded, perhaps providing better luck than previous two cabins at site.

1989–1990: Upper Gorge Brook Trail relocated to NE at easier grade, eliminating steep climb up ravine.

1991: Snapper Trail relocated off steep ski trail route, now at easier grade.

Early 1990s: Dartmouth grad Bernie Waugh hikes all the official trails on Moosilauke in a day, a feat known as "The Moose." In 2003, ultrarunner Sue Johnston becomes second to accomplish this, hiking 45 mi. and 12,000 ft. of elevation in 14½ hrs.

1993–1994: Carriage Road widened and improved by DOC and USFS, supported by federal transportation grant. New Beaver Brook Shelter built high up on Beaver Brook Trail. Upper part of Beaver Brook Trail relocated over flank of Mt. Blue, away from former route along rim of Jobildunk Ravine.

1999: Dartmouth alum and Moosilauke aficionado Dr. Robert Averill publishes two-volume *Moosilauke Reader*, superb anthology of writings about the mountain.

2007: Major reconstruction on steep part of Beaver Brook Trail by all-female DOC trail crew.

Trail Approaches

Moosilauke is blessed with a variety of scenic trail approaches from various directions. By any route the final stretch to the summit is exposed to wind and weather and should not be attempted if conditions are unfavorable. It is not as exposed or potentially dangerous as the Presidentials or upper Franconia Ridge, but this is still a big mountain that deserves respect. Please stay on marked trails to protect fragile vegetation in Moosilauke's alpine zone. When leaving summit, follow signs carefully to make sure you descend correct trail.

Southwest Approach from Glencliff

Glencliff Trail, Moosilauke Carriage Road
7.8 mi. round trip, 3300-ft. elevation gain

TRAILHEAD (1480 ft.): Take NH 25 to the tiny village of Glencliff, between Warren and Haverhill. Turn N onto High St. and drive 1.2 mi. to parking area for Glencliff Trail on R in area of fields and pastures just below Glencliff Home for the Elderly. The trail starts at a sign a few yards back down the road, though it is easier to follow an old road from the parking area, soon joining up with the trail.

This route provides a long, steady ascent to the ridge near South Peak and a final easy approach along the partly open crest. It is part of the Appalachian Trail. From parking area, easiest route is to follow old farm road ahead to E, crossing small brook on bridge, and in ca. 0.1 mi. short lower section of Glencliff Trail joins from R. Continue up old road through open pastures, passing along R edge of one large field, through a patch of woods, then along L side of another pasture. Look back for views of Owls Head and Blueberry Mtn. in Benton Range. Trail then swings L into woods to jct. R with Hurricane Trail at 0.4 mi. / 1680 ft. Glencliff Trail ascends steadily through mixed woods, then open hardwoods. At ca. 1.5 mi. / 2700 ft. enter conifer zone and slab along slope, crossing several small brooks. At 2.5 mi. / 3600 ft. trail swings R for steady, steeper climb through fir forest, a section called "The Agony" when DOC hut crews packed supplies to the Summit Camp. Good distant views W and closer views down into Tunnel Brook Notch are available from talus slope on R at 2.8 mi. / 4300 ft. Above here grade is more moderate to jct. R with side trail to South Peak at 3.0 mi. / 4460 ft. Glencliff Trail ends at Moosilauke Carriage Road a few yards beyond. (Side trip to South Peak adds 0.4 mi round trip with 100-ft. elevation gain. Beyond shallow col this narrow path rises through scrub and over rocks to open summit, with excellent views, especially N to Moosilauke summit, W to Vermont and down to slides and beaver ponds in Tunnel Brook Notch to NW.)

At end of Glencliff Trail, turn L on Moosilauke Carriage Road. This wide trail rises gradually through high scrub, with occasional smooth level sections. Partway along views to E and W start to appear over the scrub. Cross level crest of semi-open "Middle Peak" at 3.5 mi.; here side path, starting up low bank by pile of rocks, leads 15 yds. R to excellent view over Gorge Brook ravine with Ravine Lodge visible far down in valley. Main trail dips slightly with summit in sight ahead and leaves scrub at 3.7 mi.; from here to summit, except for one short section, trail is completely exposed to weather. Climb easily up footway defined by low rock walls through open, grassy terrain, with excellent views to S, and higher up to W, reaching broad summit and foundation of old Summit House at 3.9 mi. / 4802 ft. High point is on ledges just E of foundation.

Northwest Approach from Tunnel Brook Rd. (FR 700)

Benton Trail
7.2 mi. round trip, 3100-ft. elevation gain

TRAILHEAD (1700 ft.): Take NH 112 to a point 0.3 mi. E of its eastern jct. with NH 116 (this is 1.9 mi. W of WMNF Wildwood Campground) and turn S onto Tunnel Brook Rd. (FR 162), which is paved at first, then gravel. Bear L at jct. onto FR 700 at 1.4 mi. and continue to sign and parking area for Benton Trail on L at 2.9 mi.

Benton Trail provides a moderately graded climb along an old bridle path with especially attractive forests, a fine view partway up, and a final approach along open N ridge. This is one of the most lightly used approaches to Moosilauke. From trailhead, trail swings R and runs at easy grade to cross Tunnel Brook on ledges at 0.2 mi. (difficult at high water). It climbs easily to cross a logging road at 0.4 mi., then ascends moderately through open hardwoods. At ca. 2500 ft. forest changes to conifers with some birch and trail swings L to run up through woods along S edge of dropoff. At 1.3 mi. / 2800 ft. reach ledges on L with excellent view into steep Little Tunnel Ravine and N to Kinsmans; this is fine objective for a short hike. Beyond outlook, grades are easy to moderate through woods along edge of ravine, then up broad slope. Pass spring on R at 2.2 mi. / 3700 ft. and continue steadily up through beautiful boreal fir forest. At 4400 ft. is side path R to view SW. Shortly after passing short path R to wider W view, reach jct. L with Beaver Brook Trail at 3.2 mi. / 4550 ft. Benton Trail, now on Appalachian Trail and coinciding with Beaver Brook Trail, continues climbing moderately ahead, reaching treeline at 3.3 mi. and angling R up to top of open N ridge with sweeping views around northern horizon. Enjoy exhilarating stroll along broad, nearly level grassy crest following line of tall cairns, reaching summit at 3.6 mi. / 4802 ft.

WEST SIDE LOOP

For a full-day trip with great variety of scenery, one can make a traverse of Moosilauke with a return through the interesting Tunnel Brook Notch. Start at Glencliff trailhead, ascend Glencliff Trail and Carriage Road to summit at 3.9 mi., then descend Benton Trail to Tunnel Brook Rd. at 7.5 mi. Turn L and walk 0.9 mi. S along this lightly traveled gravel road, ascending easily to N end of Tunnel Brook Trail at 8.4 mi. / 1880 ft. Follow this easy-graded trail through pleasant hardwoods, passing beaver meadow and crossing Tunnel Brook just beyond at 9.2 mi., winding through area of old landslides, then recrossing brook at 9.7 mi. In short distance trail emerges on E side of string of beaver ponds and meadows, with views across to huge slides on Mt. Clough. At 10.0 mi. swing R by campsite to cross brook on beaver dam and continue S along W side of more beaver ponds, with views up to Slide Ravine and Moosilauke's South Peak, especially from edge of Mud Pond at 10.3 mi. / 2280 ft. Trail crosses over height of land, then descends moderately through hardwoods on old logging road above Slide Brook. Pass small reservoir on L at 11.7 mi. / 1800 ft., make two crossings of Slide Brook, then cross Jeffers Brook at 12.6 mi. Continue past private camp to Long Pond Rd. at 12.8 mi. / 1393 ft. Turn L and descend on this gravel road to bridge over Jeffers Brook, then rise to paved High St. at 13.2 mi. Turn L and ascend 0.2 mi. to Glencliff Trail parking. Total for loop is 13.4 mi. with 4000-ft. elevation gain.

Northeast Approach from NH 112 in Kinsman Notch

Beaver Brook Trail
7.6 mi. round trip, 3100-ft. elevation gain

TRAILHEAD (1870 ft.): Beaver Brook Trail, part of the Appalachian Trail, starts from large parking area with privy and kiosk on S/W side of NH 112 in Kinsman Notch, 0.5 mi. W of entrance to Lost River.

The Beaver Brook Trail is the steepest approach to Moosilauke and is very rugged in first 1.5 mi., both on ascent and descent, much of it climbing alongside a series of beautiful cascades on Beaver Brook. This section has many rock and triangular wooden steps, with iron handrails at several tricky spots with dropoffs, and can be dangerous if wet or icy, when the rocks can be very slippery. The upper portion is easier, providing some views along the flank of Mt. Blue, and concludes with an open walk along Moosilauke's N ridge, where it coincides with the Benton Trail.

From parking area, follow path past R side of kiosk and in a few yds. turn L onto main route of trail coming in from road. Trail runs nearly level, crossing one small brook on rocks and another on sturdy bridge, and quickly swings L at easy grade. Cross small brook on rocks and Beaver Brook on bridge at 0.2 mi., and just beyond swing R past DOC warning sign ("Take special care at cascades to avoid tragic results") and climb moderately, crossing another small stream, to nice ledges at base of first cascade at 0.4 mi. / 2025 ft. Trail climbs moderately up ledges and through woods, then swings R and L up very steep, tricky ledge scramble with dropoff at ca. 2300 ft.; iron handrails and wooden steps help here. Farther up is another scramble at edge of a cascade, then you pass nice ledge shelf on R with long view upstream to high cascade. Steep climb up rock steps leads to closeup view of the high cascade at ca. 2600 ft. Continue up more rock steps and new (2007) wooden staircase, then narrow section along ledge wall, high above stream, with iron handrail for security. Trail continues steep assault with more rock steps and wooden pin steps up ledges. At ca. 2800 ft. ascend long arc of pin steps up steep mossy ledge; at top is open ledgy area with view out to Mts. Liberty and Flume. Rugged climb continues up past more cascades, then on high slope well above brook.

At 1.1 mi. / 3200 ft. trail veers L away from main brook and climbs steeply alongside mossy tributary, with jumbled rocky footing. At ca. 3450 ft. cross small open brookbed with peek back at Kinsmans. Steady climb continues with one short switchback and at 1.5 mi. / 3750 ft. side trail R leads 80 yds. R past privy ("Bert's Bath") and two tent pads to DOC Beaver Brook Shelter, with view NE to Franconia Range; water may be found in small brook 30 yds. past shelter. After short, steep pitch, main trail climbs moderately, then eases to high plateau between Mt. Blue and Mt. Jim. Here, at 1.9 mi./4050 ft., is jct. L with Asquam–Ridge Trail. Bear R on Beaver Brook Trail at easy grade, then climb moderately. Trail next contours across S face of Mt. Blue, with some rough, rocky footing along rim of Jobildunk Ravine. At 2.5 mi./4275 ft. pass small ledge on R with standing view over wild valley of Jobildunk Ravine and out to distant mountains to E. Just beyond, sharp R turn takes you on relocated stretch of trail, away from former route that continued along edge of Jobildunk Ravine. Climb fairly steep and rough section with partial views back to E and S to point 100 ft. in elevation below summit of Mt. Blue. Grade becomes easy here in nice fir forest at 4425 ft. After slight descent, trail turns L and climbs over knob, passing three partial overlooks on L; first has view of Franconia Range and second has view to SE. Main summit looms close by to R. After short descent into col, trail rises moderately to jct. with Benton Trail at 3.4 mi./4550 ft. Turn L on Benton Trail (here coinciding with Beaver Brook Trail) for steady climb to treeline followed by final gentle approach along broad, open N ridge, reaching summit of Moosilauke at 3.8 mi./4802 ft.

Southeast Approaches from Ravine Lodge Rd.

Gorge Brook Trail
7.4 mi. round trip, 2550-ft. elevation gain

TRAILHEAD (2460 ft.): Gorge Brook Trail begins at end of Ravine Lodge Rd., which leaves NH 118 7.2 mi. from NH 112 near North Woodstock and 5.8 mi. from NH 25 near Warren. Drive 1.6 mi. up this gravel road and turn around in cul-de-sac at end (no parking here; DOC sign warns that if you do park here, "your teeny tiny car will be CRUSHED by a giant bus!!!"), then parallel park on R (W) side of road near stairway to DOC Ravine Lodge.

The Gorge Brook Trail is perhaps the easiest and most popular ascent route to Moosilauke. A 1989–90 relocation eased the grades on the upper climb and opened several fine views partway up. Two possible loop options using this trail are described in addition to the out-and-back climb.

From your car, walk back to cul-de-sac at end of road and past kiosk with view up to mountain. In 100 yds. Gorge Brook Trail turns L at sign and descends, then in another 50 yds. swings L again onto old road and drops down fairly steep, rocky pitch to footbridge over Baker River at 0.2 mi./2360 ft. as trail from Ravine Lodge joins on L. Turn L on far side of bridge as Asquam–Ridge Trail goes R, then in 60 yds. swing R away from river as old road continues ahead to Class of '97 swimming hole. At 0.3 mi. turn R where Hurricane Trail continues ahead. Gorge Brook Trail rises moderately over very rocky footway, then grade eases. Cross brook on bridge at 0.6 mi./2620 ft.; on far side is jct. L with Snapper Trail. Continue up alongside brook at easy and occasionally moderate grade with many views of stream, recrossing on bridge at 1.3 mi. At 1.6 mi. / 3250 ft. (sign: "Last Sure Water"), turn sharp R by plaque for Ross McKenney Forest and traverse E at easy grade, then swing L and climb moderately to NE through open birch and fir, with fairly rocky footing. Bear L onto old logging road at 2.1 mi. and pass fine cleared outlook S to Mt. Kineo and Carr Mtn. at 2.3 mi. / 3850 ft.

Ca. 25 yds. beyond outlook, wide-cut trail swings L off tote road and winds up slope through beautiful fern-filled fir forest. Higher up it makes several short switchbacks with some restricted views, then at sharp L turn at 2.9 mi. / 4300 ft. there is more open but still partly restricted view NE to Franconia Range and Presidentials beyond Mts. Jim and Waternomee, with Mt. Blue to L. Steady, winding climb continues, swinging L up rock steps at 3.2 / 4500 ft. mi. to traverse section called "The Balcony." At this turn there are views NE, and farther along this stretch there are standing views to E and a look down at lower Gorge Brook valley and Ravine Lodge. At 3.3 mi. turn R, then soon turn R again and briefly climb through open ledgy area with views S, then bear L on gentle shoulder known as East Peak along corridor through high scrub. Descend slightly with main summit in sight ahead, then rise easily and emerge from scrub at 3.5 mi. Enjoy beautiful easy climb along broad open, grassy shoulder, then ascend moderately to R base of summit ledges (avoiding an old trail route to L). Swing L up rock steps for steeper 50 yd. climb to summit ledges and sign at 3.7 mi. / 4802 ft. On descent, Gorge Brook Trail at first heads ENE down rock steps towards town of Lincoln, then in 50 yds. swings R and leads SE across broad, open shoulder.

CARRIAGE ROAD/SNAPPER TRAIL LOOP OPTION FOR DESCENT

An attractive option to returning down Gorge Brook Trail, with nearly same distance, is loop over S ridge via Moosilauke Carriage Rd. and Snapper Trail. From summit, descend S in open at easy to moderate grade along well-defined Carriage Road with wide views to W and S; Moosilauke's Middle and South Peaks are in sight ahead. Descend into high scrub at 3.9 mi., then rise slightly to semi-open "Middle Peak" with views back to summit. At 4.1 mi., along level crest of Middle Peak, side path, starting up low bank by pile of rocks, leads 15 yds. L to excellent view over Gorge Brook ravine with Ravine Lodge visible far down in valley. Main trail soon descends gradually along ridge with occasional flat, smooth sections. Reach jct. R with Glencliff Trail at 4.6 mi. / 4460 ft. (For visit to South Peak and more good views—highly recommended on nice day— add 0.4 mi. round trip and 100-ft.elevation gain; side path leaves a few yards down Glencliff Trail on L.)

For descent, continue down wide, reconstructed section of Carriage Road; downgrade is mostly steady with fairly good footing. At 4.7 mi.

pass row of boulders (intended to keep snowmobiles from continuing to summit), and at 4.9 mi./4225 ft. there is fine view L to Moosilauke summit and distant peaks as far as Mt. Washington. Grade steepens and trail makes several turns, with frequent views to S and E down to ca. 5.3 mi./3700 ft. Continue down through mixed woods to jct. L with Snapper Trail at 5.8 mi./3360 ft. Turn L here and descend across slope at easy to moderate grades through fine conifer and birch forest, crossing steeper, older route of Snapper Ski Trail at 6.0 mi. At 6.4 mi. trail swings R (SE) onto easy, smooth section, then swings L and R to cross small mossy brook at 6.6 mi. Trail follows this brook down at moderate grade, bearing L for sharp drop at bottom to meet Gorge Brook Trail at 6.9 mi./2620 ft. Turn R here and descend rocky section of trail, turn L at bottom and proceed upstream along Baker River, then R across footbridge over river. On far side Gorge Brook Trail turns L (route to R ascends to Ravine Lodge), ascends steadily up old road for 0.1 mi., then turns R and continues up another 50 yds. to gravel road (total 100-ft. climb). Turn R to reach end of Ravine Lodge Rd. in 100 yds. Loop total is 7.5 mi. with 2550-ft. elevation gain.

Asquam–Ridge Trail, Beaver Brook Trail
5.8 mi. one-way, 2700-ft. elevation gain

The Asquam–Ridge Trail offers a longer, easier, lightly-used ascent route to Moosilauke from Ravine Lodge Rd., with descent via Gorge Brook Trail or Carriage Road/Snapper Trail route. Grades are mostly easy, and much of the trail passes through beautiful conifer forest. From turnaround at end of Ravine Lodge Rd., continue ahead on extension of road not open to vehicles, soon passing kiosk with view of Moosilauke and then jct. where Gorge Brook Trail descends L to cross Baker River. (Although Asquam–Ridge Trail, or Ridge Trail as it appears on some signs, technically begins off Gorge Brook Trail on far side of river, hikers can save 0.2 mi. and 100 ft. of elevation loss and gain by continuing ahead on road, where there is a sign for Ridge Trail; this is route described here.) Al Merrill Loop soon diverges R; continue ahead at easy grade on road (which dates back to 1940s logging operation) and cross Baker River on footbridge at 0.5 mi. On far side turn R as lower part of Ridge Trail joins from L. Trail ascends easily along stream through fine mixed woods, passing weedy clearing on L marking site of old lumber camp.

At 1.5 mi./2900 ft. trail turns R, crosses footbridge over river, and ascends moderately to jct. R with Al Merrill Loop at 1.9 mi./3100 ft. Bear sharp L here on Ridge Trail and climb long easy-graded stretch on old logging road, first through birch and fir, then in a beautiful fir forest. Grade is somewhat steeper and footing rockier as trail ascends to crest of ridge between Mt. Waternomee and Mt. Jim. Trail heads NW up ridgecrest, passing abandoned route on L. It then makes several switchbacks as it

Cairns mark the way along the open and exposed summit ridge of Mount Moosilauke.

climbs SE side of Mt. Jim, passes framed view L through fir wave looking S to Carr Mtn. and Mt. Cardigan, and soon skirts close by wooded summit of Jim (a few yds. to R) at 3.6 mi. / 4172 ft. Trail now descends easily through nice fir forest, passes through blowdown area with view of Mt. Blue ahead, then runs through flat, densely-grown area to meet Beaver Brook Trail at 3.9 mi. / 4050 ft. From here follow Beaver Brook Trail and Benton Trail to summit of Moosilauke at 5.8 mi. / 4802 ft., as described above. Descend via Gorge Brook Trail for loop of 9.5 mi. with 2800-ft. elevation gain. Or, for grand tour of Moosilauke, descend via Carriage Road (with side trip to South Peak), Snapper Trail and lower Gorge Brook Trail; total including South Peak is 10.0 mi. with 2900-ft. elevation gain.

South Approach from Breezy Point

Moosilauke Carriage Road
10.2 mi. round trip, 3100-ft. elevation gain

TRAILHEAD (1720 ft.): The Moosilauke Carriage Road starts at a scenic spot called Breezy Point, once the site of several inns and now an area of open fields with views of Moosilauke's South and East Peaks, Mt. Kineo and Carr Mtn. Road to Breezy Point leaves NH 118 2.5 mi. N of its northern jct. with NH 25 and 3.3 mi. S of its jct. with Ravine Lodge Rd.; there is a sign for Moosilauke Carriage Road at the jct. Drive 1.6 mi. up this road to its end (paved, then dirt, then rough pavement), by old driveway on L that served Moosilauke Inn (good parking here). You may be able to drive short distance farther on grassy road, which descends slightly to sign for Carriage Road and parking area. At times the road has been closed 0.1–0.2 mi. below this point, in this case park on shoulder and walk up to end of road.

From its scenic trailhead at Breezy Point, the historic Moosilauke Carriage Road makes a long, steady ascent to the ridgecrest near the South Peak, where it meets the Glencliff Trail, then makes a scenic traverse to the summit. There are no views in the lower 3.5 mi., and the wide corridor can be monotonous at times, but nonetheless it is an interesting route, parts of which are often used for loops in combination with other trails. The Carriage Road offers generally good footing and passes through some fine forest.

From sign and parking area at end of road, walk ahead on grassy road, soon crossing Merrill Brook on wide bridge, then crossing a smaller brook and bridge. At 0.3 mi. trail swings L and skirts small clearing, then encounters first of several wet, mucky sections. Easy grade leads through nice hardwood forest, and after slight descent there is another mucky stretch. Dip to cross Little Brook on bridge at 1.2 mi., then climb to lower jct. L with Hurricane Trail at 1.3 mi. / 2125 ft. Ahead, Carriage Road coincides with Hurricane Trail, crossing Big Brook on Camp Misery Memorial Bridge; metal gate blocks vehicle access here. Carriage Road winds steadily up to upper jct. with Hurricane Trail on R at 1.6 mi. / 2380 ft. Continue ahead at easy / moderate grade through fine hardwood forest. Trail makes several sweeping switchbacks and at ca. 2800 ft. woods change to fir and birch. Several more switchbacks lead to jct. R with Snapper Trail at 3.0 mi. / 3360 ft. From here up Carriage Road is wider and more heavily used. Steady climbing leads to first views back to S at ca. 3.5 mi. / 3700 ft. As it continues its steady climb wide trail offers several more vistas looking back and at 3.9 mi. / 4225 ft. there is fine view R to Moosilauke summit and distant peaks to NE as far as Mt. Washington. At 4.1 mi. pass through row of large boulders that block snowmobile access to summit, and proceed at easier grade to jct. L with Glencliff Trail at 4.2 mi. / 4460 ft. (A few yds. along Glencliff Trail side path leads L 0.2 mi. / 100 ft. to open South Peak and unique views.)

Carriage Road now climbs at easy grade along summit ridge through high scrub, with occasional smooth level sections. Partway along views E and W start to appear over scrub. Cross level crest of semi-open "Middle Peak" at 4.7 mi.; here side path, starting up low bank by pile of rocks, leads 15 yds. R to excellent view over Gorge Brook ravine with Ravine Lodge visible far down in valley. Main trail dips slightly with summit in sight ahead and leaves scrub at 4.9 mi.; from here to summit, except for one short section, trail is completely exposed to weather. Climb easily up footway defined by low rock walls through open, grassy terrain, with excellent views to S, and higher up to W, reaching broad summit and foundation of old Summit House at 5.1 mi./4802 ft. High point is on ledges just E of foundation.

An interesting loop descent can be made by descending Gorge Brook Trail for 3.5 mi., enjoying several viewpoints in upper 1.4 mi. At jct. by Baker River where Gorge Brook Trail turns L, turn R onto Hurricane Trail, cross Gorge Brook on bridge, then descend to edge of Baker River. Hurricane Trail now ascends gently and follows level old road high above brook, with good footing. Cross small brook and enjoy more good walking to jct. with Carriage Road, 1.0 mi. from Gorge Brook Trail. Turn L on Carriage Road for 1.6 mi. descent to Breezy Point trailhead. This 6.1 mi. descent from summit creates 11.2 mi. loop with 3150-ft. elevation gain.

Winter

Moosilauke is an alluring objective in winter, but should be attempted only with favorable weather conditions. Fierce W winds often batter the upper ridge. Crampons may be required for the final open approach. The Gorge Brook Trail has excellent grades for snowshoeing and lots of views on the way up, and is largely protected from prevailing winds almost to the top. Ravine Lodge Rd. is not plowed, adding 1.6 mi. each way to the trip, plus an extra 400-ft. elevation gain (total 10.6 mi. round trip, 2950-ft. elevation gain). Plowed parking is available off NH 118 at the road entrance. Glencliff Trail is also good for snowshoeing, though the upper section of this route is more exposed to wind; the trailhead parking area is plowed. Beaver Brook Trail is sometimes used as a winter approach, but its steep grades along the cascades are quite difficult for snowshoeing and possibly dangerous in icy conditions. The road into the Benton Trail is not plowed. Skiers have long used the Carriage Road for winter ascents (and descents!) This route is shared with snowmobilers, who are supposed to turn back below Glencliff Trail jct. but sometimes ride on up the ridge.

View Guide

MAIN SUMMIT: Moosilauke has long been renowned for the breadth and variety of its views, taking in large portions of the White Mountains, central New Hampshire, the Connecticut River valley and Vermont. On very clear days several peaks in New York's Adirondacks may be spotted. Wrote one nineteenth-century visitor, Rev. Washington Gladden, "The view from the summit of Moosilauke is, on the whole, the most thoroughly satisfactory and inspiring view I have ever seen." It is a vast view indeed, and is best reserved for a clear day since many features would not be visible on a hazy day.

To the NE the blue-green jumble of the White Mountains is piled ridge upon ridge out to the Presidentials. The sharp, barren peaks of Mts.

Lafayette and Lincoln are prominent over nearby Mt. Wolf. The cliff face of Indian Head is seen low down to the R of Wolf, and close by in this direction is the broad wooded dome of Mt. Blue. South Twin is seen behind and R of Lincoln / Little Haystack, with Mts. Adams and Jefferson in the distance and farther R. The crest of the Franconia Range sweeps gracefully over to Mt. Liberty. The summit ridge of Owl's Head Mtn. just peers over the Little Haystack–Liberty col, under Adams and Jefferson. Farther R the slide-scarred Mt. Guyot peers over with Mt. Washington, 31 mi. away, towering a bit farther to the R, flanked by Mt. Clay on the L and Boott Spur on the R. In the right light, Mts. Monroe, Franklin and Eisenhower can be seen below and between Washington and Boott Spur. The striped face of Mt. Flume is to the R of Liberty, with Mt. Bond behind on the L and Bondcliff on the R. Mt. Willey is to the R of Bondcliff and (L to R) Mt. Hight, Carter Dome and Rainbow Ridge hover on the horizon farther R, with the various peaks of Wildcat Mtn. beneath. Mt. Isolation can barely be picked out below and between Carter Dome and Rainbow Ridge, and Mt. Davis extends in front to the R of Rainbow Ridge. From Mt. Flume a ridge extends R to Whaleback Mtn., marked by large gravel slides, with Big Coolidge Mtn. in front. The distant Baldfaces are seen to the R of Whaleback, and farther R Sable and Chandler Mtns. are visible beyond Stairs Mtn., with Mt. Nancy to the R. Down to the ENE are the towns of North Woodstock and Lincoln in the basin where the Pemigewasset River and its East Branch join.

Looking up the East Branch valley, the long, lumpy ridge of Mt. Hancock looms above the sprawling ridges of Mt. Hitchcock, with NW Hancock on the L, North Hancock in the middle with Mt. Carrigain peering over its L shoulder, and South Hancock on the R. Kearsarge North pops out to the R of Hancock, through Hancock Notch, with the double summits of Mt. Huntington on the R. Black Mtn., a spur of Loon, is seen under Hancock Notch. Loon Mtn. is in the foreground under Huntington, and Mt. Tremont peers over the R summit of Huntington.

To the E (L to R) Big Attitash Mtn., North Moat, Bear Mtn. and South Moat rise over the nearer Scar Ridge, with the Osceolas looming to the R. Close by in this direction are Mts. Jim (L) and Waternomee (R). Farther R the three peaks of Tripyramid are sighted through Thornton Gap, with Mt. Whiteface over Mt. Tecumseh on the R. The Sisters and part of Mt. Chocorua are seen to L of North Tripyramid, above Scaur Peak, and the tip of Mt. Passaconaway is just visible on the R of Middle Tripyramid. Farther R, Flat Mtn.'s bumpy crest is seen over Green Mtn., a S spur of Tecumseh. More to the R is the great bulk of Sandwich Dome rising above ledgy Fisher, Dickey and Welch Mtns. The distant Green Mtn. in Effingham is seen over the col between Flat and Sandwich Dome. To the R of the Dome Mt. Shaw and its Ossipee Range neighbors rise beyond Mt. Israel. Looking SE in the distance, beyond nearby ridges, are (L to R) the Moose Mtns. and Copple Crown Mtn. over the Campton Range, Red Hill beyond the Squam Range, tiny Mt. Bet, a stretch of Lake Winnipesaukee, and the long spread of the Belknap Range, with Mt. Major on its L end and the higher Belknap and Piper Mtns. on the R. Prospect Mtn. in Holderness can be seen under Belknap and Piper. Farther R, nearby Mt. Cushman is seen over the broad East Peak of Moosilauke, with the long E ridge of Mt. Kineo behind. Fort Mtn. in southern New Hampshire peeks over the middle of Kineo's E ridge.

To the S, just a few miles away, are the long, wooded ridges of Mt. Kineo (L) and Carr Mtn. (R). Hersey Mtn. and Plymouth Mtn. are behind Kineo on the L, and prominent Stinson Mtn. is behind and R of Kineo. The twin Uncanoonucs are on the horizon over the R shoulder of Stinson, with the equally distant Joe English Hill a bit farther R. Tenney Mtn. is seen in this direction and closer, with Mt. Crosby to its R. Farther R the distinctive Mt. Kearsarge is on the skyline to the L of Carr, with Ragged Mtn. to its L and closer. On clear days Crotched Mtn. may be spotted in the distance to the L of Kearsarge. To the R of and beyond Carr is the bald Mt. Cardigan. On very clear days Mt. Monadnock can be espied just to the R of Cardigan, with rounded Lovewell Mtn. and the elongated Sunapee Mtn. farther to the R.

Looking SW the spine of Moosilauke's S ridge stretches out to South Peak on the L; the sharp Croydon Peak is right above South Peak. Broad, tower-topped Smarts Mtn. is to the R of South Peak, and Vermont's Mt. Ascutney is beyond and farther R. On clear days Glebe Mtn. and the broad dome of Stratton Mtn. are visible to the R of Ascutney. The bright ledges of Mt. Cube are prominent due SW over Moosilauke's S ridge. On the horizon over Cube is the double summit of Okemo Mtn., with Bromley Mtn. beyond on the L and Peru Peak in back on the R. Farther R are the distant Dorset Peak, with a flat-topped spur on its R (visible only on very clear days) and Salt Ash Mtn. Next to the R, Lake Armington is seen over lowly Mt. Mist. Farther R, beyond the chopped-off Webster Slide Mtn., are Lake Tarleton, Piermont Mtn. and the distinctive sharp peaks of Killington and Pico on the horizon, joined by a long ridge. In the middle distance is the broad valley of the Connecticut, a patchwork of fields, woods and small towns. This wide-sweeping view continues around to the R, taking in the Bloodroot Mtn. group and many other Green Mountain summits.

Just S of W is low Blueberry Mtn., dark with spruce and spotted with ledges, nearby in front; Vermont's Breadloaf Mtn. range is in the distance over Blueberry. To the R the ridge of the Benton Range rises from Blueberry to the long crest of Jeffers Mtn. with the broad, wooded Mt. Clough (Moosilauke's near W neighbor) in front. Mts. Abraham and Ellen, joined by a long, level ridge, are on the horizon over Jeffers, and on exceptionally clear days a few peaks of the Adirondacks—Dix, Marcy, Gothics,

Algonquin, Rocky Peak Ridge and Giant, L to R,—can be picked out through Lincoln Gap to the L of Abraham, while New York's Whiteface Mtn. pops up through Appalachian Gap to the R of Ellen.

To the WNW is the N end of the Benton Range, with The Hogsback and the cone of Sugarloaf on the L and ledgy Black Mtn. on the R, with part of Long Pond visible in front. The fields of North Haverhill are beyond Sugarloaf, and farther in this direction is the prominent, humpy Signal Mtn. Range in central Vermont, with the unmistakable Camel's Hump seen over its L end. Mt. Mansfield sprawls far beyond Black, with Bolton Mtn. and the closer Worcester Range to its L and the Sterling Range to its R. Farther R are Belvidere, Tillotson and Haystack Mtns., and the twin Jay Peaks in far northern Vermont, with two peaks in Quebec's Sutton Mtns. still more to the R.

Seen to the N (in this direction the views are best enjoyed ca. 100 yds. N of the summit along the Benton Trail) are the mountains near Willoughby Lake in Vermont, including (L to R) Mts. Hor and Pisgah framing Willoughby Gap, Bald Mtn., and Burke and Umpire Mtns. Quebec's Owl's Head can be seen over a long ridge to the L of Hor. Seen in the foreground, looking NNW between the Jay Peaks and Willoughby Gap, is the small range consisting of Green Mtn., Moody Ledge and Cobble Hill. Farther R on the Vermont horizon, almost due N, are East Haven Mtn. and broad East Mtn., with prominent buildings on its top, seen beyond the nearer Cooley and Cole Hills. Between East Haven and East Mtns., Gore Mtn. peeks over in back above part of Seneca Mtn. To the NNE are the peaks of the Nash Stream region, just N of the White Mountains. On the L in this group is Goback Mtn., with Vermont's Mt. Monadnock behind on its L, then these mountains range across West Peak, Gore and Sugarloaf. Next to the R are North Whitcomb and the prominent ledgy cone of North Percy, with Long Mtn. to its R. Lowly Prospect Mtn. near Lancaster is under North Percy. To the R of Long is the Hutchins Mtn. ridge in the Pilot Range. Nearer in this direction is Bald Peak on the side of North Kinsman, with the low peaks of Mts. Agassiz and Cleveland beyond.

Swinging more to the NE, North (L) and South (R) Kinsman are dominant, with Mt. Cabot rising over North Kinsman and Cannon Mtn. poking above the R side of South Kinsman. North Terrace Mtn. (with spurs of Starr King on either side) peeks through the col between the Kinsmans, Mt. Starr King is above South Kinsman, and Mt. Waumbek's summit is above Cannon with its long E ridge extending to the R. Cherry Mtn. can be seen under Waumbek's E ridge, with Pliny Mtn. over its R shoulder, then the view swings back to the L shoulder of Mt. Lafayette.

SOUTH PEAK VIEW: This bare spur has a fine view also, sweeping much of the horizon. The view from the W edge of the summit is especially wide, extending from Carr and Kearsarge Mtns. on the L to East Mtn. in Vermont's Northeast Kingdom on the R, and including the Connecticut River valley and all the Vermont high peaks. To the N is a fine close-up view of the main summit of Moosilauke and its broad East Peak, looking like a scene from the Scottish Highlands. Also unique to South Peak is the striking view NW down into the deep Tunnel Brook Notch between Moosilauke and Mt. Clough, with good looks at several of the chocolate brown beaver ponds (including the southernmost, Mud Pond) on the floor of the gap and the huge slides on the E face of Clough. The views E from the South Peak are good but not as open, including many peaks from Mt. Washington on the L across to Sandwich Dome on the R.

NO. OF 4000-FOOTERS VISIBLE: 34 (from main summit)

SANDWICH RANGE AND WATERVILLE VALLEY

Mount Osceola and East Osceola

Mount Osceola

ELEVATION: 4340 ft. / 1323 m   ORDER OF HEIGHT: 23 (tie)
LOCATION: Town of Lincoln, Town of Waterville Valley,
    Township of Livermore
USGS MAPS: 7½′ Mt. Osecola, 7½′ Waterville Valley

East Osceola

ELEVATION: 4156 ft. / 1267 m   ORDER OF HEIGHT: 34
LOCATION: Town of Lincoln, Town of Waterville Valley,
    Township of Livermore
USGS MAP: 7½′ Mt. Osceola

Geography

Mt. Osceola and its rugged East Peak form the NW wall of the high, mountain-ringed basin of Waterville Valley. The mountain's ridgeline serves as the boundary line between the bustling tourist community of Lincoln and the unpopulated township of Livermore. It also serves as a separating line between the forested East Branch country to the N and the heavily developed Waterville Valley area to the S.

The 4340-ft. main summit, with its broad ledgy top and superb vista, has been the most popular hiking destination in the Waterville Valley region for well over a century. Flat-topped East Osceola, on the other hand, stands on the opposite spectrum as one of the White Mountains' least distinguishable high peaks. Unlike its sister peak, the summit is completely wooded, prompting one New Hampshire peakbagger to quip, "the summit view is definitely—and exclusively—coniferous."

The Osceola range runs E to W, with its cluster of four summits separated by less than two miles. Just W of the main summit are the Middle Peak (4220 ft.) and the sharp, knobby West Peak (4114 ft.), both trailless and required peaks for the "Trailwrights 72" list of 4000-footers. To the N, the ridge is drained into the valley of the Hancock Branch through steep ravines by several branches of Pine Brook. To the S, several ridges descend towards Waterville Valley, while flat-topped Breadtray Ridge ends abruptly in a bluff overlooking Thornton Gap. This 2300-ft. pass separates Osceola from Mt. Tecumseh to the S, and from here the West Branch of Mad River flows eastward while Eastman Brook flows to the W into the Pemigewasset valley. To the W of Breadtray Ridge is a broad valley, once called Breadtray Basin, drained by a nameless brook flowing SW from the slopes of Middle and West Peaks. Osceola Brook has carved a deep S-facing ravine between the main summit and East Peak; one looks straight down into this valley from the ledges of the main summit.

The broad E face of East Osceola drops off precipitously into the deep, glacier-carved hollow of Mad River Notch. The W knob of seldom-visited Mount Kancamagus (main summit, 3728 ft.) rises out of the notch on the opposite side. Just S of the 2300-ft. height-of-land in the notch rest the small, remote and very scenic Upper and Lower Greeley Ponds, headwaters of the S-flowing Mad River, offering impressive views of the East Osceola ridges from their shores. A lower spur, faced with a line of cliffs, extends NE from East Osceola at the N end of the Notch. At the S end of the pass a SE spur of East Osceola ends abruptly in the sheer Painted Cliff. Greeley Brook flows out of a broad ravine S of this precipice; the floor of this valley can be accessed by the Timber Camp Trail, which offers a close-up view of the Painted Cliff. On the next spur ridge to the S is Goodrich Rock, one of the largest glacial boulders in the region, accessible by a side trail from the Greeley Ponds Trail.

To the W of the Osceolas, beyond a 3100-ft. pass, Scar Ridge extends NW across several subsidiary summits to its main summit (3774 ft.) and then descends to Loon Mtn. above the town of Lincoln. Scenic East Pond is located on a 2600-ft. shelf just S of the Osceola–Scar Ridge col.

Over the years numerous slides have scarred the mountain on both its E and N slopes. Two prominent slides litter the slopes of East Osceola as it rises out of Mad River Notch. Several other slides, the most prominent of which came down through the ravine just NW of the main summit (drained by the main, central branch of Pine Brook) in November 1995, mark the N slopes and are best seen from various points along the Kancamagus Highway. Viewed from this angle, the Osceola ridge has an especially wild and rugged look. Another slide in a SE ravine below the main summit (drained by the W branch of Osceola Brook) is well-seen from the floor of Waterville Valley.

Split Cliff, a spectacular rock outcropping a quarter-mile N of the main summit, for many years was reached via a side trail off the main path between Osceola and East Osceola. Bushwhackers who have successfully battled their way through the scrubby ridgetop vegetation to reach this spot say its view N into the wilds of the Pemi Wilderness is unmatched.

A hiker gazes off toward Osceola's wooded East Peak from the ledges atop the main summit.

This ragged rock face can be seen from outlooks along the Kancamagus Highway.

Nomenclature

The mountain is named for the famous Seminole Indian chief who hailed from Florida's Everglades. Chief Osceola was one of the Indian leaders in the Second Seminole War against the United States, which lasted from 1835 to 1842. He employed early "guerilla warfare" tactics against government troops who were carrying out a U.S. plan to transport Seminole Indians from Florida to Oklahoma. He was taken prisoner in 1837 and died in captivity a year later.

No one knows for sure who gave the mountain its name, but Nathaniel L. Goodrich, author of a 1952 history of Waterville Valley, surmised that it might have been nineteenth-century Valley resident, E .J. Connable, formerly of Jackson, Michigan. His reasoning was that some early guidebooks mentioned a "Wisconsin tourist" as being the person to name at least one other peak (Mount Tecumseh) in the Valley. "It is tempting to surmise that Wisconsin is an error for Michigan . . . but that is just guessing," wrote Goodrich. The author also points out that on Arnold Guyot's 1860 map of the region, Mt. Osceola was listed as Mad River Peak.

Breadtray Ridge was named for its flat-topped, breadloaf-like shape.

Historical Highlights

First Ascent: Possibly by Capt. Samuel Willard, a colonist heading up an expeditionary force that was sent into the White Mountains in 1725 to look for Indian activity in the region. An expedition journal recounts a climb of a high mountain in the East Branch region, presumably Mt. Osceola.

1830: Nathaniel Greeley settles in Waterville Valley.

1850s: Greeley establishes first trail up mountain as part of network for inn he has opened (the first trail system in the White Mountains). Greeley's route (later a bridle path) ascended the "second ridge west of Osceola Brook" and climbed four and a half miles through "virgin forest never touched by the axe." In his 1952 history of Waterville Valley, Nathaniel Goodrich, himself a notable trail-builder, wrote that "until recently the remans of short corduroy ramps, built to aid horses up sloping rock, were still to be seen." Bridle path is also opened through Mad River Notch, eventually leading to Sawyer River country and lower Crawford Notch.

1874: Prof. E. T. Quimby of Dartmouth College establishes station for U.S. Coast Survey on summit, marked with iron bolt and triangle.

1881: Guidebook editor Moses Sweetser compares summit view with that of Mts. Carrigain and Willey "for its wide sweep over the Pemigewasset Forest and the surrounding peaks." He notes that path from Greeley's is "comparatively smooth and plain" and is "practicable for ladies." Guidebook includes two-page description of summit view.

1882: W. L. Hooper of AMC spends night on summit, then bushwhacks down N side of mountain to Pine Brook.

1884: A "comfortable bark-camp" is built on crest of Osceola.

1885: Privately published account—"One Night in a Mountain Camp: Story of the Ascent of Osceola in 1885"—appears in print.

1888: Waterville Valley Athletic and Improvement Association formed.

Early 1890s: Winnepiseogee Paper Company, owner of much of the forest land in and around Waterville Valley, begins timber harvesting operations in area. In 1898 this company is merged with International Paper Co. (IPC).

1890 or 1891: Southernmost slide on East Osceola comes crashing down on E-facing slopes.

1891: AMC group, sojourning in Waterville Valley, summits main peak on snowshoes.

1894–1901: Heavy cutting is undertaken on N slopes of Osceola by crews from J. E. Henry Co. in Lincoln; logs are transported back to Lincoln mills by logging railroad in valley of Hancock Branch.

1896: Rev. Julius Ward adds new chapter, "Snow-Shoeing on Osceola," to his 1890 book, *The White Mountains: A Guide to Their Interpretation*.

1897: Second slide occurs on East Osceola, creating N slide overlooking Mad River Notch.

1900: A. L. Goodrich lays out trail through steep ravine of Osceola Brook between main and east peaks. Known variously as Osceola Brook Trail and Ravine Path, it strikes ridgeline in col, then climbs via ridgecrest to main summit. This is frequently used for loop with older path up Osceola. Later, side path is opened to Split Cliff, where "the view and the cliff formation are unusual." The trail up Osceola Brook is abandoned by the 1950s.

1902: Route between main summit and East Peak is "thoroughly blazed"; rougher route descends to Greeley Ponds.

1909–1914: Woodstock & Thornton Gore logging RR operated in Eastman Brook valley by Woodstock Lumber Co. In 1912, Livermore Tripoli Co. undertakes unsuccessful operation to extract and process diatomaceous earth, or tripolite, from East Pond.

1910: New Hampshire Timberland Owners Association and state forestry department fund construction of wooden fire tower atop Osceola.

1915: State fire warden C. B. Shiffer marks out new trail from Thornton Gore to summit. Includes stretch of trail through virgin forest. Over time, path goes by name of Breadtray Basin Trail, Breadtray Trail and Osceola West. Trail follows warden's telephone line much of the way. This route is abandoned by 1960s.

1923: Wooden fire lookout tower is replaced with new steel tower featuring glass-enclosed room at top.

1926: IPC sells Waterville Valley timber holdings to Parker–Young Company, which threatens to run logging RR into Mad River Notch.

1928: U.S. Forest Service pays $1.05 million for 23,000 acres in and around Waterville Valley, saving Mad River Notch from logging. Parker–Young Co. does log on S and SE slopes of Osceola from late 1920s into 1940s. Several logging camps are established along west and main branches of Mad River. River drives are conducted on Mad River through 1933.

1933–1934: Construction of Tripoli Road, connecting Waterville Valley with Pemigewasset River valley to W, is undertaken by Forest Service, CCC. Road follows old Woodstock & Thornton Gore logging RR grade (1909–1914) on W side and former Waterville Gap Trail on E side.

1934: *AMC Guide* describes new trail up and over summit of East Osceola. East Peak Trail begins in col between two peaks, runs up to summit, and then down into Mad River Notch to Upper Greeley Pond.

Ca. 1936: East Pond Trail is extended over pass W of Osceola.

1937–1938: Hubert B. Goodrich cuts loop path, called "Nature Trail," from Greeley Ponds Trail up along base of Painted Cliff on East Osceola. Path is obliterated by 1938 hurricane.

1938: Hurricane demolishes many acres of virgin spruce on Breadtray

The former fire tower atop the main peak of Mount Osceola was manned by lookouts until the mid-1950s.

Ridge, forcing temporary closure of newly-built Breadtray Ridge Trail. Fire break along ridge from East Pond region to Upper Greeley Pond is cut by Forest Service.

1942: Forest Service replaces lookout tower with new structure.

1946: *AMC Guide* says old Breadtray Ridge, Osceola Trails have been combined into Mt. Osceola Trail.

1948: *AMC Guide* decribes bushwhack route from Mt. Osceola Trail along ridge to West Peak.

1954: Heavy rains from pair of summer hurricanes touch off three new landslides on mountain.

1955: Fire tower atop main summit is manned for final season.

1969: Greeley Ponds Scenic Area designated by Forest Service.

1985: Summit fire tower is removed by Forest Service.

Mid-1980s: North end of Mt. Osceola Trail at Mad River Notch is relocated away from base of north slide, now angles down less steeply to height-of-land in Mad River Notch. This relocation displaces proposed new trail up N ridge of East Peak, which is never built.

1995: During late fall rainstorm, huge slide falls on N slope between main summit and Middle Peak.

Trail Approaches

The Mount Osceola Trail (WMNF) is the lone trail up the mountain. Its southern terminus is along Tripoli Road (FR 30), while its northern terminus is in Mad River Notch, where it meets the Greeley Ponds Trail 1.3 mi. from the Kancamagus Highway and 3.8 mi. from the Livermore Trail from Waterville Valley. The trail runs a total distance of 5.7 mi.

Unless your hiking party has spotted vehicles at both the Tripoli Rd. and Kancamagus Highway trailheads, the only practical way to "bag" the two summits in a single trip is an over-and-back trek from either trail-head. Ascending the peaks from Tripoli Rd. is the easier of the two approaches as the total elevation gain is less and the climbing is significantly less steep than that via Mad River Notch.

Southwest Approach from Tripoli Road

MT. OSCEOLA ONLY

Mt. Osceola Trail
6.4 mi. round trip, 2050-ft. elevation gain

MT. OSCEOLA AND EAST OSCEOLA OUT AND BACK

Mt. Osceola Trail
8.4 mi. round trip, 2950-ft. elevation gain

TRAILHEAD (2280 ft.): Mt. Osceola Trail leaves from parking lot on N side of Tripoli Rd. near its height-of-land, 7.0 mi. E of I-93 at Exit 31 and 2.9 mi. W of its intersection with West Branch Rd. near Livermore Trail (Depot Camp) parking area.

The climb out of Thornton Gap is on moderate grades, never steep, and the main summit is reached in a relatively easy 3.2 mi. However, footing is very rocky in lower 1.25 mi. (tedious on descent), though much smoother at higher elevations.

From parking area trail runs NE at easy to moderate grade, becoming rocky underfoot almost immediately. In ca. 0.4 mi. it swings more to E and slabs along S slope of Breadtray Ridge, climbing gradually. At 0.9 mi. trail bends L, then L again, and soon turns R onto wide and especially gnarly section of trail, ascending moderately through slender birches and small conifers. At 1.3 mi. footing improves and trail makes another L turn, beginning series of switchbacks leading to top of Breadtray Ridge. Huge bowl separates this ridge from main summit mass, and through trees to NE Osceola's summit is seen on opposite side of the valley. In next section there are some nice stretches of gravelly walking through wild fir forest, with only an occasional rocky spot. Ascent is steadier as trail approaches main mass of Osceola, and at 2.1 mi. / 3500 ft. ledge on L offers standup view S to Sandwich Dome. Rougher climb leads to R turn by tiny brook (often dry) at 2.3 mi. / 3650 ft. Trail now ascends main ridge by switchbacks through rough terrain, crossing numerous angled slabs that may be icy in late fall. Second and third switchbacks offer partial views S to Mt. Tecumseh and distant hills from semi-open areas. At 3.0 mi., trail makes abrupt R turn for final moderate climb to flat summit crest. (At this corner, beaten path to L is long-abandoned route of Breadtray Basin Trail.) Mt. Osceola Trail first reaches small ledgy clearing, site of original fire tower and probably high point on mountain. Two concrete abutments are seen to L; next to one at edge of trail is unmarked side path leading 20 yds. to uplifted ledge in scrub with fine views to NW. Fifty yds. past first tower abutments are second set of concrete supports in large open area. Just past these, at 3.2 mi. / 4340 ft., are Osceola's main summit ledges, with wide views. A USGS benchmark is found at the NE edge of these ledges.

To reach East Osceola, trail departs L (N) from second concrete abutments. For first half-mile, as trail descends to col, grade of trail alternates between level terraces and steep, rough pitches. Especially challenging is short, steep chimney just above low point on connecting ridge. Most descending hikers will follow well-used detour L around chimney.

From col, reached at 3.8 mi. / 3820 ft., trail climbs steadily up East Osceola cone. About halfway up (at ca. 4000 ft.), look for rock ledge up on L offering nice view N and W. From ledge it is 0.2 mi. of steady climbing to trailside cairn marking flat, wooded summit (mostly viewless except for glimpses through dead trees), attained at 4.2 mi. / 4156 ft.

Northeast Approach from Kancamagus Highway (NH 112)

EAST OSCEOLA ONLY

Greeley Ponds Trail, Mt. Osceola Trail
5.6 mi. round trip, 2216-ft. elevation gain

EAST OSCEOLA AND MT. OSCEOLA OUT AND BACK

Greeley Ponds Trail, Mt. Osceola Trail
7.6 mi. round trip, 3116-ft. elevation gain

TRAILHEAD (1940 ft.): Hikers bound for the summits from the Kancamagus Highway (NH 112) should park at Greeley Ponds trailhead, small parking area marked by sign 4.5 mi. E of Lincoln Woods hiking trailhead and USFS information center. (This is 0.2 mi. E of trailhead for Greeley Ponds X-C ski trail.).

Follow Greeley Ponds Trail on gradual ascent through deep mixed woods, crossing two branches of South Fork of Hancock Branch at 0.3 mi. Trail slabs along up on E side of valley with occasional bog bridges and some muddy, rocky footing. At 0.9 mi. trail turns L on old logging road and rises at easy grades, then swings R and L to height-of-land in Mad River Notch at 1.3 mi. / 2300 ft., where Mt. Osceola Trail intersects on R. Turn R and ascend on moderate grade for first 0.8 mi., approaching and then passing under cliffs of NE spur of East Osceola. This section of trail features attractive birches in lower part and passes interesting boulders on R at base of cliffs. At sharp R turn (ca. 3000 ft.), trail joins older route and begins very steep half-mile climb alongside century-old slide. Trail skirts to R of large rock face at ca. 3300 ft. and after sustained steep, rough pitch angles L up across broken ledges on upper portion of slide at ca. 3700 ft., with fine view straight down at green-tinted Upper Greeley Pond, E to Mt. Kancamagus and NE to many distant peaks. Trail remains steep, ending with slippery scramble up eroded gully to shoulder of East Osceola; look here for side path R leading to outlook W to main ridge of Osceola, Scar Ridge and beyond. Trail turns L and after short breather continues fairly steep climb to knob at N end of ridge, then moderates as summit is approached, reaching flat, wooded, mostly viewless high point (on R, marked by cairn) at 2.8 mi. / 4156 ft.

To reach main peak, follow trail as it drops steadily past fine outlook N and W (up on R), reaching col at 3.2 mi. / 3820 ft. After negotiating steep rock chimney (or well-trodden bypass to R) at start of ascent, continue on alternating steep and easy grades 0.5 mi. to open summit ledges at 3.8 mi. / 4340 ft. For NW outlook, continue short distance ahead to second set of ledges in small clearing; look for side path R by concrete tower support at edge of woods.

Winter

Motor vehicle access to the Tripoli Rd. end of the Mount Osceola Trail is nonexistent in winter as the road is closed at both its E and W ends; the shorter approach is 2.9 mi. up the road from Livermore Trail (Depot Camp) parking on the Waterville (E) side. For that reason, most winter climbers choose to ascend the peaks from the NE by way of the Greeley Ponds Trail and Mad River Notch. The climb up East Osceola can be very difficult when there is poor snow cover, or if the track is too hard-packed; this is one of the more challenging sections on a popular route to a winter 4000-footer. Crampons should be carried for this section and also for the very steep pitch at the chimney just above the windswept, often drifted col on the Mt. Osceola side; sane hikers will use the bypass on the R (ascending) rather than the chimney itself. With deep snow, additional views open up on ridgecrest approach to main summit. One of the earliest to climb Osceola in winter (in the 1890s) was the Rev. Julius Ward, who wrote, "There is a great deal that you cannot put into words in describing such a view as I witnessed from Osceola during the brightest hours of a perfect winter day."

View Guide

MT. OSCEOLA, MAIN LEDGES: The main summit has perhaps the finest view of any major peak in the southern White Mountains. The expansive summit ledges, facing E atop a cliff, afford a grand view of the surrounding mountain landscape. A lower shelf of ledge down in front is a favorite perch for many an Osceola visitor. "I regard the panorama of mountains from this summit as the finest key to the mountains which I know," enthused the Rev. Edward Everett Hale, for whom another 4000-footer is named. A short side path through the scrub 50 yds. W of the main ledges leads to another fine outlook to the NW, with a memorable view of the jumble of forest-covered mountains around the Pemigewasset Wilderness.

The main ledges are perched above the deep ravine of Osceola Brook, whose headwall meets the crest of the ridge at the col with East Osceola, which is very prominent close by to the NE. The view starts on the far L (N) with Zeacliff at the N edge of the Pemigewasset Wilderness. In the distance to the R of Zeacliff are Mts. Starr King and Waumbek with Mt. Cabot peering over Starr King and the tip of The Horn just visible to its R. Farther R is the great sprawl of Mt. Hancock, with the NW Peak on the L, the rounded, slide-scarred North Peak in the center, and the South Peak to the R, above a minor nub on the nearby Osceola ridge. The hairpin curve on the Kancamagus Highway is below the NW summit of Mt. Hancock and to the L of the minor nub. Mt. Tom (R) and Mt. Deception (L) are seen between NW Hancock and North Hancock, and Mt. Willey is seen between North and South Hancock. Next to the R are the twin rounded summits of Mt. Huntington in the foreground, with another section of the Kancamagus Highway visible below.

The high Presidentials rise beyond Huntington: (L to R) Mt. Jefferson, Mt. Adams, Mt. Clay, Mt. Washington and Boott Spur. Mt. Eisenhower is under Clay with Mt. Pierce (L) and Mt. Jackson (R) in front of it and lower. Lower still, between Pierce and Jackson, is Mt. Webster. A dominant feature of the view, to the R of Washington and in line with Boott Spur, is the great curving dome of Mt. Carrigain. To the R of and behind Carrigain are the Giant Stairs and Mt. Resolution (with Mt. Crawford in front). To the L of Stairs are parts of Rocky Branch Ridge, and more distant are Middle and South Carter, the Wildcats, and Carter Dome, with its Rainbow Ridge rising over the Stairs. To the R of Resolution are (L to R) Jackson's Black Mtn., South and North Baldface, Sable Mtn., Chandler Mtn., Eastman Mtn. and the Doubleheads. West Royce peers over in back of Black and Maine's Mt. Blue is a dim blue pyramid farther L (over Resolution's South Peak). Mt. Parker is seen under South Baldface, with Mt. Hope below it. Several peaks near Rumford, Maine, can be spotted beyond the Doubleheads. The prominent cliff of Iron Mtn. stands out in front of and below the Doubleheads, with Hart Ledge below it. In the foreground under the Baldface Range is the long east spur of Mt. Huntington.

Continuing to the R, the view is dominated by the nearby flat-topped peak of East Osceola, with Mt. Tremont rising above; distant Mt. Tom in Maine pokes up to the L of Tremont. The sharp summit of Bartlett Haystack is to the R of East Osceola over Owls Cliff, with Greens Cliff below in front and prominent Kearsarge North above and behind. Extending L from Kearsarge North is the lower range of the Gemini, Mt. Shaw and Walter Mtn. the latter two seen over Tremont. Distant Mt. Tom in western Maine is visible over the L half of Walter Mtn. Maine's Streaked Mtn. is seen on the horizon off the R slope of Kearsarge North. Next to the R is the rolling crest of Mt. Kancamagus, with Little and Big Attitash Mtns. and Bear Mtn. beyond. North Moat pops up over the L side of Bear, and to the R of Bear are Middle and South Moat with Maine's Pleasant Mtn. on the horizon. Farther R are the Three Sisters and rocky Mt. Chocorua, with the lower peaks of Potash and Hedgehog below the Sisters. Under and just R of Chocorua is Mt. Tripyramid's Scaur Peak, with the Fool Killer and Mt. Paugus behind on its R and Flume Peak down in front to the R. Bill Merrill Mtn. and other hills in western Maine are seen in the distance to the R of Chocorua. Next to the R, rising impressively to the SE beyond a low spur ridge of East Osceola and the upper Waterville Valley, are the three towering peaks of Mt. Tripyramid, with Mt. Passaconaway peeking out just to the L of slide-scarred North Tripyramid. To the R of Tripyramid is Mt. Whiteface with the two rounded Sleepers below. Farther R the Ossipee Range, with Mt. Shaw, its highest peak, in the center, is seen over the long, low ridge of the northern Flat Mtn. In the Ossipees, Flagg Mtn. is to the L of Shaw, and Faraway Mtn. and Mt. Roberts are to the R. The Moose Mtns. can be seen between Shaw and Faraway, and Copple Crown Mtn. is to the R of Faraway. In the foreground in this direction is the long, low ridge of Snows Mtn.

The S view from Osceola's ledges takes in the developed Waterville Valley area. Massive Sandwich Dome, and its subsidiary summits, Jennings and Noon Peaks, provide a dramatic backdrop for the many condos and hotels in the Valley. The distant Blue Hills Range in southeastern New Hampshire is seen beyond Lake Winnipesaukee to the L of Sandwich, and Piper Mtn. in the Belknap Range is visible between Sandwich's summit and sharp Jennings Peak, with Nottingham and Fort Mtns. on the horizon to the R of Piper. Farther R are the low ridges of the Squam Range (L) and the Campton Range (R), with sprawling Bean Hill (L) and the twin rounded Uncanoonucs (R) far off on the horizon over the Squams. Beyond the Campton Range is wavy Hersey Mtn., and behind Hersey on the R are the far-off Pack Monadnocks (L) and Crotched Mtn. (R). To the R of the Campton Range is flat-topped Prospect Mtn. in Holderness. The summit of Osceola's nearest neighbor to the S, Mt. Tecumseh, is blocked by trees, though the Waterville Valley ski slopes are visible. On clear days the distant peak of Mt. Kearsarge may be spotted to the L of the ski slopes, with Mt. Monadnock beyond on its L.

MT. OSCEOLA, NW OUTLOOK: Osceola's NW outlook, an uplifted ledge in the scrub reached by a short side path, provides a clear view into the western Pemi Wilderness and out to many peaks farther W and E. The view is best seen standing, but part of it can be enjoyed while seated. The view begins on the far R with Sable and Chandler Mtns; the view from here across to Zeacliff is described for the main summit ledges. To the L of Zeacliff, seen beyond the sprawling, jumbled peaks of Mt. Hitchcock, are (R to L) Zealand Ridge and Zealand Mtn., Mt. Bond, Bondcliff, West Bond, lofty South Twin and lowly Galehead Mtn. To the L of the Bond Range, Mt. Garfield rises out of the western Pemi Wilderness, high over indistinct Owl's Head Mountain. The Franconia Brook valley forms a trough on the R of Owl's Head. To the R of Garfield are East Mtn. and Gore Mtn., far away in northern Vermont. To the L of Garfield are the Franconia Ridge peaks: (R to L): Lafayette, Lincoln, Little Haystack, Flume and Liberty, with Liberty appearing the sharpest from this vantage, and the gravelly Lincoln Slide well-displayed. The East Branch valley, meanwhile, is seen snaking its way between Mts. Hitchcock and Flume. To the L of Liberty, looking NW, are (R to L) Cannon, the Cannon Balls, and North and South Kinsman, with Whaleback Mtn. under Cannon and Big Coolidge Mtn. in front to the R of North Kinsman. On clear days, Haystack Mtn. near Hazen's Notch in northern Vermont can be seen through the col to the L of the Northeast Cannon Ball (the Cannon Ball closest to Cannon Mtn.) To the L of South Kinsman, the trackless Middle Peak of Osceola appears enticingly close, with broad Scar Ridge and the sharp lower Black Mtn. (under Big Coolidge) on its R. Mt. Wolf is seen above Middle Peak, and on the horizon between Middle Peak and Scar Ridge is Vermont's Mt. Mansfield, with the range extending to Mt. Whiteface on its R. To the L of Middle Peak, partly obscured by scrub, is the lumpy profile of Vermont's Signal Mtn. range, with Camel's Hump peering through one of its cols and Mt. Ethan Allen seen through the next col to the L. On the far L, just N of W and barely visible through the scrubby treetops, is the massive sprawl of Mt. Moosilauke.

EAST OSCEOLA: East Osceola's summit vista is about as lacking as they come. If not for an obstructed view to the N and W (found at the end of a short, beaten path leading W from the summit cairn), there'd be no view at all worthy of mention. In recent years, however, a partial view has opened up from a fir wave area, reached by a beaten path on the NE side of the summit plateau.

Elsewhere on the mountain there are two notable vistas. One is found a quarter-mile W of and below the summit on a trailside ledge. Standing on this rock, an unobstructed sweep of the mountains to the N—from the Kinsmans E to Mt. Carrigain—is obtained, similar to the NW outlook on the main summit (though extending farther E). Close by on the

L is the rugged, ledgy main peak of Osceola. The view into the western Pemigewasset Wilderness is especially fine, including the Franconia Range, Owl's Head, Mt. Garfield and the Bonds.

A good view to the E and N is found along the approach route via Mad River Notch, from the top of the slide that is crossed high up on East Osceola's N ridge. On the far L is North Hancock, marked by the prominent Arrow Slide, with sharp NW Hancock and Zealand Ridge on the extreme L. The sharp wooded peak of South Hancock is to the R of North Hancock, with imposing Mt. Carrigain farther to the R. The ridges of Mt. Huntington, including its cliff-faced W spur, sprawl in front of Hancock and Carrigain, while Mt. Jefferson and part of Mt. Adams are seen between them. Middle and South Carter, Wildcat and Carter Dome are seen over the R slope of Carrigain's Signal Ridge, with Giant Stairs and Mt. Resolution to the R and closer, beyond the flat ridge of Duck Pond Mtn. Black Mtn. in Jackson is to the R of and behind Resolution. Farther R the Baldfaces are seen over Mt. Parker, with Sable and Chandler Mtns. to the R—all seen beyond Huntington's long, flat E spur. Iron Mtn., showing cliffs on its R end, is to the R of and closer than the Baldface Range, with Doublehead behind to the R. Part of Maine's Pleasant Mtn. is visible to the R of Doublehead. Directly across Mad River Notch is the slide-marked W knob of Mt. Kancamagus, with Mt. Tremont over its L side and Kearsarge North popping up above its top. In this direction there is a startling look down at green-tinted Upper Greeley Pond at the base of the W knob. The main summit of Kancamagus is to the R of the W knob, with Big Attitash and North Moat seen between them. To the R of Kancamagus are Mt. Chocorua, Mt. Paugus, Scaur Peak, Mt. Passaconaway, and the three peaks of Tripyramid, rising above the remote plateau near Livermore Pass, with the great North Slide in full view.

NO. OF 4000-FOOTERS VISIBLE: from Mt. Osceola, 41; from East Osceola, 41 (by working hard for views through the trees)

Mount Passaconaway

ELEVATION: 4043 ft. / 1232 m   ORDER OF HEIGHT: 42
LOCATION: Sandwich Range, Town of Waterville
USGS MAPS: 7½′ Mount Tripyramid, 7½′ Mount Chocorua

Geography

Passaconaway is a great wooded dome in the heart of the Sandwich Range, rising majestically above the broad Albany, or Swift River Intervale to the N and the Wonalancet lowlands and Lakes Region to the S. Though cloaked in dark forest, Passaconaway's symmetrical crown offers good views S, E and N. Trail approaches can be made from several directions to this handsome and interesting mountain.

Beyond a broad, flat col (3260 ft.), a long, high ridge connects Passaconaway with Mt. Whiteface to the SW, enclosing The Bowl, a beautiful glacial cirque harboring old-growth forest and drained by the Wonalancet River. This area was never logged and was added to the WMNF in 1914 thanks to the efforts of Kate Sleeper Walden and the WODC. In 1931, 510 acres in the main (western) cirque were designated a Natural Area by the Forest Service; in the 1990s this area was expanded to include over 1500 acres and is now managed as a Research Natural Area for the study of old-growth forest. The floor of the cirque is cloaked in a virgin northern hardwood forest; some trees are reported to be more than 400 years old. The steep headwall of The Bowl, marked by a rock slab, plunges from the Passaconaway–Whiteface col. A short ridge runs S from the summit of Passaconaway, dividing The Bowl from a smaller cirque-like basin to the E, which is drained by a branch of Wonalancet River that was once called Passaconaway Brook. The W flank of the mountain falls sharply into the long valley of Downes Brook.

A major ridge runs SE over the flat-topped, wooded sub-peaks of "Nanamocomuck" (3340 ft.) and the two-tiered "Wonalancet Hedgehog" (3140 ft.) to the low gap of Paugus Pass (2220 ft.), which separates Passaconaway from Mt. Paugus to the E. These spurs give Passaconaway a trademark stair-step profile when seen from the S. Extending NE from Nanamocomuck is Square Ledge (2620 ft.), with a great E-facing cliff overlooking the broad upper valley of Oliverian Brook, described by Charles Edward Beals, Jr. as "a gigantic scarred face of perpendicular ledge." A western tributary of Oliverian Brook drains the valley between Square Ledge, Nanamocomuck and Passaconaway itself, the route traversed by Passaconaway Cutoff.

From Wonalancet Hedgehog another ridge runs S over flat-topped Hibbard Mtn. (2940 ft.) and Mt. Wonalancet (2780 ft., a spruce-clad dome once known as Toadback); these peaks along with Wonalancet Hedgehog are known as the Wonalancet Range. The S slopes of these mountains are drained by branches of Spring Brook. Another Hedgehog Mtn., sometimes called the "Albany Hedgehog" (2532 ft.) is a detached, ledgy spur to the N of Passaconaway rising beyond a broad col and dividing the lower valleys of Downes and Oliverian Brooks. It is a popular destination for a shorter hike and its summit and expansive East Ledges offer outstanding close-up views of its massive parent peak. Wonalancet Hedgehog, Hibbard Mtn., Mt. Wonalancet and Square Ledge also offer interesting views from various ledges.

Mt. Passaconaway is marked by prominent slides on its NW side (the ledgy Downes Brook Slide) and its E slope (a gravelly slide visible from the Passaconaway Cutoff), while Nanamocomuck bears its own slide on its steep N slope.

Nomenclature

The mountain was originally dubbed "North Whiteface" on Arnold Guyot's 1860 map. Its present name was bestowed in the 1870s by state geologist Charles H. Hitchcock in honor of Passaconaway, "Son of the Bear," the legendary sachem, or chief, of the Pennacook tribe, which lived in the lower Merrimack valley. He ruled a powerful confederation of tribes through much of the 1600s and was peaceably inclined to the white settlers who had established a toehold along the New England coast. He was reputed to be a great warrior, hunter and sorcerer. Legend holds that upon his death ca. 1682 he was borne to the summit of Agiochook (Mt. Washington) in a sleigh drawn by giant wolves, there to join the Council of the Gods. Among his children were the chieftains Wonalancet and Nanamocomuck, for which spurs of the mountain are named. Kancamagus, "the fearless one," was his grandson.

Like his father, Wonalancet (also spelled "Wannalancet," interpreted to mean "pleasant-breathing") tried to keep peace with the English settlers. This, despite many provocations by the whites and entreaties from other tribes who did battle with the colonists during King Philip's War. Mt. Wonalancet was first called Toadback for its hummocky shape. The Indian chief's name was applied to the mountain by the poet Lucy Larcom, who spent summer vacations in West Ossipee beginning in 1867.

Nanamocomuck was Passaconaway's elder son but did not succeed to the chieftainship and may have died young. His name was first applied to the higher SE spur of Mt. Passaconaway (previously dubbed "Unnamed Hump") on a 1920s WODC map. In the 1934 *AMC* Guide it was incorrectly spelled as "Nanamuck." A 1935 article in *Appalachia* by Ruth Gillette Hardy urged that the Nanamocomuck name be granted official status for "this spruce-dark, hidden little summit," but it remains unofficial to this day. Wonalancet Hedgehog was named for its humpish, porcupine-like shape, and for some time was known merely as Mt. Hedgehog. The Wonalancet prefix was added to distinguish it from the Hedgehog Mtn. just N of Mt. Passaconaway, only three miles away. Hibbard Mtn. was named for Judge Ellery Albee Hibbard, a lawyer from Laconia who in the 1880s represented a timber company in a lawsuit about whether a lumber haul road should be built along the Swift River to Tamworth. The name first appeared in the 1901 WODC guidebook, coauthored by Kate Sleeper, a founder of the WODC.

Historical Highlights

First Ascent: Unknown. Possibly climbed by Arnold Guyot in mid-1800s.

1778: Mark Jewell is first settler in Wonalancet Intervale. In later years several mills spring up in area, including Dicey's Mill at W base of Mt. Wonalancet/Hibbard Mtn.

Late 1700s: "Old Mast Road" is cut to haul large white pines—reserved for the King's navy—from Albany Intervale up Oliverian Brook valley, over low point of ridge between Mts. Passaconaway and Paugus, and down to lowlands to S.

1790s: First settlers clear land in Albany Intervale N of Mt. Passaconaway.

1800: Austin George and family homestead in Albany Intervale; family abandons home in 1815.

1824: Amzi Russell family moves into abandoned George house.

1837: First road is laid out from Conway into Albany Intervale, ending at settlement to N of Mt. Passaconaway. Thomas H. Shackford family is among prominent residents.

Ca. 1840: Lumbermen try driving logs down rock-strewn Swift River, but effort is soon abandoned.

Late 1860s: James M. Shackford (son of Thomas) enlarges house to take in summer boarders; inn is called "Passaconaway House" or "Shackford's." Later owners continue to operate hostelry. President Grover Cleveland is frequent guest.

1869: George L. Vose climbs Passaconaway for N.H. Geological Survey.

1873: Jack Allen, Civil War veteran, moves into Albany Intervale and becomes legendary local character as guide, hunter, angler, trapper and teller of tales.

1876: Charles E. Fay (first President of the AMC, which is formed that year) and worker from U.S. Coastal Survey traverse trailless ridge from Mt. Whiteface and ascend Passaconaway. Moses Sweetser's guidebook notes that Passaconaway "presents a remarkably massive and commanding appearance," though "it is wooded clear over the summit, and is therefore of but little interest to tourists." He suggests trailless ascent routes from Albany Intervale via Downes Brook, from Wonalancet and from summit of Mt. Whiteface.

1880: James M. Shackford, a farmer from Albany Intervale, is commissioned by AMC to cut trail cut up Oliverian Brook valley to summit of Passaconaway, but there is no record of trail being completed.

1891: Katherine (Kate) Sleeper opens inn at Wonalancet, other inns soon follow, and region becomes popular with AMC trampers. Local residents led by AMC's Charles E. Fay cut trail up Passaconaway from S from site of Dicey's Mill in Wonalancet River valley. Route climbs southern spur of mountain, then swings up E side of cone to summit, where naturalist Frank Bolles has cleared eastern viewpoint. They build shelter, Passaconaway Lodge, by E base of cone (near current junction of East Loop and Walden Trail). AMC contributes $25 to effort.

1891: Thomas Colbath, husband of Ruth Colbath, unexpectedly leaves their house in intervale to NE of Mt. Passaconaway. For 39 years she lights lantern each night in window hoping for his return—one of most poignant tales of region. He does return in 1933—three years after Ruth's death. Russell–Colbath House is now maintained as historic site by USFS.

1892: Innkeeper Kate Sleeper and others organize Wonalancet Out Door Club. AMC snowshoers make winter ascent of Passaconaway.

Early 1890s: Huge landslide falls off NW side of mountain into Downes Brook valley; later becomes route of Downes Brook Slide Trail. (Some sources say this slide fell in 1884.) In his book of poetry, *Chocorua's Tenants*, naturalist Frank Bolles writes:

> Ah, what is that sound of rending,
> Crushing, crashing, splintering timber?
> Hear the groans of breaking spruce trunks,
> Hear the moans of straining fibres,
> Hear the roar of falling boulders
> Bounding down the endless ledges.
> All of Passaconaway's bulwarks
> Seem to break before the storming.

1898: WODC cuts path from Old Mast Road up to Square Ledge, with side path L up to Wonalancet Hedgehog.

1899: AMC cuts new trail, Passaconaway Loop, up W side of cone, making loop over summit possible. New 9' × 13' open log camp is built at W base of cone to replace earlier structure on E side. Dr. William H. Rollins cuts path from eastern loop down to Square Ledge. WODC cuts path up Mt. Wonalancet.

Early 1900s: WODC opens Walden Trail, connecting Wonalancet Hedgehog with trail from Square Ledge to Mt. Passaconaway, then following upper part of original trail from Dicey's Mill. Club also cuts Wonalancet Range Trail, running from Mt. Wonalancet across Hibbard Mtn. to Walden Trail. Walden Trail is named for Arthur Walden, famed breeder of sled dogs and husband of Kate Sleeper.

1906–1916: Swift River Railroad logging operation harvests vast quantities of timber in Albany Intervale. Spur line runs a mile up Oliverian Brook valley, serving seven lumber camps. Lumber roads are extended up Downes Brook valley to W, where other camps are established. At its height, operation employs over 1500 workers with two school houses, post office and several boarding houses. At some point Passaconaway post office is featured as smallest in world in "Ripley's Be-lieve It or Not."

1906: AMC cuts trail from summit to top of Downes Brook Slide.

1912: Fire in Oliverian Brook valley burns slopes between Hedgehog Mtn., Mt. Passaconaway and Mt. Paugus. Also in this year, Jack Allen dies.

1914: Thanks to work of Kate Sleeper and WODC, The Bowl's virgin for-est is preserved from logging and added to WMNF.

1916: Charles Edward Beals, Jr. chronicles history of Albany Intervale in *Passaconaway in the White Mountains*, describes Passaconaway as "the loftiest, wildest, yet most symmetrical, most awe-inspiring mountain of the Sandwich Range." He describes ascent via Downes Brook Slide, delineates views from summit vantage points, and recalls several bear encounters on mountain.

1916: Short-lived trail, "Walden Cut-Off," is built from Dicey's Mill up to col between Nanamocomuck and Wonalancet Hedgehog. AMC trans-fers maintenance of Passaconaway Lodge and Passaconaway Loop to WODC.

1916: Passaconaway House burns; the next year it is replaced by new hos-telry, Swift River Inn.

Ca. 1917: USFS opens trail up Oliverian Brook valley from Albany Inter-vale, replacing northern section of Old Mast Road, which had been disrupted by logging.

1919: Trail from Mt. Passaconaway to Square Ledge reopened after being destroyed by logging several years earlier. About this time branch trail is opened leading from Oliverian Brook Trail up to foot of Square Ledge, where it joins route from Wonalancet.

Ca. 1920: Passaconaway Mountain Club, based at Swift River Inn in Al-bany Intervale, opens trail along approximate route of today's Pas-saconaway Cutoff. This trail discontinued ca. 1940 after flood and slides, reopened 1965. PMC also maintains several other trails in Pas-saconaway area until inn is closed in 1938 and sold to University of N.H. for forestry camp. Buildings at Dicey's Mill are gone.

1925: J. Brooks Atkinson (later to become Pulitzer Prize winner) writes about sojourn at Camp Rich and descent of Downes Brook Slide in *Skyline Promenades*.

1925: Passaconaway Lodge is rebuilt. In 1948 it is renamed Camp Rich after Edgar J. Rich, prominent WODC member. Camp is rebuilt again in 1953.

1934: Hiker Edgar Wright recalls finding sketch of "Mutt and Jeff," clad in mountain gear, left in cylinder at summit by famed cartoonist Bud Fisher.

1938: September hurricane destroys virgin spruce along Dicey's Mill Trail. Later that fall trail volunteer Rev. Frederick B. Noss marvels at the "appalling destruction" and declares that anyone attempting to follow

Dicey's Mill Trail "will lose his reason." Hurricane also unleashes two landslides on side of mountain.

Ca. 1960: Downes Brook Slide Trail abandoned.

1982: Upper part of Passaconaway Cutoff relocated away from brook.

1984: Sandwich Range Wilderness (25,000 acres) created by Congress, includes most of Mt. Passaconaway.

1980s: Upper 0.3 mi. of old Downes Brook Slide Trail is reopened as spur trail to N view.

1997–2001: WODC reconstructs badly eroded Walden Trail. Project entails over 10,000 hours of work and includes placement of 512 rock steps. E end of East Loop is relocated to higher junction with Walden Trail.

1998: January ice storm decimates second-growth hardwoods on southern slopes. Trail crews clear hundreds of fallen trees from Dicey's Mill Trail with hand tools.

2000: Camp Rich collapses and is removed.

2006: Sandwich Range Wilderness is expanded, N and E slopes of Mt. Passaconaway and more of Oliverian Brook valley are added.

Trail Approaches

North Approach from Kancamagus Highway (NH 112)

> **Oliverian Brook Trail, Passaconaway Cutoff, Square Ledge Trail, Walden Trail.**
>
> 10.2 miles round trip, 2800-ft. elevation gain

TRAILHEAD (1238 ft.): Parking area for Oliverian Brook Trail is at end of short gravel side road off S side of Kancamagus Highway (NH 112), 1.0 mi. W of Bear Notch Rd.

This is a long wooded approach with steep climbing at the end. From kiosk and gate at S end of parking area, walk 200 ft. S on gravel road, then turn L into woods at sign for Oliverian Brook Trail and meander through pines. Trail turns R onto original route at 0.1 mi. At 0.2 mi. look R across old clearcut for partial view of Mt. Passaconaway looming above Hedgehog Mtn. Trail continues S, crossing old roadbed, with gentle ups and downs. At 0.6 mi. make short descent and turn R on section of old railroad grade, used by Conway Lumber Co. ca. 1910. Just beyond, X-C ski trail splits off to R. Oliverian Brook Trail continues ahead, passes between small beaver ponds, and keeps to level, straight grade. Bear L off RR grade at 1.1 mi. and climb at easy grade along Oliverian Brook with several nice streamside vignettes, crossing two side streams.

At 1.9 mi./1500 ft., just after entering Sandwich Range Wilderness, bear R on Passaconaway Cutoff. Climbing is mostly easy to crossing of W branch of Oliverian Brook at 2.4 mi. Easy to moderate grade contin-

Mount Passaconaway as viewed from the open ledges of nearby Hedgehog Mountain.

ues through conifers, then hardwoods. At 2.8 mi./1800 ft. trail bears L for steady climb high above brook through spruces, then hardwoods and white birches, with Passaconaway looming massively to R across valley. Pass framed view N to Hedgehog Mtn. at 3.5 mi. Turn R at T-junction with Square Ledge Trail at 3.6 mi./2550 ft. Pass through dip and ascend to bottom of slide on N flank of Nanamocomuck Peak at 3.9 mi./2775 ft.; careful scramble up to L provides good view N to Hedgehog Mtn. and Mt. Washington beyond. Ascent now becomes steeper, leading up to jct.

with Walden Trail at 4.3 mi. / 3300 ft.. Bear R here at moderate grade, then swing R up steep rough pitch to jct. L with East Loop (which traverses 0.2 mi. to Dicey's Mill Trail) at 4.4 mi. Continue up steeply on reconstructed Walden Trail. Grade relaxes as trail winds up cone through wild fir woods, then becomes steep and rough again. After scrambly pitch swing L to fine S outlook on L at 4.9 mi. and make short, steep climb to E outlook on R at 5.0 mi. Trail swings L at easy grade across summit plateau and in 20 yds. side path R descends 0.3 mi. / 200 ft., at easy to moderate grade, to spectacular N outlook- well worth the side trip. Ca. 60 yds. farther is jct. with Dicey's Mill Trail; viewless wooded summit is reached by 40-yd. side path L (sign).

LOOP OPTION FROM NORTH VIA SQUARE LEDGE
11.3 mi. loop, 2950-ft. elevation gain.

Interesting descent variation can be made over great E-facing cliff of Square Ledge. At jct. of Square Ledge Trail and Passaconaway Cutoff, continue ahead on Square Ledge Trail, climbing over knoll, swinging L and descending sharply, then climbing again along base of rock face to wooded summit of Square Ledge in 0.4 mi. Here obscure side path R leads up ledge ramp and out through brushy woods to whitish outcrop with impressive view up to Mt. Passaconaway and out to Paugus Pass; use caution, as ledge drops off abruptly on L where you emerge. Back on main trail, traverse down and up along ridge to top of huge Square Ledge cliff at 0.6 mi. from jct. with Passaconaway Cutoff, with view across Oliverian Brook valley to Mt. Paugus; this spot may be posted during peregrine falcon nesting season, April 1–August 1—please heed restrictions on signage. Here trail turns R for very steep, rocky descent below wooded cliffs, then more moderate downgrade to jct. L with Square Ledge Branch Trail at 1.0 mi. / 2100 ft. Turn L on Branch Trail and descend moderately, paralleling small brook, to crossing of Oliverian Brook, and meet Oliverian Brook Trail at 1.5 mi. / 1750 ft. Turn L here for easy descent on Oliverian Brook Trail through mixed woods in remote valley. Cross Oliverian Brook at 2.1 mi. and west branch of brook at 2.7 mi. Reach jct. with Passaconaway Cutoff at 2.9 mi. and continue ahead for easy 1.9 mi. walk on Oliverian Brook Trail to trailhead.

South Approach from Wonalancet

Dicey's Mill Trail
9.2 miles round trip, 2950-ft. elevation gain

TRAILHEAD (1140 ft.): Spacious hiker's parking area off Ferncroft Rd., 0.5 mi. from NH 113A at sharp corner in Wonalancet. From the W, take Exit 24 off I-93 and follow US 3 to Holderness. Turn L on NH 113 and proceed

11.5 mi. to Center Sandwich. Turn L here, staying on NH 113 another 3.6 mi. to junction with NH 113A in North Sandwich. Continue straight on NH 113A and follow it 6.6 mi. to sharp R turn by fields of Wonalancet. Turn L onto Ferncroft Road at corner and drive 0.5 mi. to parking area on R. Parking is not allowed on Ferncroft Rd. beyond this point.

From the E, take NH 113 from NH 16 at village of Chocorua. At crossroads in Tamworth village turn R on NH 113A and follow it 6.6 mi. to where Ferncroft Rd. leaves on R at sharp L turn.

This is a steady, moderate route, wooded to the top, and is the most popular route to Mt. Passaconaway. From parking area, trail follows Ferncroft Rd. NW across private land (please stay on trail and respect owners' right to privacy). Continue straight where Blueberry Ledge Trail diverges L across Squirrel Bridge. Road soon crosses field to house on R; here trail forks L across upper part of field and soon enters woods. At 0.8 mi. pass connecting path leading L over bridge to Blueberry Ledge Cutoff and quickly enter WMNF and Sandwich Range Wilderness. Climb steadily through "S-curve" and then ascend easily through fine hardwood forest up E side of Wonalancet River valley. Slight descent leads to jct. L with Tom Wiggin Trail at 1.9 mi./1950 ft. Trail is nearly level through mature hardwoods, passing site of Dicey's Mill (sawmill in late 1800s), then swings R and L to cross E branch of Wonalancet River at 2.3 mi./2020 ft. Trail passes large boulder on R and begins long, steady ascent up E side of a ridge through ice-damaged hardwoods, then conifers, with a few steeper pitches and glimpses through the trees of Wonalancet Range to R and Mt. Passaconaway ahead.

In upper part of this section trail contours slope, then swings L and climbs to jct. L with Rollins Trail at 3.7 mi./3300 ft. at crest of ridge. Dicey's Mill Trail continues ahead up over ledge steps and crosses small brook just before jct. with East Loop on R at 3.9 mi./3400 ft. Dicey's Mill Trail continues ahead, soon passing side path L to site of Camp Rich (camping allowed, good water source), and zig-zags up summit cone through wild conifer forest. After generally easy grades, last 0.2 mi. is steep and rocky, with one ledgy scramble near top. On summit crest trail emerges on ledge with good standup view L (NW), from Mt. Tripyramid around to Willey Range, swings R, and quickly meets Walden Trail at 4.6 mi./4040 ft., where side path R (sign) leads 40 yds. to viewless wooded high point. Continue ahead on Walden Trail for 60 yds. across summit plateau for side path that descends L to spectacular N view (0.6 mi. round trip with 200 ft. of elevation gain on way back, well worth the modest effort) and 20 yds. beyond to E view. For full range of views, descend steep upper part of Walden Trail past fine S view, then turn R on East Loop and follow it 0.2 mi. at easy grade to Dicey's Mill Trail. This is only 0.1 mi. longer than direct return on upper Dicey's Mill Trail.

LOOP OPTIONS

Longer loop options over less-used trails with good views can be fashioned from Ferncroft parking area in combination with descent via Dicey's Mill Trail.

Old Mast Road and Walden Trail
9.4 mi. loop, 3400-ft. elevation gain

This loop features a pleasant approach, followed by steep, rough climbing with views. Walden Trail has been recently reconstructed by WODC, offering much better footing than before. From Ferncroft, follow easy Old Mast Road, passing jct. L with Wonalancet Range Trail at 0.1 mi., crossing Spring Brook on bridge, and passing jct. R with Kelley Trail at 0.3 mi. Old Mast Road climbs at easy to moderate grades with good footing, at first through hemlocks, then up through long stretch of hardwood forest. Trail then eases across crest of ridge to four-way jct. at 2.0 mi. / 2350 ft. Turn L here on Walden Trail, ascend rock steps, then tackle very steep, rugged section on E side of Wonalancet Hedgehog featuring several ledge scrambles, including one broken, wet ledge that requires caution. Trail levels on 2860-ft. shoulder, then climbs fairly steeply again to short spur R at 2.6 mi. / 3000 ft. that leads to ledge with fine view E including impressive look at Mt. Paugus with Mt. Chocorua beyond and Moats to NE. Easier climbing leads to 3140-ft. summit of Hedgehog at 2.7 mi., marked by large boulder on R; just before high point, side trail L descends easily for 0.1 mi. to ledge with wide view S over Wonalancet Intervale and Lakes Region.

Walden Trail descends easily along ridge to jct. L with Wonalancet Range Trail at 2.9 mi. Continue ahead on Walden Trail, dropping steeply past view N towards Mt. Washington and down to wild col at 3.2 mi. / 2900 ft. Descend briefly to L, then swing R past rock face and ascend very steep, rough section with slippery, gravelly footing. Grade eases as you ascend to flat wooded crest of Nanamocomuck Peak at 3.6 mi. / 3340 ft. Descend easily to 3180-ft. saddle, then rise moderately to jct. R with Square Ledge Trail at 4.1 mi. / 3300 ft. Walden Trail ascends moderately, then swings R up steep, rough pitch to jct. L with East Loop at 4.2 mi., It continues steeply up cone of Passaconaway, with occasional breathers, swinging L at top of sharp pitch to fine S outlook at 4.7 mi. Another steep pitch leads to E outlook at 4.8 mi. Continue short distance farther at easy grade across summit plateau, passing side trail R descending 0.3 mi. / 200 ft. at easy / moderate grade to magnificent N outlook, to jct. with Dicey's Mill Trail and side path L (sign) to wooded, viewless summit. Descend via Dicey's Mill Trail.

Wonalancet Range Trail and Walden Trail
9.8 mi. loop, 3450-ft. elevation gain

This loop offers mostly moderate climbing with good views. From parking area and kiosk, briefly follow road to NE and bear L into woods on Old Mast Road. After 0.1 mi. on level, turn L onto blue-blazed Wonalancet Range Trail. Path briefly hugs bank of Spring Brook, climbs short, steep pitch, and meanders up at easy to moderate grades through fine hemlock grove, then mixed woods. It then veers R and makes long, steady ascent slabbing NW across slope of hardwoods, entering WMNF and Sandwich Range Wilderness at 0.8 mi. Above here slope and trail become very rocky, and grade steepens. At 1.3 mi. trail enters spruce woods and soon turns L to climb two very steep, rough pitches to jct. with Short Cut trail at 1.5 mi. / 2350 ft. (Short Cut bears R and slabs up across E side of Mt. Wonalancet, rejoining Range Trail in 0.4 mi.)

At jct., Wonalancet Range Trail swings L for steep, rough, winding climb up side of Mt. Wonalancet through dense spruces. At 1.7 mi. / 2550 ft. trail climbs up large open rock slab with good view SE and E; use caution if wet or icy. Trail remains fairly steep above ledge, then eases, circles around to R and runs across broad, flat densely wooded summit of Wonalancet at 1.9 mi. / 2780 ft. Easy descent N along ridge, passing over minor secondary summit, leads to upper jct. with Short Cut in Wonalancet / Hibbard col at 2.3 mi. / 2580 ft. After crossing broad saddle, trail ascends Hibbard at easy, then moderate grade through open spruce forest. At 2.7 mi., at top of grade, short side path leads R to outlook facing S over Lakes Region; use caution as there is big drop in front. Main trail meanders up at gentle grade to open ledge at summit of Hibbard at 2.4 mi. / 2940 ft.; here there is impressive view (best if standing) W to Mt. Whiteface rising from The Bowl, with Mt. Passaconaway seen up to R.

After slight descent, trail meanders along level ridge through conifers, then climbs easily to boulder at high point and dips a few yards to T-jct. with Walden Trail at 3.3 mi. / 3100 ft. Turn L to reach Mt. Passaconaway in 1.9 mi. as described above. Descend via Dicey's Mill Trail.

EAST LOOP

This gently graded 0.2 mi. path traverses the S face of Passaconaway's cone at ca. 3400 ft., connecting the Dicey's Mill and Walden Trails, and allows one to make a loop over the summit that accesses all of the viewpoints. From Dicey's Mill Trail, 3.9 mi. from Ferncroft, East Loop leads E through fine open fir forest, then passes semi-open blowdown area on R with glimpses of Mt. Whiteface. It continues across slope, falling and rising gently, and meets Walden Trail 0.1 mi. above that trail's jct. with Square Ledge Trail.

Loops with Mt. Whiteface can be fashioned using Rollins Trail along connecting ridge. Combine N route to Passaconaway with Rollins, Kate Sleeper and Downes Brook Trails and road walk on Kancamagus Highway (15.6 mi., 3700-ft. elevation gain). With S route to Passaconaway, use Rollins and Blueberry Ledge Trails (11.9 mi., 3850-ft. elevation gain).

Winter

Parking areas are plowed at both the Oliverian Brook Trail and Ferncroft trailheads. By far the most popular winter route is the Dicey's Mill Trail, a good, moderately graded snowshoe route with a few steep pitches on the cone. Passaconaway and Whiteface are often combined via the Rollins Trail and rugged Blueberry Ledge Trail (which is better ascended than descended). The Rollins Trail is a long, tiring section and may be hard to follow. The upper part of the Walden Trail is challenging in winter and could be icy on its steep pitches; hikers approaching from the N can avoid this section by taking the East Loop to the upper Dicey's Mill Trail.

View Guide

Passaconaway's actual summit is thickly wooded and viewless, but there are four good outlooks at various points around the top.

NW OUTLOOK: This ledge is located near the top of the Dicey's Mill Trail where it emerges from the final steep climb onto the summit plateau. This is a partly restricted stand-up view to the W and N. On the far L, partly screened by trees, are the nearby dark, rounded masses of East and West Sleeper. Carr Mtn. sprawls over the R half of East Sleeper, with Mt. Cube beyond on its R and Smarts Mtn. and Stinson Mtn. to its L. On clear days the Killington Range in Vermont can be seen between Smarts and Stinson, with Salt Ash Mtn. to its L. Mt. Kineo spreads between the Sleepers, above the southern ridge of Mt. Tecumseh's spur, Green Mtn. The three peaks of Tripyramid are to the R of West Sleeper, rising impressively from the Sabbaday Brook valley, with the Waterville Valley ski trails and Tecumseh's summit seen through the col between West Sleeper and South Tripyramid. Mt. Moosilauke rises between South and Middle Tripyramid. The more open part of the view begins with Middle and North Tripyramid, with northern spurs of Moosilauke between them. Mt. Osceola and East Osceola are to the R of North Tripyramid, with the flat-topped Fool Killer in the foreground. Scaur Peak peers over the middle of the Fool Killer. Farther R and more distant is Mt. Kancamagus with South and North Kinsman over its L end. Farther R are Mts. Flume and Liberty (just peering over), then the Franconia Range stretches across to Mts. Lincoln and Lafayette rising above the sprawling Mt. Huntington (with cliffs on its W spur). The peak of Mt. Hitchcock pops out over the saddle between Huntington's W spur and its twin broad main peaks, under the Lincoln Slide. The crest of Owl's Head can be seen behind the main Huntington summits. Mt. Garfield rises well to the R of Lafayette, then the view moves onto the nearer South and North Hancock. To the R of North Hancock, over Hancock's long E ridge, are West Bond, Mt. Bond, South Twin, Mt. Guyot and North Twin. Farther R Zealand Mtn. is seen over the low, cliff-shod nubble of The Captain. On the far R is the massive bulk of Mt. Carrigain.

s outlook: This sunny white ledge located beside the Walden Trail at 3950 ft. provides a wide view over the southern spurs of Passaconaway with the Lakes Region beyond. On the L is the nearby whaleback ridge of the lower Wonlanacet Range—Hibbard Mtn. (L) and Mt. Wonalancet (R)—enclosing the valley of the E branch of the Wonalancet River. The Ossipee Range spreads wide beyond the Wonalancet Range, with Whittier and Bald Mtns. on its L end, Mt. Shaw in its center, and Mts. Faraway and Roberts above the northern Black Snout on its R end. In the distance to the L of Shaw are Copple Crown Mtn. (R) and the Moose Mtns. (L). On clear days Blue Job Mtn. can be spotted to the R of Shaw. To the R of the Ossipees, above Mt. Wonalancet and the mouth of the Wonalancet River valley, is the sprawl of Lake Winnispesaukee with the Belknap Range beyond. Belknap and Gunstock Mtns. are prominent on the R end of the Belknaps; to the L of these is distant Fort Mtn. in southern New Hampshire. Farther R is the prominent, elongated Red Hill, with Squam Lake shimmering to its R. Over the E (L) spur of Red Hill are wide-spreading Bean Hill and Joe English Hill beyond, with the twin Uncanoonucs farther L. Over the R half of Red Hill are (L to R) the Lyndeborough Mtns., Pack Monadnock and Crotched Mtn. The wavy crest of Hersey Mtn. is seen beyond Squam Lake, with Mt. Monadnock peering over its L end. Mt. Israel is to the R of Squam Lake, seen over the SE ridge of Mt. Whiteface. On the horizon over Israel is Mt. Kearsarge. In the distance to the R of Israel are Ragged Mtn. (with Lovewell Mtn. over its L end) and Sunapee Mtn. On the far R is a striking vista SE to the long, steep-sided ridge of Mt. Whiteface, just two mi. away, rising above The Bowl and a S spur ridge of Passaconaway. Over the R shoulder of Whiteface are Sandwich Dome and its sharp spur, Jennings Peak. In clear weather Vermont's Okemo Mtn. can be seen to the R of the Dome.

e outlook: A ledge beside the Walden Trail at the E end of the summit plateau opens a partly restricted but good vista, best if standing; you have to move around a bit to see the entire view. This roomy ledge is a good lunch spot. On the far L Mt. Washington, with Mt. Monroe on its L, rises above the nearer Mt. Tremont and Owl's Cliff. Boott Spur is to the R of Washington, with Mt. Isolation, Stairs Mtn. and Mt. Resolution below. Farther R the Wildcats, Middle Carter (with South Carter in front and below) and Carter Dome are seen beyond the nearer Bartlett Haystack. Distant Baldpate Mtn. is visible off the ridge descending R from Carter Dome, while the nearer Hart Ledge peers over the col to the L of the

Haystack. To the R of the Haystack is the long ridge of Bear Mtn., with Mt. Langdon (L) and ledgy Iron Mtn. (R) between them. Jackson's Black Mtn. is behind Iron on the R, with Sunday River Whitecap seen just L of its summit. The Baldfaces rise above Bear, with the Doubleheads below and to the R. In the distance to the L of the Baldfaces are the long ridges of the eastern Mahoosuc Range, with the 4000-footer Saddleback Mtn. in Maine peering over in the middle. Caribou Mtn. peers over to the L of North Doublehead, and Speckled Mtn. spreads to the R of South Doublehead, with the lower Butters–Red Rock Mtn. ridge extending to its R. The distant pyramid of Maine's Mt. Blue is to the R of Speckled. Close at hand under Bear are the white ledges of Hedgehog Mtn. To the R of Bear is fire-scarred Table Mtn., below the wooded humps of Big Attitash Mtn. Saddleback Wind and Bald Mtns. in Maine are visible over the L end of Big Attitash. Farther R Kearsarge North lifts its pyramid behind the high ridge of North Moat Mtn. North Gemini and Mt. Shaw are just L of Kearsarge, with various mountains near Rumford, Maine, in the distance. Beyond the broad Albany Intervale the Moat Range runs to the R over Middle & South Moat, with ledgy spurs thrust out into the Swift River valley. Black Cap Mtn. is behind South Moat on the R, and farther R still is Streaked Mtn. on the horizon.

Eastward the rocky crest of Chocorua dominates the view, with the rounded Three Sisters on the L and the sharp summit on the R. Over the L end of the Sisters is Maine's long, level Pleasant Mtn. Lumpy Mt. Paugus sprawls nearer and below Chocorua, spotted with ledges and crumbling granite cliffs. Below Paugus is the wooded backside of Square Ledge and a dramatic look down into the upper valley of Oliverian Brook. On the horizon above Paugus and the S ridge of Chocorua are the Burnt Meadow Mtns. and part of Sebago Lake beyond. Over the flat S spur of Paugus the city of Portland on the Maine coast, 60 mi. away, and the Atlantic Ocean beyond, may be spotted on crystal days. Farther R (SE), the view takes in Chocorua Lake, Silver Lake, and Ossipee Lake, the latter seen over the nearby Wonalancet Hedgehog and Mt. Mexico. Green Mtn. is behind Ossipee Lake on the L, and the view continues around to the distant Moose Mtns. and Copple Crown Mtn. and, on the far R, the Ossipee Range.

N OUTLOOK: Passaconaway's finest viewpoint is a small opening perched on the steep N slope, atop what Beals (1916) called a "lofty eagle-nest of a cliff." You have to descend 0.3 mi. and 200 ft. from the summit to this point, but in clear weather it's well worth the trouble. The view is a northward sweep of mountain country (including 38 4000-footers), with a tremendous dropoff below to the lower slopes of Passaconaway.

On the far L are the pointed peaks of Middle and North Tripyramid, with Mt. Moosilauke between them, the flat ridge of The Fool Killer beneath, and East Osceola and Osceola to the R. Next to the R, South & North Kinsman rise in the distance above Mt. Kancamagus. Mts. Flume and Liberty are almost in line to the R of Kancamagus, followed by Mts. Lincoln and Lafayette and the sharp pyramid of Mt. Garfield. Mt. Huntington sprawls beneath the Franconias, presenting impressive cliffs on its W spur. Mt. Hitchcock can be seen behind Huntington, under Mt. Lincoln, and farther R the ridge of Owl's Head also rises behind Huntington. To the R of Garfield is the long wooded mass of Mt. Hancock, with North Hancock peering over in back of South Hancock. To the R West Bond (barely), Mt. Bond, South Twin and North Twin poke over Hancock's long E ridge. The cliffy nubble of The Captain protrudes from the low point between Hancock and its impressive neighbor to the R, Mt. Carrigain, with Zealand Mtn. beyond The Captain. To the R of Carrigain is a beautiful look through Carrigain Notch, with Vose Spur on the L and Mt. Lowell on the R. The long W ridge of Mt. Field is seen through the notch, with Cherry Mtn. peering over in back. Below the Notch and closer is granite-faced Green's Cliff, and nearer still is ledgy Potash Mtn., seen across the lower Downes Brook valley.

Mts. Tom, Field and Willey are arrayed behind Mts. Lowell and Anderson, just R of Carrigain Notch. To the R of Willey are Mt. Nancy and Mt. Bemis; over Bemis is Mt. Waumbek with Mt. Cabot poking up behind it. Over the R shoulder of Potash is the glimmer of Church Pond on the floor of Albany Intervale. Mt. Webster rises far above and beyond the pond, and the Southern Presidentials march upward over Pierce, Eisenhower, Franklin and Monroe (with Mt. Jefferson behind on its L) to the dramatic peak of Mt. Washington, about 22 mi. to the N. Mt. Tremont is below Washington, and from here the view continues through Bear Mtn., the Carters and Moats and around to Mt. Chocorua on the eastern horizon, as described under the E outlook, but with a much more open and dramatic foreground. Of particular note is the look straight down at Hedgehog Mtn., in line with Bear Mtn.

NO. OF 4000-FOOTERS VISIBLE: 40

Mount Tecumseh

ELEVATION: 4003 ft. / 1220 m   ORDER OF HEIGHT: 47 (tie)
LOCATION: Town of Waterville Valley, Township of Livermore
USGS MAP: 7½′ Waterville Valley

Geography

Among the higher peaks of the White Mountains, Mount Tecumseh (along with Mt. Isolation) holds the dubious distinction of being the shortest of the tallest. These two peaks are overtopped by each of the other 46 White Mountain 4000-footers. Tecumseh is also among the most visited mountains in New Hampshire as it is home to Waterville Valley Ski Area, one of the state's busiest winter resorts. The ski area dominates the mountain's E-facing slopes and operates with a special use permit issued by the U.S. Forest Service. For hikers Tecumseh presents a short and moderate hike with some interesting views along the ridgetop.

Tecumseh is the culminating point of the string of mountains which stretch 5–6 mi. NNE from Thornton to the broad Waterville Valley. Tecumseh, Mt. Osceola, Mt. Kancamagus, the Tripyramids, and Sandwich Dome form a ring of peaks that almost completely surrounds the scenic resort community at Waterville. The mountain is flanked on the E and W by two great valleys. The Waterville Valley, through which the Mad River flows, opens to the E. The broader Pemigewasset River valley, with its headwaters well to the N, lies further to the W along the I-93 corridor. Mt. Osceola rises just to the N of Tecumseh, separated only by narrow Thornton Gap (or Waterville Gap, 2300 ft.), through which runs the seasonal Tripoli Road (connecting I-93 with Waterville Valley). From the gap Eastman Brook flows W to the Pemigewasset valley.

The jumble of peaks that rise from the S and extends all the way to Tecumseh's sharp, pointed summit, begins with 2132-ft. Cone Mtn. in Thornton. The ridgeline thrusts higher and higher as it rises toward Tecumseh, with prominent, ledgy Welch Mtn. (2605 ft.) and Dickey Mtn. (2734 ft.) passed first. From Dickey a long ridge extends N over unofficially named "Foss Peak" (3312 ft.) to trailless Green Mtn. (3536 ft.), Tecumseh's closest neighbor to the S along the scrubby ridge. A spur ridge runs SW from Green over rugged Hogback Mtn. (2770 ft.) and ledgy Fisher Mtn. (2609 ft.). Shattuck Brook drains the valley between Dickey and Hogback / Fisher.

The main summit of Tecumseh, which appears rather inconspicuous from some vantage points, is actually quite sharp, prompting one early White Mountain guidebook writer to say it is "one of the most interesting sections of natural architecture in the mountain region." The pyramid-shaped summit, with its "lofty pile of white rocks" (indicating that it was once more open), features a narrow ridgecrest which drops off sharply on all sides. The best profile of the summit is seen from a vantage point along the ridgetop Sosman Trail connecting the main summit with the top of the ski area.

The mountain has two subsidiary summits which are also accessible by trail. Tecumseh's wooded, flat-topped 3766-ft. West Peak, over which passes the Mt. Tecumseh Trail from Tripoli Road, was formerly considered one of New England's 100 Highest peaks, and for a time was regularly an objective of peakbaggers. The West Peak was removed from the list in 1985 after the U.S. Geological Survey determined that the mountain was 24 ft. lower than previously believed. The steep SE slope of West

Tecumseh is spotted with talus fields, and Sweetser's guide referred to this ridge as "Mt. Avalanche." West Tecumseh's long gentle ridge to the SW extends out to Bald Mtn., a prominent, ledge-spotted knob occasionally reached by bushwhacking hikers. Between this and the main Green–Tecumseh ridge is a large trailless valley drained by Haselton Brook. Three short, ledgy ridges, prominent when seen from the W, especially in winter, extend into this valley from the W side of the Green–Tecumseh ridge. The middle of these spurs was once known as Spring Mtn., and in the late 1800s there was a mineral spring-house at its base, beside Haselton Brook.

Waterville Valley Ski Area's highest chairlifts extend to the top of White Peak (3860 ft.), Tecumseh's other long and flat subsidiary summit. This area is reached from the main summit by the Sosman Trail, or from the eastern base of the mountain by a network of ski trails. A prominent spur ridge runs SE from White Peak.

In addition to Haselton Brook on the SW, major streams which flow off the mountain are Tecumseh Brook to the E (between the main summit and White Peak), Hardy Brook to the SE, and Johnson Brook to the W (off the W side of the Bald Mtn. ridge).

Nomenclature

Like a number of other southern White Mountain peaks, this mountain bears the name of a legendary Indian chief described by one historian as "the most extraordinary Indian in American history." Mt. Tecumseh is named for the great Shawnee chief who unsuccessfully tried to unite the tribes of the Ohio region in an effort to ward off encroachment of their homeland by westward bound settlers. Tecumseh's unsuccessful campaign was crushed on Nov. 7, 1811, when warriors led by his twin brother, Tenkswatawa (who was also known as the Shawnee Prophet), were routed by U.S. soldiers in the infamous Battle of Tippecanoe. Following the failed Indian campaign, Tecumseh (1768–1813) allied himself with the British during the War of 1812 and was eventually killed in the Battle of the Thames in Ontario, Canada. Coincidentally, Tecumseh's birthplace in Ohio was in a village on the Mad River. That is the same name of the river which flows S through New Hampshire's Waterville Valley.

To this day there remains a cloud of mystery over who gave the mountain its name. Early maps of the region simply referred to the peak as Waterville Mountain. But the name Tecumseh was certainly bestowed upon the mountain by 1874, when state geologist Charles H. Hitchcock issued his comprehensive report on the Geology of New Hampshire. He said the name was given to the mountain by Campton photographer E. J. Young, who produced several early stereographs of the Waterville Valley area.

It has also been speculated that E. J. Connable of Jackson, Michigan, who first came to Waterville Valley in 1859, may have come up with the permanent names for both Tecumseh and neighboring Mt. Osceola. Guidebook author Moses Sweeter added to the name-calling in early editions of his popular Osgood's White Mountains by relating that the mountain was also known locally as Kingsley's Peak, "a title recently conferred in honor of himself by a gentleman who imagined he was its discoverer."

Historical Highlights

First Ascent: Unknown

1830: Nathaniel Greeley arrives in Waterville Valley and establishes permanent residency.

1850s: Greeley orchestrates construction of network of walking paths in and around Valley in conjunction with inn he has opened. His trail system, the first in the Whites, includes paths to Tecumseh (from E and from S along ridge from Welch Mtn.), Osceola, and Sandwich Dome.

1879: AMC cuts new trail to summit via "steep north ridge of Tecumseh Brook."

1880: Sweetser describes several possible routes to summit, noting approach from Waterville is shortest and best. Other possibilities includes three routes of ascent from the Elkins farm in the Haselton Brook valley to the SW, including one over Fisher and Green Mts., another over Spring Mtn., and a third up the headwall of the Haselton Brook ravine, and also an ascent from the S over Welch Mtn. Of ridge walk between Green Mt. and main summit, Sweetser writes, "In some places the easiest way to advance is on hands and knees, so dense and spiky is the upper growth."

1881: AMC stalwarts Marian and Lucia Pychowska climb Tecumseh and marvel at view from bare summit.

1888: Waterville Valley Athletic & Improvement Association (WVAIA) is formed, becomes active trail-building group.

1891: Twenty-one AMC members take part in February excursion to Waterville Valley. Snowshoe treks include ascents of Tecumseh, Osceola, Tripyramids.

1892: A. L. Goodrich espouses virtues of Waterville Valley area in *Appalachia* (January 1892). Article includes sketch map of Valley and existing trail system.

1909: Woodstock and Thornton Gore Railroad (1909–1914), operated by Woodstock Lumber Company, begins operation along Eastman Brook valley NW of Tecumseh, following for most part grade of modern day Tripoli Rd.

1920s: Hiking trail relocated to S side of Tecumseh Brook due to logging.

1928: Forest Service pays $1.05 million for 23,000 acres in and around Waterville Valley.

1933–1934: Construction of Tripoli Rd., connecting Waterville Valley with Pemigewasset River valley to W, is undertaken by Forest Service, CCC.

1934: First ski trail on mountain is cut. Old logging camp on lower E slope is converted to public ski cabin.

1937: Forest Service approves construction of new ski trail (Tecumseh Trail) on mountain. Work is done by CCC. Trail runs two miles down to Tripoli Rd. with vertical descent of 1900 ft.

1939: In aftermath of destructive Hurricane of 1938, Forest Service establishes Tecumseh Fire Trail from height-of-land on Tripoli Road to summit. Trail mainly follows fire barrier strip on ridge leading to summit.

1940: Forest Service considers, rejects proposal for installation of ski lift on Tecumseh Trail.

1940: *AMC Guide* includes descriptions of Haselton Brook and Johnson Brook Trails. Haselton Brook Trail (formerly the Bald Mt. Trail) approaches mountain from SW and joins Mt. Tecumseh Trail 0.4 mi. N of summit. Johnson Brook Trail enters from W, 1.6 mi. N of summit. Eventually a single Mt. Tecumseh Trail is designated, using old ski trail and parts of fire barrier and Johnson Brook Trail.

1952: AMC trailman Nathaniel Goodrich chronicles region in book, *The Waterville Valley*, and notes that "when our itch for bushwhacking became unbearable, a favorite cure was to climb Tecumseh, then fight our way all down the ridge to Welch and the six-mile bridge."

1966: Former Olympic skier Tom Corcoran and his Waterville Company open new Mt. Tecmuseh Ski Area. Shortly thereafter WVAIA opens Sosman Trail along ridgecrest.

1985: West Peak of Tecumseh is removed from New England 100 Highest list as new geological survey reveals peak is 24 ft. shorter than previously thought.

1991: Lower section of Mt. Tecumseh Trail from E is re-routed away from ski slopes.

Trail Approaches

East Approach from Waterville Valley Ski Area

Mt. Tecumseh Trail
5.0 mi. round trip, 2300-ft. elevation gain

TRAILHEAD (1840 ft.): From I-93 at Exit 28, follow NH 49 for 10.6 mi. N and turn L on Tripoli Rd. (access road for Mt. Tecumseh Ski Area). In another 1.2 mi. continue straight where Tripoli Rd. bears R and continue to loop road for ski area parking lots, where you bear R. Mount Tecumseh

Trail begins at sign on upper end of R side of loop, to R of base lodge and across from entrance to northernmost parking lot (Lot 1). The Mt. Tecumseh Trail, which runs 5.6 mi. from the base of Waterville Valley Ski Area, over the summit, and on down to Tripoli Road (FR 30) just W of its height-of-land, is the lone base-to-summit hiking trail on the mountain. Because the two trailhead lots are miles apart, few trampers traverse the entire length of the trail, opting instead to climb and return from the summit via the same route. For the purposes of this guide, each approach is considered separately. When descending from summit, follow signs carefully to ensure you are on correct route. The trail from the ski area immediately strikes off into woods, crosses small stream, then continues 0.3 mi. at easy grade along S side of Tecumseh Brook. Trail then bears sharp R across brook (arrow and double-blazed) and continues along new section of trail opened in 1991. From here, trail climbs steeply over rough and rocky footway onto small ridge, which it follows nearly on level through hardwoods. Trail then ascends into conifer forest, and at 1.1 mi. / 2475 ft. it drops L back down to brook, recrosses, and climbs via switchbacks steeply out of ravine to wide old logging road, where original path is regained. Look here for sign directing hikers 20 yards to L, where beaten path leads to edge of ski slope and fine views E and NE, encompassing Mt. Osceola, Mt. Kancamagus and the Tripyramids enclosing the upper Waterville Valley. Elevation here is 2525 ft. Main trail bears R and ascends steadily, passing second side path L to ski slopes and lift.

Continuing along logging road, trail makes long, steady ascent up rough, rocky footway through birches and conifers. As elevation is gained, width of road narrows significantly. Upon reaching head of Tecumseh Brook ravine (on R), trail veers NW and steepens, then levels out before reaching intersection with Sosman Trail to top of ski area at 2.2 mi. / 3840 ft. Bear R here; for several hundred feet, the two trails coincide, before Sosman Trail forks L and in 0.2 mi. reaches summit via switchbacks from the W; halfway up, along rocky, scrubby section, there are partial views W towards Mt. Moosilauke and the S ridge of Tecumseh's West Peak. At fork, Mt. Tecumseh Trail swings R, contours along slope with rough footing, descending slightly, then circles around summit to NE, passes restricted viewpoint looking SE to Sandwich Dome, and climbs steeply to summit at 2.5 mi.; high point is uplifted ledge. There are partial views around summit area through breaks in trees.

Northwest Approach from Tripoli Road

Mt. Tecumseh Trail
6.2 mi. round trip, 2600-ft. elevation gain

TRAILHEAD (1820 ft.): From N, Mount Tecumseh Trail begins at parking lot on S side of Tripoli Road, 1.3 miles W of Mt. Osceola Trail and 5.7 mi. E of I- 93 (Exit 31) in Woodstock.

This approach offers a more interesting and secluded approach to Tecumseh, with wild and beautiful forests. From parking, trail quickly drops down to cross Eastman Brook (may be difficult in high water), then climbs up onto old logging road which is followed on easy to moderate grades for 1.3 mi., first through fine hardwoods, then white birches. After reaching 2980-ft. saddle, trail turns L and climbs easily through open forest, then steepens as it makes long, steady climb to crest of Tecumseh's West Peak. At top of climb short side trail R provides partial view NW toward Mt. Moosilauke and Kinsman Notch from blowdown area.

Trail continues over series of three knobs; true summit of West Peak is last, or easternmost, knob, reached at 2.4 mi. / 3766 ft. (High point is just to R off trail.) Beyond, drop into ferny, fir-forested 3620-ft. col between West Peak and main summit. At first, trail ascends from col at moderate grade, then quite steeply, finally reaching excellent stand-up outlook N at 3.0 mi. Continue on moderate grade another 0.1 mi. to summit.

South Approach

The Sosman Trail, established soon after Waterville Valley Ski Area opened in 1966, provides an alternative approach to the summit and offers the best views from the mountain at two cleared outlooks. It runs 0.8 mi. from the top of the ski slopes N to the main summit. From top of ski area, trail enters woods on right (N) side of tall transmission tower. First 0.4 mi. is nearly level, heading N along ridge through deep fir forest. After short climb, two fine viewpoints are passed. The first, which looks E, is marked by log bench. The second, offering vistas NW, is a bit further along on L. From here trail descends rock ledge (good views of sharp, summit cone), turns L and descends short pitch, then swings R and passes through level stretch of forest, before rising slightly to meet Mt. Tecumseh Trail 0.2 mi. from main summit. Continue straight ahead several hundred feet to fork. Bear L for approach via Sosman Trail, tackling summit cone over rock-strewn footway, or R for Mt. Tecumseh Trail approach.

Winter

As Tripoli Road is not maintained for winter auto traffic, and is closed at both the I-93 and Waterville Valley ends, it is impractical to consider the NW approach, or an end-to-end hike of Mt. Tecumseh Trail. Nearly all winter trampers will start and end their hikes up the mountain at the base of the ski area, taking the Mt. Tecumseh Trail to the ridgecrest. From there, the Sosman Trail provides the easier route to the top, with good views to the W en route. Deep snow improves views at the actual summit. Overall, this may be the easiest of the 4000-footers in winter. Since the ski area parking lot generally fills up quickly in the morning, especially on weekends, don't expect to find a space anywhere near the trailhead unless you're an early riser.

In recent years there have been numerous reports of renegade skiers and snowboarders swooping down the hiking trail between the two side paths to the ski slopes. Since they are often out of control, hikers should be prepared to get out of the way quickly along this section of trail. Hikers who wish to either ascend or descend via the ski trails should also be on the lookout for fast moving skiers and snowboarders, as well as grooming machines and blasting snowguns. Be forewarned, also, that you're likely to receive many a curious glance from those schussing down the mountain's steep slopes.

View Guide

SUMMIT AREA: The ledges atop the actual summit offer limited views, and as the trees atop the mountain continue to thrive, there's less and less to look at as time progresses. While the summit once afforded better-than-average views, especially E, one has to stand nearly tiptoe now to gain a decent perspective on the Osceolas to the N and Mt. Tripyramid and other Sandwich Range peaks to the E.

The best views NE are obtained from a ledge a few yards down from the actual summit. A well worn path leads to this stand-up viewspot. To the N and E are seen Tecumseh's closest neighbors, Mt. Osceola and its East Peak, with other peaks seen through the broad gap between them. South Hancock is just R of Osceola. Farther R and beyond is Mt. Washington, with Mts. Jefferson, Adams and Clay to its L. Mt. Pierce is under Adams, Mt. Eisenhower is under Clay and Mt. Monroe is under Washington. Mt. Carrigain looms just to the L of East Osceola. To the R of East Osceola, on the other side of the Mad River valley, is the long, dark wooded mass of Mt. Kancamagus. In the distance, starting on the L between East Osceola and Kancamagus, are Middle and South Carter over Rocky Branch Ridge, the Wildcats, Carter Dome with Giant Stairs below, Rainbow Ridge and Black Mtn. above Mt. Resolution, the Baldfaces, Sable and Chandler, Eastman Mtn., the Doubleheads, Mt. Tremont, Owls Cliff, and Bartlett Haystack. Kearsarge North is seen over Livermore Pass, the broad gap between Kancamagus and Tripyramid's Scaur Peak, and farther R is Bear Mtn. North Moat is over the R end of Bear, Black Cap Mtn. is just L of Scaur Peak, and Middle and South Moat are to the R of Scaur Peak, with Maine's Pleasant Mtn. beyond and farther R.

Partial easterly views are available from an opening just below the summit ledges. Most impressive are the three peaks and two slides of Mt. Tripyramid across the valley, with Mt. Passaconaway peeking over to the R of South Tripyramid and the Sleepers and Mt. Whiteface farther R. To the SE are the sprawling northern Flat Mtn. and the dark bulk of Sandwich Dome.

Splendid views N and W to the peaks of the Franconia Notch region and the western Pemi Wilderness, seen from a unique angle, are found from a stand-up outlook ledge along the Mt. Tecumseh Trail 0.1 mi. N of the summit. Cannon Mtn., the Cannon Balls and North and South Kinsman are to the NW. To the R of Cannon–Kinsman, poking up well above the peaks of nearby Scar Ridge, are Mts. Flume, Liberty, Lincoln and Lafayette. To their R is the sharp summit of Mt. Garfield, towering over the round dome of Owl's Head Mtn. Farther R are the peaks of the Twin–Bond Range, including Galehead, South Twin, West Bond, Bondcliff and Mt. Bond. Also seen is Tecumseh's West Peak, less than a mile away.

SOSMAN TRAIL OUTLOOKS: Arguably, the mountain's most stunning vistas are those obtained from the viewpoints established several years ago along the ridgeline Sosman Trail. If climbing Tecumseh via the E (ski area) end of the Mt. Tecumseh Trail, the short side trip to these viewpoints (0.4 mi. round trip from where the trail crests the ridge) is well worthwhile. The first outlook, attained on the R after a short scramble up a steep slope 0.4 mi. S of the summit, offers a sweeping view W and NW. On the far L is Carr Mtn.'s long ridge, with Vermont's Killington and Pico Peaks seen in the distance on clear days. Farther R is Mt. Kineo, with Mt. Cube behind on its L. Next to the R is Mt. Cushman, with Piermont Mtn. beyond and Vermont's Breadloaf Mtn. group on the horizon to the R. Mt. Moosilauke's huge bulk is farther to the R, just N of W, with its South Peak on the L and its northern spurs, Jim and Blue, on the R. Continuing to the R, the lower Kinsman Ridge leads up to Mt. Wolf. Mt. Mansfield is on the horizon over the lower Kinsman Ridge, with the Worcester Range to its L. To the R of Wolf are South and North Kinsman, the Cannon Balls, and Cannon Mtn. To the NNW the peaks of Franconia Ridge rise above the main summit of Scar Ridge. Farther R is the sharp peak of Middle Scar, with Owl's Head and Mt. Garfield to its R. On the far R and close at hand is the spruce-clad, arrow-like peak of Tecumseh.

A bit further along the trail, this time on the L, is a rustic log bench where one can sit and enjoy a sweeping vista to the E and NE of Waterville Valley. The view starts on the L with the nearby peak of Tecumseh, with Mt. Osceola seen off its R slope. Through the gap between Osceola and its East Peak are Mts. Jefferson, Adams and Clay, with Mt. Eisenhower below. To the R of East Osceola is the sprawling Mt. Kancamagus, with many peaks seen beyond, starting with the lower part of Mt. Carrigain's Signal Ridge and Slide Peak, a spur of Mt. Washington. Next to the R are Middle and South Carter, with Wildcats E and D and Rocky Branch Ridge below. Farther R are Wildcat A, Carter Dome with Giant Stairs below, and Rainbow Ridge above Mt. Resolution. Jackson's Black Mtn. is seen to the L of the main summit of Kancamagus, and to the R of the main summit are South Baldface, Sable and Chandler. Mt. Tremont is seen off the R slope of Kancamagus's E summit, with the tips of the Doubleheads to the

L and Owls Cliff and Bartlett Haystack to the R. Chatham's Mt. Shaw, The Gemini and Kearsarge North are seen over the broad Livermore Pass. Bear Mtn. is to the R of Kearsarge, and North Moat is seen in the back between Bear and Tripyramid's Scaur Peak. Farther R are the three Tripyramid peaks and the two rounded Sleepers, with Mt. Passaconaway poking up between South Tripyramid and West Sleeper. The Snows Mtn. ski slopes are seen below Middle and South Tripyramid. On the far R is Mt. Whiteface rising above upper Snows Mtn. and its own West Spur; by moving to the L, part of the northern Flat Mtn. can be added to the view.

Wide views E are also available from the ski slopes, which run approximately 1.8 mi. from top to bottom. Though highly scenic, treading down the skiways tends to be tedious and very hard on the knees and for many hikers it is not recommended as a method of descent.

NO. OF 4000-FOOTERS VISIBLE: 36

North and Middle Tripyramid

North Tripyramid

ELEVATION: 4180 ft. / 1274 m   ORDER OF HEIGHT: 32
LOCATION: Sandwich Range, Town of Waterville
USGS MAP: 7½′ Mount Tripyramid

Middle Tripyramid

ELEVATION: 4140 ft. / 1262 m   ORDER OF HEIGHT: 35
LOCATION: Sandwich Range, Town of Waterville
USGS MAP: 7½′ Mount Tripyramid

Geography

A triad of sharp peaks along its ridgecrest and two huge slides on its flanks mark Tripyramid as one of the most distinctive and rugged mountains in the Whites. It is easily recognized by what nineteenth-century writer Samuel Adams Drake called "its singularly admirable and well-proportioned architecture." Tripyramid rises in the Sandwich Range Wilderness between Waterville Valley on the SW and the Albany Intervale on the NE. North and Middle Peaks are official 4000-footers, while the South Peak (4100 ft. / 1250 m) lacks the requisite 200-ft. rise from its col. The North Peak is somewhat detached from the other two. A variety of trails provide scenic and rugged approaches to Tripyramid.

There are good views E and W from Middle Peak and restricted vistas NE and S from North Peak. The best views are found atop the North

Slide (mostly bare granite ledge on the NW flank of North Peak) and the South Slide (a slide of gravel and broken rock on the SW flank of South Peak). Two smaller slides on the E slope of the mountain are now largely revegetated.

Scaur Peak (3605 ft.) is a prominent, sharp-peaked spur connected to North Peak by a level ridge on the NW. A long, gentle ridge extends W from Scaur Peak, ending in the low rock nubble known as The Scaur (2230 ft.). The lower W part of this ridge rises from the narrow valley of Flume Brook on the N, in which is sequestered the Waterville Flume. Flume Peak (2980 ft.), a southern spur of Mt. Kancamagus, is on the N side of this valley. Livermore Pass (2900 ft.) separates Scaur Peak from the main mass of Mt. Kancamagus on the NW. The wonderfully-named, flat-topped Fool Killer (3548 ft.) juts to the E from North Peak, overlooking the valley of Sabbaday Brook. From The Fool Killer a spur ridge extends NE over a 2882-ft. hump to the Swift River valley. The high, rounded domes of West Sleeper (3881 ft.) and East Sleeper (3860 ft., one of New England's "Hundred Highest") connect South Tripyramid with Mt. Whiteface on the SE.

The N slopes of the mountain are drained by the broad basin of Pine Bend Brook. Several short, steep ridges descend into this basin from the ridge between North Tripyramid and Scaur Peak, and a prominent ridge extends NE from Scaur Peak between Pine Bend and Horne Brooks. On the E Sabbaday Brook flows down through a long, curving valley between the Tripyramids, The Fool Killer, The Sleepers, and a long N spur ridge of East Sleeper. Sabbaday Falls, a beautiful flume-like formation, is on the lower part of this brook. On the W side of the Tripyramids, Avalanche Brook flows down from a ravine (once called the "Ravine of Avalanches") between North Peak and Scaur Peak, while Slide Brook tumbles down from the base of the South Slide. For many years a landmark for Tripyramid climbers was a small flume on Slide Brook called the "V," but this feature is no longer accessible by trail. Slide and Avalanche Brooks unite at the W base of the mountain and continue downstream to the Mad River. Cold Brook, a tributary of Slide Brook, drains a deep basin below Middle Peak, enclosed by spur ridges from the North and South Peaks. To the SW of South Tripyramid is the long ridge of Snows Mtn. (3060 ft.). Cascade Brook flows down a valley between Snows and a long spur curving NW from West Sleeper. The broad, remote gap between the Sleepers, Snows Mtn. and nearby Flat Mtn. is known as Lost Pass. This mostly trailless, little-visited upland can be studied from the top of Tripyramid's South Slide.

Nomenclature

Early names for this three-headed mountain included "Saddle Mtn." and "Waterville Haystacks." One 1860 map called the mountain "Passaconaway," but that same year the geographer Arnold Guyot published his map and applied the name "Tripyramid." In 1876 state geologist Charles H. Hitchcock adopted Guyot's "Tripyramid" name in his *Geology of New Hampshire* and moved "Passaconaway" to another 4000-footer in the Sandwich Range.

The Fool Killer received its name because of its deceptive appearance when viewed from Albany Intervale, where it blends in with the main bulk of Tripyramid. On at least one occasion an exploring group reached the top of this spur ridge, only to discover that the real objective loomed much higher beyond a thickly wooded connecting ridge.

Historical Highlights

First Ascent: Unknown, possibly by Arnold Guyot in mid-1800s.

1830: Nathaniel Greeley settles in Waterville Valley.

1840s: Settlers clear two patches of land near western base of Tripyramid. Homestead of Ebenezer Swazey near junction of Cascade and Avalanche Brooks is named "Swazeytown." Frank Blanchard's homestead farther up Avalanche Brook is dubbed "Beckytown," after his wife, Rebekah.

1869: First South Slide falls in October rainstorm; it is said to be 2½ miles long and up to 1000 ft. wide at the base. Steep upper half-mile has angle of 34 degrees. Path is soon cut from Waterville to base of slide.

1874: Charles E. Fay and three others ascend South Slide and traverse the three peaks to "unveil the mysteries" of this little-known mountain. Nathaniel Greeley proclaims them to be the first persons to stand on North Peak, but Fay's group knows otherwise, having seen old axe blaze on tree.

1875: Guidebook editor Moses Sweetser and surveying party climb Tripyramid from Waterville and cross over to Mt. Whiteface to town of Sandwich. Route up South Slide (then called the "Great Slide" and considered "the most remarkable object among the curiosities of Waterville") to South Peak is written up in his 1876 guidebook. Trip is said to "occupy a long and workful day."

1879: AMC opens Livermore Trail (then called "American Institute of Instruction Path") from Beckytown through Livermore Pass and on to Sawyer River valley to N.

1880: AMC members scout Sabbaday Brook valley as route for trail to Tripyramid, but decide expense of this long route is too great to justify completion.

1885: North Slide and second South Slide fall in August downpour. One visitor writes that the South Slides have "made the fair mountain a desert of rock." Rev. Dr. J. M. Buckley makes exciting ascent up newly bared ledges of North Slide, barely escapes fall in crumbling stone near apex.

1890s: Winnipiseogee Paper Company and then International Paper Company conduct logging operations for spruce at western base of mountain; dams are built for log driving, small mills are erected, and several camps are established, including Depot Camp, Swazeytown Camp, Flume Brook Camp, and Avalanche Camp.

1892: Party of six AMC snowshoers, including two women, scale North Peak—perhaps the first winter ascent. "The climbing was of the hardest kind: the snow soft and heavy, loading the shoe at every step," writes Isaac Y. Chubbuck in *Appalachia* article. One snowshoer falls into spruce trap and requires "considerable floundering" to get out.

1900: Edgar J. Rich and other WODC members cut Sleeper Trail to connect South Slide and Mt. Whiteface.

1904: A. L. Goodrich and other Watervilleans cut trail above North Slide and soon extend it across ridge.

1906–1916: Conway Lumber Company's Swift River Railroad operation logs heavily in valleys to N of Tripyramid at far W end of rail line. Cuttings and camps extend into valleys of Sabbaday and Pine Bend Brooks. Huge white pines are taken from Pine Bend area in 1915–16.

1916: Tripyramid makes first appearance in AMC guidebook. In addition to North & South Slides and Sleeper Trail, book describes route up Sabbaday Brook valley using logging roads and slide on E side of mountain. Also mentioned is trail that climbs from Woodbury Trail (to Mt. Whiteface) over ridge between Cascade and Slide Brooks, meeting route down from South Slide at small flume called the "V."

1924: New slide falls on E slope. Sabbaday Brook Trail soon established, using older slide in upper portion.

1926: Woodstock Lumber Company, subsidiary of Parker–Young Company, acquires Waterville timberlands and renewed logging is undertaken to W of Tripyramid. Major log driving dam is located at Swazeytown on Avalanche Brook.

Mid-1930s: Pine Bend Brook Trail built from Albany Intervale to North Peak. Trail to "V" from Cascade Brook has been abandoned.

1938: Hurricane obliterates part of Sleeper Trail; remains obscure until ca. 1960 due to logging.

1944: USFS extends Livermore Rd. from Avalanche Camp to Flume Brook Camp near Livermore Pass.

Mid-1950s: Scaur Ridge Trail opened. Lower parts of routes to North and South Slides are relocated. These two routes formerly split from loop jct. near Avalanche Camp, now have separate access points off Livermore Trail one mile apart.

Mid-1980s: Sabbaday Brook Trail relocated away from lower part of E slide, now takes more moderate, switchbacking route to top of slide.

1984: Tripyramids included in newly created 25,000-acre Sandwich Range Wilderness.

North (left) and Middle Tripyramid from South Peak.

Trail Approaches

Tripyramid offers a variety of trail approaches from either side, with the option for exciting slide scrambling, mellow wooded ridge walking, and long valley walks. By any route Tripyramid is a full-day, fairly challenging hike, and a great one.

West Approach from Waterville Valley

> **Livermore Trail, Mount Tripyramid Trail via North and South Slides**
> 11.0 mi. loop, 3000-ft. elevation gain

TRAILHEAD (1580 ft.): Large parking area for Livermore Rd. (Depot Camp) near jct. of West Branch Rd. and Tripoli Rd. near Waterville Valley. From NH 49, 10.3 mi. from Exit 28 off I-93, turn L onto ski area access road and in 1.2 mi. turn R onto Tripoli Rd. In another 0.6 mi. turn R onto West Branch Rd., cross bridge, and bear L into parking area.

The loop over the Tripyramid slides is one of the most exciting and challenging hikes in the Whites. It's best to ascend the steep granite slabs of the North Slide and descend the gravelly South Slide. Some hikers will be uncomfortable on the North Slide, and it is potentially dangerous and should be avoided if wet or icy. Even on a dry day it is among the most challenging sections of trail in the Whites, and is not recommended for descent. The Scaur Ridge Trail (see below) is a safer alternative for the ascent.

From parking area, walk up the Livermore Trail, here a wide gravel road, at easy grades. Cross Depot Camp clearing at 0.3 mi. with glimpse of Tripyramid ahead and continue up road past Greeley Ponds Trail and several other junctions with local WVAIA hiking trails. Sloping meadow on R provides limited views at ca. 1.0 mi. Continue up wide, winding road, and at 2.2 mi. bear L on Livermore Trail as logging road/X-C ski trail diverges R over bridge. In another 0.1 mi. look for ledgy cascades in Avalanche Brook on R.

Trail from South Slide comes in on R at 2.6 mi./2000 ft. Continue at moderate grade up Livermore Trail, passing Avalanche Camp clearing on L at 3.1 mi. At 3.6 mi./2400 ft., at sharp L turn on Livermore Trail, bear R on trail to North Slide. Drop down bank to cross Avalanche Brook and ascend moderately up hardwood ravine with large yellow birches, entering Sandwich Range Wilderness. Gravel outwash and dense conifers signify steeper approach to base of slide, reached at 4.1˚mi./2900 ft. Scramble up dark, exposed slabs—steepest and smoothest at bottom. This is trickiest part of climb, requiring liberal use of hands; some of ledges are very slippery. Blazes are few, so choose your line carefully. Higher up, above ca. 3350 ft., footing improves on grainier, lighter rock and views open dramatically to W and N. Slide becomes very wide at ca. 3600 ft. Take care not to kick loose rock onto hikers below. Follow R fork of slide and exit top L corner at 4.6 mi./3900 ft. Climb steeply through woods to Pine Bend Brook Trail at 4.8 mi.; turn R and quickly reach 4180-ft. summit of North Peak with limited view NE on obscure side path L and partial view S from small clearing to R.

After offering glimpse of triangular Middle Peak close ahead, combined Mt. Tripyramid/Pine Bend Brook Trails descend short steep pitch, then grades are easy down to broad col and jct. L with Sabbaday Brook Trail at 5.3 mi./3860 ft. Cross ferny col and climb easily, then up steep, eroded pitch to Middle Peak at 5.6 mi./4140 ft. There is fine outlook to W across Waterville Valley on R just before reaching summit, and standup view E towards Mts. Passaconaway and Chocorua from ledge at high point, just L of trail. Descend steeply, then easily to col, then make short, steep climb to South Peak with partial view back to N (revealing Middle and North Peaks close at hand and many peaks in distance, including Lafayette on L, Carrigain in middle, and Washington on R) from ledge and reach narrow wooded summit at 6.0 mi./4100 ft. Drop easily at first, then very steeply to top of S Slide at 6.2 m/3900 ft. Descend carefully over steep gravel, ledge & broken rock with wide views W and S (including unusual look at Lost Pass area), passing jct. L with Kate Sleeper Trail; just above jct. are best viewing seats. Views remain superb on wide upper part of slide, then you descend steeply through scrub with partial views and occasional down-scrambles. Slide opens up again in lower section, and bottom is reached at 6.6 mi./3100 ft. Descend briefly through dense conifers, then swing R up through small clearing, traverse wooded slope, and pick up old logging road. Descent is now moderate to easy down along Slide Brook, at times through fine hardwoods. After bend to L pass Black Cascade (difficult to access) at 7.7 mi. / 2300 ft., just before crossing Cold Brook. From here descent is pleasant walk to crossing of Avalanche Brook at 8.4 mi. and jct. with Livermore Trail just beyond; turn L for easy 2.6 mi. walk back to car.

SCAUR RIDGE TRAIL ALTERNATE ROUTE TO NORTH PEAK

This pleasant trail climbs at moderate grades from Livermore Trail, 3.8 mi. from Depot Camp trailhead and 0.2 mi. above jct. with North Slide trail to Pine Bend Brook Trail on narrow ridge between Scaur Peak and North Tripyramid. Turning R off Livermore Trail (elevation 2450 ft.), trail climbs at easy grade through fine hardwoods, entering Sandwich Range Wilderness and angling across S slope of Scaur Peak on old logging road. Higher up, as yellow and white birch dominate forest, look R for peeks through trees at imposing North Slide. Cross brookbed at 0.8 mi. / 3075 ft. and make L turn at 0.9 mi. Steeper climb leads to Pine Bend Brook Trail at 1.2 mi. / 3440 ft. Turn R here for easy traverse followed by rugged climb to North Peak, reaching summit 2.0 mi. from Livermore Rd. This adds 1.0 mi. to loop distance over Tripyramids for total of 12.0 mi. with 3000 ft. elevation gain. Some hikers using this route prefer to ascend South Slide and descend Scaur Ridge Trail.

North Approach from Kancamagus Highway

Pine Bend Brook Trail, Mount Tripyramid Trail

NORTH PEAK ONLY

8.0 mi. round trip, 2800-ft. elevation gain

NORTH AND MIDDLE PEAKS

9.6 mi. round trip, 3450-ft. elevation gain

TRAILHEAD (1370 ft.): Pine Bend Brook Trail starts at sign (limited road-side parking) on S side of Kancamagus Highway (NH 112) 1.0 mi. W of Sabbaday Falls parking area.

This varied trail has a mix of easy and steep grades and limited views. From highway, trail leads S a short distance, then turns R onto section of old Swift River logging RR grade for 0.2 mi. Trail then turns L and leads S at easy grade through spruces and hemlocks, swings R onto old logging road, following small brook, and soon crosses it—the first of more than 10 crossings of various branches of Pine Bend Brook; some may be dry in summer. There is short relocation to R leading to second crossing. At 1.3 mi., at third crossing, trail swings R (W) and continues at easy grade over low divide. After final brook crossings, trail bends L (SW) and ascends moderately through hardwoods. At 2.2 mi./2100 ft. enter Sandwich Range Wilderness, soon cross brookbed, and turn L to climb more steeply up W side of ravine with rough rocky footing. At 2.6 mi./2550 ft. turn L for steep, rough climb out of ravine, then bear R to ascend steadily up brushy ridge with limited views N. At 3.1 mi. reach crest of ridge between Scaur Peak and North Peak. Descend slightly and bear L for easy traverse to jct. R with Scaur Ridge Trail at 3.2 mi./3440 ft. Pine Bend Brook Trail climbs briefly and traverses crest of this wild narrow ridge, with restricted view R up to North Peak and its slide and glimpses L out to N, then swings R and ascends easily at first, followed by steep, winding, ledgy climb with many slippery ledge steps to negotiate. Reach summit of North Peak at 4.0 mi./4180 ft., just beyond jct. with trail from N Slide. Limited views NE and S on short side paths; for excellent views W and N, descend 0.2 mi./300 ft. on N Slide trail to top of slide. To reach Middle Peak, continue 0.8 mi. along Mount Tripyramid Trail from North Peak as described above, then retrace steps over North Peak and descend to trailhead via Pine Bend Brook Trail.

Northeast Approach from Kancamagus Highway

Sabbaday Brook Trail, Mount Tripyramid Trail

NORTH AND MIDDLE PEAKS
11.4 mi. round trip, 3100-ft. elevation gain

TRAILHEAD (1320 ft.): Sabbaday Brook Trail starts at Sabbaday Falls picnic area on S side of Kancamagus Highway (NH 112) 3.3 mi. W of Bear Notch Rd.

This trail provides a long and beautiful walk up a secluded valley, ending with a steep climb to the ridge. Sabbaday Brook Trail starts as graded path, passing side loop L up staircases alongside picturesque Sabbaday Falls at 0.3 mi. Cross wide Sabbaday Brook 3 times from 0.7 to 0.9 mile—difficult at high water. Trail soon picks up old logging road on E bank above brook, entering Sandwich Range Wilderness at 1.3 mi., and undertakes lovely walk up remote hardwood valley, with glimpses R to Fool Killer, West Sleeper and South Tripyramid. Swing R to recross brook at 2.8 mi./2100 ft., wind W and then NW up floor of valley through hardwood and birch forest interspersed with miniature meadows, and cross mossy brook twice more. At 3.7 mi. trail passes base of small slide off Fool Killer on R; short scramble up provides views up to high ridges of Sleepers and Tripyramid. Trail swings L (S) at final brook crossing at 4.1 mi./2900 ft. and cuts across E slope of Tripyramid. Turn R near top of old slide at 4.5 mi./3300 ft; from top of slab there is view E to Fool Killer, Passaconaway and Chocorua. From here climb is very steep and rough, reaching crest of ridge and Mount Tripyramid Trail at 4.9 mi./3860 ft.

Turn L (S) for Middle Peak (0.3 mi., 300 ft. elevation gain), or R (N) for North Peak (0.5 mi., 320 ft. elevation gain).

OTHER OPTIONS

A nice loop hike over the Middle and North Peaks can be done by combining the Pine Bend Brook Trail, Mount Tripyramid Trail, and Sabbaday Brook Trail, then adding a 1.0 mi. road walk on the Kancamagus Highway back to your starting point. Total distance of loop is 11.0 mi. with 3100-ft. elevation gain.

The Tripyramids can also be approached from the SE via the Kate Sleeper Trail. This remote ridgecrest path runs through beautiful boreal forest from the jct. between the two summits of Mt. Whiteface 0.8 mi. down to a 3400-ft. col and jct. with Downes Brook Trail. From here it traverses Sleeper Ridge, climbing moderately over its two rounded, wooded summits, East Sleeper (reached by 0.1 mi. side path) and West Sleeper (summit is just to N of trail). After rough section along Sleeper–Tripyramid saddle it ascends steeply to cross slide (good views SW) and meet Mt. Tripyramid Trail near top of South Slide, 2.5 mi. from Downes Brook Trail with 900 ft. elevation gain. Strong hikers can use Kate Sleeper Trail with Downes Brook Trail and Sabbaday Brook Trail to make long, tough loop that includes Whiteface and all Tripyramid summits: 18.0 mi. (including 1.3 mi. road walk) with 4500-ft. elevation gain.

Winter

Pine Bend Brook Trail is the most popular approach, though it has several challenging steep sections that will test snowshoe or crampon technique. There is limited roadside parking—bring a shovel! The L turn out of the ravine at 2.6 mi. is easy to miss. Sabbaday Brook Trail is a scenic winter approach if brook crossings are frozen, with nice views through the trees as you ascend the long valley, but the upper part is very steep. The loop over the slides is hazardous in winter and not recommended for the great majority of winter trampers. Livermore and Scaur Ridge Trails provide a long but safer and relatively easy approach in winter (13.2 mi. round trip to both peaks, 3250-ft. elevation gain); there is ample plowed parking at the Depot Camp trailhead. Hikers are not required to pay a Waterville Valley trail fee for using the first two groomed miles of Livermore Trail, but you should not walk on set ski tracks and should yield to skating skiers. Views from the North Peak are much improved with deep snowpack.

View Guide

By far the best views from Tripyramid are from atop the North and South Slides. Even if you opt not to do the slides loop on the Mount Tripyramid Trail, in clear weather the side trip down to the North Slide from North

Peak is well worth the 0.4 mi. round trip from the summit of North Peak, with a steep 300-ft. climb on the way back.

NORTH SLIDE VIEW: The widest section of the North Slide, a short distance below its apex, overlooks a grand sweep of mountain country to W and N. There are some rock seats to be found here.

On the far L, looking W, is the distinctive cone of Mt. Tecumseh, with part of Waterville Valley Ski Area on the L and its West Peak on the R. Mt. Moosilauke fills the horizon through Thornton Gap, the pass between Tecumseh and Osceola. Flat-topped Breadtray Ridge forms the R (N) side of the gap. The rugged, slide-scarred Osceolas are WNW across the upper basin of Mad River, with nearby Flume Peak closer and far below East Osceola. The distant Kinsmans are seen over the cliffy NE arm of Osceola, with Big Coolidge beneath. Whaleback, Liberty and Flume are to the R.

To the NW is the long, darkly wooded bulk of Mt. Kancamagus, with Mts. Lafayette and Lincoln over its middle, and Mt. Hitchcock and Owl's Head over the highest Kanc summit on the R. Mt. Garfield's pyramid is over the R shoulder of Kancamagus. The double summit of Mt. Huntington is next to the R, with Bondcliff and West Bond above and beyond. Mt. Bond is to the R of West Bond, with South Twin between them. Just R of the Bonds and closer are the Hancocks, with Scaur Peak close at hand and below. Massive Carrigain rises to the R of Hancock's long E ridge and the nubble of The Captain. Whitewall Mtn. and Cherry Mtn. are sighted through the gap between Hancock and Carrigain. On Carrigain's R, over Signal Ridge, is Mt. Willey, and farther R, on the E side of Carrigain Notch, is slide-streaked Mt. Lowell. Between Willey and Lowell are Mt. Weeks (L) and Mt. Dartmouth (R).

To the R of Lowell are Mt. Nancy and the Webster Cliffs. Next to the R are the Presidentials, including Jackson, Pierce, Eisenhower, Jefferson, Monroe, and Mt. Washington soaring above Oakes Gulf. A bit farther down the slide the view opens out more to the R to Boott Spur, Montalban Ridge, the Wildcats and the Carters.

NORTH PEAK VIEW: Standing only, there is a limited vista NE over the trees to the Presidentials, Carters, Baldfaces, Moats and nearer peaks such as Bear, and Church Pond down on the Albany Intervale. An obscure side path leads from the summit rock to an expanded view in this direction, including a peek down at the Fool Killer. Another short path leads to a restricted view S to Middle and South Peaks with Mt. Whiteface to the L and Sandwich Dome to the R.

MIDDLE PEAK, W VIEW: A small outlook ledge a few yards W of the trail, just N of the summit, overlooks the Waterville Valley region. On the far L (S) is nearby South Tripyramid, with the distant Uncanoonuc Mtns.

and Red Hill above the southern Flat Mtn. on its L. Distant, wavy Hersey Mtn. and massive Sandwich Dome are to the R of South Peak, with sharp Jennings Peak to the R of Sandwich and the northern Flat Mtn. beneath. Mts. Monadnock and Kearsarge can be seen in the distance over the L shoulder of Sandwich. Sunapee Mtn. can be seen over the R slope of Sandwich. Of the many distant hills to the R of Jennings Peak, Mt. Cardigan (with Tenney Mtn. beneath), Croydon Peak and Vermont's Mt. Ascutney stand out. The long, low ridge of Snows Mtn. is close by in this direction, beyond which are the Mad River valley and the ledgy peaks of Welch and Dickey. Stinson Mtn. is to the L of and beyond Welch, with the Moose Mtns. in Hanover and Winslow Ledge to its R. The long flat ridge of Green Mtn. joins Dickey with Tecumseh to the R. Carr Mtn.'s spread is over the L end of Green, with Smarts Mtn. and Vermont's Killington and Pico in the distance a bit farther L. Over the R shoulder of Green is the long crest of Mt. Kineo. Between Carr and Kineo is Mt. Cube.

W across the valley are Mt. Tecumseh and the Waterville Valley ski trails, with Tecumseh's West Peak to the R. Massive Moosilauke is perfectly framed by Thornton Gap. To the R, over Osceola's Breadtray Ridge, are lower Kinsman Ridge, and the Signal Mtn. range and Camel's Hump in Vermont. The view NW to the Osceolas is especially fine from this angle. The crumbling Painted Cliff is prominent on a spur of East Peak, with the Kinsmans and two Cannon Balls to the R. On the far R are Whaleback, the four Franconia Ridge peaks, Mt. Hitchcock, Owl's Head, and Garfield, all seen over the nearer ridge of Mt. Kancamagus. From the lower ledge here (use caution) it is possible to expand the view to Mt. Huntington, South Twin and the Bonds.

MIDDLE PEAK, E VIEW: From the summit ledge of Middle Peak is an interesting view over the trees NE to distant peaks and E along the Sandwich Range. On the far L Middle Carter is seen over the Wildcats, then Carter Dome is visible above the bumpy ridge of Mt. Tremont, with Mt. Parker behind Tremont on the L and Owl Cliff in front and to the R. Farther R is Bartlett Haystack; in between this peak and Tremont are Black and Iron Mtns. in Jackson, the latter with prominent cliffs. The Baldface Range is seen above Bartlett Haystack. Farther R, through the broad gap of Bear Notch, are the low peaks of Mts. Stanton and Pickering, with the Doubleheads above and beyond. Speckled Mtn. is seen between the Baldface Range and the Doubleheads, and the twin peaks of Eastman Mtn. are on either side of North Doublehead. The distant pyramid of Maine's Mt. Blue can be spotted to the R of South Doublehead. Farther R Kearsarge North rises over Bear Mtn. and Big Attitash. Close at hand and far below is the ledgy knob of Potash Mtn., with the Fool Killer down to the L. Beyond the Swift River valley the long ridge of the Moats fills the horizon; Maine's Streaked Mtn. is on the horizon to the R of North Moat and

Black Cap peers over Middle Moat. Close in to the R of the Moats is dark, bristling Hedgehog Mtn.

Eastward is a fine view of Mt. Chocorua, with Maine's Pleasant Mtn. in the distance to the L and the N ridges of Paugus beneath. Farther R and most striking is the great wooded dome of Passaconaway, rising above a N spur ridge of East Sleeper. To the R of Passaconaway a long ridge runs up to Mt. Whiteface. Between these peaks are glimpses of Silver Lake, Green Mtn. in Effingham and Ossipee Lake. Through gaps in the trees to the R (SE) are the Ossipee Range, Lake Winnipesauke and the Belknap Range over the nearby humps of the Sleepers.

SOUTH SLIDE VIEW: The top of the South Slide offers an unusual vista over the wild, mostly trailless region between Tripyramid and Sandwich Dome and out to distant southern horizons. There's an excellent rock seat just below the top of the slide. On the far L (SE) the top of the West Spur of Mt. Whiteface peers over the L end of the long, massive WSW arm of East Sleeper, with Mt. Shaw in the Ossipee Range in the distance. Flagg Mtn. is connected to Shaw on the L, with the distant Moose Mtns. in Brookfield visible between them. More of the Ossipee Range is seen to the R of Shaw, including the pyramid of Black Snout under Faraway Mtn. and Mt. Roberts on the R end of the range. Distant summits in the Blue Hills Range are visible on either side of Roberts. Farther R the Belknap Range spreads beyond Lake Winnispesaukee, with Mt. Major on its L end and Belknap, Gunstock and Piper Mtns. on its R end. Next to the R the sprawling, tower-topped Red Hill rises beyond the nearby dome of the southern Flat Mtn. Red Hill Pond (L) and Garland Pond (R) can be spotted in front of Red Hill on the L.

Farther R and close by is the S end of Flat Mountain Pond on a high tableland. At your feet is a broad spruce-wooded plateau holding two beaver ponds. Above is the wild cut of Lost Pass, the gap between the SW arm of Sleeper Ridge on the L and the broad bulk of the northern Flat Mtn. on the R, with Mt. Israel seen through the pass. The distant spread of Bean Hill is seen between Red Hill and Mt. Israel, with the two rounded Uncanoonuc Mtns. rising still farther away. The wavy crest of Hersey Mtn. rises far beyond the northern Flat. The Flat Mtn. ridge extends R to the massive double summit of Sandwich Dome, with the sharp Jennings Peak on its R. On clear days Mt. Monadnock (L) and Mt. Kearsarge (R) are visible over the ridge extending L from Sandwich's summit, and Mt. Cardigan is prominent to the R of Jennings. Ski-trailed Tenney Mtn. is under Cardigan, and to the R is Cardigan's prominent northern spur, Cataloochee Mtn. The sharp Croydon Peak pops up between Cardigan and Cataloochee. Farther R is Vermont's Mt. Ascutney. Nearby to the SW is the long, low ridge of Snows Mtn., with Stinson Mtn. beyond and Welch & Dickey Mtns. to the R. South and North Moose Mtn. in Hanover are to the R of Stinson, and the broad Winslow Ledge is seen between Welch and Dickey. To the R of Dickey is the elongated Carr Mtn. with Smarts Mtn.'s bulky mass beyond to the L of Carr's summit crest. On clear days Vermont's Killington Peak can be espied to the L of Smarts. Farther R is the long southern crest that leads up to Green Mtn. and Mt. Tecumseh. Above and beyond this ridge are Mt. Cube (on the L and farther) and Mt. Kineo (on the R and closer). From the L (E) edge of the slide, by the Kate Sleeper Trail jct., Mt. Moosilauke can be seen to the R of Mt. Tecumseh and Tecumseh's West Peak.

NO. OF 4000-FOOTERS VISIBLE: from North Tripyramid, 36 (somewhat theoretical, perhaps in winter only); from Middle Tripyramid, 36

Mount Whiteface

ELEVATION: 4020 ft. / 1225 m   ORDER OF HEIGHT: 45
LOCATION: Sandwich Range, Town of Waterville
USGS MAP: 7½′ Mount Tripyramid

Geography

With its great S cliff and long, steep-sided ridgecrest to the N, Whiteface strikes a bold and commanding pose in the center of the Sandwich Range Wilderness. The precipitous face of the mountain thrusts southward from the main line of the range and looms, sphinx-like, 3000 ft. above the lowlands of Wonalancet (once known as Birch Intervale) and Whiteface Intervale to the S. It is the southernmost of the White Mountain 4000-footers. Though the true summit is viewless, from the ledgy S summit (ca. 4000 ft.), just 0.3 mi. away, there are wide views over the lake country, and other vantages just below on the Blueberry Ledge Trail provide vistas in other directions. A good trail system offers several varied and interesting approaches.

From the true summit a narrow, humpy ridge, traversed by the Rollins Trail, extends nearly two mi. N to a broad col with Mt. Passaconaway, enclosing on its E side the beautiful glacial cirque known as The Bowl, managed as a 1556-acre Research Natural Area by the WMNF. In this secluded valley, drained by the Wonalancet River, are woods that have never been logged—a rarity in the White Mountains. Some of the trees are reported to be over 400 years old. The broad floor of the valley is forested with mature hardwoods, while spruce and fir dominate on the steep walls. Several slides have fallen off the N ridge of Mt. Whiteface into The Bowl. To the E, across The Bowl, is the lower Wonalnacet Range; from Hibbard Mtn.

on this range, and from the S outlook on Mt. Passaconaway, there are striking profile views of the steep E side of the Whiteface ridge. On the W side of the N ridge is the long, remote upper valley of Downes Brook, a major tributary of the Swift River. Two large slides have fallen off the steep side of this ridge into Downes Brook.

Bold ridges run S from either side of the S summit; the basin between them, below the S cliff, is drained by White Brook. The Blueberry Ledge Trail tackles the rocky SE ridge, while the McCrillis Trail climbs the SW ridge. The Blueberry Ledges are an extensive area of gently sloping open rock slabs, fringed with scrubby spruce, low down on the mountain's SE ridge. Interesting features on the S cliff include a small overhang cave and a naturally-formed set of stairs in a foot-wide dike, accessible only to trained rock climbers.

To the SW are the ravines of Whiteface River (separating Whiteface and East Sleeper from the southern of the two Flat Mtns.) and its East Branch (the basin between the McCrillis Trail ridge and the S ridge of the Whiteface West Spur), and beyond that is the remote plateau around picturesque Flat Mountain Pond. Just to the W of the main summits is the broad, flat-topped West Spur (3580 ft.), with a cliff-faced ridge running S. Beyond West Spur to the NW the Whiteface massif is connected to Mt. Tripyramid by the high, rolling Sleeper Ridge (East Sleeper, 3860 ft.; West Sleeper, 3881 ft.), named for Kate Sleeper, a community leader, innkeeper and trails activist from Wonalancet. A high, conifer-clad plateau with several beaver meadows divides Whiteface from East Sleeper, at the head of Downes Brook.

Nomenclature

"Whiteface" is an obvious reference to the prominent cliff on the S slope of the mountain. Guidebook editor Moses Sweetser averred that the rock face was bared by a great landslide in October 1820. However, the name predates that slide, appearing in Jeremy Belknap's 1784 journal and on Philip Carrigain's 1816 map. Timothy Dwight referred to it as "White-Faced Mtn." in his 1831 *Northern Traveller*, while geographer Arnold Guyot labeled the peak "South Whiteface" on his 1860 map, distinguishing it from "North Whiteface"—today's Passaconaway.

Historical Highlights

First ascent: Unknown. The mountain was mentioned as early as 1784 in Dr. Jeremy Belknap's journal. The geographer Arnold Guyot probably climbed it in the mid-1800s.

Ca. 1820: Landslide strips soil and vegetation off steep south face of mountain. Reads one account of the slide, "Oh! What a scene was there! Huge rocks, uprooted trees and oceans of sand had come down from the mountain filling the beautiful interval to the depth of several feet."

1842: Members of Charles T. Jackson's geological survey team ascend mountain from Neal McCrillis property. In reporting on trip two years later, Jackson writes that mountain "is very abrupt, and its summit is a naked rock."

1850s: Path is built to south summit from McCrillis Farm in Whiteface Intervale, later becomes known as McCrillis Trail.

1869: George L. Vose ascends Whiteface and makes detailed observations for second N.H. Geological Survey. Work of survey moves mountain from town of Albany to Waterville.

1871: U.S. Coast Survey erects signal station on summit.

1875: Moses Sweetser and party traverse Tripyramid and Whiteface while researching new guidebook.

1875: The poet Lucy Larcom, regular summer visitor to West Ossipee and Sandwich Range, publishes sonnet, "Clouds on Whiteface," in her *An Idyl of Work*:

> So lovingly the clouds caress his head—
> The mountain-monarch; he, severe and hard,
> With white face set like flint horizon-ward . . ."

1876: Sweetser's guidebook describes summit view as "one of the most beautiful in the state" and notes that parties occasionally spend night in "rude camp" there, with spring close by. Path from McCrillis farm is obscure in places, but one can procure guide at farm for $2.00 a day. Guidebook offers detailed view description.

1891: Katherine Sleeper opens inn at Wonalancet Farm. Charles E. Fay and J. Rayner Edmands of AMC and two Tamworth men traverse Mt. Whiteface, the Sleepers (then nameless), and Mt. Tripyramid. On second day they descend W side of N ridge of Whiteface to Downes Brook, negotiating very rough and rocky terrain. Ascending up valley towards East Sleeper, they note large new slide coming down off Whiteface ridge.

1892: Community leader Katherine Sleeper and other trails enthusiasts found Wonalancet Out Door Club (WODC).

1895: Thomas S. Wiggin cuts Wiggin Trail from Dicey's Mill Trail up SE ridge to summit.

1899: Gordon H. Taylor blazes Blueberry Ledge Trail (initially called Gordon Taylor Trail), joining Wiggin Trail below upper ridge; route is specifically marked for snowshoeing. Dr. William H. Rollins cuts Rollins Trail along N ridge towards Mt. Passaconaway. McCrillis Trail is restored. Camp Shehadi built between main and south summits using proceeds from lecture by Shehadi Abdullah Shehadi, a native of Syria then living in Providence, Rhode Island; is intended largely for use by snowshoeing parties. (Rebuilt in 1929.)

1900: Sleeper Trail is cut by Edgar J. Rich across Sleeper Ridge from Whiteface to Mt. Tripyramid.

1902–1907: Woodbury Trail built from Waterville Valley to summit by W. R. Woodbury, Paul R. Jenks and Charles W. Blood. Long route climbs over SW spur of Sleeper Ridge.

1908: Ferncroft Inn is opened near base of Blueberry Ledge Trail by Sarah Elizabeth and Elliot Fisher; remains in operation into 1950s. Main house and assortment of cottages and cabins could accommodate 115 guests.

1912: Camp Heermance built near south summit, under direction of Edgar Laing Heermance, a trail-building minister, who pioneered Blue Trails system in Connecticut. (Rebuilt in 1933.)

1914: The Bowl is added to WMNF through efforts of Kate Sleeper and WODC; virgin forest is saved from logging. Land is acquired from Louis S. Tainter of Publishers Paper Co.

Ca. 1916: Logging disrupts Sleeper and Woodbury Trails.

1917: Beebe River logging railroad begins operation out of Campton, is eventually extended for 22 mi., past Flat Mountain Pond to Camp 12 at SW base of Whiteface.

1920: Ashes of lumber baron Louis S. Tainter are cemented in ledge at S summit and marked by plaque, still present today.

1920s: Downes Brook Trail opened by WMNF. Large slides fall off N ridge of Whiteface into Downes Brook.

1923: Fire sparked by Beebe River logging railroad burns 3,500 acres in Flat Mtn. Pond region and lower SW slopes of Whiteface. Firefighter John Gray is trapped by blaze and perishes.

1931: The Bowl is designated as Research Natural Area by Forest Service.

1938: Hurricane obliterates part of Sleeper Trail; subsequent logging further obscures path.

1950s: Woodbury Trail abandoned except for W end near Snows Mtn.

1968: Plaque honoring Rev. Martin Luther King, Jr. is placed on S summit, but is later removed "for reasons and by persons unknown to us" (1979 *AMC Guide*).

1984: Congress creates 25,000 acre Sandwich Range Wilderness, includes Mt. Whiteface.

1987: Bottom section of McCrillis Trail is closed, new connector opened from Flat Mountain Pond Trail.

Early 1990s: WODC reclaims maintenance of Sleeper Trail from Sub Sig Outing Club, renames it "Kate Sleeper Trail," including former section of Downes Brook Trail leading from head of Downes Brook to Rollins Trail between main and south summits of Whiteface.

2002: Having deteriorated beyond repair, Camps Shehadi and Heermance are removed.

Trail Approaches

Southeast Approach from Wonalancet

Blueberry Ledge Trail, Rollins Trail
8.4 mi. round trip, 3050-ft. elevation gain

TRAILHEAD (1140 ft.): Spacious hiker's parking area off Ferncroft Rd., 0.5 mi. from NH 113A at sharp corner in Wonalancet. From the W, take Exit 24 off I-93 and follow US 3 to Holderness. Turn L on NH 113 and proceed 11.5 mi. to Center Sandwich. Turn L here, staying on NH 113 another 3.6 mi. to junction with NH 113A in North Sandwich. Continue straight on NH 113A and follow it 6.6 mi. to sharp R turn by fields of Wonalancet. Turn L onto Ferncroft Road at corner and drive 0.5 mi. to parking area on R.

From the E, take NH 113 from NH 16 at village of Chocorua. At crossroads in Tamworth village turn R on NH 113A and follow it 6.6 mi. to where Ferncroft Rd. leaves on R at sharp L turn.

This is the shortest and most popular approach to Whiteface, following a bold SE ridge. It is a varied and very scenic trail, but the upper part is steep and difficult with several challenging ledge scrambles. It can be dangerous if wet or icy. There are several fine viewpoints. The lower part of the trail is on private land in proximity to several homes; please respect residents' privacy. From hiker's parking, return to Ferncroft Rd., turn R and walk 0.3 mi. up road, then at sign for Blueberry Ledge Trail turn L across Squirrel Bridge and follow another road to edge of woods at 0.5 mi., where Pasture Path diverges L. Blueberry Ledge Trail continues ahead on old woods road, passing jct. R with Blueberry Ledge Cutoff at 0.6 mi. (This attractive trail, 1.4 mi. long, leads along Wonalancet River past small gorge, then ascends steadily to rejoin Blueberry Ledge Trail at top of Blueberry Ledges, 2.0 mi. from trailhead.) Trail soon enters WMNF and Sandwich Range Wilderness, and at 0.9 mi. McCrillis Path (not to be confused with McCrillis Trail) diverges L; in recent years this trail has been closed W of the WMNF boundary. Blueberry Ledge Trail climbs easily and traverses level area, then ascends moderately, mostly through spruces, to lower end of gentle, semi-open Blueberry Ledges at 1.6 mi. At top of ledges, at 2.0 mi. / 2150 ft., where Blueberry Ledge Cutoff rejoins from R, there is restricted view S to Ossipee Range. Trail now ascends easily through hardwoods and mixed forest, then rather steeply to Wonalancet Outlook (ca. 3000 ft., originally cut by Edgar J. Rich), with a partial view SE. After long, steady climb in conifers, trail levels on densely wooded shoulder and dips to jct. R with Tom Wiggin Trail at 3.2 mi. / 3350 ft. (This steep trail, nicknamed "The Fire Escape," provides alternate 3.0 mi. approach to this point via lower Dicey's Mill Trail. It leaves from that trail at 1.9 mi./1950 ft., descends to cross Wonalancet River, and climbs moderately and then very steeply with gravelly footing through fine hardwood forest. It passes small cliff on L at 2.6 mi./2600 ft. and continues stiff climb into conifers, with occasional glimpses R to Mt. Passaconaway and The Bowl, and meets Blueberry Ledge Trail in small saddle. WODC has posted signs at both ends of this steep and loose trail to discourage incidental use. Wiggin Trail ascends 1450 ft. in 1.1 mi.)

Above Wiggin jct., Blueberry Ledge Trail climbs moderately, makes brief traverse, then tackles steep upper ridge. First open ledge is reached at 3600 ft., with view of Lakes Region to S and Sandwich Dome to SW. Just above here is one of more difficult scrambles on trail, steep slab that once sported wooden steps, but removed years ago. Steep climb continues with several more vistas interspersed with winding ledge scrambles. One ledge on L looks across S cliff to Sandwich Dome and Flat Mountain Pond. Look for exceptional flat ledge viewpoint and lunch spot on R, looking N into The Bowl, at 3.8 mi./3900 ft.; see view description below. After passing site of old Camp Heermance on R (removed, camping not allowed) reach ledgy S summit and jct. with Rollins and McCrillis Trails (signs are at N end of ledges) at 3.9 mi./3990 ft. Highest knob, with broken iron pin and old triangle from U.S. Coast and Geodetic Survey chiseled into ledge, is on E side of rather large ledgy area. Views are excellent from this knob and also from ledges down in front a few yds. to SW. For true summit, continue N on Rollins Trail, crossing ledgy wooded knob with glimpse ahead to Osceola, Tripyramid, and true summit, then drop steeply over ledge steps to 3940-ft. col and jct. L with Kate Sleeper Trail at 4.0 mi. (Camp Shehadi has been removed from this site and camping is not allowed.) Continue ahead on Rollins Trail, which makes short climb, then traverses easily along ridge to unmarked and viewless wooded summit at 4.2 mi./4020 ft. If you start descending, you've gone past the high point.

Southwest Approach from Whiteface Intervale

Flat Mountain Pond Trail, McCrillis Trail, Rollins Trail
10.4 mi. round trip, 3250-ft. elevation gain

TRAILHEAD (968 ft.): Start at E trailhead for Flat Mountain Pond Trail off Whiteface Intervale Rd., which leaves NW side of NH 113A at a point 2.9 mi. N of the junction of NH 113 and NH 113A in North Sandwich and 3.7 mi. SW of the sharp corner in Wonalancet at the jct. with Ferncroft Rd. Follow Whiteface Intervale Rd. for 0.4 mi. (passing jct. L with Bennett St. at 0.1 mi.) to trailhead parking on L.

This is a longer and less-used approach up Whiteface's SW ridge, with

A viewpoint along the McCrillis Trail gives hikers a sneak peek at the south summit of Mount Whiteface.

a couple of good outlooks en route. There is a long, gentle approach followed by a fairly steep climb over the last 1.2 mi. McCrillis Trail may be obscure in its lower hardwood section—follow with care. From parking area, follow gravel road past beaver meadow L with view of Sandwich Dome. Road bears L at 0.5 mi., and at 0.6 mi. trail turns R off road into woods. Turn L at 0.7 mi. and R at 0.8 mi.—all turns are marked with arrows. Path now runs through hemlocks along bank above Whiteface River through private conservation land, passing view up to Mt. Whiteface at 0.9 mi. Continue over minor ups and downs, then descend switchbacks to cross river on large rocks (no bridge, difficult at high water) at 1.6 mi., entering Sandwich Range Wilderness. Turn L here, then R onto McCrillis Trail at 1.7 mi. / 1250 ft. After short climb, traverse to E, then bear L on old road at 2.1 mi. and begin long, easy climb through gently sloping hardwood forest. In places saplings crowd trail where canopy was opened by 1998 ice storm. Climb steepens at 3.7 mi. / 2700 ft. into spruce-fir forest. At 4.3 mi. / 3300 ft. pass first of several ledgy, scrubby outlooks, from ledge up on L of trail (requiring short scramble) looking SW towards Lakes Region and Sandwich Dome. Then look for viewpoint on R looking up to S cliff of Whiteface and SE to Ossipee Lake and Ossipee Range. Trail plunges into deep fir woods for stiff climb to S summit, ending with short, fairly difficult scramble and traverse of ledges with views SW to Flat Mt. Pond and Sandwich Dome. At 4.9 mi. McCrillis Trail meets Blueberry Ledge and Rollins Trails behind S summit ledges. Continue 0.3 mi. N on Rollins Trail for true summit.

Northeast Approach via Rollins Trail

The Rollins Trail runs along the long, rough N ridge of Whiteface, allowing loop trip with Dicey's Mill Trail and two-peak day with side trip to Mt. Passaconaway. There are two good outlooks down into the Bowl. From point 3.7 mi. up Dicey's Mill Trail, head W (L) on Rollins Trail (elevation 3300 ft.). Descend briefly and traverse broad col above headwall of The Bowl, with easy ups and downs and one partial view of Mt. Whiteface, then start climbing first hump on N ridge of Whiteface at 0.8 mi. Fairly steep climb leads to open ledge on L with fine view into Bowl and out to SE at 1.1 mi. / 3600 ft. Continue up ridge over several wooded humps, short steep pitches alternating with easier sections and two short descents. At 1.9 mi. look for dramatic standup view down into Bowl on L. Reach unmarked wooded summit of Whiteface at 2.2 mi. / 4020 ft. Good views at S summit are 0.3 mi. farther S on Rollins Trail—descend easily, then moderately to col and jct. R with Kate Sleeper Trail and then make short steep climb to ledgy S summit. Loop over Whiteface via Dicey's Mill, Rollins and Blueberry Ledge Trails: 10.1 mi., 3100-ft. elevation gain. With side trip to Mt. Passaconaway: 11.9 mi., 3850-ft. elevation gain.

North Approach from Kancamagus Highway

Downes Brook Trail, Kate Sleeper Trail, Rollins Trail
12.6 mi. round trip, 2800-ft. elevation gain

TRAILHEAD (1250 ft.): Parking area for UNH, Mt. Potash and Downes Brook Trails is at end of short side road on S side of Kancamagus Highway (NH 112), across from Passaconaway Campground and 2 mi. W of Bear Notch Rd.

This is a long, less-used approach up the isolated valley of Downes Brook. It's a pretty woods walk through remote country, but with 10 brook crossings it should be avoided in high water. Grades are easy to moderate nearly the entire distance. Trail starts up old gravel road for 100 yds., turns R at top of bank and traverses through scrubby woods, then turns L onto original route of trail at 0.3 mi. In short distance Mt. Potash Trail diverges R. Easy walking through nice hemlocks leads to first crossing at 0.7 mi., with three more in next 0.7 mi. After fourth crossing trail makes short climb and descent, then swings L for long easy section on E side of brook, entering Sandwich Range Wilderness at ca. 1.7 mi. and crossing slide outwash at 2.2 mi. / 1840 ft. After three more crossings, trail stays on W side for long stretch. Make two more crossings, with sidehill section on high bank between them, then at 4.5 mi. / 2850 ft. there are views L across valley to two large slides on side of N ridge of Whiteface.

Ascent steepens to tenth crossing near head of brook (which is here very small), above which you reach swampy plateau and jct. with Kate Sleeper Trail at 5.2 mi./3400 ft., with small beaver meadow visible ahead. Turn L (SE) and follow Kate Sleeper Trail on moderate climb to junction with Rollins Trail in col at 6.0 mi/3900 ft. True summit is 0.2 mi. L (N); view ledges on S summit are 0.1 mi. R (S).

Another possible trip from the Kancamagus Highway, this one entailing a loop hike over Whiteface and Passaconaway, can be made via Downes Brook, Kate Sleeper, Rollins, Dicey's Mill, Walden, Square Ledge, Passaconaway Cutoff and Oliverian Brook Trails. The loop distance is 15.6 mi. (including 1.0 mi. road walk), with a 3700-ft. elevation gain.

Winter

Blueberry Ledge Trail is the most popular approach; the Ferncroft Rd. parking area is plowed. The upper section of this trail is very challenging and possibly dangerous if icy; crampons are often required for the steep ledgy scrambles. Many winter peakbaggers make the long loop over both Whiteface and Passaconaway; it is generally considered easier to ascend rather than descend the Blueberry Ledge Trail. The Rollins Trail may be hard to follow along the N ridge; expect many slaps in face from fir branches. The Tom Wiggin Trail is rarely broken out in winter. The Flat Mountain Pond/McCrillis Trail and Downes Brook/Kate Sleeper Trail approaches avoid the tricky ledges on Blueberry Ledge Trail, but these routes are seldom used in winter and may require miles of trail-breaking. Downes Brook Trail is feasible only after prolonged cold weather freezes up the brook crossings.

View Guide

SOUTH SUMMIT: The open S summit of Whiteface presents several tiers of ledges with a 180-degree view S over the broad, low-lying Lakes Region. The best loafing and viewing spots are on the highest knob (on the E side of the summit area) and the lower ledges a few yards SW on the McCrillis Trail.

On the far L (NE) there is a glimpse of Mt. Passaconaway over the trees. Big Attitash Mtn. is seen off the R slope of Passaconaway, with Maine's Bald and Saddleback Wind Mtns. on the skyline. Farther R is the Moat Range, with Kearsarge North rising over North Moat at the L end of the range. Mt. Shaw in Chatham is off the L slope of North Moat, and farther away various peaks near Rumford, Maine, can be seen on either side of Kearsarge North. Distant Mt. Tom in Maine is seen over Middle Moat. Black Cap Mtn. is behind South Moat on the R, and farther R on the horizon are Maine's Streaked and Singepole Mtns. Nanamocomuck Peak, a spur of Passaconaway, is close by in this direction. Next to the R, looking ENE, the Three Sisters are seen above the main summit of Mt. Paugus, and farther R the distinctive rocky cone of Mt. Chocoura rises above the S knob of Mt. Paugus and Paugus's crumbling SW cliffs. Part of Maine's Pleasant Mtn. can be seen beyond Chocorua, with Conway Lake to the R. Below Paugus and close by are humpy Wonalancet Hedgehog (L) and Hibbard Mtn.(R). From Hibbard the rounded hump of Mt. Wonalancet juts out on the R, seen down through the trees, with lowly Mt. Mexico behind and many low ranges in western Maine on the horizon, and farther still is the glimmer of Sebago Lake. Chocorua Lake is seen over Mts. Wonalancet and Mexico and Silver Lake is beyond to the R.

To the SE, past a shoulder of Whiteface, are the fields of Wonalancet, with Ossipee Lake and Green Mtn. in Effingham beyond. To the R, looking SSE, are the long, jumbled ridges of the Ossipee Range. At the L end of the range, just R of Ossipee Lake, are the Nickerson Mtns., with Great Hill and Great Hill Pond in front. Farther R are Whittier and Bald Mtns. and then the pyramid of Mt. Shaw, highest peak in the range, with Flagg Mtn. extending to its L. Behind Shaw on the L are the more distant Copple Crown and Moose Mtns. Farther R the Ossipees extend across Faraway Mtn. and Mt. Roberts with the sharp Black Snout in front and Blue Job Mtn. and other peaks in the distant Blue Hills Range in the distance.

Due S and below are the fields of Whiteface Intervale and far beyond, 22 mi. away, is the great spread of Lake Winnipesaukee, unfolding between the Ossipee Range on the L and Red Hill, bearing a fire tower, on the R. The Belknap Range spreads behind the lake, with the prominent Belknap and Gunstock Mtns. on its R end. The twin rounded Uncanoonuc Mtns. can be spotted over the over the L (E) spur of Red Hill. Squam Lake stretches to the R of Red Hill, with double-peaked Mt. Israel flanking it on the R and conical little Young Mtn. in the foreground. Mt. Kearsarge is seen over the R shoulder of Israel, with wavy Hersey Mtn. to its L. On very clear days, the dim, broad-shouldered peak of Mt. Monadnock may be espied over Hersey. To the R of Israel are the long wooded ridges of the Squam Range, with Ragged Mtn. (L) and Sunapee Mtn. (R) in the distance. Farther R and nearby to the SW is the wooded cone of Flat Mtn., the southern of two adjacent peaks bearing that name, with flat-topped Prospect Mtn. beyond. On the far R is the SE ridge of Sandwich Mtn. leading up to the summit, with Mt. Cardigan far away over its L shoulder, and, to the R and even more distant, Vermont's Mt. Ascutney.

A few yards SW and down on the McCrillis Trail is an interesting view of Flat Mountain Pond and Sandwich Dome. The knobby Jennings Peak is to the R of Sandwich, with Stinson Mtn. beyond and between them. On clear days Vermont's Killington and Pico Peaks are visible on the horizon over Jennings. To the R of Jennings are Smarts Mtn. and Carr Mtn.

UPPER OUTLOOK ON BLUEBERRY LEDGE TRAIL: This flat-topped crag at 3900 ft. offers an extended and wide-open view NE and E across the deep ravine of The Bowl to Mt. Passaconaway and many distant peaks, and around to Lake Winnipesaukee on the S. To the L, looking N, a jumble of mountains is seen through the gap between the N ridge of White-face and the summit cone of Passaconaway. On the L Mt. Nancy and Mt. Bemis rise beyond the E end of Green's Cliff. In the distance South Weeks and the E end of Mt. Waumbek are visible over the Nancy–Bemis col, and Mt. Webster (L) and Mt. Jackson (R) are seen in the distance over Bemis. The Southern Presidentials rise from Jackson over Mts. Pierce, Eisenhower, Franklin and Monroe up to Mt. Washington, soaring above the gaping Oakes Gulf, just E of N and 24 mi. away. Mt. Jefferson peers over to the L of Monroe, Mt. Clay peeks over Monroe, and Boott Spur juts out to the R of Washington. In front of Washington on the R are Owl's Cliff and ledgy Mt. Tremont, Giant Stairs and Mt. Resolution, and Rocky Branch Ridge. In the right light it may be possible to pick out Mt. Isolation under Boott Spur. Bartlett Haystack is to the R of Tremont, with Mt. Parker to its L and Wildcats E and D in the distance over Parker. Wild-cat A and Carter Dome rise far beyond the Haystack, with Middle Carter (and South Carter below) between them. Extending R from Carter Dome is its rounded spur, Rainbow Ridge, with lowly Mt. Langdon low down in front and to the R.

Two miles NE across the beautiful, hardwood-draped Bowl is the shapely wooded dome of Passaconaway. A great slab of rock shines near The Bowl's headwall. Between the L slope of Passaconaway and Carter Dome is Black Mtn., with far-off Sunday River Whitecap on its L. Over the R shoulder of Passaconaway is Big Attitash Mtn, (part of Table Mtn.'s cliff is in front), with Maine's Bald and Saddleback Wind on the horizon. Farther R is North Moat, with Kearsarge North rising above and behind. Chatham's Mt. Shaw is behind Kearsarge on the L, with Spruce Mtn. near Rumford, Maine, between them. Middle and South Moat are seen above nearby Nanamocomuck Peak, with Black Cap Mtn. and the lower Green Hills behind to the R. Maine's Mt. Tom is on the horizon over Middle Moat, and Streaked and Singepole Mtns. are off to the R of the Green Hills. Mts. Paugus and Chocorua are viewed above Wonalancet Hedgehog, with part of Pleasant Mtn. behind Chocorua. Under Nanamo-comuck and Wonalancet Hedgehog is the descending S spur of Passacon-away, which the Dicey's Mill Trail follows on its far (E) side. From here the view extends SE and S around to the Ossipee Range, Lake Winnipe-saukee, and the Belknap Range, as described under the South Summit view, the main difference being the more open view SE, especially down to Hibbard Mtn. and Mt. Wonalancet.

NO. OF 4000-FOOTERS VISIBLE: 40 (combined for S summit, Blueberry Ledge Trail upper outlook, and through trees around true summit)

NORTH COUNTRY

Mount Cabot

ELEVATION: 4170 ft. / 1271 m   ORDER OF HEIGHT: 33
LOCATION: Pilot Range, Township of Kilkenny, Town of Lancaster
USGS MAPS: 7½′ Jefferson, 7½′ Stark

Geography

Bulky, whale-shaped Mt. Cabot and its train of Pilot Range peaks stand guard on the northern fringe of the White Mountains, looming over the town of Lancaster on the W and the Kilkenny region and the headwaters of the Upper Ammonoosuc River to the E. Its broad, wooded summit is the major peak of the wild Pilot Range. This northernmost of the 4000-footers has a real North Country feel to it, with fern-filled fir forests and far fewer hikers than the more popular ranges to the S.

On the S, remote Bunnell Notch (3041 ft.) separates Cabot's broad and slightly lower SE summit (4080 ft.) from the 3638-ft. North Peak of neighboring Terrace Mtn. Cabot's upper S face features a broad band of talus (broken rock), a distinctive landmark from afar. A high ridge runs NE from Cabot down to a 3710-ft.col, then over The Bulge (3950 ft., a wooded, rounded summit with no views) and The Horn (3905 ft., a sharp rocky peak and spectacular open viewpoint). The very top of The Horn is a table-like ledge that requires a short scramble for access, and it is only from this perch that the widest views are obtained. Both The Bulge and The Horn are among the New England Hundred Highest peaks. From The Bulge the long, trailless Pilot Ridge extends NW over a series of wooded peaks culminating in Hutchins Mtn. (3730 ft., also known as Pilot Mtn.). The secluded upper valley of Mill Brook drains the E slopes of this ridge and the N slopes of the Bulge and The Horn. To the NE of The Horn is a highland plateau cradling Unknown Pond (3177 ft.) and tiny, trailless Bishop's Pond. These picturesque tarns are guarded on the E by 3510-ft. Unknown Pond Ridge and are drained SE via Unknown Pond Brook. Just to the S the West Branch of the Upper Ammonoosuc River rises in the SE-facing ravine enclosed by Mt. Cabot, The Bulge, The Horn and the latter's long SE ridge.

A long ridge runs W from the summit of Cabot; between it and the Pilot Ridge is the deep valley of Fox Brook. Bunnell Brook (which drains from Bunnell Notch) and Bone Brook flow off the SW slopes of the mountain to the flatlands of Lancaster.

Though Cabot's broad summit is heavily wooded with no views, good vistas are found on the way up the Mt. Cabot Trail at Bunnell Rock on the SW slope of the S summit; from the cabin and clearing at the site of a former fire tower, located at the N end of the S summit crest; and from a side path on the W side of the summit itself.

Nomenclature

The mountain was named "Mt. Sebastian Cabot" about 1886 by William H. Peek, an enthusiastic explorer of the White Mountains, in honor of an English sea captain who was the grand pilot of Henry VII. Cabot explored along the coast of New England in the sixteenth century. The peak was also known as "Grand Pilot," "Pilot Dome," and "Kilkenny Peak." Peek also applied the name "Mons Ovium" to the lower S summit of Cabot, and dubbed the great talus slope as the "Sheep-Fold," for the resemblance of the boulders to sheep huddled in an enclosure. He also named "The Bulge" (sometimes called "Turtle-Back") and called The Horn, "South Peak."

The Pilot Range was named by early visitors to the upper Connecticut River valley, who used the mountains as landmarks and called them the "Land Pilot Hills." Local legend offers a different origin for the name, averring that the range was named after a dog called Pilot, who lived in the Kilkenny forest with a reclusive settler named Jonathan Willard in the late 1700s. The range was also called "Little Moosehillock" by Timothy Dwight, who twice traveled through this area around 1800.

The unincorporated township of Kilkenny, a name now often applied in general to the northern part of the WMNF, shares its name with the county of Kilkenny in Ireland. The name was presumably applied here by an Irish settler.

Unknown Pond was probably named for its remoteness, while Bishop's Pond was named for the Rt. Rev. Robert McConnell Hatch, a bishop in the Episcopal Church and a longtime Kilkenny enthusiast. He wrote several pieces about the region for *Appalachia* from 1956–1965, including a lyrical description of his namesake pond.

Historical Highlights

First Ascent: Unknown

1823: In *Gazetteer of the State of New Hampshire*, John Farmer and Jacob B. Moore describe the few residents of town of Kilkenny: "They are poor, and for aught that appears to the contrary, must always remain so, as they may be deemed actual trespassers on that part of creation, destined by its author for the residence of bears, wolves, moose and other animals of the forest."

1876: Moses Sweetser's guide includes section on Pilot Mtns., "a great congregation of low mountains covered, for the most part, with forests, and diversified by several high, bold peaks." He notes that "parts of it have never been visited." Section gives directions for climbing Pilot (Hutchins) Mtn. and describes view therefrom.

1885: AMC group (William H. Peek, Eugene B. Cook, George A. Sargent and Hubbard H. Hunt) traverses Pilot Range. They climb Pilot (Hutchins) Mtn. from Lost Nation Rd., where they enjoy "bewitching, entrancing" panorama. They descend into deep valley and camp, then climb over spur ridges next day and ascend "Grand Pilot" (Mt. Cabot). After leaving Hutchins they find no axe marks or other sign of human intrusion, but predict that "it will probably not be long before the iron horse itself will penetrate these wilds, and carry off the spoils of these hitherto inviolate solitudes." On summit of Cabot, Cook climbs tree to make sure they are on highest point, which is measured at 4230 ft. Peek publishes account and sketches of views from Hutchins and Cabot in March 1886 *Appalachia*.

1886: The Peek group returns for another exploration. Cook, Peek, Hunt and Charles E. Lowe ascend S summit of Cabot from Lancaster Gore, enjoy the "charming" view from the "Sheep-Fold" talus slope, then descend into Bunnell Notch, where they rendezvous with Sargent, who has come from Randolph over Round (Weeks) and Terrace Mtns. They camp in notch for two nights, then Sargent and Cook traverse Cabot S summit, Cabot summit, and Bulge across to Horn, while Peek and Hunt take lower route across E slopes of Cabot and valley between Cabot and Horn. They rendezvous on Horn, where view is described, then return over Cabot in rainstorm. Measurements give elevations of 4220 ft. for Cabot, 3950 ft. for Bulge and 3917 ft. for Horn. Another account appears in Dec. 1887 *Appalachia*.

1892–1903: Upper Ammonoosuc Lumber Company builds logging railroad and conducts intensive timbering operations in lower Kilkenny region on E side of Cabot.

1903: In wake of logging, huge fire in May scorches 25,000 acres in Kilkenny region, lapping up E slopes of Pilot Range. Present birch forest in area is legacy of fire. Today, line of birch growth on NE slope of Cabot is clearly visible from Horn.

1906: AMC group of four climbs Cabot in winter, starting at Lost Nation and proceeding up Fox Brook valley, thence up NW spur of Cabot. At top they find the "mountain-top forest, all deep-muffled in untrodden snow" and savor "the absolute stillness of perfect winter." Account by Raymond M. Dow Adams, "Pilot Dome in Winter," is published in May 1906 *Appalachia*.

1911: Fire tower is built near summit of Cabot by N.H. Timberland Owners Association.

1916: *AMC Guide* notes that "of the little-known mountain ranges in New Hampshire, perhaps none have received such scant attention in the public prints as the Pilot Range. . . . The range . . . is included in that vague title, now seldom heard, the Kilkenny Mountains." As for Cabot, guide describes "excellent path, traversed by horses its entire length," from Terrence White farm in East Lancaster (largely the route of today's Mt. Cabot Trail). On S slope of mountain, trail passes view into "bare, fire-swept Bunnell Notch." Guide notes observation tower and firewarden's cabin near summit; camp is connected by telephone with Lancaster. Warden is F. C. Leavitt; water source near summit is later named "Bishop–Leavitt Spring" in honor of this and another fire warden.

1924: New 50-ft. steel fire tower is built.

1925: New trail from York Pond through Bunnell Notch opens route to Cabot from E.

1940: USFS assumes management of fire tower, which is manned through 1949. Unknown Pond Trail makes first appearance in *AMC Guide*; new trail connects York Pond Rd. with Mill Brook Trail.

1948: *AMC Guide* notes that "Lookout's Trail" up to summit of Cabot is no longer maintained, though trail through Bunnell Notch is retained.

1958: With creation of AMC 4000-Footer Club previous year, directions for climbing Cabot, officially trailless, are published in June issue of *Appalachia*.

1960: Short-lived trail is cut across Terrace Mtn. WMNF resumes maintenance on trail to Cabot summit. *AMC Guide* makes first mention of climbing routes to Horn, noting that it's been climbed from SW from Mt. Cabot and from NE via Unknown Pond. Trip is "not recommended except for experienced parties."

1962: Lancaster Explorer Post begins several-year tradition of "Lighting of Cross" high on side of Cabot during Easter Season. This is done on fire tower until its removal, then continued on ledges to N using railroad flares placed in trees ca. 50 ft. apart.

1965: Cabot fire tower is dynamited in November as part of training for U.S. Army Special Forces.

1968: Horn is one of peaks on new list of New England Hundred Highest developed by AMC peakbagging enthusiasts. In time, herd path develops across ridge from Cabot.

1969: *AMC Guide* gives more detailed descriptions of routes to trailless Horn. One can follow ridge across from Cabot, with hardwoods on S-facing slopes and spruce on N-facing slopes, or approach from valley of Unknown Pond Brook, following stream up to Bishop's Pond, then swinging L around cliffs on climb to summit. These hints remain in guide through 1983 edition.

Late 1980s: Kilkenny Ridge Trail built N from Cabot over The Bulge, The Horn (side trail) and past Unknown Pond to Rogers Ledge and South Pond, and S across Terrace Mtn., Willard Notch, Mt. Weeks to Mt. Waumbek.

2000: Legal access to lower Mt. Cabot Trail is closed due to landowner dispute. Bulge is added to New England Hundred Highest list, reflecting revised USGS map.

2004: USFS upgrades and partially relocates E section of Bunnell Notch Trail; shorter W section is abandoned.

Trail Approaches

East Approach from York Pond Rd.

York Pond Trail, Bunnell Notch Trail, Kilkenny Ridge/
Mt. Cabot Trail
9.6 mi. round trip, 2900-ft. elevation gain

TRAILHEAD (1670 ft.): Parking for York Pond Trail is at end of York Pond Rd. by Berlin Fish Hatchery. From NH 110, 7.1 mi. W of NH 16 in Berlin, turn S on York Pond Rd. At 5.0 mi. from NH 110 a gate marks entrance to hatchery. In past, as sign indicates, this has been closed from 4 PM to 8 AM. In recent years, with increased usage of this trailhead, gate has been left open later in evening, and in winter it is left open through the season. To check status of gate, call hatchery at 603–449–3412. If gate is open, continue driving on York Pond Rd. past hatchery facilities and York Pond (on L, view of North Weeks across water). Pavement gives way to dirt 1.0 mi. beyond gate, and at 2.1 mi. from gate park on L at sign for York Pond Trail; room for several cars here. Additional parking is available at Unknown Pond trailhead, 0.1 mi. back along road. York Pond trailhead is total of 7.1 mi. from NH 110.

With W approach closed (see below), this is the shortest and probably most popular approach to Cabot. Formerly notorious for its obscurity and muddy footing, the Bunnell Notch Trail underwent major improvement by the Forest Service in 2004 and now provides a pleasant, moderate approach up a secluded valley. From parking spot, follow York Pond Trail along logging road for 0.2 mi., crossing brook on bridge, to clearing with view of Mt. Cabot. Bear R here on Bunnell Notch Trail (as York Pond Trail bears L) and follow grassy, weed-grown logging road at easy upgrade. At 0.5 mi. cross clearing where spur road bears L; stay straight here and descend gradually, with more glimpses of Cabot ahead, crossing two small brooks and then larger brook that drains E from Bunnell

Notch at 0.9 mi. At 1.1 mi. trail turns L off logging road onto recently built section, ascending rock staircase and climbing up onto high bank. At 1.3 mi. trail bends R where former route joins from L, climbs steadily a short way, then runs level along L edge of old clearcut. After passing glimpse of North Weeks and South Terrace through trees to L, trail dips to edge of brook and climbs along its R side through hardwoods. Trail crosses several small side streams while following tumbling main brook. At 1.9 mi. / 2250 ft. trail swings R and climbs away from brook, traverses along slope, comes briefly back down beside stream, then ascends slope again. In this section several small cascades are visible when leaves are down. Trail comes back near brook once more, then climbs above it again through glades of yellow and white birch. Stiff climb leads high up slope, easing at ca. 2800 ft. as Bunnell Notch is approached. Trail now climbs at easy to moderate grade through darker woods along N side of this wild pass.

After slight descent, at 3.0 mi. / 3040 ft. southbound Kilkenny Ridge Trail departs L for Terrace Mtn. Continue ahead, descending easily, and at 3.1 mi. turn R on northbound Kilkenny Ridge Trail. (Section of Bunnell Notch Trail ahead is abandoned.) This connecting section descends gently, then traverses through open, fern-filled birch glades. After slight rise meet Mt. Cabot Trail coming from L at 3.4 mi. / 2950 ft.; from here to summit Kilkenny Ridge and Mt. Cabot Trails are combined. Turn R here and climb moderately up fairly eroded trail that once served as tractor road for firetower. Trail swings R into area of scrubby firs with partial view back to SW, and at 3.8 mi. / 3350 ft. pass short spur R (sign: VIEW) to Bunnell Rock—open, sunny ledge perch with good view S over Bunnell Notch to North Peak of Terrace Mtn. and more distant ranges. Trail now makes long, steady climb through conifer forest, with several switchbacks. Final L turn leads to old firewarden's cabin at N end of S summit ridge at 4.4 mi. / 4070 ft.; this is maintained by WMNF and Jefferson Boy Scouts and is open to public for overnight use. (Wood stove has been removed for safety reasons.) Just beyond is clearing at site of former fire tower with good views NE and SW. Dip into small col and ascend easily through open, ferny forest of old balsam fir. At 4.6 mi. side trail R (sign: SPRING) descends steeply for 0.2 mi. / 250 ft. to spring once used by firewardens; this path was fairly overgrown in 2007. Main trail continues easy / moderate ascent to flat, wooded summit area, marked by sign, at 4.8 mi. / 4170 ft. Here there are two short side paths. First path, on L 15 yds. before summit sign, leads 30 yds. to partly restricted standup view to W and SW from scrubby blowdown area. Just past summit sign, where Kilkenny Ridge Trail swings R to descend towards Bulge, second path continues straight for 30 yds. to slightly higher point that is true summit of Cabot.

LOOP OPTION

Descent via Kilkenny Ridge Trail, Unknown Pond Trail
11.6 mi. loop, 3300-ft. elevation gain

A long and very scenic loop can be made from end of York Pond Rd. including Mt. Cabot, The Bulge, The Horn and Unknown Pond. After climbing to Cabot summit via Bunnell Notch route (4.8 mi.), follow Kilkenny Ridge Trail N for steady 460-ft. descent to broad col, then climb 240 ft. to summit of The Bulge in deep fir forest at 5.6 mi. / 3950 ft. (summit cairn, no views). Descend 300 ft. to jct. with side trail R to The Horn, at 5.9 mi. / 3650 ft. Side path to Horn climbs at easy to moderate grade through open fir forest. Near top trees become scrubbier and you must negotiate several short ledge scrambles in succession as views begin to appear. Bare rocks of summit are reached at 0.3 mi. from jct. with 255-ft. climb. You must make short, fairly difficult scramble (best done on E side) to get up on uppermost ledge, which is flat on top. Views of Kilkenny region and many distant peaks are nearly panoramic, though partly screened to NE. Only partial views are available from lower ledges around the summit rock, so it is worth the effort to get to the very top. This 0.6 mi. round trip is a must in good weather and is included in mileage total. See view description below and panorama in *Scudder's White Mountain Viewing Guide.*

From jct. with Horn side trail (6.5 mi., including side trip to Horn), Kilkenny Ridge Trail makes moderate slabbing descent through firs along W slope of Horn, with rocky footing. At 7.0 mi. trail swings R (E) around N slope through ferny birch forest, then swings L and winds down to wet sag. Trail now climbs ca. 125 ft., then meanders to jct. with Unknown Pond Trail near picturesque Unknown Pond at 8.2 mi. / 3177 ft. Turn R on combined Unknown Pond/Kilkenny Ridge Trails, in 60 yds. passing side path R to shore of Unknown Pond with nice view of Horn across water. In another 25 yds., northbound Kilkenny Ridge Trail turns L while S half of Unknown Pond Trail continues ahead 35 yds. to another side path R to a shoreside viewpoint and rest spot. In another 30 yds. a spur leads L and up to several designated tentsites and privy. Continue ahead on S section of Unknown Pond Trail, soon beginning steady, winding descent down upper valley through birch forest. Trail briefly levels on plateau, then resumes sidehill descent. Steep pitch with rock steps leads down near brook, then grade eases. When well down valley, trail crosses Unknown Pond Brook at 9.4 mi., then crosses tributary, and recrosses main brook at 9.6 mi. / 2350 ft. Trail now continues down lower valley at easy to moderate grade. At bottom of downgrade trail hops across small brook and follows old logging railroad grade across swampy lowlands, passing view of Terrace Mtn. At 11.3 mi. trail turns R off RR grade and final stretch through logged areas leads to parking area for Unknown Pond Trail off York Pond Rd., 3.3 mi. from Unknown Pond. Turn R on road and walk 0.1 mi. to York Pond trailhead at 11.6 mi.

North Approach from Mill Brook Rd. (FR 11) in Stark

Unknown Pond Trail, Kilkenny Ridge Trail
10.6 mi. round trip, 3250-ft. elevation gain

TRAILHEAD (1755 ft.): From NH 110 7.4 mi. E of Groveton and 0.5 mi. E of the Stark covered bridge, turn S onto gravel Mill Brook Rd. (FR 11) and drive 4.5 mi. to sign for Unknown Pond Trail on L, just before bridge; parking is available on R just beyond bridge. (This road is not plowed in winter.)

This remote northern out-and-back approach leads you up through gleaming birch forests to picturesque Unknown Pond, from which you circle around The Horn, climb over The Bulge, and continue up to the summit of Cabot. The mileage given above includes the side trip to the summit of The Horn.

From parking spot, cross plank bridge onto Unknown Pond Trail and ascend easily through hardwoods along tributary brook, with occasionally muddy footing. Trail soon pulls away from brook as easy ascent continues. Along nearly level stretch, pass post on L marking Stark/Kilkenny town line at 1.0 mi./2230 ft. Trail comes briefly beside small brook, then white birches take over and grade steepens. Climb is now steady along side of slope, with mostly good footing, through acres of beautiful birch forest. There are occasional glimpses back to R through trees to chain of Pilot Range peaks. At ca. 2900 ft. grade eases and woods darken with conifers. You cross small, wet opening with luxuriant fern growth and tiny stream, reach height-of-land in another 0.2 mi., and dip slightly to jct. with Kilkenny Ridge Trail at 2.2 mi./3170 ft. At this jct. southbound Kilkenny Ridge Trail leaves R for The Horn and Mt. Cabot, but it is worthwhile to continue ahead for 60 yds. on combined Unknown Pond Trail/northbound Kilkenny Ridge Trail to side path that descends 30 yds. R to shore of Unknown Pond with nice view of Horn across water.

Retrace steps 60 yds. to where southbound Kilkenny Ridge Trail diverges L for Horn. Trail soon passes obscure side path L to small viewpoint on shore of pond with superb view of Horn, then meanders across plateau, swings L and descends ca. 125 ft. to wet saddle. It soon swings R up NE slope of Horn through ferny birch forest, then R again to contour around N side. At 1.1 mi. from Unknown Pond Trail, you swing L and make slabbing climb through firs with rocky footing up to jct. in 3650-ft. col between Horn and Bulge, reached at 1.7 mi. from Unknown Pond Trail. From jct. in col, side path to Horn diverges sharp L and climbs at easy to moderate grade through open fir forest. Near top trees become scrubbier and you must negotiate several short ledge scrambles in succession as views begin to appear. Bare rocks of summit are reached at 0.3 mi. from col, with 255-ft. climb. You must make short, fairly difficult scramble (best done on E side) to get up on topmost ledge, which is flat on top. Views are nearly panoramic, though partly screened to NE. Only partial views are available from lower ledges around the summit rock, so it is worth the effort to get to the very top. See view description below.

From jct. with Horn spur, Kilkenny Ridge Trail continues ahead (R) 0.3 mi. for stiff 300-ft. climb through nice fir woods to viewless summit of The Bulge, marked by cairn. Trail now descends to broad 3710-ft. col, then makes steady 460-ft. ascent to summit sign for Mt. Cabot, 1.1 mi. from jct. with Horn spur. True high point is 30 yds. R on side path at point where main trail bends L to summit sign. In another 15 yds. along main trail there is second side path leading 30 yds. R to partial view W from scrubby blowdown area. To continue S on Kilkenny Ridge Trail to viewpoint at fire tower site and adjacent cabin, and return, add another 0.8 mi. round trip and 100 ft. of climbing.

West Approach from Arthur White Road in East Lancaster

Access to the lower part of this route was closed by a landowner in February 2000. As of this writing in 2008, there is still no legal access here, and this approach should not be used until the issue is resolved. A brief description is included here in case the situation does change. For current status, check with WMNF Androscoggin District at 603–466–2713.

Mt. Cabot Trail
7.8 mi. round trip, 2750-ft. elevation gain

TRAILHEAD (1510 ft.): Small parking area near end of Arthur White Rd. in East Lancaster. From US 2, 0.2 mi. W of its junction with NH 116 near the village of Jefferson, turn N onto North Rd. and follow it for 2.3 mi., then turn R on Gore Rd., which changes to Garland Rd. at a L turn. At 4.0 mi. from US 2 turn R onto Pleasant Valley Rd., and at 4.8 mi. turn R again on Arthur White Rd. and continue to parking area on L at 5.2 mi., just before end of road at Heath's Gate.

Until access was closed, this was the shortest and most popular approach to Cabot. From parking area, trail follows logging road at easy upgrade through logged areas. At 0.4 mile York Pond Trail splits R on bed of old Kilkenny logging railroad. Continue straight on Mt. Cabot Trail at moderate grade on logging road, badly eroded in places. Trail becomes more of a footpath and enters WMNF at 1.3 mi. Continue at easy grades through hardwoods to crossing of Bunnell Brook and jct. R with abandoned W section of Bunnell Notch Trail at 2.2 mi. / 2650 ft. Trail now zigzags up through birches, and Kilkenny Ridge Trail joins from R at 2.5 mi. / 2950 ft. Continue up as described under east approach, reaching

Bunnell Rock at 2.9 mi. / 3350 ft., cabin and fire tower site at 3.5 mi. / 4070 ft., and wooded summit at 3.9 mi. / 4170 ft.

Winter

Cabot is a wonderful climb in winter, with reliably deep snow and moderate grades ideal for snowshoeing. With the W approach closed and access to the N approach from Stark unplowed, the E approach is by far the best choice. The York Pond Rd. is plowed all the way to the York Pond Trail trailhead, and a parking area for several cars usually is plowed there on the L. There may be additional plowed parking at the Unknown Pond Trail trailhead 0.1 mi. back along the road. The gate at the fish hatchery entrance has been kept open throughout the winter. Blazing is fairly sparse on the Bunnell Notch Trail, so some care may be required to follow it up the valley in the hardwoods. Scrubby areas along the upper Mt. Cabot Trail may offer some bonus views with deep snow. The cabin offers a nice place for a break out of the wind, but note that the wood stove has been removed for safety reasons. The trail across to The Bulge and The Horn is used much less frequently and may require strenuous trail breaking. Ditto for the Unknown Pond Trail from York Pond Road, which also has some significant sidehilling in its upper section.

View Guide

BUNNELL ROCK: This great S-facing ledge perch soaks up the sun and looks across Bunnell Notch to the nearby North Peak of Terrace Mtn., a rounded and wooded mass. On the far L, in the distance to the L of North Terrace, are the southern Mahoosucs, including (L to R) Mt. Carlo, Mt. Success, Bald Cap with Jericho Mtn. below, Cascade Mtn., Peabody Mtn. through the gap to the R of Cascade, and Gammon and Caribou Mtns. above Mt. Hayes, seen over the slope of Black Crescent. Next to the R and closer are the twin summits of Black Crescent Mtn. To the R of Black Crescent, off the L slope of North Terrace, are Shelburne Moriah, Middle Moriah and Mt. Moriah. Over the R shoulder of North Terrace are Mt. Waumbek (L) and Mt. Starr King (R). South and North Twin peer over the col to the R of Starr King. To the R of the next spur of Starr King and above Haystack Mtn., a lower spur, are the tip of Mt. Liberty, Mt. Garfield, and Mts. Lincoln and Lafayette.

Farther R, behind and R of another, cone-shaped Starr King spur, are Cannon Mtn. and South and North Kinsman, with Mt. Moosilauke peering over behind the Kinsmans. Mt. Clough is farther R and beyond the Kinsmans, and continuing to the R are several lower summits in the Benton Range: the long crests of Jeffers Mtn. and The Hogsback, the bump of Sugarloaf, and the prominent peak of Black Mtn. in the Benton Range.

In the foreground are the low, rounded Mt. Cleveland (in line with Jeffers) and Mt. Agassiz (to the R of Hogsback). Farther R, about SW, is Cole Hill near Easton. Farther R, on clear days, Vermont's Killington and Pico Peaks can be spotted on the horizon. Continuing to the R, you see Dalton Mtn. in the mid-distance and then a nearer trio of low, rounded summits rising from the flatlands of the Whitefield–Lancaster area: Prospect Mtn., Mt. Pleasant and Orne Mtn. On the horizon in this direction is the bumpy Signal Mtn. range in west-central Vermont, with sharp Spruce Mtn. on its R end. The long ridge joining Mt. Abraham and Mt. Ellen is on the horizon to the R of the Signal range. Continuing across the horizon to the R are Ethan Allen Mtn. and the distinctive Camel's Hump, the closer Miles Mtn. with the Worcester Range beyond, and Mt. Mansfield on the far R, just N of W, with Kirby Mtn. to its R and closer.

CLEARING AT FIRE TOWER SITE: This opening, 0.4 mi. below the true summit of Cabot, provides good views NE and SW, though in recent years tree growth has increasingly restricted them. More aspects of the western view can be seen from the porch of the nearby cabin and from the viewpoint on the side path near the true summit.

The NE view, quite different from any other New Hampshire 4000-footer vista, looks over the Kilkenny region and far beyond into Maine. You must move down in front to see the more northerly part of the view. On the L the beautiful pyramid of The Horn rises close by to the NNE, with Stub Hill and Bosebuck Mtn. on the horizon to its L. Above The Horn many ridges and peaks in far northwestern Maine are seen on the horizon. To the R of The Horn the top of the cliff of Rogers Ledge peers over the L shoulder of the gentle mountain called Unknown Pond Ridge. Just L of Rogers Ledge are the sharp peak of Mt. Dustan (L) and the double rounded summit of Aziscohos Mtn. (R), with West Kennebago Mtn. on the horizon. Over the crest of Unknown Pond Ridge is the distant sprawl of East Kennebago Mtn., and just over the R shoulder of Unknown Pond Ridge is the nearby cliff of Greens Ledge. On the horizon to the R of Greens Ledge are several distant high peaks in the Rangeley Lakes area, including (L to R) Bigelow, Crocker, Sugarloaf, Saddleback and Abraham. A bit farther R, over the southern knob of Unknown Pond Ridge and the broad mass of Cambridge Black Mtn., are Bemis and Elephant Mtns. (L) and Old Blue Mtn. (R) in the distance. Extending R from behind the S end of Unknown Pond Ridge is the level crest of Deer Ridge, with the summit of Deer Mtn., showing a large old clearcut patch, on its R end. Jackson Mtn. near Weld, Maine, is seen on the horizon to the L of Deer Mtn., over the L end of the mid-distance Red Ridge. The double summit of Baldpate Mtn. is prominent above Deer Mtn., with bulky Old Speck to the R.

Looking E, the Mahoosuc Range runs in a long chain to the R from

Old Speck with the broad Androscoggin River valley in the foreground. The peaks to the R of Old Speck include Mahoosuc Arm, Mahoosuc Mtn. and Fulling Mill Mtn. framing Mahoosuc Notch (with Sunday River Whitecap seen through the notch), the North Peak of Goose Eye, the sharp main peak of Goose Eye, broad Mt. Carlo with Jericho Lake seen in front, Mt. Success, and the Bald Cap group. Bear Mtn. in the eastern Mahoosucs can be seen between Success and Bald Cap, and Jericho Mtn. is in front of and below Bald Cap, with the lower Mt. Forist to its L. Part of the city of Berlin can be seen behind Mt. Forist on the L. Mt. Abram and two neighbors poke up over the ridge between the summit of Bald Cap and its S (R) spur, Bald Cap Peak. On the far R, to the R of Bald Cap, is Cascade Mtn., with Streaked Mtn. on the horizon and Peabody Mtn. behind on the R.

The SW view includes some of the central White Mtns. and a wide lowland sweep. On the far L, looking SSE, the Presidentials can be seen over the trees, above the rounded dome of South Weeks. Mts. Madison, Adams, Jefferson and Washington are to the L of South Weeks, and Mt. Monroe is directly above South Weeks. To the R is the long, gentle E ridge of Mt. Waumbek, with the Presidentials continuing across, peering over its L end: Mt. Franklin, Mt. Eisenhower, Mt. Pierce, the nub of Mt. Jackson, and Mt. Webster. The tip of Mt. Passaconaway just peers over to the R of Webster. Farther R, Mts. Willey, Field and Carrigain appear above the twin summit knobs of Waumbek with Mt. Tom to the R of the true summit. Farther R the ridge leads from Waumbek across to Starr King, with the Hancocks and Osceolas in the distance. Zealand Ridge and Mt. Bond are above the summit of Starr King, then a long ridge leads R from Bond across Mt. Guyot to South and North Twin, with Mt. Hale below Guyot and Cherry Mtn. in front of and below the Twins. The pinprick of West Bond can be spotted to the R of Guyot. The ridge of Starr King descends R to its lower spurs, revealing more peaks in the distance: the tip of Mt. Flume, the sharp peak of Mt. Liberty, Mt. Garfield, and Mts. Lincoln and Lafayette. Farther R, looking SSW, are the Kinsmans with Mt. Moosilauke behind and Cannon Mtn. in front to the L. Closer in this direction is the low crest of Beech Hill. Mt. Clough is farther R and beyond the Kinsmans, and continuing to the R are several lower summits in the Benton Range: the long crests of Jeffers Mtn. and The Hogsback, the bump of Sugarloaf, and the prominent peak of Black Mtn. in the Benton Range. In the foreground are the low, rounded Mt. Cleveland (in line with Jeffers) and Mt. Agassiz (to the R of Hogsback).

Swinging around to the SW and W, the view opens out across a vast expanse of lower country and beyond to the Connecticut River valley and Vermont, a landscape quilted with fields and woods and dotted with houses. To the R of the Benton Range, looking about SW, is Cole Hill near Easton. Farther R, on clear days, Vermont's Killington and Pico

Peaks can be spotted on the horizon. Continuing to the R, you see Dalton Mtn. in the mid-distance and then a nearer trio of low, rounded summits rising from the flatlands of the Whitefield–Lancaster area: Prospect Mtn., Mt. Pleasant and Orne Mtn. On the horizon in this direction is the bumpy Signal Mtn. range in west-central Vermont, with sharp Spruce Mtn. on its R end. The long ridge joining Mt. Abraham and Mt. Ellen is on the horizon to the R of the Signal range. Continuing across the horizon to the R are Ethan Allen Mtn. and the distinctive Camel's Hump, the closer broad mass of Miles Mtn. with the Worcester Range beyond, and Mt. Mansfield on the far R, just N of W, with the nearer mass of Kirby Mtn. to its R.

THE HORN SUMMIT: The sharp, rocky top of The Horn is the best viewpoint in the Kilkenny region and one of the finest in all the White Mountains. Especially noteworthy are the intimate views around the Pilot Range and the distant perspectives on the Presidentials, Mahoosucs and other mountain assemblages. There is a panorama for The Horn in *Scudder's White Mountain Viewing Guide*.

Rising massively and close by to the SW is the double-humped bulk of Mt. Cabot, with a great wooded bowl carved into its flank. To the R of Cabot and even closer is the rounded, wooded summit of The Bulge. To the R of The Bulge, looking W over a broad saddle, a wide prospect opens out over the town of Lancaster and the Connecticut River valley towards Vermont, with (L to R) sharp-peaked Spruce Mtn. off the R slope of The Bulge, Mts. Abraham and Ellen, Camel's Hump, the Worcester Range beyond Miles Mtn., and Mt. Mansfield on the horizon. Farther R is the prominent pyramid of Burke Mtn. in Vermont's Northeast Kingdom. The lower Stone Mtn.–Burnside Mtn. Range is in front of Burke. To the R of Burke and farther away are Belvidere Mtn. (L) and East Haven Mtn. (R). Close at hand in this direction is a wooded knob that is a minor NW spur of The Bulge. Extending to the R from this bump are the several wooded peaks of the wild, trailless Pilot Ridge, with the remote upper basin of Mill Brook at their base. The pointed summit of Hutchins Mtn., the high point of this ridge, is set back in the center, with a long spur trailing out to the R. Over the flat-topped Pilot peak to the L of Hutchins is Vermont's East Mtn., sporting a prominent building (an old Air Force base) on top, with the sharp Jay Peak on its L and the top of Bald Mtn. peering over on its R. Mts. Hor and Pisgah, forming Willoughby Gap, can be seen to the L of Jay and a bit closer.

On clear days two peaks in the far-off Sutton Mtns. of Quebec are visible over the nearer West Mtn. in Vermont, above a saddle just to the R of Hutchins. A long ridge leading across Bluff and Middle Mtns. and up to distant, massive Gore Mtn. in Vermont is prominent over the ridge that descends to the R from a rounded N spur of Hutchins. Over the lower end of this descending ridge is the double peak of Goback Mtn. in

Stratford, New Hampshire, with a pair of lower spurs on its R. Vermont's Brousseau Mtn. is seen in the distance off the L slope of Goback. Next to the R is the long Sugarloaf Mtn. range in the Nash Stream Forest: (L to R) West Peak, Sugarloaf Mtn., Bunnell (formerly Blue) Mtn. peering over in the back, and Gore Mtn., with the ledgy Percy Peaks seen under Gore. Farther R, looking due N, is the broad mass of Long Mtn. The low dark cliff of the Devil's Slide can be seen under the saddle between the Percys and Long, with the ledgy knob of Victor Head up behind it on the right. The tip of North Whitcomb Mtn. (Muise Mtn.) peers over the Long ridge, and Dixville Peak is seen in back off the R end of Long, with Mill Mtn. down in front in this direction. Farther R on the horizon (you must stand to see this part of the view) is the long ridge of Rice Mtn., with Magalloway Mtn. (dropping sharply on its R side) popping up on its L and Stub Hill in back on its R. More to the R, the mountains on the Quebec border can be seen on clear days.

Continuing to the R, the double summit of Aziscohos Mtn. can be seen to the NE, with the sharp peak of Mt. Dustan closer and to the L, and the nearby North Peak of Rogers Ledge down in front. Next to the R are the main peak of Rogers Ledge and Square Mtn., both fronted with granite cliffs. Maine's sprawling East Kennebago Mtn, is on the horizon above these two peaks, and distant West Kennebago can be spotted just L of Rogers Ledge. Next to the R and just a mile away across the valley of Unknown Pond Brook is the birch-wooded crest known as Unknown Pond Ridge. Its summit is just R of Square Mtn., and there are two smaller peaks on its R end, with Deer Ridge (including Deer Mtn. on its R end) just behind.

Many Maine peaks are seen on the horizon over Unknown Pond Ridge. Saddleback Mtn. is right over the main summit, with the Bigelow Range and the Redington–Crocker Range behind on the L. Sugarloaf Mtn. pops up off the R slope of Saddleback. Farther R and somewhat closer are Bemis and Elephant Mtns. (L) and Old Blue Mtn. (R). The summit of Mt. Abraham rises beyond the col between Bemis and Elephant, and anther part of Mt. Abraham is glimpsed through the broad gap between Elephant and Old Blue. The isolated Cambridge Black Mtn. is seen under Old Blue. Peering over a distant ridge above the R end of Cambridge Black are the peaks of the Jackson Mtns. near Weld, Maine. Just to the R of and behind Cambridge Black is a broad mass known as Red Ridge. Next to the R is Baldpate Mtn., showing three distinct peaks; the pointed Mt. Blue sticks up over Baldpate's lower L slope. Extending for many miles to the R of Baldpate is the Mahoosuc Range, starting with its highest peak, Old Speck, seen over the L of the two lower S peaks of Unknown Pond Ridge. From Old Speck the range runs to the R over Mahoosuc Arm, then Mahoosuc Mtn. and Fulling Mill Mtn., with Sunday River Whitecap seen through the gap of Mahoosuc Notch between them.

To the R of Fulling Mill, looking E, are the North Peak of Goose Eye, Goose Eye's sharp main peak, squat Mt. Carlo, and the broad crest of Mt. Success (with Jericho Lake on the flats below). Bear Mtn. in the eastern Mahoosucs is seen through the gap to the R of Success, then the main Mahoosuc Range continues R over the long ridge of Bald Cap Mtn., with Mt. Forist seen under its middle and Jericho Mtn. beneath its R end. Distant Streaked Mtn. is seen over the R end of Bald Cap. To the R of Bald Cap are the lower, elongated summits of Cascade Mtn. and Mt. Hayes. Peabody Mtn. is over Cascade, Caribou Mtn. rises prominently through the gap between Cascade and Hayes, and the flat crest of Butters Mtn. is seen above Hayes. To the R of Butters are Durgin and Speckled Mtns., the latter seen over a shoulder of Shelburne Moriah Mtn. Next to the R the three Moriah peaks—Shelburne Moriah, Middle Moriah and Mt. Moriah—rise beyond Black Crescent Mtn. The lower, ledgy bump of Imp Mtn. is to the R of the Moriahs, then that range abruptly rises to the high Carter peaks, (L to R) North, Middle and South Carter, Mt. Hight and Carter Dome. Mt. Crescent is seen beneath Hight and Carter Dome.

To the R of the Carters the Presidential Range rises majestically. Mt. Madison is on the L, with the tip of Wildcat A peeking over Osgood Ridge on its L. Mt. Adams soars to the R of Madison, with the great gouge of King Ravine well-displayed. Mt. Washington is next to the R and highest, with Mt. Jefferson and Castle Ravine below and in front, and descending on Washington's R are Mts. Monroe, Franklin, Eisenhower and Pierce. Under these peaks are the rounded summits of North Weeks (on the L, with a spur ridge extending L) and South Weeks (R). The long, level ridge of Mt. Waumbek extends to the R from South Weeks. About ⅓ from the R end of the Waumbek ridge, keen eyes can spot the summit of Mt. Carrigain just poking up behind, and a bit farther L is the tip of, we presume, Mt. Willey. Mt. Pierce is seen above the South Weeks–Waumbek col, and the South Peak of Terrace Mtn. is below it. The Middle Peak of Terrace is under the double peak of Waumbek, then the view swings back to the nearby bulk of Mt. Cabot. East Osceola and Mt. Osceola can be espied in the distance through the gap where the ridgelines of Waumbek and Cabot meet.

NO. OF 4000-FOOTERS VISIBLE: from Mt. Cabot, 39 (including 5 visible only through trees at summit); from The Horn, 18

Mount Waumbek

ELEVATION: 4006 ft. / 1221 m   ORDER OF HEIGHT: 46
LOCATION: Pliny Range, Township of Kilkenny, Town of Jefferson
USGS MAP: 7½′ Jefferson

Geography

Poking barely above the 4000-ft. mark, the wooded summit of Mt. Waumbek is the culminating point of the Pliny Range, an arc of North Country ridges overlooking the Israel River valley and town of Jefferson to the S and the wild Kilkenny region to the N. The climb up Waumbek via the Starr King Trail is one of the mellowest hikes in the high peaks. The open, lichen-draped fir forest that cloaks the ridgecrest is especially enchanting.

Waumbek's summit is heavily wooded, but 50 yds. E along the Kilkenny Ridge Trail a blowdown area offers a partial view of the Presidentials, and a knob 0.2 mi. farther E, about equal in height to the main summit, provides a restricted but interesting view N. Waumbek's close neighbor to the W, Mt. Starr King (3907 ft.), offers restricted views W and S near its summit; its vistas have been increasingly obscured by tree growth in recent years. A notable feature of both summits is that typically tame and ravenous gray jays are often encountered there.

The semicircular Pliny Range is noted by geologists as an unusual "ring-dike" created when molten magma welled up into a circular crack in the earth's crust and later cooled and solidified into resistant rock. The range begins on the NW with trailless Haystack Mtn. (3330 ft.), then runs SE over a shoulder to Starr King and, with only a slight dip to a 3750-ft. col, on to Waumbek. A long, nearly level ridge runs about 1.5 mi. E from Waumbek over the E knob and four minor bumps, then the range swings N, dropping to a 3533-ft. col and continuing over the wooded, rounded summits of South Weeks (3885 ft.), Middle Weeks (3684 ft.) and North Weeks (3901 ft.) before ending at Willard Notch (2707 ft.), a beautiful upland plateau that divides the Pliny and Pilot Ranges. North and South Weeks are among New England's Hundred Highest peaks, and all three Weeks summits are traversed by the Kilkenny Ridge Trail.

On the N the Pliny Range encloses a broad hardwood valley known as Willard Basin, drained by Garland Brook, which takes its rise at Willard Notch, and its SE tributary, Great Brook. The headwaters of Great Brook rise in a deep bowl between Waumbek and South Weeks. Willard Notch and Willard Basin are bordered on the N by Terrace Mtn. (3655 ft.), with its bold, slide-scarred South Peak being the southernmost summit of the Pilot Range.

Mt. Pliny (3606 ft.) is a symmetrical, trailless spur peak projecting S from the E ridge of Waumbek beyond a 3159-ft. col. The basin between Waumbek and Pliny is drained by the headwaters of Priscilla Brook. A second spur ridge extends SE from Waumbek's E ridge, eventually ending at Pond Hill (2805 ft.) NW of the Pond of Safety. The Waumbek Slide, in a S-facing ravine between the peaks, is a prominent landmark. Crawford Brook flows S through this deep basin between the S ridges of Waumbek and Starr King. To the S and SW of the range are the expansive lowlands of Jefferson, from which the high ridge of Starr King and Waumbek dominates the landscape.

Nomenclature

As the highest peak in the Pliny Range, Waumbek was originally known as "Pliny Major." The Pliny name may have been in use as early as 1784 and appeared on Philip Carrigain's 1816 map. It commemorates a Roman poet and naturalist of the first century.

The Native American terms "waumbekket-methna," meaning "white or snowy mountains," and "waumbik," or "white rocks," were originally associated with the Mt. Washington Range. Sometime in the late 1800s the name "Mt. Waumbek" came to replace "Pliny Major," and "Mt. Pliny" slid down to the SE spur. In 1861 the peak W of the main summit was named in honor of the Rev. Thomas Starr King, a Unitarian minister from Boston whose classic 1859 book, *The White Hills: Their Legends, Landscape and Poetry*, introduced thousands of readers to the beauties of the White Mountains and paid special tribute to the beauty of the mountain vistas in the town of Jefferson. The name was applied by innkeeper Benjamin H. Plaisted, who at Starr King's urging had built the Waumbek House at the base of the mountain in 1860.

Mt. Weeks, originally called Round Mtn., was renamed for New Hampshire's Senator John W. Weeks, whose 1911 Weeks Act laid the legislative foundation for the creation of the White Mountain National Forest. Willard Notch and Basin were supposedly named for Jonathan Willard, an eccentric settler from southern New Hampshire who lived in the Kilkenny woods with his dog, Pilot.

Historical Highlights

First Ascent: Unknown.

1773: Col. Joseph Whipple establishes settlement at Jefferson (then known as Dartmouth).

1859: In his *The White Hills: Their Legends, Landscape and Poetry*, Rev. Thomas Starr King gives effusive praise to the setting and views found in the town of Jefferson, calling it "the ultima thule in grandeur in an artist's pilgrimage among the New Hampshire mountains, for at no other point can he see the White Hills themselves in such array and force."

1860: At urging of Thomas Starr King, innkeeper Benjamin H. Plaisted builds Waumbek House hotel at S base of mountain. Building is enlarged in 1865 and 1879, and starting in 1888 it undergoes major remodeling and expansion, becoming one of largest and most luxurious grand hotel complexes in the mountains. Peak capacity is 500–600 guests. Meanwhile, several smaller inns open in Jefferson in 1870s.

1864: Samuel Eastman's guidebook notes that Mt. Starr King is "easily ascended" from Waumbek House, suggesting trail had been built up mountain.

1875: Starr King summit is established as station for U.S. Coastal Survey, ledge is marked with bolt and triangle.

1876: Moses Sweetser's guidebook describes well-trodden path from Waumbek House up Starr King, used by "hundreds of visitors every year," and gives elaborate description of view. Recommends visiting in afternoon "when the great ravines are filled with light."

1883: AMC explorer E. B. Cook ascends Pliny Mtn. from Stag Hollow to SE, climbs trees to get views, notes unique vista into Castle and Cascade Ravines on Presidentials.

1885: Nathan Matthews of Boston blazes route from Starr King to Waumbek.

1885: E. B. Cook ascends trail to Starr King, follows newly blazed line to Waumbek, continues E on trailless ridge, drops to headwaters of Garland Brook, then ascends Round Mtn. (now North Weeks). He descends S from Round but strays off course on logging roads and spends night in deserted lumber camp in Upper Ammonoosuc valley, returning to Randolph next morning.

1887: Lancaster & Kilkenny Railroad Co. extends logging railroad E from Lancaster into Willard Basin on N side of Waumbek. By 1893 virgin conifers on N and W slopes of Pliny Range have been cut and hauled to mills. Engineer is killed in 1890 when engine jumps tracks. After abandoning plan to extend line through Willard Notch into Upper Ammonoosuc basin, company closes operation in 1897 and removes tracks. Today western part of York Pond Trail follows this railroad grade.

1890: In his book, *The White Mountains: A Guide to Their Interpretation*, Rev. Julius Ward extols view from Starr King: "the Presidential Range from this point is grander and more inspiring than from any other quarter in the west or north."

1916: Second edition of *AMC Guide* describes obscure trail, "which follows deer runs to some extent," leading from Starr King to Waumbek.

1928: Main building of Waumbek House burns to ground in May fire. Remaining buildings on property, largest of which is Waumbek Hall, re-open for guests in 1929 and are operated by several different owners into 1970s.

Mid-1930s: Through trail from Jefferson to York Pond in Kilkenny opened, passing over col between Waumbek and Pliny. This is later named Keenan Brook Trail, then Priscilla Brook Trail. Path abandoned in 1980s. 1936 *AMC Guide* description for Starr King mentions USGS tower on summit with views in all directions.

1940s: Shelter built near summit of Starr King. Rebuilt 1968, removed ca. 1980. Remnants of fireplace still visible today.

1944: Randolph Mountain Club assumes responsibility for maintenance of trail to Starr King.

1948: *AMC Guide* reports trail from Starr King to Waumbek "extremely obscure."

1957: Waumbek Slide falls on S slope during July 22 rainstorm; that evening Jefferson resident Ralph Hunt reports hearing roar and then long rumble of slide behind his house. *AMC Guides* in 1960s and 1970s describe slide as bushwhack ascent route.

1960: With recent founding of 4000-Footer Club, trail from Starr King to Waumbek is "cleared and well-marked," says *AMC Guide*. 1963 edition notes that "views have been cleared in several directions."

Early 1960s: Major ski development, "Willard Basin Ski Area," proposed for N slopes of Starr King and Waumbek. Plans call for six chairlifts, two T-bar lifts, and 9000-ft. tramway, with 2100-ft. vertical drop. Lease on 1800 acres of land is obtained from Forest Service, field surveys begin, and open house held Jan. 1965 is attended by 1,300, who enjoy free hot dogs and ski-doo rides, but lack of financing eventually scuttles project.

1966: *AMC Guide* notes possible confusion on trail between Starr King and Waumbek due to blazing for proposed ski development.

Early 1970s: Path between Starr King and Waumbek becomes officially maintained trail as extension of Starr King Trail.

1980: Waumbek House property closes for good and remaining largest building, Waumbek Hall, is razed.

Late 1980s: Kilkenny Ridge Trail opened from Waumbek across E ridge and over three peaks of Mt. Weeks to Willard Notch, and beyond to Mt. Cabot, Rogers Ledge and South Pond.

Trail Approaches

Southwest Approach from Starr King Rd. in Jefferson

Starr King Trail
7.2 miles round trip, 2700-ft. elevation gain

TRAILHEAD (1600 ft.): Located at end of Starr King Rd., which leaves N side of US 2 in Jefferson, 0.2 mi. E of jct. with NH 115A and 3.7 mi. W of jct. with NH 115. Follow this rough dirt road, bearing L at 0.1 mi. and passing private driveways on R. At 0.25 mi. from US 2 swing R into small hiker's parking area.

The vast majority of hikers climb Waumbek via the Starr King Trail, enjoying moderate grades and attractive forests. Though not the shortest, this is considered one of the easier 4000-footers. Trail begins at E end of parking area, following old logging road for 100 yds., then bears L and climbs to higher road at 0.1 mi. Turn R here for easy climb above small brook, soon passing old stone well on R. At 0.4 mi./1800 ft. turn R off road and climb moderately to another R turn at 0.8 mi./2100 ft. Trail now ascends steadily up broad SW ridge of Starr King through beautiful mature hardwood forest, gaining crest at ca. 2500 ft.

At 1.5 mi./2900 ft. trail swings L to begin long traversing climb along W slope of ridge as woods abruptly change to darker mix of spruce, fir and birch. Look L for occasional glimpses of parallel ridge across valley. Footing gets rockier at times in this section. Pass spring on L, marked by sign and issuing from base of large rock, at 2.1 mi./3400 ft. Higher up pass through open fir forest and blowdown areas, then swing R and climb steadily to wooded summit of Starr King at 2.6 mi./3907 ft. High point is ledge with USGS benchmark disk on R. Trail descends slightly for 40 yds. to ledgy spot where, by standing on outcrop up on R, one may obtain distant vista to SW and W, and also partial view of nearby Presidentials to SE. Trail turns L here and descends 20 yds. to clearing at site of former shelter, where fireplace and chimney still stand at back edge. Partial views of peaks to S can be enjoyed by standing on ledges at back, upper edge of opening.

Continuation of trail to Mt. Waumbek leaves clearing to R of chimney and descends easily NE, then E down broad ridge between the peaks, leading through beautiful, open ferny fir forest. It dips to N side of ridge, then crosses to S side, passing below col and dipping to low point at ca. 3750 ft. Trail then meanders back to crest of ridge at open blowdown area and soon makes moderately steep climb for ca. 0.2 mi. It levels for final 100 yds., reaching clearing at wooded summit, marked by large cairn, at 3.6 mi./4006 ft. Here Kilkenny Ridge Trail continues ahead (E), leading to the best views from Waumbek. By descending 50 yds. on this trail, you can enjoy partial view of Presidentials from blowdown area on R, accessed by side path 10 yds. long. For restricted but interesting view to N towards Mt. Cabot and other peaks of the Kilkenny region, continue 0.2 mi. E on Kilkenny Ridge Trail, descending to minor col and ascending to blowdown-ravaged E knob of Waumbek, about equal in height to main summit.

Northeast Approach from York Pond Rd.

York Pond Trail, Kilkenny Ridge Trail
8.7 mi. one way, 3700-ft. elevation gain

TRAILHEAD (1670 ft.): This route begins at small parking area for York Pond Trail near end of York Pond Rd. by Berlin Fish Hatchery. York Pond

Rd. leaves S side of NH 110, 7.1 mi. from its jct. with NH 16 in Berlin. In 5.0 mi. it passes gate at entrance to hatchery. In past gate has been closed between 4:00 pm and 8:00 am; however, with increased usage of Bunnell Notch Trail approach to Mt. Cabot in recent years, gate has been left open later in evening. For current status call hatchery at 603–449–3412. From gate, continue another 2.1 mi. on road (paved for another 1.0 mi.) and park on L at sign for York Pond Trail, which starts on gated logging road.

Though not often used for a day hike approach to Waumbek, the York Pond and Kilkenny Ridge Trails can be followed to Willard Notch, over the three rounded summits of Mt. Weeks, and across the long, flat E ridge of Waumbek to the summit. There are no open views along this route, but plenty of fine woods walking in a remote setting. A peakbagger's bonus is the ascent of two New England Hundred Highest peaks — North Weeks and South Weeks — along the way. With a car spotted at the Starr King trailhead (and a long car spot it is), one can descend that way for a total hike of 12.3 mi. with 3850-ft. elevation gain. Retracing steps from the summit of Waumbek to the York Pond trailhead adds 1300 ft. of elevation for a total of 17.4 mi. / 5000 ft.

From trailhead, walk around gate and follow York Pond Trail at easy grade on logging road, crossing brook on bridge. At 0.2 mi., in overgrown clearing, bear L on York Pond Trail as Bunnell Notch Trail diverges R. In 100 yds. trail crosses brook on small dam, and continues at easy grades. At 0.5 mi. make two brook crossings 75 yds. apart, possibly difficult in high water. Trail follows brook, then crosses extensive wet area with numerous plank walkways. Beyond, trail continues to follow brook up on bank through birch and hardwood, comes briefly back to it at small cascade at 1.3 mi., then climbs moderately away from brook on old logging road. Some recent logging is evident on L, then above 2100 ft. trail ascends through beautiful open hardwood forest. At 1.8 mi. / 2400 ft. trail swings R up valley towards Willard Notch. Soon white birches predominate, and grades eases as trail passes through open, fern-filled birch glades. Woods darken with conifers as you approach height-of-land in Willard Notch. Reach jct. with southbound Kilkenny Ridge Trail in conifer grove at 2.4 mi. / 2750 ft.

Turn L here and ascend through spruce woods, then begin long switchbacking climb up lower slope of North Weeks, passing through mixed birch and conifer forest. At a L turn at ca. 3050 ft., just after passing through glade of old, gnarled yellow birches, look for small view of The Horn, framed by another old yellow birch, a few yds. to R of trail. Continue moderate winding climb, with occasional steeper pitches, through open mixed woods, which give way to mostly balsam fir higher up. At ca. 3400 ft. look for glimpse of Mt. Cabot and its talus slope through gap in trees to R. Higher up there are more peeks at The Horn. At ca. 3500 ft. begin long, moderate climb more or less directly up slope through open, lichen-draped firs, easing off before reaching flat, wooded summit at 3.7 mi. / 3901 ft. Spur paths lead R and L to campsites. Trail now descends at easy grade down S side of summit; in less than 0.1 mi. a blowdown patch to L provides a partial view E to Goose Eye Mtn. in the Mahoosucs. At 3.9 mi. swing L (E) for fairly steep descent across slope, passing spring flowing from L partway down. Trail swings R at 3550 ft. and makes slabbing descent to col between North and Middle Weeks, passing one limited vista towards Mt. Madison. Drop into col at 4.5 mi. / 3278 ft., then make winding climb, with some muddy spots near bottom, to broad, flat crest of Middle Weeks, reached at 5.1 mi. / 3684 ft. Enjoy level stroll along crest, then descend at easy to moderate grades, traversing muddy area, cross broad 3494-ft. col, and ascend easily, then more steeply over a fairly rocky footway with several turns. Trail eases on shoulder before short final climb to summit of South Weeks, reached at 6.1 mi. / 3880 ft.

High point is on spur leading 15 yds. to R. Here main trail bends L and descends gradually, then moderately, swinging L at bottom to 3533-ft. col at 6.7 mi. Here it turns R and runs briefly through S side of col, then begins moderate climb to SW up onto Waumbek's E ridge. Near top of ascent it swings L and traverses easily across slope, then at 7.1 mi. / 3800 ft. it turns sharp R (W) and begins long, gently ascending section along Waumbek's E ridge. Interspersed with gradual climbs and level sections are several short descents off minor knobs. This is beautiful stretch of woods walking through old balsam fir forest, with occasional peeks at distant peaks to L (S) through blowdown openings. More significant climb leads to E knob of Waumbek at 8.5 mi. / 4000 ft., where there are interesting restricted views to R (N) of Terrace Mtn., Mt. Cabot and The Horn. Trail descends to minor col, then ascends moderately to true summit at 8.7 mi. / 4006 ft.; 50 yds. before top, side path leads 10 yds. L to view of Presidentials from blowdown area

Winter

The Starr King Trail is excellent for snowshoeing and is frequently packed out. Starr King Rd. is not plowed to the trailhead; park at a plowed pulloff on the S side of US 2 diagonally across from the entrance of Starr King Rd. This adds 0.3 mi. each way to hike. Deep snow improves views on both Starr King and Waumbek; the ridge between is a delightful snowshoe ramble through the firs. In deep untracked snow this section of trail may be hard to follow. The NE approach from York Pond Rd. is very seldom tracked out in winter and getting all the way to Waumbek would most likely be a major epic. The road is plowed to the trailhead, and a parking area is usually plowed there.

View Guide

MT. STARR KING VIEW: Starr King was long famous for its view of the Presidential Range, but in recent years the vistas near the summit have become considerably more restricted due to ongoing tree growth. The two primary view spots are an uplifted ledge on the R of the trail, just beyond the actual summit, at the point where the trail turns L to descend to the clearing at the old shelter site, and from ledges at the back of the old shelter clearing. In both spots you must stand to obtain a decent panorama; views are very limited if seated.

From the uplifted ledge just past the summit, the primary view is SW over the expansive lowlands of Jefferson and Whitefield to distant peaks in Vermont and some of the western peaks of the White Mountains. From here there is also a partial framed view of the Presidentials looking L (SE) along the trail towards the clearing.

The SW view starts on the L with glimpses through the trees of the Willey Range, Twin Range, Cherry Mtn. and Mt. Liberty. The clear SW view begins with Mt. Garfield, then Mts. Lincoln and Lafayette cutting the skyline. A long ridge runs down to the R from Lafayette, and through the gap to the R of Lafayette are Mt. Waternomee (L) and Mt. Jim (R), both spurs of Mt. Moosilauke. Next to the R is Cannon Mtn., with South Kinsman and Mt. Moosilauke above and behind it on the R. Farther R is North Kinsman, with the broad mass of Mt. Clough to its R and farther away. Low-rising Beech Hill in Twin Mountain is in front below North Kinsman and Clough. To the R of and beyond Clough are the Benton Range peaks of (L to R) Jeffers Mtn. and the Hogsback (both with long, flat crests), the bump of Sugarloaf Mtn., and the prominent, ledgy Black Mtn. The little hump of Mt. Cleveland is in front of Black, and in the foreground in this direction is beautiful Cherry Pond, down on the flats. Next to the R is Cole Hill, with little Mt. Agassiz (Mt. Cleveland's near neighbor) in front to its R. Farther R the distant Killington Range in the Green Mountains sprawls on the horizon, with sharp Killington Peak in the middle and Pico Peak on the R end. Little Cherry Pond can be spotted down below in line with Pico. More Green Mountain ridges extend R across the skyline, then the nearer, humpy Signal Range in east-central Vermont is prominently seen. On the far R end of this range is the sharp peak of Spruce Mtn., seen beyond the nearer Dalton Mtn. The long ridge joining Mts. Abraham and Ellen can be seen to the R of and beyond Spruce, and continuing to the R one can spot Mt. Ethan Allen and distinctive Camel's Hump in the Green Mountain chain, then the somewhat nearer Worcester Range, and, on the far R, glimpsed through the trees, is Mt. Mansfield.

Looking L (SE) from this ledge, by moving around you can see (R to

L) Mt. Jefferson, Mt. Adams (with Castle, Cascade and King Ravines well-displayed), Mt. Madison, Mt. Hight through the col to the R of the highest Howk on Mt. Madison's Howker Ridge, South Carter and Middle Carter.

By standing and moving around on the upper ledges (starting on the R and moving across the ledges to the L) at the back side of the clearing by the old fireplace and chimney, one can spot a decent number of peaks to the S in the Crawford Notch and Pemigewasset Wilderness regions. Seen on the far L (while standing on the R-most ledge) are Mts. Bemis and Nancy over the middle humps of Mt. Deception. Mt. Passaconaway pokes up between Bemis and Nancy. Next to the R are Mts. Willey, Field and Tom, with the W peak of Deception under the Willey–Field ridge and Mt. Carrigain popping up between Field and Tom. Next to the R is the long E ridge of Mt. Hancock leading across to South Hancock. Farther R is the dome of North Hancock seen above Whitewall Mtn., and continuing to the R one sees NW Hancock with East Osceola poking up in back to its L. In the foreground in this direction are Mt. Rosebrook and the ski trails of Bretton Woods. (To continue the panorama to the R, one must move across the ledges to the L.) Through the gap to the R of the Hancock ridges is Mt. Osceola, then the nearer truncated ridge of Zeacliff. Middle and West Osceola are seen over the flat crest to the R of Zeacliff, with Mt. Oscar seen below in front. Zealand Ridge extends R to the summit of Zealand Mtn., with Mt. Bond rising above and Mt. Guyot to the R. The tip of West Bond pokes up over a low point to the R of Guyot. Mt. Hale and its spur ridges sprawl below and in front of Zealand, Bond and Guyot. To the R of Guyot a long ridge runs R to the sharp peak of South Twin, with North Twin on its R.

MT. WAUMBEK SUMMIT VIEW: Although there is no view from the wooded summit, about 50 yds. E along the Kilkenny Ridge Trail a short side path leads R (S) to a spot with an interesting view SE from a blow-down area, partly restricted by dead snags. On the far L, partly screened, is Mt. Moriah, with Pine Mtn. just peering over part of the Crescent Range in front. To the R of Moriah is the lower, cliff-faced Imp Mtn., then the sharply rising North Carter is seen above Mt. Randolph, and farther R are Middle and South Carter and Mt. Hight, seen over Mt. Madison's Howker Ridge. Farther to the R, looking SE, the Presidentials take center stage—a long line of craggy peaks filling the sky. On the L Howker Ridge leads up to Mt. Madison. Close by and down below in this direction is the wooded cone of Mt. Pliny. Next to the R is lofty Mt. Adams, with King Ravine in front under John Quincy Adams, and a long ridge running R down to Edmands Col, at the head of Castle Ravine. Nelson Crag is seen through the col. Next comes Mt. Jefferson, with lowly Mt. Bowman crouching at its foot. Behind and R of Jefferson is Mt. Washington, with Mt. Clay beneath. To the R of Washington are craggy Mt. Monroe, the low swell of

Mt. Franklin, and the bald dome of Mt. Eisenhower. Mt. Pierce is seen over Mt. Dartmouth, with the nubble of Mt. Jackson to its R. On the far R there are glimpses of Mt. Webster and then distant Mt. Passaconaway rising over Mt Bemis, with the E hump of Mt. Deception below.

MT. WAUMBEK EAST KNOB VIEW: This secondary summit of Waumbek, 0.2 mi. E of the main summit on the Kilkenny Ridge Trail, is about equal in height and offers a unique if partly restricted stand-up view N over the peaks of the Kilkenny region. You must move around and peer through gaps in the trees to see everything described here; with deep snow this view is much improved. On the far L is distant, sharp-peaked Sable Mtn. in NE Vermont, with cliff-faced Brousseau Mtn. behind on its L. Next to the R and closer is Goback Mtn. in Stratford, New Hampshire, with the prominent peak of Hutchins Mtn. in the Pilot Range farther R and closer. To the R of Hutchins a long ridge rises R to the broad, rounded summit of Mt. Cabot. Over the broad gap between Hutchins and Cabot are several peaks in the Nash Stream Forest, including (L to R) West Peak, Sugarloaf Mtn. with Bunnell Mtn. rising behind, and the tip of Gore Mtn. Vermont's Monadnock Mtn. peers over in back to the L of West, and in front of and to the R of West is a lesser peak of the Pilot Range.

To the R of Cabot's summit is its slightly lower S summit, displaying an extensive talus slope, with the Middle and North Peaks of Terrace Mtn. in front. The sharp peak of The Horn juts out to the R of Cabot, with the E end of Long Mtn. behind on its R. Next to the R and farther away is the broad mass of Dixville Peak, and continuing to the R the summit of Unknown Pond Peak is seen behind and L of the nearby peak of South Terrace, which is marked by a gravelly slide. On the horizon are Cave Mtn. to the L of Unknown Pond Peak, part of Crystal Mtn. in the back and directly above Unknown Pond Peak, and Rice Mtn. over the summit of South Terrace. To the R of South Terrace is the S ridge of Unknown Pond Peak, with Stub Hill on the horizon. Farther R the great cliff of Square Mtn. peers over the lower R slope of Unknown Pond Ridge. To the R of Square and closer is the long, level crest of Deer Ridge seen through the wide gap of Willard Notch, with distant ridges in NW Maine on the horizon. Towards the R end of Deer Ridge, Mt. Dustan (L) and Aziscohos Mtn. (R) are prominent; Deer Mtn. and West Kennebago in NW Maine are on the horizon beyond Aziscohos. To the R of Willard Notch there is a partial view of the nearby rounded bulk of North Weeks. To the R of North Weeks it is possible to obtain glimpses of distant peaks in the Rangeley Lakes area beyond the broad ridge of Cambridge Black Mtn., including (L to R) the Bigelows, Crocker, Bemis Mtn. with Saddleback beyond on the R, Sugarloaf Mtn., and Elephant and Old Blue Mtn. with Mt. Abraham beyond and between them.

NO. OF 4000-FOOTERS VISIBLE: 36 (from Waumbek, through trees)

APPENDIXES

4000-Footer Feats and Oddities

Over the years a number of unusual twists have been put on the goal of climbing all the high peaks in the White Mountains. Those that we know of are listed below; undoubtedly there are more we have not heard of, and some we probably don't want to know. These are presented not to encourage compulsive/obsessive readers to duplicate these feats, but to show to what lengths mountain-lovers and devoted peakbaggers will go to pursue their passion.

"Diretissima"

In the summer of 1970 the Rev. Henry Folsom of Old Saybrook, Conn., worked out the shortest continuous route of walking on trails and roads to climb all the peaks "diretissima"—in the most direct manner. In 19 days (not consecutive) and 244.05 miles (including 22.8 miles on roads and an inadvertent one mile bushwhack on Kinsman Ridge) he bagged them all, starting with Mt. Cabot on the N and finishing with Mt. Moosilauke to the SW. His tale is told in the December 1971 issue of *Appalachia*. The feat was reprised in 2007 by hiker Mats Roing, who climbed all the peaks in one continuous, unsupported 11-day backpacking trip, starting with Mt. Moosilauke and ending with Mt. Cabot. Adding his own twist, Roing dropped down for 10 push-ups atop each peak.

Every Month of the Year

Gene Daniell, longtime editor of the *AMC White Mountain Guide* and Secretary of the Four Thousand Footer Club, was the first to climb each peak in every month of the year—12 rounds of the 48. He deemed April, with its deep, rotten snow and high water crossings, the toughest month. As of this writing seven others have completed this goal and several more are closing in. Well-known hiker Ed Hawkins has completed the "48 × 12" (or "The Grid") twice and has developed a website for completers and aspirants. Remarkably, in April 2008 Hawkins also completed his 48th round of the peaks for "48 × 48," and as this was being written he hoped to complete his fiftieth round in July 2008.

At Night in Winter

In the 1990s, Fred Hunt, a noted Adirondack peakbagger, completed his goal of climbing all the White Mountain peaks at night in winter. On the night of March 6–7, 1999 Mike Bromberg, the cartographer who created the wonderful Wonalancet Out Door Club trail map of the Sandwich Range, achieved his goal of standing atop the summit of every 4000-footer at midnight in winter. Mt. Garfield was the final summit in his quest.

Speed Records

While most hikers climbing the forty-eight peaks are content to complete the list in whatever time frame it takes them—typically over the course of several summers—there have been those who strive to be the fastest. Lately, it seems, they're going faster than ever.

In 1973, teenage brothers George and Tom Fitch of Concord, Masachusetts, made the first planned "speed-hike" of the then-46 White Mountain high peaks in 6 days, 15 hours and 30 minutes. They averaged 27 miles a day over carefully planned routes, stashing a bicycle at each day's ending point and then driving to their starting point in their parents' station wagon. They carried all their own gear, food and water and had no support team assisting them. Sometimes they hiked on into darkness, but they did sleep each night.

In the summer of 1991 Doug Mayer, Al Sochard and Bill Parlette, fueled by Oreos, jumbo Milky Ways, Pop-Tarts, bananas and Gatorade, went on an eight-day rampage in the Whites. By the time the dust had cleared the quirky trio had hiked 250 miles and nabbed all forty-eight 4000-footers. You can read about their knee-shattering adventure in the June 1992 issue of *Appalachia*.

Having previously set "speed peakbagging" records in Colorado and the Adirondacks, 35-year-old Ted "Cave Dog" Keizer came to the White Mountains in August 2002 and blazed through the 48 White Mountain high peaks in 3 days, 17 hours and 21 minutes. His trek was carefully planned, scouted and organized, with transportation and support provided by friends. Trained in sleep deprivation, he hiked through much of the night. One unusual twist of his itinerary was his off-trail descent of the Lincoln Slide off Franconia Ridge to access Owl's Head.

Cave Dog's record stood for less than a year before it was bested by Tim Seaver, a 41-year-old Vermont hiker and photographer. From July 6 through July 9, 2003, Seaver turned in a time of 3 days, 15 hours and 51 minutes for scaling the 48 peaks. He stashed water bottles in advance of his marathon and was aided by a small support team. Like Keizer, he slept only for short intervals, and persevered despite injuring a tendon partway through the marathon trek. Seaver's total route covered 184.4 miles with 62,436 feet of elevation gain.

From December 26, 2003 to January 6, 2004, Sue "Stinkyfeet" Johnston of Waterford, Vermont, and Bob "Frodo" Williams of Wilmington, Massachusetts, both 38, made winter ascents of the forty-eight 4000-footers in 10 days, 22 hours and 37 minutes—the first "Winter 4000" speed record. On their final day they hiked Owl's Head, Mt. Carrigain and Mt. Waumbek—a total of 39 miles with 9,500 feet of elevation gain—and finished early in the morning. Overall they hiked 227 miles (71 miles at night) with 71,000 feet of elevation gain, 60 water crossings and 9 refueling stops at Dunkin' Donuts.

That record was broken in the winter of 2005–2006 by Tim Seaver and Cathy Goodwin, with Andrew Hawley and/or Jeff Vieno coming along on most of the peaks. This team pared the time down to 9 days, 23 hours and 13 minutes. *Their* final day marathon featured 7 peaks, 36.3 miles and 11,850 feet of elevation gain. Overall they covered 230.7 miles with 71,396 feet of elevation gain.

All the Peaks in One Winter

In the winter of 1994–1995, Cindy DiSanto, Cathy Goodwin and Steve Martin became the first to scale all the high peaks in one calendar winter—a feat which requires favorable weather and snow conditions and an understanding boss. They made it even though it took them three tries to reach the summit of Mt. Isolation. In recent years a number of other hikers have accomplished this feat, including Tim Muskat, who climbed them solo in five consecutive winters from 2003–2004 through 2007–2008. Goodwin did it every winter for six years from 2001–2002 through 2006–2007, and in the winter of 2004–2005 she completed two rounds. She has developed a website for completers and aspirants of the "all in one winter."

Two canines are honored to be members of that club. Brutus, a 150-lb. Newfoundland who hiked the Whites for several years with his owner, Kevin Rooney, became the first canine to complete the 4000-footers overall in January 2004. The next winter, accompanied by a regular group of trampers known as the "Brutus Brigade," the big friendly Newfie did them all in a single winter. That feat was matched in the winter of 2006–2007 by Atticus M. Finch, a 20-lb. miniature schnauzer who hiked with his human companion, Tom Ryan. In that winter season the duo came close to completing two rounds, finishing with 81 peaks overall.

Ascents from All Four Points of the Compass, in Winter

The late Guy Waterman, a well-known writer, climber and peakbagger, crafted what may forever rank as the most amazing peakbagging feat in the White Mountains. Sometimes accompanied by his wife Laura or hiking friends, at other times alone, he climbed each peak from all four compass directions—east, south, west and north—no matter what obstacles loomed en route. This involved some of the most difficult bushwhack routes one could conceive of in the Whites, a maelstrom of spruce traps, blowdown, cliffs, slides, scrub and bottomless snow. We remember a chance encounter with Guy one summer day atop Mt. Garfield. As we stood and gazed at the Twin Mtns. to the east, Guy matter-of-factly pointed out the route he had navigated on Christmas Eve up the impossibly steep and tangled west slope of North Twin. Look at a trail map and you'll see dozens of equally astounding off-trail routes up the various 4000-footers. Amazing! We believe Guy also once climbed the 4000-footers in alphabetical order.

Skiing to the Peaks

In April 2005, avid backcountry skier Todd G. ("el-bagr" on hiking websites) completed an amazing journey by skiing to the remote summit of Mt. Isolation—the forty-eighth peak he reached on his boards.

Juggling on the Summits

Peakbagger June Gutowski, accompanied by her husband John, has the distinction of being the first person known to have *juggled* on each of the 48 summits.

Youngest and Oldest

According to Gene Daniell, longtime record-keeper for the 4000-Footer Club, the youngest to complete the peaks was a 4½-year-old boy, while the oldest were two 79-year-old gentlemen.

The Dartmouth Outing Club Seventy-fifth Anniversary Peakbag

To celebrate its seventy-fifth Anniversary, the Dartmouth Outing Club synchronized ascents of all 48 peaks on October 6, 1984, with some 350 club members taking part. All reached their respective summits by noon.

Flags on the Forty-eight

A few days after the September 11, 2001, terrorist attacks, a group of six hikers climbed Mt. Liberty and unfurled a large American flag at the summit in a display of sympathy and support. Every September since then, hundreds of hikers have participated in the "Flags on the 48," carrying flags to each peak and flying them for two hours on improvised flagpoles. This has become a large and well-organized event, with hikers signing up for their favorite summits well in advance. For more information see www.flagsonthe48.org.

Other Oddities

We have heard of others who have attempted to climb the 4000-footers barefoot, walking backwards, and in other odd ways, but can't say whether they succeeded. One hiker, John A. Pennuci, even calculated the 4000-footers by weight loss (*Appalachia*, Dec. 1975), with the Bonds ranking first and Tecumseh last. If you know of any unusual peakbagging ventures involving the 4000-footers, please let us know so that we may include them in future editions.

How Many 4000-Footers Can You See?

It's a question often asked when standing atop an open White Mountain summit, gazing out at a panoramic view. Once the peaks become familiar, it's great fun to identify them from different perspectives near and far.

A few years ago I began tabulating the 4000-footers visible from some of the better White Mountain viewpoints. When I read in *Adirondack* magazine that Joe Coughlin, an ardent peakbagger from Watertown, New York, was surveying the views from the "Adirondack 46" 4000-footers, I was inspired to do the same for the "White Mountain 48."

For "viewbagging" purposes, the New Hampshire 4000-footers fall into five categories:

1. Those with an open summit, a tower, or viewpoints in each necessary direction. On these twenty-three peaks, all visible 4000-footers can be seen with no trouble on a clear day.
2. Those nine peaks with partial open views in several directions, sufficient to spot all visible 4000-footers with a little walking around.
3. Those with an open view in one direction. To see in all directions from these six summits, you have to bushwhack around to find openings through the trees.
4. Summits with severely restricted views. You have to work harder on these three.
5. Those that are completely wooded. On these seven summits, you must be ready to search diligently for even the slightest view, though there may be good views en route.

The views listed here represent what could be seen if each summit was open. Thus the views for the wooded summits are somewhat theoretical, though with patient bushwhacking nearly all the potentially visible 4000-footers can be spotted.

One peak being visible from another is taken to mean from true summit to true summit, even if it's only the thinnest slice. Secondary summits and other portions of the summit ridge don't count. For mountains with ill-defined summits (e.g. Zealand, Owl's Head), this can be somewhat of a judgment call, especially since it's so hard to see from these "peaks."

This was a project that required clear, crisp days, for distances between mutually visible peaks range up to about 40 miles (e.g. Mts. Whiteface and Cabot). I enjoyed many glorious days on the finer viewpoints, mixed in with some thrashing through the firs and peering between branches and tree trunks on the wooded summits. In some cases the deep snows of winter gave a welcome lift for seeing over the trees.

The most spectacular view was from Mt. Carrigain on a crystal September day. The most frustrating viewless mountain was Owl's Head— its level crest yielded no satisfactory openings through the trees near the marked summit.

There's no peak from which you can see all of the other forty-seven New Hampshire 4000-footers, though some come reasonably close. Sharing top honors are Mts. Washington and Carrigain with 43 peaks visible. Low mountain on the totem pole is Mt. Moriah, tucked away up behind the Presidentials in the northeast corner of the Whites, with only eight 4000-footers visible.

One thing is apparent: location is far more important than height. Of the 20 highest White Mountain summits, only eight are in the top 20 in number of 4000-footers visible. The peaks in the south-central area of the Whites are more favorably positioned in this regard than those in the eastern and western ranges. Thus lowly Mt. Tecumseh reveals 36 peaks to the viewbagger, while lofty Mt. Adams yields only 31 because of its towering Presidential neighbors.

Number of New Hampshire 4000-Footers Visible From . . .

Carrigain	43*	Passaconaway	40	Lincoln	38
Washington	43†	Whiteface	40	Bond	38
Osceola	41	Jefferson	40	South Hancock	37
East Osceola	41	Cabot	39	No. Tripyramid	36
North Hancock	41	Lafayette	38	Tecumseh	36

*Peaks not visible from Carrigain include Moriah, Madison, Cannon, and Galehead.

†Peaks not visible from Washington include Cannon, North Kinsman, South Kinsman, and Galehead. Cannon Tramway building is visible from Washington, but the true summit of Cannon, slightly higher, is not. Only the very tip of West Bond is visible from Washington, in good light.

Mid. Tripyramid	36	Garfield	30	Middle Carter	22
Waumbek	36	Pierce	30	Owl's Head	22
South Twin	35	Isolation	29	North Kinsman	22
Moosilauke	34	Carter Dome	29	South Kinsman	21
Flume	33	Bondcliff	28	Tom	21
Willey	33	Field	28	Zealand	20
Liberty	32	North Twin	27	South Carter	19
Eisenhower	32	Wildcat	26	Cannon	16
Monroe	32	Wildcat D	24	Galehead	11
Adams	31	Hale	23	Madison	10
Jackson	30	West Bond	23	Moriah	8

4000-footer Summits—View Types

1. OPEN SUMMIT OR TOWER WITH 360-DEGREE VIEW

Adams	Garfield	Madison
Bond	Isolation	Monroe
Bondcliff	Jackson	Moosilauke
West Bond	Jefferson	Moriah
Cannon	South Kinsman	South Twin
Carrigain	Lafayette	Washington
Eisenhower	Liberty	Wildcat D
Flume	Lincoln	

2. SUMMIT WITH VIEWS IN SEVERAL DIRECTIONS

Middle Carter	Pierce	Tecumseh
Osceola	Middle Tripyramid	Tom
Passaconaway	North Twin	Willey

3. SUMMIT WITH VIEW IN ONE DIRECTION

Carter Dome	North Hancock	North Kinsman
Field	South Hancock	Wildcat

4. SUMMIT WITH RESTRICTED VIEW

Hale	North Tripyramid*	Waumbek

5. SUMMIT WITH NO VIEW

Cabot*	East Osceola[†]	Whiteface*
South Carter	Owl's Head[†]	Zealand[†]
Galehead*		

*Views available near, but not at summit area.
[†]Views available on approach trail.

4000-Footer Checklist

RANK	PEAK	HEIGHT	DATE CLIMBED
1.	Washington	6288 ft. / 1916.6 m	_____
2.	Adams	5799 ft. / 1768 m	_____
3.	Jefferson	5716 ft. / 1742 m	_____
4.	Monroe	5372 ft. / 1637 m	_____
5.	Madison	5366 ft. / 1636 m	_____
6.	Lafayette	5260 ft. / 1603 m	_____
7.	Lincoln	5089 ft. / 1551 m	_____
8.	South Twin	4902 ft. / 1494 m	_____
9.	Carter Dome	4832 ft. / 1473 m	_____
10.	Moosilauke	4802 ft. / 1464 m	_____
11.	North Twin	4761 ft. / 1451 m	_____
12.	Eisenhower	4760 ft. / 1451 m	_____
13.	Carrigain	4700 ft. / 1433 m	_____
14.	Bond	4698 ft. / 1432 m	_____
15.	Middle Carter	4610 ft. / 1405 m	_____
16.	West Bond	4540 ft. / 1384 m	_____
17.	Garfield	4500 ft. / 1372 m	_____
18.	Liberty	4459 ft. / 1359 m	_____
19.	South Carter	4430 ft. / 1350 m	_____
20.	Wildcat	4422 ft. / 1348 m	_____
21.	Hancock	4420 ft. / 1347 m	_____
22.	South Kinsman	4358 ft. / 1328 m	_____
23. (T)	Field	4340 ft. / 1323 m	_____
23. (T)	Osceola	4340 ft. / 1323 m	_____
25.	Flume	4328 ft. / 1319 m	_____
26.	South Hancock	4319 ft. / 1316 m	_____
27.	Pierce	4312 ft. / 1314 m	_____
28.	North Kinsman	4293 ft. / 1309 m	_____
29.	Willey	4285 ft. / 1306 m	_____
30.	Bondcliff	4265 ft. / 1300 m	_____
31.	Zealand	4260 ft. / 1298 m	_____
32.	North Tripyramid	4180 ft. / 1274 m	_____
33.	Cabot	4170 ft. / 1271 m	_____
34.	East Osceola	4156 ft. / 1267 m	_____
35.	Middle Tripyramid	4140 ft. / 1262 m	_____
36.	Cannon	4100 ft. / 1250 m	_____
37.	Wildcat D	4062 ft. / 1238 m	_____
38.	Hale	4054 ft. / 1236 m	_____
39.	Jackson	4052 ft. / 1235 m	_____
40.	Tom	4051 ft. / 1235 m	_____

RANK	PEAK	HEIGHT	DATE CLIMBED
41.	Moriah	4049 ft. / 1234 m	_____
42.	Passaconaway	4043 ft. / 1232 m	_____
43.	Owl's Head	4025 ft. / 1227 m	_____
44.	Galehead	4024 ft. / 1227 m	_____
45.	Whiteface	4020 ft. / 1225 m	_____
46.	Waumbek	4006 ft. / 1221 m	_____
47. (T)	Isolation	4003 ft. / 1220 m	_____
47. (T)	Tecumseh	4003 ft. / 1220 m	_____

Bedrock Types of the 4000-Footers

Adams: *Metamorphic*—interbedded mica schist and quartzite
Bond, Bondcliff and West Bond: *Igneous*—Mt. Lafayette granite porphyry
Cabot: *Igneous*—Hastingite and riebeckite granite (The Bulge and The Horn—syenite)
Cannon: *Igneous*—Conway granite, including Cannon Cliffs
Carrigain: *Igneous*—Carrigain syenite porphyry on upper mountain, including summit and crest of Signal Ridge; Mt. Osceola granite on lower W slopes; Conway granite on lower N slopes and in Carrigain Notch; Moat volcanics on S and E slopes of Signal Ridge
Carter Dome, Middle Carter and South Carter: *Metamorphic*—gray paragneiss
Eisenhower: *Metamorphic*—Littleton gray gneiss
Field: *Igneous*—Conway granite on W side, Albany porphyritic quartz syenite on E side, Moat volcanics on N ridge
Flume: *Igneous*—Mt. Lafayette granite porphyry at summit; three other granitic rocks on W slopes
Galehead: *Metamorphic*—Talford schist at summit and on S ridge; *Igneous*—Mt. Lafayette granite porphyry at Galehead Hut
Garfield: *Igneous*—Mt. Garfield porphyritic quartz syenite at summit, part of a ring-dike; Kinsman quartz monzonite on NW and SE slopes; Mt. Lafayette granite porphyry on NE slopes
Hale: *Igneous*—Moat volcanics at summit; rest of mountain is a mix of various igneous and *metamorphic* rocks; Sugarloaves are Conway granite
North and South Hancock: *Igneous*—Mt. Osceola granite
Isolation: *Metamorphic*—Littleton gray gniess on W side, interbedded mica schist and micaceous quartzite on E side

Jackson: *Metamorphic*—Littleton gray gneiss

Jefferson: *Metamorphic*—interbedded mica schist and quartzite

North and South Kinsman: *Igneous*—Kinsman quartz monzonite

Lafayette: *Igneous*—Mt. Lafayette granite porphyry at summit; Mt. Garfield porphyritic syenite on upper E slopes; Kinsman quartz monzonite on lower E slopes and W slopes, including Greenleaf Hut and Old Bridle Path

Liberty: *Igneous*—Mt. Lafayette granite porphyry at summit and on upper W slopes; Kinsman quartz monzonite and Mt. Garfield porphyritic quartz syenite on upper E slopes; Conway granite at The Flume

Lincoln: *Igneous*—Mt. Lafayette granite porphyry at summit and along ridge S to Little Haystack; other granitic rocks as on Lafayette

Madison: *Metamorphic*—interbedded mica schist and quartzite

Monroe: *Metamorphic*—Littleton gray gneiss at summit and on N and W slopes; interbedded mica schist and quartzite at Lakes of Clouds and to E; between Monroe and hut is a narrow band of metamorphic rock known as the Boott member, formed from limestone

Moosilauke: *Metamorphic*—mica schist and micaceous quartzite

Moriah: *Metamorphic*—gray paragneiss on E slopes, along ridgecrest and on upper W slopes; mica schist and quartzite along NW ridge, including Mt. Surprise

Osceola and East Osceola: *Igneous*—Mt. Osceola granite

Owl's Head: Primarily *igneous*—Kinsman quartz monzonite on N and W, Mt. Lafayette granite porphyry on S and E; small circular area of Moat volcanics on SE spur; *metamorphic* band of Talford schist slices across ridge, including summit

Passaconaway: *Igneous*—Passaconaway syenite at summit and on S slopes; Conway granite on lower N and E slopes, including Square Ledge and Albany Hedgehog; small areas of *metamorphic* schist NW and NE of summit

Pierce: *Metamorphic*—littleton gray gneiss

Tecumseh: *Metamorphic*—schist at summit and West Peak; *Igneous*—Conway granite on E side and S down ridge to Dickey and Welch Mtns.

Tom: *Igneous*—Moat volcanics on summit ridge, Conway granite on W slopes; three bands of igneous rock and one band of *metamorphic* rock on E slopes

North and Middle Tripyramid: *Igneous*—quartz syenite along ridge, exposed at top of North and South Slides; surrounded by several circular bands of other igneous rocks; part of a ring-dike

North and South Twin: *Igneous*—Mt. Lafayette granite porphyry

Washington: *Metamorphic*—interbedded mica schist and quartzite

Waumbek: *Igneous*—quartz syenite; part of a ring-dike
Whiteface: *Igneous*—Passaconaway syenite on main ridge and upper S
　ledges; Conway granite on SE slopes, including Blueberry Ledges;
　Kinsman quartz monzonite on SW slopes
Wildcat and Wildcat D: *Metamorphic*—mostly gray paragneiss; at sum-
　mit of "A" Peak is intrebedded mica schist and micaceous quartzite
Willey: *Metamorphic*—andalusite schist and micaceous quartzite on N
　and NE part of mountain; *Igneous*—Conway granite on W, S and SE
　slopes; boundary between rock types is just W of summit
Zealand: *Igneous*—Mt. Lafayette granite porphyry W of Zeacliff Pond,
　Conway granite E to Zeacliffs and Zealand Notch

Useful Websites and Phone Numbers

Trail Information

Views from the Top—Northeast. www.viewsfromthetop.com
　"Trail Conditions—New Hampshire" section carries reports submit-
ted by hikers—a great way in winter to check up on snow depth and conditions. More detailed accounts are found in the "Trip Reports."

Hike the Whites! www.hikethewhites.com
　David Metsky's site is a terrific resource for White Mountain hiking,
with many illustrated trip reports on 4000-footers.

Peakbagging in the Mountains of New England. http://home.earthlink
.net/~ellozy/
　Excellent site maintained by FTFC committee member Mohamed Ellozy, with emphasis on peakbagging in the Northeast. Features route summaries, GPS coordinates for trailheads and lots of other information.

Weather

Mt. Washington Observatory. www.mountwashington.org
　Excellent site includes Higher Summits and Valley forecasts, weather
report, live summit cameras, avalanche forecast, snow depths and, in winter, conditions at Pinkham Notch, Crawford Notch and other locations.

National Weather Service. www.weather.gov

General Information

AMC Four Thousand Footer Club. www.amc4000footer.org
Official site of the FTFC, with mountain lists, application forms, FAQ, awards dinner info and more.

Appalachian Mountain Club. www.outdoors.org
The AMC website has a useful trip planning page for the 4000-footers, bulletin boards for trail conditions, gear and general hiking information, plus a wealth of general information about the Whites. It also features the White Mountain Guide online (by subscription).

Pinkham Notch Visitor Center, Gorham, N.H. 603–466–2721

HikeSafe. www.hikesafe.com
Informative website on safe hiking, co-sponsored by NH Fish and Game and WMNF.

Leave No Trace. www.lnt.org
Provides the principles and knowledge for minimizing impact on the land and on other hikers.

White Mountain National Forest.
www.fs.fed.us/r9/forests/white_mountain/
Among many other things, the WMNF website has updates on important trail projects such as bridge repair, and has a road status page for updates on openings and closures of seasonal forest roads.
WMNF Supervisor's Office, Laconia, N.H. 603–528–8721
Androscoggin Ranger District, Gorham, N.H. 603–466–2713
Pemigewasset Ranger District, Plymouth, N.H. office 603–536–1310
Pemigewasset Ranger District, Bethlehem, N.H. office 603–869–2626
Saco Ranger District, Conway, N.H. 603–447–5448

Randolph Mountain Club. www.randolphmountainclub.org
Lots of info for the Northern Presidentials.

Wonalancet Out Door Club. www.wodc.org
Good source of info on the Sandwich Range.

The Waterman Fund. www.watermanfund.org
Established in honor of Laura and the late Guy Waterman, this nonprofit distributes grants for alpine stewardship projects in the Northeastern mountains.

Emergency Numbers

Dial 9–1–1 or 1–800–525–5555

Selected Bibliography

Abbott, Karl P. *Open for the Season.* Garden City, N.Y.: Doubleday & Company, Inc., 1950.

Among the Clouds. Mount Washington, N.H.

Appalachia. Journal of the Appalachian Mountain Club, Boston.

Averill, Robert E., ed. *The Moosilaukee Reader, Vol. I & Vol. II.* Warren, N.H.: Moose Country Press, 1999.

Baird, Iris W., and Chris Haartz. *A Field Guide to New Hampshire Firetowers.* 2nd edition, 2005.

Baird, Iris W. *Looking Out for Our Forests.* Lancaster, N.H.: Baird Backwoods Construction Publications, 2005.

Beals, Charles Edward, Jr. *Passaconaway in the White Mountains.* Boston: Richard G. Badger, 1916.

Bean, Grace H. *The Town at the End of the Road: A History of Waterville Valley.* Canaan, N.H.: Phoenix Publishing, 1983.

Belcher, C. Francis. *Logging Railroads of the White Mountains.* Boston: Appalachian Mountain Club, 1980.

Belknap, Jeremy. *The History of New Hampshire, Vol. III.* Boston, 1792.

Blaisdell, Katharine. *Over the River and Through the Years: Book Five.* Bradford, Vt.: The Journal Opinion, 1983.

Bliss, L. C. *Alpine Zone of the Presidential Range.* Edmonton, Canada, 1963.

Bolles, Frank. *At the North of Bearcamp Water: Chronicles of a Stroller in New England From July to December.* Boston: Houghton Mifflin Company, 1893.

Bolnick, Bruce, Doreen Bolnick, and Daniel Bolnick. *Waterfalls of the White Mountains.* Woodstock, Vt.: Countryman Press, 2nd edition, 1999.

Burt, F. Allen. *The Story of Mount Washington.* Hanover, N.H.: Dartmouth Publications, 1960.

Burt, Frank H. *Mount Washington: A Handbook for Travellers.* Boston, 1904.

Crawford, Lucy. *The History of the White Mountains, From the First Settlement of Upper Coos and Pequaket.* Portland, Maine: B. Thurston & Company, 1886.

Cross, George N. *Dolly Copp and the Pioneers of the Glen.* 1927.

Cross, George N. *Randolph: Old and New.* Randolph, N.H.: Town of Randolph, 1924.

Daniell, Eugene S., III, and Steven D. Smith, eds. *AMC White Mountain Guide.* 28th edition. Boston: Appalachian Mountain Club, 2007. With six trail maps, cartography by Larry Garland. All previous editions of Guide used back to 1st edition, 1907.

Dartmouth Outing Club. *A Trail Guide to Mount Moosilauke.* Hanover, N.H., 1978.

Dickerman, Mike. *Along the Beaten Path.* Littleton, N.H.: Bondcliff Books, 2nd edition, 2000.

Dickerman, Mike. *Why I'll Never Hike the Appalachian Trail.* Littleton, N.H.: Bondcliff Books, 1997.

Dickerman, Mike, et alia. *A Guide to Crawford Notch.* Littleton, N.H.: Bondcliff Books, 1997.

Dickerman, Mike, ed. *Mount Washington: Narratives and Perspectives.* Littleton, N.H.: Bondcliff Books, 1999.

Dickerman, Mike, ed. *The White Mountain Reader.* Littleton, N.H.: Bondcliff Books, 2000.

Doan, Daniel, and Ruth Doan MacDougall. *50 Hikes in the White Mountains.* Woodstock, Vt.: Countryman Press, 6th edition, 2004.

Doan, Daniel, and Ruth Doan MacDougall. *50 More Hikes in New Hampshire.* Woodstock, Vt.: Countryman Press, 5th edition, 2006.

Drake, Samuel A. *The Heart of the White Mountains, Their Legend and Scenery.* New York: Harper and Brothers, 1881.

Eastman, Samuel C. *The White Mountain Guidebook.* 7th edition. Boston: Lee and Shepard, 1867.

English, Ben Jr., and Jane English, eds. *Our Mountain Trips: Part I—1899 to 1908.* Littleton, N.H.: Bondcliff Books, 2005.

English, Ben Jr., and Jane English, eds. *Our Mountain Trips: Part II—1909 to 1926.* Littleton, N.H.: Bondcliff Books, 2007.

Evans, George. *Jefferson, New Hampshire, 1773–1927.* Jefferson, N.H., 1927.

Federal Writers' Project. *Skiing in the East.* New York: M. Barrows & Company, 1939.

Geology Quadrangle Series published by N.H. Department of Resources and Economic Development, Concord, N.H.

    Geology of the Crawford Notch Quadrangle, by Donald M. Henderson et alia, 1977.

    Geology of the Franconia Quadrangle, by Marland P. Billings and Charles R. Williams, 1935.

    Geology of the Gorham Quadrangle, by Marland P. Billings and Katharine Fowler-Billings, 1975.

    Geology of the Mt. Chocorua Quadrangle, by Althea Page Smith et alia, 1939.

    Geology of the Mt. Washington Quadrangle, by Marland P. Billings et alia, 1979.

    Geology of the Percy Quadrangle, by Randolph W. Chapman, 1949.

    Geology of the Plymouth Quadrangle, by Charles B. Moke, 1946.

Goodale, Christine L. "Fire in the White Mountains: A Historical Perspective," in *Appalachia,* Winter / Spring 2004, pp. 60–75.

Goodman, David. *Backcountry Skiing Adventures: Maine and New Hampshire.* Boston: Appalachian Mountain Club Books, 2nd edition, 1999.

Goodrich, Nathaniel L. *The Waterville Valley*. Lunenburg, Vt.: North Country Press, 1952.

Gove, Bill. J. E. *Henry's Logging Railroads: The History of the East Branch & Lincoln and Zealand Valley Railroads*. Littleton, N.H.: Bondcliff Books, 1998.

Gove, Bill. *Logging Railroads of the Saco River Valley*. Littleton, N.H.: Bondcliff Books, 2001.

Gove, Bill. *Logging Railroads Along the Pemigewasset River*. Littleton, N.H.: Bondcliff Books, 2006.

Granite Monthly, The. Concord, N.H.

Hitchcock, C. H., and Joshua Huntington. *The Geology of New Hampshire*. Concord, N.H.: Vol. I, 1874, and Vol. II, 1877.

Hooke, David O. *Reaching That Peak: 75 Years of the Dartmouth Outing Club*. Canaan, N.H.: Phoenix Publishing, 1987.

Howe, Nicholas. *Not Without Peril*. Boston: Appalachian Mountain Club Books, 2000.

Hudson, Judith Maddock. *A History of Trails in the Northern Presidentials and the Randolph, N.H. Region*. Randolph, N.H., RMC Archive, 2004.

Jackson, Charles T. *Final Report on the Geology and Mineralogy of the State of New Hampshire*. Concord, N.H.: Carroll & Baker, 1844.

Johnson, Christopher. *This Grand and Magnificent Place*. Durham, N.H.: University of New Hampshire Press, 2006.

Julyan, Robert, and Mary Julyan. *Place Names of the White Mountains*. Revised Edition. Hanover, N.H.: University Press of New England, 1993.

Kidder, Glenn M. *Railway to the Moon*. Littleton, N.H., 1969.

Kilbourne, Frederick W. *Chronicles of the White Mountains*. Boston: Houghton Mifflin Company, 1916.

King, Thomas Starr. *The White Hills: Their Legends, Landscape and Poetry*. Boston: Crosby and Ainsworth, 1859.

Kostecke, Diane M., ed. *Franconia Notch: An In-Depth Guide*. Concord, N.H.: Society for the Protection of N.H. Forests, 1975.

Little, William. *The History of Warren: A Mountain Hamlet Located Among the White Hills of New Hampshire*. Manchester, N.H., 1870.

Littleton Courier, The, Littleton, N.H.

Map Adventures. *White Mountains Waterproof Map Trail Map*. Cartography by Steven Bushey. 3rd edition, 2006.

Marchand, Peter. *North Woods*. Boston: Appalachian Mountain Club Books, 1987.

McAvoy, George E. *And Then There Was One*. Littleton, N.H.: The Crawford Press, 1988.

Mount Washington Observatory News Bulletin and *Windswept*. North Conway, N.H.

Mudge, John T. B. *The White Mountains: Names, Places & Legends*. Etna, N.H.: The Durand Press, 1992.

Putnam, William Lowell. *Joe Dodge: One New Hampshire Institution.* Canaan, N.H.: Phoenix Publishing, 1986.

Putnam, William Lowell. *The Worst Weather on Earth.* Gorham, N.H.: Mount Washington Observatory, 1991.

Ramsey, Floyd W. *Shrouded Memories: True Stories from the White Mountains of New Hampshire.* Littleton, N.H., 1994.

Randall, Peter E. *Mount Washington: A Guide and Short History.* Third Edition. Woodstock, Vt.: Countryman Press, 1992.

Randolph Mountain Club. *Randolph Paths.* Randolph, N.H., 8th edition, 2005.

Randolph Mountain Club Newsletter. Randolph, N.H.

Reifsnyder, William E. *High Huts of the White Mountains.* Boston: Appalachian Mountain Club Books, 2nd edition, 1993.

Rowan, Peter, and June Hammond. *Mountain Summers.* Gorham, N.H.: Gulfside Press, 1995.

Scudder, Brent E. *Scudder's White Mountain Viewing Guide.* North Sutton, N.H.: High Top Press, 2nd edition, 2005.

Slack, Nancy B., and Allison W. Bell. *A Field Guide to the New England Alpine Summits.* Boston: Appalachian Mountain Club Books, 2nd edition, 2006.

Smith, Steven D. *Ponds and Lakes of the White Mountains: A Four-Season Guide for Hikers and Anglers.* Woodstock, Vt.: Backcountry Publications, 2nd edition, 1998.

Smith, Steven D. *Snowshoe Hikes in the White Mountains.* Littleton, N.H.: Bondcliff Books, 2000.

Smith, Steven D. *Wandering Through the White Mountains.* Littleton, N.H.: Bondcliff Books, 2004.

Spaulding, John H. *Historical Relics of the White Mountains, Also a Concise White Mountain Guide.* Boston, 1855.

Stier, Maggie, and Ron McAdow. *Into the Mountains.* Boston: Appalachian Mountain Club Books, 1995.

Sweetser, Moses F. *The White Mountains: A Handbook for Travellers.* Fourth edition. Boston: James R. Osgood and Company, 1881.

Sweetser, Moses F. *Chisholm's White Mountain Guide.* Portland, Maine: Chisholm Brothers, 1902 edition.

Sykes, Jon. *Secrets of the Notch.* Burlington, Vt.: Huntington Graphics, 2001.

Tolles, Bryant F., Jr. *The Grand Resort Hotels of the White Mountains: A Vanishing Architectural Legacy.* Boston: David R. Godine, 1998.

Underhill, Miriam. *Give Me the Hills.* Riverside, Conn.: Chatham Press, Inc., 1971.

Van Diver, Bradford B. *Roadside Geology of Vermont and New Hampshire.* Missoula, Mont.: Mountain Press, 1987.

Ward, Julius H. *The White Mountains: A Guide to Their Interpretation.* New York: D. Appleton and Co., 1890.

Waterman, Guy. *An Outline of Trail Development in the White Mountains, 1840–1980.* Randolph, N.H., RMC Archive, 2005.

Waterman, Laura, and Guy Waterman. *Forest and Crag: A History of Hiking, Trail Blazing and Adventure in the Northeast Mountains.* Boston: Appalachian Mountain Club, 1989.

Waterman, Laura, and Guy Waterman. *Backwoods Ethics: Environmental Issues for Hikers and Campers.* Woodstock, Vt.: The Countryman Press, 2nd Edition, 1993.

Waterman, Laura, and Guy Waterman. *Wilderness Ethics: Preserving the Spirit of Wildness.* Woodstock, Vt.: The Countryman Press, 1993.

Waterman, Laura, and Guy Waterman. *Yankee Rock and Ice: A History of Climbing in the Northeastern United States.* Harrisburg, Pa.: Stackpole Books, 1993.

Webster, Ed. *Rock Climbs in the White Mountains of New Hampshire.* Eldorado Springs, Co.: Mountain Imagery, 3rd edition, 1996.

Welch, Sarah N. *A History of Franconia, New Hampshire.* Franconia, N.H., 1972.

White Mountain Echo and Tourists' Register. Bethlehem, N.H.

Wight, D. B. *The Wild River Wilderness.* Littleton, N.H., 1971.

Wilcox, Rick, and S. Peter Lewis. *An Ice Climber's Guide to Northern New England.* Conway, N.H.: TMC Books, 3rd edition, 2002.

Willey, Benjamin G. *Incidents in White Mountain History.* Boston: Nathaniel Noyes, 1856.

Wonalancet Out Door Club. *Trail Map & Guide to the Sandwich Range Wilderness and Environs.* Cartography by Mike Bromberg. Wonalancet, N.H., 3rd edition, 2007.

Wonalancet Out Door Club Newsletter. Wonalancet, N.H.

Wroth, Katherine, ed. *White Mountain Guide: A Centennial Retrospective.* Boston: Appalachian Mountain Club Books, 2007.

About the Authors

STEVEN D. SMITH has been exploring New Hampshire trails for over 30 years, has nearly completed his seventh round of the White Mountain 4000-Footer list (including once in winter), and is a member of the Appalachian Mountain Club's Four Thousand Footer Committee. He is co-editor of the *AMC White Mountain Guide* and is the author or co-editor of several previously published White Mountain guidebooks. He is an AMC / WMNF trail adopter and a volunteer with Pemigewasset Valley Search & Rescue. He owns The Mountain Wanderer Map and Book Store in Lincoln, New Hampshire, specializing in New England outdoors and travel. Steve and his wife, Carol, who completed her 4000-footers in 2002, reside in Lincoln.

MIKE DICKERMAN is an award-winning journalist whose popular hiking column, "The Beaten Path," appears regularly in several New Hampshire newspapers. He has successfully climbed all the White Mountain 4000-Footers in both summer and winter. He is the author and/or editor of six previously published books, *Along the Beaten Path*, *A Guide to Crawford Notch*, *Why I'll Never Hike the Appalachian Trail*, *Mount Washington: Narratives and Perspectives*, *The White Mountain Reader*, and *Lincoln & Woodstock, New Hampshire*. He is the owner of Bondcliff Books in Littleton, New Hampshire, a publishing company specializing in White Mountain and regional interest titles. He and his wife, Jeanne, live and work year-round in Littleton.

Corrections and updates to guide (May 2015)

Mount Adams

p. 29 (Geography), *p. 32* (Nomenclature) and *p. 43* (Lowe's Path): Adams 4 has been renamed by the U.S. Board on Geographic Names as Mt. Abigail Adams, after the wife of President John Adams.

Mount Eisenhower

p. 55: Round-trip elevation gain via Crawford Path and Mount Eisenhower Loop is 3300 ft.

pp. 56-58: After being closed for several years due to damage from Tropical Storm Irene, the trails in the Dry River valley were reopened in fall 2014. The Dry River Trail has been relocated away from washed-out areas; follow with care as the footway is primitive and markings are minimal.

Mount Isolation

p. 68: In fall 2014, the approach via Dry River Trail and Isolation Trail from US 302 was reopened; in relocated sections the footway is primitive and markings are minimal – follow with care. The Rocky Branch Trail from Stairs Col Trail to Isolation Trail east remains closed due to severe damage from Tropical Storm Irene. Repairs are scheduled for 2015. For updates, contact the WMNF Saco Ranger District at 603-447-5448.

Mount Jackson

pp. 73-75: Round-trip elevation gains are changed as follows. Mt. Jackson via Webster-Jackson Trail, 2250 ft.; Mt. Jackson & Mt. Webster, 2550 ft.; Mt. Jackson & Mizpah Spring Hut, 2450 ft.; approach via Webster Cliff Trail, 3500 ft.

Mount Jefferson

p. 88: In the last line of the first paragraph, the ascent of the Link from the Castle Ravine Trail to the Castle Trail is 700 ft.

p. 88: In the first sentence of the second paragraph, on two of the brook crossings the trail crosses debris from a 2010 avalanche; caution is advised.

Mount Monroe

p. 118: Hiker parking is available for a fee at the Cog Railway lower lot; the 0.3 mi. connector to Ammonoosuc Ravine Trail begins up to the right above the Base Station buildings. There is no fee for winter parking at the Cog.

pp. 120-121: In fall 2014, the ascent route via Dry River Trail was reopened. The Dry River Trail has been relocated away from washed-out areas; follow with care as the footway is primitive and markings are minimal.

Mount Pierce

pp. 130-131: In fall 2014 the ascent route via Dry River Trail and Mount Clinton Trail was reopened. The Dry River Trail has been relocated away from washed-out areas; follow with care as the footway is primitive and markings are minimal. The Mount Clinton Trail requires great care to follow.

Mount Washington

p. 140: The rocky hump between Nelson Crag and Ball Crag has been named "Agiochook Crag" by the U.S. Board on Geographic Names.

p. 151: Hiker parking is available for a fee at the Cog Railway lower lot; the 0.3 mi. connector to Ammonoosuc Ravine Trail begins up to the right above the Base Station buildings. There is no fee for winter parking at the Cog. Before reaching Gem Pool, Ammonoosuc Ravine Trail passes through an area of damage from a 2010 avalanche and from Tropical Storm Irene.

p. 152: The 0.4 mi. connector from the Cog Railway Base Station to Jewell Trail begins behind the ticket office, crosses the tracks and a bridge over the Ammonoosuc River, then ascends to the main trail.

p. 163: The Great Gulf Trail requires much care to follow on the headwall, especially in an area where a rock slide occurred during Tropical Storm Irene.

Carter Dome

p. 179: A bridge on the lower part of the Nineteen Mile Brook Trail was washed out by Tropical Storm Irene; replacement is planned.

p. 181: The trailhead for Bog Brook Trail has been moved to a new parking area 0.1 mi. to the west, at the start of FR 233. A new connecting path leads from here to Bog Brook Trail.

Middle and South Carter

p. 194: The summit signs on Middle and South Carter have been removed. There is now a SE view from South Carter, reached by an unmarked, 15-yd. spur path on the E side of the trail, 10 yds. S of the summit spur path. The view includes the Royces, Speckled Mtn., Streaked Mtn. on the horizon, Mt. Meader, the Baldfaces and Pleasant Mtn. over the E ridge of Mt. Hight, Mt. Hight and Carter Dome.

p. 195: Most of the road walk between the Imp and Nineteen Mile Brook trailheads can be avoided by using a logging road that connects the south branch of Imp Trail (2.1 mi. down from the junction with North Carter Trail, where it makes a prominent bend from NW to N, descending), with the AMC's Camp Dodge on NH 16. Turn left (west) onto the road, which leads 0.2 mi. to the upper field at Camp Dodge. From there the Camp Dodge access road is followed another 0.2 mi. to NH 16. Turn left and walk 0.4 mi. S on NH 16 to the Nineteen Mile Brook trailhead. If using this option park at Nineteen Mile Brook Trail. With this option, the total loop over South and Middle Carter is 10.6 mi. with 3550-ft. elevation gain.

Mount Moriah

p. 203: Additional parking for the Carter-Moriah Trail is available where the powerline crosses Bangor St. 0.1 mi. N of the trailhead.

Wildcat Mountain (A Peak) and Wildcat D

p. 217: A bridge on the lower part of the Nineteen Mile Brook Trail was washed out by Tropical Storm Irene; replacement is planned.

pp. 217-218: The trailhead for Bog Brook Trail has been moved to a new parking area 0.1 mi. to the west, at the start of FR 233. A new connecting path leads from here to Bog Brook Trail.

p. 218: Hikers ascending or descending via the ski trails during the ski season must purchase a pass at Wildcat Skier Services and follow a designated route, only during operating hours; for details see www.skiwildcat.com.

Mount Tom

p. 238, p. 241, pp. 243-244: New tree growth continues to obscure the western and southern view from the blowdown area near the summit, though it is still good in winter.

Mount Carrigain

p. 288: The trailhead elevation for the Signal Ridge Trail is 1380 ft. With this change, and the relocation described below, the round trip from Sawyer River Rd. to Mt. Carrigain via Signal Ridge Trail is now 10.6 mi. with 3500 ft. of elevation gain. The loop hike using the Carrigain Notch, Desolation and Signal Ridge Trails is now 13.9 mi. with 3900 ft. of elevation gain.

Several relocations were made on the Signal Ridge Trail in 2012. The first 0.25 mi. of the trail now follows a new route on the south side of White-face Brook, avoiding a potentially difficult brook crossing. At 0.6 mi. the trail turns L onto a relocation along the bank above the old route on the edge of Whiteface Brook, which was washed out by Tropical Storm Irene; it rejoins the older route in 0.2 mi. There has been a major relocation at the junction with the Carrigain Notch Trail. The Signal Ridge Trail now follows the route of the Carrigain Notch Trail north for 0.25 mi., crossing Carrigain Brook in a short distance, and skirting the shore of a beaver pond/meadow. At a new trail intersection, the Signal Ridge Trail turns L onto a new section of trail 0.3 mi. long that runs level for 90 yd., then turns L and climbs up over a small ridge. It dips to cross a small brook, and meanders SW back to the older route of the Signal Ridge Trail, about 0.25 mi. NW of the former junction with Carrigain Notch Trail. This relocation adds 0.3 mi. and 50 ft. of elevation gain in each direction for the Signal Ridge Trail.

p. 289: The observation tower was refurbished in 2013. The USFS plans to install a small radio repeater and antenna on the summit in the near future.

Galehead Mountain

p. 298: Round-trip distance for north approach via Gale River Trail is 10.4 mi. and elevation gain is 2550 ft.

p. 298: A major relocation of the Gale River Trail was completed in 2011, avoiding two potentially difficult crossings of the North Branch of the Gale River. The relocation leaves on the right 1.7 mi. from the parking area, climbs easily southward high above the river, dips to cross Garfield Stream at 2.2 mi., climbs again, then descends gradually to rejoin the older route at 2.8 mi.

Mount Garfield

p. 304: Round-trip elevation gain for Garfield Trail approach is 3100 ft.

North and South Hancock

p. 315: The bypass of the first two crossings of the North Fork is now the official route of the trail.

Owl's Head Mountain

p. 325: There are now well-beaten but braided herd paths between the "old summit" and the "new summit."

p. 326: Most winter peakbaggers now use the Black Pond and Brutus bushwhack routes; both of these vary slightly from year-to-year depending on how they are initially broken out.

North and South Twin Mountain

p. 332-333: For northwest approach via Gale River Trail, round-trip distances and elevation gains are changed as follows: South Twin only, 11.0 mi., 3500 ft.; South and North Twin, out and back, 13.6 mi., 4250 ft.; South and North Twin, loop with carspot, 11.1 mi., 3700 ft.

p. 333: A major relocation of the Gale River Trail was completed in 2011, avoiding two potentially difficult crossings of the North Branch of the Gale River. The relocation leaves on the right 1.7 mi. from the parking area, climbs easily southward high above the river, dips to cross Garfield Stream at 2.2 mi., climbs again, then descends gradually to rejoin the older route at 2.8 mi.

p. 334: Parking is no longer available at the Seven Dwarves Motel. However, hiker parking is available at the end of Little River Rd., except during snowfall (snowplow turnaround); do not block gates or driveways. Cross the bridge and immediately turn L and follow old railroad grade about 1 mi. to end of Haystack Rd. and summer trailhead.

Mount Lafayette

p. 360: A section of the Old Bridle Path a short distance from the parking lot has been relocated to bypass damage from Tropical Storm Irene.

p. 361: Round-trip elevation gain for the Greenleaf Trail approach is 3500 ft.

p. 362: Round-trip elevation gain for the Skookumchuck Trail approach is 3650 ft.

Mount Liberty

p. 373: Under "Other Options," walking distance from Liberty Spring Trail/Whitehouse Trail junction back to Lafayette Place is 2.5 mi. Distance for Lafayette, Lincoln and Liberty is 14.3 mi. With addition of Mt. Flume, distance is 16.5 mi.

Mount Lincoln

p. 381: A section of the Old Bridle Path/Falling Waters Trail a short distance from the parking lot has been relocated to bypass damage from Tropical Storm Irene.

North and South Kinsman

p. 409: The trailhead for the Mt. Kinsman Trail has been relocated 0.3 mi. south of the former trailhead (which was at the Franconia/Easton town line), and just south of the Tamarack Tennis Camp. This is 4.7 mi. south of NH 18 in Franconia and 1.7 mi. north of the Easton town hall. A short driveway leads into a large dirt parking area. A new (2009) section of trail, 0.5 mi. long, ascends eastward to join the original route of the trail. It turns R onto a woods road where it joins the old route; descending, turn L off the woods road at an arrow. Distances and elevation gains for the Kinsmans are the same as for the older route. This parking area is sometimes, but not always, partly plowed in winter.

Mount Moosilauke

pp. 435-436: Tunnel Brook Rd. was badly washed out by Tropical Storm Irene in 2011. Though it has been restored, it is no longer open to vehicle traffic beyond a gate at the jct. 1.4 mi. from NH 112 (elevation 1410 ft.). Hikers must proceed on foot from this point, following the road for 1.5 mi. to the start of the Benton Trail on the L. Round-trip to the summit is now 10.2 mi. with 3400-ft. elevation gain.

pp. 438-440: A section of the Gorge Brook Trail has been relocated due to damage from Tropical Storm Irene. After crossing the bridge over Gorge Brook at 0.6 mi., the Gorge Brook Trail coincides with the Snapper Trail for 0.15 mi., then diverges R (sign for Carter-Wales Connection) onto a relocated section that climbs gradually for 0.3 mi. before rejoining the older route 0.15 mi. below the second crossing of Gorge Brook. Distances and elevation gains are the same as for the original route.

p. 440: The lower 0.5 mi. of the Asquam-Ridge Trail, from its junction with the Gorge Brook Trail to the bridge over the Baker River from the extension of Ravine Lodge Rd., has been closed due to a washout from Tropical Storm Irene. The Asquam-Ridge Trail now follows the old logging road ahead from the end of Ravine Lodge Rd.

Mount Passaconaway

p. 466: Round-trip distance for north approach from Kancamagus Highway is 10.0 mi., elevation gain is 2900 ft.

p. 468: Elevation gain for loop option via Square Ledge is 3050 ft.

p. 471: In 30 yd. from its junction with the Old Mast Road, the Wonalancet Range Trail turns L onto a relocation, then soon turns L again onto the older route.

Mount Tecumseh
p. 480: A short distance in from the Waterville Valley trailhead, a 0.1 mi. section of the Mt. Tecumseh Trail has been relocated to the L to bypass a washout from Tropical Storm Irene.

p. 480: Trailhead elevation for the Mt. Tecumseh Trail on Tripoli Rd. is 1880 ft. Round-trip elevation gain for the Tripoli Rd. approach is 2500 ft.

p. 481-484: The eastward summit view has been greatly expanded in recent years by (illegal) removal of trees. Trees now restrict much of the eastern view from the Sosman Trail, and the bench is no longer present.

North and Middle Tripyramid
p. 490: elevation gain for Pine Bend Brook Trail route is 2900 ft. for North Tripyramid and 3550 ft. for North and Middle.

p. 492: In 2012 Hurricane Sandy flattened a large area of conifers along the Kate Sleeper Trail on the E side of East Sleeper. These were cleared with hand tools in 2013 by WODC but care is still required to follow the trail.

Mount Whiteface
p. 500: On the Blueberry Ledge Trail, starting about 1.1 mi. from the trailhead, two relocations – one on the R, and then a longer one to the L – have been cut to avoid a wet area.

Mount Cabot
p. 512: The summit sign on Mt. Cabot has been removed. In the near future the USFS will install a small radio repeater near the summit of Mt. Cabot and will construct a wooden helicopter landing platform at the old fire tower site.

p. 515: The Mt. Cabot Trail remains unmaintained and officially closed by the Forest Service, and No Trespassing signs are sometimes posted by the landowner. Its use is not recommended.

Mount Waumbek
p. 522, p. 526, p. 529: The viewpoint at the clearing near the summit of Mt. Starr King was partially cleared and reopened in 2012. The view just east of Waumbek's summit has expanded, with 27 NH 4000-footers visible.

p. 525: The round-trip elevation gain via the Starr King Trail is 2800 ft.

Appendices

p. 533: In late summer 2014, on separate journeys, Taylor Radigan and Arlette Laan became the first known women to complete a Diretissima of the 4000-footers.

As of early 2015 Ed Hawkins had completed 75 rounds and five grids. Tim Muskat of Sandwich, NH had also completed five grids.

p. 534: In July 2014 a new men's 4000-footer speed record was set by Andrew Thompson with a time of 3 days, 14 hours, 59 minutes, breaking Tim Seaver's record of 3:15:51. In September 2014 a new women's 4000-footer speed record was set by Brianna Tidd with a time of 4 days, 19 hours, 40 minutes, breaking Cath Goodwin's record of 4:19:58.

p. 535: The men's winter speed record is currently held by Ryan Welts with a time of 7 days, 17 hours and 7 minutes in January 2009.

The women's winter speed record is currently held by Sue Johnston with a time of 8 days, 4 hours and 2 minutes from March 10-18, 2010.

p. 536: In 2010 George Pullman of Clifton, NJ finished the 4000-footers on Mts. Adams and Madison at the age of 83. In August 2014, on Mt. Jefferson, Stephen Maddock of Randolph, NH completed his goal of climbing all the 4000-footers after reaching the age of 80.

Under "Juggling on the Summits," "June Gutowski" should be "June Rogier."

In 2014 J. R. Stockwell of Gilmanton, NH completed his goal of bushwhacking to the summit of each 4000-footer in each of the four seasons, an epic achievement mostly done solo.